★ **San Clemente** ⑫
See pages 186–7

★ **Trajan's Markets** ⑩
See pages 88–9

Piazza di Spagna

Via Veneto

Piazza della Rotonda

Quirinal

★ **Santa Maria del Popolo** ⑥
See pages 138–9

★ **Santa Maria Maggiore** ⑬
See pages 172–3

⑧

⑩

Esquiline

⑨

Capitol

Forum

⑪

⑫

Palatine

Lateran

⑭

Caracalla

★ **San Giovanni in Laterano** ⑭
See pages 182–3

Aventine

Santa Maria in Trastevere ⑤
See pages 212–13

★ **Colosseum** ⑪
See pages 92–5

DK TRAVEL GUIDES

ROME

DORLING KINDERSLEY *TRAVEL GUIDES*

ROME

DORLING KINDERSLEY, INC.
LONDON • NEW YORK • SYDNEY • MOSCOW • DELHI
www.dk.com

DORLING KINDERSLEY, INC

www.dk.com

PROJECT EDITOR Fiona Wild
ART EDITOR Annette Jacobs
EDITORS Ferdie McDonald, Mark Ronan, Anna Streiffert
US EDITORS Mary Ann Lynch, Mary Sutherland
DESIGNER Lisa Kosky
DESIGN ASSISTANT Marisa Renzullo

MAIN CONTRIBUTORS
Olivia Ercoli, Ros Belford, Roberta Mitchell

MAPS
Andrew Heritage, James Mills-Hicks, John Plumer,
Chez Picthall (Dorling Kindersley Cartography)

PHOTOGRAPHERS
John Heseltine, Mike Dunning, Kim Sayer

ILLUSTRATORS
Studio Illibill, Kevin Jones Associates,
Martin Woodward, Robbie Polley

This book was produced with the assistance of
Websters International Publishers.

Reproduced by Colourscan (Singapore)
Printed and bound in China by L.Rex Printing Co., Ltd.

First American Edition, 1993
4 6 8 10 9 7 5
Published in the United States by
Dorling Kindersley Publishing, Inc.,
95 Madison Avenue, New York, New York 10016
Reprinted with revisions 1996, 1997, 1999 (twice), 2000

Copyright © 1993, 2000 Dorling Kindersley Limited, London

Library of Congress Cataloging-in-Publication Data
Belford, Ros.
Rome / Ros Belford, Rodney Palmer.
p.   cm. – – (Eyewitness travel guides)
Includes index.
ISBN 0-7894-4891-2
1. Rome (Italy) – – Aerial photographs.   2. Rome (Italy) – – Guidebooks.
I. Palmer, Rodney.   II. Title.   III. Series.
DG806.8.B45   1993
914.5'63204929– –dc20   92-53473
                                               CIP

THROUGHOUT THIS BOOK, FLOORS ARE REFERRED TO IN ACCORDANCE WITH
EUROPEAN USAGE, I.E. THE "FIRST FLOOR" IS ONE FLIGHT UP.

**The information in every
Dorling Kindersley Travel Guide is checked annually**.
Every effort has been made to ensure that this book is as up-to-date as
possible at the time of going to press. Some details, however, such as
telephone numbers, opening hours, prices, gallery hanging arrangements
and travel information are liable to change. The publishers cannot accept
responsibility for any consequences arising from the use of this book.
We value the views and suggestions of our readers very highly. Please write
to: Editorial Director, Dorling Kindersley Travel Guides, Dorling Kindersley,
9 Henrietta Street, London WC2E 8PS.

CONTENTS

Colosseum

INTRODUCING ROME

***Moses* by Michelangelo in
San Pietro in Vincoli**

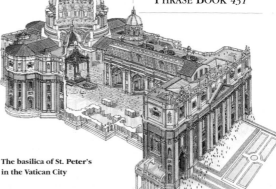

The basilica of St. Peter's
in the Vatican City

HOW TO USE THIS GUIDE

THIS EYEWITNESS TRAVEL GUIDE helps you get the most from your stay in Rome with the minimum of practical difficulty. The opening section, *Introducing Rome*, locates the city geographically, sets modern Rome in its historical context and explains how Roman life changes through the year. *Rome at a Glance* is an overview of the city's attractions. The main sightseeing section is section two, *Rome Area by Area*, starting on page 62. It describes all the important sights with maps, photographs and detailed illustrations. In addition, six planned walks take you step by step through special areas of Rome.

Carefully researched tips for hotels, shops and markets, restaurants and cafés, sports and entertainment are found in section three, *Travelers' Needs*, and section four, *Survival Guide* has advice on everything from mailing a letter to catching the Metro.

ROME AREA BY AREA

The city has been divided into the 16 central sight-seeing areas, each separately color-coded. Each chapter opens with a portrait of the area and a list of the sights to be covered. These are located by numbers on an *Area Map*. This is followed by a large-scale *Street-by-Street Map* focusing on the most interesting part of the area. The main body of the chapter consists of detailed descriptions of all the listed sights. Finding your way around the chapter is made simple by the numbering system used throughout. This refers to the order in which the sights are described in the chapter.

Sights at a Glance lists the sights in the area by category: Churches and Temples, Museums and Galleries, Historic Streets and Piazzas, Historic Buildings, Arches and Gates, Columns, Obelisks and Statues, Fountains, Ancient Sites and Parks and Gardens.

The area covered in greater detail on the *Street-by-Street Map* is shaded red.

Numbered circles pinpoint all the listed sights on the *Area Map*. Palazzo Doria Pamphilj, for example, is **❻**.

1 Area Map

For easy reference, the sights in each area are numbered and located on a map of the area. To help the visitor, the map also shows Metro stations and parking areas.

Photographs of distinctive details of buildings help you identify the sights.

Color-coding on each page makes the area easy to find in the book.

2 Street-by-Street Map

This gives a bird's-eye view of the heart of each sightseeing area. To help you locate and identify important sights as you walk around, these are highlighted in stronger color.

A locator map shows you exactly where you are in relation to surrounding areas. The area shown in the *Street-by-Street Map* is marked in red.

Palazzo Doria Pamphilj ❻ is shown on this map as well.

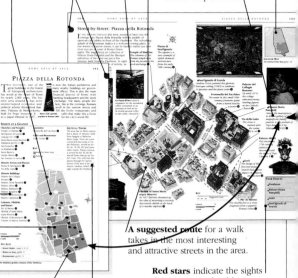

A suggested route for a walk takes in the most interesting and attractive streets in the area.

Red stars indicate the sights that no visitor should miss.

Travel tips help you to reach the area quickly.

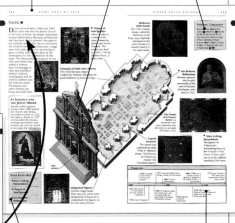

ROME AT A GLANCE

Each map in this section covers a specific theme: *Churches and Temples, Museums and Galleries, Fountains and Obelisks, Celebrated Visitors and Residents.* The top sights are shown on the map; other sights are described on the two pages following.

Each sightseeing area is color-coded.

The theme is explored in greater detail on the two pages following the map.

3 Detailed information on each sight

All the important sights in each area are described individually. They are listed in order, following the numbering on the Area *Map. Practical information is also provided.*

4 Rome's major sights

These are given two or more full pages in the sightseeing area in which they are found. Historic buildings are dissected to reveal their interiors; and museums and galleries have color-coded floor plans to help you find important exhibits.

PRACTICAL INFORMATION

Each entry provides all the information needed to visit the sight. A key to the symbols used is inside the back cover.

Map reference to *Street Finder* **at back of book**   **Sight number**

                              Address   **Telephone number**

Palazzo Doria Pamphilj 6

Piazza del Collegio Romano 1A.
Map 5 A4 & 12 E3. (679 43 65.
56, 60, 62, 70, 85, 95, 160, 492.
Open 10am–1pm Tue, Fri, Sat & Sun.
Closed public hols. **Adm charge.**
compulsory for private apartments;
notify attendant if you want tour.

Opening hours

Useful bus routes   **Services and facilities available**

The Visitors' Checklist provides the practical information you will need to plan your visit.

The facade of each major sight is shown to help you spot it quickly.

Red stars indicate the most interesting architectural details of the building, and the most important works of art or exhibits on display inside.

A timeline charts the key events in the history of the building.

INTRODUCING
ROME

Putting Rome on the Map

Since its foundation over 2,700 years ago on seven hills near the banks of the River Tiber, Rome has grown into a city of three million people covering 580 sq miles (1,500 sq km) of central Italy. Within this area is the independent Vatican City State. Rome was made capital of the newly united Italy in 1870. It is about 17 miles (28 km) from the sea and has good rail and road links to many other historic Italian towns and cities.

KEY

- ☐ Rome and Environs
- ― Main railway
- ✈ Airport
- ▬ Motorway
- ═ A road

0 kilometers   50

0 miles   25

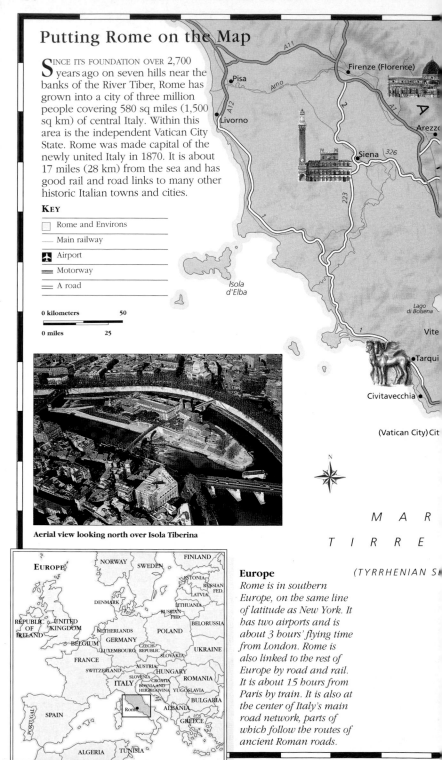

Aerial view looking north over Isola Tiberina

Pisa

Arno

Firenze (Florence)

Livorno

Arezzo

Siena   326

223

Isola
d'Elba

Lago
di Bolsena

Vite

Tarqui

Civitavecchia

(Vatican City) Cit

N

M A R

T I R R E

(TYRRHENIAN S

Europe

Rome is in southern Europe, on the same line of latitude as New York. It has two airports and is about 3 hours' flying time from London. Rome is also linked to the rest of Europe by road and rail. It is about 15 hours from Paris by train. It is also at the center of Italy's main road network, parts of which follow the routes of ancient Roman roads.

EUROPE

NORWAY   SWEDEN   FINLAND

ESTONIA

RUSSIAN
FED.

LATVIA

DENMARK

LITHUANIA

RUSSIAN
FED.

BELORUSSIA

REPUBLIC
OF
IRELAND

UNITED
KINGDOM

NETHERLANDS

GERMANY

POLAND

BELGIUM

LUXEMBOURG

CZECH
REPUBLIC

UKRAINE

FRANCE

SLOVAKIA

SWITZERLAND

AUSTRIA

HUNGARY

SLOVENIA

CROATIA

ROMANIA

ITALY

BOSNIA AND
HERZEGOVINA

YUGOSLAVIA

Rome

BULGARIA

ALBANIA

PORTUGAL

SPAIN

GREECE

ALGERIA   TUNISIA

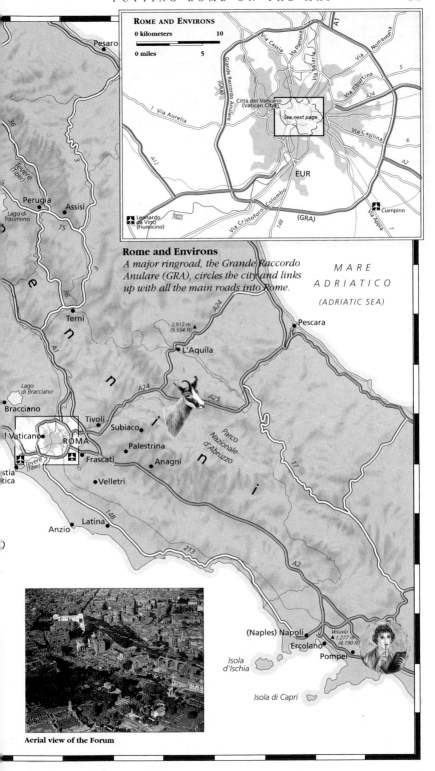

ROME AND ENVIRONS

0 kilometers   10

0 miles   5

Via Cassia

Via Flaminia

Via Salaria

Via Nomentana

Via Tiburtina

A1

A24

Grande Raccordo Anulare (GRA)

1 Via Aurelia

Città del Vaticano
(Vatican City)

See next page

Via Casilina

A12

EUR

6

Leonardo
da Vinci
(Fiumicino)

Tevere
(Tiber)

Via Cristoforo Colombo

148

(GRA)

Ciampino

Via Appia

Rome and Environs

*A major ringroad, the Grande Raccordo
Anulare (GRA), circles the city and links
up with all the main roads into Rome.*

M A R E
A D R I A T I C O

(ADRIATIC SEA)

Pesaro

Tevere
(Tiber)

36

3

Perugia

Assisi

Lago di
Trasimeno

75

e

36

3

A1

Terni

n

A24

2,912 m
(9,554 ft)

L'Aquila

A25

Pescara

Lago
di Bracciano

Bracciano

Tivoli

Subiaco

n

Parco
Nazionale
d'Abruzzo

l Vaticano

ROMA

Tevere
(Tiber)

Frascati

Palestrina

Anagni

i

n

n

stia
tica

Velletri

i

Anzio

Latina

148

17

213

A2

(Naples) Napoli

Vesuvio
1,277 m
(4,190 ft)

Ercolano

Pompei

Isola
d'Ischia

Isola di Capri

Aerial view of the Forum

Central Rome

MOST OF THE SIGHTS described in this book lie within the old city wall in 16 areas shown on the map below. Each of the areas has its own chapter. If you are on a short visit, you may have to restrict yourself to just a few of the central areas: the Forum to see ancient Rome; the Capitol, Piazza della Rotonda and Piazza Navona for the historic centre of the city; Campo de' Fiori for its grand Renaissance palazzi; Piazza di Spagna for its reminders of the 18th-century Grand Tour and its smart modern shops; and the Vatican to see St Peter's and the center of Roman Catholicism.

PAGES 128–41
Street Finder maps
4, 5

0 meters   500

0 yards   500

N

Vatican

Piazza di Spagna

Piazza della Rotonda

Piazza Navona

Campo de' Fiori

Janiculum

Trastevere

PAGES 222–49
Street Finder maps
3, 4

PAGES 116–27
Street Finder maps
4, 11, 12

PAGES 142–53
Street Finder maps
4, 8, 11, 12

PAGES 214–21
Street Finder maps
3, 4, 7, 11

PAGES 206–13
Street Finder maps
4, 7, 8, 11

PAGES 102–15
Street Finder maps
4, 5, 12

PAGES 198–205
Street Finder maps
7, 8, 12

PAGES 154–65
Street Finder maps
5, 6, 12

PAGES 250–55
Street Finder maps
5, 6

PAGES 64–75
Street Finder maps
5, 12

PAGES 166–75
Street Finder maps
5, 6

PAGES 76–95
Street Finder maps
5, 8, 9, 12

PAGES 96–101
Street Finder map 8

PAGES 188–97
Street Finder maps
8, 9

PAGES 176–87
Street Finder maps
6, 9, 10

Via Veneto

Quirinal

Esquiline

pitol

Forum

Palatine

Lateran

entine

Caracalla

THE HISTORY OF ROME

ONE OF THE most ancient cities in Europe, Rome was founded over 2,700 years ago. Since then, it has been continuously inhabited, and, as the headquarters first of the Roman Empire and then of the Catholic Church, it has had an immense impact on the world. Many European languages are based on Latin; many political and legal systems follow the ancient Roman model; and buildings all around the world utilize styles and techniques perfected in ancient Rome. The city itself retains layers of buildings spanning over two millennia. Not surprisingly, all this history can seem a little overwhelming.

Rome began as an Iron Age hut village, founded in the mid-8th century BC. In 616, the Romans' sophisticated Etruscan neighbors seized power but were ousted in 509, when Rome became a Republic. It conquered most of the rest of Italy, then turned its attentions overseas, and by the 1st century BC, it ruled Spain, North Africa and Greece. The expansion of the Empire provided opportunities for power-hungry individuals, and the clashing of egos led to the collapse of democracy. Julius Caesar ruled for a time as dictator, and his nephew, Octavian, became Rome's first emperor, assuming the title Augustus. During the reign of Augustus, Christ was born, and though Christians were persecuted until the 4th century, the new religion took hold, and Rome became its main center.

Even though it was the seat of the papacy, during the Middle Ages Rome went into decline. The city recovered spectacularly in the mid-15th century and for over 200 years was embellished by the greatest artists of the Renaissance and the Baroque. Finally, in 1870, Rome became the capital of the newly unified Italy.

Roman eagle (2nd century AD)

15th-century map of Rome from the north

Detail from 2nd-century AD Roman mosaic from the Temple of Fortune in Palestrina

Rome's Early Development

ACCORDING TO THE HISTORIAN Livy, Romulus founded
Rome in 753 BC. Sometime later, realizing his tribe
was short of females, he invited the neighboring
Sabines to a festival and orchestrated the mass
abduction of their women. Although Livy's account is
pure legend, there is evidence that Rome was founded
around the middle of the 8th century BC, and that the
Romans and Sabines united shortly afterward. Historical
evidence also gives some support to Livy's claim that
after Romulus's death Rome was ruled by a series of
kings, and that in the 7th century BC it was conquered
by the Etruscans and ruled by the Tarquin family. Last
of the dynasty was Tarquinius Superbus (Tarquin
the Proud). His despotic rule led to the Etruscans
being expelled and the founding of a Republic
run by two annually elected consuls. The uprising
was led by Lucius Junius Brutus, the model of the
stern, patriotic Roman Republican.

EXTENT OF THE CITY
☐ 750 BC   ☐ Today

Ceremonial trumpets

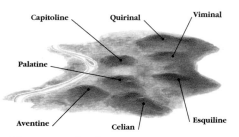

The Seven Hills of Rome
*By the 8th century BC, shepherds and
farmers lived on four of Rome's seven hills.
As the population grew, huts were built in the
marshy valley later occupied by the Forum.*

Capitoline — Quirinal — Viminal
Palatine
Aventine — Celian — Esquiline

Iron Age Hut
*Early settlers lived
in crude thatch
huts. Traces of
their original
foundations
have been
found on the
Palatine.*

Augur, digging
foundation

TEMPLE OF JUPITER
*This Renaissance painting by Perin del
Vaga shows Tarquinius Superbus
founding the Temple of Jupiter on the
Capitol, the sacred citadel of Rome.*

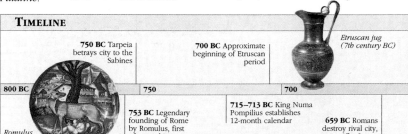

TIMELINE

750 BC Tarpeia
betrays city to the
Sabines

700 BC Approximate
beginning of Etruscan
period

Etruscan jug
(7th century BC)

800 BC   750   700   6

*Romulus
and Remus*

753 BC Legendary
founding of Rome
by Romulus, first
of seven kings

715–713 BC King Numa
Pompilius establishes
12-month calendar

659 BC Romans
destroy rival city,
Alba Longa

☐ **Rome's Early Development**

The Legend of the She-Wolf
The evil King of Alba threw his baby nephews, Romulus and Remus, into the Tiber but they were washed ashore and suckled by a she-wolf.

Raven, guardian of the citadel

Apollo of Veio
Etruscan culture and religion were influenced by the Greeks. This 5th- or 6th-century statue of the Greek god Apollo comes from Veio, a powerful, wealthy Etruscan city.

King Tarquin, holding the stone worshiped as a thunderbolt

The Legend of Aeneas
Some Roman legends make the Trojan hero Aeneas the grandfather of Romulus and Remus.

WHERE TO SEE ETRUSCAN ROME

The Cloaca Maxima sewer still functions, but there are few other traces of Etruscan Rome. Most finds come from Etruscan sites outside Rome like Tarquinia, with its tomb paintings of sumptuous banquets *(see p271)*, but there are good collections in the Villa Giulia *(pp262–3)* and Vatican Museums *(p238)*. The most famous object, however, is a bronze statue of the legendary she-wolf in the Capitoline Museums *(p73)*. The Antiquarium Forense *(p87)* displays objects from the necropolis that once occupied the site of the Roman Forum.

Funeral urns shaped like huts were used for cremation starting in the mid-8th century BC.

Etruscan jewelry, like this 7th-century BC gold filigree brooch, was lavish. Treasures of this kind have given the Etruscans a reputation for luxurious living.

600 BC Possible date of construction of Cloaca Maxima sewer

578 BC Servius Tullius Etruscan King

565 BC Traditional date of the Servian Wall around Rome's seven hills

Statue of Jupiter

510 BC Temple of Jupiter consecrated on Capitoline

600   550   500

616 BC Tarquinius Priscus, first Etruscan king. Forum and Circus Maximus established

534 BC King Servius murdered

509 BC L.J. Brutus expels Etruscans from Rome and founds the Republic

L.J. Brutus

507 BC War against Etruscans. Horatius defends wooden bridge across Tiber

Kings, Consuls and Emperors

R OME HAD OVER 250 RULERS in the 1,200 years between its foundation by Romulus and AD 476, when the last emperor was deposed by the German warrior Odoacer. Romulus was the first of seven kings, overthrown in 509 BC when Rome became a Republic. Authority was held by two annually elected consuls, but provision was made for the appointment of a dictator in times of crisis. In 494 BC, the office of Tribune was set up to protect the plebeians from injustice at the hands of their patrician rulers. Roman democracy, however, was always cosmetic. It was discarded completely in 27 BC, when absolute power was placed in the hands of the emperor.

70–63 BC Pompey

107–87 BC Marius is consul seven times

205 BC Scipio Africanus

218 BC Quintus Fabius Maximus

Romulus; his twin Remus; and the she-wolf who suckled them

456 BC Lucius Quintus Cincinnatus

c753–715 BC Romulus

800 BC	700	600	500	400	300	200	10
SEVEN KINGS			**REPUBLIC**				
800 BC	700	600	500	400	300	200	10

c715–673 BC Numa Pompilius

396 BC Marcus Furius Camillus

c673–641 BC Tullus Hostilius

c509 BC Lucius Junius Brutus and Horatius Pulvillus

133 BC Tiberius Gracchus

122–121 BC Gaius Gracchus

c641–616 BC Ancus Marcius

c534–509 BC Tarquinius Superbus

82–80 BC Sulla

c579–534 BC Servius Tullius

63 BC Cicero

616–579 BC Tarquinius Priscus

60–50 BC Triumvirate of Julius Caesar, Pompey and Crassus

45–44 BC Juli Caesar is sole rule

Tarquinius Priscus consulting an augur

Julius Caesar, whose rise to power marked the end of the Roman Republic

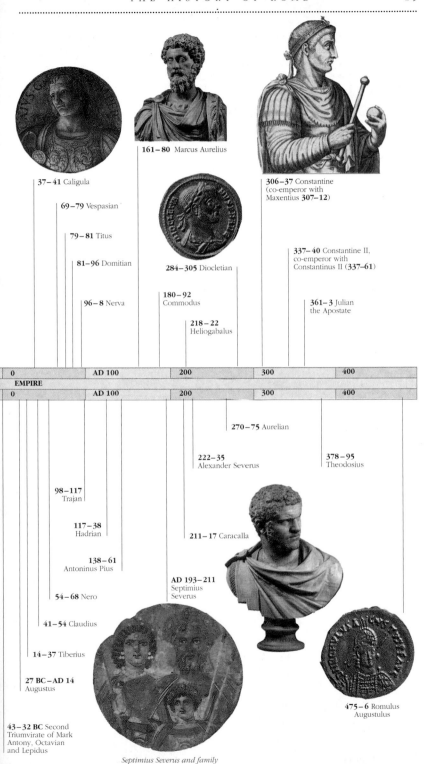

161–80 Marcus Aurelius

37–41 Caligula

69–79 Vespasian

79–81 Titus

81–96 Domitian

96–8 Nerva

306–37 Constantine
(co-emperor with
Maxentius **307–12**)

284–305 Diocletian

337–40 Constantine II,
co-emperor with
Constantinus II (**337–61**)

180–92
Commodus

218–22
Heliogabalus

361–3 Julian
the Apostate

| 0 | AD 100 | 200 | 300 | 400 |

EMPIRE

| 0 | AD 100 | 200 | 300 | 400 |

270–75 Aurelian

222–35
Alexander Severus

378–95
Theodosius

98–117
Trajan

117–38
Hadrian

211–17 Caracalla

138–61
Antoninus Pius

AD 193–211
Septimius
Severus

54–68 Nero

41–54 Claudius

14–37 Tiberius

27 BC–AD 14
Augustus

43–32 BC Second
Triumvirate of Mark
Antony, Octavian
and Lepidus

475–6 Romulus
Augustulus

Septimius Severus and family

The Roman Republic

BY THE MID-2ND CENTURY BC, Rome controlled the west Mediterranean, policing and defending it with massive armies. The troops had more loyalty to the generals than to distant politicians, giving men like Marius, Sulla, Pompey and Caesar the muscle to seize political power. Meanwhile, peasants whose land had been destroyed during the invasion

Bronze coin, showing Temple of Vesta (c 57 BC)

of Hannibal in 219 BC had flooded into Rome. They were followed by slaves and freedmen from conquered lands such as Greece, swelling the population to half a million. There was plenty of work for immigrants: constructing roads, aqueducts, markets and temples, all financed by taxes on Rome's expanding trade.

EXTENT OF THE CITY

▢ *400 BC*   ▢ *Today*

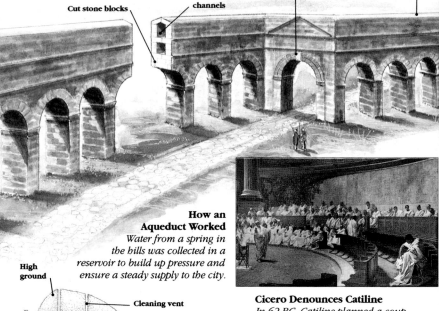

Cut stone blocks

Covered water channels

Arch spanning road

The gradient of an aqueduct was about 1 in 1,000.

How an Aqueduct Worked
Water from a spring in the hills was collected in a reservoir to build up pressure and ensure a steady supply to the city.

High ground

Cleaning vent

Reservoir

Underground water channel

Arches carrying water across low ground

Cicero Denounces Catiline
In 62 BC, Catiline planned a coup. Cicero discovered the plot and persuaded the Senate to condemn the conspirators to death.

TIMELINE

499 BC Battle against Latin tribes; Temple of Castor and Pollux built to commemorate the victory

Via Appia

380 BC Servian Wall rebuilt

396 BC Definitive victory over rival Etruscan city, Veio

312 BC Construction of Via Appia and Rome's first aqueduct, the Aqua Appia

500 BC	450 BC	400 BC	350 BC	300 B

Relief of Capitoline geese

390 BC Rome invaded by Celtic Gauls: quacking geese on Capitoline hill warn of impending attack

264–241 BC First Punic War (against Carthage)

▢ **Roman Republic**

Roman Street
In the 1st century BC, most buildings in Rome were made from brick and concrete. Only a few public buildings were of marble.

AQUEDUCT (2ND CENTURY BC)

Rome owed much of its prosperity to its skilled civil engineers. When the city's wells were no longer sufficient, aqueducts were built to bring water from surrounding hills. Some were over 50 miles (80 km) long.

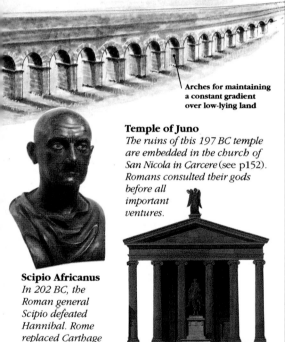

Arches for maintaining a constant gradient over low-lying land

Temple of Juno
The ruins of this 197 BC temple are embedded in the church of San Nicola in Carcere (see p152). Romans consulted their gods before all important ventures.

Scipio Africanus
In 202 BC, the Roman general Scipio defeated Hannibal. Rome replaced Carthage as master of the Mediterranean.

WHERE TO SEE REPUBLICAN ROME

This fresco depicting a group of slaves building a wall can be seen at the Museo Nazionale Romano (see p163).

The Temple of Saturn, first built in 497 BC, now consists of eight majestic columns overlooking the Forum at the end of the Via Sacra (see p83).

Rome's loveliest Republican buildings are the two Temples of the Forum Boarium (see p203). Four more temples can be seen in the Area Sacra of Largo Argentina (p150). Most monuments from this period, however, lie underground. Only a few, like the Tomb of the Scipios (p195), have been excavated. One of the bridges leading to Tiber Island (p152), the Ponte Fabricio, dates from the 1st century BC and is still used by pedestrians.

---

220 BC Via Flaminia built, linking Rome to the Adriatic coast

168 BC Victory in Macedonian War completes Roman conquest of Greece

133–120 BC Gracchi brothers killed for trying to introduce land reforms

51 BC Caesar conquers Gaul

Ponte Fabricio, built in 62 BC

250 BC	200 BC	150 BC	100 BC

218–202 BC Second Punic War; Scipio Africanus defeats Carthaginians

Hannibal

149–146 BC Third Punic War; Carthage destroyed

71 BC Spartacus's slave revolt crushed by Crassus and Pompey

60 BC Rome has three joint rulers: Pompey, Crassus and Caesar

Imperial Rome

IN 44 BC, Caesar became dictator for life, only to be assassinated a month later. The result was 17 years of civil war, which ended in 27 BC, when Augustus became Rome's first emperor. The Empire expanded in fits and starts, but by the late 3rd century it was so huge that Diocletian decided to place it under the rule of four emperors.

Statue of Bacchus, god of wine

Thanks to trade and taxes from its vast domains, Rome was the most magnificent city in the world, studded with the lavish buildings of emperors advertising their civic munificence and military triumphs.

EXTENT OF THE CITY

AD 250   Today

Cross-vaulted ceiling with mosaic decoration

Natatio (swimming pool)

Apotheosis of Augustus
The first and perhaps the greatest Roman emperor, Augustus ruled for 27 years and was deified by the Senate after his death.

ROMA CAPVT MVNDI

The baths could hold up to 3,000 people. They met to gossip in the central *frigidarium* (cold room).

Area for exercise and gymnastics

The Roman Empire under Trajan
By the 2nd century AD, the Roman Empire stretched from Britain to Syria, and Rome was known as the Caput Mundi, *the head of the world.*

TIMELINE

49 BC Caesar crosses the Rubicon and takes Rome

27 Augustus becomes first emperor

Emperor Nero

64 Fire during Nero's rule destroys much of city

65 First persecution of Christians under Nero

72 Colosseum begun

50 BC	0	AD 50	100

44 Caesar becomes dictator for life and is murdered by Brutus and Cassius

AD 42 St. Peter the Apostle comes to Rome

13 Ara Pacis is erected to celebrate the peace Augustus has secured in the Empire

67 St. Peter is crucified and St. Paul executed in Rome

Statue of St. Peter in San Paolo fuori le Mura

Imperial Rome

Roman Revelry
Banquets could last for ten hours, with numerous courses. In order to continue eating, guests would retire to a small room to vomit between courses.

BATHS OF DIOCLETIAN (AD 298)
Rome's public baths were not just places to keep clean. They also had bars, libraries, barbershops, brothels and sports facilities.

Tepidarium (warm room)

Virgil (70–19 BC)
Virgil was Rome's greatest epic poet. His most famous work is the Aeneid, *the story of the Trojan hero, Aeneas, and his journey to the future site of Rome.*

WHERE TO SEE IMPERIAL ROME
There are relics of Imperial Rome throughout the city center, some hidden below churches and palazzi, others – like the Forum *(see pp76–87)*, the Palatine *(pp97–101)* and the Imperial Fora *(pp88–91)* – fully excavated. The magnificence of the era, however, is best conveyed by the Pantheon *(pp110–11)* and the Colosseum *(pp92–5)*.

The Arch of Titus *(p87)*, erected in the Forum in AD 81, commemorates Emperor Titus's sack of Jerusalem in AD 70.

A relief of Mithras, a popular Persian god (3rd century AD), can be seen beneath the church of San Clemente *(pp186–7)*.

164–80 Plague rages in Roman Empire	**212** Citizenship granted to virtually all inhabitants of the Empire	**270** Aurelian Wall begun

Section of Aurelian Wall

150	200	250
125 Hadrian redesigns the Pantheon	**216** Baths of Caracalla completed	**247** Rome's Millennium is celebrated
		284 Empire divided into West and East

Mosaic from the Baths of Caracalla

Early Christian Rome

Crucifixion in Santa Maria Antiqua

IN THE 1ST CENTURY AD, during the reign of Tiberius, a rebellious pacifist was crucified in a distant corner of the Empire. This was nothing unusual, but within a few years, the followers of that man – Jesus Christ – became notorious in Rome, and they and Christ's teachings were perceived as a threat to public order, and many Christians were executed. Even so, the new religion spread through all levels of Roman society. When the Apostles Peter and Paul arrived in Rome, there was a small Christian community, and in spite of persecution by the state, Christianity flourished. In AD 313, the Emperor Constantine issued an edict granting Christians freedom of worship and soon after founded a shrine on the site of St. Peter's tomb. This secured Rome's position as a center of Christianity, but in the 5th century Rome's political importance declined, and the city fell to Goths and other invaders.

EXTENT OF THE CITY

AD 395	Today

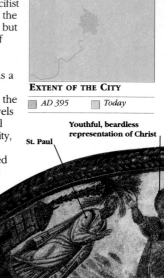

St. Paul

Youthful, beardless representation of Christ

Classical-style border decorated with fruit

4TH-CENTURY MOSAIC, SANTA COSTANZA

Beautiful mosaics, often with palm trees and other Oriental motifs suggesting Jerusalem, helped spread the message of early Christianity.

Santo Stefano Rotondo
This 17th-century engraving shows how a Roman temple (top) might have been transformed (above) into the 5th-century round church of Santo Stefano.

The Good Shepherd
The pagan image of a shepherd sacrificing a lamb became a Christian symbol.

TIMELINE

c320 Building of first St. Peter's	**356** Legendary founding of Santa Maria Maggiore		*Gold solidus of Theodosius*	**410** Rome sacked by Alaric's Goths		**455** Rome sacked again by Vandals
300		**350**		**400**		**450**
312 Control of Empire won by Constantine after battle at Milvian Bridge		*Battle of the Milvian Bridge*	**380** Emperor Theodosius makes Christianity the official religion of the Roman Empire	**395** Division of the Empire between Ravenna and Constantinople	**422** Founding of Santa Sabina	

☐ **Early Christian Rome**

Epigraph of Peter and Paul
This is one of hundreds of early Christian graffiti housed in the Lapidary Gallery of the Vatican (see p237).

Crucifixion, Santa Sabina
This 5th-century panel on the door of Santa Sabina (see p204) is one of the earliest known representations of the Crucifixion. Interestingly, Christ's cross is not actually shown.

WHERE TO SEE EARLY CHRISTIAN ROME
There are traces of early Christianity all over Rome. Many ancient churches were built over early Christian meeting places and sites of martyrdoms: among them are San Clemente *(see pp186–7),* Santa Pudenziana *(p171)* and Santa Cecilia *(p211).* Outside the walls of the old city are miles of underground catacombs *(pp265–6),* many decorated with Christian frescoes, while the Vatican's Pio-Christian Museum *(p240)* has the best collection of early Christian art.

This statuette, carved out of bone, is embedded in the rock of the Catacombs of San Panfilo, just off the Via Salaria (**map** 2 F4).

St. Peter receiving peace from the Savior

Lambs symbolizing the Christian flock

Constantine's Cross
Constantine's vision of the True Cross during the Battle of the Milvian Bridge made him convert to Christianity.

The Cross of Justin, in the Treasury of St. Peter's *(p232),* was given to Rome by the Emperor Justin in AD 578.

475 Fall of Western Roman Empire; Byzantium becomes seat of Empire

A Byzantine image of St. Paul

609 Pantheon is consecrated as a Christian church

500

550

600

496 Anastasius II is first pope to assume title *Pontifex Maximus*

590–604 Pope Gregory the Great strengthens the papacy

630 Sant'Agnese fuori le Mura is built in Roman Byzantine style

The Papacy

THE POPE is considered Christ's representative on earth, claiming his authority from St. Peter, the first Bishop of Rome. Though some popes have been great thinkers and reformers, the role has rarely been purely spiritual. In the Middle Ages, many popes were involved in power struggles with the Holy Roman Emperor. Renaissance popes like Julius II and Leo X, the patrons of Raphael and Michelangelo, lived as luxuriously as any secular prince. The popes listed here include all those who exercised significant political or religious influence, up as far as the end of the Counter Reformation, when the power of the papacy began to wane.

St. Ludovic Kneels before Boniface VIII *by Simone Martini*

314–35 St. Sylvester I

222–30 St. Urban I

217–22 St. Callixtus I

590–604 St. Gregory the Great

496–8 Anastasius II

Gregory the Great leading a procession to end the plague

931–5 John XI

891–6 Formosus

955–64 John XII

1227–41 Gregory IX

1216–27 Honorius III Savelli

0	200	400	600	800	1000	1200

PAPACY BASED IN ROME

0	200	400	600	800	1000	1200

336 St. Mark

352–66 Liberius

88–97 St. Clement

42–67 St. Peter

579–90 Pelagius II

608–15 St. Boniface IV

731–41 St. Gregory III

772–95 Adrian I

1032–44, 1047–8 Benedict IX

1073–85 St. Gregory VII

1099–1118 Paschal II

1130–43 Innocent II

1154–9 Adrian IV

847–55 St. Leo IV

817–24 St. Paschal I

1198–1216 Innocent III

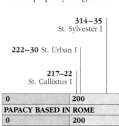

St. Peter, from a mosaic in Santa Prassede (see p171)

795–816 St. Leo III

Innocent III's Vision of the Church, *from a fresco by Giotto*

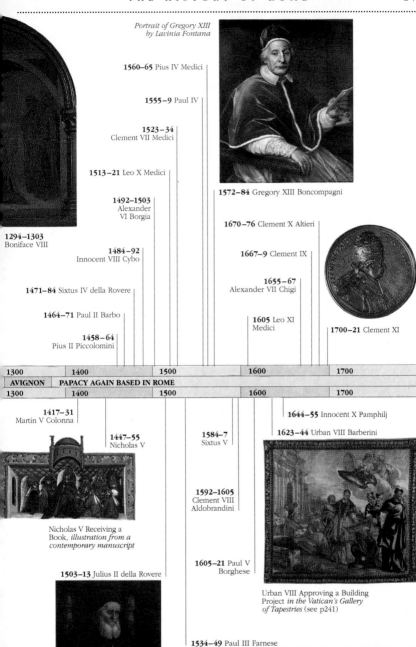

Portrait of Gregory XIII by Lavinia Fontana

1560–65 Pius IV Medici

1555–9 Paul IV

1523–34 Clement VII Medici

1513–21 Leo X Medici

1492–1503 Alexander VI Borgia

1572–84 Gregory XIII Boncompagni

1670–76 Clement X Altieri

1294–1303 Boniface VIII

1667–9 Clement IX

1484–92 Innocent VIII Cybo

1655–67 Alexander VII Chigi

1471–84 Sixtus IV della Rovere

1464–71 Paul II Barbo

1605 Leo XI Medici

1700–21 Clement XI

1458–64 Pius II Piccolomini

1300	1400	1500	1600	1700
AVIGNON	**PAPACY AGAIN BASED IN ROME**			
1300	1400	1500	1600	1700

1417–31 Martin V Colonna

1644–55 Innocent X Pamphilj

1447–55 Nicholas V

1584–7 Sixtus V

1623–44 Urban VIII Barberini

Nicholas V Receiving a Book, illustration from a contemporary manuscript

1592–1605 Clement VIII Aldobrandini

1503–13 Julius II della Rovere

1605–21 Paul V Borghese

Urban VIII Approving a Building Project in the Vatican's Gallery of Tapestries (see p241)

Raphael's portrait of Julius II

1534–49 Paul III Farnese

Paul III Gives his Approval to the Capuchin Order by Sebastiano Ricci

Medieval Rome

Mosaic, San Clemente

Supplanted by Constantinople as capital of the Empire in the 4th century, Rome was reduced to a few thousand inhabitants by the early Middle Ages; its power just a memory. In the 8th and 9th centuries, the growing importance of the papacy revived the city and made it once more a center of power. But continual conflicts between the Pope and the Holy Roman Emperor soon weakened the papacy. The 10th, 11th and 12th centuries were among the bleakest in Roman history: violent invaders left Rome poverty-stricken, and the constantly warring local barons tore apart what remained of the city. Despite this, the first Holy Year was declared in 1300 and thousands of pilgrims arrived in Rome. But by 1309, the papacy was forced to move to Avignon, leaving Rome to slide into further squalor and strife.

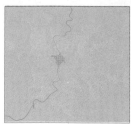

EXTENT OF THE CITY

| ▨ 1300 | ▨ Today |

Charlemagne Crowned in St. Peter's
On Christmas Day in 800, Charlemagne was made emperor of the Holy Roman Empire, a new Christian dominion to replace that of ancient Rome.

Column of Trajan

Column of Marcus Aurelius

San Giovanni in Laterano

Aurelian Wall

Madonna and Child Mosaic
The Chapel of St. Zeno (817–24) in the church of Santa Prassede (see p171) has some of the best examples of Byzantine mosaics in Rome.

MEDIEVAL PLAN OF ROME
Maps like this one, illustrating the principal features of the city, were produced for pilgrims, the tourists of the Middle Ages.

TIMELINE

Emperor Otto I

700	800	900	100
725 King Ine of Wessex founds the first hostel for pilgrims in the Borgo	**852** The Vatican is fortified with walls following a raid by Saracens		**961** King Otto the Great becomes first German Holy Roman Emperor
778 Charlemagne, King of the Franks, conquers Italy	**800** Charlemagne crowned emperor in St. Peter's	**880–932** Rome is ruled by two women, Theodora and then her daughter, Marozia	

 Medieval Rome

Stefaneschi Triptych *(1315)*
Giotto and his pupils painted this triptych for Cardinal Stefaneschi as an altarpiece for St. Peter's. It is now in the Vatican Museums (see p240).

WHERE TO SEE MEDIEVAL ROME

Among the most interesting churches of the period are San Clemente, with a fine apse mosaic and Cosmati floor *(see pp186–7)*, Santa Maria in Trastevere *(pp212–13)* and Santa Maria sopra Minerva, Rome's only Gothic church *(p108)*. Santa Cecilia in Trastevere *(p211)* has a Cavallini fresco, and there is fine Cosmati work in Santa Maria in Cosmedin *(p202)*.

Colosseum Capitol **Pyramid of Caius Cestius**

Pantheon **Castel Sant'Angelo** **Old St. Peter's**

Charlemagne's Dalmatic in the Treasury of St. Peter's *(p232)* was supposedly worn by the Holy Roman Emperor at his coronation. In fact, the richly embroidered vestment probably dates from the 14th century.

Cosmati Tabernacle
Marblework by the Cosmati family, like this tabernacle in Santa Sabina (see p204), decorates many of Rome's medieval churches.

Santa Sabina *(p204)* on the Aventine Hill has a medieval bell-tower.

1084 Rome is attacked by Normans	1108 San Clemente is rebuilt	1200 Rome an independent commune under Arnaldo di Brescia	1309 Pope Clement V moves the papacy to Avignon	1348 Black Death strikes Rome
			1300 First Holy Year proclaimed by Pope Boniface VIII	
	1100	**1200**		**1300**
Mosaic facade, Santa Maria in Trastevere (pp212–13)	1232 Cloister of San Giovanni in Laterano completed			1347 Cola di Rienzo – an Italian patriot – tries to restore the Roman Republic
	1140 Santa Maria in Trastevere is restored	*Cola di Rienzo*		

Renaissance Rome

POPE NICHOLAS V came to the throne in 1447 determined to make Rome a city fit for the papacy. Among his successors, men like Julius II and Leo X eagerly followed his lead, and the city's appearance was transformed. The Classical ideals of the Renaissance inspired artists, architects and craftsmen, such as Michelangelo, Bramante, Raphael and Cellini, to build and decorate the churches and palaces of a newly confident Rome.

Detail of Botticelli's *Youth of Moses* (1480s)

EXTENT OF THE CITY

▢ 1500   ▢ Today

Hemispherical dome

Balustrade of small columns

Classical colonnade of 16 Doric columns

School of Athens by Raphael
In this fresco (see p243), Raphael complimented many of his peers by representing them as ancient Greek philosophers. The building shown is based on a design by Bramante.

THE TEMPIETTO
The Tempietto (1502) at San Pietro in Montorio (see p219) was one of Bramante's first works in Rome. A simple, perfectly proportioned miniature Classical temple, it is a model of High Renaissance architecture.

Cosmati-style mosaic floor

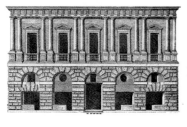

Palazzo Caprini
Bramante's design had a strong influence on later Renaissance palazzi. Parts of the building survive in Palazzo dei Convertidi (see p227).

TIMELINE

1377 Papacy returns to Rome from Avignon under Pope Gregory XI

1409–15 Papacy moves to Pisa

1452 Demolition of old St. Peter's basilica begins

1444 Birth of Bramante

1350	1400	14

1378–1417 The Great Schism, a division in the papacy in Avignon

1417 Pope Martin V ends the Great Schism in the papacy

Pope Martin V, reigned 1417–31

▢ **Renaissance Rome**

Sack of Rome
*In 1527, the unruly troops of
Charles V of Spain pillaged
the city, destroying countless
works of art. Pope Clement VII
took refuge in Castel
Sant'Angelo.*

Pope Nicholas V
*Nicholas ordered
the demolition of
the old St.
Peter's.*

Statue of St. Peter,
believed to have
been crucified
on this site

Underground chapel

WHERE TO SEE RENAISSANCE ROME

The Campo de' Fiori area *(see
pp142–53)* is full of grand
Renaissance palazzi, especially
along Via Giulia *(pp276–7)*.
Across the river stands the
delightful Villa Farnesina
(pp220–21). The most typical
church of the period is Santa
Maria del Popolo *(pp138–9)*,
and the best collection of
Renaissance art is in the
Vatican Museums *(pp234–47)*.
These include the Sistine
Chapel *(pp244–7)* and the
Raphael Rooms *(pp242–3)*.

The Madonna di Foligno by
Raphael (1511–12) is one of the
fine Renaissance paintings in
the Vatican Pinacoteca *(p241)*.

The Pietà, commissioned for
St. Peter's in 1501, was one of
Michelangelo's first sculptures
executed in Rome *(p233)*.

	1483 Birth of Raphael	**1486** Building of Palazzo della Cancelleria	**1519** Frescoes completed in Villa Farnesina	**1527** Troops of Emperor Charles V sack Rome	

1500   **1550**

1475 Birth of
Michelangelo

1506 Pope Julius II
orders start of work
on new St. Peter's

1508 Michelangelo
begins painting the
Sistine Chapel ceiling

Cumaean Sibyl, Sistine Chapel

1547 Pope Paul III
appoints Michelangelo
architect of St. Peter's

Emperor
Charles

Baroque Rome

BY THE 16TH CENTURY, the Catholic Church had become immensely rich – one of the chief criticisms of the Protestant reformers. The display of grandeur and extravagance by the papal court contrasted sharply with the poverty of the people, and **Baroque** wealthy Roman society was characterized by **putto** sumptuous luxury and a ceaseless round of entertainment. To make the Catholic faith more appealing than Protestantism, scores of churches were built, and monuments and fountains were erected to glorify the Holy See. The finest architects in the ornate, dramatic style of the Baroque were Bernini and Borromini.

EXTENT OF THE CITY

| 1645 | Today |

Ceiling portraying heavenly scenes

Monument to Pope Alexander VII
This Bernini tomb in St. Peter's (pp230–33) *includes a skeleton brandishing an hourglass.*

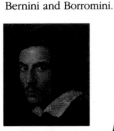

Gian Lorenzo Bernini *(1598–1680)*
The favorite artist of the papacy, Bernini transformed Rome with his churches, palaces, statues and fountains.

Holy Family fresco

Tapestry of Pope Urban VIII
Bernini's most devoted patron, Pope Urban VIII Barberini (1623–44), is shown here receiving the homage of the nations.

A marble rose marks the best place to stand to appreciate the illusion of space created by the artist.

TIMELINE

1568 The Jesuits build the Gesù, prototypical church of the early Baroque

Altar carving from the Gesù

1595 Annibale Carracci begins to fresco Palazzo Farnese

1624 Bernini's sculpture of *Apollo and Daphne*

1626 Work on St. Peter's is completed

1550	1575	1600	1625

1571 Birth of Caravaggio

1585 Pope Sixtus V plans new streets

1600 Philosopher Giordano Bruno is burned at the stake for heresy

Galileo

1633 Galileo condemned to death in Rome for heresy

☐ **Baroque Rome**

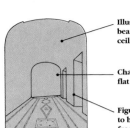

Illusionistic
beams in
ceiling

Chapel painted on
flat slanting wall

Figures painted
to be viewed
from an angle

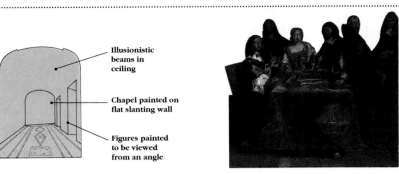

Queen Christina of Sweden
*In a coup for Catholicism, Christina
renounced Protestantism and abdicated
her throne. In 1655, she moved to
Rome, where she became the center of
a lively literary and scientific circle.*

St. Ignatius,
founder of
the Jesuits

**San Carlo alle
Quattro Fontane**
*One of Borromini's
most influential designs
was this tiny oval
church (see
p161) on the
Quirinal
Hill.*

Francesco Borromini
*(1599–1667)
In the many churches
he built in Rome,
Borromini made
use of revolutionary
geometric forms.*

POZZO CORRIDOR
*The use of perspective
to create an illusion of
depth and space was a
favorite Baroque device.
Andrea Pozzo painted
this illusionistic corridor
in the 1680s in the Rooms
of St. Ignatius near the
Gesù (see pp114–15).*

1651 Bernini
redesigns
much of
Piazza
Navona

*Bernini's Fontana
dei Fiumi in
Piazza Navona*

1694 Palazzo di
Montecitorio is
completed

1735 Spanish Steps are designed

1732 Works start on
Trevi Fountain

1650	1675	1700	1725

1657 Borromini completes
Sant'Agnese in Agone

*Bonnie Prince
Charlie, pretender
to the throne
of England*

1721 Bonnie
Prince Charlie
is born in
Rome

1734 Clement XII
makes Palazzo
Nuovo world's first
public museum

1656 Work starts on Bernini's
colonnade for St. Peter's square

Understanding Rome's Architecture

Arch of Titus

THE ARCHITECTURE of Imperial Rome kept alive the Classical styles of ancient Greece, at the same time developing new, uniquely Roman forms based on the arch, the vault and the dome. The next important period was the 12th century, when many Romanesque churches were built. The Renaissance saw a return to Classical ideals, inspired by the example of Florence, but in the 17th century Rome found a style of its own again in the flamboyance of the Baroque.

The entablature above these columns has both straight and arched sections (Hadrian's Villa).

CLASSICAL ROME

Most Roman buildings were of concrete faced with brick, but from the 1st century BC, the Romans started to imitate earlier Greek models, using marble to decorate temples and other public buildings.

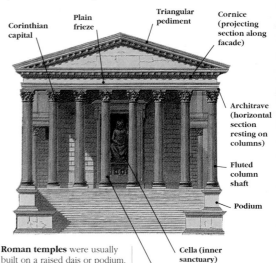

Corinthian capital · Plain frieze · Triangular pediment · Cornice (projecting section along facade) · Architrave (horizontal section resting on columns) · Fluted column shaft · Podium · Cella (inner sanctuary) · Colonnade enclosing portico

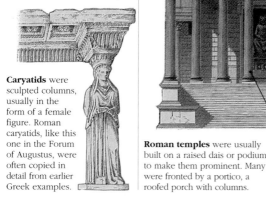

Caryatids were sculpted columns, usually in the form of a female figure. Roman caryatids, like this one in the Forum of Augustus, were often copied in detail from earlier Greek examples.

Roman temples were usually built on a raised dais or podium, to make them prominent. Many were fronted by a portico, a roofed porch with columns.

The orders of Classical architecture were building styles, each based on a different column design. The three major orders were borrowed by the Romans from the Greeks.

Doric order   Ionic order   Corinthian order

Aedicules were small shrines, framed by two pillars, usually containing a statue of a god.

Coffers were decorative sunken panels that reduced the weight of domed and vaulted ceilings.

EARLY CHRISTIAN AND MEDIEVAL ROME

The first Christian churches in Rome were based on the basilica: oblong, with three naves, each usually ending in an apse. From the 10th to the 13th centuries, most churches were built in the Romanesque style, which used the rounded arches of ancient Rome.

Basilicas in Rome have, in most cases, kept their original rectangular shape. The nave of San Giovanni in Laterano retains its 4th-century floor plan.

The triumphal arch divides the nave of a church from the apse. Here, in San Paolo fuori le Mura, it is decorated with mosaics.

RENAISSANCE AND BAROQUE ROME

Renaissance architecture (15th–16th centuries) drew its inspiration directly from Classical models. It revived the use of strict geometric proportions. The Baroque age (late 16th–17th centuries) broke many established rules, favoring grandiose decoration over pure Classical forms.

Putti were a popular decorative feature in the Baroque. A *putto* is a painting or sculpture of a child like a Cupid or cherub.

A loggia is an open-sided gallery or arcade. It may be a separate structure or part of a building, as here at San Saba.

A tabernacle is used to house the Sacrament for the mass. This 13th-century Gothic wall tabernacle is in San Clemente.

A baldacchino is a canopy, supported on columns, rising over the main altar. This Baroque example is in St. Peter's.

Rusticated masonry decorates the exterior of many Renaissance palazzi. It consists of massive blocks divided by deep joints.

COSMATESQUE SCULPTURE AND MOSAICS

The Cosmati family, active in Rome during the 12th and 13th centuries, have given their name to a particularly Roman style of decoration. They worked in marble, producing various elements for churches, including cloisters, episcopal thrones, tombs, pulpits, fonts and candlesticks. These were often decorated with

Cosmatesque floor, Santa Maria in Cosmedin

bands of colorful mosaic. They also left many fine floor mosaics, usually of white marble with an inlay of red and green porphyry. Ancient Roman columns were cut up to provide the materials. Several other families of stonemasons used a similar style, and their work is also described as Cosmatesque.

Rome during Unification

U NDER NAPOLEON, Italy had a brief taste of unity, but by 1815 it was once more divided into many small states, and papal rule was restored in Rome. Over the next 50 years, patriots – led by Mazzini, Garibaldi and others – struggled to create an independent, unified Italy. In 1848, Rome was briefly declared a Republic, but Garibaldi's forces were driven out by French troops. The French continued to protect the pope, while the rest of Italy was united as a kingdom under Vittorio Emanuele of Savoy. In 1870, troops stormed the city, and Rome became capital of Italy.

Garibaldi in his distinctive red shirt

EXTENT OF THE CITY

■ *1870*   ■ *Today*

Porta Pia

Tricolored flag of the new Italian kingdom

Plumed hat of the Bersaglieri, crack troops from Savoy

Allegory of Italy's Liberty
This patriotic poster from 1890 shows the king; his chief minister, Cavour; Garibaldi; and Mazzini. The woman in red represents Italy.

Vittorio Emanuele II
Vittorio Emanuele, King of Piedmont, became the first King of Italy in 1861.

ROYALISTS STORM PORTA PIA
On September 20, 1870, troops of the kingdom of Italy put an end to the papal domination of Rome. They breached the city walls near Porta Pia; the pope retreated, and Rome was made the Italian capital.

TIMELINE

1751 Piranesi's *Views of Rome* revive interest in Classical ruins

1762 Trevi Fountain is completed

Napoleon Bonaparte

1797 Napoleon captures Rome

1799 Napoleon expelled from Italy by Austrians and Russians

1750		1775		1800

Piranesi etching of Trajan's Forum

1792 Canova creates the Tomb of Pope Clement XIII, St. Peter's

1800–1801 Napoleon takes Italy again

1807 Birth of Garibaldi

☐ **Rome during Unification**

Garibaldi and Rome

The charismatic leader Giuseppe Garibaldi had taken much of Italy from foreign rule by 1860. Rome still remained a crucial problem. Here he declares "O Roma o morte" (Rome or Death).

Giuseppe Verdi (1813–1901)

Verdi, the opera composer, supported unification and in 1861 became a member of Italy's first national parliament.

Villa Paolina

Breach in Aurelian Wall

A Freed City

This marble plaque was set up at Porta Pia to commemorate the liberation of Rome.

Victor Emmanuel Monument

A vast monument to Italy's first king (see p74) stands in Piazza Venezia.

· S · P · Q · R ·
VRBE · ITALIAE · VINDICATA
INCOLIS · FELICITER · AVCTIS
GEMINOS · FORNICES · CONDIDIT

1816 Work begins on Piazza del Popolo

Fountain in Piazza del Popolo

1848 Nationalist uprising in Rome. Pope flees and a Republic is formed

1860 Garibaldi and his 1,000 followers take Sicily and Naples

1870 Royalist troops take Rome, completing the unification of Italy

1825

1850

1820 Revolts throughout Italy

1821 Keats dies in Piazza di Spagna

1849 Pope is restored to power, protected by a French garrison

Pope Pius IX

1861 Kingdom of Italy founded with capital in Turin

Twentieth-Century Rome

World Cup mania

T HE FASCIST DICTATOR, Mussolini, dreamed of recreating the immensity, order and power of the old Roman Empire: "Rome", he said, "must appear wonderful to the whole world." He began to build a grandiose new complex, EUR, in the suburbs, and razed 15 churches and many medieval houses to create space for wide new roads. Fortunately most of the old center has survived, leaving the city with one of Europe's most picturesque historic cores. To mark the Holy Year and the new Millennium, crumbling churches and monuments have been given a thorough facelift.

EXTENT OF THE CITY

▢ *1960s*   ▢ *Today*

Placido Domingo | José Carreras | Luciano Pavarotti

Mussolini's Plans for Rome
This propaganda poster reflects Mussolini's grandiose projects such as Via dei Fori Imperiali in the Forum area (see p76), and EUR (p267).

Pope John Paul II
John Paul II is the first non-Italian pope since the 1520s. A traditionalist, he exerts a tremendous influence on the lives of the world's Catholics.

THREE TENORS CONCERT (1990)
Combining Italy's love for music and soccer, this opera recital at the Baths of Caracalla was broadcast live during the World Cup.

TIMELINE

1900	1915	1930	1945
1911 Victor Emmanuel Monument is completed	**1915** Italy enters World War I	**1929** Lateran Treaty creates a separate Vatican state	**1946** National referendum establishes Italy as a Republic; King Umberto II exiled
	1922 Fascists march on Rome. Mussolini becomes Prime Minister	**1926** Opposition parties banned	**1944** Allies liberate Rome from Germans
		1940 Italy enters World War II; work begins on EUR zone	

Poster for EUR

Religion Today
Rome has attracted pilgrims for centuries, and they continue to come, especially at Easter, for beatifications and for the Holy Year of 2000. The city also hosts a large, cosmopolitan religious community.

Conductor Zubin Mehta

Poster for La Dolce Vita
In the 1950s and '60s Rome was Europe's Hollywood. Ben Hur, Quo Vadis?, *and* Cleopatra *were made at the Cinecittà studios, as well as Italian films like Fellini's* La Dolce Vita.

Valentino Model
While not as important as Milan for fashion, Rome is still home to some of the industry's leading designers.

City-Centre Traffic
Rome's streets are congested, and many buildings have been damaged by pollution. There are plans to close the historic center to traffic.

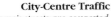

1960 Olympic Games are held in Rome

1978 Premier Aldo Moro kidnapped, then killed by Red Brigades; Karol Wojtyla is elected Pope John Paul II

1990 Rome hosts several World Cup games.

1993 Francesco Rutelli of the Green Party is elected mayor

1960	1975	1990	2000	2010

1962 Second Vatican Council brings about Church reforms

1957 Treaty of Rome initiates European Common Market

1981 Assassination attempt on Pope John Paul II in St Peter's Square

2000 Rome enters the 21st century with millions of pilgrims celebrating the Holy Year, known as the Jubilee

ROME AT A GLANCE

ROM ITS EARLY DAYS as a simple settlement of shepherds on the Palatine Hill, Rome grew to rule a vast empire that stretched from northern England to North Africa. Later, after the empire had collapsed, Rome became the center of the Christian world, and artists and architects flocked to work for the popes.

The legacy of this history can be seen throughout the city. The following pages are a timesaving summary of the best Rome has to offer. There are sections on churches and temples, museums and galleries, fountains and obelisks, and celebrated visitors and residents. Below are the top attractions no visitor should miss.

ROME'S TOP TOURIST ATTRACTIONS

Capitoline Museums
See pp70–73.

Colosseum
See pp92–5.

Sistine Chapel
See pp244–7.

Spanish Steps
See p134.

Raphael Rooms
See pp242–3.

Trevi Fountain
See p159.

Castel Sant'Angelo
See pp248–9.

Pantheon
See pp110–11.

St. Peter's
See pp230–33.

Roman Forum
See pp78–87.

Piazza Navona
See p120.

Interior of the Pantheon, by Giovanni Paolo Pannini (1691–1765)

Rome's Best: Churches and Temples

As the center of Christianity, Rome has a vast wealth of beautiful and interesting churches. These range from magnificent great basilicas built to assert the importance of the medieval and Renaissance Catholic church, to smaller, humbler buildings where the first Christians gathered, often in secret. Among the most fascinating early churches are those converted from ancient Roman temples. Additions to these over the years have resulted in some intriguing many-layered buildings. A more detailed historical overview of Rome's churches is on pages 44 to 45.

Pantheon
This monumental 2,000-year-old building is one of the largest surviving temples of ancient Rome.

St. Peter's
At 450 ft (136 m) high, Michelangelo's dome is the tallest in the world. Sadly, the artist died before seeing his work completed.

Santa Maria in Trastevere
Built over a very early Christian foundation, this church is famous for its ornate mosaics.

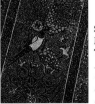

Santa Cecilia in Trastevere
This statue of Cecilia, showing her as she lay when her tomb was uncovered, was sculpted in 1599 by Stefano Maderno.

Santa Maria in Cosmedin
The decorations in this 6th-century church are 12th century and earlier. A restored painting in the apse shows the Virgin, Child and saints.

Sant'Andrea al Quirinale
Bernini made maximum use of strong, dynamic curves in this oval interior (1658–70), creating a small masterpiece of the Roman Baroque.

Santa Maria Maggiore
Rich mosaics and relics contrast with the sober interior form of Santa Maria Maggiore. Among its treasures are vestments bearing the Borghese coat of arms.

Santa Prassede
Magnificent Byzantine mosaics cover the walls and ceilings of this 9th-century church. This Christ with angels is in the Chapel of St. Zeno.

Santa Croce in Gerusalemme
Saints adorn the facade of Santa Croce. Inside are relics of the Cross, brought from Jerusalem by St. Helena.

Via Veneto

Quirinal

Forum

Palatine

Esquiline

Aventine

Caracalla

Lateran

0 meters   500

0 yards   500

San Clemente
Many archaeological layers lie beneath the 12th-century church. This sarcophagus dates from the 4th century.

San Giovanni in Laterano
The original church was built by Constantine, the first Christian emperor. The Chapel of St. Venantius mosaics include the figure of St. Venantius himself.

Exploring Churches and Temples

THERE ARE MORE CHURCHES in Rome than there are days of the year, so you'll have to be selective. Catholic pilgrims have always been drawn to the seven major basilicas: **St. Peter's**, the heart of the Roman Catholic church; **San Giovanni in Laterano**; **San Paolo fuori le Mura**; **Santa Maria Maggiore**; **Santa Croce in Gerusalemme**; **San Lorenzo fuori le Mura** and **San Sebastiano**. These have a wealth of relics, tombs and magnificent works of art from many different periods. Smaller churches can be equally fascinating, especially those that have preserved their original character.

ANCIENT TEMPLES

ONE PAGAN TEMPLE survives virtually unaltered since it was erected in the 2nd century AD. The **Pantheon**, "Temple of all the Gods," has a domed interior quite different in structure from any other church in Rome. It was reconsecrated as a Christian church in the 7th century.

Other Roman temples have been incorporated into Christian churches at various times. Two of these are in the Forum: **Santi Cosma e Damiano** was established in the Temple of Romulus in 526, while San Lorenzo in Miranda

was built onto the ruins of the **Temple of Antoninus and Faustina** in the 11th century. The Baroque facade, built in 1602, looms behind the columns of the temple.

Another church that clearly shows its ancient Roman origins is **Santa Costanza**, built as a mausoleum for Constantine's daughter. It is a round church with some splendid 4th-century mosaics.

EARLY CHRISTIAN AND MEDIEVAL CHURCHES

SOME EARLY BASILICAS, the 5th-century **Santa Maria Maggiore** and **Santa Sabina**, for example, retain much of their original structure. Other, even earlier, churches such as the 4th-century **San Paolo fuori le Mura** and **San Giovanni in Laterano** preserve their original basilica shape. San Paolo was rebuilt after an 1823 fire destroyed the original building, and the San Giovanni of today dates from a 1646 reconstruction by Borromini. Both these churches still have their medieval cloisters.

13th-century fresco by Pietro Cavallini in Santa Cecilia

Santa Maria in Trastevere and **Santa Cecilia in Trastevere** were built over houses where the earliest Christian communities met and worshiped in secret, to avoid persecution. One church where the different layers of earlier structures can clearly be seen is **San Clemente**. At its lowest level, it has a Mithraic temple of the 3rd century AD. Other early churches include **Santa Maria in Cosmedin,** with its impressive Romanesque bell tower, and the fortified convent of **Santissimi Quattro Coronati**. Many Roman churches, most notably **Santa Prassede**, contain fine early Christian and medieval mosaics.

Cloister of San Giovanni in Laterano

The impressive domed interior of the Pantheon, which became a church in 609

UNUSUAL FLOOR PLANS

The design of Rome's first churches was based on the ancient basilica, a rectangular building divided into three naves. Since then, there have been many bold departures from this plan – including round churches, square churches based on the shape of the Greek cross, as in Bramante's plan for St. Peter's and, in the Baroque period, even oval and hexagonal ones.

Pantheon (2nd century)

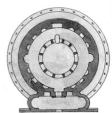

Santa Costanza (4th century)

RENAISSANCE

The greatest undertaking of the Renaissance popes was the rebuilding of **St. Peter's**. Disagreements on the form it should take meant that, although work started in 1506, it was not completed until well into the 17th century. Fortunately, this did not prevent the building of Michelangelo's great dome. In addition to working on St. Peter's, Michelangelo provided the **Sistine Chapel** with its truly magnificent frescoes.

On a completely different scale, another key work of Renaissance architecture is Bramante's tiny **Tempietto** (1499) on the Janiculum. **Santa Maria della Pace** has a Bramante cloister, some frescoes by Raphael and a charming portico by Pietro da Cortona. Also of interest is Michelangelo's imaginative use of the great vaults of the Roman Baths of Diocletian in the church of **Santa Maria degli Angeli**.

There are other churches worth visiting for the sake of

Michelangelo's dramatic dome crowns St. Peter's interior

their outstanding paintings and sculptures. **Santa Maria del Popolo**, for example, has two great paintings by Caravaggio, the Chigi Chapel designed by Raphael and a series of 15th-century frescoes by Pinturicchio. **San Pietro in Vincoli**, besides having the chains with which St. Peter was bound in prison, boasts Michelangelo's awe-inspiring statue of Moses, while **San Luigi dei Francesi** contains three Caravaggios depicting St. Matthew plus frescoes by Domenichino.

BAROQUE

Interior of Rosati's dome in San Carlo ai Catinari (1620)

The Counter Reformation inspired the exuberant, lavish style of such churches as the **Gesù** and **Sant' Ignazio di Loyola**. The best-loved examples of Roman Baroque are the later works associated with Bernini, such as the great colonnade and baldacchino he built for **St. Peter's**. Of the smaller churches he designed, perhaps the finest is **Sant' Andrea al Quirinale**, while **Santa Maria della Vittoria** houses his truly astonishing Cornaro Chapel with its dramatic sculpture, *Ecstasy of St. Teresa*. The late Baroque was not all Bernini, however. You should also look for such churches as **San Carlo ai**

Catinari, with a beautiful dome by Rosato Rosati, and the many churches by Bernini's rival, Borromini. **Sant'Agnese in Agone** and **San Carlo alle Quattro Fontane** are famed for the dramatic concave surfaces of their facades, while **Sant'Ivo alla Sapienza's** complex structure makes it one of the small-scale Baroque masterpieces.

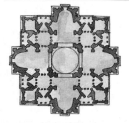

Bramante's St. Peter's (1503)

Sant'Andrea al Quirinale (1658)

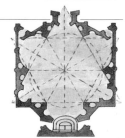

Sant'Ivo alla Sapienza (1642)

Rome's Best: Museums and Galleries

THE MUSEUMS OF ROME are among the richest in the world; the Vatican alone contains incomparable collections of Egyptian, Etruscan, Greek, Roman and Early Christian artifacts, as well as frescoes by Michelangelo and Raphael, priceless manuscripts and jewels. Excavations in the 19th century added treasures from ancient Rome that are now displayed in museums throughout the city. The finest Etruscan collections in the world can be enjoyed in the Villa Giulia. More details on Rome's museums and galleries are given on pages 48 and 49.

Villa Giulia
Etruscan treasures from Rome's early history are displayed in this beautiful Renaissance villa.

Vatican Museums
The galleries and long corridors hold priceless artifacts, such as this 9th-century mosaic showing scenes from the life of Christ.

Galleria Spada
This collection's strength lies in its 17th- and 18th-century paintings. Earlier works include a Visitation *by Andrea del Sarto (1486–1530).*

Palazzo Corsini
Included here are works by Caravaggio, Rubens and Van Dyck, as well as a painting of the Baroque sculptor Bernini – a rare portrait by Il Baciccia (1639–1709).

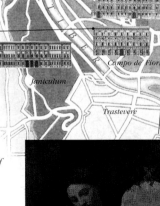

Galleria Doria Pamphilj
Most of the great names of the Renaissance are represented on this gallery's crowded walls. Titian (1485–1576) painted Salomé *early in his career.*

Museo e Galleria Borghese
The ground-floor museum houses ancient Greek and Roman sculpture as well as early Bernini master-pieces, such as his David *(1619). Upstairs are paintings by Titian, Rubens and other masters.*

Museo Nazionale Romano
This fresco, from Livia's Villa (1st century AD) outside Rome, is one of a huge collection of finds from archaeological sites throughout the city.

Palazzo Barberini
The works of art here date mainly from the 13th to the 16th century. This figure of Providence comes from Pietro da Cortona's The Triumph of Divine Providence *(1633–9).*

Palazzo Venezia
The highlights of Rome's most important museum of decorative arts are its Byzantine and medieval collections, including this Byzantine enamel of Christ dating from the 13th century.

Via Veneto

Quirinal

Esquiline

tol

Forum

Palatine

Caracalla

Lateran

tine

Capitoline Museums: Palazzo dei Conservatori
Pietro da Cortona's Rape of the Sabine Women *(1629) is one of many Baroque paintings in the picture gallery.*

Capitoline Museums: Palazzo Nuovo
Among the sculptures is this head of Giulia Domna (wife of Septimius Severus) from the 2nd century AD.

Exploring Museums and Galleries

R OME'S MUSEUMS and galleries boast two major strengths: Greek and Roman archaeological treasures and paintings and sculpture of the Renaissance and the Baroque. The Vatican Museums have superb collections of both, as do, on a smaller scale, the Capitoline Museums. Fine paintings can also be found scattered throughout Rome in museums, galleries and churches (see pp44–5).

Etruscan clay head, Villa Giulia

ETRUSCAN ARTIFACTS

finds are Etruscan; some of the pottery, statuettes and other artifacts are relics of the Faliscans, Latins and other tribes who inhabited central Italy before the Romans.

The Gregorian Etruscan Museum in the **Vatican Museums** was opened in 1837 to house Etruscan finds from tombs on church-owned land. The Museo Barracco in the **Piccola Farnesina** has statues from the much-older civilizations of ancient Egypt and Assyria.

ANCIENT ROMAN ART

T HE ARCHAEOLOGICAL zone in Rome forms a huge open-air museum of evidence of ancient Roman life, while the porticoes and cloisters of the city's churches are filled with ancient sarcophagi and fragments of statuary. The largest important collection can be seen in the **Museo Nazionale Romano** at the Baths of Diocletian and its new branch Palazzo Massimo. The museum's many ancient artifacts include, most notably, a sarco-phagus from Livia's Villa at Prima Porta, just north of Rome. Also on display is some wonderfully well-preserved mosaics. The museum's great collection of Roman statues is now housed in the newly restored **Palazzo Altemps**.

The most important statues are in the **Vatican Museums**, which also have the best of the great Greek works, such as the *Laocoön*, brought to Rome around

5th-century BC Etruscan gold plate with inscription, Villa Giulia

T HE ETRUSCANS inhabited an area stretching from Florence to Rome from the 8th century BC and ruled Rome from the late 7th century BC (see pp16–17). It was the Etruscan custom to bury the dead along with their possessions, and as a result Etruscan artifacts have been excavated from tombs all over central Italy. Three main collections can be seen in Rome. The **Villa Giulia** has been the home of the Museo Nazionale Etrusco since 1889. The villa, designed by Vignola for Pope Julius III's summer outings, is one of Rome's prettiest Renaissance buildings. Its gardens contain a reconstructed Etruscan temple. Not

Victory banner, Museo della Civiltà Romana

the 1st century AD. It had tremendous influence on the subsequent development of Roman art. Splendid copies of Greek originals can be seen in the **Capitoline Museums**.

In the Forum, occupying two floors of the church of Santa Francesca Romana, **Antiquarium Forense** with restored finds from the excavations. For those who enjoy history, the large-scale model at the **Museo della Civiltà Romana** in EUR gives an excellent idea of what ancient Rome looked like in the 4th century AD.

Centurion's breast-plate, Museo della Civiltà Romana

ART GALLERIES

Muses in Raphael's *Parnassus* (1508–11), Vatican Museums

I N THE PAST, many of Rome's great aristocratic families owned magnificent private collections of painting and sculpture. Some of these are still housed in ancestral palazzi that are open to the public. One is the **Galleria Doria Pamphilj**, which has the greatest concentration of paintings of any palazzo in Rome. It's well worth searching through the dimly lit rooms to find the pearls of the collection, which include works by Raphael,

Filippo Lippi, Caravaggio, Titian and Claude Lorrain, and a portrait of Pope Innocent X Pamphilj by the Spanish artist Velázquez. The **Galleria Spada** collection, begun by Bernardino Spada in 1632, is still in the fine original gallery built for it. The paintings demonstrate 17th-century Roman taste and include works by Rubens, Guido Reni, Guercino, and Jan Brueghel the Elder. The **Galleria Colonna** houses a collection of art from the same period.

Hellenistic faun, Museo Borghese

Other old family residences are now showcases for state art collections. The Galleria Nazionale d'Arte Antica is divided between **Palazzo Barberini** and **Palazzo Corsini**. Palazzo Barberini, built between 1625 and 1633 by Bernini and others for the Barberini family, houses paintings from the 13th to the 16th century. It also has objets d'art acquired by the state from various private collections. At some future date, the 17th- and 18th-century paintings exhibited in the Palazzo Corsini, on the south side of the Tiber, will

be transferred to join the Palazzo Barberini collection. Another wonderful private collection was that of the Borghese family, also now managed by the state. **Museo e Galleria Borghese** contains the sculpture collection, including the technically amazing *Apollo and Daphne* by the youthful genius Bernini and the famous statue of Pauline Borghese by Canova. On the first floor is the picture collection with paintings by Titian, Coreggio and others.

The **Capitoline Museums** hold collections that were gifts of the popes to the people of Rome. The Pinacoteca (art gallery) in the **Palazzo dei Conservatori** contains works by Titian, Guercino and Van Dyck. There is an art gallery at the **Vatican Museums**, but lovers of Renaissance art will head straight for the Sistine Chapel and the Raphael Rooms. Rome's main modern art collection is in the **Galleria Nazionale d'Arte Moderna**.

SMALLER MUSEUMS

THE MOST IMPORTANT of the smaller collections is the beautifully laid-out medieval museum in **Palazzo Venezia**, which has exhibits ranging from ceramics to sculpture. Rome has a wealth of small specialist museums, including a **Museum of Musical Instruments**; a **Museo del Folklore**, with tableaux showing life in Rome during the last century; and the **Burcardo Theater Museum**.

For those with an interest in the English Romantic poets who lived in Rome in the 19th century, there is the **Keats-Shelley Memorial House**, a museum in the house where John Keats died. Focusing on the French Empire, the **Museo Napoleonico** has relics and paintings

Laocoön (1st century AD) in the Vatican's Pio-Clementine Museum

of Napoleon and his family members, many of whom lived in Rome.

The Deposition (1604) by Caravaggio, the Vatican

Portrait of Pauline Borghese painted by Kinson (c1805), now in the Museo Napoleonico

Rome's Best: Fountains and Obelisks

ROME HAS SOME of the loveliest fountains in the world.
Many of them are the work of the greatest sculptors of
the Renaissance and Baroque eras. Some fountains are
flamboyant displays, others quiet trickles of water. Many
are simply drinking fountains, while a few cascade from
the sides of buildings. Obelisks date from far earlier
in the city's history. Although some of them were
commissioned by Roman emperors, many are even
older and were brought to Rome by triumphant conquering armies. A detailed overview of the city's
fountains and obelisks is on pages 52 and 53.

Piazza San Pietro
*Twin fountains give
life to the splendid
monumental piazza
of St. Peter's. Maderno
designed the one on
the Vatican side in
1614; the other was
later built to match.*

Piazza del Popolo
*19th-century massive
marble lions and
fountains surround an
ancient obelisk in the
center of the piazza.*

Fontana dei Quattro Fiumi
*The fountain of the four
rivers is the work of Bernini.
The four figures represent
the Ganges, the Plate, the
Danube and the Nile.*

**Obelisk of Santa Maria
sopra Minerva**
*This Egyptian obelisk,
held up by Bernini's
marble elephant, dates
from the 6th century BC.*

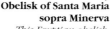

Fontana delle Tartarughe
*One of Rome's more secret fountains,
this jewel of Renaissance sculpture
shows youths helping tortoises into a basin.*

Fontana della Barcaccia
This elegant 1627 fountain is probably the work of Pietro Bernini, father of the more famous Gian Lorenzo.

N

0 meters 500

0 yards 500

Trevi Fountain
The Trevi, inspired by Roman triumphal arches, was designed by Nicola Salvi in 1732. Tradition has it that a coin thrown into the water guarantees a visitor's return to Rome.

zza agna *Via Veneto*

Quirinal

Esquiline

pitol

Forum

Palatine

Lateran

Caracalla

entine

Fontana delle Naiadi
When this fountain was unveiled in 1901, the realistically sensual bronze nymphs caused a storm of protest.

Obelisk of Piazza San Giovanni in Laterano
The oldest obelisk in Rome dates from the 15th century BC. It came to Rome in AD 357, brought here on the orders of Constantine II.

Piazza della Bocca della Verità Fountain
In this 18th-century fountain, built by Carlo Bizzaccheri for Pope Clement XI, water spills over a craggy rock formation where two Tritons hold aloft a large shell.

Exploring Fountains and Obelisks

Fountain of the Amphorae (1920s)

THE POPES who restored the ancient Roman aqueducts used to build fountains to commemorate their deeds of munificence. As a result, fountains of all sizes and shapes punctuate the city, drawing grateful crowds on hot summer evenings. Ancient obelisks provide powerful reminders of the debt Roman civilization owed to the Egyptians. Architects have learned to incorporate them into Roman piazzas in fascinating ways.

FOUNTAINS

THE TREVI FOUNTAIN is one of the most famous of all. It is a *mostra*, a monumental fountain built to mark the end of an aqueduct – in this case the Acqua Vergine, built by Marcus Agrippa in 19 BC, although the Trevi itself was not erected until 1762. Other *mostre* are the **Fontana dell'Acqua Paola,** built for Pope Paul V in 1612 on the Janiculum, and the **Moses Fountain**, commemorating the opening of the Acqua Felice by Pope Sixtus V in 1587.

Almost all Rome's famous piazzas have fountains. In **Piazza San Pietro** there is a matching pair of powerful fountains. Piazza Navona has Bernini's wonderful Baroque **Fontana dei Quattro Fiumi** (fountain of the four rivers) as its main attraction. The fountain's four figures each represent one of the four principal rivers then known. To the south of this is the smaller **Fontana del Moro** (the Moor), also by Bernini, showing an Ethiopian struggling with a dolphin. At the north end, Neptune

wrestles with an octopus on a 19th-century fountain. In Piazza Barberini is the magnificent Bernini creation of 1642–3: the **Fontana del Tritone** with its sea god blowing through a shell.

More recently, large piazzas have been redesigned around fountains. Valadier's great design for **Piazza del Popolo** (1816–20) has marble lions and fountains surrounding the

Fountain of the Four Tiaras located behind St Peter's

The Pantheon Fountain

central obelisk plus two more fountains on the east and west sides of the square. The turn of the century saw the opening of the **Fontana delle Naiadi** (nymphs), in Piazza della Repubblica; its earthy figures were a great scandal at the time. The highly original **Fountain of the Amphorae** (map 8 D2) was erected in Piazza dell'Emporio during the 1920s. The same designer, Pietro Lombardi, also created the **Fountain of the Four Tiaras** (map 3 C3) behind the colonnade of St. Peter's.

The city also has a number of smaller, and often very charming fountains. At the foot of the Spanish Steps is the **Fontana della Barcaccia** (the leaking boat) of 1627; the **Fontana delle Tartarughe**

THE TREVI FOUNTAIN

Appropriately for a fountain resembling a stage set, the theatrical Trevi has been the star of many films set in Rome, including romantic films like *Three Coins in a Fountain* and *Roman Holiday*, but also *La Dolce Vita*, Fellini's satirical portrait of Rome in the 1950s. Whatever liberties Anita Ekberg took then, paddling in the fountains of Rome is now forbidden, however tempting it could be in the summer heat.

Anita Ekberg in *La Dolce Vita* (1960)

Fontana dei Cavalli Marini

(the tortoise fountain) has been in the tiny Piazza Mattei since 1581, and by Santa Maria in Domnica is the **Fontana della Navicella** (little boat), created out of an ancient Roman sculpture in the 16th century. In the forecourt of **Santa Sabina** (map 8 D2) water gushes from a huge mask set in an ancient basin. The **Pantheon Fountain** (map 4 F4), from 1575, is by Jacopo della Porta. **Le Quattro Fontane** (four fountains) have stood at the Quirinal hill crossroads since 1593.

Fountains in parks and gardens include the **Galleon Fountain** (1620–21) at the Vatican, and the **Fontana dei Cavalli Marini** (seahorses), of 1791, at Villa Borghese. The somewhat decayed 16th-century terraced gardens of the **Villa d'Este,** with their display of over 500 fountains, are still worth the journey.

Piazza Navona with Fontana dei Fiumi, by Pannini (1691–1765)

The Ovato Fountain at Villa d'Este

OBELISKS

T HE MOST ANCIENT and tallest of Rome's obelisks is the **Obelisk of Piazza di San Giovanni in Laterano**. Built of red granite, 100 ft (31 m) high, it came from the Temple of Ammon at Thebes, erected in the 15th century BC. It was brought to Rome in AD 357 by the order of Constantine II and put up in the Circus Maximus. In 1587 it was rediscovered, broken into three pieces, and re-erected in the following year. Next in age is the obelisk in **Piazza del Popolo**, from the 12th or 13th century BC. It was brought to Rome in the

time of Augustus and also erected in the Circus Maximus. The slightly smaller **Obelisk of Piazza Montecitorio** was another of Augustus's trophies.

Other obelisks, such as the one at the top of the Spanish Steps, are Roman imitations of Egyptian originals. The **Obelisk of Piazza dell' Esquilino** and the one in **Piazza del Quirinale** (map 5 B4) first stood at the entrance to the Mausoleum of Augustus. When reerected, most obelisks were mounted on decorative bases, often with statues and fountains at their foot. Others became parts of sculptures. Bernini was the creator of the marble elephant balancing the Egyptian **Obelisk of Santa Maria sopra Minerva** on its back, and the **Fontana dei Quattro Fiumi**, its obelisk

Obelisk in Piazza del Popolo

from the Circus of Maxentius. Another obelisk was added to the remodeled Pantheon Fountain in 1711. The obelisk in **Piazza San Pietro** is Egyptian but does not have the usual hieroglyphics.

The **Obelisk of Axum** was brought by Mussolini's army from Ethiopia in 1937 as a war trophy. It now stands by the UN Food and Agriculture Organization building near the Circus Maximus.

Wall fountain at Villa d'Este

Celebrated Visitors and Residents

ROME EXERTS a powerful fascination, and foreigners throughout history have succumbed to its charms, often staying for long periods or even taking up permanent residence. The list of famous visitors is almost endless: painters, sculptors and architects from Rome's very earliest days; writers, poets and musicians; and exiles, pilgrims, religious teachers, philosophers, aesthetes and archaeologists – all have passed through. Their orchestral works, operas, paintings, drawings, drama and literary journals testify to Rome's inspirational effect.

J.W. von Goethe *(1749–1832)*
The German poet, philosopher, artist, playwright, botanist and courtier lived at 20 Via del Corso, now a museum.

Martin Luther *(1483–1546)*
The religious reformer from Germany came to the convent at Santa Maria del Popolo in 1511. His horror at the corruption he saw led to the Reformation.

Sant'Ignazio di Loyola *(1491–1556)*
He came to Rome from Spain in 1537 and founded the Jesuits near what is now the Gesù, the first Jesuit church.

Queen Christina *(1626–89)*
The Swedish queen abdicated in 1654 and came to live in Palazzo Corsini on Via Lungara.

St. Dominic *(1170–1221)*
Founder of the Dominican order, St. Dominic was born in Spain. The order's headquarters were at Santa Sabina on the Aventine.

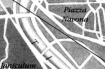

Map labels:
Vatican
Piazza Pop(o)
Piazz(a) della Rot(onda)
Piazza Navona
Janiculum
Campo de' Fi(ori)
T I B E R
Trastevere

Jean Auguste Ingres *(1780–1867)*
The 19th-century French painter, leader of the Neoclassical tradition, lived in Rome from 1806 until 1820. He returned in 1834 as director of the French Academy at Villa Medici.

Pauline Borghese *(1780–1825)*
Napoleon's sister was the subject of scandal in 1805, when she posed semi-nude for a statue by Canova, which is now in Museo Borghese.

The Exiled Stuarts
James Stuart (1688–1766), unsuccessful claimant to the British throne, came to Rome as an exile. He was presented with Palazzo Balestra by Pope Clement XI and died here.

Via Veneto

Quirinal

Esquiline

Capitol

Forum

Palatine

Lateran

Caracalla

Aventine

Lord Byron *(1788–1824)*
Though the English poet's stay in the city was brief, the influence on his work was long-lasting. Stanzas in Childe Harold's Pilgrimage *and* Manfred *were inspired by his seeing the Colosseum in moonlight.*

0 meters 500
0 yards 500

Percy Bysshe Shelley *(1792–1822)*
The great English Romantic poet wrote his drama Prometheus Unbound *in the calm of the ruined Baths of Caracalla in 1819.*

Artists and Writers Inspired by Rome

ARTISTS AND WRITERS have been attracted to Rome since Classical times. Many came to work for the emperors; the poets Horace, Virgil and Ovid, for example, all enjoyed the patronage of Emperor Augustus. Later on, especially in the Renaissance and Baroque periods, the greatest artists and architects came to Rome to compete for commissions from the popes. However, patronage was not the only magnet. Since the Renaissance, Rome's Classical past and its picturesque ruins have drawn artists, architects and writers from all over Italy and abroad.

The prolific love poet Ovid (43 BC–AD 17)

Self-portrait by the 18th-century artist Angelica Kauffmann, c 1770

PAINTERS, SCULPTORS AND ARCHITECTS

Diego Velázquez, one of many great 17th-century artists to visit Rome

IN THE EARLY 16th century, artists and architects were summoned from all parts of Italy to realize the grandiose building projects of the popes. From Urbino came Bramante (1444–1514) and Raphael (1483–1520); from Perugia came Perugino (1450–1523); from Florence came Michelangelo (1475–1564) and many others. They worked in the Vatican, on the new St. Peter's and on the decoration of the Sistine Chapel. Artists were often well rewarded, but they also lived in dangerous times. Florentine sculptor and goldsmith Benvenuto Cellini (1500–71) helped defend Castel Sant' Angelo *(see pp248–9)* during the Sack of Rome (1527) but was later imprisoned there and made a dramatic escape. His memoirs tell the story.

Toward the end of the 16th century, church patronage was generous to the Milanese-born Caravaggio (1571–1610), despite his violent character and unruly life. The Carracci family from Bologna also flourished – especially brothers Annibale (1560–1609) and Agostino (1557–1602).

The work of Gian Lorenzo Bernini (1598–1680) can be seen all over Rome. He succeeded Carlo Maderno (1556–1629) as architect of St. Peter's and created its great bronze baldacchino; the splendid colonnade *(see pp230–31);* and numerous fountains, churches and sculptures. His rival for the title of leading architect of the Roman Baroque was Francesco Borromini (1599–1667), whose highly original genius can be appreciated in many Roman churches and palazzi.

In the 17th century, it became common for artists from outside Italy to work in Rome. Diego Velázquez (1599–1660), King Philip IV of Spain's court painter, came in 1628 to study the treasures of the Vatican. Rubens (1577–1640) came from Antwerp to study and carry out commissions. The French artists Nicolas Poussin (1594–1665) and Claude Lorrain (1600–82) lived here for many years.

The Classical revival of the 18th century attracted artists to Rome in unprecedented numbers. From Britain came the Scottish architect Robert Adam (1728–92) and the Swiss artist Angelica Kauffmann (1741–1807), who settled here and was buried with honor in Sant'Andrea delle Fratte. After the Baroque excesses, sculpture turned to the simplicity of Neoclassicism. A leader of this movement was Antonio Canova (1757–1821). Sculptors from all over Europe were influenced by him, including the Dane Bertel Thorvaldsen (1770–1844), who lived in Rome for many years.

Claude Lorrain's view of the Forum, painted in Rome in 1632

WRITERS

DANTE (1262–1321) visited Rome during his exile from Florence, and in the *Inferno* he describes the great influx of pilgrims for the first Holy Year (1300). The poet Petrarch (1304–74), born in Arezzo, came to the city in much-happier circumstances to be crowned with laurels on the Capitol in 1341. The poet Torquato Tasso (1544–95), from Sorrento, was invited to receive a similar honor, but died soon after his arrival. He is buried in Sant'Onofrio *(see p219)* on the Janiculum.

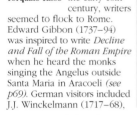

Torquato Tasso

Two of the first writers from abroad to visit Rome were the French essayist Montaigne (1533–92) and English poet John Milton (1608–74). Then, by the early 18th century, writers seemed to flock to Rome. Edward Gibbon (1737–94) was inspired to write *Decline and Fall of the Roman Empire* when he heard the monks singing the Angelus outside Santa Maria in Aracoeli *(see p69)*. German visitors included J.J. Winckelmann (1717–68),

who wrote influential studies of ancient art, and the poet J.W. von Goethe (1749–1832).

In the Romantic period Rome teemed with English writers: poets Keats, Shelley and Byron, followed by the Brownings and the novelist Charles Dickens. Travel writers in the 19th century included Augustus Hare (1834–1903) and the German historian Ferdinand Gregorovius (1821–91). Much of *The Portrait of a Lady* by American Henry James (1843–1916) is set in Rome.

Modern life in Rome is brilliantly captured by the Roman-born novelist and short-story writer Alberto Moravia (1907–90).

Portrait of the poet John Keats painted by his friend Joseph Severn in 1819

MUSICIANS

GIOVANNI LUIGI da Palestrina (1525–94), from the town of that name, became choir-master and organist to the Vatican and composed some of the greatest unaccompanied choral music ever written. In 1770, the 14-year-old Mozart heard Gregorio Allegri's unpublished *Miserere* in the Sistine Chapel and wrote it down from memory. Arcangelo

Corelli (1653–1713), the great violinist and composer of the Baroque age, worked in Rome under the patronage of Cardinal Ottoboni. One of his first commissions was to provide a festival of music for Queen Christina of Sweden.

During the 19th century, the Prix de Rome brought many French musicians to study here at the Villa Medici *(see p135)*. Hector Berlioz (1803–69) owed the inspiration for his popular *Roman Carnival,* the overture to his opera *Benvenuto Cellini,* to his two-year stay in Rome. Georges Bizet (1838–75) and Claude Debussy (1862–1918) were also Prix de Rome winners. Franz Liszt (1811–86), after his 50th year, settled in Rome, took minor orders and became known as Abbé Liszt. He wrote *Fountains of the Villa d'Este* while staying at the villa in Tivoli.

Giacomo Puccini

More recent, 20th-century musical associations with Rome include the popular works by Ottorino Respighi (1870–1936), *The Fountains of Rome* and *The Pines of Rome,* while Giacomo Puccini (1858–1924) used Roman settings when creating his dramatic tragic opera, *Tosca.*

ROMAN CINEMA

The Cinecittà studios, built in 1937 just outside Rome, are most famous for the films made here in the 1940s, classics of Italian Neorealism such as Roberto Rossellini's *Roma Città Aperta* and Vittorio De Sica's *Sciùscià* and *Ladri di Bicicletta.* In the 1950s, Cinecittà became a center for international productions including the epics *Ben Hur* and *Spartacus.*

The director most strongly associated with Roman cinema is Federico Fellini, whose films *La Dolce Vita* (1960) and *Roma* (1972) present a highly idiosyncratic portrait of the follies of the city. Perhaps the most famous film-maker associated with Rome is the controversial writer Pier Paolo Pasolini (1922–75), who became internationally known with his films *Teorema* (1968) and *Il Decamerone* (1971).

Pier Paolo Pasolini

ROME THROUGH THE YEAR

THE BEST TIMES to visit Rome are spring and autumn, when the weather is usually warm and sometimes even hot enough to sunbathe and swim at the beaches and lakes outside the city. November is best avoided since the weather tends to be gray and extremely rainy, while in high summer, most people (including Romans, who leave the city in droves) find the heat unbearable. Easter and Christmas are obviously very special in Rome, but there are other religious festivals worth seeing at other times in the year, as well as some enjoyable secular events, like the Festa de Noàntri in Trastevere and the Flower Festival in Genzano. In villages outside Rome, local celebrations are held to welcome new crops, such as strawberries and beans in the spring, and grapes and truffles in the autumn.

SPRING

EASTER, falling in March or April, marks the official beginning of the tourist season in Rome. Catholics from all over the world flock into the city to make their pilgrimages to the main basilicas and to hear the Pope's Easter Sunday address outside St. Peter's; the less devout come simply to take advantage of the mild weather. Meanwhile, Romans pile into their cars and head for the coast and countryside, so you can expect the roads, the beaches, and the restaurants of the Castelli Romani and Lake Bracciano to be busy.

Temperatures tend to be around 66° F (18° C), but can hit 82° F (28° C), so by mid-May it's usually possible to lunch and dine outside. However, there can still be sudden downpours and temperature swings, so do bring warm

Crowds gathering in St. Peter's square at Easter

clothes and an umbrella. In April, tubs full of colorful azaleas are arranged on the Spanish Steps and along Via Veneto, and once the roses start to flower in the city's Rose Garden overlooking the Circus Maximus, it is opened to the public.

For two weeks from mid-May, Via dei Coronari is lit by candles, lined with plants and hung with banners for the street's antiques fair, while Via Margutta hosts an outdoor art show. In the first week of May, the International Horse Show is held in the Villa Borghese, and toward the end of the month many world-class tennis players flock to Rome to compete in the International Tennis Championships at Foro Italico.

EVENTS

Festa di Santa Francesca Romana *(March 9)*, Santa Francesca Romana. Blessing of the city's cars, buses and trams *(see p87)*.
Festa di San Giuseppe *(March 19)*, Trionfale area. St. Joseph's (and Father's) Day. Street stalls, food and music.
Good Friday *(March/April)*, Colosseum. Procession of the Cross at 9pm led by the pope.
Easter Sunday *(March/April)*, St. Peter's square. Address made by the pope *(see p231)*.
Rome's Birthday *(Sunday before April 21)*, Piazza del Campidoglio.
Festa della Primavera *(March/April)*, Spanish Steps and Trinità dei Monti. Azaleas in the street and concerts.
Art exhibition *(April/May)*, Via Margutta *(see p339)*.
International Horse Show *(early May)*, Villa Borghese *(see p350)*.
Antiques Fair *(mid–late May)*, Via dei Coronari *(see p324)*.
International Tennis Championships *(late May)*, Foro Italico *(see p350)*.

International Horse Show in Villa Borghese in May

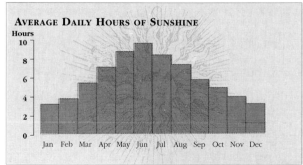

AVERAGE DAILY HOURS OF SUNSHINE
Hours

10
8
6
4
2
0

Jan Feb Mar Apr May Jun Jul Aug Sep Oct Nov Dec

Sunshine Chart
Rome is famous for its light. June is the sunniest month, but very dry, and without the occasional shower the bright heat can feel intense. In autumn, Rome's southerly position makes the midday sun enjoyably warm.

SUMMER

IN JUNE, a summer season of concerts begins, with performances in some of the city's most beautiful palaces, churches and courtyards. In July and August, opera and classical drama is staged at Ostia Antica and in various outdoor locations. Throughout the summer there are also contemporary cultural events – film, music of all kinds, dance and theater – staged as part of the Cineporto and Massenzio film festivals *(see p346)* and RomaEuropa. On midsummer evenings, there are stalls and amusements on the Tiber embankments by Castel Sant'Angelo, while in the last two weeks of July

Summer vegetables

Trastevere becomes an open-air party, as the Noantri festival is celebrated with trinket stalls, dining in the street and fireworks. Mid-July is good for shoppers because the sales *(saldi)* begin.

Many Romans leave the city at the end of June, when schools close, but since June and July are busy for tourists, hotels, restaurants and cafés and sights are packed. In

Flower-carpeted streets in Genzano

August, when the temperature often soars to over 104° F (40° C), virtually all Romans flee the city for the sea, and many restaurants,cafés and shops close for the month.

EVENTS

Flower Festival *(June, the Sunday after Corpus Domini)*, Genzano, Castelli Romani, south of Rome. Streets are carpeted with flowers.
Festa di San Giovanni *(June 23–24)*, Piazza di Porta San Giovanni. Celebrated with meals of snails in tomato sauce, suckling pig, a fair and fireworks display.
RomaEuropa *(late June–autumn)*, mainly in Villa Medici. Films, dance, theater and concerts *(see p341)*.
Festa di San Pietro *(June 29)*, many churches. Celebrations mark the feast of St. Peter.

Tevere Expo *(end June–mid-July)*, along the Tiber. Arts and crafts, food and wine, music and fireworks *(see p339)*.
Festa de Noantri *(last two weeks in July)*, the streets of Trastevere. Feasting, processions and entertainment *(see p339 and p341)*.
Estate Romana *(July/ August)*, Baths of Caracalla, Villa Ada, Ostia Antica, by the Tiber, in parks. Opera, concerts, drama and film *(see p341)*.
Festa della Madonna della Neve *(August 5)*, Santa Maria Maggiore. Legendary 4th-century fall of snow re-enacted with showers of white flower petals *(see p172)*.
Ferragosto *(August 15)*, Santa Maria in Trastevere. Midsummer Roman holiday. Almost everything closes down. Celebrations are held for the Feast of the Assumption.

The heat of an August afternoon in front of St. Peter's

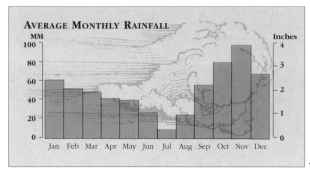

AVERAGE MONTHLY RAINFALL

MM   Inches
100   4
 80   3
 60   2
 40   1
 20
  0   0
   Jan Feb Mar Apr May Jun Jul Aug Sep Oct Nov Dec

Rainfall Chart
Autumn is Rome's rainiest season, with heavy downpours, sometimes lasting for days, especially in November. Rain in summer tends to come in violent – but often extremely refreshing – storms. In winter and early spring, expect a few dull, drizzly days.

AUTUMN

SEPTEMBER AND OCTOBER are the best – and among the most popular – months to visit Rome. The fiery heat of July and August will have cooled a little, but midday can be very hot, and you can still eat and drink outside without feeling chilly until late at night. Visiting Rome in November is not recommended: it is the wettest month of the year, and Roman rainstorms are often very strong and heavy.

At the beginning of October, an artisans' fair is held on Via dell'Orso and adjacent streets, while nearby the antiques galleries of Via dei Coronari hold open house. There are also October antiques fairs in Orvieto and Perugia, two of the loveliest Umbrian hill towns, which are about an hour's drive north of Rome. In November, there's yet another prestigious antiques fair at the papal palace of Viterbo, 40 miles (65 km) north of Rome *(see p271).*

Autumn is, of course, the season of harvest festivals, and it can be fun to head out to the small towns around Rome to sample delicacies such as local cheeses,

A roast chestnut stall in autumn

sausages, chestnuts and mushrooms. Another reason for taking a trip out of Rome is the wine festival in Marino (in the Castelli Romani, south of Rome). There are plenty of opportunities to sample the wines of this region that was once the home to luxurious 16th- and 17th-century country residences but now is renowned particularly for its white wines.

Throughout the autumn and winter, freshly roasted chestnuts can be bought from vendors on street corners, and there is usually a stand on Campo de' Fiori where you can sample the new season's wine, *vino novello,* for free. On All Souls and All Saints days,

which fall on November 1 and 2 respectively, the Romans make pilgrimages to the tombs of relatives who are buried in the cemeteries of Prima Porta and Verano. Chrysanthemums are then traditionally placed on their graves, and for this reason they should definitely not be given to friends, hosts and hostesses as thank-you presents for their hospitality.

On a much happier note, the classical concert and opera seasons begin again in October and November.

Details of performances can be found in various listing magazines such as *Trovaroma* and *Roma c'è (see p340)* and on posters dotted around the city.

EVENTS

Art fair *(September)*, Via Margutta *(see p339).*
Crafts fair *(last week September/first week October)*, Via dell'Orso, near Piazza Navona *(see p339).*
Marino Wine Festival *(first Sunday in October)*, Marino. Celebrations include tastings and street entertainment.
Antiques Fair *(mid-October)*, Via dei Coronari *(see p339).*
All Souls and All Saints Days *(November 1, 2)*, Prima Porta and Verano cemeteries. Witness the Pope usually celebrating Mass in the extensive Verano cemetary.
Festa di Santa Cecilia *(November 22)*, Santa Cecilia in Trastevere and Catacombs of San Callisto.
Vino Novello tasting *(late November)*, Campo de' Fiori.

Autumn in the Villa Doria Pamphilj park

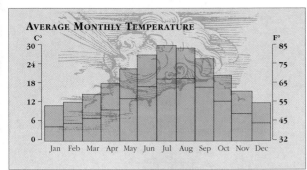

AVERAGE MONTHLY TEMPERATURE

Temperature Chart
The chart shows the average minimum and maximum monthly temperatures. July and August can be unbearably hot, making sightseeing a chore. The cooler days of spring and autumn are ideal to visit Rome, but there are some dull and rainy spells.

WINTER

DURING THE WINTER, Rome is bracingly chilly, but the temperature rarely drops below freezing. Not all buildings are centrally heated, so if you're staying in a small hotel bring warm clothes and request extra blankets as soon as you arrive, because they are often in short supply. Warm up in cafés with hot chocolate or a cappuccino.

The run-up to Christmas is great fun in Rome, especially if you have children. Manger scenes, *presepi*, are set up in many churches, piazzas and public places and from mid-December to Twelfth Night,

The Befana on Piazza Navona

Piazza Navona hosts a market where you can buy manger scenes, decorations and toys.

If you don't have friends in Rome, Christmas can be lonely, since it is such a family event. On New Year's Eve, however, everyone is out on the street to drink sparkling wine and let off fireworks.

Befana, on January 6, is a traditional holiday when a witch, called La Befana, delivers sweets to children. The Carnival season runs from late January through to February, celebrated largely by children with costume

Rome during one of its rare snowfalls

parties and parades along Via Nazionale, Via Cola di Rienzo and the Pincio. Keep out of the way of teenagers with shaving cream sprays and water balloons.

EVENTS

Festa della Madonna Immacolata *(December 8)*, Piazza di Spagna. Firemen climb up a ladder to place a wreath on the statue of the Virgin Mary.
Christmas Market *(mid-December – mid-January)*, Piazza Navona. Christmas and children's market *(see p120)*.
Nativity scenes *(mid-December – mid-January)*, many churches. Life-size scene in St. Peter's square, collection at Santi Cosma e Damiano.
Midnight Mass *(December 24)*, at most churches.
Christmas Day *(December 25)*, St. Peter's square. Blessing by the pope.
New Year's Eve *(December 31)*, all over city. Fireworks displays, furniture thrown out.
Befana *(January 6)*, all over the city. Parties for children.

PUBLIC HOLIDAYS
New Year's Day (Jan 1)
Epiphany (Jan 6)
Easter Monday
Liberation Day (Apr 25)
Labor Day (May 1)
SS Peter and Paul's day (Jun 29)
Ferragosto (Aug 15)
All Saints (Nov 1)
Immaculate Conception (Dec 8)
Christmas Day (Dec 25)
Santo Stefano (Dec 26)

Via Condotti at Christmas

ROME AREA
BY AREA

CAPITOL

THE TEMPLE OF JUPITER on the Capitol, the southern summit of the Capitoline Hill, was the center of the ancient Roman world. Reached by a zig-zagging path up from the Forum, the temple was the scene of all the most sacred religious and political ceremonies. The hill and its temple came to symbolize Rome's authority as *caput mundi*, head of the world, and the concept of a "capital" city is derived from the Capitol. Throughout the city's history, the Capitol, or Campidoglio as it is called in Italian, has remained the

Hand of colossal statue in Palazzo dei Conservatori

seat of municipal government. Today's city council, the Comune di Roma, meets in the Renaissance splendor of Palazzo Senatorio. Rome's position as a modern capital is seen in the enormous Victor Emmanuel Monument, which blots out the view of the Capitol from Piazza Venezia. The present arrangement of the buildings on the hill dates from the 16th century, when Michelangelo created a beautiful piazza reached by a dramatic flight of steps, the Cordonata. Two of the three buildings around the piazza are now home to the Capitoline Museums.

SIGHTS AT A GLANCE

Churches and Temples
Santa Maria in Aracoeli **7**
Temple of Jupiter **8**
San Marco **12**

Museums and Galleries
*Capitoline Museums:
Palazzo Nuovo pp70–71* **1**
*Capitoline Museums:
Palazzo dei Conservatori
pp72–3* **2**
Palazzo Venezia
and Museum **11**

Historic Buildings
Roman Insula **5**

Historic Streets and Piazzas
Piazza del Campidoglio **3**
Cordonata **4**
Aracoeli Staircase **6**

Ancient Sites
Tarpeian Rock **9**

Monuments
Victor Emmanuel
Monument **10**

GETTING THERE
All the sights in this area are within walking distance of Piazza Venezia. Bus routes converge here from all parts of the city, as do many thousands of motorists. From Termini station you can catch the 64, 70, 75, or 170; from Piazza Barberini the 56, 60 or 492. From St. Peter's and the Vatican the only bus is the 64. Other useful routes include the 44, 46, and 628.

SEE ALSO

• *Street Finder*, maps 5, 12

Statue of Marcus Aurelius on Michelangelo's Piazza del Campidoglio

Street by Street: The Capitol and Piazza Venezia

THE CAPITOL, citadel of ancient Rome, is a must stop for every visitor. A broad flight of steps (the Cordonata) leads up to Michelangelo's spectacular Piazza del Campidoglio. This is flanked by the Palazzo Nuovo and the Palazzo dei Conservatori, housing the Capitoline Museums with their fine collections of sculpture and painting. The absence of cars makes the hill a welcome retreat from the squeal of brakes below, but visitors should brave traffic to visit Palazzo Venezia and its museum.

Victor Emmanuel Monument
This huge white marble monument to Italy's first king was completed in 1911 ⑩

PIAZZA VENEZIA

PIAZZA VENEZIA

San Marco
The church of the Venetians in Rome has a fine 9th-century apse mosaic ⑫

Palazzo Venezia
The museum's finest exhibits, such as this 13th-century gilded angel decorated with enamel, date from the late Middle Ages ⑪

Roman Insula
This is a ruined apartment block dating from imperial Rome ⑤

VIA DEL TEATRO DI MA

Cordonata
Michelangelo's great staircase shifted the orientation of the Capitol to the west ④

Aracoeli Staircase
When it was built in 1348, the staircase became a center for political debate ⑥

★ Palazzo dei Conservatori
Displayed in the courtyard in this part of the Capitoline Museums is a fine series of reliefs from the Temple of Hadrian (see p106) ②

Santa Maria in Aracoeli
The treasures hidden behind the church's brick facade include this 15th-century fresco, The Funeral of St. Bernardino *by Pinturicchio* ❼

★ Palazzo Nuovo
This bust of Augustus in the Hall of the Emperors is one of many fine classical sculptures in the Capitoline Museums ❶

LOCATOR MAP
See Central Rome Map pp12–13

Palazzo Senatorio was used by the Roman Senate from about the 12th century. It now houses the offices of the mayor.

★ Piazza del Campidoglio
Michelangelo designed both the geometric paving and the facades of the buildings ❸

Temple of Jupiter
This artist's impression shows the gold-and-ivory statue of Jupiter that stood in the temple ❽

Tarpeian Rock
In ancient Rome traitors were thrown to their death from this cliff on the Capitol ❾

STAR SIGHTS

★ **Piazza del Campidoglio**

★ **Palazzo dei Conservatori**

★ **Palazzo Nuovo**

Capitoline Museums: Palazzo Nuovo ❶

See pp70–71.

Capitoline Museums: Palazzo dei Conservatori ❷

See pp72–3.

Piazza del Campidoglio ❸

Map 5 A5 & 12 F5. 🚌 *See **Getting There** p65.*

WHEN EMPEROR Charles V visited Rome in 1536, Pope Paul III Farnese was so embarrassed by the muddy state of the Capitol that he asked Michelangelo to draw up plans for repaving the piazza and for renovating the facades of Palazzo dei Conservatori and Palazzo Senatorio.

Michelangelo proposed adding the Palazzo Nuovo to form a piazza in the shape of a trapezium, embellished with Classical sculptures chosen for their relevance to Rome. Building started in 1546 but progressed so slowly that Michelangelo only lived to oversee the double flight of steps at the entrance of Palazzo Senatorio. The piazza was completed in the 17th

century, the design remaining largely faithful to the original. Pilasters two-stories high and balustrades interspersed with statues link the buildings thematically. The piazza faces west toward St. Peter's, the Christian equivalent of the Capitol. At it center stands a replica of a statue of Marcus Aurelius. The original is in the Palazzo Nuovo *(see pp70–71)*.

Cordonata ❹

Map 5 A5 & 12 F5. 🚌 *See **Getting There** p65.*

FROM PIAZZA VENEZIA, the Capitol is approached by a gently rising, subtly widening ramp – the Cordonata. At the foot is a pair of granite Egyptian lions, and a 19th-century monument to Cola di Rienzo is on the left, close to where the 14th-century tyrant was executed. The top of the ramp is guarded by restored Classical statues of the Dioscuri, Castor and Pollux.

Roman *Insula* ❺

Piazza d'Aracoeli. **Map** 5 A5 & 12 F4. 📞 67 10 30 65. 🚌 *See **Getting There** p65.* **Open** *by appt only: permit needed* (see p367).

TWO THOUSAND YEARS ago the urban poor of Rome used to make their homes in *insulae* – apartment blocks.

One of the statues of the Dioscuri at the top of the Cordonata

These were often badly maintained by landlords and expensive to rent in a city where land costs were high. This 2nd-century AD tenement block, of barrel-vault construction, is the only survivor from that era. The fourth and fifth stories and part of the sixth remain above current ground level.

In the Middle Ages, a section of these upper stories was converted into a church; its bell tower and 14th-century Madonna in a niche are visible from the street.

During the Fascist years, the area was cleared, and three lower floors emerged. Some 380 people may have lived in the tenement, in the squalid conditions described by the 1st-century AD satirical writers Martial and Juvenal. The latter mentions that he had to climb 200 steps to reach his garret.

This *insula* may once have had more stories. The higher you lived, the more dismal the conditions, as the cramped spaces of the building's upper levels testify.

The Cordonata in an 18th-century painting by Antonio Canaletto

Aracoeli Staircase ❻

Piazza d'Aracoeli. **Map** 5 A5 & 12 F4.
🚌 See **Getting There** p65.

THE ARACOELI Staircase contains 124 marble steps (122 if you start from the right) and was completed in 1348, some say in thanks for the passing of the Black Death, but more probably in preparation for the 1350 Holy Year.

The 14th-century tribune-turned-tyrant Cola di Rienzo harangued the masses from the Aracoeli Staircase; 17th-century foreigners slept on the steps, until Prince Caffarelli, who lived on the hill, scared them off by rolling stone-filled barrels down upon them.

Popular belief has it that by climbing the steps on your knees you can win the national lottery. From the top is a good view of Rome, with the domes of Sant' Andrea della Valle and St. Peter's slightly to the right.

Aracoeli Staircase

Santa Maria in Aracoeli ❼

Piazza d'Aracoeli (entrances via Aracoeli Staircase and door behind Palazzo Nuovo). **Map** 5 A5 & 12 F4.
📞 06-679 81 55. 🚌 See **Getting There** p65. **Open** 7am–6:30pm daily.

DATING FROM AT LEAST the 6th century, the church of Santa Maria in Aracoeli, or St. Mary of the Altar in the Sky, stands on the northern summit of the Capitoline, on the site of the ancient temple

Ceiling commemorating Battle of Lepanto in nave of Santa Maria in Aracoeli

to Juno. Its 22 columns were taken from various ancient buildings; the inscription on the third column to the left explains that it comes *"a cubiculo Augustorum"* – from the bedroom of the emperors.

The church of the Roman senators and people, Santa Maria in Aracoeli has been used to celebrate many triumphs over adversity. Its ceiling, with naval motifs, commemorates the Battle of Lepanto (1571) and was built under Pope Gregory XIII Boncompagni, whose family crest, the dragon, can be seen towards the altar end.

Many other Roman families and individuals are honored by memorials in the church. To the right of the entrance door, the tombstone of archdeacon Giovanni Crivelli, rather than being set into the floor of the church, stands eternally at attention, partly so that the signature "Donatelli" (by Donatello) can be read at eye level.

The frescoes in the first chapel on the right, painted by Pinturicchio in the 1480s in the beautifully clear style of the early Renaissance, relate the life and death of St. Bernardino of Siena. On the left wall, the perspective of *The Burial of the Saint* actually slants to the right, taking into account the position of the viewer standing just outside the chapel.

The church is most famous, however, for an icon with apparently miraculous powers, the *Santo Bambino*, a 15th-century olive-wood figure of the Christ child which was carved out of a tree from the garden of Gethsemane. Its powers are said to include resurrecting the dead, and it is sometimes summoned to the bedsides of the gravely ill. The original figure was stolen in 1994 but has now been replaced by a replica.

At Christmas the Christ Child is moved to a picturesque crèche (second chapel to the left), but usually it is located in the sacristy, as is the panel of the *Holy Family* from the workshop of Giulio Romano.

The miraculous olive-wood Christ Child at Santa Maria in Aracoeli

Capitoline Museums: Palazzo Nuovo ❶

A COLLECTION of Classical statues has been kept on the Capitoline hill since the Renaissance. The first group of bronze sculptures was given to the city by Pope Sixtus IV in 1471 and more additions were made by Pope Pius V in 1566. The Palazzo Nuovo was designed by Michelangelo as part of the renovation of the Piazza del Campidoglio, and after its completion in 1655, a number of the statues were transferred there. In 1734 Pope Clement XII Corsini decreed that the building be turned into the world's first public museum.

MUSEUM GUIDE

The two floors of the Palazzo Nuovo are devoted chiefly to sculpture. Most of the finest works, such as the Capitoline Venus, are Roman copies of Greek masterpieces. There are also two collections of busts assembled in the 18th century for visitors keen to identify all the philosophers and poets of ancient Greece and the rulers of ancient Rome. The price of entry includes admission to the Palazzo dei Conservatori, which is directly opposite.

Hall of the Philosophers
The hall contains a rich mix of portraits of Greek politicians, scientists and literary figures. They are Roman copies that decorated the libraries, villas and gardens of the wealthy in ancient times.

Portrait of a Flavian Lady
The woman wears the fanciful and elaborate hairstyle popular among the female aristocracy of the 1st century AD.

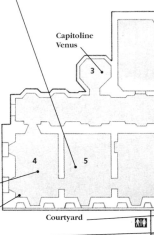

Capitoline Venus

3

4   5

First floor

Courtyard

★ **Marcus Aurelius**
This bronze equestrian statue of the emperor dates from the 2nd century AD. It used to stand on a pedestal in the centre of the Campidoglio, but has now been restored and is housed in the Palazzo Nuovo. A copy stands on the square.

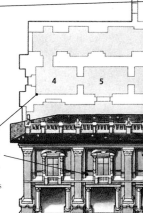

4   5

Ground floor

The facade of Palazzo Nuovo was designed by Michelangelo, but the work was actually finished in 1655 by the brothers Carlo and Girolamo Rainaldi.

STAR SCULPTURES

★ **Marcus Aurelius**

★ **Discobolus**

★ **Dying Galatian**

KEY TO FLOORPLAN

☐ Non-exhibition space

☐ Exhibition space

Mosaic of the Doves
This charming naturalistic mosaic once decorated the floor of Hadrian's Villa at Tivoli (see p269). It shows doves drinking water from a vase.

★ **Discobolus**
The twisted torso was part of a Greek statue of a discus thrower. An 18th-century French sculptor, Monnot, made the additions that turned him into a wounded warrior.

Red Faun
Found at Tivoli, the famous red marble satyr is a 2nd-century AD version of a Greek original – an example of Hadrian's fondness for all things Greek.

— Stairs to ground floor

7 8

— Stairs to first floor

3

9 8 7

★ **Dying Galatian**

Great compassion is conveyed in this Roman copy of an original Greek work of the 3rd century BC.

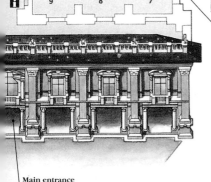

Alexander Severus as Hunter
In this marble of the 3rd century AD, the emperor is posed as Perseus, holding up the head of Medusa the Gorgon after he had killed her in her sleep.

— Main entrance

Capitoline Museums: Palazzo dei Conservatori ❷

T HE PALAZZO DEI CONSERVATORI was the
seat of the city's magistrates during
the late Middle Ages. Its frescoed halls
are still used occasionally for political
meetings, and the ground floor houses
the municipal registry office. The palazzo
was built by Giacomo della Porta, who
carried out Michelangelo's designs for the
Piazza del Campidoglio in the mid-16th
century. While much of the
palazzo is given over to
sculpture, the art galleries
on the second floor hold
works by Veronese,
Guercino, Tintoretto,
Rubens, Caravaggio,
Van Dyck and Titian.

Facade of Palazzo dei Conservatori
*Work began on this Michelangelo design
in 1563, the year before his death.*

MUSEUM GUIDE
*The whole museum is now
open after restoration, but
is still being reorganized,
why objects might move.
The rooms on the first floor
are remarkable for their
original 16th- and 17th-
century decoration and
Classical statues. The
second-floor gallery
houses paintings and a
collection of porcelain.*

**Burial and Glory
of St. Petronilla**
*This huge Baroque altar-
piece was painted from
1622–3 by Guercino to
hang in St. Peter's.*

Stairs to
second floor

★ **St. John the Baptist**
*Painted in 1595–6,
Caravaggio's sensual
portrait of the young
saint presents a highly
unorthodox image of the
forerunner of Christ.*

Stairs to
first floor

Second-floor
art gallery

Court

Main
entrance

The Horatii and Curatii
*D'Arpino's fresco was painted
in 1613 and depicts a duel
taken from early Roman legend.*

KEY TO FLOOR PLAN

■	Garden
☐	Non-exhibition space
☐	Re-opened after restoration
☐	Exhibition space

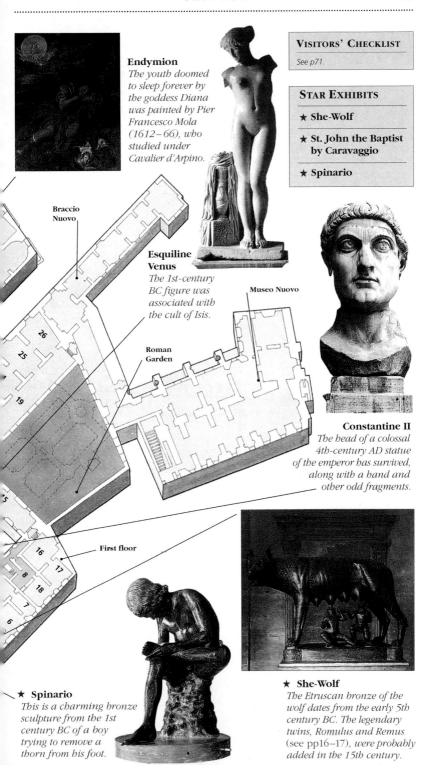

Endymion
*The youth doomed
to sleep forever by
the goddess Diana
was painted by Pier
Francesco Mola
(1612–66), who
studied under
Cavalier d'Arpino.*

VISITORS' CHECKLIST

See p71.

STAR EXHIBITS

★ **She-Wolf**

★ **St. John the Baptist
by Caravaggio**

★ **Spinario**

Braccio
Nuovo

**Esquiline
Venus**
*The 1st-century
BC figure was
associated with
the cult of Isis.*

Museo Nuovo

Roman
Garden

26

25

19

Constantine II
*The head of a colossal
4th-century AD statue
of the emperor has survived,
along with a hand and
other odd fragments.*

First floor

16 17

8
18

7

6

★ **Spinario**
*This is a charming bronze
sculpture from the 1st
century BC of a boy
trying to remove a
thorn from his foot.*

★ **She-Wolf**
*The Etruscan bronze of the
wolf dates from the early 5th
century BC. The legendary
twins, Romulus and Remus
(see pp16–17), were probably
added in the 15th century.*

Temple of Jupiter ❽

Via del Tempio di Giove. **Map** 5 A5 & 12 F5. 🚌 *See* **Getting There** *p65.*

THE TEMPLE of Jupiter, the most important in ancient Rome, was built in honor of the arch god around 509 BC on the southern summit of the Capitoline Hill. From the few traces that remain, archaeologists have been able to reconstruct the rectangular Greek appearance of the temple as it once stood. In places are remnants of its particularly Roman feature, the podium. Most of this lies beneath the Museo Nuovo wing of the Capitoline Museums *(see pp72–3).*

By walking around the site, from the podium's south-western corner in Via del Tempio di Giove to its south-eastern corner in Piazzale Caffarelli, visitors can see that the temple was about the same size as the Pantheon.

Sabine soldiers crushing the treacherous Tarpeia with their shields

Ancient coin showing the Temple of Jupiter

Tarpeian Rock ❾

Via di Monte Caprino and Via del Tempio di Giove. **Map** 5 A5 & 12 F5. 🚌 *See* **Getting There** *p65.*

THE SOUTHERN TIP of the Capitoline is called the Tarpeian Rock (Rupe Tarpea), after Tarpeia, the young daughter of Spurius Tarpeius, defender of the Capitol in the 8th-century BC Sabine War.

The Sabines, bent on vengeance for the rape of their women by Romulus and his men, bribed Tarpeia to let them up to the Capitol. As the Augustan historian Livy records, Tarpeia's reward for her treachery was to be what the sabines wore on their shield arms: heavy gold bracelets and jeweled rings.

The Sabines kept to the letter of the bargain if not to its spirit – they repaid Tarpeia not with their jewelry but by crushing her to death between their shields.

Tarpeia was possibly the only casualty of her act of treachery – as the invading warriors met the Roman defenders, the Sabine women leapt between the two opposing armies, and forced them to become reconciled. All traitors and other condemned criminals were subsequently executed by being thrown over the sheer face of the rock.

The place has been considered dangerous and used to be fenced off, but restoration work is now under way.

Victor Emmanuel Monument ❿

Piazza Venezia. **Map** 5 A5 & 12 F4. 🚌 *See* **Getting There** *p65.* **Open** *for temporary exhibitions only.*

KNOWN AS Il Vittoriano, this monument was begun in 1885 and inaugurated in 1925 in honor of Victor Emmanuel II of Savoy, the first king of a unified Italy. The king is depicted here in a gilt bronze equestrian statue, oversized like the monument itself – the statue is 39 ft (12 m) long.

The edifice contains a museum of the Risorgimento, the events that led to unification *(see pp36–7).* It has, however, been closed since the early 1980s. Built in austere white Brescian marble, the "wedding cake" or "typewriter" (two of the many insulting nicknames given to this unloved white elephant) will never mellow into the ocher tones of surrounding buildings. It is widely held to be the epitome of self-important, insensitive architecture.

Victor Emmanuel Monument in Piazza Venezia

Palazzo Venezia and Museum ⓫

Via del Plebiscito 118. **Map** 5 A4 & 12 E4. **[** 06-79 88 65. **]** See **Getting There** p65. **Open** 9am– 1.30pm Tue–Sat, 9am–12.30pm Sun (last adm: 30 mins before closing). **Closed** Jan 1, May 1, Dec 25. **Adm charge**. **[**&**]** Temporary exhibitions.

Palazzo Venezia with Mussolini's balcony in the center

Pope Paul II

ONE OF THE first Renaissance civic buildings in Rome, this palazzo has arched windows and doors that are so harmonious the facade was once attributed to the great Humanist architect Leon Battista Alberti (1404–72). It was more probably designed by Giuliano da Maiano, who carved the fine doorway to the piazza.

Palazzo Venezia was built in 1455–64 for the Venetian cardinal Pietro Barbo, who later became Pope Paul II. It was at times a papal residence, but also the Venetian Embassy before passing into French hands in 1797. Since 1916 it has belonged to the state. In the Fascist era Mussolini used it as his headquarters, addressing crowds from the balcony.

The interior is best seen on a visit to the Museo del Palazzo Venezia, Rome's most underrated museum, which holds first-class collections of early Renaissance painting; painted wood sculptures and Renaissance chests from throughout Italy; tapestries from all over Europe; majolica; silver; Neapolitan ceramic figurines; Renaissance bronzes; arms and armor; Baroque terra-cotta sculptures by Bernini, Algardi and others; and 17th- and 18th-century Italian paintings. There is a marble screen from the Aracoeli convent, which was destroyed to make way for the Victor Emmanuel Monument, and a bust of Paul II, showing him to rank with Martin V and Leo X among the fattest popes. The building also hosts major temporary exhibitions.

San Marco ⓬

Piazza San Marco 48. **Map** 5 A4 & 12 F4. **[** 679 52 05. **]** See **Getting There** p65. **Open** 8am–12:30pm, 4pm–7pm Tue, Thu–Sun, 4pm–7pm Mon, 8am–12:30pm Wed. **[**✝**]** **[**Ø**]**

THE CHURCH of San Marco was founded in 336 by Mark, then pope, in honor of St. Mark the Evangelist. The relics of Pope Mark lie under the altar. The church was restored by Pope Gregory IV in the 9th century – the magnificent apse mosaics date from this period.

Further major rebuilding took place from 1455 –1471, when Pope Paul II Barbo made San Marco the church of the Venetian

Coat of arms of Pope Paul II

community in Rome. The blue-and-gold coffered ceiling is decorated with Pope Paul's heraldic crest, the lion rampant, recalling the lion of St. Mark, the patron saint of Venice. The appearance of the rest of the interior, with its colonnades of Sicilian jasper, was largely the creation of Filippo Barigioni in the 1740s. Complemented by an interesting array of funerary monuments in the aisles, the taste is typical of the late Roman Baroque.

Leon Battista Alberti, whose name is also mentioned tentatively in connection with Palazzo Venezia, may have been the architect of the elegant travertine arcade and loggia of the facade.

San Marco's apse mosaic of Christ, with Gregory IV on the far left

FORUM

THE FORUM was the center of political, commercial and judicial life in ancient Rome. The largest buildings were the basilicas, where legal cases were heard. According to the playwright Plautus, the area teemed with "lawyers and litigants, bankers and brokers, shopkeepers and strumpets, good-for-nothings waiting for a tip from the rich." As

Figure of barbarian on the Arch of Constantine

Rome's population boomed, the Forum became too small. In 46 BC Julius Caesar built a new one, setting a precedent that was followed by emperors from Augustus to Trajan. In addition to the Imperial Forums, emperors erected triumphal arches to themselves, and just to the east Vespasian built the Colosseum, center of entertainment after the business of the day.

SIGHTS AT A GLANCE

Churches and Temples
Temple of Saturn **5**
Temple of Castor and Pollux **8**
Temple of Vesta **9**
Temple of Antoninus and Faustina **11**
Temple of Romulus and Santi Cosma e Damiano **12**
Santa Francesca Romana **14**
Temple of Venus and Rome **17**

Historic Buildings
Basilica Aemilia **1**
Curia **2**
Basilica Julia **7**

House of the Vestal Virgins **10**
Basilica of Constantine and Maxentius **13**
Trajan's Markets pp88–9 **18**
Torre delle Milizie **20**
Casa dei Cavalieri di Rodi **21**
Mamertine Prison **24**
Colosseum pp92–5 **27**

Museums
Antiquarium Forense **15**

KEY

| | Tour of the Forum maps |
| **M** | Metro station |

Arches and Columns
Arch of Septimius Severus **4**
Column of Phocas **6**
Arch of Titus **16**
Column of Trajan **19**
Arch of Constantine **26**

Ancient Sites
Rostra **3**
Forum of Augustus **22**
Forum of Caesar **23**
Forum of Nerva **25**

GETTING THERE
The simplest way to reach the area is by Metro to Colosseo on line B. The Forum's main entrance is on Via dei Fori Imperiali, served by buses 75, 85, 87, 117, 175, 186, 810 and 850. Many more routes go to Piazza Venezia. For Trajan's Markets, take such buses as the H, 64, 65 and 70 that stop in Via IV Novembre.

SEE ALSO

• *Street Finder*, maps 5, 8, 9, 12

• *Where to Stay* pp294–5

• *Triumphal Arches Walk* pp278–9

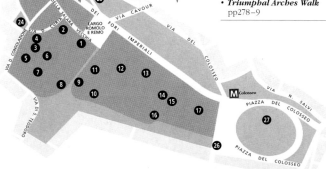

View of the Forum with the Colosseum rising behind the bell tower of Santa Francesca Romana

A Tour of the Roman Forum: West

To APPRECIATE THE LAYOUT of the Forum before visiting its confusing patchwork of ruined temples and basilicas, it is best to view the whole area from above, from the back of the Capitol. From there you can make out the Via Sacra (the Sacred Way), the route followed through the Forum by religious and triumphal processions towards the Capitol. Up until the 18th century when archaeological excavations began, the Arch of Septimius Severus and the columns of the Temple of Saturn lay half buried underground. Excavation of the Forum continues, and the ruins uncovered date from many different periods of Roman history.

The Temple of Vespasian was the point from where Piranesi made this 18th-century engraving of the Forum. Its three columns were then almost completely buried.

Temple of Concord

Portico of the Dii Consentes

Temple of Saturn
The eight surviving columns of this temple stand close by the three columns of the Temple of Vespasian **5**

Rostra
These are the ruins of the platform used for public oratory in the Forum **3**

Basilica Julia
Named after Julius Caesar, who ordered its construction, the basilica housed important law courts **7**

Column of Phocas
One of the very last monuments erected in the Forum, this single column dates from AD 608 **6**

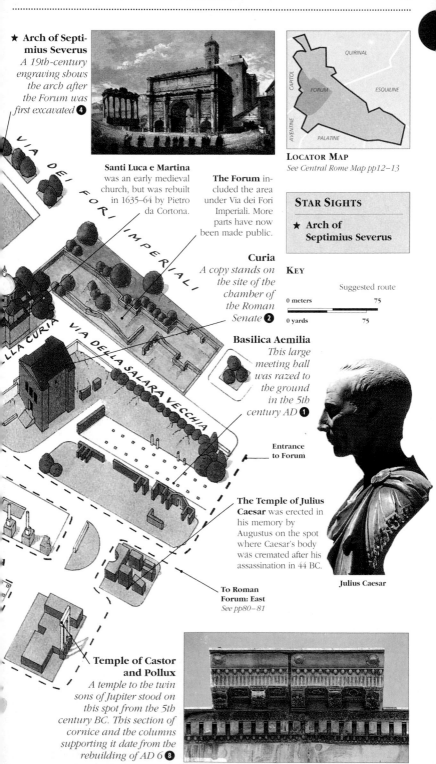

★ **Arch of Septimius Severus**
A 19th-century engraving shows the arch after the Forum was first excavated ❹

LOCATOR MAP
See Central Rome Map pp12–13

Santi Luca e Martina
was an early medieval church, but was rebuilt in 1635–64 by Pietro da Cortona.

The Forum included the area under Via dei Fori Imperiali. More parts have now been made public.

STAR SIGHTS

★ **Arch of Septimius Severus**

Curia
A copy stands on the site of the chamber of the Roman Senate ❷

KEY

Suggested route

0 meters 75

0 yards 75

Basilica Aemilia
This large meeting hall was razed to the ground in the 5th century AD ❶

Entrance to Forum

The Temple of Julius Caesar was erected in his memory by Augustus on the spot where Caesar's body was cremated after his assassination in 44 BC.

Julius Caesar

To Roman Forum: East
See pp80–81

Temple of Castor and Pollux
A temple to the twin sons of Jupiter stood on this spot from the 5th century BC. This section of cornice and the columns supporting it date from the rebuilding of AD 6 ❽

A Tour of the Roman Forum: East

THE EASTERN END of the Roman Forum is dominated by the massive barrel-vaulted ruins of the Basilica of Constantine. To picture the building as it was in the 4th century AD, you must imagine marble columns, floors and statues, as well as glittering tiles of gilt bronze. The remains of the other important buildings are scanty, though the garden and ponds in the center of the House of the Vestal Virgins make it a very attractive spot. The two churches in this part of the Forum cannot be reached from within the archaeological area but are accessible from the road outside.

The Regia was the office of the Pontifex Maximus, the chief priest of ancient Rome.

To Forum entrance

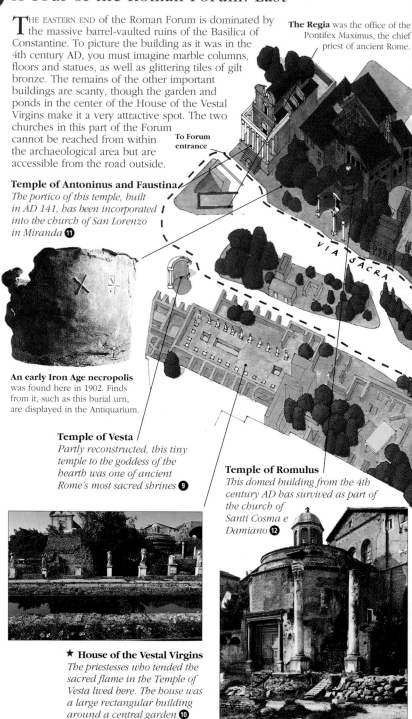

VIA SACRA

Temple of Antoninus and Faustina
The portico of this temple, built in AD 141, has been incorporated into the church of San Lorenzo in Miranda ⑪

An early Iron Age necropolis was found here in 1902. Finds from it, such as this burial urn, are displayed in the Antiquarium.

Temple of Vesta
Partly reconstructed, this tiny temple to the goddess of the hearth was one of ancient Rome's most sacred shrines ⑨

Temple of Romulus
This domed building from the 4th century AD has survived as part of the church of Santi Cosma e Damiano ⑫

★ **House of the Vestal Virgins**
The priestesses who tended the sacred flame in the Temple of Vesta lived here. The house was a large rectangular building around a central garden ⑩

★ **Basilica of Constantine and Maxentius**
The stark remains of the basilica's huge arches and ceilings give some idea of the original scale and grandeur of the Forum's public buildings 🔞

LOCATOR MAP
See Central Rome Map pp12–13

Santa Francesca Romana
The church takes its name from a saint who cared for the Roman poor in the 15th century 🔞

VIA DEI FORI IMPERIALI

Antiquarium Forense
A small museum houses archaeological finds made in the Forum. They include this frieze of Aeneas and the Founding of Rome *from the Basilica Aemilia* 🔞

Colonnade surrounding Temple of Venus and Rome

Temple of Venus and Rome
These extensive ruins are of a magnificent temple built here in AD 121 by the Emperor Hadrian, largely to his own design 🔞

VIA SACRA

Ruined Baths

To the Palatine

Arch of Titus
This 19th-century reconstruction shows how the arch may have looked when it spanned the flag-stoned roadway of the Via Sacra 🔞

STAR SIGHTS

★ **Basilica of Constantine**

★ **House of the Vestal Virgins**

KEY

‒ ‒ ‒   Suggested route

0 meters	75
0 yards	75

could and keep the difference.
This is why tax collectors in
the Bible were so loathed.

The basilica was
rebuilt many times; it
was finally burned
down when the Visi-
goths sacked Rome in
AD 410. Business seems
to have carried on
until the last moment,
for the pavement is
splashed with tiny
lumps of coins that
melted in the fire.

**Melted coins embedded in the
floor of the Basilica Aemilia**

Basilica Aemilia ❶

See Visitors' Checklist.

ORIGINALLY this building was
a rectangular colonnaded
hall, with a multicolored
marble floor and a bronze-
tiled roof. It was built by the
consuls Marcus Aemilius
Lepidus and Marcus Fulvius
Nobilor in 179 BC. The two
consuls, who were elected
annually, exercised supreme
power over the Republic.

Basilicas in ancient Rome
served no religious purpose;
they were meeting halls for
politicians, moneylenders and
publicani (businessmen con-
tracted by the state to collect
taxes). A consortium of *publicani* agreed to hand over a
specified sum to the state, but
its members were allowed to
collect as much as they

Curia ❷

See Visitors' Checklist.

A MODERN REPLICA has been
built over the ruins of the
hall where Rome's Senate
(chief council of state) used
to meet. The first Curia stood
on the site now occupied
by the church of Santi
Luca e Martina, but
after the building
was destroyed by
fire in 52 BC, Julius
Caesar built a new
Curia at the edge
of the Forum. This
was restored by
Domitian in AD 94
and, after another
fire, rebuilt by
Diocletian in the 3rd
century. The replica you see
today is based on Diocletian's
Curia. Inside are two relief
panels commissioned by
Trajan to decorate the Rostra.
One shows Trajan destroying
records of unpaid taxes to
free citizens from debt; in the
other he sits on a throne
receiving a mother and child.

Replica of the Curia

Rostra ❸

See Visitors' Checklist.

Ruins of the Imperial Rostra

SPEECHES WERE delivered from
this dais, the most famous –
thanks to Shakespeare –
being Mark Antony's "Friends,
Romans, Countrymen" oration
after the assassination of Julius
Caesar in 44 BC. Caesar
himself had just reorganized
the Forum and this speech
was made from the newly
sited Rostra, which is now
in ruins. In the
following year the
head and hands of
Cicero were put
on display after he
had been put to
death by the
second Triumvirate
(Augustus, Mark
Antony and Marcus
Lepidus). Fulvia,
Mark Antony's
wife, stabbed the
great orator's tongue with a
hairpin. It was also here that
Julia, Augustus's daughter, was
said to have played the
prostitute – one of many
scandalous acts that led to
her banishment.

The dais took its name from
the ships' prows *(rostra)* with
which it was decorated.
Sheathed in iron (for ramming
enemy vessels), these came
from ships captured at the
Battle of Antium in 338 BC.

Honorary
statue

Relief panel
in balustrade,
showing
Trajan's acts
of charity

Prows of ships
(rostra)

ROSTRA
*This reconstruction
shows the platform for
public speaking in the Forum,
as it looked in Imperial times.*

Arch of Septimius Severus ❹

See Visitors' Checklist.

THIS TRIUMPHAL ARCH, one of the most striking and best-preserved monuments of the Forum, was erected in AD 203 to celebrate the tenth anniversary of the accession of Septimius Severus. The relief panels – largely eroded – celebrate the emperor's victories in Parthia (modern-day Iraq and Iran) and Arabia.

"Barbarian" captives, Arch of Severus

Originally, the inscription along the top of the arch was to Septimius and his two sons, Caracalla and Geta, but after Septimius died, Caracalla murdered Geta and had his brother's name removed. Even so, the holes in which the letters of his name were pegged are still visible.

During the Middle Ages the central arch, half-buried in earth and debris, was used to shelter a barber's shop.

Triumphal arch of the Emperor Septimius Severus

Temple of Saturn ❺

See Visitors' Checklist.

THE MOST PROMINENT of the ruins in the fenced-off area between the Forum and the Capitoline Hill is the Temple of Saturn. It consists of a high platform, eight columns and a section of entablature. There was a temple dedicated to

Ionic capitals on the surviving columns of the Temple of Saturn

Saturn here as early as 497 BC, but it had to be rebuilt many times and the current remains date only from the 42 BC.

Saturn was the mythical god-king of Italy, said to have presided over a prosperous and peaceful Golden Age from which slavery, private property, crime and war were absent. As such, he appealed particularly to the lower classes and slaves. Every year, between December 17 and December 23, Saturn's reign was remembered in a week of sacrifices and feasting known as the Saturnalia.

As long as the revels lasted, the normal social order was turned upside down. Slaves were permitted to drink and dine with (and sometimes even be served by) their masters. Senators and other high-ranking Romans would abandon the aristocratic togas that they usually wore to distinguish them from the lower classes and put on more democratic, loose-fitting gowns. During the holidays all the law courts and schools in the city were closed. No prisoner could be punished, and no war could be declared.

People also celebrated the Saturnalia in their own homes: they exchanged gifts, in particular special wax dolls and wax tapers, and played lighthearted gambling games, the stakes usually being nuts, a symbol of fruitfulness. Much of the spirit and many of the rituals of the festival have been preserved in the Christian celebration of Christmas.

Column of Phocas ❻

See Visitors' Checklist.

THIS COLUMN, 44 ft (13.5 m) high, is one of the few to have remained upright since the day it was put up. Until 1816, when an inquisitive Englishwoman, Lady Elizabeth Foster, widow of the fifth duke of Devonshire, decided to excavate its pedestal, nobody knew what it was. It turned out to be the youngest of the Forum's monuments, erected in AD 608 in honor of the Byzantine emperor Phocas, who had just paid a visit to Rome. The column may have been placed here as a mark of gratitude to Phocas for giving the Pantheon to the pope *(see pp110–11)*.

Slender, fluted Column of Phocas

Remains of the Basilica Julia, a Roman court of civil law

Basilica Julia **❼**

See Visitors' Checklist, p82.

THIS IMMENSE basilica, which occupied the area between the Temple of Saturn and the Temple of Castor and Pollux, was begun by Julius Caesar in 54 BC and completed after his death by his great nephew Augustus. It was damaged by fire almost immediately afterward in 9 BC, but was subsequently repaired and dedicated to the emperor's grandsons, Gaius and Lucius.

After numerous sackings and pilferings, only the steps, pavement and column stumps remain. Nevertheless, the ground plan is fairly clear. The basilica had a central hall, measuring 260 ft by 59 ft (82 m by 18 m), surrounded by a double portico. The hall was on three floors, while the outer portico had only two.

The Basilica Julia was the seat of the *centumviri*, a body of 180 magistrates who tried civil law cases. They were split into four chambers of 45 men, and unless a case was particularly complicated, they would all sit separately.

The four courts were, however, divided only by screens or curtains, and the voices of lawyers and cheers and boos of spectators in the upper galleries echoed through the building. Lawyers used to hire crowds of spectators, who would applaud every time the lawyer who was paying them made a point and jeer at his opponents. The clappers and booers must have had a good deal of time on their hands: scratched into the steps are checkerboards where they played dice and other gambling games to while away the time between cases.

Temple of Castor and Pollux **❽**

See Visitors' Checklist, p82.

THE THREE SLENDER fluted columns of this temple form one of the Forum's most beautiful ruins. The first temple here was probably dedicated in 484 BC in honor of the mythical twins and patrons of horsemanship, Castor and Pollux. During the battle of Lake Regillus (499 BC) against the ousted Tarquin kings, the Roman dictator Postumius promised to build a temple to the twins if the Romans were victorious. Some said the twins appeared on the battlefield, helped the Romans to victory and then materialized in the Forum – the temple marks the spot – to announce the news.

The temple, like most buildings in the Forum, was rebuilt many times. The three surviving columns date from the last occasion on which it was rebuilt – by the future Emperor Tiberius after a fire in 6 BC. For a long period the temple housed the city's office of weights and measures, and it was also used at times by a number of bankers.

Corinthian columns of the
Temple of Castor and Pollux

Temple of Vesta **❾**

See Visitors' Checklist, p82.

THE FORUM'S most elegant temple, a circular building originally surrounded by a ring of 20 fine fluted columns, dates from the 4th century AD, though there had been a temple on the site for far longer. It was partially reconstructed in 1930.

The cult of the Vestals was one of the oldest in Rome, and centered on six Vestal Virgins, who were required to

TEMPLE OF VESTA
The temple preserved the shape of the original primitive structure made of wooden posts with a thatched roof.

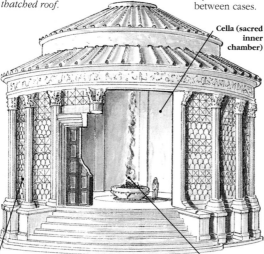

Cella (sacred
inner
chamber)

Ring of Corinthian columns

Sacred flame

keep alight the sacred flame of Vesta, the goddess of the hearth. This responsibility was originally entrusted to the daughters of the king, but it then passed to the Vestals, the only group of women priests in Rome. It was no easy task, as the flame was easily blown out by the wind. Any Vestal who allowed the flame to die was whipped by the high priest and dismissed.

The girls, who had to belong to noble families, were selected when they were between six and ten years old. They served for 30 years: the first ten were spent learning their duties, the next ten performing them and the final ten teaching novices. They enjoyed high status and financial security, but were compelled to remain virgins. The penalty for transgressing was to be buried alive, although only ten Vestals are recorded as ever having suffered this fate. The men concerned were whipped to death. When Vestals retired, they were free to live the rest of their lives as ordinary citizens. If they wished they could marry, but few ever did.

Another of the Vestals' duties was to guard the Palladium, a sacred statue of the goddess Pallas Athena. The irreverent Emperor Heliogabalus burgled the temple in the 3rd century AD. He thought he had succeeded in stealing the Palladium, but the Vestals had been warned of his intention and had replaced it with a replica.

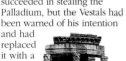

Central courtyard of the House of the Vestal Virgins

Honorary statue of a Vestal Virgin

House of the Vestal Virgins ❿

See Visitors' Checklist, p82.

As soon as a girl became a Vestal she came to live in the House of the Vestal Virgins. Originally this was an enormous complex with about 50 rooms on three stories. The only substantial remains today are some of the rooms around the central courtyard. This space is perhaps the most evocative part of the Forum. Overlooking ponds of water lilies and plump goldfish is a row of eroded, and mostly headless, statues of senior Vestals, dating from the 3rd and 4th centuries AD. The better-preserved examples were transferred to the Museo Nazionale Romano (see p163). On one of the pedestals the inscription has been removed because the Vestal in question suffered some disgrace. It is thought she may have been a certain Claudia, known to have betrayed the cult by converting to Christianity.

Though many of the rooms surrounding the courtyard are well preserved – some even retain flights of steps leading to an upper floor – you are not allowed inside them. If you look into the series of rooms along the south side, however, you might be able to see the remains of a mill,

used for grinding the grain with which the Vestals made a special sacrificial cake. The bakery was next door.

Temple of Antoninus and Faustina ⓫

See Visitors' Checklist, p82. **Church open** 10am–noon Thu; ring the bell.

One of the forum's oddest sights is the Baroque facade of the church of San Lorenzo in Miranda rising above the porch of a Roman temple. First dedicated in AD 141 by the Emperor Antoninus Pius to his late wife Faustina, the temple was rededicated to them both on the death of the emperor. In the 11th century it became a church because it was thought San Lorenzo (St. Lawrence) had been condemned to death there. The current church dates from 1601.

Temple of Antoninus and Faustina

Restored section of Temple of Vesta

Temple of Romulus and Santi Cosma e Damiano ⓬

See Visitors' Checklist, p82. **Santi Cosma e Damiano** ☎ *06-99 15 40.* **Open** *Apr–Sep: 9am–1pm, 4–7pm daily. Oct–Mar: 7am–1pm, 3–7pm daily.* **Crèche** *9:30am–12:30pm, 3pm–6:30pm daily.* **Adm charge** *for crèche.*
✝ ♿

N O ONE IS SURE to whom the so-called Temple of Romulus was dedicated, but it was probably to the son of the Emperor Maxentius and not to Rome's founder. It is a circular brick building, topped by a cupola, with two rectangular side rooms and a concave porch. The heavy, dull bronze doors are original.

Since the 6th century the temple has acted as a vestibule to the church of Santi Cosma e Damiano, which itself occupies an ancient building – a hall in Vespasian's Forum of Peace. The entrance is on Via dei Fori Imperiali. The beautiful carved figures of its 18th-century Neapolitan *presepio* (crèche or Nativity scene) are back on view now, and the church has a vivid Byzantine apse mosaic with Christ pictured against orange clouds.

Roof of the Temple of Romulus

Basilica of Constantine and Maxentius ⓭

See Visitors' Checklist, p82.

T HE BASILICA'S three vast, coffered barrel vaults are powerful relics of what was the largest building in the Forum. Work began in AD 308 under the Emperor Maxentius. When he was deposed by Constantine after the Battle of the Milvian Bridge in AD 312, work on the massive project continued under the new regime. The building, which like other Roman basilicas was used for the administration of justice and for carrying on business, is often referred to simply as the Basilica of Constantine.

The area covered by the basilica was roughly 330 ft by 215 ft (100 m by 65 m). It was originally designed to have a long nave and aisles running from east to west, but Constantine switched the axis around to create three short broad aisles with the main entrance in the center of the long south wall. The height of the building was 115 ft (35 m). In the apse at the western end, where it could be seen from all over the building, stood a 39 ft (12 m) statue of the emperor, made partly of wood and partly of marble. The giant head, hand and foot are on display in the courtyard of the Palazzo dei Conservatori *(see pp72–3).* The basilica's roof glittered with gilded tiles until the 7th century, when they were removed and re-used to cover the roof of the old St. Peter's.

The three barrel-vaulted aisles of the basilica were used as law courts.

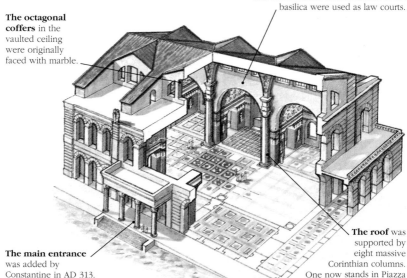

The octagonal coffers in the vaulted ceiling were originally faced with marble.

The main entrance was added by Constantine in AD 313.

The roof was supported by eight massive Corinthian columns. One now stands in Piazza Santa Maria Maggiore *(see p173).*

Santa Francesca Romana ⑭

Piazza di Santa Francesca Romana. **Map** 5 B5. **☎** 06-679 55 28. **🚌** 85, 87, 117, 175, 673, 810 **🚋** 30b. **Ⓜ** Colosseo. **Open** 9:30am–12:30pm, 3:30pm–7pm daily. **✝ 🏛**

EVERY YEAR on March 9, devout Roman drivers try to park as close as possible to this Baroque church with a Romanesque bell tower. The aim of their pilgrimage is to have their vehicles blessed by Santa Francesca Romana, the patron saint of motorists. During the 15th century, Francesca of Trastevere founded a society of pious women devoted to helping the less fortunate. After her canonization in 1608, the church, originally called Santa Maria Nova, was rededicated to Francesca.

Bell tower of Santa Francesca

The most curious sight inside the church is a flagstone with what are reputed to be the imprints of the knees of St. Peter and St. Paul. The story goes that a magician, Simon Magus, decided to prove that his powers were superior to those of the Apostles by levitating himself above the Forum. As Simon was in midair, Peter and Paul fell to their knees and prayed fervently for God to show his divine force. Simon instantly plummeted to his death.

Antiquarium Forense ⑮

See Visitors' Checklist, p82.

THE FORMER CONVENT of Santa Francesca Romana now houses a small museum and the offices of those in charge of the excavations of the Forum. The museum is currently being reorganized, and only one or two rooms are open. They contain Iron Age burial urns and graves

Dedication to Titus and Vespasian on the Arch of Titus

and their skeletal occupants, along with some ancient bric-a-brac exhumed from the Forum's drains. Fragments of statues, capitals, friezes and other architectural decoration taken from the Forum's buildings will be on exhibit when the museum reopens.

Frieze of Aeneas in the Antiquarium Forense

Arch of Titus ⑯

See Visitors' Checklist, p82.

THIS TRIUMPHAL ARCH was erected in AD 81 by the Emperor Domitian in honor of the victories of his brother, Titus, and his father, Vespasian, in Judea. In AD 68 the Jews, weary of being exploited by unscrupulous Roman officials, rebelled. A bitter war broke out, ending two years later in the fall of Jerusalem and the start of Jewish Diaspora.

Although the reliefs inside the arch are badly eroded, you can make out a triumphant procession of Roman soldiers carrying off spoils from the Temple of Jerusalem. The booty includes the altar, silver trumpets and a golden seven-branched menorah.

Temple of Venus and Rome ⑰

See Visitors' Checklist, p82.

THE EMPEROR Hadrian designed this temple to occupy what had been the vestibule to Nero's Golden House. Many of the columns have been reerected, and though there is no access, there is a good view as you leave the Forum and also from the upper tiers of the Colosseum. The temple, the largest in Rome, was dedicated to Roma, the personification of the city, and to Venus because she was the mother of Aeneas, father of Romulus and Remus. Each goddess had her own *cella* (shrine). When the architect Apollodorus pointed out that the seated statues in the niches were too big (had they tried to "stand," their heads would have hit the vaults), Hadrian had him put to death.

Statue of goddess   **Porphyry column**

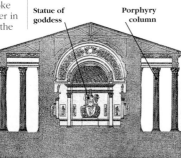
Cross-section of Temple of Venus and Rome

Trajan's Markets 🔞

ORIGINALLY CONSIDERED among the wonders of the Classical world, Trajan's Markets now show only a hint of their former splendor. Emperor Trajan and his architect, Apollodorus of Damascus, built this visionary new complex of 150 shops and offices (probably used for administering the corn ration) in the early 2nd century AD. It was the ancient Roman equivalent of the modern shopping center, selling everything from silks and spices imported from the Middle East to fresh fish, fruit and flowers.

The Markets Today
Above the facade stands the 13th-century Torre delle Milizie, built for defensive purposes.

Cross vaulting

Trajan
The emperor was a benevolent ruler and a successful general.

Main Hall
Twelve shops were built on two floors, and the corn ration was shared out on the upper story. This was a free corn ration given to Roman men to prevent hunger.

Via Biberatica
The main street that runs through the market is named after the drinking inns which once lined it.

Small semicircle of shops

Staircase

TIMELINE

AD 100–112 Building of Trajan's Markets	**472** Invasion by Ricimer the Suevian. Some of his Germanic troops stationed here	**1200s** Torre delle Milizie built on top of the markets	**1572** Convent of Santa Caterina da Siena built over part of markets	**1924** Many medieval houses demolished

AD 100	AD 500	1000	1300	1800	1950

AD 117 Death of Trajan **AD 98** Trajan succeeds Nerva as emperor	**552** Byzantine takeover of Rome. Markets occupied and fortified by the army	**1300s** Annibaldi and Caetani families vie for control of the area	**1828** First tentative excavations, but importance of site not recognized	**1911–14** Convent demolished **1930–33** Markets finally excavated

VISITORS' CHECKLIST

Mercati Traianei, Via IV Novembre.
Map 5 B4. *06-679 00 48.*
*64, 65, 70 to Via IV Novembre
and many routes to Piazza Venezia.*
Open *Apr–Sep: 9am–6.30pm
Tue–Sat; Oct–Mar: 9am–1pm
(last adm: 30 mins before closing).*
Closed *Mon, public hols.* **Adm
charge** *except last Sun of month;
ticket incl Forum of Augustus.*

The Markets in the 16th Century
*This fanciful fresco depicts a gladiatorial combat
taking place in front of the partly buried remains
of Trajan's Markets.*

A Market Shop
*Shops were built with
arched entrances, their
jambs and lintels
creating rectangular
portals and windows.
A wooden mezzanine
was used for storage.*

Upper Corridor
*Shops on this upper level
were thought to have sold
wine and oil, because
storage jars were
discovered here.*

**Large hall with
semidomed
ceiling**

MARKET SHOPPING
Shops opened early and closed about
noon. The best ones were decorated
with mosaics of the goods they sold.
Almost all the shopping was done
by men, though women visited the
dressmaker and cobbler. The
tradespeople were almost all
male. In employment records
for the period AD 117 to 193,
the only female shopkeepers
mentioned are three wool-
sellers, two jewelers, a
greengrocer and a
fishwife.

Fish mosaic

**Wall dividing
market area from
Forum of Trajan**

Forum of Trajan, built in front
of the markets in AD 107–113,
was flanked by the Basilica
Ulpia. The basilica, measuring
170 m (558 ft) by 60 m (197
ft), was the largest in Rome.

The terrace
over the archway
spanning Via
Biberatica has
a good view of
the Forum of
Trajan below.

Trajan's Markets ⑱

See pp88–9.

Column of Trajan ⑲

Via dei Fori Imperiali. **Map** 5 A4 & 12 F4. See Visitors' Checklist for Trajan's Markets, p89.

Detail of Trajan's Column

THIS ELEGANT marble column was inaugurated by Trajan in AD 113, and celebrates his two campaigns in Dacia (Romania) in AD 101–103 and AD 105–106. The column, base and pedestal are 131 ft (40 m) tall – precisely the same height as the spur of the Quirinal Hill, which was excavated to make room for Trajan's Forum. Spiraling up the column are minutely detailed scenes from the campaigns, beginning with the Romans preparing for war and ending with the Dacians being ousted from their homeland. The column is pierced with small windows to illuminate its internal spiral staircase (closed to the public). If you wish to see the reliefs in detail, there is a complete set of casts in the Museo della Civiltà Romana at EUR (see p267).

When Trajan died in AD 117, his ashes, and those of his wife, Plotina, were placed in a golden urn in the column's hollow base. The column's survival was largely thanks to the intervention of Pope Gregory I ("the Great") who reigned from 590 to 604. He was so moved by a relief showing Trajan helping a woman whose son had been killed that he begged God to release the emperor's soul

from hell. God duly appeared to the pope to say that Trajan had been rescued, but asked him not to pray for the souls of any more pagans.

According to legend, when Trajan's ashes were exhumed, his skull and tongue were not only intact, but his tongue told of his release from Hell. The land around the column was then declared sacred and the column spared. The statue of Trajan remained on top of the column until 1587, when it was replaced with one of St. Peter.

Torre delle Milizie ⑳

Mercati Traianei, Via IV Novembre. **Map** 5 B4. *Closed* for restoration.

FOR CENTURIES this massive brick tower was thought to have been the one in which Nero stood watching Rome burn, after he had set it alight in order to clear the city's slums. It is uncertain whether arson was among Nero's crimes, but it is certain that he did not watch the fire from this tower – it was built in the 13th century.

Casa dei Cavalieri di Rodi ㉑

Piazza del Grillo 1. **Map** 5 B5. 06-679 00 48. 85, 87, 115, 117, 175, 186. **Open** by appt only.

Loggia, Casa dei Cavalieri di Rodi

SINCE THE 12TH CENTURY, the crusading order of the Knights of St. John, also known as the Knights of Rhodes (Rodi) or Malta, have had their priorate in this medieval house above the Forum of Augustus. If you are lucky enough to get inside, ask to see the beautiful Cappella di San Giovanni (Chapel of St. John).

Forum of Augustus ㉒

Piazza del Grillo 1. **Map** 5 B5 & 12 F5. See Visitor' Checklist for Trajan's Markets, p89.

Podium of the Temple of Mars in the Forum of Augustus

THE FORUM of Augustus was built to celebrate Augustus's victory over Julius Caesar's assassins, Brutus and Cassius, at the Battle of Philippi in 41 BC. The temple in its center was dedicated to Mars the Avenger. The forum stretched from a high wall at the foot of the sleazy Suburra quarter to the edge of the Forum of Caesar. At least half of it is now concealed below Mussolini's Via dei Fori Imperiali. The temple is easily identified, with its cracked steps and four Corinthian columns. Originally it had a statue of Mars that looked very like Augustus. In case anyone failed to notice the resemblance, a giant statue of Augustus himself was placed against the Suburra wall.

Forum of Caesar ㉓

Via del Carcere Tulliano. **Map** 5 A5. 06-67 10 30 65. 85, 87, 115, 117, 175, 186. **Open** by appt only; permit needed (see p367).

THE FIRST of Rome's Imperial forums was built by Julius Caesar. He spent a fortune – most of it booty from his conquest of Gaul – buying up and demolishing houses on the site. The best of these was a temple dedicated in 46 BC to the goddess Venus Genetrix, from whom Caesar claimed descent. The temple contained statues of Caesar and Cleopatra as well as of Venus. All that remains of this temple to vanity is a platform and three Corinthian columns. The forum was enclosed by a double colonnade that sheltered a row of shops, but this burned down in AD 80 and was rebuilt by Domitian and Trajan. Trajan also added the Basilica Argentaria (an important financial exchange) and a heated public lavatory. The forum is only open for visits by appointment, but parts are visible from above in Via dei Fori Imperiali.

Mamertine Prison ㉔

Clivo Argentario 1. **Map** 5 A5. *06-679 29 02.* *85, 87, 115, 117, 175, 186.* ***Open*** *9am–noon, 2–6pm daily.* ***Donation*** *expected.*

19th-century engraving of guards visiting prisoners in the Mamertine

BELOW THE 16th-century church of San Giuseppe dei Falegnami (St. Joseph of the Carpenters) is a dank dungeon in which, according to Christian legend, St. Peter was imprisoned. He is said to have caused a spring to bubble up into the cell, and used the water to baptize his guards.

The prison, also known as Tullianum, was in an old cistern with access to the city's main sewer (the *cloaca maxima*). The lower cell was used for executions, and bodies were thrown into the sewer. Among the enemies of Rome to be executed here was the Gaulish leader Vercingetorix, defeated by Julius Caesar in 52 BC.

17th-century view of the ruined Forum of Nerva

Forum of Nerva ㉕

Piazza del Grillo 1 (reached through Forum of Augustus). **Map** 5 B5. *06-67 10 30 65.* *87, 186.* ***Closed*** *for excavations.*

THE FORUM of Nerva was begun by Nerva's predecessor, Domitian, and completed in AD 97. Little more than a long corridor with a colonnade along the sides and a Temple of Minerva at one end, it was also known as the Forum Transitorium because it lay between the Forum of Peace built by the Emperor Vespasian in AD 70 and the Forum of Augustus. Vespasian's forum is almost completely covered by Via dei Fori Imperiali, as is much of the Forum of Nerva itself. Excavations have unearthed Renaissance shops and taverns, and part of the forum, including the base of the temple and two columns that were part of the original colonnade. These support a relief of Minerva above a frieze of young girls learning to sew and weave.

Arch of Constantine ㉖

Between Via di San Gregorio and Piazza del Colosseo. **Map** 8 F1. *81, 85, 87, 117, 175, 673, 810.* *30b.* M *Colosseo.*

THIS TRIUMPHAL ARCH was dedicated in AD 315 to celebrate Constantine's victory three years before over his co-emperor, Maxentius. Constantine claimed he owed his victory to a vision of Christ, but there is nothing Christian about the arch – in fact, most of the medallions, reliefs and statues were scavenged from earlier monuments. There are statues of Dacian prisoners taken from Trajan's Forum and reliefs of Marcus Aurelius, including one where he distributes bread to the poor. Inside the arch are reliefs of Trajan's victory over the Dacians. These were probably by the artist who worked on the Column of Trajan.

Medallion on the Arch of Constantine

Colosseum ㉗

See pp92–5.

North side of the Arch of Constantine, facing the Colosseum

Colosseum 🟤

ROME'S GREATEST amphitheater was commissioned by the Emperor Vespasian in AD 72 on the marshy site of a lake in the grounds of Nero's palace, the Domus Aurea *(see p175)*. Deadly gladiatorial combats and wild animal fights were staged free of charge by the emperor and wealthy citizens for public viewing. The Colosseum was built to a practical design, with its 80 arched entrances allowing easy access to 55,000 spectators, but it is also a building of great beauty. The drawing here shows how it looked at the time of its opening in AD 80. It was one of several similar amphitheaters built in the Roman Empire, and some survive at El Djem in North Africa, Nîmes and Arles in France and Verona in northern Italy. Despite being damaged over the years by neglect and theft, it remains a majestic sight.

Outer Wall of the Colosseum
Stone plundered from the facade in the Renaissance was used to build several palaces, bridges and parts of St. Peter's.

The Founder of the Colosseum
Vespasian was a professional soldier who became emperor in AD 69, founding the Flavian dynasty.

The outer walls are made of travertine.

FLORA OF THE COLOSSEUM

By the 19th century, the Colosseum was heavily overgrown. Different microclimates in various parts of the ruin had created an impressive variety of herbs, grasses and wild flowers. Several botanists were inspired to study and catalog them, and two books were published, one listing 420 different species.

Borage, a herb

The bollards anchored the velarium.

The velarium was a huge awning that shaded spectators from the sun. Supported on poles attached to the upper story of the building, it was then hoisted into position with ropes anchored to bollards outside the stadium.

TIMELINE

80 Vespasian's son, Titus, stages inaugural festival in the amphitheater. It lasts 100 days.

AD 70	100
72 Emperor Vespasian begins work on the Colosseum	**81–96** Amphitheater completed in reign of Domitian

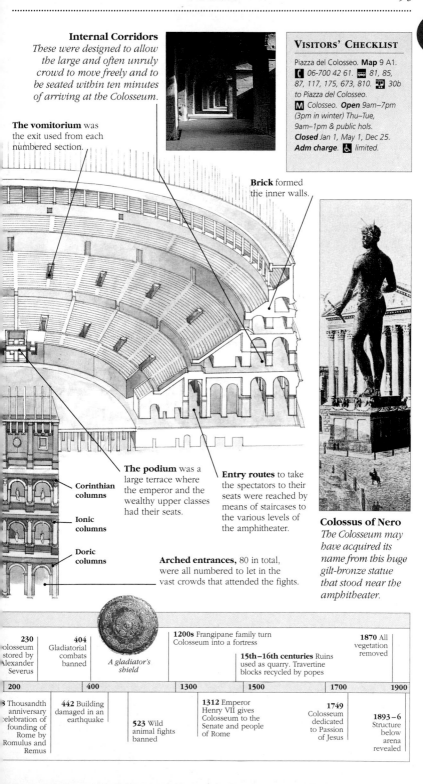

Internal Corridors
These were designed to allow the large and often unruly crowd to move freely and to be seated within ten minutes of arriving at the Colosseum.

The vomitorium was the exit used from each numbered section.

VISITORS' CHECKLIST

Piazza del Colosseo. **Map** 9 A1.
06-700 42 61. 81, 85, 87, 117, 175, 673, 810. 30b to Piazza del Colosseo.
Colosseo. **Open** 9am–7pm (3pm in winter) Thu–Tue, 9am–1pm & public hols.
Closed Jan 1, May 1, Dec 25.
Adm charge. limited.

Brick formed the inner walls.

Corinthian columns

Ionic columns

Doric columns

The podium was a large terrace where the emperor and the wealthy upper classes had their seats.

Entry routes to take the spectators to their seats were reached by means of staircases to the various levels of the amphitheater.

Arched entrances, 80 in total, were all numbered to let in the vast crowds that attended the fights.

Colossus of Nero
The Colosseum may have acquired its name from this huge gilt-bronze statue that stood near the amphitheater.

230 Colosseum restored by Alexander Severus	404 Gladiatorial combats banned	*A gladiator's shield*	1200s Frangipane family turn Colosseum into a fortress		1870 All vegetation removed
			15th–16th centuries Ruins used as quarry. Travertine blocks recycled by popes		
200	**400**	**1300**	**1500**	**1700**	**1900**
8 Thousandth anniversary celebration of founding of Rome by Romulus and Remus	442 Building damaged in an earthquake	523 Wild animal fights banned	1312 Emperor Henry VII gives Colosseum to the Senate and people of Rome	1749 Colosseum dedicated to Passion of Jesus	1893–6 Structure below arena revealed

How Fights Were Staged in the Arena

T HE EMPERORS HELD shows here that often began with animals performing circus tricks. Then on came the gladiators, who fought one another to the death. When one was killed, attendants dressed as Charon, the mythical ferryman of the dead, carried his body off on a stretcher; sand was raked over the blood to make ready for the next bout. A badly wounded gladiator would surrender his fate to the crowd. The "thumbs up" sign from the emperor meant he could live, "thumbs down" that he die, and the victor became an instant hero. Animals were brought here from as far away as North Africa and the Middle East. The games held in AD 248 to mark the 1,000th anniversary of the founding of Rome saw the death of a host of lions, elephants, zebras and elks.

Beneath the Arena
Late 19th-century excavations exposed the network of underground rooms where the animals were kept.

Interior of the Colosseum
The stadium was built in the form of an ellipse, with tiers of seats around a vast central arena.

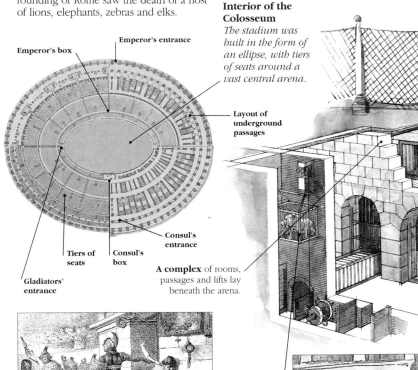

Emperor's box

Emperor's entrance

Layout of underground passages

Tiers of seats

Consul's box

Consul's entrance

Gladiators' entrance

A complex of rooms, passages and lifts lay beneath the arena.

Dramatic Entrances
Below the sand was a wooden floor through which animals, men and scenery appeared in the arena.

Roman Gladiators
These were usually slaves, prisoners of war or condemned criminals. Most were men, but there were a few female gladiators.

**The Colosseum by
Antonio Canaletto**
*This 18th-century view of
the Colosseum shows the
Meta Sudans fountain
(now demolished). Water
"sweated" from a metal
ball on top of its brick cone.*

Metal fencing
kept animals
penned in,
while archers
stood by just
in case any
escaped.

Seating was tiered, and
different social classes
were segregated.

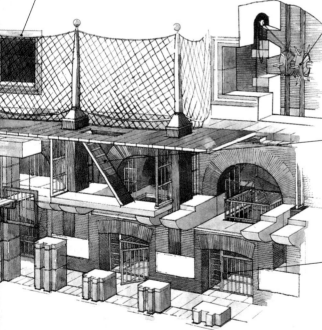

A winch
brought the
animal cages
up to arena
level when
they were
due to fight.

**A ramp and
trap door**
enabled the
animal to reach
the arena after
walking along
a corridor.

Cages were actually
three-sided lifts that
were hoisted to the
level where the
animals were
released.

SEA BATTLES IN THE ARENA

The historian Dion Cassius,
writing in the 4th century AD,
relates how, 150 years earlier,
the Colosseum's arena was
flooded to stage a mock sea
battle. Scholars now believe
that he was mistaken. The
spectacle probably took place
in the Naumachia of Augustus,
a water-filled arena situated
across the Tiber in Trastevere.

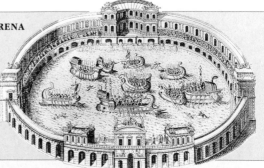

PALATINE

ACCORDING TO LEGEND, Romulus and Remus were brought up here by a wolf in a cave. Traces of Iron Age huts, dating from the 10th century BC, have been found on the Palatine Hill, providing archaeological support for the area's legendary links with the founding of Rome. The Palatine was a very desirable place to live, becoming home to some of the city's most famous inhabitants. The great orator Cicero had a house here, as did the lyric poet Catullus. Augustus was born on the hill and continued to live here in very modest

Fresco of mask in the House of Augustus

circumstances even when he became emperor. The two buildings identified as the House of Augustus and the House of Livia, his second wife, are among the best preserved. The first emperor's example of frugality was ignored by his successors, Tiberius, Caligula and Domitian, who all built extravagant palaces here. The ruins of Tiberius's palace lie beneath the 16th-century Farnese Gardens. The most extensive ruins are those of the Domus Augustana and Domus Flavia, the two wings of Domitian's palace, and the later extension built by Septimius Severus.

SIGHTS AT A GLANCE

Temples
Temple of Cybele 6

Historic Buildings
Domus Flavia 1
Domus Augustana 3
House of Livia 5

Ancient Sites
Cryptoporticus 2
Stadium 4
Huts of Romulus 7

Parks and Gardens
Farnese Gardens 8

SEE ALSO
• *Street Finder*, map 8

GETTING THERE
There are two ways of getting on to the Palatine hill; through either the Roman Forum (from Via dei Fori Imperiali) or through the entrance in Via di San Gregorio. A separate ticket for the Palatine is needed, even if you come from the Forum. The best buses are the 85, 87 and 175; all stop in Via dei Fori Imperiali near the main entrance. Tram 30b and Colosseo Metro station *(see p77)* are also handy.

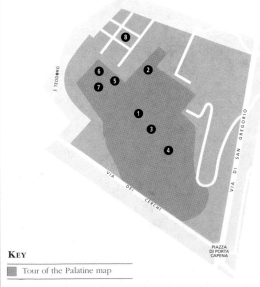

KEY

Tour of the Palatine map

0 meters 200
0 yards 200

Towering ruins of the Palace of Septimius Severus on the Palatine Hill

A Tour of the Palatine

SHADED ON ITS LOWER SLOPES with pines, and scattered in spring with wild flowers, the Palatine is the most pleasant and relaxing of the city's ancient sites. You can reach the hill by walking up from the Roman Forum *(see pp76–7)*. The area is dominated by the ruins of the Domus Flavia and the Domus Augustana, two parts of Domitian's huge palace built at the end of the 1st century AD. What you are able to see depends on where excavations are taking place at the time.

Huts of Romulus
These are traces of a 9th-century BC village on the Palatine ➐

To Farnese Gardens
See p101

House of Augustus

Temple of Cybele
Also known as the Temple of the Magna Mater, this was the center of an important fertility cult ➏

★ House of Livia
Many of the wall paintings have survived in the house where Augustus lived with his wife Livia ➎

STAR SIGHTS

★ **Domus Flavia**

★ **House of Livia**

KEY

- - - Suggested route

0 meters   75

0 yards   75

★ Domus Flavia
This oval fountain was designed to be seen from the dining hall of the palace ➊

Domus Augustana
The Roman emperors lived in this part of the palace, wh[...] the Domus Flavia was used f[...] public functions ➌

Cryptoporticus
In this long underground gallery, built by Nero, the stuccoes that decorated the walls and vault have been replaced with copies ②

LOCATOR MAP
See Central Rome Map pp12–13

Octagonal fountain of the Domus Flavia

The Palatine Antiquarium is housed in a former convent, and houses artifacts from ancient Rome.

Stadium
Part of the Imperial palace, this enclosure may have been used by the emperors as a private garden ④

Entrance

The exedra of the Stadium may have housed a balcony for emperors to view races.

Baths of Septimius Severus

The Palace of Septimius Severus (reigned AD 193–211) was an extension of the Domus Augustana. It projected beyond the hillside, requiring enormous arched supports.

Substructure of palace

Domus Flavia ●

See Visitors' Checklist.

**Marble pavement in the courtyard
of the Domus Flavia**

I N AD 81, DOMITIAN, the third
of the Flavian dynasty of
emperors, decided to build a
splendid new palace on the
Palatine Hill. But the western
peak, the Germalus, was
covered with houses and
temples, while the eastern
peak, the Palatium, was very
steep. So the emperor's
architect, Rabirius, flattened
the Palatium and used the
soil to fill in the cleft between
the two peaks, burying (and
thus preserving) a number of
Republican-era houses.

The palace had two wings –
one official (the Domus
Flavia), the other private (the
Domus Augustana). It was
the main imperial palace for
300 years. At the front of the
Domus Flavia, the surviving
stubs of columns and fragments of walls trace the
shapes of three adjoining
rooms. In the first of these, the
Basilica, Domitian dispensed
his personal brand of justice.

The central Aula Regia was a
throne room decorated with
12 black basalt statues. The
third room (now covered
with corrugated plastic) was
the Lararium, a shrine for the
household gods known as
Lares (usually the owner's
ancestors). It may have been
used for official ceremonies
or by the palace guards.

Fearing assassination,
Domitian had the walls of the
courtyard covered with shiny
marble slabs designed to act
as mirrors so that he could
see anyone lurking behind
him. Ironically, he was
assassinated in his bedroom,
possibly on the orders of his
wife, Domitia. The courtyard
is now a pleasant place to
pause; the flower beds in the
center follow the maze pattern
of a sunken fountain pool.

Cryptoporticus ●

See Visitors' Checklist.

T HE CRYPTOPORTICUS, a series
of underground corridors,
was built by Nero to connect
his Golden House (see p175)
with the palaces of earlier
emperors on the Palatine. A
branch leading to the Palace
of Domitian was added later.
Its vaults are decorated with
delicate stucco reliefs – copies
of originals, now kept in the
Palatine's closed museum.

Domus
Augustana ●

See Visitors' Checklist.

T HIS PART of Domitian's
palace was called the
Domus Augustana because it
was the private residence of
the "august" emperors. On
the upper level, a high brick

wall remains, and visitors can
make out the shape of its two
courtyards. The far better
preserved lower level is closed
to the public, though visitors
can look down on its sunken
courtyard with the geometric
foundations of a fountain in its
center. Sadly, not visible are
the stairs linking the two levels
(once lit by sunlight falling on
a mirror-paved pool), or the
surrounding rooms, paved
with colored marble.

Stadium ●

See Visitors' Checklist.

Stadium viewed from the south

T HE STADIUM on the Palatine
was laid out at the same
time as the Palace of Domitian.
It is not clear whether it was a
public stadium, a private track
for exercising horses or simply
a large garden. The alcove in
the eastern wall looks as
though it may have held a box
from which the emperor could
have watched races. It is
known, however, that the
stadium was used for foot
races by the Ostrogothic king
Theodoric in the 6th century –
he added the small oval-
shaped enclosure at the
southern end of the site.

Remains of the Domus Augustana and the Palace of Septimius Severus

House of Livia ❺

See Visitors' Checklist. If closed, see the custodian.

Fresco in the House of Livia

THIS HOUSE dating from the 1st century BC is one of the best preserved on the Palatine. It was probably part of the house in which the Emperor Augustus and his second wife, Livia, lived. Compared with later Imperial palaces, it is a modest home. According to Suetonius, the biographer of Rome's early emperors, Augustus slept in the same small bedroom for 40 years on a low bed that had "a very ordinary coverlet." He wore home-made clothes

Detail of floor mosaic

(woven by Livia; his sister, Octavia; and daughter, Julia), but he was vain enough to wear shoes with extremely thick soles to conceal the fact that he was rather short.

The ground level of the Palatine is now above the house, so visitors walk down steps and along a mosaic-paved corridor into a courtyard. Its imitation marble wall frescoes have been detached in order to preserve them, but they still hang in situ. Though they are very faded, the veining patterns are still visible. Leading off the courtyard are three small reception rooms. The frescoes in the central one include a faded scene of Hermes coming to the rescue of Zeus's beloved Io, who is guarded by the 100-eyed Argos. In the left-hand room are faint frescoes of griffins and other beasts, while the decor in the right-hand room includes colorful landscapes and cityscapes.

Temple of Cybele ❻

See Visitors' Checklist.

OTHER THAN a platform with a few column stumps and capitals, there is little to see of the Temple of Cybele, a popular Roman fertility goddess of Asian origin. The priests of the cult castrated themselves in the belief that the sacrifice of their own fertility would guarantee that of the natural world. The annual festival of Cybele, in early spring, culminated with frenzied eunuch-priests slashing their bodies to offer blood to the goddess, and the ceremonial castration of novice priests.

Statue of the goddess Cybele

Huts of Romulus ❼

See Visitors' Checklist.

ACCORDING TO LEGEND, after killing his brother, Remus, Romulus founded a village on the Palatine. In the 1940s a series of holes was found filled with earth lighter in color than the surrounding soil. Archaeologists deduced that these holes must originally have held the supporting poles of three Iron Age huts – the first foundations of Rome (*see pp16–17*).

Farnese Gardens ❽

See Visitors' Checklist.

IN THE MID-16TH century Cardinal Alessandro Farnese, grandson of Pope Paul III, bought the ruins of Tiberius's palace on the Palatine. He filled in the ruined building and had Vignola, architect of the interior of the Gesù church, design a garden. The result was one of the first botanical gardens in Europe, its terraces linked by steps stretching from the House of the Vestal Virgins in the Forum to the Palatine's Germalus peak. The gardeners introduced a number of plants to Italy and Europe, among them *Acacia farnesiana*. Farnese was at the center of a flamboyant set that included a number of courtesans, so the parties here were likely to have been somewhat unholy.

The area was dug up during the excavation of the Palatine and relandscaped afterward. Nevertheless, the tree-lined avenues, rose gardens and glorious views still make it an ideal place to unwind.

Farnese pavilions, relics of the age when the Palatine was a private garden

PIAZZA DELLA ROTONDA

THE PANTHEON, one of the great buildings in the history of European architecture, has stood at the heart of Rome for nearly 2,000 years. The historic area around it has seen uninterrupted economic and political activity throughout that time. Palazzo di Montecitorio, built for Pope Innocent XII as a papal tribunal in 1694,

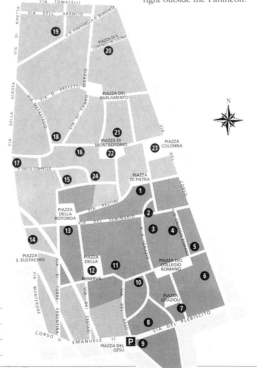

Bitter-style apéritif, popular in Roman cafés

is now the Italian parliament and many nearby buildings are government offices. This is also the main financial district of Rome with banking headquarters and the stock exchange. Not many people live here, but in the evenings, Romans stroll in the narrow streets and fill the lively restaurants and cafés that make this a focus for the city's social life.

SIGHTS AT A GLANCE

Churches and Temples
Temple of Hadrian **1**
Sant'Ignazio di Loyola **3**
Gesù pp114–15 **9**
Santa Maria sopra Minerva **11**
Pantheon pp110–11 **13**
Sant'Eustachio **14**
La Maddalena **15**
Santa Maria in
Campo Marzio **18**
San Lorenzo in Lucina **20**

Historic Streets and Piazzas
Piazza di Sant'Ignazio **2**
Via della Gatta **7**

Historic Buildings
Palazzo del Collegio
Romano **4**
Palazzo Doria Pamphilj **6**
Palazzo Altieri **8**
Palazzo Baldassini **17**
Palazzo Borghese **19**
Palazzo di Montecitorio **21**
Palazzo Capranica **24**

Columns, Obelisks and Statues
Pie' di Marmo **10**
Obelisk of Santa Maria
sopra Minerva **12**
Obelisk of Montecitorio **22**
Column of Marcus Aurelius **23**

Fountains
Fontanella del Facchino **5**

Cafés and Restaurants
Caffè Giolitti **16**

KEY

▨	Street-by-Street map
🅿	Parking

GETTING THERE
The area has no Metro station, but is about 15 minutes' walk from Spagna or Barberini Metro stops. There are some convenient bus stops in Via del Plebiscito, served by the 56, 64, 70, 492 and many other routes. Piazza Colonna is served by the 56, 60, 85 and all buses that go up Via del Corso. The only bus that passes through the narrow streets of the area is the 116 electric minibus, which stops right outside the Pantheon.

```
0 meters      200
0 yards       200
```

Piazza della Rotonda seen through the granite columns of the Pantheon

Street by Street: Piazza della Rotonda

IF YOU WANDER THROUGH this area, sooner or later you will emerge into Piazza della Rotonda, with its jumble of open-air café tables in front of the Pantheon. The refreshing splash of the fountain makes it a welcome resting place. In this warren of narrow streets, it can be hard to imagine just how close you are to some of Rome's finest sights. The magnificent art collection of Palazzo Doria Pamphilj and the Baroque splendor of the Gesù are just a few minutes' walk from the Pantheon. At night there is always a lively buzz of activity as people dine in style or enjoy the coffee and ice creams for which the area is famous.

Temple of Hadrian
The columns of this Roman temple now form the facade of the stock exchange ❶

Piazza di Sant'Ignazio
The square is a rare example of stylish domestic architecture from the early 18th century ❷

La Tazza d'Oro enjoys a reputation for the wonderful coffee consumed on its premises as well as for its freshly ground coffee to take out. *(See p319.)*

Santa Maria sopra Minerva
The rich decoration of Rome's only Gothic church was added in the 19th century ⓫

★ **Pantheon**
The awe-inspiring interior of Rome's best-preserved ancient temple is only hinted at from the outside ⓭

Obelisk of Santa Maria sopra Minerva
In 1667, Bernini dreamed up the idea of mounting a recently discovered obelisk on the back of a marble elephant ⓬

★ Sant'Ignazio di Loyola
Andrea Pozzo painted this glorious Baroque ceiling (1685) to celebrate St. Ignatius and the Jesuit order ❸

Palazzo del Collegio Romano
Up until 1870, the college educated many leading figures in the Catholic Church ❹

LOCATOR MAP
See Central Rome Map pp12–13

Fontanella del Facchino
The water in this small 16th-century fountain spurts from a barrel held by a porter ❺

★ Palazzo Doria Pamphilj
Among the masterpieces in the art gallery of this magnificent family palazzo is this portrait of Pope Innocent X by Velázquez (1650) ❻

Via della Gatta
The street is named after the statue of a cat ❼

Palazzo Altieri
This enormous 17th-century palazzo is decorated with the arms of Pope Clement X ❽

★ Gesù
The design of the very first Jesuit church had a great impact on religious architecture ❾

STAR SIGHTS

★ Pantheon

★ Palazzo Doria Pamphilj

★ Gesù

★ Sant'Ignazio di Loyola

KEY
– – – Suggested route

0 meters 75
0 yards 75

Pie' di Marmo
This marble foot is a stray fragment from a gigantic Roman statue ❿

Temple of Hadrian ❶

La Borsa, Piazza di Pietra. **Map** 4 F3 & 12 E2. 🚌 *60, 81, 85, 116, 117 and many other routes along Via del Corso.* **Not open** to the public.

THIS TEMPLE honors the Emperor Hadrian as a god, was dedicated by his son and successor Antoninus Pius in AD 145. The remains of the temple are visible on the southern side of Piazza di Pietra, incorporated in a 17th-century building. This was originally a papal customs house, completed by Carlo Fontana and his son in the 1690s. Today the building houses the Roman Stock exchange (La Borsa).

Eleven marble Corinthian columns 49 ft (15 m) high stand on a base of *peperino*, a volcanic rock quarried from the Alban Hills to the south of Rome. The columns decorated the northern flank of the temple, enclosing its inner shrine, the *cella*. The *peperino* wall of the *cella* is still visible behind the columns, as is part of the coffered portico ceiling.

A number of reliefs from the temple representing conquered Roman provinces are now in the courtyard of the Palazzo dei Conservatori *(see pp72–3)*. They reflect the mostly peaceful foreign policy of Hadrian's reign.

Remains of Hadrian's Temple

Piazza di Sant'Ignazio ❷

Map 4 F4 & 12 E3. 🚌 *60, 81, 85, 116, 117 and many other routes along Via del Corso.*

ONE OF THE MAJOR works of the Roman Rococo, the piazza (1727–8) is Filippo Raguzzini's masterpiece. It offsets the imposing facade of the church of Sant'Ignazio

Illusionistic ceiling in the crossing of Sant'Ignazio

with the intimacy of the houses of the bourgeoisie. The theatrical setting, the curvilinear design and the playful forms of its windows, balconies and balusters mark the piazza as one of a highly distinct group of structures. Along with Palazzo Doria Pamphilj (1731), the facade of La Maddalena (1735) and the aristocratic Spanish Steps (1723), it belongs to the moment when Rome's bubbly Rococo triumphed over conservative Classicism.

Sant'Ignazio di Loyola ❸

Piazza di Sant'Ignazio. **Map** 4 F4 & 12 E3. 📞 *06-679 44 06.* 🚌 *60, 81, 85, 116, 117 and many other routes along Via del Corso.* **Open** *7:30am–12:30pm & 4pm–7:15pm daily.* 🛈

THE CHURCH was built by Pope Gregory XV in 1626 in honor of St. Ignatius of Loyola, founder of the Society of Jesus and the man who most embodied the zeal of the Counter-Reformation.

Together with the Gesù *(see pp114–15)*, Sant'Ignazio forms the center of the Jesuit area in Rome. Its vast interior, lined with precious stones, marble, stucco and gilt, creates a sense of theater. The church has a Latin-cross plan, with an apse and many side chapels.

A cupola was planned but never built, so the space it would have filled was covered by a fake perspective painting. The piers built to uphold the cupola support the observatory of the Collegio Romano.

Palazzo del Collegio Romano ❹

Piazza del Collegio Romano. **Map** 5 A4 & 12 E3. 🚌 *60, 81, 85, 116, 117 and many other routes along Via del Corso.* **Not open** to the public.

ON THE SAME BLOCK as the church of Sant'Ignazio is the palazzo used by Jesuits as a college where many future bishops, cardinals and popes studied. The college was confiscated in 1870 and turned into an ordinary school. The portals bear the coat of arms of its founder, Pope Gregory XIII Boncompagni (reigned from 1572–85). The facade is also adorned with a bell, two sundials and a clock. On the right is a tower built in 1787 as a meteorological observatory. Until 1925 its time signal regulated all the clocks in the city.

Portal of the Collegio Romano

Fontanella del Facchino ❺

Via Lata. **Map** 5 A4 & 12 E3.
🚌 *60, 64, 70, 81, 85, 117 and many other routes.*

I L FACCHINO (the Porter), once in the Corso, now set into the wall of the Banco di Roma, was one of Rome's "talking statues" like Pasquino *(see p124)*. Created around 1590, the fountain may have been based on a drawing by painter Jacopino del Conte. The statue of a man holding a barrel probably represents a member of the Università degli Acquaroli (Fraternity of Water Carriers), though it is also said to be of Martin Luther, or of the porter Abbondio Rizzio, who died carrying a barrel.

The Facchino drinking fountain

Palazzo Doria Pamphilj ❻

Piazza del Collegio Romano 1/A.
Map 5 A4 & 12 E3. ☎ 06-679 73 23.
🚌 *56, 60, 62, 85, 95, 160, 492 and many other routes.* **Open** 10am–5pm Fri–Wed. **Closed** Aug 15–30, public hols. **Adm charge.** ♿ limited. 🎥 compulsory for private apartments, otherwise ask. 📷

P ALAZZO DORIA PAMPHILJ is a great island of stone in the heart of Rome, the oldest parts dating from 1435. Through the Corso entrance you can see the 16th-century porticoed courtyard with the coat of arms of the della Rovere family. The Aldobrandini were the next owners. Between 1601 and 1647 the mansion acquired a second courtyard and flanking wings at the expense of a public bath that stood nearby.
   When the Pamphilj family took over, they completed the Piazza del Collegio Romano facade and the Via della Gatta

wing, a splendid chapel and a theater inaugurated by Queen Christina of Sweden in 1684.
   In the first half of the 18th century, Gabriele Valvassori created the gallery above the courtyard and a new facade along the Corso, using the highly decorative style of the period known as the *barocchetto*, which now dominates the building. The stairways and salons, the Mirror Gallery and the picture gallery all radiate a joyous sense of light and space.
   The family collection in the Doria Pamphilj gallery has over 400 paintings dating from the 15th to the 18th century, including the famous portrait of Pope Innocent X Pamphilj by Velázquez. There are also important works by Titian, Caravaggio, Lorenzo Lotto, Guercino and Claude Lorrain. The rooms in the private apartment have many of their original furnishings on display including splendid Brussels and Gobelins tapestries.

Via della Gatta ❼

Map 5 A4 & 12 E3. 🚌 *56, 60, 62, 85, 95, 160, 492 and many other routes along Corso Vittorio Emanuele II.*

T HIS NARROW STREET runs between the Palazzo Doria Pamphilj and the smaller Palazzo Grazioli. The ancient

marble sculpture of a cat *(gatta)* that gives the street its name is on the first cornice on the corner of Palazzo Grazioli.

Via della Gatta's marble cat

Palazzo Altieri ❽

Via del Gesù 93. **Map** 4 F4 & 12 E3.
🚌 *46, 56, 60, 64, 70, 81, 186 and many other routes along Corso Vittorio Emanuele II.* 🚊 *8.*

T HE ALTIERI FAMILY is first mentioned in Rome's history in the 9th century. This palazzo was built by the last male heirs, the brothers Cardinal Giambattista di Lorenzo Altieri and Cardinal Emilio Altieri, later Pope Clement X (reigned 1670–76). Many surrounding houses had to be demolished, but an old woman called Berta refused to leave, so her hovel was incorporated into the building. Its windows are still visible on the west end of the palazzo. Part of the palazzo is occupied by Mirabilia, a ticket agency *(see p341)*.

Gesù ❾

See pp114–15.

Caravaggio's *Rest During the Flight into Egypt* in Palazzo Doria Pamphilj

Marble foot from a Roman statue

Pie' di Marmo ❿

Via di Santo Stefano del Cacco. **Map** 4 F4 & 12 E3. 🚌 *60, 64, 70, 81, 85, 116 and other routes along Via del Corso and Corso Vittorio Emanuele II.*

IT WAS POPULARLY believed in the Middle Ages that half the population of ancient Rome was made up of bronze, gold and marble statues. Fragments of these giants, usually gods or emperors, are scattered over the city. This piece, a marble foot (*Pie' di marmo*), comes from an area dedicated to the Egyptian gods Isis and Serapis and was probably part of a statue in one of the temples. These statues were painted and covered with jewels and clothes given by the faithful – a great fire hazard with unattended burning tapers.

Santa Maria sopra Minerva ⓫

Piazza della Minerva 42. **Map** 4 F4 & 12 E3. 🅒 *06-679 39 26.* 🚌 *116 and many other routes along Via del Corso and Corso Vittorio Emanuele II.* **Open** *7am–7pm daily.* **Cloister open** *8:30am–1pm, 4pm–7pm Mon–Sat, ask in the church.* 🚻 🔯 **Concerts.**

FEW OTHER CHURCHES display such a complete and impressive record of Italian art. Dating from the 13th century, the Minerva is one of the few examples of Gothic architecture in Rome. It was the traditional stronghold of the Dominicans, whose anti-heretical zeal earned them the nickname of *Domini Canes* (the hounds of the Lord).

Built on ancient ruins, supposed to have been the Temple of Minerva, the simple T-shaped vaulted building acquired rich chapels and works of art by which its

many patrons wished to be remembered. Note the Cosmatesque 13th-century tombs and the exquisite works of 15th-century Tuscan and Venetian artists. Native Roman talent of the period can be admired in Antoniazzo Romano's *Annunciation*, featuring Cardinal Juan de Torquemada, uncle of the infamous Spanish Inquisitor.

The more monumental style of the Roman Renaissance is well represented in the tombs of the 16th-century Medici popes, Leo X and his cousin Clement VII, and in the richly decorated Aldobrandini Chapel. Near the steps of the choir is the celebrated sculpture called *Risen Christ*, started by Michelangelo but completed by Raffaele da Montelupo in 1521.

There are also splendid works of art from the Baroque period, including a tomb and a bust by Bernini. The church is visited not only for its art, but also because it contains the tombs of many famous Italians: St. Catherine of Siena, who died here in 1380; the Venetian sculptor Andrea Bregno (died 1506); the Humanist Cardinal Pietro Bembo (died 1547); and Fra Angelico, the Dominican friar and painter, who died in Rome in 1455.

Obelisk of Santa Maria sopra Minerva ⓬

Piazza della Minerva. **Map** 4 F4 & 12 D3. 🚌 *116 and routes along Via del Corso and Corso Vittorio Emanuele II.*

ORIGINALLY MEANT to decorate Palazzo Barberini as a joke, this exotic elephant and obelisk sculpture is typical of Bernini's inexhaustible imagination. (The elephant was actually sculpted by Ercole Ferrata to Bernini's design.) When the ancient obelisk was found in the garden of the monastery of Santa Maria sopra Minerva, the friars wanted the monument erected in their piazza. The elephant was provided with its enormous saddlecloth because of a friar's insistence that the gap under the animal's abdomen would undermine its stability. Bernini knew better: you need only look at the Fontana dei Fiumi (*see p120*) in Piazza Navona to appreciate his use of empty space. The elephant, an ancient symbol of intelligence and piety, was chosen as the embodiment of the virtues on which Christians should build true wisdom.

Bernini's Egyptian obelisk and marble elephant

Nave of Santa Maria sopra Minerva

Pantheon 🔞

See pp110–11.

Sant'Eustachio 🔞

Piazza Sant'Eustachio. **Map** 4 F4 & 12 D3. 📞 *06-686 53 34.* 🚌 *116 and many routes along Corso Vittorio Emanuele II.* **Open** *4pm–8pm daily.* 🚻

THE ORIGINS of this church go back to early Christian times, when it offered relief to the poor. In medieval times many charitable brotherhoods elected Sant'Eustachio as their patron and had chapels here.

The Romanesque bell tower is one of the few surviving remnants of the medieval church, which was totally redecorated in the 17th and 18th centuries.

Nearby is the excellent Caffè Sant'Eustachio *(see p319).*

Bell tower of Sant'Eustachio

La Maddalena 🔞

Piazza della Maddalena. **Map** 4 F3 & 12 D2. 📞 *06-679 77 96.* 🚌 *116 and many routes along Via del Corso and Corso Vittorio Emanuele II.* **Open** *7:30am–noon, 5pm–7:30pm daily.* 🚻

SITUATED IN a small piazza near the Pantheon, the Maddalena's Rococo facade built in 1735, epitomizes the love of light and movement of the late Baroque. Its curves are reminiscent of Borromini's San Carlo alle Quattro Fontane *(see p161).* The facade has been lovingly restored, despite the protests of diehard Neoclassicists who dismiss its painted stucco as sugar icing.

The small size of the Maddalena did not deter the

The old-fashioned *salone* of the Caffè Giolitti

17th- and 18th-century decorators, who filled the interior with ornament from the floor to the top of the elegant cupola. The organ loft and choir are particularly powerful examples of the Baroque desire to fire the imagination of the faithful.

Many of the paintings and sculptures employ the new Christian imagery of the Counter Reformation. In the niches of the nave, for example, the statues are personifications of virtues such as Humility and Simplicity. There are also scenes from the life of San Camillo, who died in the adjacent convent in 1614. The church belonged to his followers, the Camillians, a preaching order active in Rome's hospitals. Like the Jesuits, they commissioned works of art to convey the force of their religious message.

La Maddalena's stuccoed facade

Caffè Giolitti 🔞

Via degli Uffici del Vicario 40. **Map** 4 F3 & 12 D2. 📞 *06-699 12 43.* 🚌 *116 and many routes along Via del Corso and Corso Rinascimento.* **Open** *7am–1:30am Tue–Sun.*

FOUNDED IN 1900, the Caffè Giolitti is the heir to the *Belle Époque* cafés that lined the nearby Corso in Rome's first days as capital of the new Italian state. Its *salone* holds tourists in summer and Roman families on weekends, while on weekdays it is frequented by office workers, construction workers and officials from the nearby parliament *(see p112).*

Palazzo Baldassini 🔞

Via delle Coppelle 35. **Map** 4 F3 & 12 D2. 🚌 *116 and many routes along Via del Corso and Corso Rinascimento.* **Not open** to the public.

MELCHIORRE BALDASSINI commissioned Antonio da Sangallo the Younger to build his home in Florentine Renaissance style in 1514–20. With its cornices marking the different floors and wroughtiron window grilles, this is one of the best examples of an early 16th-century Roman palazzo. It stands in the part of Rome still known as the Renaissance Quarter, which flourished around the long straight streets such as Via di Ripetta and Via della Scrofa built at the time of Pope Leo X (reigned 1513–21).

Pantheon ⑬

IN THE MIDDLE AGES, the Pantheon, the Roman "temple of all the gods," became a church; in time this magnificent building with its awe-inspiring domed interior became a symbol of Rome itself. The rectangular portico screens the vast hemispherical dome: only from inside can its true scale and beauty be appreciated. The rotunda's height and diameter are equal: 140 ft (43.3 m). The opening at the top of the dome, the *oculus*, provides the only light. We owe this marvel of Roman engineering to the Emperor Hadrian (AD 118–125), who designed it to replace an earlier temple built by Marcus Agrippa, son-in-law of Augustus. The shrines that now line the wall of the Pantheon range from the Tomb of Raphael to those of the kings of modern Italy.

★ **Interior of the Dome**
The dome was cast by pouring concrete mixed with tufa and pumice over a temporary wooden framework.

The walls of the drum supporting the dome are 19 ft (6 m) thick.

The portico, enclosed by granite columns

The immense portico is built on the foundations of Agrippa's temple.

STAR FEATURES

★ **Interior of the Dome**

★ **Tomb of Raphael**

Bell Towers
This 18th-century view by Bernardo Bellotto shows Bernini's much-ridiculed turrets, which were removed in 1883.

Floor Patterning
The marble floor, restored in 1873, preserves the original Roman design.

RAPHAEL AND LA FORNARINA

Raphael, at his own request, was buried here when he died in 1520. He had lived for years with his model, La Fornarina *(see p210)*, seen here in a painting by Giulio Romano, but she was excluded from the ceremony of his burial. To the right of his tomb is a memorial to his fiancée, Maria Bibbiena, niece of the artist's patron, Cardinal Dovizi di Bibbiena.

VISITORS' CHECKLIST

Piazza della Rotonda. **Map** 4 F4 & 12 D3. ☎ 06-68 30 02 30.
🚌 116 and many routes along nearby Via del Corso, Corso del Rinascimento and Corso Vittorio Emanuele II. **Open** 9am–6:30pm daily. **Closed** Jan 1, May 1 & Dec 25. 🚻 ♿ **Concerts**. 📷

Oculus

Coffering
Constructing the dome from hollow decorative coffers reduced its weight.

Relieving Arches
Brick arches embedded in the structure of the wall act as internal buttresses, distributing the weight of the dome.

★ **Tomb of Raphael**
The artist's body rests below a Madonna by Lorenzetto (1520).

TIMELINE

Inscription on pediment

27–25 BC Marcus Agrippa builds first Pantheon		**735** Gregory III roofs the Pantheon in lead	**1305–77** While papal seat is in Avignon, Pantheon is used as fortress and poultry market	**1888** Tomb of King Vittorio Emanuele II completed
30 BC	**AD 100**	**600**	**1100**	**1600**
AD 118 Hadrian builds new Pantheon	**609** Pope Boniface IV consecrates Pantheon as church of Santa Maria ad Martyres	**663** Byzantine Emperor Constans II strips gilded tiles from the roof	**1632** Urban VIII melts down bronze from portico for Bernini's baldacchino in St. Peter's	

Bernini's curving southern facade of Palazzo di Montecitorio

Santa Maria in Campo Marzio ®

Piazza in Campo Marzio 45.
Map 4 F3 & 12 D2. ▦ *116 and many routes on Via del Corso and Corso del Rinascimento.* **Closed** *for renovation.*

AROUND the courtyard through which you enter the church, there are fascinating remnants of medieval houses, once the property of the original monastery. The church itself was rebuilt in 1685 by Antonio de Rossi, using a square Greek-cross plan with a cupola. Above the altar is a 12th-century painting of the Madonna, which gives the church its name.

Palazzo Borghese ®

Largo della Fontanella di Borghese.
Map 4 F3 & 12 D1. ▦ *70, 81, 117, 492, 628.* **Not open** *to the public.*

THE PALAZZO was acquired in about 1605 by Cardinal Camillo Borghese, just before he became Pope Paul V. Flaminio Ponzio was hired to enlarge the building and give it the grandeur appropriate to the residence of the pope's family. He added a wing overlooking Piazza Borghese and the delightful porticoed courtyard inside. Subsequent enlargements included the building and decoration of a great *nympheum* known as the Bath of Venus. For more than two centuries this palazzo housed the Borghese family's renowned collection of paintings, which was bought

by the Italian state in 1902 and transferred to the Galleria Borghese *(see pp260– 61).*

Pope Paul V, who commissioned Palazzo Borghese for his family

San Lorenzo in Lucina ®

Via in Lucina 16A. **Map** 4 F3 & 12 E1. ℂ *06-687 14 94.* ▦ *81, 115, 117, 492, 628.* **Open** *8am–noon, 5pm– 7:30pm daily.* ♦ ♦ *last Sat of each month at 4:30pm (phone to book).*

THE CHURCH is one of Rome's oldest Christian places of worship, and was probably built on a well sacred to Juno, protectress of women. It was rebuilt in the 12th century, and today's external appearance is typical of

the period: a portico with re-used Roman columns crowned by medieval capitals, a plain triangular pediment and a Romanesque bell tower with colored marble inlay.

The interior was totally rebuilt in 1856–8. The old basilica plan was destroyed and the two side naves were replaced by Baroque chapels. Don't miss the fine busts in the Fonseca Chapel, designed by Bernini, or the *Crucifixion* by Guido Reni above the main altar. There is also a 19th-century monument honoring French painter Nicolas Poussin, who died in Rome in 1655 and was buried in the church.

Palazzo di Montecitorio ®

Piazza di Montecitorio. **Map** 4 F3 & 12 E2. ▦ *56, 60, 62, 81, 95, 116, 117, 160, and many other routes.* **Not open** *to the public (visits 10am–4.30pm 1st Sun each month can be booked in adv* ℂ *06-67601).*

THE PALAZZO's first architect, Bernini, got the job after he presented a silver model of his design to the wife of his patron, Prince Ludovisi. The building was completed in 1694 by Carlo Fontana and became the Papal Tribunal of Justice. In 1871 it was chosen to be Italy's new Chamber of Deputies, and by 1927 it had doubled in size with a second grand facade. The 630 members of parliament are elected by a majority system with proportional representation

The church of San Lorenzo in Lucina

Emperor Augustus's obelisk

Obelisk of Montecitorio ㉒

Piazza di Montecitorio. **Map** 4 F3 & 12 E2. 🚌 56, 60, 62, 85, 95, 116, 117, 160, and many other routes.

THE MEASUREMENT of time in ancient Rome was always a rather hit-and-miss affair: for many years the Romans relied on an imported (and therefore inaccurate) sundial, a trophy from the conquest of Sicily. In 10 BC, the Emperor Augustus laid out an enormous sundial in the Campus Martius. Its center was roughly in today's Piazza di San Lorenzo in Lucina. The shadow was cast by a huge granite obelisk that he had brought back from Heliopolis in Egypt. Unfortunately, this sundial also became inaccurate after only 50 years, possibly due to subsidence.

The obelisk was still in the piazza in the 9th century but then disappeared until it was rediscovered in the reign of Pope Julius II (1503–13). The pope was intrigued by its Egyptian hieroglyphs, which were thought to hold the key to the wisdom of Adam before the Fall, but it was only under Pope Benedict XIV (reigned 1740–58) that the obelisk was finally unearthed. It was erected in its present location in 1792 by Pope Pius VI.

Column of Marcus Aurelius ㉓

Piazza Colonna. **Map** 5 A3 & 12 E2. 🚌 56, 60, 62, 81, 95, 116, 117, 160 and many other routes.

CLEARLY AN IMITATION of the Column of Trajan (see p90), this monument was erected after the death of Marcus Aurelius in AD 180 to commemorate his victories over the barbarian tribes of the Danube. Made 80 years after the original column, this one is very different artistically: the wars of Marcus Aurelius are rendered in simplified pictures in stronger relief, sacrificing Classical proportions for the sake of clarity and immediacy. The spirit of the work is more akin to the 4th-century Arch of Constantine (see p91) than to Trajan's monument. Gone are the heroic qualities of the Roman soldiers, by now mostly barbarian mercenaries, and a sense of respect for the vanquished. A new emphasis on the supernatural points to the end of the Hellenistic tradition and the beginning of Christian culture.

Composed of 28 drums of marble, the column was restored in 1588 by Domenico Fontana on the orders of Pope Sixtus V. The emperor's statue on the summit was replaced by a bronze of St. Paul. The 20 spirals of the low relief chronicle the German war of AD 172–3 and (above) the Sarmatic war of AD 174–5. The column is almost 100 ft (30 m) high and 12 ft (3.7 m) in diameter. An internal spiral staircase leads to the top. The easiest way to appreciate the sculptural work, however, is to visit the Museo della Civiltà Romana at EUR (see p267) and study the casts of the reliefs.

Palazzo Capranica ㉔

Piazza Capranica. **Map** 4 F3 & 12 D2. 🚌 56, 60, 62, 81, 95, 116, 117, 160.

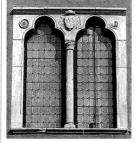

Windows of Palazzo Capranica

ONE OF ROME'S small number of surviving 15th-century buildings, the palazzo was commissioned by Cardinal Domenico Capranica both as his family residence and as a college for higher education. Its fortresslike appearance is a patchwork of subsequent additions, not unusual in the late 15th century when Rome was still hovering between medieval and Renaissance taste. The Gothic-looking windows on the right of the building show the cardinal's coat of arms, and the date 1451 is inscribed on the doorway underneath. The palazzo now houses a popular movie theater.

Relief of the emperor's campaigns on the Column of Marcus Aurelius

Gesù ❾

DATING FROM BETWEEN 1568 and 1584, the Gesù was the first Jesuit church to be built in Rome. Its design epitomizes Counter Reformation Baroque architecture and has been much imitated throughout the Catholic world. The layout proclaims the church's two major functions: a large nave with side pulpits for preaching to great crowds, and a main altar as the centerpiece for the celebration of the mass. The illusionistic decoration in the nave and dome was added a century later. Its message is clear and confident: faithful Catholic worshipers will be joyfully uplifted into the heavens, while Protestants and heretics will be flung into hell's fires.

★ Chapel of Sant'Ignazio
Above its altar is a statue of the saint, framed by gilded lapis lazuli columns. The chapel was built in 1690 to 1700 by Andrea Pozzo, a Jesuit artist.

Triumph of Faith Over Idolatry
This vivid Baroque allegory sculpted by Théudon illustrates the great ambition of Jesuit theology.

ST. IGNATIUS AND THE JESUIT ORDER

The Spanish soldier Ignatius Loyola (1491–1556) joined the Church after being wounded in battle in 1521. He came to Rome in 1537 and founded the Jesuits, sending missionaries and teachers all over the world to win souls for Catholicism.

Main entrance

STAR FEATURES

★ **Nave Ceiling Decorations**

★ **Chapel of Sant'Ignazio**

★ **Tomb of San Roberto Bellarmino**

Allegorical Figures
Antonio Raggi made these stuccoes, which were designed by Il Baciccia to complement the figures on his own nave frescoes.

Madonna della Strada
This 15th-century image, the Madonna of the Road, was originally displayed on the facade of Santa Maria della Strada which once stood on this site.

VISITORS' CHECKLIST

Piazza del Gesù. **Map** 4 F4 & 12 E4. 06-69 70 01.
H, 44, 46, 56, 60, 62, 64, 70, 75, 81, 87, 170, 492, 628, 719 and other routes. 8.
Open 6am–12:30pm, 4pm–7:15pm daily.

★ **San Roberto Bellarmino**
Bernini captured the forceful personality of this anti-Protestant theologian, who died in 1621.

The Chapel of St. Francis Xavier is a memorial to the great missionary who died alone on an island off China in 1552.

★ **Nave Ceiling Decorations**
The figures in Il Baciccia's astonishing fresco of the Triumph of the Name of Jesus *spill out onto the coffered vaulting of the nave.*

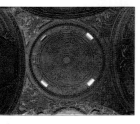

Cupola Frescoes
The cupola was completed by della Porta to Vignola's design. The frescoes, by Il Baciccia, feature Old Testament figures.

TIMELINE

1540 Founding of the Society of Jesus (the Jesuits)	**1571** Giacomo della Porta's design chosen for the facade	**1696–1700** The Chapel of Sant' Ignazio is designed by Andrea Pozzo, a Jesuit artist	**1773** Pope Clement XIV orders the suppression of the Jesuit order
	1584 Church's consecration		
1500	**1600**		**1700**
1545–63 Council of Trent defines the new Catholic orthodoxy	**1568–71** Vignola builds the church up to the crossing under the patronage of Cardinal Alessandro Farnese		**1670–83** Giovanni Battista Gaulli (Il Baciccia) paints the nave vault, dome and apse
1556 Death of Ignatius		**1622** Ignatius Loyola is canonized	

PIAZZA NAVONA

THE FOUNDATIONS of the buildings surrounding the elongated oval of Piazza Navona were the ruined grandstands of the vast Stadium of Domitian. The piazza still provides a dramatic spectacle today with the obelisk of the Fontana dei Quattro Fiumi in front of the church of Sant'Agnese in Agone as its focal

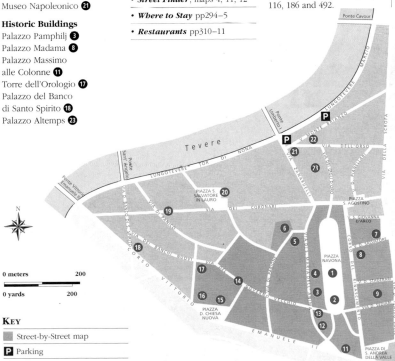

Lion on Fontana dei Quattro Fiumi

point. The predominant style of the area is Baroque, many of its finest buildings dating from the reign of Innocent X Pamphilj (1644–55), patron of Bernini and Borromini. Of special interest is the complex of the Chiesa Nuova, headquarters of the Filippini, the order founded by San Filippo Neri, the 16th-century "Apostle of Rome".

SIGHTS AT A GLANCE

Churches and Temples
Sant'Agnese in Agone **4**
Santa Maria dell'Anima **5**
Santa Maria della Pace **6**
San Luigi dei Francesi **7**
Sant'Ivo alla Sapienza **9**
Sant'Andrea della Valle **10**
Chiesa Nuova **15**
Oratorio dei Filippini **16**
San Salvatore in Lauro **20**

Museums
Palazzo Braschi **12**
Museo Napoleonico **21**

Historic Buildings
Palazzo Pamphilj **3**
Palazzo Madama **8**
Palazzo Massimo
alle Colonne **11**
Torre dell'Orologio **17**
Palazzo del Banco
di Santo Spirito **18**
Palazzo Altemps **23**

Fountains and Statues
Fontana dei Quattro Fiumi **1**
Pasquino **13**

Historic Streets and Piazzas
Piazza Navona **2**
Via del Governo Vecchio **14**
Via dei Coronari **19**

Restaurants
Hostaria dell'Orso **22**

SEE ALSO

• **Street Finder**, maps 4, 11, 12

• **Where to Stay** pp294–5

• **Restaurants** pp310–11

GETTING THERE
This central area is within walking distance of many parts of the city. Much of the area itself is closed to traffic, but it is easily reached by bus. The principal routes along Corso Vittorio Emanuele II are the 64 from Termini station to St Peter's and the 46. Corso del Rinascimento, which runs parallel to Piazza Navona, is served by several useful routes, including the 70, 81, 116, 186 and 492.

KEY

▨ Street-by-Street map

P Parking

0 meters   200
0 yards   200

Piazza Navona, with the Fontana del Moro and church of Sant'Agnese in Agone

Street by Street: Piazza Navona

NO OTHER PIAZZA in Rome can rival the theatricality of Piazza Navona. Day and night, there is always something going on in the pedestrian area around its three flamboyant fountains. The Baroque is also represented in many of the area's churches. To discover an older Rome, walk along Via del Governo Vecchio and admire the facades of its Renaissance buildings and browse in the fascinating antiques shops.

Oratorio dei Filippini
The musical term oratorio *comes from this place of informal worship* **⑯**

Torre dell' Orologio
This clock tower by Borromini (1648) is part of the Convent of the Filippini **⑰**

Chiesa Nuova
This church was rebuilt in the late 16th century for the order founded by San Filippo Neri **⑮**

VIA DEL CORALLO

VIA DEL GOVERNO VECCHIO

VIA DI PARIONE

To Corso Vittorio Emanuele II

Via del Governo Vecchio
This street preserves a large number of fine Renaissance houses **⑭**

Santa Maria della Pace
The medallion shows Pope Alexander VII, who had the church restored by Pietro da Cortona in 1656 **⑥**

CORSO VITTORIO EMANUELE II

Pasquino
Romans hung satirical verses and dialogues on this weatherbeaten statue **⑬**

PIAZZA DI PASQUINO

Palazzo Pamphilj
This grand town house was built for Pope Innocent X and his family in the mid-17th century **③**

PIAZZA DI SAN PANTALEO

Palazzo Braschi
A late 18th-century building with a splendid balcony, the palazzo houses the Museo di Roma **⑫**

Palazzo Massimo alle Colonne
The magnificent curving colonnade (1536) is by Baldassarre Peruzzi **⑪**

STAR SIGHTS

★ **Sant'Andrea della Valle**

★ **San Luigi dei Francesi**

★ **Piazza Navona**

KEY

– – – Suggested route

0 meters   75
0 yards   75

Sant'Agnese in Agone
Borromini's startling concave facade (1657) dominates one side of Piazza Navona ❹

Santa Maria dell'Anima
For four centuries this has been the German church in Rome ❺

Fontana dei Quattro Fiumi
This fountain supporting an Egyptian obelisk was designed by Bernini ❶

Palazzo Madama
A spread-eagled stone lionskin decorates the central doorway of the palazzo, now the Italian Senate ❽

LOCATOR MAP
See Central Rome Map pp12–13

★ **San Luigi dei Francesi**
An 18th-century statue of St. Louis stands in a niche in the facade ❼

★ **Piazza Navona**
This unique piazza owes its shape to a Roman racetrack and its stunning decor to the genius of the Roman Baroque ❷

The Fontana del Moro was remodeled in 1653 by Bernini, who designed the central sea god.

Sant'Ivo alla Sapienza
This tiny domed church is one of Borromini's most original creations. He worked on it between 1642 and 1650 ❾

To Campo de' Fiori

★ **Sant'Andrea della Valle**
The church, with its grandiose facade by Carlo Rainaldi (1665), has gained fame outside Rome as the setting of the first act of Puccini's Tosca ❿

Fontana dei Quattro Fiumi ❶

Piazza Navona. **Map** 4 E4 & 11 C3. 🚌
46, 62, 64, 70, 81, 87, 116, 492, 628.

B UILT FOR POPE Innocent X
Pamphilj, this magnificent
fountain in the center of
Piazza Navona was unveiled
in 1651. The pope's coat of
arms, the dove and the olive
branch, decorate the bold
pyramid rock formation
supporting the Roman
obelisk, which once stood in
the Circus of Maxentius on
the Appian Way. Bernini
designed the fountain, which
was paid for by means of
highly unpopular taxes on
bread and other staples. The
great rivers then known – the
Ganges, the Danube, the Nile
and the Plate – are
represented by four giants.

The Nile's veiled head
symbolizes the river's
unknown source, but there is
also a legend that the veil
conveys Bernini's dislike for
the nearby Sant'Agnese in
Agone, designed by his rival,
Borromini. Similarly, the

View of Palazzo Pamphilj across Piazza Navona

athletic figure of the Plate,
cringing with arm upraised, is
supposed to express Bernini's
fear that the church will
collapse. Sadly, these widely
believed stories have no basis
in actual fact: Bernini had
completed the fountain before
Borromini even started work
on the church.

Piazza Navona ❷

Map 4 E3 & 11 C2. 🚌 *46, 62, 64,
70, 81, 87, 116, 492, 628.*

R OME'S MOST beautiful
Baroque piazza follows
the shape of Domitian's
stadium, which once stood on
this site – some of its arches
are still visible below the
church of Sant'Agnese in
Agone. The *agones* were
athletic contests held in the
1st-century stadium, which
could seat 33,000. The word
Navona is thought to be
a corruption of *in
agone*. The piazza's
unique appearance and
atmosphere were
created in the 17th
century with the add-
ition of the Fontana dei
Quattro Fiumi. The

other fountains, the Fontana
di Nettuno and the Fontana
del Moro, date from the previous century but have been
altered several times since.
The figure known as Il Moro
is a late work by Bernini.

Up until the 19th century,
Piazza Navona was flooded
during August by stopping
the fountain outlets. The rich
moved around in carriages,
while street urchins paddled
after them.

Today the piazza is a
favorite in all seasons. Each
January 6, it fills with colorful
stalls selling toys and sweets
for the feast of the Befana.

Palazzo Pamphilj ❸

Piazza Navona. **Map** 4 E4 & 11 C3.
🚌 *46, 62, 64, 70, 81, 87, 116, 492,
628.* **Not open** to the public.

**Family dove and olive branch on
the facade of Palazzo Pamphilj**

I N 1644 Giovanni Battista
Pamphilj became Pope
Innocent X. During his ten-
year reign, he heaped riches
on his own family, especially
his domineering sister-in-law,
Olimpia Maidalchini. The
"talking statue" Pasquino *(see
p124)* gave her the nickname
"Olim-Pia," Latin for "formerly
virtuous." She lived in the
grand Palazzo Pamphilj,
which has frescoes by Pietro
da Cortona and a gallery by
Borromini. The building is
now the Brazilian embassy
and cultural center.

Symbolic figure of the River Ganges in Bernini's Fontana dei Quattro Fiumi

Sant'Agnese in Agone ➍

Piazza Navona. **Map** 4 E4 & 11 C3.
[06-679 44 35. 46, 62, 64, 70,
81, 87, 116, 492, 628. **Open** 4:30pm–
6:30pm Mon–Sat, 10am–noon Sun &
religious hols. 🕇 🛴

THIS CHURCH IS believed to
have been founded on the
site of the brothel where, in
AD 304, the young St. Agnes
was exposed naked to force
her to renounce her faith. A
marble relief in the crypt
shows the miraculous growth
of her hair, which fell around
her body to protect her
modesty. She was martyred
on this site and is buried in
the catacombs that bear her
name along the Via
Nomentana *(see p264).*

Today's church was
commissioned by Pope
Innocent X in 1652. The first
architects were a father and
son, Girolamo and Carlo
Rainaldi, but they were
replaced by Borromini,
who worked on the
church from 1653 to
1657. He stuck largely
to the Rainaldi
scheme, except
for the concave
facade designed
to emphasize
the dome. A statue
of St. Agnes on the
facade is said to
be reassuring the
Fontana dei Fiumi's
statue of the River
Plate that the
church is stable.

**Statue of St. Agnes
on Sant'Agnese
facade**

Carlo Saraceni's *Miracle of St. Benno and the Keys of Meissen Cathedral*

tomb by Baldassarre Peruzzi
in Santa Maria dell'Anima. It
stands to the right of
Giulio Romano's
damaged altarpiece and
is redolent of the
pagan Renaissance
spirit the pope had so
condemned during
his brief, rather
gloomy reign, when
patronage of the arts
ground to a halt. Santa
Maria dell'Anima is
the German church in
Rome, and some of its
paintings, such as the
Miracle of St. Benno by
Carlo Saraceni (1618),
illustrate events connected
with the history of Germany.

Santa Maria dell'Anima ➎

Via della Pace 24. **Map** 4 E4 & 11 C2.
[06-682 81 81. 46, 62, 64, 70,
81, 87, 116, 492, 628. **Open**
8am–7pm Mon–Sat, 8am–1pm,
3pm–7pm Sun. 🕇 📷 🛴

POPE ADRIAN VI (reigned
1522–3), son of a ship-
builder from Utrecht, was the
last non-Italian pope before
John Paul II. He would have
disapproved of his superb

Santa Maria della Pace ➏

Vicolo dell'Arco della Pace 5. **Map** 4 E3
& 11 C2. [06-686 11 56. 46,
62, 64, 70, 81, 87, 116, 492, 628.
Closed for restoration. 🕇 🛴 2 steps.

A DRUNKEN SOLDIER allegedly
pierced the breast of a
painted Madonna on this site,
causing it to bleed. Pope
Sixtus IV della Rovere

(reigned 1471–84) placated
the Virgin by ordering Baccio
Pontelli to build her a church
if she would bring the war
with Turkey to an end. Peace
was restored, and the church
was named Santa Maria della
Pace (St. Mary of Peace).

The cloister was added by
Bramante in 1504. As in his
famous Tempietto *(see p219),*
he scrupulously followed
Classical rules of proportion
to produce a thoroughly
original result, achieving a
really monumental effect in a
relatively small space.

Pietro da Cortona may have
had Bramante's Tempietto in
mind when he added the
church's charming semi-
circular portico in 1656. The
interior, a short nave ending
under an octagonal cupola,
houses Raphael's famous
frescoes of four *Sybils,* plus
four *Prophets* by his pupil
Timoteo Viti, painted for the
banker Agostino Chigi in 1514.
Baldassarre Peruzzi also did
some work in the church (the
fresco in the first chapel on
the left), as did the architect
Antonio da Sangallo the
Younger, who designed the
second chapel on the right.

San Luigi dei Francesi ❼

Via Santa Giovanna d'Arco.
Map 4 F4 & 12 D2. **[** 06-688 27 1.
🚌 70, 81, 87, 116, 492, 628.
Open 8am–12:30pm, 3:30pm–7pm
daily. **Closed** Thu pm. 🚪 🏛

THE FRENCH national church
was founded in 1518, but
took until 1589 to complete,
with contributions by Giacomo
della Porta and Domenico
Fontana. The church serves as
a last resting place for many
illustrious French people,
including Chateaubriand's
lover Pauline de Beaumont.

Three Caravaggios hang in
the fifth chapel on the left,
dedicated to St. Matthew.
Painted between 1597 and
1602, these were Caravaggio's
first great religious works: the
Calling of St. Matthew, the
Martyrdom of St. Matthew and
St. Matthew and the Angel.
The first version of this last
painting was rejected because
of its vivid realism – never
before had a saint been
shown as a tired
old man with
dirty feet. All
three works
display very
disquieting
realism and
highly
dramatic use
of light.

**Shield linking symbols of France
and Rome on facade of San Luigi**

Palazzo Madama ❽

Corso del Rinascimento. **Map** 4 F4 &
12 D3. **[** 06-670 61. 🚌 70, 81, 87,
116, 186, 492, 628. **Open** 10am–6pm
first Sat of month.

THIS 16TH-CENTURY palazzo
was built for the Medici
family, who had owned a bank
here in the previous century.
It was the residence of the
Medici cardinals and cousins,
Giovanni and Giuliano. Both
later became popes: Giovanni
as Leo X and Giuliano as
Clement VII. Caterina de'
Medici, Clement VII's niece,
also lived here before she was
married to Henry, son of King
Francis I of France in 1533.

Caravaggio, whose paintings of St. Matthew hang in San Luigi dei Francesi

The palazzo takes its name
from Madama Margherita of
Austria, illegitimate daughter
of Emperor Charles V, who
married Alessandro de' Medici
and, after his death, Ottavio
Farnese. Thus part of the art
collection of the Florentine
Medici famile was inherited
by the Roman Farnese family.

The spectacular facade, with
its ornate cornice and
whimsical roof details, was
built in the 17th century by
Paolo Maruccelli. Since 1871
the palazzo has been the seat
of the Senate, the upper
house of the Italian parliament.

Cornice of Palazzo Madama

Sant'Ivo alla Sapienza ❾

Corso del Rinascimento 40.
Map 4 F4 & 12 D3. **[** 06-686 49 87
🚌 46, 64, 70, 81, 87, 116, 186,
492, 628. **Open** for mass 9am–noon
Sun. **Closed** Jul & Aug. 🚪

THE CHURCH'S lantern
is crowned with a
cross on top of a
dramatic twisted
spiral – a highly
distinctive landmark
from Rome's roof
terraces. Seen up
close, this
Borromini
church is
even more   **Lantern and spire**
striking. No   **of Sant'Ivo**
other Baroque
church is quite like it. The
church is based on a design
of astonishing geometrical
complexity, with walls that are
a breathtaking combination of
concave and convex surfaces.
It stands in the small
courtyard of the Palazzo della
Sapienza, seat of the old
University of Rome from the
15th century until 1935.

Sant'Andrea della Valle ⑩

Piazza Sant'Andrea della Valle. **Map 4**
E4 & 12 D4. 📞 *06-686 13 39.* 🚌 *H,*
46, 56, 60, 62, 64, 70, 75, 81, 87, 116,
170, 492, 628. 🚋 *8.* **Open** *8:30am–*
noon, 4:30pm–7:30pm daily. 🚻

Dome of Sant'Andrea della Valle

T HIS CHURCH is the scene of
the first act of Puccini's
opera *Tosca*, though opera
fans will not find the Attavanti
chapel, which is a poetic
invention. The real church has
much to recommend it – the
recently restored facade
shows the flamboyant
Baroque style at its best.
Inside, a golden light filters
through the high windows,
showing off the gilded
interior. Here lie the two
popes of the Sienese
Piccolomini family: on the left
of the central nave is the
tomb of Pius II, the first
Humanist pope (reigned
1458–64); Pope Pius III lies
opposite – he reigned for less
than a month in 1503.

The church is famous for its
beautiful dome, the largest in
Rome after St. Peter's. It was
built by Carlo Maderno from
1622 to 1625 and was painted
with splendid frescoes by
Domenichino and Giovanni
Lanfranco. The latter's
extravagant style, seen in the
dome fresco *Glory of
Paradise*, won him most of
the commission, and the
jealous Domenichino is said
to have tried to kill him. He
failed, but Domenichino's
jealousy was unnecessary, as
shown by his two beautiful
paintings of scenes from the
life of St. Andrew around the
apse and altar. In the Strozzi
Chapel, built in the style of
Michelangelo, the altar has
copies of the *Leah and Rachel*
by Michelangelo in San Pietro
in Vincoli *(see p170)*.

Palazzo Massimo alle Colonne ⑪

Corso Vittorio Emanuele II 141.
Map 4 F4 & 11 C3. 🚌 *46, 62, 64, 70,*
81, 87, 116, 186, 492, 628. **Chapel**
open *7am–noon Mar 16 every year.*

Roman column, Palazzo Massimo

D URING THE LAST two years
of his life, Baldassarre
Peruzzi built this palazzo for
the Massimo family, whose
home had been destroyed in
the sack of Rome in 1527.
Peruzzi displayed great
ingenuity in dealing with an
awkwardly shaped site. The
previous building had stood
on the ruined Theater of
Domitian, which created a
curve in the great processional
Via Papalis. Peruzzi's convex
colonnaded facade follows
the line of the street. His
originality is also evident in
the small square upper
windows, the courtyard
and the stuccoed
vestibule. The entrance
in Piazza de'
Massimi has a
Renaissance-style
frescoed facade. A
single column from the
theater has been set up
in the piazza.

The Massimo family,
Quintus Fabius
Maximus, traced its
origins to the
conqueror of Hannibal in the
3rd century BC, and their proud
coat of arms is borne by an
infant Hercules. Over the years
the family produced many
great Humanists; in the 19th
century a Massimo nego-tiated
peace with Napoleon. On
March 16 each year the family
chapel opens to the public to
celebrate Paolo Massimo's
resurrection from the dead by
San Filippo Neri in 1538.

Palazzo Braschi ⑫

Piazza San Pantaleo 10. **Map** 4 E4 &
11 C3. 📞 *06-687 53 45.* 🚌 *46, 62,*
64, 70, 81, 87, 116, 186, 492, 628.
🚋 *8. Reopens after restoration spring
2000 – phone for opening hours.*

O N ONE SIDE of Piazza San
Pantaleo is the last
Roman palazzo to be built
for the family of a pope.
Palazzo Braschi was built in
the late 18th century for Pope
Pius VI Braschi's nephews by
the architect Cosimo Morelli.
He gave the building its
imposing facade, which looks
out on to the piazza.

The palazzo now houses
the municipal Museo di Roma.
It holds collections of pictures,
drawings and everyday
objects illustrating life
in the city from
medieval times
until the 19th
century.

**Angel with raised wing by Ercole Ferrata,
flanking the facade of Sant'Andrea della Valle**

Pasquino ⓭

Piazza di Pasquino. **Map** 4 E4 & 11 C3. 🚌 *46, 62, 64, 70, 81, 87, 116, 492, 628.*

Pasquino, the most famous of Rome's satirical "talking statues"

THIS ROUGH CHUNK of marble is all that remains of a Hellenistic group, probably representing the incident in Homer's *Iliad* in which Menelaus shields the body of the slain Patroclus. For years it lay as a stepping stone in a muddy medieval street until it was erected on this corner in 1501, near the shop of an outspoken cobbler named Pasquino. Freedom of speech was not encouraged in papal Rome, so the cobbler wrote out his satirical comments on current events and attached them to the statue.

Other Romans were quick to follow suit, hanging their maxims and verses by the statue by night to escape punishment. Despite the wrath of the authorities, the sayings of the "talking statue" (renamed Pasquino) were part of popular culture right up until the 19th century. Other statues started to "talk" in the same satirical vein; Pasquino used to conduct dialogues with the statue Marforio in Via del Campidoglio (now in the courtyard of Palazzo Nuovo, *see pp70–71*) and with the Babuino in Via del Babuino *(see p135)*. One of Rome's few English-language cinemas is named after Pasquino *(see p347)*.

Via del Governo Vecchio ⓮

Map 4 E4 & 11 B3. 🚌 *46, 62, 64.*

THE STREET TAKES its name from Palazzo del Governo Vecchio, the seat of papal government in the 17th and 18th centuries. Once part of the Via Papalis, which led from the Lateran to St. Peter's, the street is lined with 15th- and 16th-century houses and small workshops. Particularly interesting are the 15th-century houses at Nos. 104 and 106. The small palazzo at No. 123 was once thought to have been the home of Bramante. Opposite is Palazzo del Governo Vecchio. It is also known as Palazzo Nardini, after its founder, whose name is inscribed on the first-floor windows along with the date 1477.

Via del Governo Vecchio

Chiesa Nuova ⓯

Piazza della Chiesa Nuova.
Map 4 E4 & 11 B3. ☎ *06-687 52 89.* 🚌 *46, 62, 64.* **Open** *7:30am–noon, 4:30pm–7pm daily.* ✝

Facade of the Chiesa Nuova

SAN FILIPPO NERI (St. Philip Neri) is the most appealing of the Counter Reformation saints. A highly unconventional reformer, he required his noble Roman followers to humble themselves in public. He made aristocratic young men parade through the streets of Rome in rags or even with a fox's tail tied behind them and set noblemen to work as laborers building his church. With the help of Pope Gregory XIII, his church was built in place of an old medieval one, Santa Maria in Vallicella, and it has been known ever since as the Chiesa Nuova (new church).

Begun in 1575 by Matteo da Città di Castello and continued by Martino Longhi the Elder, it was consecrated in 1599, although the facade, by Fausto Rughesi, was finished only in 1606. Against San Filippo's wishes, the interior was decorated after his death; Pietro da Cortona frescoed the nave, dome and apse, taking nearly 20 years. There are also three paintings by Rubens: *Madonna and Angels* above the altar; *Saints Domitilla, Nereus and Achilleus* on the right of the altar; and *Saints Gregory, Maurus and Papias* on the left. San Filippo is buried in his own chapel, to the left of the altar.

Borromini's facade of the Oratorio

Oratorio dei Filippini 16

Piazza della Chiesa Nuova. **Map** 4 E4 & 11 B3. **☎** 06-686 93 74. **🚌** 46, 62, 64. **Admission** by appt only; call the caretaker. **📷** **Concerts.**

W ITH THE ADJOINING church and convent, the oratory formed the center of Filippo Neri's religious order, founded in 1575. Its members are commonly known as Filippini. The musical term *oratorio* (a religious text sung by solo voices and chorus) derives from the services held here.

Filippo Neri came to Rome at 18 to work as a tutor. The city was undergoing a period of religious strife and an economic slump after the sack of Rome in 1527. There was also an outbreak of the plague. It was left to newcomers like Neri and Ignazio di Loyola to revive the spiritual life of the city.

Neri formed a brotherhood of laymen who worshiped together and helped pilgrims and the sick *(see Santissima Trinità dei Pellegrini, p146).* He founded the Oratory as a center for religious discourse. Its conspicuous curving brick facade was built by Borromini between 1637 and 1643.

Torre dell' Orologio 17

Piazza dell'Orologio. **Map** 4 E4 & 11 B3. **🚌** 46, 62, 64.

B ORROMINI BUILT this clock tower to decorate one corner of the Convent of the Oratorians of San Filippo Neri from 1647 to 1649. It is typical of Borromini in that the front and rear are concave and the

sides convex. The mosaic of the Madonna beneath the clock is by Pietro da Cortona, while on the corner of the building is a small tabernacle to the Madonna flanked by angels in the style of Bernini.

Pietro da Cortona (1596–1669)

Palazzo del Banco di Santo Spirito 18

Via del Banco di Santo Spirito. **Map** 4 D4 & 11 A2. **🚌** 46, 62, 64. **Open** normal banking hours.

F ORMERLY THE MINT of papal Rome, this palazzo is often referred to as the Antica Zecca (old mint). The upper stories of the facade, built by Antonio da Sangallo the Younger in the 1520s, are in the shape of a Roman triumphal arch. Above the arch stand two Baroque statues symbolizing Charity and Thrift, and in the center of the arch above the main entrance an inscription records the founding of the Banco di Santo Spirito by Pope Paul V Borghese in 1605.

Pope Paul was a very shrewd financier who encouraged Romans to deposit their money at the bank by offering the vast estates of the Hospital of Santo Spirito *(see p226)* as security. The system provided for only the rudimentary banking requirements of the population, but business was brisk as people deposited money here, secure in the knowledge that they could get it out simply by presenting a chit. The hospital coffers also gained from the system. The Banco di Santo Spirito still exists but is now part of the Banca di Roma.

Facade of the Banco di Santo Spirito, built to resemble a Roman arch

Via dei Coronari ⑲

Map 4 D3 & 11 B2. 🚌 46, 62, 64, 70, 81, 87, 115, 116, 186, 280, 492.

LARGE NUMBERS of medieval pilgrims making their way to St. Peter's walked along this street to cross over the Tiber at Ponte Sant'Angelo. Of the businesses that sprang up to try to part the pilgrims from their money, the most enduring was the selling of rosaries, and the street is still named after the rosary sellers (coronari). The street followed the course of the ancient Roman Via Recta (straight street), which originally ran from today's Piazza Colonna to the Tiber.

Making one's way through the people in Via dei Coronari could be hazardous. In the Holy Year of 1450, some 200 pilgrims died, crushed by the crowds or drowned in the Tiber. Following the tragedy, Pope Nicholas V demolished the Roman triumphal arch that stood at the entrance to Ponte Sant'Angelo. In the late 15th century, Pope Sixtus IV encouraged the building of private houses and palaces along the street.

Although the rosary sellers have been replaced by antiques dealers, the street still has many original buildings from the 15th and 16th centuries. One of the earliest, at Nos. 156–7, is known as the House of Fiammetta, the mistress of Cesare Borgia.

Antiques shop, Via dei Coronari

Cloister, San Salvatore in Lauro

San Salvatore in Lauro ⑳

Piazza San Salvatore in Lauro 15. **Map** 4 E3 & 11 B2. 📞 06-687 51 87. 🚌 70, 81, 87, 115, 116, 186, 280. **Open** 8.30am– noon Mon, Wed, Sat, Sun, 4–7pm (summer; 5–8pm) daily. ✝

THE CHURCH is named "in Lauro" after the laurel grove that grew here in ancient times. The church standing here today was constructed at the end of the 16th century by Ottaviano Mascherino. The bell tower and sacristy were 18th-century additions by Nicola Salvi, famous for the Trevi Fountain (see p159).

The church contains the first great altarpiece by the 17th-century artist Pietro da Cortona, *The Birth of Jesus*, in the first chapel to the right.

The adjacent Convent of San Giorgio, to the left, has a pretty Renaissance cloister, a frescoed refectory and the monument to Pope Eugenius IV (reigned 1431–47), moved here when old St. Peter's was pulled down. An extravagant Venetian, Eugenius would willingly spend thousands of ducats on his gold tiara but requested a "simple, lowly burial place" near his predecessor, Pope Eugenius III. His portrait, painted by Salviati, is in the refectory.

In 1669 the church became the seat of a pious association, the Confraternity of the Piceni, inhabitants of the Marche region. Fanatically loyal to the pope, the Piceni were traditionally employed as papal soldiers and tax collectors.

Museo Napoleonico ㉑

Piazza di Ponte Umberto 1. **Map** 4 E3 & 11 C1. 📞 06-68 80 62 86. 🚌 70, 81, 87, 116, 186, 280, 492. **Open** 9am– 7pm Tue–Sat, 9am–1.30pm Sun. **Closed** Jan 1, May 1, Dec 25. **Adm charge.** 🚫

THIS MUSEUM contains memorabilia and portraits of Napoleon Bonaparte and his family. Personal relics of Napoleon himself include an Indian shawl he wore during his exile on St. Helena.

After his death in 1821, the pope allowed many of the Bonaparte family to settle in Rome, including his mother Letizia, who lived in Palazzo Misciattelli on Via del Corso, and his sister Pauline who married the Roman Prince Camillo Borghese. The museum has a cast of her right breast, made by Canova in 1805 as a study for his statue of her as a reclining Venus, now in the Museo Borghese (see p261). Portraits and personal effects of other members of the family are on display, including uniforms, court dresses, and a penny-farthing bicycle that belonged to Prince Eugène, the son of Emperor Napoleon III.

The last male of the Roman branch of the family was Napoleon Charles, portrayed in a late 19th-century painting by Guglielmo de Sanctis. The collection was assembled in 1927 by the Counts Primoli, the sons of Charles's sister, Carlotta Bonaparte.

Facade of San Salvatore in Lauro

The palace next door, in Via Zanardelli, houses the Racolta Praz, an impressive selection of over 1,000 *objets d'art*, paintings and pieces of furniture. Dating from the 17th and 18th century, they were collected by the art historian Mario Praz, who died in 1981.

Side relief of the Ludovisi Throne, Palazzo Altemps

Entrance to Museo Napoleonico

Hostaria dell'Orso ㉒

Via dei Soldati 25. **Map** 4 E3 & 11 C2. 🚌 70, 81, 87, 116, 186, 280, 492, 628. **Not open** to the public.

THIS ANCIENT INN has a 15th-century portico and loggia built with columns taken from Roman ruins. Legend has it that Dante once stayed here. Later visitors to Rome known to have used the inn include the 16th-century French writers Rabelais and Montaigne.

Palazzo Altemps ㉓

Via di Sant'Apollinare 44. **Map** 4 E3 & 11 C2. 📞 06-683 37 59. 🚌 70, 81, 87, 115, 116, 280, 492, 628. **Open** 9am–10pm Tue–Sat, 9am–2pm Sun. **Adm charge**.

AN EXTRAORDINARY collection of Classical sculpture is housed in this branch of the Museo Nazionale Romano.

Restored as a museum during the 1990s, the palazzo was originally built for Girolamo Riario, nephew of Pope Sixtus IV in 1480. The Riario coat of arms can still be seen in the janitor's room. In the popular uprising that followed the pope's death in 1484, the building was sacked and Girolamo fled the city. .

In 1568 the palazzo was bought by Cardinal Marco Sittico Altemps. His family was of German origin – the name is an Italianization of Hohenems – and influential in the church. The palazzo was renovated by Martino Longhi the Elder in the 1570s. He added the great belvedere, crowned with obelisks and a marble unicorn.

The Altemps family were ostentatious collectors; the courtyard and its staircase are lined with ancient sculptures. These form part of the museum's collection, together with the Ludovisi collection of ancient sculptures, which was previously housed in the Museo Nazionale Romano in the Terms of Diocletian (see p163). Located on the ground floor is the Greek statue of Athena Parthenos and the Dionysious group, a Roman copy of the Greek original. On the first floor, at the far end of the courtyard, visitors can admire the beautifully decorated Painted Loggia, dating from 1595. The Ludovisi throne, a Greek original

carved in the 5th century BC, is located on the same floor.

It is decorated with reliefs, one of which shows a young woman rising from the sea, who is thought to represent Aphrodite. In the room which is known as the Salone del Camino is the powerful statue *Galata's Suicide*, a marble copy of a group originally made in bronze. Nearby is the Ludovisi Sarcophague, dating from the 3rd century AD.

Galata's Suicide in the Palazzo Altemps

PIAZZA DI SPAGNA

BY THE 16th century, the increase in numbers of visiting pilgrims and ecclesiastics was making life in Rome's already congested medieval center unbearable. A new triangle of roads was built (and is still in place today), to help channel pilgrims as quickly as possible from the city's north gate, the Porta del Popolo, to the Vatican. By the 18th century, hotels had sprung up

Lion fountain in Piazza del Popolo

throughout the district. Today this attractive area offers much more: the superb works of Renaissance and Baroque art in Santa Maria del Popolo and Sant' Andrea delle Fratte; the magnificent reliefs of the restored Ara Pacis; art exhibits in the Villa Medici; views of the city from the Spanish Steps and the Pincio Gardens; plus Rome's most famous shopping streets, centered around Via Condotti.

SIGHTS AT A GLANCE

Churches
Sant'Andrea delle Fratte ❶
Trinità dei Monti ❿
All Saints ⓬
Santa Maria dei Miracoli and
Santa Maria in Montesanto ⓮
Santa Maria del
Popolo pp138–9 ⓱
San Rocco ㉑
Santi Ambrogio e Carlo
al Corso ㉒

Museums and Galleries
Keats-Shelley
Memorial House ❼
Casa di Goethe ⓭

Historic Buildings
Palazzo di Propaganda
Fide ❷
Villa Medici ⓫

Arches, Gates and Columns
Colonna dell'Immacolata ❸
Porta del Popolo ⓲

Historic Streets and Piazzas
Via Condotti ❹
Piazza di Spagna ❻

Spanish Steps ❾
Piazza del Popolo ⓰

Monuments and Tombs
Ara Pacis ⓳
Mausoleum of Augustus ⓴

Parks and Gardens
Pincio Gardens ⓯

Café and Restaurant
Caffè Greco ❺
Babington's Tea Rooms ❽

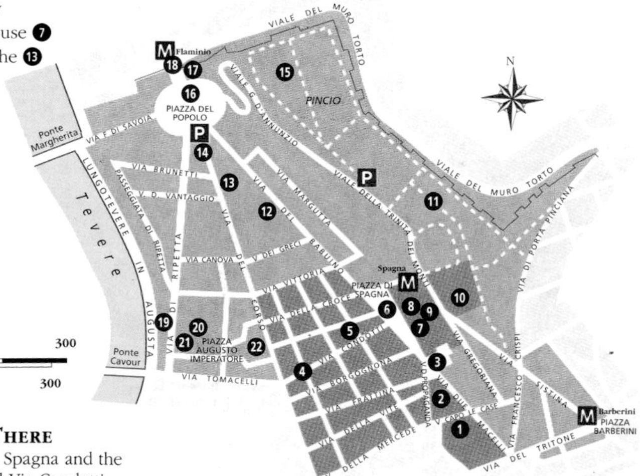

GETTING THERE

For Piazza di Spagna and the shops around Via Condotti, the Spagna Metro station on line A is more convenient than the main bus routes along Via del Corso and Via del Tritone. Stay on until Flaminio Metro if you want to visit Piazza del Popolo. For getting around locally, the 117 minibus, which goes up Via del Babuino, is very handy.

KEY

Street-by-Street map

M Metro station

P Parking

— City Wall

SEE ALSO

• *Street Finder*, maps 4, 5

• *Where to Stay* pp294–5

• *Restaurants* pp310–11

• *Shops* pp322–37

The Spanish Steps leading up to the church of Trinità dei Monti

Street by Street: Piazza di Spagna

THE NETWORK of narrow streets between Piazza di Spagna and Via del Corso is one of the liveliest areas in Rome, drawing throngs of tourists and Romans to its discreet and elegant shops. In the 18th century, the area was full of hotels for frivolous English aristocrats doing the Grand Tour, but there were also artists, writers and composers, who took the city's history and culture more seriously.

Caffè Greco
Busts and portraits recall the café's former artistic patrons ⑤

★ **Piazza di Spagna**
For almost three centuries, the square with its curious Barcaccia fountain in the center has been the chief meeting place for visitors to Rome ⑥

Via delle Carrozze took its name from the carriages of wealthy tourists that used to line up there for repairs.

Via Condotti
This shadowy narrow street has the smartest shops in one of the smartest shopping areas in the world ④

Bulgari sells very expensive jewelry behind an austere shopfront in Via Condotti.

0 meters   75
0 yards   75

KEY

– – – Suggested route

Ⓜ Metro station

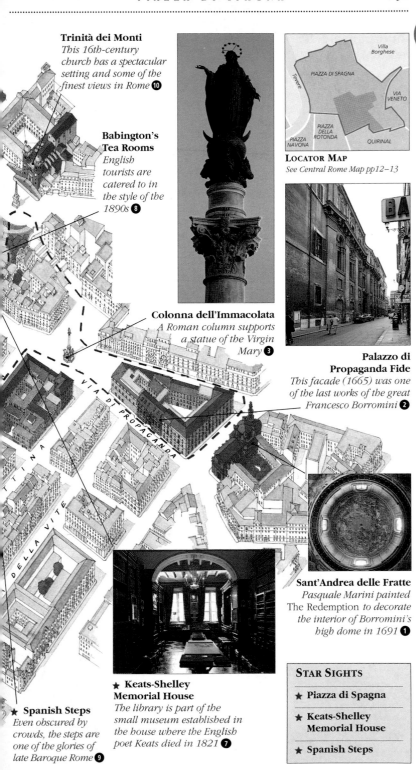

Trinità dei Monti
This 16th-century church has a spectacular setting and some of the finest views in Rome ❿

Babington's Tea Rooms
English tourists are catered to in the style of the 1890s ❽

Colonna dell'Immacolata
A Roman column supports a statue of the Virgin Mary ❸

LOCATOR MAP
See Central Rome Map pp12–13

Palazzo di Propaganda Fide
This façade (1665) was one of the last works of the great Francesco Borromini ❷

Sant'Andrea delle Fratte
Pasquale Marini painted The Redemption *to decorate the interior of Borromini's high dome in 1691* ❶

★ Keats-Shelley Memorial House
The library is part of the small museum established in the house where the English poet Keats died in 1821 ❼

★ Spanish Steps
Even obscured by crowds, the steps are one of the glories of late Baroque Rome ❾

STAR SIGHTS

★ Piazza di Spagna

★ Keats-Shelley Memorial House

★ Spanish Steps

Sant'Andrea delle Fratte ●

Via Sant'Andrea delle Fratte 1.
Map 5 A3. 06-679 31 91. 117.
Spagna. **Open** 6:30am–12:30pm,
4pm–7pm daily.

WHEN SANT'ANDREA delle Fratte was built in the 12th century, this area was the northernmost edge of Rome. Though the church is now firmly embedded in the city, its name (*fratte* means "thickets") recalls its old setting.

The church was completely rebuilt in the 17th century, partly by Borromini. His bell tower and dome, best viewed from the higher ground farther up Via Capo le Case, are remarkable for the complex arrangement of concave and convex surfaces. The bell tower is particularly fanciful, with angel caryatids, flaming torches, and exaggerated

scrolls like semifolded hearts supporting a spiky crown.

In 1842, the Virgin Mary appeared in the church to a Jewish banker, who promptly converted to Christianity and became a missionary. Inside, the chapel of the Miraculous Madonna is the first thing visitors notice. The church is better known, however, for the angels that Borromini's rival, Bernini, carved for the Ponte Sant'Angelo. Pope Clement IX declared they were too lovely to be outside, so they remained with Bernini's family until 1729, when they were moved to the church.

Palazzo di Propaganda Fide ●

Via di Propaganda 1. **Map** 5 A2.
06-69 88 01 01. 116, 117.
Spagna. **Open** by appt; write to
Mons. Mottola, Piazza di Spagna 48.

THE POWERFUL JESUIT Congregation for the Propagation of the Faith was founded in 1622. Their headquarters had to be a remarkable building, and Bernini was commissioned. But Innocent X, who became pope in 1644, preferred the style of Borromini who was asked to continue. His extraordinary west facade facade, completed in 1662, must have outstripped everyone's expectations. It is striped with broad pilasters, between which the first-floor windows bend in, and the central bay bulges. A rigid band divides its floors, and the cornice above the convex central bay swerves inwards. The more you look at it, the more restless it seems; a sign perhaps of the increasing unhappiness of the architect who committed suicide in 1667.

**Angel by Bernini,
Sant'Andrea delle Fratte**

Entrance to the Jesuit College

Colonna dell'Immacolata ●

Piazza Mignanelli. **Map** 5 A2.
116, 117, 492. Spagna.

INAUGURATED IN 1857, the column commemorates Pope Pius IX's proclamation of the doctrine of the Immaculate Conception, holding that the Virgin Mary was the only human being ever to have been born "without the stain of original sin." The column itself dates from ancient Romebut is crowned with a statue of the Virgin Mary.

On December 8 the fire brigade places a wreath at the foot of the column (*see p61*).

**Portrait of Pope Pius IX
(reigned 1846–78)**

Via Condotti

Map 5 A2. 🚍 *81, 115, 116, 117.*
M *Spagna. See* **Shops and Markets**
pp322–33.

NAMED AFTER the conduits
that carried water to the
Baths of Agrippa near the
Pantheon, Via Condotti is
now home to the most
traditional of Rome's designer
clothes shops. Stores selling
shoes and other leather goods
are also well represented. The
street is extremely popular for
early evening strolls, when
elegant perfumed ladies and
men in immaculate suits and
trench coats mingle with
tourists in shorts and sneakers.

Slightly younger designers
such as Laura Biagiotti,
Gianfranco Ferrè and the
Fendi sisters have shops on
the parallel Via Borgognona,
while Valentino and Giorgio
Armani both have stores on
Via Condotti itself. Valentino
has a second branch on Via
Bocca di Leone, which crosses
Via Condotti just below Piazza
di Spagna, and Versace also
has a shop here. Giorgio
Armani has a second store
on nearby Via del Babuino,
among the discreet art
galleries, exclusive antiques
shops and furniture stores.

**View along Via Condotti toward
the Spanish Steps**

Caffè Greco ❺

Via Condotti 86. Map 5 A2.
☎ 06-679 17 00. 🚍 *117.*
M *Spagna.* **Open** *8am–8:30pm
daily.* **Closed** *Jan 1, May 1, two weeks
in August, Dec 25–26.* ♿

THIS CAFE was opened by a
Greek (hence *Greco*) in
1760, and throughout the 18th

Caffè Greco, nearly 250 years old

century it was a favorite
meeting place for
foreign artists. Writers
such as Keats, Byron
and Goethe and
composers Liszt,
Wagner and Bizet all
breakfasted and drank
here. So, too, did
Casanova and mad
King Ludwig of
Bavaria. Today, locals
often stand in the
crowded foyer to sip
espresso; there are also
tables in a cozy back
room, against walls studded
with the portraits of the café's
famous customers.

**Pope Urban VIII's arms,
with the Barberini bees**

Piazza di Spagna ❻

Map 5 A2. 🚍 *117.* M *Spagna.*

SHAPED LIKE a crooked bow
tie and surrounded by tall
shuttered houses painted in
muted shades of ocher, cream
and russet, Piazza di Spagna
(Spanish Square) is crowded
all day and (in summer) most
of the night. The most famous
square in Rome, it has long
been the haunt of foreign
visitors and expatriates.

In the 17th century, Spain's
ambassador to the Holy See
had his headquarters on the
square, and the area around it
was deemed to be Spanish
territory. Foreigners who
unwittingly trespassed were
liable to be dragooned into
the Spanish army. In the 18th
and 19th centuries, Rome was
almost as popular with
visitors as it is today, and the

square stood at the heart of
the city's main hotel district.
Some travelers came in search
of knowledge and artistic
inspiration, but most were
more interested in gambling,
collecting ancient statues to
adorn their family homes and
conducting love affairs with
Italian women.

Not surprisingly, wealthy
travelers attracted hordes of
beggars, who often produced
letters describing their plight,
written by scribes who
worked in the square.

The Fontana della Barcaccia
in the square is the least
showy of Rome's Baroque
fountains, and it is often
completely screened from
view by
people resting
on its rim. It
was designed
either by the
famous Gian
Lorenzo
Bernini or by
his father,
Pietro.
Because the
pressure from
the aqueduct
that feeds the
fountain is
extremely low, there are no
spectacular cascades or spurts
of water. Instead, Bernini
constructed a leaking boat –
barcaccia means "useless
old boat" – which lies half-
submerged in a shallow pool.

The bees and suns that
decorate the Fontana della
Barcaccia are taken from the
family coat of arms of Pope
Urban VIII Barberini, who
commissioned the fountain.

**The Fontana della Barcaccia at
the foot of the Spanish Steps**

Bust of Shelley by Moses Ezekiel

Keats-Shelley Memorial House 7

Piazza di Spagna 26. **Map** 5 A2.
06-678 42 35. 117.
Spagna. **Open** 9am–1pm,
3pm–6pm (Oct–Mar: 2.30pm–
5.30pm) Mon–Fri. **Closed** public
hols, 10 days in Aug. **Adm charge**.
book in advance.

IN NOVEMBER 1820 the English
poet John Keats came to
stay with the painter Joseph
Severn in a dusty pink house,
the Casina Rossa, on the
corner of the Spanish Steps.
Suffering from consumption,
Keats had been sent to Rome
by his doctor, in the hope
that the mild, dry climate
would help the young man's
recovery. Depressed because
of scathing criticism of his
work and tormented by his
unrequited love for a young
girl named Fanny Brawne,
Keats died at 25 the following February.

His death inspired his friend
and fellow poet Percy Bysshe
Shelley to write the poem
"Mourn not for Adonais." In
July 1822 Shelley himself was
drowned in a boating accident
in the Gulf of La Spezia off
the coast of Liguria. Keats,
Shelley and Severn are all
buried in Rome's Protestant
Cemetery (see p205).

In 1906 the house was
bought by an Anglo-American
association and preserved as
a memorial and library to
honor English Romantic

poets. The relics include a
lock of Keats's hair, some
fragments of Shelley's bones
in a tiny urn and a garish
Carnival mask picked up by
Lord Byron as a souvenir of a
trip to Venice. You can visit
the room where Keats died,
though all the original
furniture was burned after his
death, on papal orders.

Babington's Tea Rooms 8

Piazza di Spagna 23. **Map** 5 A2.
06-678 60 27. 117.
Spagna. **Open** 9am–8.30pm
daily. **Closed** Dec 25.

THESE AUGUST, old-fashioned
tea rooms were opened in
1896 by two Englishwomen,
Anna Maria and Isabel Cargill
Babington, to serve homesick
British tourists scones, preserves, and pots of Earl Grey
tea. The food remains homey
– shepherd's pie and chicken
supreme for lunch, muffins
and cinnamon toast for tea –
though these days the menu
offers for breakfast pancakes
with maple syrup as well as the
traditional bacon and eggs.

**Purveyors of English breakfasts to
homesick exiles since 1896**

Spanish Steps 9

Scalinata della Trinità dei Monti,
Piazza di Spagna. **Map** 5 A2. 117.
Spagna.

IN THE 17TH century the
French owners of Trinità dei
Monti decided to link the
church with Piazza di Spagna
by building a magnificent
new flight of steps. They also
planned to place an equestrian
statue of King Louis XIV at the
top. Pope Alexander VII Chigi
was not very happy at the

The Spanish Steps in spring with azaleas in full bloom

prospect of erecting a statue of a French monarch in the papal city, and the arguments continued until the 1720s, when an Italian architect, Francesco de Sanctis, produced a design that satisfied both parties. The steps, completed in 1726, combine straight sections, curves and terraces to create one of the city's most dramatic and distinctive landmarks.

When the Victorian novelist Charles Dickens visited Rome, he reported that the Spanish Steps were the meeting place for artists' models, who would dress in colorful traditional costumes, hoping to catch the attention of a wealthy artist. The steps are now a popular place to sit, write postcards, take photos, flirt or just watch the passers-by but eating there is no longer allowed.

Trinità dei Monti ⑩

Piazza della Trinità dei Monti. **Map** 5 A2.
📞 06-679 41 79. 🚌 117. Ⓜ *Spagna.*
Open 7am–7pm daily (4–8pm in summer). 🏛

Trinità dei Monti's bell towers

T HE VIEWS of Rome from the platform in front of the facade of Trinità dei Monti, with its twin bell towers, are so beautiful that the church itself is often ignored. It is, however, unusual for Rome, for it was founded by the French in 1495, and although it was later badly damaged, there are still traces of attractive late Gothic latticework in the vaults of the transept. The interconnecting side chapels are decorated with Mannerist paintings, including two fine

19th-century engraving of the inner facade of the Villa Medici

works by Daniele da Volterra. A pupil of Michelangelo, Volterra had to paint clothes on the nudes in the *Last Judgment* in the Sistine Chapel, in response to the objections of Pope Pius IV.

Michelangelo's influence is obvious in the muscled bodies shown in the *Deposition* (second chapel on the left). The circles of figures and dancing angels around the Virgin Mary in the *Assumption* (third chapel on the right), have more in common with the graceful style of Raphael.

Villa Medici ⑪

Accademia di Francia a Roma, Viale della Trinità dei Monti 1. **Map** 5 A2.
📞 06-676 11. 🚌 117. Ⓜ *Spagna.*
Accademia and gardens open spring & autumn: Sun am. Otherwise variable, so phone first. **Exhibitions, concerts. Adm charge.** 🏛

S UPERBLY POSITIONED on the Pincio Hill above Piazza di Spagna, this 16th-century villa has kept the name it assumed when Cardinal Ferdinando de' Medici bought it in 1576. From the terrace visitors can look across the city to Castel Sant'Angelo, from where Queen Christina of Sweden is said to have fired the large cannonball that now sits in the basin of the fountain.

The villa is now home to the French Academy, which was founded by Louis XIV in 1666 to give select painters the

chance to study in Rome. Nicolas Poussin was one of the first advisers to the Academy, Ingres was a director and ex-students include Fragonard and Boucher.

After 1803, when the French Academy moved to the Villa Medici, musicians were also admitted; both Berlioz and Debussy came to Rome as students of the Academy.

All Saints ⑫

Via del Babuino 153B. **Map** 4 F2.
📞 06-360 01 881. 🚌 117. **Open** 9am–noon, 5.30–6.30pm daily (phone to check). 🏛

I N 1816 THE POPE gave English residents and visitors the right to hold Anglican services in Rome, but it wasn't until the early 1880s that they acquired a site to build their own church. The architect was G E Street, best known in Britain for his Neo-Gothic churches and the London Law Courts. All Saints is also built in Victorian Neo-Gothic, and the interior, though splendidly decorated with different colored Italian marbles, has a very English air. Street also designed St-Paul's-within-the-Walls in Via Nazionale, whose interior is a jewel of British Pre-Raphaelite art.

The street on which All Saints stands got its name from the Fontana del Sileno, known as Babuino (baboon) due to the sad condition in

Fontana del Sileno, on Via del Babuino since 1957

which it was found.

Casa di Goethe ⓭

18–20 Via del Corso. **Map** 4 F1. 📞
06-32 65 04 12. 🚌 95, 117, 490,
495, 628, 926. 🚋 225. Ⓜ *Flamino*.
Open 11am–6pm Wed–Mon. **Adm
Charge.** 🏛

THE GERMAN POET, dramatist
and novelist Johann
Wolfgang von Goethe (1749–
1832) lived in this house from
1786 until 1788, working on
the journal that eventually
formed part of his travel book
The Italian Journey. Rome's
noisy street life irritated him,
especially during Carnival
time. He was a little perturbed
by the number of murders in
his neighborhood, but Rome
energized him and his book
became one of the most influential ever written about Italy.

Santa Maria dei Miracoli and Santa Maria in Montesanto ⓮

Piazza del Popolo. **Map** 4 F1. 🚌 95,
117, 490, 495, 628, 926. 🚋 225. Ⓜ
Flamino. **Santa Maria dei Miracoli**
📞 06-361 02 50. **Open** 6am–1pm,
5–7:30pm Mon–Sat, 8:30am–
1:30pm, 5–8pm Sun & public hols.
🏛 ♿ **Santa Maria in Montesanto**
📞 06-361 05 94. **Open** Jul–Sep
5–7pm daily. **Closed** Aug. 🏛

THE TWO CHURCHES at the
south end of Piazza del
Popolo were designed by the
architect Carlo Rainaldi
(1611–91), proof that he could
be as ingenious as his peers,
Bernini and Borromini. To
provide a focal point for the
piazza, the churches had to
look symmetrical, but
the site on the

Portrait of Goethe in the Roman countryside by Tischbein (1751–1821)

left was narrower than that on
the right. Rainaldi solved the
problem by giving Santa Maria
dei Miracoli (on the right) a
circular dome and Santa Maria
in Montesanto an oval one,
cleverly squeezing it into the
narrower site; while the sides
of the supporting drums that
face the piazza are identical.

Pincio Gardens ⓯

Il Pincio. **Map** 4 F1. 🚌 95, 117, 490,
495, 628, 926. 🚋 225. Ⓜ *Flaminio*.
♿

THE PINCIO GARDENS lie
above Piazza del Popolo,
on a hillside that has been so
skillfully terraced and richly
planted with trees that, from
below, the zigzagging road
climbing to the gardens is
virtually invisible. In ancient
Roman times, there
magnificent gardens on the
Pincio hill, but the present
gardens were designed
in the early 19th century
by Giuseppe Valadier
(who also
redesigned
the Piazza

The Pincio Gardens water clock

del Popolo). The broad
avenues, lined with umbrella
pines, palm trees and
evergreen oaks, soon became
a fashionable place to stroll,
and even this century such
diverse characters as Gandhi
and Mussolini, Richard Strauss
and King Farouk of Egypt
patronized the Casina
Valadier, an exclusive café
and restaurant on the grounds.
 From the Pincio's main
square, Piazzale Napoleone I,
the panoramic views of Rome
stretch from the Monte Mario
to the Janiculum. For full
effect, approach the gardens
from the grounds of Villa
Borghese *(see pp258–9)*
above the Pincio or along
Viale della Trinità dei Monti.

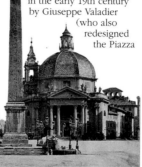

**The twin churches of Santa Maria di Montesanto (left) and Santa Maria
dei Miracoli in a 19th-century view of Piazza del Popolo**

The panorama is particularly beautiful at sunset, the traditional time for tourists to take a stroll in the gardens.

One of the most striking features of the park itself is an Egyptian-style obelisk that Emperor Hadrian erected on the tomb of his favorite, the beautiful male slave Antinous. After the slave's premature death (according to some accounts he died saving the emperor's life), Hadrian deified him.

The 19th-century water clock on Via dell'Orologio was designed by a Dominican monk. It was displayed at the Paris Exhibition of 1889.

Traditional Carnival band in Piazza del Popolo

The Casina Valadier restaurant in the Pincio Gardens

Piazza del Popolo ⑯

Map 4 F1. 🚌 *95, 117, 490, 495, 628, 926.* 🚋 *225.* Ⓜ *Flaminio.*

A VAST COBBLED OVAL standing at the apex of the triangle of roads known as the Trident, Piazza del Popolo forms a grand symmetrical antechamber to the heart of Rome. Twin Neoclassical facades stand on either side of the Porta del Popolo; an Egyptian obelisk rises in the center; and the matching domes and porticoes of Santa Maria dei Miracoli and Santa Maria di Montesanto flank the beginning of Via del Corso.

Although it is now one of the most unified squares in Rome, Piazza del Popolo evolved gradually over the centuries. In 1589 the great town-planning pope, Sixtus V, had the obelisk erected in the center by Domenico Fontana.

Over 3,000 years old, the obelisk was originally brought to Rome by Augustus to adorn the Circus Maximus after the conquest of Egypt. Almost a century later Pope Alexander VII commissioned Carlo Rainaldi to build the twin Santa Marias.

In the 19th century the piazza was turned into a grandiose oval by Giuseppe Valadier, the designer of the Pincio Gardens. He also encased Santa Maria del Popolo in a Neoclassical shell to make its south facade fit in better with the overall appearance of the piazza.

In contrast to the piazza's air of ordered rationalism, many of the events staged here were barbaric. In the 18th and 19th centuries, public executions were held in Piazza del Popolo, often as part of the celebration of Carnival. Condemned men were sometimes hammered to death by repeated blows to the temples. The last time a criminal was executed in this way was in 1826, even though the guillotine had by then been adopted as a more scientific means of execution.

The riderless horse races from the piazza down Via del Corso were scarcely more humane: the performance of the runners was enhanced by feeding the horses stimulants, wrapping them in nail-studded ropes and letting off fireworks at their heels.

Santa Maria del Popolo ⑰

See pp138–9.

Porta del Popolo ⑱

Between Piazzale Flaminio and Piazza del Popolo. **Map** 4 F1. 🚌 *95, 117, 490, 495, 628, 926.* 🚋 *225.* Ⓜ *Flaminio.*

T HE VIA FLAMINIA, built in 220 BC to connect Rome with Italy's Adriatic coast, enters the city at Porta del Popolo, a grand 16th-century gate built on the orders of Pope Pius IV Medici. The architect, Nanni di Baccio Bigio, modeled it on a Roman triumphal arch. The outer face has statues of St. Peter and St. Paul on either side and a huge Medici coat of arms above.

A century later, Pope Alexander VII commissioned Bernini to decorate the inner face to celebrate the arrival in Rome of Queen Christina of Sweden. Lesser visitors were often held up while Customs officers rifled their luggage. The only way to speed things up was with a bribe.

Porta del Popolo's central arch

Santa Maria del Popolo ⑰

ONE OF ROME'S greatest stores of artistic treasures, this early Renaissance church was commissioned by Pope Sixtus IV della Rovere in 1472. Among the artists who worked on the building were Andrea Bregno and Pinturicchio. Later additions were made by Bramante and Bernini. Many illustrious families have chapels here, all decorated with appropriate splendor. The Della Rovere Chapel has delightful Pinturicchio frescoes; the Cerasi Chapel has two Caravaggio masterpieces, the *Conversion of St. Paul* and the *Crucifixion of St. Peter*, but the finest of all is the Chigi Chapel designed by Raphael for his patron, the banker Agostino Chigi. The most striking of the church's many Renaissance tombs are the two by Andrea Sansovino behind the main altar.

★ **Chigi Chapel**
Raphael designed this chapel, which has an altarpiece by Sebastiano del Piombo. Niches on either side of the altar house sculptures by Bernini and Lorenzetto. Mosaics in the dome show God as creator of the seven heavenly bodies.

Kneeling Skeleton
This floor mosaic of the figure of death was added to the Chigi Chapel in the 17th century.

NERO'S GHOST

Nero lived on in the imagination of the people long after the fall of the Roman Empire. In the Middle Ages, a legend arose that a walnut tree growing here on the spot where his ashes were buried was haunted by the emperor. Ravens roosting in the tree were thought to be demons tormenting him for his hideous crimes. When the first church was built here in 1099 by Pope Paschal II, the tree was cut down, supposedly putting an end to the supernatural events that had terrified local people.

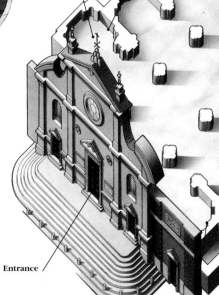

Entrance

Cybc
Chap

STAR FEATURES

★ **Chigi Chapel**

★ **Caravaggio Paintings in Cerasi Chapel**

★ **Delphic Sibyl**

Della Rovere Chapel
Pinturicchio painted the frescoes in the lunettes and the Nativity above the altar from 1490.

VISITORS' CHECKLIST

Piazza del Popolo 12. **Map** 4 F1.
📞 06-361 08 36. 🚌 95, 117,
490, 495, 628, 926. 🚋 225.
Ⓜ Flaminio. **Open** 7am–noon,
4pm–7pm Mon–Sat, 8am–2pm,
4:30pm–7:30pm Sun. ✝

The altarpiece of *The
Assumption* is by Annibale
Carracci (1540–1609).

★ Caravaggio Paintings in Cerasi Chapel

*One of two Caravaggios
in the Cerasi Chapel,* The
Crucifixion of St. Peter
*uses dramatic fore-
shortening to highlight
the sheer effort involved
in turning the saint's
crucifix upside down.*

Stained Glass

*In 1509, French
artist Guillaume de
Marcillat was invited to
provide Rome's first two
stained-glass windows.*

The Tomb of Ascanio
Sforza, who died in 1505,
is by Andrea Sansovino.

★ Delphic Sibyl

*This is one of a series of frescoes by
Pinturicchio, some Classical and
others biblical, painted from 1508–10
to decorate the apse ceiling.*

The altar
houses the 13th-
century painting
known as the
*Madonna del
Popolo.*

The Tomb of Giovanni
della Rovere (1483) is by
pupils of Andrea Bregno.

TIMELINE

1213–27 Church
enlarged under
Gregory IX

*Pinturicchio
(c 1454–1513)*

1485–9 Della
Rovere Chapel
painted by
Pinturicchio

1513–16
Raphael designs
and executes
Chigi Chapel

1090	1200	1300	1400	1500

1099 Paschal II builds
chapel over tombs of
the Domitia family
(which included
Nero) in honor of the
Madonna

*Pope Paschal II
(reigned
1099–1118)*

1472–8 Sixtus IV builds
church (one of the
first Renaissance
churches in Rome)

1473 Main altar built

1530–34
Chigi Chapel
altarpiece
built by
Sebastiano
del Piombo

Ara Pacis ⑲

Via di Ripetta. **Map** 4 F2.
📞 06-68 80 68 48. 🚌 70, 81, 115,
186. **Open** 9am–4:30pm Tue–Sat,
9am–1pm Sun. **Adm charge**.

R ECONSTRUCTED at great
expense over a period
of many years, the Ara Pacis
(Altar of Peace) is one of the
most significant monuments
of ancient Rome. It celebrates
the peace created throughout
the Mediterranean area by
Emperor Augustus after his
victorious campaigns in Gaul

Frieze on south wall showing a procession with the family of Augustus

Marcus Agrippa *(right)*

and Spain. The monument was
commissioned by the Senate in
13 BC and completed four
years later. It was positioned so
that the shadow of the huge
obelisk sundial on Campus
Martius (*see p113*) would fall
upon it on Augustus' birthday.
It is a square enclosure on a
low platform with the altar in
the center. All the surfaces are
decorated with magnificent
friezes and reliefs carved
in Carrara marble, most
likely by Greek craftsmen.
The reliefs on the north
and south walls depict a
procession that took
place on July 4 in 13 BC;

in which the members of the
emperor's family can be
can be identified, ranked by
their position in the succession.
The heir apparent at the time
was Marcus Agrippa, husband
of Augustus' daughter, Julia.
All the portraits in the relief
are carved with extraordinarily
effective realism, even the
innocent toddler clinging to
his mother's skirts.

The tale of the rediscovery
of the Ara Pacis dates back
to the 16th century, when the
first panels were unearthed.
One section ended up in
Paris, another in Florence.
Other discoveries were
made in the late 19th century,

when archaeologists finally
realized just what they had
found. What we see today
has all been pieced together
since 1938, in part original, in
part facsimile. In 1999 work
began to further organize the
whole archeological area.

Livia *(right)*, **Augustus's second
wife and mother of Tiberius, with
an unidentified family member**

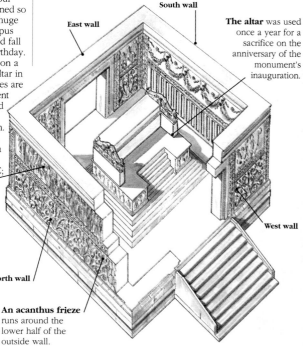

South wall

East wall

The altar was used
once a year for a
sacrifice on the
anniversary of the
monument's
inauguration.

West wall

North wall

An acanthus frieze
runs around the
lower half of the
outside wall.

**Augustus's young
grandson, Lucius**

Mausoleum of Augustus 20

Piazza Augusto Imperatore.
Map 4 F2. 🚌 *32, 81, 117, 492, 628, 913, 926.* **Open** *by appt only: permit needed. (see p367).*

NOW JUST a weedy mound, ringed with cypresses and sadly strewn with litter, this was once the most prestigious burial place in Rome. Augustus had the mausoleum built in 28 BC, the year he became sole ruler, as a tomb for himself and his descendants. The circular building was 270 ft (87 m) in diameter with two obelisks (now in Piazza del Quirinale and Piazza dell' Esquilino) at the entrance.

Inside were four concentric passageways (linked by corridors) where the urns containing the ashes of the imperial family were placed. The first to be buried there was Augustus's favorite nephew, Marcellus, who had married Julia, the emperor's daughter. He died in 23 BC, possibly poisoned by Augustus's second wife, Livia, who felt that her son Tiberius would make a more reliable emperor. When Augustus died in AD 14, his ashes were placed in the mausoleum, Tiberius duly became emperor and dynastic poisonings continued to fill the family vault with urns.

This sinister monument was later used as a medieval fortress, a vineyard, a private garden and, even, in the 18th century, as an auditorium and a theater.

Augustus, the first Roman emperor

Madonna, San Rocco and Sant'Antonio with Victims of the Plague by Il Baciccia (1639–1709)

San Rocco 21

Largo San Rocco 1. **Map** 4 F2.
📞 *06-689 64 16.* 🚌 *32, 81, 117, 492, 628, 913, 926.* **Open** *7:30am–9am, 5–7:45pm Mon–Sat, 9am–1pm, 5–7:45pm Sun. **Closed** Aug 17–31.* 🚹

THIS CHURCH, with a restrained Neoclassical facade by Giuseppe Valadier, the designer of Piazza del Popolo, began life as the chapel of a 16th-century hospital with beds for 50 men – San Rocco was a healer of the plague-stricken. A maternity wing was added for the wives of Tiber bargemen to save them from having to give birth in the insanitary conditions of a boat. The hospital came to be used by unmarried mothers, and one section was set aside for women who wished to be unknown. They were even permitted to wear a veil for the duration of their stay. Unwanted children were sent to an orphanage, and if any mothers or children died they were buried in anonymous graves. The hospital was abandoned at the turn of the 20th century and demolished in the 1930s during the excavation of the Mausoleum of Augustus.

In the church sacristy has an interesting Baroque altarpiece (c.1660) by Il Baciccia, the artist who decorated the ceiling of the Gesù *(see pp114–15).*

Santi Ambrogio e Carlo al Corso 22

Via del Corso 437. **Map** 4 F2.
📞 *06-687 83 35.* 🚌 *32, 81, 117, 492, 628, 913, 926.* **Open** *7:30am–12:30pm & 5–7pm (Oct–Mar: 7:30pm) daily. Ring porter's door to left of church if closed.* 📷

THIS CHURCH belonged to the Lombard community in Rome and is dedicated to two canonized bishops of Milan, Lombardy's capital. In 1471, Pope Sixtus IV gave the Lombards a church that they dedicated to Sant'Ambrogio, who died in 397. Then in 1610, when Carlo Borromeo was canonized, the church was rebuilt in his honor. Most of the new church was the work of father and son Onorio and Martino Longhi, but the fine dome is by Pietro da Cortona. The altarpiece by Carlo Maratta (1625–1713) is *Gloria dei Santi Ambrogio e Carlo.* An ambulatory leads behind the altar to a chapel housing the heart of San Carlo in a richly decorated reliquary.

Statue of San Carlo by Attilio Selva (1888–1970) behind the apse of Santi Ambrogio e Carlo

CAMPO DE' FIORI

ETWEEN Corso Vittorio Emanuele II and the Tiber, the city displays many distinct personalities. The open-air market of Campo de' Fiori preserves the lively bohemian atmosphere of the medieval inns that once flourished here, while the area also contains Renaissance palazzi, such as Palazzo Farnese and Palazzo Spada, where powerful Roman families built

18th-century Madonna in Campo de' Fiori

their fortresslike houses near the route of papal processions. Close by, overlooking the picturesque Tiber Island, lies the former Jewish Ghetto, where many traces of daily life from past centuries can still be seen. The Portico of Octavia and the Theater of Marcellus are spectacular examples of the city's many-layered history, built up over the half-ruined remains of ancient Rome.

SIGHTS AT A GLANCE

Churches and Temples
Santissima Trinità
dei Pellegrini ❺
Santa Maria dell'Orazione
e Morte ❼
San Girolamo della Carità ❾
Sant'Eligio degli Orefici ❿
Santa Maria in Monserrato ⓫
San Carlo ai Catinari ⓲
Santa Maria in Campitelli ⓴
San Nicola in Carcere ㉑
San Giovanni dei Fiorentini ㉙

Museums and Galleries
Palazzo Spada ❻
Piccola Farnesina ⓮
Burcardo Theater Museum ⓯

Historic Buildings
Palazzo Pio Righetti ❷
Palazzo del Monte di Pietà ❸
Palazzo Farnese ❽
Palazzo Ricci ⓬
Palazzo della Cancelleria ⓭
Casa di Lorenzo Manilio ㉕
Palazzo Cenci ㉖

Fountains
Fontana delle Tartarughe ⓳

Historic Streets and Piazzas
Campo de' Fiori ❶
Tiber Island ㉗
Ghetto and Synagogue ㉔
Via Giulia ㉘

Famous Theatres
Teatro Argentina ⓰

Ancient Sites
Sotterranei di San Paolo
alla Regola ❹
Area Sacra dell'Argentina ⓱
Theatre of Marcellus ㉒
Portico of Octavia ㉓

GETTING THERE
Only bus 116 can manage the narrow streets around Campo de' Fiori, but many routes, including the 46, 56, 60 and 64, and tram 8, converge on Largo Argentina. This is a useful starting point for exploring the area. Only the 46, 62 and 64 go along the full length of Corso Vittorio Emanuele II while 23 and 280 travel along Lungotevere.

SEE ALSO
- **Street Finder**, maps 4, 8, 11, 12
- **Where to Stay** pp294–5
- **Restaurants** pp310–11
- **Via Giulia Walk** pp276–7

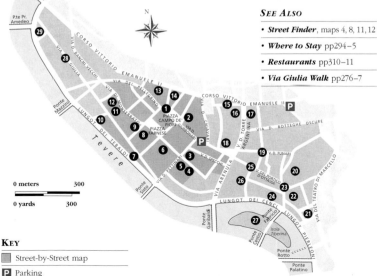

KEY
Street-by-Street map
P Parking

0 meters 300
0 yards 300

Fruit stalls beneath the statue of Giordano Bruno in the Campo de' Fiori market

Street by Street: Campo de' Fiori

THIS FASCINATING PART of Renaissance Rome is also an exciting area for shopping and night-life, centered on the market square of Campo de' Fiori. Its stalls supply many nearby restaurants, and young people shop for clothes in Via dei Giubbonari. Popular reasonably priced restaurants and pizzerias keep the area alive late into the night. By day, there are great buildings to admire, though few are open to the public. Two exceptions are the Piccola Farnesina, with its collection of Classical statues, and Palazzo Spada, home to many important paintings.

Sant'Eligio degli Orefici
A small Renaissance church designed by Raphael is concealed behind a later facade ❿

Palazzo Ricci
Painted Classical scenes were a favorite form of decoration for the facades of Renaissance houses ⓬

San Girolamo della Carità
The chief attraction of this church is Borromini's fabulous Spada Chape ❾

Santa Maria di Monserrato
This church, which has strong connections with Spain, houses a Bernini bust of Cardinal Pedro Foix de Montoya ⓫

Santa Maria dell'Orazione e Morte
A pair of dramatic winged skulls flank the doorway to this church dedicated to the burial of the dead ❼

Palazzo Farnese
Michelangelo and other great artists helped to create this monumental Renaissance palazzo ❽

KEY

– – – Suggested route

0 meters   75
0 yards   75

Palazzo della Cancelleria
The papal administration ran the affairs of the church from this vast building ⑬

Piccola Farnesina
This plaque honors Giovanni Barracco. His sculpture collection is housed in the palazzo ⑭

LOCATOR MAP
See Central Rome Map pp12–13

★ **Campo de' Fiori**
The colorful market makes this one of the city's most entertaining squares ❶

Palazzo Pio Righetti
Heraldic eagles stare down from the pediments of the palazzo's windows ❷

Palazzo del Monte di Pietà
This was a papal institution, where the poor pawned their possessions in order to borrow small sums of money ❸

Sotterranei di San Paolo alla Regola
Remains of a Roman house have survived in the basement of an old palace ❹

★ **Palazzo Spada**
The picture gallery houses a collection started by two wonderfully eccentric 17th-century cardinals ❻

Santissima Trinità dei Pellegrini
The principal role of this church was one of charity, looking after poor pilgrims arriving in Rome ❺

STAR SIGHTS

★ **Campo de' Fiori**

★ **Palazzo Spada**

Campo de' Fiori ❶

Piazza Campo de' Fiori. **Map** 4 E4 & 11 C4. 🚌 *116 and routes to Largo di Torre Argentina. See **Markets** p338.*

THE CAMPO DE' FIORI (field of flowers), once a meadow, occupies the site of the open space facing the Theater of Pompey. Cardinals and noblemen used to rub shoulders with fishmongers and foreigners in the piazza's market, thus it was one of the liveliest areas of medieval and Renaissance Rome. Today's market retains much of the traditional atmosphere.

In the center of the square is a statue of a hooded figure. This is the philosopher Giordano Bruno, who was burnt at the stake for heresy on this spot in 1600 – a grim reminder of the executions that were held here.

The piazza was surrounded by inns for pilgrims and other travelers. Many of these were once owned by the successful 15th-century courtesan Vannozza Catanei, mistress of Pope Alexander VI Borgia. On the corner between the piazza and Via del Pellegrino is Catanei's shield, which she had decorated with her own coat of arms and those of her husband and her lover, the Borgia pope.

Market stalls in Campo de' Fiori

Palazzo Pio Righetti ❷

Piazza del Biscione 89. **Map** 4 E5 & 11 C4. 🚌 *116 and routes to Largo Torre Argentina. **Not open** to the public.*

THE VAST 17th-century Palazzo Pio Righetti was built over the ruined Theater of Pompey. The windows of

Window pediment with heraldic lion and pine cones, Palazzo Pio Righetti

the palazzo are decorated with lions and pine cones from the coat of arms of the Pio da Carpi family who lived here.

The curve of the Theater of Pompey, completed in 55 BC, is followed by Via di Grotta Pinta. This was Rome's first permanent theater built of stone and concrete. In places, for example, the basement of the Pancrazio restaurant, you can see early examples of *opus reticulatum* – small square blocks of tufa (porous rock) set diagonally as a facing for a concrete wall.

Palazzo del Monte di Pietà ❸

Piazza del Monte di Pietà 33. **Map** 4 E5 & 11 C4. ☎ *06-51 72 66 10.* 🚌 *116 and routes to Largo di Torre Argentina.* 🚊 *8.* **Chapel open** *7.40am–2pm Tue–Fri.* **Closed** *public hols.* **Adm** *by appt or on request to porter.*

THE MONTE, as it is known, is a public institution founded in 1539 by Pope Paul III Farnese as a pawnshop to staunch the usury then rampant in the city. The building still has offices and auction rooms for the sale of unredeemed goods.

The stars with diagonal bands on the huge central plaque decorating the facade are the coat of arms of Pope Clement VIII Aldobrandini, added when Carlo Maderno enlarged the palace in the 17th century. The clock on the left was added later.

Within, the chapel is a jewel of Baroque architecture, adorned with gilded stucco, marble paneling and reliefs. The decoration makes a perfect setting for the sculptures by Domenico Guidi – a bust of San Carlo Borromeo and a

relief of the *Pietà.* There are also splendid reliefs by Giovanni Battista Théudon and Pierre Legros of biblical scenes illustrating the charitable nature of the institution.

Relief by Théudon of *Joseph Lending Grain to the Egyptians* in Palazzo del Monte di Pietà

Sotterranei di San Paolo alla Regola ❹

Via di San Paolo alla Regola. **Map** 11 C5. ☎ *06-67 10 38 19.* 🚌 *23, 116, 280 and routes to Largo di Torre Argentina.* 🚊 *8.* **Adm** *by request in advance to Ripartizione del Comune di Roma (06-67 10 38 19).*

AN OLD PALACE hides the perfectly conserved remains of an ancient Roman house, dating from the 2nd–3rd centuries. Restoration works are being carried out in order to open this site to the public, but at present it is only possible to visit by special arrangement.

A ramp leads down well below today's street level, to reveal the locations of shops of the time. One level above is the Stanza della Colonna, at one time an open courtyard, with traces of frescoes and mosaics on its walls.

Guido Reni's *Holy Trinity,* **in Santissima Trinità dei Pellegrini**

Santissima Trinità dei Pellegrini ❺

Piazza della Trinità dei Pellegrini. **Map** 4 E5 & 11 C5. 📞 *06-686 84 51.* 🚌 *23, 116, 280 and routes to Largo di Torre Argentina.* 🚋 *8.* **Currently closed** *for restoration; phone to check.*

Tʜᴇ ᴄʜᴜʀᴄʜ ᴡᴀꜱ donated in the 16th century to a charitable organization founded by San Filippo Neri to care for the poor and sick, in particular the thousands of paupers who flocked in pilgrimage to Rome during the special holy years known as Jubilees.

The 18th-century facade has niches with statues of the Evangelists by Bernardino Ludovisi. The interior, with Corinthian columns, ends in a horseshoe vault and apse, dominated by Guido Reni's striking altarpiece titled *Holy Trinity* (1625). The frescoes in the lantern are also by Reni.

Other interesting paintings include *St. Gregory the Great Freeing Souls from Purgatory*, by Baldassarre Croce (third chapel to the left); Cavalier d'Arpino's *Virgin and Saints* (second chapel to the left); and a painting by Borgognone (1677) showing the Virgin and recently canonized saints, including San Carlo Borromeo and San Filippo Neri. In the sacristy are depictions of the nobility washing the feet of pilgrims, a custom that was started by San Filippo.

Palazzo Spada ❻

Piazza Capo di Ferro 13. **Map** 4 E5 & 11 C4. 📞 *06-686 11 58.* 🚌 *23, 116, 280 and routes to Largo di Torre Argentina.* 🚋 *8.* **Gallery open** *9am–7pm Tue–Sat, 9am–1.30pm Sun.* **Adm charge.** 🚫 🎥 📷 **Adm** *to other rooms on written request to Ufficio Personale, Consiglio di Stato (at Palazzo Spada).* 🚫

Tʜɪꜱ ᴍᴀᴊᴇꜱᴛɪᴄ ᴘᴀʟᴀᴢᴢᴏ, built around 1550 for Cardinal Capo di Ferro, has an elegant stuccoed courtyard and a facade decorated with reliefs evoking Rome's glorious past.

Cardinal Bernardino Spada, who lived here in the 17th century with his brother, Virginio (also a cardinal), hired Bernini and Borromini to work on the building. The brothers' whimsical delight in false perspectives resulted in a colonnaded gallery by Borromini that appears four times longer than it really is.

The cardinals also amassed a superb private collection of paintings. These are now displayed in the Galleria Spada together with some Classical statues and 18th-century furniture. The wide range of artists represented includes Rubens, Dürer and Guido Reni. Works to look for by lesser artists include *The Visitation* by Andrea del Sarto (1486–1530), *Cain and Abel* by Giovanni Lanfranco (1582–1647) and *The Death of Dido* by Guercino (1591–1666).

Santa Maria dell'Orazione e Morte ❼

Via Giulia. **Map** 4 E5 & 11 B4. 📞 *06-68 80 27 15.* 🚌 *23, 116, 280.* **Open** *for mass 6pm Sun, public hols.* ✝

A ᴘɪᴏᴜꜱ ᴄᴏɴꜰʀᴀᴛᴇʀɴɪᴛʏ was formed here in the 16th century to collect the bodies of the unknown dead and give them a Christian burial. The theme of death is stressed in this church, dedicated to St. Mary of Prayer and Death. The doors and windows of Ferdinando Fuga's dramatic Baroque facade are decorated with winged skulls. Above the central entrance is a *clepsydra* (an ancient hourglass) – symbolic of death.

Offertory box in Santa Maria dell'Orazione e Morte

Palazzo Farnese ❽

Piazza Farnese. **Map** 4 E5 & 11 B4. 🚌 *23, 116, 280 and routes to Largo di Torre Argentina.* 🚋 *8.* **Not open** *to the public.*

Tʜᴇ ᴘʀᴏᴛᴏᴛʏᴘᴇ for many princely palaces, the imposing Palazzo Farnese was originally built for Cardinal Alessandro Farnese (who became Pope Paul III in 1534). He commissioned the greatest artists to work on it, starting with Antonio da Sangallo the Younger as architect in 1517. Michelangelo, who took over after him, contributed the great cornice and central window of the main facade, and the third level of the courtyard.

Michelangelo had a plan for the Farnese gardens to be connected by a bridge to the Farnese home in Trastevere, Villa Farnesina *(see pp220–21)*. The elegant arch spanning Via Giulia belongs to this sadly unrealized scheme. The palazzo was completed in 1589, on a less ambitious scale, by Giacomo della Porta. It is now the home of the French Embassy, which moved in already in 1635.

Majestic facade of Palazzo Farnese

Spada Chapel in San Girolamo

San Girolamo della Carità ⑨

Via di Monserrato 62A. **Map** 4 E5 & 11 B4. [C] *06-687 97 86.* ▤ *23, 46, 62, 64, 116, 280.* **Open** *10am–noon Wed, 10:30–11:30am Sun.* 🔧

THE CHURCH was built on the site of the home of San Filippo Neri, the 16th-century saint from Tuscany. This warm, patient man renewed Rome's spiritual and cultural life with his friendly, open approach to religion. He would have loved the frolicking putti shown surrounding his statue in his chapel, reminding him of the Roman urchins he had cared for during his lifetime.

The breathtaking Spada Chapel was designed by Borromini and is unique both

as a work of art and as an illustration of the spirit of the Baroque age. All architectural elements are concealed so that the space of the chapel's interior is defined solely by decorative marblework and statues. Veined jasper and precious multicolored marbles are sculpted to imitate flowery damask and velvet hangings. Even the altar rail is a long swag of jasper drapery held up by a pair of kneeling angels with wooden wings.

Although there are memorials to former members of the Spada family, oddly, there is no indication as to which of the Spadas was responsible for endowing the chapel. It was probably art lover Cardinal Virginio Spada, a follower of San Filippo Neri.

Sant'Eligio degli Orefici ⑩

Via di Sant'Eligio 8A. **Map** 4 D4 & 11 B4. [C] *06-686 82 60.* ▤ *23, 46, 62, 64, 116, 280.* **Open** *10:30am–noon Mon–Wed, Fri (call to check).* **Closed** *Aug & Sep.* 🔧

THE NAME of the church records the fact that it was commissioned by a rich corporation of goldsmiths *(orefici)* in the early 16th century. The original design was by Raphael, who, like his master, Bramante, had acquired a sense of the grandiose from the remains of Roman antiquity. The influence of some of Bramante's works, such as the choir of Santa Maria del Popolo *(see p138–9)*, is evident in the simple way the arches and pilasters define the structure of the walls.

The cupola of Sant' Eligio is attributed to Baldassarre Peruzzi, while the facade was added in the early 17th century by Flaminio Ponzio. Among the various 16th-century painters who decorated the interior was Taddeo Zuccari, who worked on Palazzo Farnese *(see p147).*

Statue of San Filippo Neri by Pierre Legros

Santa Maria in Monserrato ⑪

Via di Monserrato. **Map** 4 E4 & 11 B3. [C] *06-686 58 61.* ▤ *23, 46, 62, 64, 116, 280.* **Not Open** *to the public except by special permission: apply to the rector at Via Giulia, 151.* 🔧

An early bust by Bernini of Cardinal Pedro Foix de Montoya

THE ORIGINS of the Spanish national church in Rome go back to 1506, when a hospice for Spanish pilgrims was begun by a brotherhood of the Virgin of Montserrat in Catalonia. Inside is Annibale Carracci's painting *San Diego de Alcalà* and, in the third chapel on the left, a copy of a Sansovino statue of St. James. Some beautiful 15th-century tombs by Andrea Bregno and Luigi Capponi are in the courtyard and side chapels. Don't miss Bernini's bust of Pedro Foix de Montoya, the church's benefactor, in the annex.

San Diego by Annibale Carracci

Palazzo Ricci ⑫

Piazza de' Ricci. **Map** 4 D4 & 11 B4.
🚌 *23, 46, 62, 64, 65, 116, 280, 870.*
Not open *to the public.*

Part of the frescoed facade of Palazzo Ricci

PALAZZO RICCI was famous for its frescoed facade – now rather faded – originally painted in the 16th century by Polidoro da Caravaggio, a follower of Raphael.

In Renaissance Rome it was common to commission artists to decorate the outsides of their houses with heroes of Classical antiquity. A fresco by a leading artist such as Polidoro, reputedly the inventor of this style of painting, was a conspicuous status symbol, in the nobility's attempts to outshine each-other with their palazzi.

Palazzo della Cancelleria ⑬

Piazza della Cancelleria. **Map** 4 E4 & 11 C3. 📞 *06-69 88 48 16.* 🚌 *46, 62, 64, 70, 81, 87, 116, 492.* **Open** *with permit from Vatican only.*

THIS PALAZZO, a supreme example of the confident architecture of the Early Renaissance, was begun in 1485. It was financed partly with the gambling winnings of Cardinal Raffaele Riario. Roses, the emblem of the Riario family, adorn the vaults and capitals of the beautiful Doric courtyard. The palazzo's interior was decorated after the Sack of Rome in 1527. Giorgio Vasari boasted that he had completed work on one enormous room in just 100 days; Michelangelo allegedly retorted: "It looks like it." Other Mannerist artists, Perin del Vaga and Francesco Salviati, frescoed the rooms of the cardinal in charge of the Papal Chancellery, the office that gave the palazzo its name when it was installed here by Pope Leo X. On the right of the main entrance is the unobtrusive and rather quaint church of San Lorenzo in Damaso, founded by Pope Damasus who reigned 366–384. It was

Lily on facade of the Piccola Farnesina

reconstructed in 1495 and although Bernini made alterations to the transept and apse in 1638, it was later restored to its 15th-century lines.

Its surrounding porticoes housed libraries that held the first Papal Archives.

Piccola Farnesina ⑭

Corso Vittorio Emanuele II 166. **Map** 4 E4 & 11 C3. 📞 *06-68 80 68 48.* 🚌 *46, 62, 64, 70, 81, 87, 116, 492.* **Open** *9am–7pm Tue–Sat, 9am–1pm Sun & public hols.* **Closed** *Jan 1, May 1, Dec 25.* **Adm charge**. 🚫

THIS DELIGHTFUL miniature palazzo acquired its name from the lilies decorating its cornices. These were mistakenly identified as part of the Farnese family crest. In fact, they were part of the coat of arms of a French clergyman, Thomas Le Roy, for whom the palazzo was built in 1523.

The entrance is in a new facade, built to overlook Corso Vittorio Emanuele II when the road was constructed at the turn of the century. The original facade on the left of today's entrance is attributed to Antonio da Sangallo the Younger. Note the asymmetrical arrangement of its windows and ledges. The elegant central courtyard also retains its original appearance. The Piccola Farnesina now houses the Museo Barracco, a collection of ancient sculpture assembled during the last century by the politician Barone Giovanni Barracco. A bust of the baron

can be seen in the courtyard. The collection includes an ancient Egyptian relief of the scribe Nofer, some Assyrian artifacts and, among the Etruscan exhibits, a delicate ceramic female head. On the first floor is the Greek collection with a head of Apollo.

Inner courtyard, Piccola Farnesina

Burcardo Theater Museum ⑮

Via del Sudario 44. **Map** 4 F4 & 12 D4. 📞 *06-681 94 71.* 🚌 *46, 56, 60, 62, 64, 70, 81, 186, 492.* 🚋 *8.* **Closed** *for restoration until further notice.* **Library open** *9am–4pm Tue & Thu, 9am–1:30pm Mon, Wed & Fri.*

THIS LATE 15th-century house belonged to Johannes Burckhardt, chamberlain to Pope Alexander VI Borgia and author of a diary of Rome under the Borgias. His house now holds Rome's most complete collection of theater literature, plus Chinese puppets and comic masks from the various regions of Italy.

Teatro Argentina 🔟

Via di Torre Argentina. **Map** 4 F4 & 12 D4. 📞 06-68 40 00 11. 🚌 46, 56, 60, 62, 64, 70, 81, 87, 186, 492. 🚊 8. **Plays** performed Oct–Jun. See **Entertainment** pp346–7.

O NE OF ROME'S most important theaters was founded by the powerful Sforza Cesarini family in 1732, though the facade dates from a century later. Many famous operas were first performed here. In 1816, for example, the theater saw the ill-fated début of Rossini's *Barber of Seville*, during which the composer insulted the unappreciative audience. Enraged, the audience pursued him through the streets of Rome. Many of Verdi's masterpieces were first produced here.

Detail of facade, Teatro Argentina

Area Sacra dell'Argentina 🔟

Largo di Torre Argentina. **Map** 4 F4 & 12 D4. 🚌 46, 56, 60, 62, 64, 70, 81, 87, 186, 492. 🚊 8. **Open** by appt only: permit needed (see p367).

T HE REMAINS of four temples were discovered here during rebuilding in the 1920s. Dating from the Republican era, they are among the oldest to have been found in Rome. They are known as A, B, C and D. The oldest (temple C) dates from the early 3rd century BC. It was placed on a high platform preceded by an altar and is typical of Italic temple plans as opposed to the Greek model. Temple A is from later on in the 3rd century BC. In medieval times the small church of San Nicola de' Cesarini was built over its podium. The remains of its two apses are still visible.

San Carlo at Prayer by Guido Reni

The north column stumps belonged to a great portico, the Hecatostylum (portico of 100 columns). In Imperial times two marble lavatories were built here – the remains of one are visible behind temple A. Behind temples B and C are remains of a great platform of tufa blocks. These have been identified as part of the Curia of Pompey, a rectangular building with a statue of Pompey, where the Senate met and Julius Caesar was murdered on 15 March 44 BC.

Area Sacra, with circular ruins of temple B in the foreground

San Carlo ai Catinari 🔟

Piazza B Cairoli. **Map** 4 F5 & 12 D4. 📞 06-689 38 74. 🚌 see Area Sacra. 🚊 8. **Open** 7.30am–noon, 4.30–7pm Mon–Sat (opens 8.30am Sun). 🔟

I N 1620, ROME'S Milanese congregation decided to honour Cardinal Carlo Borromeo, with this great

church. It is called "ai Catinari" on account of the bowl-makers' *(catinari)* shops in the area. The solemn travertine facade was completed in 1638 by the Roman architect Soria. The 16th-century basilican plan is flanked by chapels. The St. Cecilia chapel was designed and decorated by Antonio Gherardi, who added a family portrait.

The church's paintings and frescoes by Pietro da Cortona and Guido Reni are confident, mature works of the Counter Reformation, depicting the life and acts of the recently canonized San Carlo. Make sure you also see the ornate crucifix, inlaid with marble, glass and mother-of-pearl, by the 16th-century sculptor Algardi on the sacristy altar.

Sacristy altar, San Carlo ai Catinari

Fontana delle Tartarughe 🔟

Piazza Mattei. **Map** 4 F5 & 12 D4. 🚌 H, 23, 56, 60, 280. 🚊 8.

T HE DELIGHTFUL Fontana delle Tartarughe – *tartarughe* are tortoises – was commissioned by the Mattei family to decorate "their" piazza between 1581 and 1588. The design was by Giacomo della Porta, but the fountain owes much of its grace and charm to the four slender bronze youths each resting one foot on the head of a dolphin, sculpted by Taddeo Landini. Nearly a century later an unknown

Della Porta's graceful Fontana delle Tartarughe

sculptor was inspired to add the struggling tortoises to complete the composition.

Santa Maria in Campitelli ⑳

Piazza di Campitelli. **Map** 4 F5 & 12 E5. [06-68 80 39 78. 44, 81, 95, 160, 628, 715, 716, 780. **Open** 7am–noon, 4pm–7pm daily.

IN 17TH-CENTURY ROME the plague could still strike fiercely and there were no reliable, effective remedies. Many Romans simply prayed for a cure to a sacred medieval icon of the Virgin, the Madonna del Portico. When a particularly lethal outbreak of plague abated in 1656, popular gratitude was so strong that a new church was built to house the icon in appropriate splendor.

Lavish altar tabernacle in Santa Maria in Campitelli

The church, designed by a pupil of Bernini, Carlo Rainaldi, was completed in 1667. The main elements of the lively Baroque facade are the graceful columns, symbolizing the supporters of the true faith.

Inside the church stands a fabulously ornate, gilded altar tabernacle with spiral columns which was designed by Giovanni Antonio de Rossi to contain the image of the Virgin. The side chapels are decorated by some of Rome's finest Baroque painters: Sebastiano Conca, Giovanni Battista Gaulli (known as Il Baciccia) and Luca Giordano.

Facade and medieval bell tower of San Nicola in Carcere

San Nicola in Carcere ㉑

Via del Teatro di Marcello 46. **Map** 5 A5 & 12 E5. [06-68 30 71 98. 44, 81, 95, 160, 170, 628, 715, 716, 780. **Open** 7am–noon, 4pm–7pm Mon–Sat, 9.30am–1pm Sun & public hols. **Closed** Aug.

THE MEDIEVAL CHURCH of San Nicola in Carcere stands on the site of three Roman temples of the Republican era which were converted into a prison (carcere) in the Middle Ages. The temples of Juno, Spes and Janus faced a city gate leading from the Forum Holitorium, the city's vegetable and oil market, to the road down to the port on the Tiber. The columns embedded in the walls of the church belonged to two flanking temples whose platforms are now marked by

grass lawns. The church was rebuilt in 1599 and restored in the 19th century, but the bell tower and Roman columns are part of the original design.

The Theater of Marcellus by Thomas Hartley Cromek (1809–73)

Theater of Marcellus ㉒

Via del Teatro di Marcello. **Map** 4 A5 & 12 E5. [06-481 48 00. 23, 44, 81, 95, 160, 170, 280, 628, 71, 716, 780. **Closed** except for concerts. See **Entertainment** p343.

THE CURVED OUTER WALL of this vast amphitheater has supported generations of Roman buildings. It was built by Emperor Augustus (27 BC–AD 14), who dedicated it to Marcellus, his nephew and son-in-law, who had died aged 19 in 23 BC.

The Middle Ages were a turbulent time of invasions and local conflicts (see p28) and by the 13th century the theatre had been converted into the fortress of the Savelli family. In the 16th century Baldassarre Peruzzi built a great palace on the theater ruins for the Orsini family, including a garden facing the Tiber. The lower arches were later occupied by humble dwellings and workshops.

Close to the theater stand three beautiful Corinthian columns and a section of frieze. These are from the Temple of Apollo, which housed many great works of art that the Romans had plundered from Greece in the 2nd century BC.

Portico of Octavia ㉓

Via del Portico d'Ottavia. **Map** 4 F5 & 12 E5. ▥ *23, 44, 81, 95, 160, 280, 628, 715, 716, 780.*

BUILT IN HONOR of Octavia, (the sister of Augustus and the abandoned wife of Mark Antony) this is the only surviving portico of what used to be the monumental piazza of Circus Flaminius. The rectangular portico enclosed temples dedicated to Jupiter and Juno, decorated with bronze statues. The part we see today is the great central atrium originally covered by marble facings.

In the Middle Ages a great fish market and a church, Sant'Angelo in Pescheria, were built in the ruins of the portico. Because the church was associated with the fishing activities of the nearby river port, aquatic flora and fauna feature in many of its inlays. Links with the Tiber are also apparent in the stucco facade on the adjacent Fishmonger's Oratory, built in 1689. The church has a fresco of the Madonna and angels by the school of Benozzo Gozzoli.

Narrow lane in the Jewish Ghetto

Ghetto and Synagogue ㉔

Synagogue, *Lungotevere dei Cenci.* **Map** 4 F5 & 12 E5. ▐ *06-68 40 06 61.* ▥ *23, 44, 56, 60, 160, 170, 186, 280, 710, 774, 780.* ▣ *8.* **Open** *9am– 4.30pm Mon–Thu, 9am–1.30pm Fri, 9am–12.30pm Sun.* **Closed** *public hols.* **Adm charge.** ⊘ ▣ ▣ **Ghetto,** main street is Via del Portico d'Ottavia.

THE FIRST Jews came to Rome as traders in the 2nd century BC and there has been a Jewish community in Rome ever since. Jews were much appreciated for their financial

Synagogue overlooking the Tiber

and medical skills during the time of the Roman Empire.

Systematic persecution began in the 16th century. From 25 July 1556 all Rome's Jews were forced to live inside a high-walled enclosure erected on the orders of Pope Paul IV. The Ghetto was in a unhealthy part of Rome. Inhabitants were only allowed out during the day, and on Sundays they were driven into the Church of Sant'Angelo in Pescheria to listen to Christian sermons – a practice abolished only in 1848.

Persecution started again in 1943 with the German occupation. Although many Jews were helped to escape or hidden by Roman citizens, thousands were deported to German concentration camps.

Today many Jews still live in the former Ghetto and the medieval streets, with shops selling typical Roman kosher food, retain much of their old character. The imposing Synagogue on Lungotevere was completed in 1904. It houses a Jewish museum which describes the history of the community through plans, torahs and other artifacts.

Casa di Lorenzo Manilio ㉕

Via del Portico d'Ottavia 1D. **Map** 4 F5 & 12 D5. ▥ *See Ghetto.* **Not open** *to the public.*

BEFORE THE RENAISSANCE, most Romans had only vague, confused ideas of their city's glorious past, but after the 15th-century revival of interest in the philosophy and arts of antiquity, some were even building houses to recall the splendor of ancient Rome. In 1468 a certain Lorenzo Manilio built a great house for his family, decorating it with an elegant Classical plaque. The

Latin inscription dates the building according to the ancient Roman method – 2,221 years after the foundation of the city – and mentions the owner's name. Original reliefs are embedded in the facades as well as a fragment of an ancient sarcophagus.

The Piazza Costaguti facade features windows patriotically inscribed with the legend *Ave Roma* (Hail Rome).

Balcony of Palazzo Cenci

Palazzo Cenci ㉖

Vicolo dei Cenci. **Map** 4 F5 & 12 D5. ▥ *See Ghetto.* **Not open** *to the public.*

PALAZZO CENCI belonged to the family of Beatrice Cenci, who was accused, together with her brothers and stepmother, of witchcraft and the murder of her tyrannical father. She was condemned to death and beheaded at Ponte Sant'Angelo in 1599.

Row of Roman busts decorating the Casa di Lorenzo Manilio

Tiber Island, with Ponte Cestio linking it to Trastevere

Most of the original medieval palazzo has been demolished, and the building you see today dates back to the 1570s, though its rather forbidding appearance seems medieval. Heraldic half-moons decorate the main facade on Via del Progresso while pretty balconies open on the opposite side where a medieval arch joins the palace to Palazzetto Cenci, designed by Martino Longhi the Elder. Inside is a traditional courtyard with an Ionic-style loggia; many of the rooms retain the original 16th-century decoration that the unfortunate Beatrice would have known as a child.

Tiber Island 🄴

Isola Tiberina. **Map** 8 D1 & 12 D5.
🚌 H, 23, 44, 280. 🚊 8.

IN ANCIENT TIMES the island, which lay opposite the city's port, had large structures of white travertine at either end built to resemble the stern and prow of a ship.

Since 293 BC, when a temple was dedicated here to Aesculapius, the god of healing and protector against the plague, the island has been associated with the sick and there is still a hospital here.

San Bartolomeo all'Isola, the church in the island's central piazza, was built on the ruins of the Temple of Aesculapius in the 10th century. Its Roman-esque bell tower is, clearly visible from across the river.

From the Ghetto area you can reach the island by a footbridge, the Ponte Fabricio. The oldest original bridge over the Tiber still in use, it was built in 62 BC. In medieval times the Pierleoni,

and then the Caetani, two powerful families, controlled this strategic point by means of a tower, still in situ. The other bridge to the island, the Ponte Cestio, is inscribed with the names of the Byzantine emperors associated with its restoration in AD 370.

Via Giulia 🄳

Map 4 D4 & 11 A3. 🚌 23, 116, 280.

THIS PICTURESQUE street was laid out by Bramante for Pope Julius II della Rovere. Lined with aristocratic palazzi dating from the 16th–18th centuries, as well as fine churches and antique shops, Via Giulia makes a fascinating walk *(see pp276–7).*

Mask fountain in Via Giulia

San Giovanni dei Fiorentini 🄴

Via Acciaioli 2. **Map** 4 D4 & 11 A2.
📞 06-68 89 20 59. 🚌 23, 46, 62, 64, 116, 280, 870. **Open** 8am–8pm daily. 🛉

THE CHURCH of St John of the Florentines was built for the large Florentine community living in this area. Pope Leo X wanted it to be an expression of the cultural superiority of Florence over Rome. Started in the early 16th century, the church took over a century to build. The principal architect was Antonio da Sangallo the Younger, but many others contributed before Carlo Maderno's elongated cupola was finally completed in 1620. The present facade was added in the 18th century.

The church was decorated mainly by Tuscan artists. One interesting exception is the 15th-century statue of San Giovannino by the Sicilian Mino del Reame in a niche above the sacristy. The spectacular high altar houses a marble group by Antonio Raggi, the *Baptism of Christ.* The altar itself is by Borromini, who is buried in the church along with Carlo Maderno.

This and San Lorenzo in Lucina *(see p112)* are the only churches in Rome which admit animals: the faithful can bring their pets, and an Easter lamb-blessing takes place.

Antonio Raggi's *Baptism of Christ* in San Giovanni dei Fiorentini

QUIRINAL

ONE OF THE original seven hills of Rome, the Quirinal was a mainly residential area in Imperial times. To the east of the hill were the vast Baths of Diocletian, still standing in front of Rome's main railroad station. Abandoned in the Middle Ages, the district returned to favour in the late 16th century. The prime

1st-century BC stucco in the Museo Nazionale Romano

site was taken by the popes for Palazzo del Quirinale. Great families such as the Colonna and the Aldobrandini had their palazzi lower down the hill. With the end of papal rule in 1870, the surrounding area, especially Via Nazionale, was redeveloped as the Quirinal became the residence of the kings of Italy, then of the President.

SIGHTS AT A GLANCE

Churches
Santi Apostoli ❹
San Marcello al Corso ❺
Santa Maria in Trivio ❼
Santi Vincenzo e Anastasio ❾
Sant'Andrea al Quirinale ⓫
San Carlo alle Quattro Fontane ⓬
Santa Maria degli Angeli ⓰
Santa Maria dei Monti ⓴
Sant'Agata dei Goti ㉑
Santi Domenico e Sisto ㉓

Museums and Galleries
Accademia Nazionale di San Luca ❽
Museo Nazionale Romano ⓱
Museo delle Paste Alimentari ❿
Palazzo delle Esposizioni ⓳

Historic Piazzas
Piazza della Repubblica ⓲

Historic Buildings
Palazzo del Quirinale ❷
Palazzo Colonna ❸
Baths of Diocletian ⓯

Fountains and Statues
Castor and Pollux ❶
Trevi Fountain ❻
Le Quattro Fontane ⓭
Moses Fountain ⓮

Parks and Gardens
Villa Aldobrandini ㉒

GETTING THERE
The area has Metro stops at Repubblica and Cavour. Useful buses include the 64, 65 and 70 along Via Nazionale and the 71, 115 and 117, which go under the Quirinal through the Traforo Umberto I tunnel. Many buses travel along Via del Tritone but there is no bus to the top of the Quirinal. You have to walk up Via XXIV Maggio.

KEY
- Street-by-Street map
- **M** Metro station
- **P** Parking

0 meters 300
0 yards 300

SEE ALSO

Fontana delle Naiadi in Piazza della Repubblica

Street-by-Street: The Quirinal Hill

EVEN THOUGH Palazzo del Quirinale is closed to the public, it is well worth walking up the hill to the palace to see the giant Roman statues of Castor and Pollux in the piazza and enjoy fine views of the city below. Come down the hill by way of the narrow streets and stairways that lead to one of Rome's unforgettable sights, the Trevi Fountain. Many small churches lie hidden away in the back streets. Towards Piazza Venezia there are grand palazzi, including that of the Colonna, one of Rome's most ancient and powerful families.

Santa Maria in Via is famous for its medieval well and miraculous 13th-century icon of the Madonna.

Santa Maria in Trivio
The attractive facade of this tiny church conceals a rich Baroque interior ⑦

Accademia Nazionale di San Luca
The art academy has works by famous former members, such as Canova and Angelica Kauffmann ⑧

Santi Vincenzo e Anastasio
The grand facade of this small Baroque church is on a corner facing the Trevi Fountain ⑨

★ **Trevi Fountain**
Rome's grandest and best-known fountain almost fills the tiny Piazza di Trevi ⑥

San Marcello al Corso
This stark Crucifixion by Van Dyck hangs in the sacristy of the church ⑤

Palazzo Odescalchi has a Bernini facade from 1664, with a balustrade and richly decorated cornice. The building faces Santi Apostoli.

Museo delle Cere, a wax museum opened in 1953, places its emphasis on horror.

To Piazza Venezia

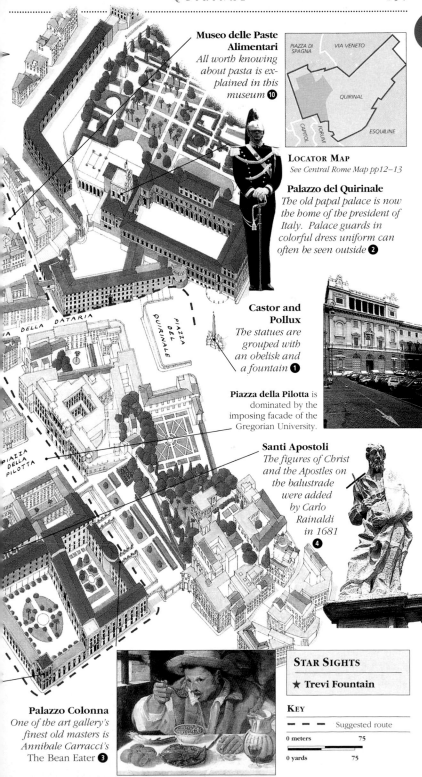

Museo delle Paste Alimentari
All worth knowing about pasta is explained in this museum ⑩

LOCATOR MAP
See Central Rome Map pp12–13

Palazzo del Quirinale
The old papal palace is now the home of the president of Italy. Palace guards in colorful dress uniform can often be seen outside ❷

Castor and Pollux
The statues are grouped with an obelisk and a fountain ❶

Piazza della Pilotta is dominated by the imposing facade of the Gregorian University.

Santi Apostoli
The figures of Christ and the Apostles on the balustrade were added by Carlo Rainaldi in 1681 ❹

Palazzo Colonna
One of the art gallery's finest old masters is Annibale Carracci's The Bean Eater ❸

STAR SIGHTS

★ Trevi Fountain

KEY

- - - Suggested route

0 meters 75

0 yards 75

Castor and Pollux ❶

Piazza del Quirinale. **Map** 5 B4.
🚌 *H, 64, 70, 170, 640 and many routes along Via del Tritone.*

Quirinal fountain and obelisk with Roman statues of Castor and Pollux

CASTOR AND POLLUX – the patrons of horsemanship – and their prancing horses stand in splendor in the Piazza del Quirinale. Over 18 ft (5.5 m) high, these statues are huge Roman copies of 5th-century BC Greek originals. They once stood at the entrance to the nearby Baths of Constantine. Pope Sixtus V had them restored and placed here in 1588. Formerly known as the "horse tamers," they gave the square its familiar name of Monte Cavallo (Horse Hill).

The obelisk that stands between them was brought here in 1786 from the Mausoleum of Augustus. In 1818 the composition was completed by the addition of a massive granite basin, once a cattle trough in the Forum.

Palazzo del Quirinale ❷

Piazza del Quirinale. **Map** 5 B3.
📞 *06-469 91.* 🚌 *H, 64, 70, 170, 175, 640 and many routes along Via del Tritone.* **Open** *8.30am–12.30pm 2nd and 4th Sun of each month.*

BY THE 1500s, the Vatican had a reputation as an unhealthy location because of the high incidence of malaria, so Pope Gregory XIII chose this superb site on the highest of Rome's seven hills as a papal summer residence. Work began in 1574. Piazza del Quirinale has buildings on three sides, while the fourth is open, with a splendid view of the city to the dome of St. Peter's.

Many great architects worked on the palace before it assumed its present form in the 1730s. Domenico Fontana designed the main facade; Carlo Maderno, the huge chapel and Bernini the narrow wing running the length of Via del Quirinale.

Following the unification of Italy in 1870, it became the official residence of the king; then in 1947 of the president of the republic. For security reasons, the palace and gardens are closed to the public apart from two Sundays each month.

Palazzo del Quirinale, official residence of the president of Italy

Palazzo Colonna ❸

Via della Pilotta 17. **Map** 5 A4 & 12 F3. 📞 *06-679 43 62.* 🚌 *H, 64, 70, 170, 640 and many routes to Piazza Venezia.* **Open** *9am–1pm Sat only (last adm: noon).* **Closed** *Aug & public hols.* **Adm charge.** 🚫

POPE MARTIN V Colonna (reigned 1417–31) began building the palazzo, but most of the structure dates from the 18th century. The art gallery, built by Antonio del Grande between 1654 and 1665, is the only part open to the public. The pictures are numbered but unlabeled, so pick up a guide on the way in. Go up the stairs

Canova's monument to Pope Clement XIV in Santi Apostoli, with figures of Humility and Modesty

and through the antechamber leading to a series of three gleaming marble rooms with prominent yellow columns, the Colonna family emblem (*colonna* means "column").

The ceiling frescoes celebrate Marcantonio Colonna's victory over the Turks at the Battle of Lepanto (1571). On the walls are 16th- to 18th-century paintings, including Annibale Carracci's *Bean Eater (see p157).* The room of landscape paintings, many by Poussin's brother-in-law, Gaspare Dughet, reflects the 18th-century taste of Cardinal Girolamo Colonna. Beyond is a room with a ceiling fresco, the *Apotheosis of Martin V.* The throne room has a chair reserved for visiting popes and a copy of Pisanello's portrait of Martin V. The gallery also offers a fine view of the private palace garden, site of the ruined Temple of Serapis.

Santi Apostoli ❹

Piazza dei Santi Apostoli. **Map** 5 A4 & 12 F3. 📞 *06-679 40 85.* 🚌 *64, 65, 70, 170 and many other routes to Piazza Venezia.* **Open** *6.30am–noon, 4pm–7.15pm daily.* ✝

THE ORIGINAL 6th-century church on this site was rebuilt in the 15th century by Popes Martin V Colonna and

Sixtus IV della Rovere, whose oak-tree crest decorates the capitals of the late 15th-century portico. Inside the portico on the left is Canova's 1807 memorial to the engraver Giovanni Volpato. The church itself contains a much larger monument by Canova, his Tomb of Clement XIV (1789).

The Baroque interior by Francesco and Carlo Fontana was completed in 1714. Note the 3D effect of Giovanni Odazzi's painted *Rebel Angels*, who appear to be really falling from the sky. A huge 18th-century altarpiece by Domenico Muratori shows the martyrdom of the Apostles James and Philip, whose tombs are in the crypt.

Detail of Triton and sea-horse at Rome's grandest fountain, the Trevi

San Marcello al Corso ❺

Piazza San Marcello 5. **Map** 5 A4 & 12 F3. 〖 06-69 93 01. 〘 56, 60, 62, 70, 81, 85, 95, 117, 492, 628. **Open** 8.30am–noon, 4–6pm Mon–Sat, 8.30am–11am, 4–6pm Sun. 🔒

THIS CHURCH was originally one of the first places of Christian worship in Rome, which were known as *tituli*. A later Romanesque building

burned down in 1519, and was rebuilt by Jacopo Sansovino with a single nave and many richly-decorated private chapels on either side. The imposing travertine facade was designed by Fontana in late Baroque style.

The third chapel on the right has fine frescoes of the Virgin Mary by Francesco Salviati. The decoration of the next chapel was interrupted by the Sack of Rome in 1527. Raphael's follower Perin del Vaga fled, leaving the ceiling frescoes to be completed by

Daniele da Volterra and Pellegrino Tibaldi when peace returned to the city. In the nave stands a splendid Venetian-style double tomb by Sansovino, a memorial to Cardinal Giovanni Michiel (victim of a Borgia poisoning in 1503) and his nephew, Bishop Antonio Orso.

Trevi Fountain ❻

Fontana di Trevi. **Map** 5 A3 & 12 F2. 〘 52, 53, 58, 60, 61, 62, 71, 95, 116, 492 and many other routes along Via del Corso and Via del Tritone.

MOST VISITORS gathering around the coin-filled fountain assume that it has always been there, but by the standards of the Eternal City, the Trevi is a fairly recent creation. Nicola Salvi's theatrical design for Rome's largest and most famous fountain *(see p52)* was completed only in 1762. The central figures are Neptune, flanked by two Tritons. One struggles to master a very unruly "sea-horse", the other leads a far more docile animal. These symbolize the two contrasting moods of the sea.

The site originally marked the terminal of the Aqua Virgo aqueduct built in 19 BC. One of the first-story reliefs shows a young girl (the legendary virgin after whom the aqueduct was named) pointing to the spring from which the water flows.

Chapel in San Marcello al Corso, decorated by Francesco Salviati

Facade of Santa Maria in Trivio

Santa Maria in Trivio ❼

Piazza dei Crociferi 49. **Map** 5 A3 & 12 F2. 📞 *06-678 96 45.* 🚌 *52, 53, 56, 58, 60, 61, 62, 71, 95, 115, 116, 160, 175, 492, 628.* **Open** *8am–12.30pm, 3.30–7.30pm daily.* 🕈

IT HAS BEEN SAID that Italian architecture is one of facades, and nowhere is this clearer than in the 1570s facade of Santa Maria in Trivio, delightfully attached to the building behind it. Note the false windows. There is illusion inside, too, particularly in the ceiling frescoes, which show scenes from the New Testament by Antonio Gherardi (1644–1702).

The name of the tiny church probably means "St. Mary-at-the-meeting-of-three-roads."

Accademia Nazionale di San Luca ❽

Piazza dell'Accademia di San Luca 77. **Map** 5 A3 & 12 F2. 📞 *06-679 88 50.* 🚌 *52, 53, 56, 58, 60, 61, 62, 71, 95, 115, 116, 160, 175, 492, 628.* **Open** *10am–1pm Mon, Wed, Fri & last Sun of month (last adm: 12.15pm).* **Closed** *Jul, Aug, public hols & Mon after last Sun of month.*

ST LUKE IS supposed to have been a painter, hence the name of Rome's academy of fine arts. Appropriately, the gallery contains a painting of *St. Luke Painting a Portrait of the Virgin* by Raphael and his followers. The academy's heyday was in the 17th and

18th centuries, when many members gave their work to the collection. Canova donated a model for his famous marble group, the *Three Graces*.

Of particular interest are three fascinating self-portraits by women: the 17th-century Italian Lavinia Fontana; the 18th-century Swiss Angelica Kauffmann, whose painting is copied from a portrait of her by Joshua Reynolds; and Elisabeth Vigée-Lebrun, the French painter of the years before the 1789 Revolution.

Santi Vincenzo e Anastasio ❾

Vicolo dei Modelli 73. **Map** 5 A3 & 12 F2. 📞 *06-678 30 98.* 🚌 *52, 53, 56, 58, 60, 61, 62, 71, 95, 115, 116, 160, 175, 492, 628.* **Open** *7.30am–12.30pm, 3.30pm–7.30pm daily.* 🕈

OVERLOOKING the Trevi Fountain is one of the most over-the-top Baroque facades in Rome. Its thickets of columns are crowned by the huge coat of arms of Cardinal Raimondo Mazzarino, who commissioned Martino Longhi the Younger to build the church in 1650. The female

bust above the door is of one of the cardinal's famous nieces, either Louis XIV's first love, Maria Mancini (1639–1715), or her younger sister, Ortensia. In the apse, memorial plaques record the popes whose *praecordia* (a part of the heart) are enshrined behind the wall. This gruesome tradition was started at the end of the 16th century by Pope Sixtus V and continued until Pius X stopped it in the early 20th century.

Museo delle Paste Alimentari ❿

Piazza Scanderberg 117. **Map** 5 A3 & 12 F2. 📞 *06-699 11 19.* 🚌 *52, 53, 56, 58, 60, 61, 62, 71, 95, 115, 116, 160, 175, 492, 628.* **Open** *9am–6pm daily.* **Closed** *public hols.*

THE ROLE OF PASTA in Italian cuisine cannot be exaggerated, and this entertaining museum presents everything there is to know about the beloved staple. Its rooms focus on various aspects, such as the history of pasta, how it is made and the background of the different shapes, while others exhibit photography and art with a pasta theme.

Self-portrait by Lavinia Fontana in the Accademia Nazionale di San Luca

Interior of Bernini's oval Sant'Andrea al Quirinale

Sant'Andrea al Quirinale ⓫

Via del Quirinale 29. **Map** 5 B3.
06-489 031 87. 71, 115, 116T, 117. **Open** 9am–noon, 4–7pm Wed–Mon (closed in the afternoon in August). **Gratuity** expected by sacristan for showing St. Stanislas's rooms.

KNOWN AS the "Pearl of the Baroque" because of its beautiful roseate marble interior, Sant'Andrea was designed by Bernini and executed by his assistants between 1658 and 1670. It was built for the Jesuits, hence the many IHS emblems (*Iesus Hominum Salvator* – Jesus Saviour of Mankind).

The site for the church was wide but shallow, so Bernini pointed the long axis of his oval plan not towards the altar, but towards the sides; he then leads the eye round to the altar end. Here he ordered works of art in various media which function not in isolation, but together. The crucified St.

Andrew (Sant' Andrea) of the altarpiece looks up at a stucco version of himself, who in turn ascends towards the lantern and the Holy Spirit.

Do not miss the rooms of St. Stanislas Kostka in the adjacent convent. The quarters of the Jesuit novice, who died in 1568 aged 19, reflect not his own spartan taste, but the richer style of the 17th-century Jesuits. The Polish saint has been brilliantly immortalized in marble by Pierre Legros (1666–1719).

San Carlo alle Quattro Fontane ⓬

Via del Quirinale 23. **Map** 5 B3.
06-488 32 61. 116T and many routes to Piazza Barberini.
Open 9.30am–12.30pm daily.

IN 1634, the Spanish Trinitarians, an order whose role was to pay the ransom of Christian hostages to the Arabs, commissioned Borromini to design a church and convent at the Quattro Fontane crossroads. The church, so small it would fit inside one of the piers of St. Peter's, is also known as "San Carlino".

Although dedicated to Carlo Borromeo, the 16th-century Milanese cardinal canonized in 1620, San Carlo is as much a monument to Borromini. Both the facade and the interior employ bold, fluid curves that give light and life to a small, cramped site. The oval dome and tiny lantern are particularly ingenious. The undulating lines of the facade are decorated with angels and a statue of San Carlo. Finished in 1667, the facade is one of Borromini's very last works.

There are further delights in the playful inverted shapes in the cloister and the stucco work in the refectory (now the sacristy), which houses a painting of San Carlo by Orazio Borgianni (1611).

In a small room off the sacristy hangs a portrait of Borromini himself wearing the Trinitarian cross. Borromini committed suicide in 1667, and in the crypt (which may soon be opened to the public) a small curved chapel reserved for him remains empty.

Dome of San Carlo alle Quattro Fontane, lit by concealed windows

Fountain of Strength (or Juno)

Le Quattro Fontane ⑬

Intersection of Via delle Quattro
Fontane and Via del Quirinale.
Map 5 B3. 🚌 116T and many routes
to Piazza Barberini. Ⓜ Barberini.

THESE FOUR small fountains
are attached to the corners
of the buildings at the intersection of two narrow, busy
streets. They date from the
great redevelopment of Rome
in the reign of Sixtus V
(1585–90). Each fountain has
a statue of a reclining deity.
The river god accompanied
by the she-wolf is clearly the
Tiber; the other male figure
may be the Arno. The female
figures represent Strength and
Fidelity or the goddesses,
Juno and Diana.

The crossroads is at the
highest point of the Quirinal
hill and commands splendid
views of three distant landmark
obelisks: those placed by
Sixtus V in front of Santa
Maria Maggiore and Trinità dei
Monti, and the one that stands
in Piazza del Quirinale.

Moses Fountain ⑭

Fontana dell'Acqua Felice, Piazza San
Bernardo. **Map** 5 C2. 🚌 60, 61, 62,
136, 137, 492. Ⓜ Repubblica.

OFFICIALLY KNOWN as the
Fontana dell'Acqua
Felice, this fountain owes its
popular name to the grotesque
statue of Moses in the central
niche. The massive structure
with its three elegant arches
was designed by Domenico
Fontana to mark the terminal
of the Acqua Felice aqueduct,
so-called because it was one
of the many great improve-
ments commissioned by
Felice Peretti, Pope Sixtus V.
Completed in 1587, it brought
clean piped water to this
quarter of Rome for the
first time.

The notorious statue of
Moses striking water from
the rock is larger than life
and the proportions of
the body are obviously
wrong. Sculpted either
by Prospero Bresciano
or Leonardo Sormani, it
is a clumsy attempt at
recreating the awesome
appearance of Michelangelo's
Moses in the church of San
Pietro in Vincoli (see p170).
As soon as it was unveiled,
it was said to be frowning at
having been brought into
the world by such an
inept sculptor.

Fontana's Moses Fountain

The side reliefs also illustrate
water stories from the Old
Testament: Aaron leading the
Israelites to water and Joshua
pointing the army towards the
Red Sea. The fountain's four
lions are copies of Egyptian
originals (now in the Vatican
Museums), which Sixtus V
had put there for public
"convenience" and "delight".

**Gold coin with head of the
Emperor Diocletian (AD 285–305)**

Baths of Diocletian ⑮

Terme di Diocleziano, Piazza della
Repubblica. **Map** 6 D3. 🚌 H, 60, 61,
62, 70, 115, 136, 137, 170, 175, 492,
640, 910. Ⓜ Repubblica, Termini.

BUILT IN AD 298–306 under
the infamous Emperor
Diocletian, who murdered
thousands of Christians, the
baths (see pp22–3) occupied
well over a hectare (2.5 acres)
of ground between the present
Piazza dei Cinquecento and
Piazza della Repubblica. The
baths, the most extensive in
Rome, could accommodate
up to 3,000 bathers at a time.

Fidelity (or Diana) with her attendant dog, one of the Quattro Fontane

Part of the Museo Nazionale Romano, the baths include a former Carthusian monastery which has a cloister designed by Michelangelo.

Part of the Museo Nazionale Romano in the Baths of Diocletian

Santa Maria degli Angeli **16**

Piazza della Repubblica. **Map** 5 C3.
06-488 08 12. H, 60, 61, 62, 70, 115, 136, 137, 170, 175, 492, 640, 910. Repubblica, Termini. **Open** 8am–12.30pm, 4pm–7pm (6.30pm in winter).

Parts of the ruined Baths of Diocletian provided both building material and setting for this church, constructed by Michelangelo in 1563. The church was so altered in the 18th century by Luigi Vanvitelli it unfortunately has lost most of its original character.

The most striking works of art inside are a fresco of the *Martyrdom of St. Sebastian* by Domenichino and a gigantic statue of St. Bruno by Jean-Antoine Houdon.

An exhibition in the sacristy gives a detailed account of Michelangelo's original design.

Museo Nazionale Romano **17**

Palazzo Massimo, Piazza dei Cinquecento. **Map** 6 D3. 06-481 75 45. H, 3, 36, 38, 38b, 64, 115, 170, 175 and many other routes to Piazza dei Cinquecento. Repubblica, Termini. **Open** 9am–10pm Tue–Sat, 9am–8pm Sun. **Closed** Jan 1, May 1, Dec 25. **Adm charge**.

Founded in 1889, the Museo Nazionale Romano holds most of the antiquities found in Rome since 1870 as well as pre-existing collections, and is one of the world's leading museums of Classical art. During the 1990s it underwent a major reorganization and it now has three branches; one in the Palazzo Altemps *(see p127)*, one in its original site, occupying the part of the Baths of Diocletian not taken up by the church of Santa Maria degli Angeli, and one in the nearby Palazzo Massimo. The palace, built in 1883–7 on the site of a 16th-century villa which belonged to Sixtus V, used to be a Jesuit college. In 1981–97 it was restored to house a significant proportion of the museum's collections.

The exhibits in Palazzo Massimo, displayed on three floors, are originals dating from the 2nd century BC to the end of 4th century AD.

On the ground floor, Room 1 has a statue known as the *Generale de Tivoli*, by a Greek artist, which depicts a Roman soldier from the period of the Asian wars. Room 2 is devoted to funeral steles while a coin collection is in Room 3. Room 4 represents the golden period of the Imperial era with portraits of Octavian (Augustus), Drusus and Tiberius. Room 5, dedicated to Augustus, displays the famous statue of the emperor found on Via Labicana, and a series of frescoes from a grave on the Esquiline showing scenes from the history of Rome. Rooms 6, 7 and 8 display statues of Greek origins, including a splendid Niobid and the muse Melpomene.

The statues on the first floor date from the era of the successors of the Augustan dynasty, including a portrait of Vespasian in Room 1. In room 6 is the Discobolos Ex-Lancelotti and other athletes, while following rooms focus on divinities, mythology, historical celebrations and theater.

The second floor display concentrates on decorations from public buildings, including beautiful frescoes and exquisitely detailed mosaics such as the Quattro Aurighe mosaics found in a villa in Baccano in northern Rome.

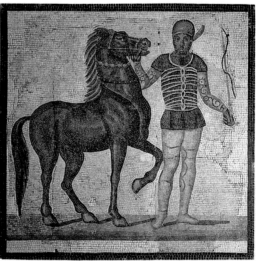

One of the Quattro Aurighe mosaics, Museo Nazionale Romano

Piazza della Repubblica ⑱

Map 5 C3. 🚌 *60, 61, 62, 64, 115, 170, 175, 492, 640, 910.*
Ⓜ *Repubblica.*

ROMANS OFTEN refer to the piazza by its old name, Piazza Esedra, which it was given because it follows the shape of an *exedra* (a semicircular recess) that was part of the Baths of Diocletian. The piazza was part of the redevelopment program undertaken when Rome became capital of a unified Italy. Under its sweeping 19th-century colonnades were once elegant shops, but they have been replaced by banks, travel agencies and cafés.

In the middle of the piazza stands the Fontana delle Naiadi. Mario Rutelli's four naked bronze nymphs caused something of a scandal when they were unveiled in 1901. Each reclines on an aquatic creature symbolizing water in its various forms: a seahorse for the oceans, a water snake for rivers, a swan for lakes and a curious frilled lizard for subterranean streams. The middle figure, added in 1911, is of the sea god Glaucus, who represents man victorious over hostile nature.

Piazza della Repubblica and the Fontana delle Naiadi

Palazzo delle Esposizioni ⑲

Via Nazionale 194 (second entrance in Via Milano). **Map** 5 B4. 📞 *06-474 59 03.* 🚌 *64, 70, 170, 175, 640.*
Open *10am–9pm Wed–Mon (last adm: 8:30pm).* **Closed** *Jan 1, May 1, Dec 25.* **Adm charge.** 🚫 ♿ *from Via Piacenza entrance only.* **Concerts, lectures, films.** See **Entertainment** *pp346–7.* 🔲 🖥 📷

Facade of the Palazzo delle Esposizioni

THIS SOMEWHAT grandiose building, with wide steps, Corinthian columns and statues, was designed as an exhibition center by the architect Pio Piacentini and built by the city of Rome in 1882 during the reign of Umberto I. The main entrance looks like a triumphal arch.

The Palazzo is still used to house exhibitions today and the exhibition space has recently been modernized. The exhibitions are changed every three months, and include a variety of sculpture and paintings. Live performances, films and lectures also take place here. Foreign films are usually shown in the original language.

Santa Maria dei Monti ⑳

Via Madonna dei Monti 41. **Map** 5 B4. 📞 *06-48 55 31.* 🚌 *64, 70, 75, 170, 175, 640.* Ⓜ *Cavour.* **Open** *7am–12:30pm, 4:30–8pm daily.* 🔲 ♿

DESIGNED BY Giacomo della Porta, this church, dating from 1580, has a particularly splendid dome. Over the high altar is a medieval painting of the Madonna, patroness of this quarter of Rome. The altar in the left transept houses the tomb and effigy of the unworldly French saint Benoît-Joseph Labre, who died here in 1783, having spent his life as a solitary pilgrim. He slept rough in the ruins of the Colosseum, gave away any charitable gifts he received and came regularly to Santa Maria dei Monti to worship. His faith could not sustain his body: when he was only in his mid-thirties, he collapsed and died outside the church. The foul rags he wore are preserved as relics.

One of the bronze nymphs of the fountain in Piazza della Repubblica

Sant'Agata dei Goti ㉑

Via Mazzarino 16 and Via Panisperna.
Map 5 B4. 06-488 80 61. 64,
70, 75, 170, 175. **Open** 7am–9am,
5pm–7pm Mon–Fri, 10:30am–
12:30pm, 4:30pm–7pm Sat, 8:30am–
12:30pm, 4:30pm–7pm Sun.

THE GOTHS who gave their
name to this church (*Goti*
are Goths) occupied Rome in
the 6th century AD. They were
Arian heretics who denied the
divinity of Christ. The church
was founded between AD 462
and 470, shortly before the
main Gothic invasions, and the
beautiful granite columns date
from this period. The main altar
has a well-preserved 12th-cen-
tury Cosmatesque tabernacle,
but the most delightful part of
the church is the charming
18th-century courtyard built
around an ivy-draped well.

Villa Aldobrandini ㉒

Via Panisperna. Entrance to gardens:
Via Mazzarino 1. **Map** 5 B4.
64, 70, 75, 115, 170.
Gardens open dawn–dusk daily.
Villa not open to the public.

BUILT in the 16th century for
the dukes of Urbino and
acquired for his family by Pope
Clement VIII Aldobrandini
(reigned 1592–1605), the
villa is now government
property and houses an
international law library.

The villa itself, decorated
with the family's six-starred
coat of arms, is closed to the
public, but the gardens and
terraces, hidden behind a
high wall that runs along Via
Nazionale, can be reached
through an iron gate in Via
Mazzarino. Steps lead up past
2nd-century AD ruins into the
recently renovated gardens,
highly recommended as an
oasis of tranquillity in the
center of the city. Gravel
paths lead between formal
lawns and clearly marked
specimen trees, and benches
are provided for the weary.
Since the garden is raised
some 30 ft (10 m) above street
level, the views are excellent.

18th-century courtyard of Sant'Agata dei Goti

Santi Domenico e Sisto ㉓

Largo Angelicum 1. **Map** 5 B4.
06-670 21. 64, 70, 75,
170, 175. **Open** by appt only.
Closed Jul–Sep.

Chapel in Santi Domenico e Sisto

THIS CHURCH has a tall,
slender Baroque facade
rising above a steep flight of
steps. This divides into two

curving flights that sweep up
to the terrace in front of the
entrance. The pediment of the
facade is crowned by eight
flaming candlesticks.

The interior has a vaulted
ceiling with a large
fresco, the *Apotheosis of
St. Dominic*, by
Domenico Canuti
(1620–84). The
first chapel on
the right was
decorated by
Bernini, who
may also have
designed the
sculpture of Mary
Magdalene
meeting the
risen Christ in
the Garden of
Gethsemane.
This fine marble
group was
executed by

**Facade of Santi
Domenico
e Sisto**

Antonio Raggi (1649). Above
the altar is a 15th-century
terra-cotta plaque of the
Madonna and Child. On the
left over a side altar is a large
painting of the Madonna from
the same period, attributed to
Benozzo Gozzoli (1420–97), a
pupil of Fra Angelico.

ESQUILINE

THE ESQUILINE is the largest and highest of Rome's seven hills. In Imperial Rome the western slopes overlooking the Forum housed the crowded slums of the Suburra. On the eastern side there were a few villas belonging to wealthy citizens like Maecenas, patron of the arts and adviser to Augustus. The essential character of the place has persisted through two millennia; it is still one of the poorer quarters

Michelangelo's *Rachel* in San Pietro in Vincoli

of the city. The area is now heavily built up, except for a rather seedy park on the Colle Oppio, a smaller hill to the south of the Esquiline, where you can see the remains of the Baths of Titus, the Baths of Trajan and Nero's Golden House. The area's main interest, however, lies in its churches. Many of these were founded on the sites of private houses where Christians met to worship secretly in the days when the religion was banned.

SIGHTS AT A GLANCE

Churches
San Martino ai Monti **1**
San Pietro in Vincoli **2**
Santa Pudenziana **3**
Santa Maria Maggiore pp172–3 **4**
Santa Prassede **5**
Santa Bibiana **7**

Museums
Museo Nazionale d'Arte Orientale **9**

Historic Piazzas
Piazza Vittorio Emanuele II **8**

Ancient Sites
Auditorium of Maecenas **10**
Nero's Golden House **12**
Sette Sale **11**

Arches
Arch of Gallienus **6**

GETTING THERE
This area is close to Termini station and has several other Metro stops: Vittorio Emanuele and Manzoni on line A, Cavour and Colosseo on line B. Bus routes here are a little confusing. Among the most useful are the 4, 9, 16 and 75 from Stazione Termini. Tram 30b goes along Via Labicana.

SEE ALSO
• *Street Finder*, maps 5, 6
• *Restaurants* pp310–11
• *Mosaics Walk* pp280–81

KEY
	Street-by-Street map
FS	Railway station
M	Metro station
P	Parking

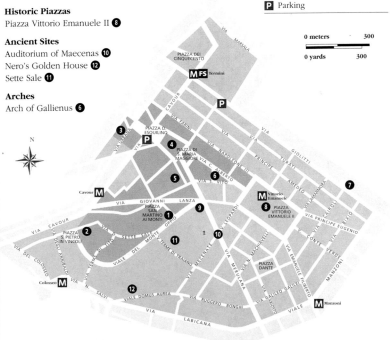

0 meters 300
0 yards 300

Southern facade of Santa Maria Maggiore by night

Street by Street: The Esquiline Hill

THE SIGHT that draws most people to this unkempt part of Rome is the great basilica of Santa Maria Maggiore. But it is also well worth searching out some of the smaller churches on the Esquiline: Santa Pudenziana and Santa Prassede, with their celebrated mosaics, and San Pietro in Vincoli, home to one of Michelangelo's most famous sculptures. To the south, in the Colle Oppio park, are the scattered remains of the Baths of Trajan.

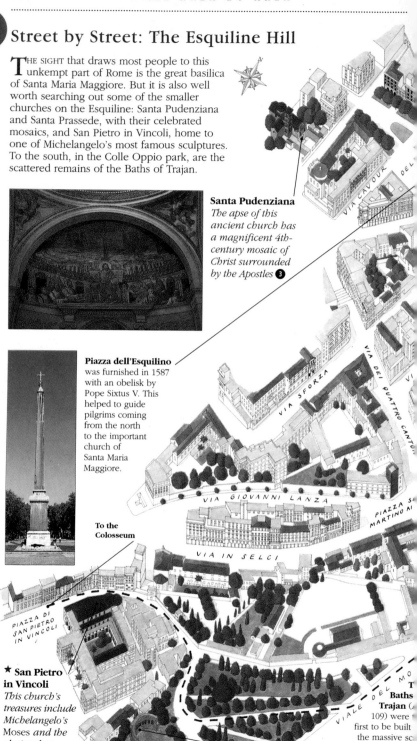

Santa Pudenziana
The apse of this ancient church has a magnificent 4th-century mosaic of Christ surrounded by the Apostles ③

Piazza dell'Esquilino
was furnished in 1587 with an obelisk by Pope Sixtus V. This helped to guide pilgrims coming from the north to the important church of Santa Maria Maggiore.

To the Colosseum

★ **San Pietro in Vincoli**
This church's treasures include Michelangelo's Moses *and the chains that bound St. Peter* ②

T
Baths
Trajan (
109) were
first to be built
the massive sc
later used in the Ba
of Diocletian and of Caraca

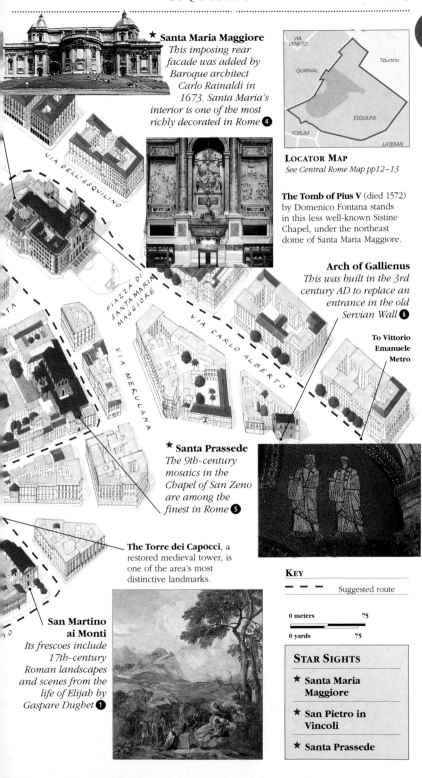

★ Santa Maria Maggiore
This imposing rear facade was added by Baroque architect Carlo Rainaldi in 1673. Santa Maria's interior is one of the most richly decorated in Rome ❹

LOCATOR MAP
See Central Rome Map pp12–13

VIA VENETO

QUIRINAL

Tiburtino

FORUM

ESQUILINE

LATERAN

The Tomb of Pius V (died 1572) by Domenico Fontana stands in this less well-known Sistine Chapel, under the northeast dome of Santa Maria Maggiore.

Arch of Gallienus
This was built in the 3rd century AD to replace an entrance in the old Servian Wall ❻

To Vittorio Emanuele Metro

VIA DELL'ESQUILINO

PIAZZA DI SANTA MARIA MAGGIORE

VIA CARLO ALBERTO

VIA MERULANA

★ Santa Prassede
The 9th-century mosaics in the Chapel of San Zeno are among the finest in Rome ❺

The Torre dei Capocci, a restored medieval tower, is one of the area's most distinctive landmarks.

San Martino ai Monti
Its frescoes include 17th-century Roman landscapes and scenes from the life of Elijah by Gaspare Dughet ❶

KEY

– – – Suggested route

| 0 meters | 75 |
| 0 yards | 75 |

STAR SIGHTS

★ Santa Maria Maggiore

★ San Pietro in Vincoli

★ Santa Prassede

San Martino ai Monti ❶

Viale del Monte Oppio 28. **Map** 6 D5.
☎ 06-487 31 66. 🚌 4, 9, 16, 70,
71, 714. Ⓜ Cavour, Vittorio
Emanuele. **Open** 7.30am–11.30am,
4.30pm–6.30pm Mon–Sat, 8.30am–
12.30pm, 6pm–7.30pm Sun. 🔒 ♿

Fresco of old San Giovanni in Laterano in San Martino ai Monti

CHRISTIANS have been worshipping on the site of this church since the 3rd century, when they used to meet in the house of a man named Equitius. In the 4th century, after Constantine had legalized Christianity, Pope Sylvester I built a church, one of very few things he did during his pontificate. In fact he was so insignificant that in the 5th century a more exciting life was fabricated for him – which included tales of him converting Constantine, curing him of leprosy and forcing him to close all pagan temples. Pope Sylvester's fictional life was further enhanced in the 8th century, with the forgery of a document in which Constantine offered him the Imperial crown.

Pope Sylvester's church was replaced in about AD 500 by St. Symmachus, rebuilt in the 9th century and then transformed completely in the 1630s. The only immediate signs of its age are the ancient Corinthian columns dividing the nave and aisles. The most interesting interior features are a series of frescoed landscapes of the Campagna (the countryside around Rome) by the 17th-century French artist Gaspare Dughet, Poussin's brother-in-law, in the right aisle. The frescoes by Filippo Gagliardi, at either end of the left aisle, show old St. Peter's and the interior of San Giovanni in Laterano before Borromini's redesign. If you can find the sacristan, you can go beneath the church to see the remains of Equitius's house.

San Pietro in Vincoli ❷

Piazza di San Pietro in Vincoli 4A.
Map 5 C5. ☎ 06-488 28 65. 🚌
75, 115, 117. Ⓜ Cavour, Colosseo.
Open 7am–12.30pm, 3.30pm–7pm
(Oct–Mar: 6pm) daily. 🔒 ♿ 📷

ACCORDING TO TRADITION, the two chains (vincoli) used to shackle St. Peter while he was being held in the depths

Reliquary with St. Peter's chains

of the Mamertine Prison (see p91) were subsequently taken to Constantinople. In the 5th century, Empress Eudoxia deposited one in a church in Constantinople and sent the other to her daughter Eudoxia in Rome. She in turn gave hers to Pope Leo I, who had this church built to house it. Some years later the second chain was brought to Rome, where it linked miraculously with its partner.

The chains are still here, displayed below the high altar, but the church is now best known for Michelangelo's Tomb of Pope Julius II. When it was commissioned in 1505, Michelangelo spent eight months searching for perfect blocks of marble at Carrara in Tuscany, but Pope Julius became more interested in the building of a new St. Peter's and the project was laid aside. After the pope's death in 1513, Michelangelo resumed work on the tomb, but had only finished the statues of Moses and the Dying Slaves when Pope Paul III persuaded him to start work on the Sistine Chapel's Last Judgment. Michelangelo had planned a vast monument with over 40 statues, but the tomb that was built – mainly by his pupils – is simply a facade with six niches for statues.

The Dying Slaves are in Paris and Florence, but the tremendous bearded Moses is here. The horns on Moses' head should really be beams of light – they are the result of the Hebrew original from the Old Testament being wrongly translated.

Michelangelo's Moses in San Pietro

Santa Pudenziana ❸

Via Urbana 160. **Map** 5 C4.
📞 06-481 46 22. 🚌 4, 9, 16, 70, 71, 714. Ⓜ *Cavour.* **Open** *8am–noon, 3pm–6pm daily.* ⛪

CHURCHES tend to be dedicated to existing saints, but in this case, the church, through a linguistic accident, created a brand new saint. In the 1st century AD a Roman senator called Pudens lived on this site, and, according to legend, allowed St. Peter to lodge with him. In the 2nd century a bath house was built on this site and in the 4th century a church was established inside the baths, known as the *Ecclesia Pudentiana* (the church of Pudens). In time it was assumed that "Pudentiana" was a woman's name and a life was created for her – she became the sister of Prassede and was credited with caring for Christian victims of persecution. In 1969 both saints were declared invalid, though their churches both kept their names.

The 19th-century facade of the church retains an 11th-century frieze depicting both Prassede and Pudenziana dressed as crowned Byzantine empresses. The apse has a remarkable 4th-century mosaic, clearly influenced by Classical pagan art in its use of subtle colors. The Apostles are represented as Roman senators in togas. Unfortunately, a clumsy attempt at restoration in the 16th century destroyed two of the Apostles and left other figures without their legs.

Apse mosaics in Santa Prassede, showing the saint with St. Paul

Santa Maria Maggiore ❹

See pp172–3.

Santa Prassede ❺

Via Santa Prassede 9A. **Map** 6 D4.
📞 06-488 24 56. 🚌 4, 9, 16, 70, 71, 714. Ⓜ *Vittorio Emanuele.* **Open** *7.30am– noon, 4pm–6.30pm daily.* ⛪ ♿

THE CHURCH was founded by Pope Paschal II in the 9th century, on the site of a 2nd-century oratory. Although the interior has been altered and rebuilt, the structure of the original design of the 9th-century church is clearly visible. Its three naves are separated by rows of granite columns. In the central nave, there is a round stone slab covering the well where, according to the legend, St. Prassede would have buried the remains of 2,000 martyrs.

Artists from Byzantium decorated the church with glittering, jewel-colored mosaics. Those in the apse and choir depict stylized white-robed elders, the haloed elect looking down from the gold and blue walls of heaven, spindly-legged lambs, feather-mop palm trees and bright red poppies.

In the apse, Santa Prassede and Santa Pudenziana stand on either side of Christ, with the fatherly arms of St. Paul and St. Peter on their shoulders. Beautiful mosaics of saints, the virgin and Christ and the Apostles also cover the walls and vault of the Chapel of St. Zeno, built as a mausoleum for Pope Paschal's mother, Theodora. Part of a column brought back from Jerusalem, allegedly the one to which Christ was bound and flogged, also stands here.

11th-century frieze and medallions on the facade of Santa Pudenziana

Santa Maria Maggiore ❹

O F ALL THE GREAT Roman basilicas, Santa Maria has the most successful blend of different architectural styles. Its colonnaded triple nave is part of the original 5th-century building. The Cosmatesque marble floor and delightful Romanesque bell tower, with its blue ceramic roundels, are medieval. The Renaissance saw a new coffered ceiling, and the Baroque gave the church twin domes and its imposing front and rear facades. The mosaics are Santa Maria's most famous feature. From the 5th century come the Biblical scenes in the nave and the spectacular mosaics on the triumphal arch. Medieval highlights include a 13th-century enthroned Christ in the loggia.

★ Cappella Paolina
Flaminio Ponzio designed this richly decorated chapel (1611) for Pope Paul V Borghese.

Obelisk in Piazza dell'Esquilino
The Egyptian obelisk was erected by Pope Sixtus V in 1587 as a landmark for pilgrims.

LEGEND OF THE SNOW

In 356, Pope Liberius had a dream in which the Virgin told him to build a church on the spot where he found snow. When it fell on the Esquiline, on the morning of August 5 in the middle of a baking Roman summer, he naturally obeyed. The miracle of the snow is commemorated each year by a service during which thousands of white petals float down from the ceiling of Santa Maria. Originally roses were used, but nowadays the petals are more usually taken from dahlias.

Coffered Ceiling
The gilded ceiling, possibly by Giuliano da Sangallo, was a gift of Alexander VI Borgia at the end of the 15th century. The gold is said to be the first brought from America by Columbus.

TIMELINE

356 Virgin appears to Pope Liberius

432–40 Sixtus III completes church

Pope Gregory VII

1347 Cola di Rienzo crowned Tribune of Rome in Santa Maria

1673 Carlo Rainaldi rebuilds apse

300 AD	600	900	1200	1500	1800

420 Probable founding date

1075 Pope Gregory VII kidnapped by opponents while reading Christmas mass in Santa Maria

Coat of arms of Gregory VII

1288–92 Nicholas IV adds apse and transepts

1743 Ferdinando Fuga adds main facade on orders of Benedict XIV

VISITORS' CHECKLIST

Piazza di Santa Maria Maggiore.
Map 6 D4. 📞 *06-48 31 95.*
🚌 *4, 9, 16, 70, 71, 714.*
🚊 *14.* Ⓜ *Termini, Cavour.*
Open *7am–6:30pm daily.* 🚻 🛍
of frescoes in loggia every 30 mins,
9am–5pm.

Baldacchino *(1740s)*
Its columns of red
porphyry and bronze
were the work of
Ferdinando Fuga.

★ **Coronation of the Virgin Mosaic**
This is the central image of a series
of wonderful apse mosaics of the
Virgin by Jacopo Torriti (1295).

★ **Tomb of**
Cardinal
Rodriguez
The Gothic
tomb (1299)
contains
magnificent
Cosmatesque
marblework.

★ **Cappella Sistina**
The chapel was built for
Pope Sixtus V (1584–87) by
Domenico Fontana and
houses the pope's tomb.

Column in Piazza
Santa Maria Maggiore
A bronze of the Virgin and Child was
added to this ancient marble column
in 1615. The column came from the
Basilica of Constantine in the Forum.

STAR FEATURES

★ **Cappella Sistina**

★ **Coronation of the**
Virgin Mosaic

★ **Cappella Paolina**

★ **Tomb of Cardinal**
Rodriguez

Arch erected in memory of Emperor Gallienus

Arch of Gallienus ❻

Via Carlo Alberto. **Map** 6 D4. 🚌 *4, 9, 16, 71.* Ⓜ *Vittorio Emanuele.*

Squashed between two buildings just off Via Carlo Alberto is the central arch of an originally three-arched gate erected in memory of Emperor Gallienus, who was assassinated by his Illyrian officers in AD 262. It was built on the site of the old Esquiline Gate in the Servian Wall, parts of which are visible nearby.

Santa Bibiana ❼

Via Giovanni Giolitti 154. **Map** 6 F4. 🆃 *06-446 10 21.* 🚌 *70, 71, 105.* Ⓜ *Vittorio Emanuele.* **Open** *7am–10am, 4.30pm–7.30pm daily (phone first).* 🚻 ♿

The deceptively simple facade of Santa Bibiana was Bernini's first foray into architecture. It is a clean, economic design with superimposed pilasters and deeply shadowed archways. The church itself was built on the site of the palace belonging to Bibiana's family. This is where the saint was buried

after being flogged to death with leaded cords during the brief persecution of the Christians that took place in the reign of Julian the Apostate (361–3). Just inside the church is a small column against which Bibiana is said to have been whipped. Her remains, along with those of her mother Dafrosa and her sister Demetria, who also suffered martyrdom, are preserved in an alabaster urn below the altar. In a niche above the altar stands a statue of Santa Bibiana by Bernini – the first fully-clothed figure he ever sculpted. He depicts her standing beside a column, holding the cords with which she was whipped, apparently on the verge of a deadly swoon.

Early sculpture by Bernini of the martyr Santa Bibiana (1626)

Piazza Vittorio Emanuele II ❽

Map 6 E5. 🚌 *4, 9, 71.* 🚊 *14, 516.* Ⓜ *Vittorio Emanuele. See* **Markets** *p338.*

Piazza Vittorio, as it is called for short, is one of the city's main open-air food markets. The arcaded square was built in the urban development undertaken after the unification of Italy in 1870. It was named after Italy's first king, but there is nothing regal about its appearance today. The shabby stalls selling cheap shoes and clothes are however about to be moved.

However, the garden area in the centre of the square has recently been restored. It contains a number of mysterious ruins, including a large mound, part of a Roman fountain from the 3rd century AD and the Porta Magica, a curious 17th-century doorway inscribed with alchemical signs and formulae.

Museo Nazionale d'Arte Orientale ❾

Via Merulana 248. **Map** 6 D5. 🆃 *06-487 44 15.* 🚌 *16, 70, 71, 714.* Ⓜ *Vittorio Emanuele.* **Open** *9am– 7pm Tue–Thu, 9am–2pm Fri, Sat & Mon, 9am–1pm Sun.* **Closed** *1st & 3rd Mon of month.* **Adm charge**.

The museum occupies part of the late 19th-century Palazzo Brancaccio, home of the Italian Institute of the Middle and Far East since 1957. The collection ranges from prehistoric Iranian ceramics, sculpture from Afghanistan, Nepal, Kashmir and India to 18th-century Tibetan paintings on vellum. From the Far East there are collections of Japanese screen paintings and Chinese jade.
The most unusual exhibits are the finds from the Italian excavation of the ancient civilization of

4th-century relief from Kashmir

Nepalese Bodhisattva in the Museo Nazionale d'Arte Orientale

Swat in northeast Pakistan. This fascinating Gandhara culture lasted from the 3rd century BC to about the 10th century AD. Its wonderfully exotic, sensual reliefs show an unusual combination of Hellenistic, Buddhist and Hindu influences.

Auditorium of Maecenas ⑩

Largo Leopardi. **Map** 6 D5.
🚌 *16, 71, 714.* Ⓜ *Vittorio Emanuele.* **Open** *9am–1.30pm Sun.* 🚫 ♿

MAECENAS, fop, gourmet and patron of the arts, was also an astute adviser and colleague of the Emperor Augustus. He was fabulously rich, and spent some of his wealth creating a fantastic villa and gardens on the Esquiline hill, most of which has long disappeared beneath the modern city. The partially reconstructed auditorium, isolated on a traffic island, is all that remains.

Inside, a semicircle of tiered seats suggests that it may have been a place for readings and performances. If it was, then Maecenas would have been entertained here by his protégés, the lyric poet Horace and Virgil, author of the *Aeneid,* reading their latest works. However, water ducts have also been discovered and it may well have been a *nympheum* – a kind of summerhouse – with

fountains. Traces of frescoes remain on the walls: you can make out garden scenes and a procession of miniature figures – including one of a characteristically drunken Dionysus (the Greek god of wine) being propped upright by a satyr.

Sette Sale ⑪

Via delle Terme di Traiano. **Map** 5 C5.
📞 *06-67 10 38 19.* 🚌 *85, 87, 117, 186, 850.* 🚇 *30b.* Ⓜ *Colosseo.*
Open *only by request; phone in advance.*

NOT FAR FROM Nero's Golden House is the cistern of the Sette Sale. It was built there to supply the enormous quantities of water needed for the Baths of Trajan. These were built for Emperor Trajan in AD 104 on parts of the Golden House damaged by a fire.

A set of stairs leads down into the cistern, well below street level. There is not much to see there now, but a walk through the huge, echoing cistern where light rays illuminates the watery surfaces is still an evocative experience. The nine sections, 98 ft (30 m) long and 16 ft (5 m) wide, had a capacity of 8 million litres.

Nero's Golden House ⑫

Domus Aurea, Via Labicana 136.
Map 5 C5. 📞 *06-699 01 10.* 🚌 *85, 87, 117, 186, 850.* 🚇 *30b.* Ⓜ *Colosseo.* **Closed** *for restoration; phone the Soprintendenza Archeologica at the above number (8am–1.30pm) to arrange a visit.*

AFTER ALLEGEDLY setting fire to Rome in AD 64, Nero decided to build himself an outrageous new palace. It occupied part of the Palatine, and most of the Celian and Esquiline hills – an area approximately 25 times the size of the Colosseum. The vestibule on the Palatine side of the complex contained a colossal gilded statue of Nero. There was an artificial lake, with gardens and woods

where imported wild beasts were allowed to roam free. According to Suetonius in his life of Nero, the palace walls were adorned with gold and mother-of-pearl, rooms were designed with ceilings that showered guests with flowers or perfumes, the dining hall rotated and the baths were fed with both sulphurous water and sea-water.

Tacitus described Nero's debauched garden parties, with banquets served on barges and lakeside brothels serviced by aristocratic women, though as Nero killed himself in AD 68, he did not have long to enjoy his new home.

Nero's successors, anxious to distance themselves from the monster-emperor, did their utmost to erase all traces of the palace. Vespasian drained the lake and built the Colosseum *(see pp92–5)* in its place, Titus and Trajan each erected a complex of baths over the palace, and Hadrian placed the Temple of Venus and Rome *(see p87)* over the vestibule.

Rooms from one wing of the palace have survived, buried beneath the ruins of the Baths of Trajan on the Oppian hill. Recent excavations have revealed large frescoes and mosaics which are thought be a panorama of Rome from a birds-eye perspective. Hopefully it will open to the public when considered safe from landslides.

Frescoed room in the ruins of Nero's Golden House

LATERAN

I N THE MIDDLE AGES, the Lateran Palace was the residence of the popes, and the basilica of San Giovanni beside it rivaled St. Peter's in splendor. After the return of the popes from Avignon at the end of the 14th century, the area declined in importance. Pilgrims still continued to visit San Giovanni and Santa

Cherub from San Giovanni in Laterano

Croce in Gerusalemme, but the area remained sparsely inhabited. Ancient convents slumbered amid gardens and vineyards until Rome became Italy's capital in 1870, and a network of residential streets was laid out to house the influx of newcomers. The main sites of archaeological importance are the Aurelian Wall and the ruins of the Aqueduct of Nero.

SIGHTS AT A GLANCE

Churches
San Giovanni in Laterano pp182–3 **1**
Santa Croce in Gerusalemme **5**
Santi Quattro Coronati **11**
San Clemente pp186–7 **12**
Santo Stefano Rotondo **13**

Shrines
Scala Santa and Sancta Sanctorum **2**

Arches and Gates
Porta Asinaria **3**
Porta Maggiore **7**

Ancient Sites
Amphiteatrum Castrense **4**
Baker's Tomb **8**
Aqueduct of Nero and the Freedmen's Tombs **9**

Museums
Museum of Musical Instruments **6**

Historic Buildings
Villa Wolkonsky **10**

SEE ALSO

GETTING THERE
San Giovanni Metro station on line A is just outside the city wall but handy for many of the sights in the area. The 16, 81, 87 and 186 are among the many buses to Piazza di San Giovanni in Laterano. This can also be reached by the 30b trams. This is slow, but its route makes it useful for exploring this part of Rome.

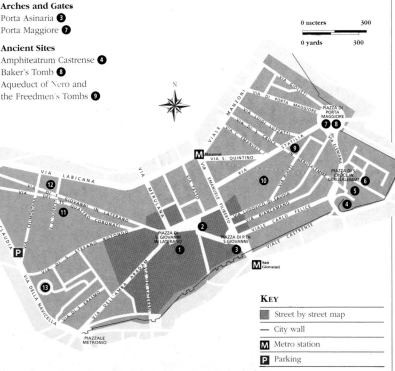

0 meters	300
0 yards	300

KEY
▨	Street by street map
—	City wall
M	Metro station
P	Parking

15th-century apse fresco in Santa Croce in Gerusalemme

Street by Street: Piazza di San Giovanni

BOTH THE BASILICA of San
Giovanni and the Lateran
Palace look out over a huge
open area, the Piazza di San
Giovanni, laid out at the end
of the 16th century with an
Egyptian obelisk, the oldest
in Rome, in the center. Sadly,
the traffic streaming in and
out of the city through Porta
San Giovanni tends to detract
from its grandeur. Across
the square is the building
housing the Scala Santa (the
Holy Staircase), one of the
most revered relics in Rome
and the goal for many
pilgrims. The area is also
a venue for political rallies,
and the feast of St. John
on June 23 is celebrated
with a fair at which
Romans consume
roast *porchetta*
(*see p59*).

**The Chapel of
Santa Rufina**,
originally the
portico of the
baptistry, has
a 5th-century
mosaic of spiraling
foliage in the apse.

VIA DI SANTO S

VIA DELL'AMBA ARADAM

VIA DEI LATERANI

**The Cloister of San
Giovanni** fortunately
survived the two fires
that destroyed the early
basilica. A 13th-century
masterpiece of mosaic
work, the cloister now
houses fragments from
the medieval basilica.

**Piazza di San
Giovanni in Laterano**
boasts an ancient obelisk
and parts of Nero's Aqueduct.
This 18th-century painting by Canaletto
shows how the piazza once looked.

STAR SIGHT

★ **San Giovanni in
Laterano**

KEY

- − − Suggested route

0 meters   75

0 yards   75

The Chapel of San Venanzio is decorated with a series of 7th-century mosaics on a gold background. This detail from the apse shows one of the angels beside the central figure of Christ. San Venanzio was an accomplished 6th-century Latin poet.

LOCATOR MAP
See Central Rome Map pp12–13

The Lateran Palace, residence of the popes until 1309, was rebuilt by Domenico Fontana in 1586.

★ San Giovanni in Laterano
Borromini's interior dates from the 17th century, but the grand facade by Alessandro Galilei, with its giant statues of Christ and the Apostles, was added in 1735 ❶

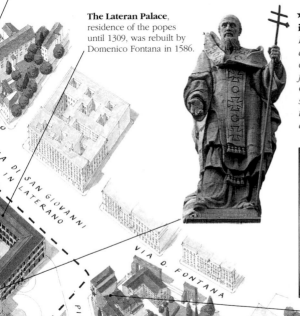

Scala Santa
This door at the top of the holy stair-case leads to the Sancta Sanctorum ❷

Porta Asinaria
This minor gateway, no longer in use, is as old as the Aurelian Wall, dating back to the 3rd century AD ❸

The Triclinio Leoniano is a piece of wall and a mosaic from the dining hall of 8th-century Pope Leo III.

San Giovanni in Laterano **❶**

See pp182–3.

Scala Santa and Sancta Sanctorum **❷**

Piazza di San Giovanni in Laterano 14.
Map 9 C1. 06-70 49 44 89.
16, 81, 85, 186 and other routes
to Piazza di San Giovanni in Laterano.
30b. San Giovanni. **Open**
6:30am–11:50am, 3:30pm–6:45pm
(Oct–Mar 3pm– 6:45pm) daily.

Devout Christians climbing the Scala Santa on their knees

ON THE EAST SIDE of Piazza di San Giovanni in Laterano, a building designed by Domenico Fontana (1589) houses two surviving parts of the old Lateran Palace. One is the Sancta Sanctorum, the other the holy staircase, the Scala Santa. The 28 steps, said to be those that Christ ascended in Pontius Pilate's house during his trial, are supposed to have been brought from Jerusalem by St. Helena, mother of the Emperor Constantine. This belief, however, cannot be traced back any earlier than the 7th century.

The steps were moved to their present site by Pope Sixtus V (reigned 1585–90) when the old Lateran Palace was destroyed. No foot may touch the holy steps, so they are covered by wooden boards. They may be climbed only by the faithful on their knees, a penance that is performed especially on Good Friday. In the vestibule

are various 19th-century sculptures, including an *Ecce Homo* by Giosuè Meli (1874).

The Scala Santa and two side stairways lead to the Chapel of St. Lawrence or Sancta Sanctorum (Holy of Holies), built by Pope Nicholas III in 1278. Decorated with fine Cosmatesque marble-work, the chapel contains many important relics, the most precious being an image of Jesus – the *Acheiropoeton,* or "picture painted without hands," said to be the work of St. Luke, assisted by an angel. The image was taken on procession in medieval times to ward off plagues.

On the walls and in the vault, restoration work has revealed 13th-century frescoes which for 500 years had been covered by later paintings. The frescoes, representing the legends of St. Nicholas, St. Lawrence, St. Agnes and St. Paul, show signs of the style that would characterize the frescoes of Giotto in Assisi, made a few years later.

Porta Asinaria **❸**

Between Piazza di Porta San Giovanni and Piazzale Appio. **Map** 10 D2.
4, 16, 81, 85, 87, 850. 30b.
San Giovanni. See **Markets** p339.

THE PORTA ASINARIA (Gate of the Donkeys) is one of the minor gateways in the Aurelian Wall *(see p196)*. Twin circular

Porta Asinaria from inside the wall

towers were added and a small enclosure built around the entrance; the remains are still visible today. From outside the walls visitors can see the gate's white travertine facade and two rows of small windows, giving light to two corridors built into the wall above the gateway. In AD 546 treacherous barbarian soldiers serving in the Roman army opened this gate to the hordes of the Goth Totila, who mercilessly looted the city. In 1084 the Holy Roman Emperor Henry IV entered Rome via Porta Asinaria with the antipope Guibert to oust Pope Gregory VII. The gateway was badly damaged in the conflicts that followed. .

The area close to the gate, especially in the Via Sannio, is the home of a popular flea-market *(see p339)*.

Amphiteatrum Castrense **❹**

Between Piazza di Santa Croce in Gerusalemme and Viale Castrense.
Map 10 E1. 9. 13, 30b.
Not open to the public.

Columns and bricked-up arches of the Amphiteatrum Castrense

THIS SMALL 3rd-century amphitheater was used for games and baiting animals. It owes its preservation to the fact that it was incorporated into the Aurelian Wall *(see p196)*, which included several existing high buildings in its fortifications. The graceful arches framed by brick semicolumns were blocked up. The amphitheater is best seen from outside the walls, where there is also a very good view of the bell tower of Santa Croce in Gerusalemme.

Discovery and Triumph of the Cross, attributed to Antoniazzo Romano, in Santa Croce in Gerusalemme

Santa Croce in Gerusalemme **⑤**

Piazza di Santa Croce in Gerusalemme 12. **Map** 10 E1. **06-701 47 69.** 9. 30b. **Open** 6:30am–12:30pm & 3:30–7:30pm daily.

E MPEROR CONSTANTINE'S mother, St. Helena, founded this church in AD 320 on the grounds of her private palace. Although the church stood at the edge of the city, the relics of the Crucifixion that St. Helena had brought back from Jerusalem made it a center of pilgrimage. Most important were the pieces of Christ's Cross (*croce* means "cross") and part of Pontius Pilate's inscription in Latin, Hebrew and Greek: "Jesus of Nazareth King of the Jews."

In the crypt is a Roman statue of Juno, found at Ostia (*see pp270–71*); it was transformed into a statue of St. Helena by replacing the head and arms and adding a cross. The 15th-century apse fresco shows the medieval legends that arose around the Cross. Helena is shown holding it over a dead youth and restoring him to life. Another episode shows its recovery from the Persians by the Byzantine Emperor Heraclitus after a bloody battle. In the center of the apse is a magnificent tomb by Jacopo Sansovino made for Cardinal Quiñones, Emperor Charles V's confessor (died 1540).

Museum of Musical Instruments **⑥**

Museo degli Strumenti Musicali, Piazza di Santa Croce in Gerusalemme. **Map** 10 E1. **06-701 47 96.** 9. 30b. **Open** 9am–2pm Tue–Sun. **Closed** Jan 1, May 1, Dec 25. **Adm charge**.

O NE OF ROME'S lesser-known museums, this building stands on the site of the Sessorianum, the great Imperial villa belonging to Empress St. Helena, later included in the Aurelian Wall. Opened in 1974, the museum has a collection of over 3,000 instruments from all over the world. It includes instruments typical of the various regions of Italy, and wind, string and percussion instruments of all ages (including Egyptian, Greek and Roman). There are also sections dedicated to church and military music.

The greater part of the collection is composed of Baroque instruments: do not miss the gorgeous Barberini harp, remarkably well preserved, on the first floor in Room 13. There are spinets, harpsichords and clavichords of many different kinds, plus one of the first pianos ever made, dating from 1722.

18th-century statue of St. Helena on the facade of Santa Croce

Art Nouveau entrance to the Museum of Musical Instruments

San Giovanni in Laterano ❶

EARLY IN THE 4th century, the Laterani family were disgraced and their land taken by Emperor Constantine to build Rome's first Christian basilica. Today's church retains the original shape, but has been destroyed by fire twice and rebuilt several times. Borromini undertook the last major rebuild of the interior in 1646, and the main facade is an 18th-century addition. Before the pope's move to Avignon in 1309, the adjoining Lateran Palace was the official papal residence, and until 1870 all popes were crowned in the church. The pope is the Bishop of Rome and here in the city's main cathedral he celebrates Maundy Thursday mass and attends the annual blessing of the people.

Cappella di San Venanzio
This chapel is attached to the baptistry and is decorated with 7th-century mosaics.

Entrance to museum

Apse

Papal Altar
Only the Pope can celebrate mass at this altar. The Gothic baldacchino, decorated with frescoes, dates from the 14th century.

★ Cloisters
Built by the Vassalletto family in about 1220, the cloisters are remarkable for their twisted twin columns and inlaid marble mosaics.

TIMELINE

AD 313 Constantine gives Laterani site to Pope Melchiades for a church

314–18 Five-aisled basilical church is built

896 Church damaged in earthquake

1144 Church dedicated to San Giovanni in Laterano

1309 Papacy moves to Avignon

1377 Return of popes from Avignon

1646 Borromini rebuilds interior

AD 300	800	1000	1400

324 Basilica consecrated by Pope Sylvester I and dedicated to the Redeemer

904–911 Church rebuilt under Pope Sergius III

1300 First Holy Year proclaimed

1308 Church destroyed by fire

1360 Church burnt down for second time

1586 Domenico Fontana builds north facade

1730–40 Alessandro Galilei constructs main facade

★**Baptistry**
Though much restored, the domed baptistry dates back to Constantine's time. It assumed its present octagonal shape in AD 432 and the design has served as the model for baptistries throughout the Christian world.

North Facade
This was added by Domenico Fontana in 1586. The pope gives his blessing from the upper loggia.

STAR FEATURES

★ **Baptistry**

★ **Cloisters**

The original Lateran Palace was almost destroyed by the fire of 1308 which devastated San Giovanni. Pope Sixtus V commissioned Fontana to replace it in 1586.

Statues of Christ and the Apostles

Boniface VIII Fresco
This fragment showing the pope proclaiming the Holy Year of 1300 is attributed to Giotto.

A side door is opened every Holy Year.

The main entrance's bronze doors originally came from the Curia *(see p82)*.

TRIAL OF A CORPSE

Fear of rival factions led the early popes to extraordinary lengths. An absurd case took place at the Lateran Palace in 897 when Pope Stephen VI tried the corpse of his predecessor, Formosus, for disloyalty to the Church. The corpse was found guilty, its right hand was mutilated and it was thrown into the Tiber.

Pope Formosus

Corsini Chapel
This chapel was built in the 1730s for Pope Clement XII. The altarpiece is a mosaic copy of Guido Reni's painting of Sant'Andrea Corsini.

Porta Maggiore ❼

Piazza di Porta Maggiore. **Map** 6 F5.
🚃 105, 516, 517. 🚋 14, 19, 30b.

ORIGINALLY the two arches of Porta Maggiore were not part of the city wall but part of an aqueduct built for the Emperor Claudius in AD 52. They carried the water of the Aqua Claudia over the Via Labicana and Via Prenestina, two of ancient Rome's main southbound roads. You can still see the original roadway beneath the gate. In the large slabs of basalt – a hard volcanic rock used in all old Roman roads – are the great ruts created by generations of cartwheels. On top of the arches, separate conduits carried the water of two aqueducts, the Aqua Claudia, and its offshoot, the Aqueduct of Nero. They bear inscriptions from the time of the Emperors Claudius, Vespasian and Titus, who restored them in the years AD 71 and AD 81, respectively. In all, six aqueducts from different water sources entered the city at Porta Maggiore.

The Aqua Claudia was 43 miles (68 km) long, with more than 9 miles (15 km) above ground. Its majestic arches are a strong feature of the Roman countryside, and a brand of mineral water still bears its name. Some arches of the Aqua Claudia were bricked up when it was joined to the 3rd-century Aurelian Wall *(see p196)*.

Relief showing breadmaking on the tomb of the baker Eurysaces

Baker's Tomb ❽

Piazzale Labicano. **Map** 6 F5. 🚃 105, 516, 517. 🚋 14, 19, 30b.

IN THE MIDDLE of the tram junction near Porta Maggiore stands the tomb of the rich baker Eurysaces and his wife, Atistia, built in 30 BC. Roman custom forbade burials within city walls, and the roads leading out of cities became lined with tombs and monuments for the middle and upper classes. This tomb is shaped like a baking oven: a low-relief frieze at the top shows Eurysaces presiding over his slaves in the various phases of breadmaking. The inscription proudly asserts his origins and reveals him as a freed slave, probably of Greek origin. Many men like him saved money from their meager slave salaries to earn their freedom and set up businesses, becoming the backbone of Rome's economy.

Aqueduct of Nero and the Freedmen's Tombs ❾

Intersection of Via Statilia and Via di Santa Croce in Gerusalemme. **Map** 10 D1. 🚃 9, 105, 516, 517. 🚋 14, 19, 30b. **Open** by appt only: permit needed (see p367).

THE AQUEDUCT was built for Nero in the 1st century AD as an extension of the Aqua Claudia. to supply Nero's Golden House *(see p175)*. It was later extended to the Imperial residences on the Palatine. Partly incorporated into later buildings, the imposing arches make their way via the Lateran to the Celian Hill. Along the first section of the aqueduct, in Via Statilia, is a small tomb in the shape of a house, dating from the 1st century BC, and bearing the names and likenesses of a group of freed slaves. Their name, Statilii, indicates that they had been freed by the Statilii, the family of Claudius's notorious wife, Messalina. Servants of families often pooled funds in this way to pay for a dignified burial in a common resting place.

Relief on the Tomb of the Statilii freedmen

Porta Maggiore, a city gate formed by the arches of an aqueduct

Well-preserved section of Nero's Aqueduct near San Giovanni

Villa Wolkonsky ⑩

Via Conte Rosso. **Map** 10 D1.
🚌 *4, 81, 590.* 🚊 *30b.* **Not open to**
the public.

NOW THE RESIDENCE of the
British ambassador, the
villa has a beautiful garden
strewn with Roman remains,
including arches of the Aqua
Claudia and a columbarium,
or collective grave, of the 2nd
century AD. Sadly, garden
parties for British residents
are no longer given here on
the Queen's official birthday.

Santi Quattro Coronati ⑪

Via dei Santi Quattro Coronati 20.
Map 9 B1. 📞 *06-70 47 54 26.*
🚌 *81, 85, 87, 117, 175, 673, 810.*
🚊 *30b.* **Open** *9.30am–noon,*
3.30pm–6pm daily. ✝ ⛪

Cloister of Santi Quattro Coronati

THE NAME of this fortified
convent (Four Crowned
Saints) refers to four Christian
soldiers martyred after they
refused to worship a pagan
god. For centuries it was the
bastion of the pope's
residence, the Lateran Palace.
Its high apse still looms over
the houses below, while a
Carolingian tower dominates
the entrance. Erected in the
4th century AD, it was rebuilt
after the invading Normans
set fire to the neighborhood
in 1084. Hidden within is the
garden of the delightful inner
cloister (admission on request),
one of the earliest of its kind,
built around 1220.
    The remains of medieval
frescoes can be seen in the
Chapel of Santa Barbara, but
the convent's main feature is
the Chapel of St. Sylvester –
its remarkable frescoes (1246)
recount the legend of the
conversion to Christianity of

the Emperor Constantine by
Pope Sylvester I (reigned 314–
35), then living as a hermit on
Monte Soratte, north of Rome.
    Stricken by the plague,
Constantine is prescribed a
bath in children's blood, to
the horror of the matrons of
Rome. Unable to bring himself
to obey, Constantine is
visited in a dream by St. Peter
and St. Paul. They advise him
to find Sylvester, who cures
him and baptizes him. The
final scene shows the emperor
kneeling before the pope.
The implied idea of the pope
as heir to the Roman Empire
would affect the whole course
of medieval European history.

San Clemente ⑫

See pp186–7.

Santo Stefano Rotondo ⑬

Via di Santo Stefano Rotondo 7.
Map 9 B2. 📞 *06-70 49 37 17.*
🚌 *81, 117, 673.* **Open** *9am–1pm,*
3.30pm–6pm (summer), 9am–noon,
2pm–4pm (winter). 📷

ONE OF ROME'S earliest
Christian churches, Santo
Stefano Rotondo was built
between 468 and 483. It has an
unusual circular plan with four
chapels in a cruciform. The

Distinctive circular outline
of Santo Stefano Rotondo

round inner area was
surrounded by concentric
corridors with 22 Ionic
supporting columns. The high
drum in the center is 72 ft (22
m) high and just as wide. It is
lit by 22 high windows, a few
of them restored or blocked by
restorations carried out under
Pope Nicholas V (reigned
1447–55), who consulted the
Florentine architect Leon
Battista Alberti. The archway in
the center of the church may
have been added during this
period, when the outer
corridor was eliminated.
    In the 16th century the
church walls were frescoed
by Niccolò Pomarancio, with
particularly gruesome
illustrations of the martyrdom
of innumerable saints. Some
of the medieval decor remains
in the chapels: in the first
chapel to the left of the
entrance is a 7th-century
mosaic of Christ with San
Primo and San Feliciano.

Fresco of St. Sylvester and Constantine in Santi Quattro Coronati

San Clemente ⓬

SAN CLEMENTE PROVIDES an opportunity to travel back through three layers of history. At street level, there is a 12th-century church; underneath this lies a 4th-century church; and below that are ancient Roman buildings, including a Temple of Mithras. Mithraism, an all-male fertility cult imported from Persia in the 1st century BC, was a rival to Christianity during the age of Imperial Rome.

The upper levels are dedicated to St. Clement, the fourth pope, who was exiled to the Crimea and martyred by being tied to an anchor and drowned. His life is illustrated in some of the frescoes in the 4th-century church. The site was taken over in the 17th century by Irish Dominicans, who still continue the excavating work begun by Father Mullooly in 1857.

Entrance to the church is through a door in Via di San Giovanni in Laterano.

Paschal Candlestick
This 12th-century spiraling candlestick, striped with glittering mosaic, is a magnificent example of Cosmati work.

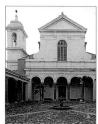

18th-Century Facade
Twelfth-century columns were used in the arcade.

★ **Cappella di Santa Caterina**
The restored frescoes by the 15th-century Florentine artist Masolino da Panicale show scenes from the life of the martyred St. Catherine of Alexandria.

12th-century church

4th-century church

Piscina
This deep pit was discovered in 1967. It could have been used as a font or fountain.

1st- to 3rd-century temple and buildings

TIMELINE

2nd century Site possibly used for secret Christian worship

Late 2nd century Temple of Mithras built

867 Reputed transfer of remains of San Clemente to Rome

1108 New church built over 4th-century church

1857 Original 4th-century church rediscovered by Father Mullooly

AD 10   500   1000   1500   1900

90–99 Papacy of St. Clement

4th century First church built over courtyard of earlier Roman building

1667 Church and convent given to Irish Dominicans

1084 Church destroyed during Norman invasion led by Robert Guiscard

AD 64 Nero's fire destroys area

1861 Church is excavated. Roman ruins discovered

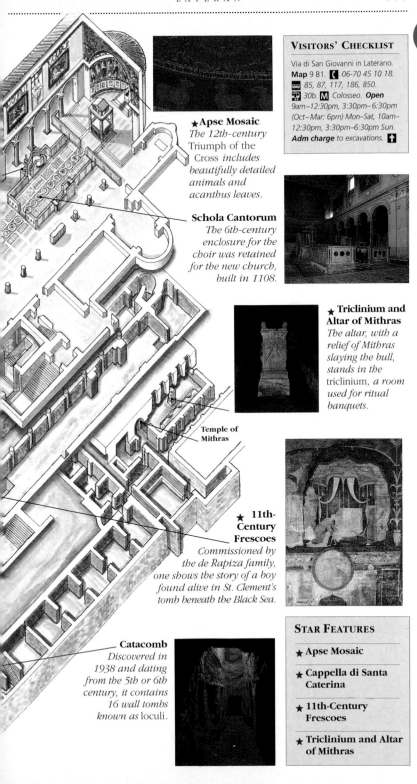

★**Apse Mosaic**
The 12th-century
Triumph of the
Cross *includes
beautifully detailed
animals and
acanthus leaves.*

Schola Cantorum
*The 6th-century
enclosure for the
choir was retained
for the new church,
built in 1108.*

**Temple of
Mithras**

★ **Triclinium and
Altar of Mithras**
*The altar, with a
relief of Mithras
slaying the bull,
stands in the
triclinium, a room
used for ritual
banquets.*

★ **11th-
Century
Frescoes**
*Commissioned by
the de Rapiza family,
one shows the story of a boy
found alive in St. Clement's
tomb beneath the Black Sea.*

Catacomb
*Discovered in
1938 and dating
from the 5th or 6th
century, it contains
16 wall tombs
known as* loculi.

Via di San Giovanni in Laterano.
Map 9 B1. ☎ *06-70 45 10 18.*
🚌 *85, 87, 117, 186, 850.*
🚋 *30b.* Ⓜ *Colosseo.* **Open**
*9am–12:30pm, 3:30pm–6:30pm
(Oct–Mar: 6pm) Mon–Sat, 10am–
12:30pm, 3:30pm–6:30pm Sun.*
Adm charge *to excavations.* ✝

★ **Apse Mosaic**

★ **Cappella di Santa
Caterina**

★ **11th-Century
Frescoes**

★ **Triclinium and Altar
of Mithras**

CARACALLA

THE CELIAN HILL over-looking the Colosseum takes its name from Caelius Vibenna, the legendary hero of Rome's struggle with the Tarquins *(see pp16–17)*. In Imperial Rome, this was a fashionable place to live, and some of its vanished splendor is still apparent in the vast ruins of the Baths of Caracalla. Today, thanks to the

Capital from ruins of Baths of Caracalla

Archaeological Zone established at the turn of the century, it is a delightfully peaceful area, a green wedge stretching from the Aurelian Wall to the heart of the city. Through it runs the cobbled Via di Porta San Sebastiano, part of the old Via Appia. It leads to Porta San Sebastiano, one of the best-preserved gates in the ancient city wall.

SIGHTS AT A GLANCE

Churches
Santi Giovanni e Paolo **1**
San Gregorio Magno **2**
Santa Maria in Domnica **4**
San Sisto Vecchio **6**
Santi Nereo e Achilleo **7**
San Cesareo **8**
San Giovanni a Porta Latina **9**
San Giovanni in Oleo **10**
Santa Balbina **16**

Arches and Gates
Arch of Dolabella **3**
Arch of Drusus **13**
Porta San Sebastiano and the Aurelian Wall **14**
Sangallo Bastion **15**

Historic Buildings
UN Food and Agriculture Organization **17**
Baths of Caracalla **18**

Tombs
Columbarium of Pomponius Hylas **11**
Tomb of the Scipios **12**

Parks and Gardens
Villa Celimontana **5**

GETTING THERE
Circo Massimo Metro station is handy if you are visiting the churches and parks on the Celian Hill. For the Baths of Caracalla and other sights closer to Porta San Sebastiano, take the 628 or 670 along Viale delle Terme di Caracalla.

SEE ALSO
• *Street Finder*, maps 8, 9
• *Where to Stay* pp294–5
• *Restaurants* pp310–11

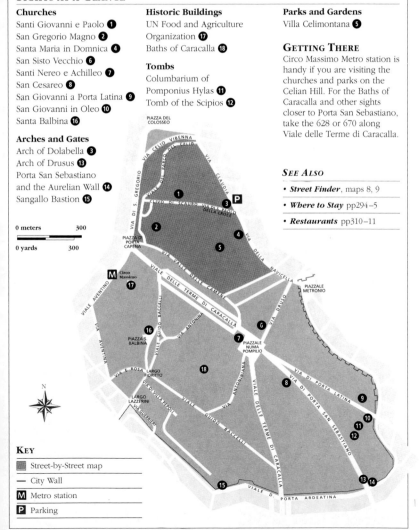

KEY

	Street-by-Street map
—	City Wall
M	Metro station
P	Parking

0 meters 300
0 yards 300

Mosaic of an athlete from the Baths of Caracalla

Street by Street: The Celian Hill

IN THE COURSE OF A MORNING exploring the green slopes of the Celian Hill, you will see a fascinating assortment of archaeological remains and beautiful churches. A good starting point is the church of San Gregorio Magno, from where the Clivo di Scauro leads up to the top of the hill. The steep narrow street passes the ancient porticoed church of Santi Giovanni e Paolo, with its beautiful Romanesque bell tower soaring above the surrounding medieval monastery buildings. Of the parks on the hill, the best-kept and most peaceful is the Villa Celimontana, with its formal walks and avenues. It is a good place for a picnic, because few bars or restaurants are nearby.

Clivo di Scauro, the Roman *Clivus Scauri*, leads up to Santi Giovanni e Paolo, passing under the flying buttresses that support the church.

VIA DI SAN GREGORIO

CLIVO DI SCAURO

La Vignola is a delightful Renaissance pavilion, reconstructed here in 1911 after it had been demolished during the creation of the Archaeological Zone around the Baths of Caracalla.

To Circo Massimo Metro

San Gregorio Magno
A monastery and a chapel were founded here by Pope Gregory the Great at the end of the 6th century ❷

★ **Santi Giovanni e Paolo**
The nave of the church, lit by a blaze of chandeliers, has been restored many times and assumed its present appearance in the 18th century ❶

★ **Villa Celimontana**
The delightful 16th-century villa built for the Mattei family is now the center of a public park ❺

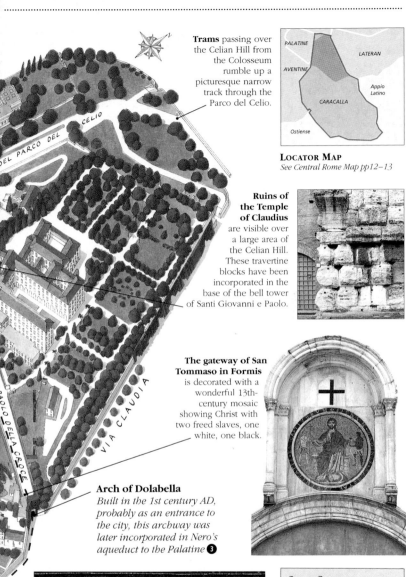

Trams passing over the Celian Hill from the Colosseum rumble up a picturesque narrow track through the Parco del Celio.

LOCATOR MAP
See Central Rome Map pp12–13

Ruins of the Temple of Claudius are visible over a large area of the Celian Hill. These travertine blocks have been incorporated in the base of the bell tower of Santi Giovanni e Paolo.

The gateway of San Tommaso in Formis is decorated with a wonderful 13th-century mosaic showing Christ with two freed slaves, one white, one black.

Arch of Dolabella
Built in the 1st century AD, probably as an entrance to the city, this archway was later incorporated in Nero's aqueduct to the Palatine ❸

★ **Santa Maria in Domnica**
This church is famed for its 9th-century mosaics. These Apostles appear on the triumphal arch above the apse, flanking a medallion containing the figure of Christ ❹

STAR SIGHTS

★ Santi Giovanni e Paolo

★ Santa Maria in Domnica

★ Villa Celimontana

KEY

– – – Suggested route

0 meters 75

0 yards 75

Santi Giovanni e Paolo ❶

Piazza Santi Giovanni e Paolo 13. **Map**
9 A1. 📞 *06-700 57 45.* 🚌 *75, 81,
175, 673.* 🚋 *30b.* Ⓜ *Colosseo or
Circo Massimo.* **Open** *8:30am–noon,
3:30pm–7pm (Oct–Mar: 6:30pm)
daily (for Roman House phone in adv).*
🚻 ♿ *church only.*

S ANTI GIOVANNI E PAOLO is
dedicated to two martyred
Roman officers whose house
stood on this site. Giovanni
(John) and Paolo (Paul) had
served the first Christian
emperor, Constantine. When
they were later called to arms
by the pagan emperor Julian
the Apostate, they refused
and were beheaded in their
own house in AD 362.

Built toward the end of the
4th century, the church
retains many elements of its
original structure. The Ionic
portico dates from the 12th
century, and the apse and bell
tower were added by
Nicholas Breakspeare, the
only English pope, who
reigned as Adrian IV (1154–59).
The base of the superb 13th-
century bell tower was part of
the Temple of Claudius
that stood on this site. In
common with many
Romanesque bell
towers, it has inlaid
marble and ceramic
roundels decorating
the brickwork.

The interior,
remodelled in 1718,
has granite piers and
columns. A tomb slab in the
nave marks the burial place of
the martyrs, whose relics are
preserved in an urn under the
high altar. In a tiny room near
the altar, a magnificent 13th-
century fresco depicts the
figure of Christ flanked by his
Apostles (ask the sacristan to
unlock the door for you).

Excavations beneath the
church have revealed two
Roman houses, of the 2nd and
3rd centuries, united and used
as a Christian burial place. The
two-story construction, with
20 rooms and a labyrinth of
corridors, has well-preserved
pagan and Christian paintings.
The arches to the left of the
church were part of a 3rd-
century street of shops.

Fresco of Christ and the Apostles in Santi Giovanni e Paolo

San Gregorio Magno ❷

Piazza di San Gregorio. **Map** 8 F2.
📞 *06-700 82 27.* 🚌 *75, 81, 175, 673.*
🚋 *30b.* Ⓜ *Circo Massimo.* **Open**
*8:30am–12:30pm, 1:45–6:30pm
daily.* 🚻

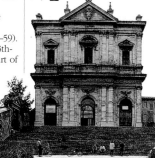

Facade of San Gregorio Magno

T O THE ENGLISH, this is one
of the most important
churches in Rome, for it was
from here that St. Augustine
was sent on his mission to
convert England to Christianity.
The church was founded in AD
575 by San Gregorio Magno (St.
Gregory the Great), who turned
his family home on this site into
a monastery. It was rebuilt in
medieval times and restored in
1629–33 by Giovanni Battista
Soria. The church is reached via
a flight of steps from the street.

The forecourt contains some
interesting tombs. To the left
is that of Sir Edward Carne,
who came to Rome several
times between 1529 and 1533
as King Henry VIII's envoy to
gain the pope's consent to the
annulment of Henry's marriage
to Catherine of Aragon.

The interior, remodeled by
Francesco Ferrari in the mid-
18th century, is Baroque, apart
for the fine mosaic floor and
some ancient columns. At the
end of the right aisle is the
chapel of St. Gregory. Leading
off it, another small chapel, believed to have been the saint's
own cell, houses his episcopal
throne – a Roman chair of
sculpted marble. The Salviati
Chapel on the left contains a
picture of the Virgin said to
have spoken to St. Gregory.

Outside, amid the cypresses
to the left of the church, stand
three small chapels, dedicated
to St. Andrew, St. Barbara and
St. Sylvia (Gregory the Great's
mother). Recently restored,
they contain frescoes by
Domenichino and Guido Reni.

**Marble throne of Gregory the Great
from the 1st century BC**

Arch of Dolabella ❸

Via di San Paolo della Croce.
Map 9 A2. 🚌 81, 117, 673.
🚃 30b. Ⓜ Colosseo.

THE ARCH was built in AD 10 by consuls Caius Junius Silanus and Cornelius Dolabella, possibly on the site of one of the old Servian Wall's gateways. It was made of travertine blocks and later used to support Nero's extension of the Claudian aqueduct, built to supply the Imperial palace on the Palatine hill.

The restored Arch of Dolabella

Santa Maria in Domnica ❹

Piazza della Navicella 12. **Map** 9 A2.
📞 06-700 15 19. 🚌 81, 117, 673.
🚃 30b. Ⓜ Colosseo. **Open**
9am–noon, 3:30pm–7pm (Oct–Mar:
6pm) daily. 🕇 ♿

THE CHURCH overlooks the Piazza della Navicella (little boat) and takes its name from the 16th-century fountain.

Dating from the 7th century, the church was made from an ancient stone galley, which was probably a temple offering of a Roman traveler for his safe return to the city. In the 16th century Pope Leo X added the portico and the coffered ceiling.

In the apse behind the modern altar is a superb 9th-century mosaic commissioned by Pope Paschal I. Wearing the square halo of the living, the Pope appears at the feet of the Virgin and Child. The Virgin, surrounded by a throng of angels, holds a handkerchief in the manner of a fashionable lady at a Byzantine court.

Villa Celimontana ❺

Piazza della Navicella. **Map** 9 A2.
🚌 81, 117, 673. **Park open**
7am–dusk daily.

THE DUKES OF MATTEI bought this land in 1553 and transformed the vineyards that covered the hillside into a formal garden. As well as palms and other exotic trees, the garden even has its own Egyptian obelisk. Villa Mattei, built in the 1580s, is now known as Villa Celimontana and houses the Italian Geographical Society.

The Mattei family used to open the park to the public on the day of the Visit of the Seven Churches, an annual event instituted by San Filippo Neri in 1552. Starting from the Chiesa Nuova (see p124), Romans went on foot to the city's seven major churches.

When they reached Villa Mattei, they were given a meal of bread, wine, salami, cheese, an egg and two apples. The garden, now owned by the city of Rome, still makes an ideal place for a picnic.

Park of Villa Celimontana

San Sisto Vecchio ❻

Piazzale Numa Pompilio 8.
Map 9 A3. 📞 06-77 20 51 74.
🚌 628, 760, 714. **Open** by appt
only. **Closed** Aug. 📷

THIS SMALL CHURCH is of great historical interest, for it was granted to St. Dominic in 1219 by Pope Honorius III. The founder of the Dominican order soon moved his own headquarters to Santa Sabina (see p204), San Sisto becoming the first home of the order of Dominican nuns. The church with its 13th-century bell tower and frescoes, is also a popular church for weddings.

Apse mosaic of the Virgin and Child in Santa Maria in Domnica

Santi Nereo e Achilleo 🕖

Via delle Terme di Caracalla 28.
Map 9 A3. 📞 *06-575 79 96.*
🚌 *160, 628, 760.* **Open** *10am–noon, 4pm–6pm Sat–Thu.* ♿

ACCORDING to legend, St. Peter, after escaping from prison, was fleeing the city when he lost a bandage from his wounds. The original church was founded here in the 4th century on the spot where the bandage fell, but later it was rededicated to the 1st-century martyrs St.

Detail of mosaic, Santi Nereo e Achilleo

Nereus and St. Achilleus.
  Restored at the end of the 16th century, the church has retained many medieval features, including some fine 9th-century mosaics on the triumphal arch. A magnificent pulpit rests on an enormous porphyry pedestal that was found nearby in the Baths of Caracalla. The walls of the side naves are decorated with a series of rather grisly 16th-century frescoes by Niccolò Pomarancio, showing in clinical detail how each of the Apostles was martyred.

Fresco by Niccolò Pomarancio of the *Martyrdom of St. Simon* in Santi Nereo e Achilleo

San Cesareo 🕗

Via di Porta San Sebastiano. **Map** 9 A3. 📞 *06-58 23 01 40.* **Open** *by appointment 9am–1pm Sun.*

THIS SPLENDID old church, built over Roman ruins of the 2nd century AD, has been closed since 1988. You can still admire Giacomo della Porta's fine Renaissance facade, but by phoning ahead to book a visit, you can also see Cosmatesque mosaic work and carving to rival that of any church in Rome. The episcopal throne, altar and pulpit are decorated with delightful birds and beasts. The church was restored in the 16th century by Pope Clement VIII, whose coat of arms decorates the ceiling.

San Giovanni a Porta Latina 🕘

Via di San Giovanni a Porta Latina.
Map 9 B3. 📞 *06-70 49 17 77.*
🚌 *4, 218, 628.* **Open** *7am–noon, 3–7pm daily.* ✝ ♿

THE CHURCH of "St. John at the Latin Gate" was founded in the 5th century, rebuilt in 720 and restored in 1191. This is one of the most picturesque of the old Roman churches. Classical columns support the medieval portico, and the 12th-century bell tower is superb. A tall cedar tree shades an ancient well standing in the forecourt. The interior has recently been restored, but it preserves the rare simplicity of its early origins, with ancient columns of varying styles lining the aisles. Traces of early medieval frescoes can still be seen. There are 12th-century frescoes

showing 46 different biblical scenes from both the Old and New Testaments, which are among the finest of their kind in Rome.

Fresco, San Giovanni a Porta Latina

San Giovanni in Oleo 🕙

Via di Porta Latina. **Map** 9 C4. 🚌 *4.*
Adm *ask at S. Giovanni a Porta Latina.*

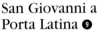

Frieze of San Giovanni in Oleo

THE NAME of this charming octagonal Renaissance chapel means "St. John in Oil." The tiny building marks the spot where, according to legend, St. John was boiled in oil – and came out unscathed, or even refreshed. An earlier chapel is said to have existed on the site; the present one was built in the early 16th century. The design has been attributed to Baldassare Peruzzi or Antonio da Sangallo the Younger. It was restored by Borromini, who altered the roof, crowning it with a cross supported by a sphere decorated with roses. He also added a terra-cotta frieze of roses and palm leaves. The wall paintings inside the chapel include one of St. John in a cauldron of boiling oil.

Niches for funerary urns in the Columbarium of Pomponius Hylas

Columbarium of Pomponius Hylas ⑪

Via di Porta Latina 10. **Map** 9 B4.
🚌 4, 218, 628. **Open** by appt only:
permit needed (see p 367).

KNOWN AS a columbarium because it resembles a dovecote (*columba* is the Latin word for dove), this kind of vaulted tomb was normally built by rich Romans to house the cremated remains of their freedmen. Many similar tombs have been uncovered in this part of Rome, which up until the 3rd century AD lay outside the city wall. This one, excavated in 1831, dates from the 1st century AD. An inscription informs us that it

Mosaic inscription in the Columbarium of Pomponius Hylas

is the Tomb of Pomponius Hylas and his wife, Pomponia Vitalinis. Above her name is a "V," which indicates that she was still living when the inscription was made. The tomb was probably a commercial venture. Niches in the interior walls of the columbarium were sold to people who could not afford to build vaults of their own.

Tomb of the Scipios ⑫

Via di Porta San Sebastiano 9.
Map 9 B4. 📞 06-70 49 00 53.
🚌 218. **Closed** for restoration.

THE SCIPIOS were a family of conquering generals. Southern Italy, Corsica, Algeria, Spain and Asia Minor all fell to their victorious Roman armies. The most famous of these generals was Publius Cornelius Scipio Africanus, who defeated the great Carthaginian general Hannibal at the Battle of Zama in 202 BC (see p21). Scipio Africanus himself was not buried here in the family tomb, but at Liternum near Naples, where he owned a favorite villa.

The Tomb of the Scipios was discovered in 1780. It contained various sarcophagi,

statues and niches with terracotta burial urns. Many of the originals have now been moved to the Vatican Museums, and copies stand in their place.

The earliest sarcophagus was that of Cornelius Scipio Barbatus, consul in 298 BC, for whom the tomb was built. Members of his illustrious family continued to be buried here up to the middle of the 2nd century BC. Excavations in the area have revealed many other archaeological finds: a columbarium similar to that of Pomponius Hylas, a Christian catacomb and a three-story house dating from the 3rd century AD, which was built over the Tomb of the Scipios.

Arch of Drusus ⑬

Via di Porta San Sebastiano.
Map 9 B4. 🚌 218.

Arch of Drusus, part of the Aqua Antoniniana aqueduct

ONCE MISTAKENLY identified as a triumphal arch, the Arch of Drusus merely supported the branch aqueduct that supplied the Baths of Caracalla. It was built in the 3rd century AD and so had no connection with Drusus, a stepson of the Emperor Augustus. Monumental in size, it supported the aqueduct across the important main route, Via Appia. The arch still spans right over the old cobbled road, just 160 ft (50 m) short of the well-known gateway Porta San Sebastiano.

Fortified gateway of Porta San Sebastiano

Porta San Sebastiano and the Aurelian Wall ⑭

Museo delle Mura, Via di Porta San Sebastiano 18. **Map** 9 B4. 🚌 *218.*
📞 *06-70 47 52 84.* **Open** *9am–7pm Tue–Sun (last adm: 30 mins before closing).* **Closed** *public hols.* **Adm charge.** ⌀

Most of the Aurelian Wall, begun by the Emperor Aurelian (AD 270–75) and completed by his successor, Probus (AD 276–82), has survived. Aurelian ordered its construction as a defense against marauding Germanic tribes, whose raids were penetrating deeper and deeper into Italy. Some 11 miles (18 km) round, with 18 gates and 381 towers, the wall took in all the seven hills of Rome. It was raised to almost twice its original height by Maxentius (AD 306–12).

Porta San Sebastiano, the gate that leads to the Via Appia Antica *(see p284)* is the largest and best-preserved gateway. It was rebuilt by the Emperor Honorius in the 5th century AD. Originally the Porta Appia, in Christian times it gradually became known as the Porta San Sebastiano, because the Via Appia led to the Basilica and Catacombs of San Sebastiano, which were popular places of pilgrimage.

It was at this gate that the last triumphal procession to enter the city by the Appian Way was received in state – that of Marcantonio Colonna after the victory of Lepanto over the Turkish fleet in 1571. Today the gate's towers house a museum containing prints and models illustrating the walls' history. From here you can take a short walk along the restored walls. The views are spectacular, especially out over the Via Appia.

The wall continued to be Rome's main defense until 1870, when it was breached by Italian artillery just by Porta Pia, close to today's British Embassy. Many of the gates are still in use, and although the city has spread, most of its noteworthy historical and cultural sights still lie within the walls.

Sangallo Bastion ⑮

Viale di Porta Ardeatina. **Map** 9 A4.
🚌 *160, 218, 671, 714.* **Closed** *for restoration.*

Pope Paul III Farnese

Haunted by the memory of the Sack of Rome in 1527 and fearing attack by the Turks, Pope Paul III asked Antonio da Sangallo the Younger to reinforce the Aurelian Wall. Work on the huge projecting bastion began in 1537. For the moment its massive bulk can be admired only from outside.

Santa Balbina ⑯

Piazza di Santa Balbina 8. **Map** 8 F3.
📞 *06-578 02 07.* 🚌 *81, 160, 175, 628, 673.* 🚋 *30b.* Ⓜ *Circo Massimo.*
Open *8am–6pm daily.* ✝

Overlooking the Baths of Caracalla, this isolated church framed by cypresses is dedicated to Santa Balbina, a 2nd-century virgin martyr. Dating back to the 4th century, this is one of the city's oldest churches. Inside stands the magnificent sculpted and inlaid tomb of Cardinal Stefanus de Surdis, signed by Giovanni di Cosma (1303).

UN Food and Agriculture Organization ⑰

Viale delle Terme di Caracalla.
Map 8 F2. 🚌 *81, 160, 175, 628, 673.* 🚋 *30b.* Ⓜ *Circo Massimo.*
Not open *to public.*

Obelisk of Axum (4th century AD)

The food and Agriculture Organization of the United Nations is based here in a modern building completed in 1952. Before it stands the obelisk of Axum, looted from Ethiopia by Mussolini, who originally commissioned the building to house the Ministry of Italian Africa.

Baths of Caracalla ⑱

Viale delle Terme di Caracalla 52.
Map 9 A3. 06-575 86 26. 81, 160, 175, 628, 673. 30b. M Circo Massimo. **Open** Apr–Sep: 9am–6pm; Oct–Mar: 9am–1pm. **Closed** Jan 1, May 1, Dec 25. **Adm charge**.

COMPLETED by the Emperor Caracalla in AD 217, the baths functioned for about 300 years, until the "plumbing" was destroyed by invading Goths. Over 1,600 bathers at a time could enjoy the facilities. A Roman bath was a long and complicated business, beginning with a sort of Turkish bath, followed by a spell in the *calidarium*, a large, hot room with pools of water to moisten the atmosphere. Then came the lukewarm *tepidarium*, a visit to the large central meeting place, known as the *frigidarium*, and finally a plunge into the *natatio*, an open-air swimming

Part of one of the gymnasia in the Baths of Caracalla

pool. For the rich, this was followed by a rubdown with scented woolen cloths. In addition to the baths, there were spaces for exercise, libraries, art galleries and gardens – creating a true leisure center. Most of the rich marble decorations of the baths were removed by the Farnese family in the 16th century to adorn the interior of Palazzo Farnese *(see p147)*.

Fragment of mosaic pavement

Until recently, open-air operas were staged here – the vocal exertions of the performers are now thought to pose a threat to the structure of this ancient monument.

KEY

- Calidarium (very hot)
- Tepidarium (lukewarm)
- Frigidarium (cold)
- Natatio (pool)
- Garden

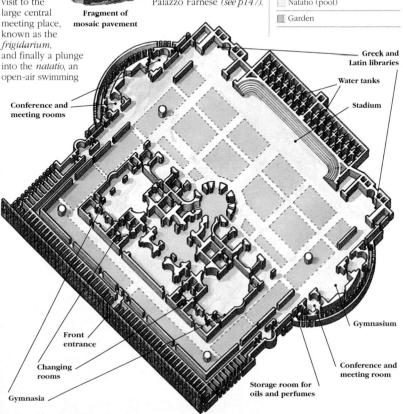

Greek and Latin libraries

Water tanks

Stadium

Conference and meeting rooms

Gymnasium

Front entrance

Changing rooms

Conference and meeting room

Storage room for oils and perfumes

Gymnasia

AVENTINE

THIS IS ONE of the most peaceful areas within the walls of the city. Although it is largely residential, there are some unique historic sights. From the top of the Aventine Hill, crowned by the magnificent basilica of Santa Sabina, there are exceptional views across the river to Trastevere and St. Peter's. At the

Mask fountain in courtyard of Santa Sabina

foot of the hill, ancient Rome is preserved in the two small Temples of the Forum Boarium and the Circus Maximus. The liveliest streets are in Testaccio, with its many stores, restaurants and clubs, while to the south, beside Rome's solitary pyramid, the Protestant Cemetery is a lovely oasis of calm.

SIGHTS AT A GLANCE

Churches and Temples
Santa Maria in Cosmedin ❶
San Giorgio in Velabro ❸
San Teodoro ❹
Santa Maria della Consolazione ❺
San Giovanni Decollato ❻
Temples of the Forum Boarium ❽
Santa Sabina ❾
Santi Bonifacio e Alessio ❿
San Saba ⓯

Historic Buildings
Casa dei Crescenzi ❼

Arches
Arch of Janus ❷

Historic Streets and Piazzas
Piazza dei Cavalieri di Malta ⓫

Ancient Sites
Monte Testaccio ⓬
Circus Maximus ⓰

Monuments and Tombs
Protestant Cemetery ⓭
Pyramid of Caius Cestius ⓮

GETTING THERE
The quickest way is by Metro line B to Piramide or Circo Massimo. For a more interesting trip, take a tram – the 30b. Several buses go down Viale Aventino to Piramide, and the 23, 81, 160, 628 and 810 all travel up Aventine Hill.

KEY

▨	Street-by-Street map
—	City Wall
Ⓜ	Metro station
Ⓟ	Parking

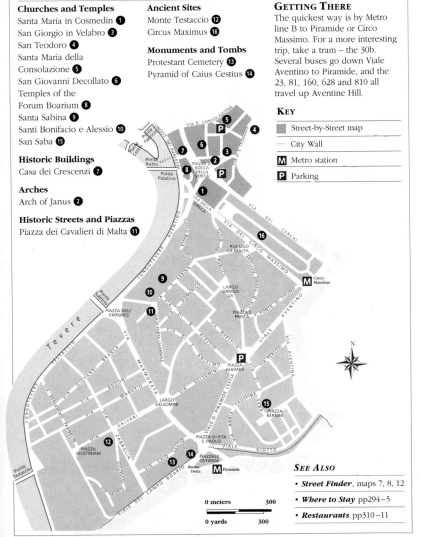

SEE ALSO
• **Street Finder**, maps 7, 8, 12
• **Where to Stay** pp294–5
• **Restaurants** pp310–11

Pines and orange trees on the Aventine Hill with dome of St. Peter's in the distance

Street by Street: Piazza della Bocca della Verità

THE AREA ATTRACTS VISITORS eager to place their hands inside the Bocca della Verità (the Mouth of Truth) in the portico of Santa Maria in Cosmedin. There are many other sights to see in this quiet corner of the city beside the Tiber, which was the site of ancient Rome's first port and its busy cattle market. Substantial Classical remains include two small temples from the Republican age and the Arch of Janus from the later Empire. In the 6th century, the area became home to a Greek community from Byzantium, who founded the churches of San Giorgio in Velabro and Santa Maria in Cosmedin.

Sant'Omobono, a late 16th-century church, now stands in isolation in the middle of an important archaeological site. The remains of sacrificial altars and two temples from the 6th century BC have been discovered.

Casa dei Crescenzi
This 11th-century building used columns and capitals from ancient Roman temples ❼

Ponte Rotto, as this forlorn ruined arch in the Tiber is called, means simply "broken bridge." It was built in the 2nd century BC, and originally named the Pons Aemilius.

★ Temples of the Forum Boarium
The tiny round Temple of Hercules and its neighbor, the Temple of Portunus, are the best preserved of Rome's Republican temples ❽

PONTE PALATINO

LUNGOTEVERE DEI PIERLEONI

TEVERE

KEY

– – – Suggested route

0 meters 75

0 yards 75

★ Santa Maria in Cosmedin
This medieval church has a mosaic floor and a Gothic altar canopy ❶

Santa Maria della Consolazione
This 16th-century church used to serve a hospital nearby **5**

San Teodoro
The 15th-century portal of this ancient round church is decorated with the arms of Pope Nicholas V **4**

LOCATOR MAP
See Central Rome Map pp12–13

San Giovanni Decollato
The plain Renaissance facade was completed in about 1504 **6**

San Giorgio in Velabro
The simple 12th-century portico of Ionic columns was destroyed by a bomb in 1993 but has been restored **3**

Arch of Janus
This square structure with arches on each side dates from the 4th century AD **2**

The Arco degli Argentari, dedicated to the Emperor Septimius Severus in AD 204, is decorated with scenes of religion and war.

The Fontana dei Tritoni by Carlo Bizzaccheri was built here in 1715. The style shows the powerful influence of Bernini.

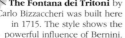

Bocca della Verità

Santa Maria in Cosmedin **❶**

Piazza della Bocca della Verità 18.
Map 8 E1. **(** 06-678 14 19. ▦ *23, 44, 75, 81, 160, 175, 280, 628, 715.*
Open *9am–1pm, 2.30pm–6pm (5pm winter) daily. (Phone to check first).*

T HIS BEAUTIFUL unadorned church was built in the 6th century on the site of the ancient city's food market. The elegant Romanesque bell tower and portico were added during the 12th century. In the 19th century a Baroque facade was removed and the church restored to its original simplicity. It contains many fine examples of Cosmati work, in particular the mosaic pavement, the raised choir, the bishop's throne and the canopy over the main altar.

Set into the wall of the portico is the Bocca della Verità (Mouth of Truth). This may have been a drain cover dating from before the 4th century BC. Medieval tradition had it that the formidable jaws would snap shut over the hands of those who told lies – a useful trick for testing the faithfulness of spouses.

Arch of Janus **❷**

Via del Velabro. **Map** 8 E1. ▦ *23, 44, 75, 81, 160, 175, 280, 628, 715.*

P ROBABLY DATING from the reign of Constantine, this imposing four-faced marble arch stood at the bustling crossroads on the edge of the Forum Boarium, near the ancient docks. Merchants and customers did business in its shade. On the keystones above the four arches you can see small figures of the goddesses Roma, Juno, Ceres and Minerva. In medieval times the arch used to form the base of a tower fortress. It was restored to its original shape in 1827.

San Giorgio in Velabro **❸**

Via del Velabro 19. **Map** 8 E1.
(06-683 29 30. ▦ *23, 44, 75, 81, 160, 175, 280, 628, 715.* **Open** *10am–12.30pm, 4.30–7pm Tue–Fri.*

San Giorgio in Velabro after its restoration in 1999

I N THE HOLLOW of the street named after the Velabrum, the swamp where Romulus and Remus are said to have been found by the she-wolf, is a small church dedicated to St. George, whose bones lie under the altar.

The 7th-century basilica has suffered over the centuries from periodic floods, and in 1993 a bomb caused extensive damage to the front of the church. Careful restoration has however returned it to its original appearance.

A double row of assorted granite and marble columns (taken from ancient Roman temples) divide the triple nave. The austerity of the cool grey interior is relieved by golden frescoes in the apse (attributed to Pietro Cavallini, 1295). The facade and the bell tower date from the 12th century.

San Teodoro **❹**

Via di San Teodoro. **Map** 8 E1.
(06-678 66 24. ▦ *81, 95, 160, 175, 204, 628.* **Open** *9.30am–6.30pm daily (to 5.30pm in winter).*

I F YOU HAPPEN to be in the area on a Sunday morning, you will find this small round 6th-century church at the foot of the Palatine a truly delightful place to visit for a weekly mass. Inside, the 6th-century mosaics in the apse are breathtaking, as is the Florentine cupola (1454). The fetching outer courtyard was designed by Carlo Fontana in 1705.

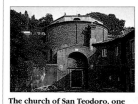

The church of San Teodoro, one of Rome's hidden treasures

The Arch of Janus, where cattle dealers sheltered from the midday sun

Facade of Santa Maria della Consolazione

Santa Maria della Consolazione ⑤

Piazza della Consolazione 84.
Map 5 A5. ☎ 06-678 46 54.
🚌 44, 81, 95, 160, 170, 628, 715.
Open 6am– noon, 3.30pm–6.30pm
(6pm winter) daily. ✝ ♿

THE CHURCH STANDS near the foot of the Tarpeian Rock, the site of numerous public executions since the time of the Sabine War.

In 1385, Giordanello degli Alberini, a condemned nobleman, paid two gold florins for an image of the Virgin Mary to be placed here, to provide some consolation to prisoners in their final moments. From this came the name of the church built here in 1470. It was reconstructed between 1583 and 1606 by Martino Longhi, who provided the early Baroque facade.

The church's 11 side chapels are owned by noble families and local crafts guild members. In the presbytery is the famed image of Mary attributed to Antoniazzo Romano.

San Giovanni Decollato ⑥

Via di San Giovanni Decollato 22.
Map 8 E1. ☎ 06-699 07 28.
🚌 44, 81, 95, 160, 170, 628, 715.
Open by appointment only.

THE MAIN ALTAR is dominated by Giorgio Vasari's *Beheading of St. John* (1553), from which the church takes its name, San Giovanni

Decollato. In 1490, Pope Innocent VIII gave this church site to a very specialized Florentine fraternal order. Ghoulishly attired in black robes and hoods, their task was to encourage condemned prisoners to repent and to give them a decent burial after they had been hanged. In the cloisters are seven manholes (one is reserved for women), which received the bodies.

The oratory contains a cycle of frescoes describing the life of St. John the Baptist, by the leading Florentine Mannerists Jacopino del Conte and Francesco Salviati. In style, the figures resemble some of those in the Sistine Chapel.

Casa dei Crescenzi ⑦

Via Luigi Petroselli. **Map** 8 E1.
🚌 44, 81, 95, 160, 170, 628, 715.

STUDDED WITH archaeological fragments, the house is what remains of a 12th-century tower fortress. It was built by the powerful Crescenzi family so they could see both the old docks of Rome (today the site of the Anagrafe or Public Records Office) and the bridge where the family collected a toll.

Ancient Roman fragments in the Casa dei Crescenzi

Temples of the Forum Boarium ⑧

Piazza della Bocca della Verità. **Map** 8 E1. 🚌 44, 81, 95, 160, 170, 628, 715.

Temple of Portunus

THESE MIRACULOUSLY well preserved Republican temples, set in a grassy enclave under the umbrella pines beside the Tiber, are particularly appealing by moonlight. They date from the 2nd century BC and were saved for posterity when they were reconsecrated as Christian churches in the Middle Ages. They offer rare examples of combined elements from Greek and Roman architecture.

The rectangular temple (formerly known as the Temple of Fortuna Virilis) was in fact dedicated to Portunus, the god of rivers and ports – a reference to the nearby port of ancient Rome. Set on a podium, the temple has four Ionic travertine columns fluted at the front and 12 pilasters, embedded in the tufa wall of the *cella* – the room that housed the image of the god. Nearby is the small circular Temple of Hercules. It is often referred to as the Temple of Vesta because of its similarity to the one in the Forum.

Luminous interior of Santa Sabina

Santa Sabina **9**

Piazza Pietro d'Illiria 1. **Map** 8 E2. **C** 06-574 35 73. **H** 23, 44, 81, 95, 160, 170, 628. **M** Circo Massimo. **Open** 10am–noon, 3:30–6pm daily. **&**

H IGH ON the Aventine stands an early Christian basilica, founded by Peter of Illyria in AD 425 and restored to its original simplicity in the early 20th century. Light filters through 9th-century windows onto a wide nave framed by white Corinthian columns supporting an arcade decorated with a marble frieze. Over the main door is a 5th-century blue and gold mosaic dedicatory inscription. The pulpit, carved choir and bishop's throne are from the 9th century.

The church was given to the Dominicans in the 13th century and in the nave is the magnificent mosaic tombstone of one of the first leaders of the order, Muñoz de Zamora (died 1300).

The side portico has 5th-century paneled doors carved from cypress wood, representing scenes from the Bible, including one of the earliest crucifixions in existence.

Santi Bonifacio e Alessio **10**

Piazza di Sant'Alessio 23. **Map** 8 D2. **C** 06-574 34 46. **H** 23, 44, 81, 95, 160, 170, 628, 715. **M** Circo Massimo. **Open** 8:30am–noon, 3:30–6:30pm (Nov–Mar: 5pm) daily. **&** ·

T HE CHURCH is dedicated to two early Christian martyrs, whose remains lie under the main altar. Legend has it that

Alessio, son of a rich senator living on the site, fled to the East to become a pilgrim and avoid an impending marriage. Returning home after many years, he died as a servant, unrecognized, under the stairs of the family entrance hall, clutching the manuscript of his story for posterity.

The original 5th-century church has undergone substantial changes over the centuries. Noteworthy are the 18th-century facade, with its five arches; the restored Cosmati doorway and pavement; and the magnificent Romanesque five-story bell tower (1217). An 18th-century Baroque chapel by Andrea Bergondi houses part of the famous staircase. Other relics include the well from Alessio's family home and the glowing Byzantine Madonna of the Intercession, brought to Rome from Damascus at the end of the 10th century.

Piazza dei Cavalieri di Malta **11**

Map 8 D2. **H** 23, 44, 81, 95, 160, 170, 628. **M** Circo Massimo.

S URROUNDED BY cypress trees, this ornate walled piazza decorated with obelisks and military trophies was designed by Piranesi in 1765. It is named after the Order of the Knights of Malta (Cavalieri di Malta) whose priory (at No. 3) is famous for the bronze keyhole through which there is a miniature view of St. Peter's, framed by a tree-lined avenue. The priory church, Santa Maria del Priorato, was restored in Neoclassical style by Piranesi in the 18th century. To visit the church ask permission in person at the Order's building at 48 Via Condotti. At the southwest corner of the square is Sant'Anselmo, the

international Benedictine church, where Gregorian chants may be heard on Sundays at 9:30am.

Doorway of the Priory of the Knights of Malta

Monte Testaccio **12**

Via Galvani. **Map** 8 D4. **H** 23, 44, 75, 280. **P** 30b. **Not open** to the public.

F ROM ABOUT 140 BC to AD 250, this hill was created by the dumping of millions of testae (hence Testaccio) – fragments of the amphorae used to carry goods to the nearby warehouses. The artificial hill is 120 ft (36 m) high, but its full archaeological significance was not realized until the late 18th century.

Facade of Santi Bonifacio e Alessio

Protestant Cemetery ⓭

Cimitero Acattolico, Via Caio Cestio 6. **Map** 8 D4. [C] *06-574 19 00.* 🚌 *23, 280, 716.* 🚊 *30b.* Ⓜ *Piramide.* **Open** *9am–6pm (Oct–Mar: 5pm) Tue–Sun (last adm: 30 mins before closing).* **Donation** *expected.* 🚻

Tᴴᴇ ᴘᴇᴀᴄᴇ of this well-tended cemetery beneath the Aurelian Wall is profoundly moving. Non-Catholics, mainly English and German, have been buried here since 1738.

In the oldest part are the graves of John Keats (died 1821 – his epitaph reads: "Here lies One Whose Name was writ in Water"), and his friend Joseph Severn (died 1879); not far away are the ashes of Percy Bysshe Shelley (died 1822). Goethe's son, Julius, is also buried here.

Tombstone of John Keats

Pyramid of Caius Cestius ⓮

Piazzale Ostiense. **Map** 8 E4. 🚌 *23, 280.* 🚊 *30b.* Ⓜ *Piramide.*

Detail of carving on sarcophagus in the portico of San Saba

Memorial pyramid of Caius Cestius

Cᴀɪᴜs ᴄᴇsᴛɪᴜs, a wealthy *praetor* (senior Roman magistrate), died in 12 BC. His one claim to fame is his tomb, an imposing pyramid faced in white marble set in the Aurelian Wall near Porta San Paolo. It stands 118 ft (36 m) high and, according to an inscription, took 330 days to build. Unmistakable as a landmark, it must have looked almost as incongruous when it was built as it does today.

San Saba ⓯

Via di San Saba. **Map** 8 F3. [C] *06-574 33 52.* 🚌 *75, 673.* 🚊 *30b.* **Open** *7am–noon, 4–7pm daily.* 🚻

Tᴜᴄᴋᴇᴅ ᴀᴡᴀʏ in a residential street on the Little Aventine Hill, San Saba began life as an oratory for Palestinian monks fleeing from Arab invasions in the 7th century. The existing church dates from the 10th century and has undergone much restoration. The portico houses a fascinating collection of archaeological remains.

The church has three naves in the Greek style and a short fourth 11th-century nave with vestiges of 13th-century frescoes of the life of St. Nicholas of Bari. Particularly intriguing is a scene of three naked young ladies laying in bed; they are saved from penury by the gift of a bag of gold from St. Nicholas, the future Santa Claus. The beautiful marble inlay in the main door, the floor and the remains of the choir are all 13th-century Cosmati work.

Circus Maximus ⓰

Via del Circo Massimo. **Map** 8 F2. 🚌 *75, 81, 160, 175, 628, 715, 716.* 🚊 *30b.* Ⓜ *Circo Massimo.*

Wʜᴀᴛ ᴡᴀs ᴏɴᴄᴇ ancient Rome's largest stadium is today little more than a long grassy esplanade. Set in the valley between the Palatine and Aventine hills, the Circus Maximus was continually embellished and expanded from the 4th century BC until AD 549, when the last races were held. The grandstands held some 300,000 spectators, cheering wildly at the horse and chariot races, athletic contests and animal fights, and betting furiously throughout.

The Circus had a central dividing barrier *(spina)* with seven large egg-shaped objects on it used for counting the laps of a race. These were joined in 33 BC by seven bronze dolphins that served a similar purpose. In 10 BC, Augustus built the Imperial box under the Palatine and decorated the *spina* with the obelisk that now stands in the center of Piazza del Popolo *(see p137)*. A second obelisk, which was added in the 4th century by Constantius II, is now in Piazza di San Giovanni in Laterano *(see pp178–9)*.

Reconstruction of the Circus Maximus in its heyday

TRASTEVERE

T**HE PROUD** and aggressively independent inhabitants of Trastevere, the area "across the Tiber", consider themselves the most authentic Romans. In one of the most picturesque old quarters of the city, it is still possible to glimpse scenes of everyday life that seem to belong to bygone centuries. There are, however, signs that much of the earthy, proletarian character of the place may soon be destroyed by the proliferation of fashionable restau-

Romanesque bell tower

rants, clubs and boutiques. Some of Rome's most fascinating medieval churches lie hidden away in the patchwork of narrow, cobbled backstreets, the only clue to their location an occasional glimpse of a Romanesque bell tower. Santa Cecilia was built on the site of the martyrdom of the patron saint of music, San Francesco a Ripa commemorates St. Francis of Assisi's visit to Rome, and Santa Maria in Trastevere is the traditional center of the spiritual and social life of the area.

SIGHTS AT A GLANCE

Churches
Santa Maria della Scala ❸
Santa Maria in Trastevere pp212–13 ❺
San Crisogono ❻
Santa Cecilia in Trastevere ❽
San Francesco a Ripa ❿

Museums and Galleries
Sant'Egidio and Museo del Folklore ❹

Historic Buildings
Casa della Fornarina ❶
Caserma dei Vigili della VII Coorte ❼
San Michele a Ripa Grande ❾

Bridges
Ponte Sisto ❷

Parks and Gardens
Villa Sciarra ⓫

SEE ALSO
• *Street Finder*, maps 4, 7, 8, 11
• *Where to Stay* pp294–5
• *Restaurants* pp310–11
• *Tiber Walk* pp274–5

KEY

	Street-by-Street map
—	City Wall
P	Parking

GETTING THERE
The most convenient way is to take tram 8 which starts from Largo di Torre Argentina, crosses the river and go along the broad, busy Viale di Trastevere. The H bus follows the same route but starts at Stazione Termini. From the Vatican it is best to take a 23 or 280 along Lungotevere. The 44 and 75 cross over to Trastevere at Porta Portese and run along Via Dandolo.

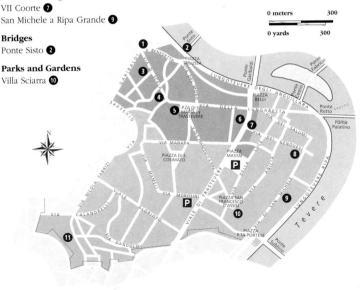

A typical *vicolo* (narrow alleyway) between the densely packed buildings of Trastevere

Street-by-Street: Trastevere

ALL YEAR ROUND TRASTEVERE is a major attraction both for its restaurants, clubs and cinemas, and for its picturesque maze of narrow cobbled alleyways. On summer evenings the streets are packed with jostling groups of pleasure seekers, especially during the noisy local festival, the Festa de Noantri *(see p59)*. Everywhere café and restaurant tables spill out over pavements, especially around Piazza di Santa Maria in Trastevere and outside the pizzerias along Viale di Trastevere. There are also kiosks selling slices of watermelon and *grattacbecca*, a mixture of syrup and grated ice. It is usually easier to appreciate the antique charm of Trastevere's narrow streets in the more tranquil atmosphere of the early morning.

Casa della Fornarina
Raphael's beautiful mistress is said to have lived here. There is now a flourishing restaurant in the back garden ❶

Santa Maria dei Sette Dolori
This church (1643) is a minor work by Borromini

Santa Maria della Scala
The church's unassuming facade conceals a rich Baroque interior ❸

Sant'Egidio and Museo del Folklore
This 17th-century fresco of Sant' Egidio by Pomarancio decorates the left-hand chapel in the church. The convent next door is a museum of Roman life and customs ❹

★ **Santa Maria in Trastevere**
The church is famous for its mosaics by Pietro Cavallini but it also has earlier works such as this mosaic of the prophet Isaiah to the left of the apse ❺

STAR SIGHTS

★ Santa Maria in Trastevere

KEY

‒ ‒ ‒ Suggested route

0 meters   75

0 yards   75

The fountain of Piazza di Santa Maria in Trastevere by Carlo Fontana (1692) is a popular meeting place. At night it is floodlit and dozens of young people sit on the steps around its octagonal base.

Ponte Sisto
This bridge was built on the orders of Sixtus IV in 1474 to link Trastevere to central Rome ②

LOCATOR MAP
See Central Rome Map pp12–13

Piazza Belli is named after Giuseppe Gioacchino Belli (1791–1863), who wrote satirical sonnets in Roman dialect rather than academic Italian. At the centre of the piazza stands a statue of the poet (1913).

Vicolo del Piede is one of the picturesque narrow streets lined with restaurant tables leading off Piazza di Santa Maria in Trastevere.

The Torre degli Anguillara (13th century) is the only survivor of the many medieval towers that once dominated the Trastevere skyline.

Caserma dei Vigili della VII Coorte
The courtyard of this antique Roman fire station still stands ⑦

San Crisogono
The Romanesque bell tower dates from the early 12th century. The plain portico is a later addition (1626), but is in keeping with the spirit of this ancient church ⑥

Casa della Fornarina ❶

Via di Santa Dorotea 20. **Map** 4 D5 & 11 B5. 📷 *23, 280. See* **Restaurants** *p316*.

N OT MUCH is known about Raphael's model and lover, La Fornarina, yet over the centuries she has acquired a name, Margherita, and even a biography. Her father was a Sienese baker (*La Fornarina* means the baker's girl) and his shop was here in Trastevere near Raphael's frescoes in the Villa Farnesina (*see pp220–21*).

Margherita earned a reputation as a "fallen woman" and Raphael, wishing to be absolved before dying, turned her away from his deathbed. After his death she took refuge in the convent of Santa Apollonia in Trastevere.

She is assumed to have been the model for Raphael's famous portrait *La Donna Velata* in the Palazzo Pitti in Florence.

Ponte Sisto ❷

Map 4 E5 & 11 B5. 📷 *23, 280*.

N AMED AFTER Pope Sixtus IV della Rovere (reigned 1471–84), who commissioned it, this bridge was built by Baccio Pontelli to replace an ancient Roman bridge. The enterprising pope also built the Sistine Chapel (*see pp244–7*), the Hospital of Santo Spirito (*see p226*) and restored many churches and monuments. This put him in great financial difficulties and he had to sell personal collections in order to finance his projects.

Another method of financing projects was to levy a tax on the city's prostitutes. Several popes are known to have resorted to this unpopular form of taxation.

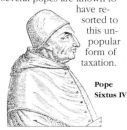

Pope Sixtus IV

Gilded Baroque altar of Santa Maria della Scala

Santa Maria della Scala ❸

Via della Scala. **Map** 4 D5 & 11 B5. 📞 *06-580 62 33*. 📷 *23, 280*. **Church open** *7–8am, 5.30–6.30pm daily*. 🕇 *7am, 5pm daily, 7am, 11.30am, 5pm Sun*.

T HIS CHURCH belongs to a time of great building activity that lasted about 30 years from the end of the 16th to the early 17th century. Its rather simple facade contrasts with a rich interior decorated with multicoloured marbles and a number of spirited Baroque altars and reliefs.

Sant'Egidio and Museo del Folklore ❹

Piazza Sant'Egidio 1. **Map** 7 C1. 📷 *H, 23, 280*. 📱 *8*. **Museo del Folklore** 📞 *06-589 59 45*. **Open** *9am–1pm Tue–Sun, also 5–7pm Tue & Thu*. **Church open** *for services only*. 🕇 *8.30pm daily*.

B UILT IN 1630, Sant'Egidio was the church of the adjoining Carmelite convent, one of many founded in the area to shelter the poor and destitute. The convent is now a folklore museum, containing a wealth of material relating to the festivals, pastimes, superstitions and customs of the Romans when they lived under papal rule.

There are old paintings and prints of the city and tableaux showing scenes of everyday life in 18th- and 19th-century Rome, including reconstructions of shops and a tavern.

The museum also has manuscripts by the much-loved poets Belli and Trilussa who wrote in local dialect.

Watercolour of public scribe (1880) in the Museo del Folklore

Santa Maria in Trastevere ❺

See pp212–13.

San Crisogono ❻

Piazza Sonnino 44. **Map** 7 C1. 📞 *06-581 82 25*. 📷 *H, 23, 280*. 📱 *8*. **Open** *7am–11am, 4pm–7pm Mon–Sat, 8am–1pm Sun*. **Adm charge** *for excavations*. 🕇 ♿

T HIS CHURCH was built on the site of one of the city's oldest *tituli* (private houses used for Christian worship). An 8th-century church with 11th-century frescoes can still be seen beneath the present church. This dates from the early 12th century, a period of intense building activity in the popular quarters of Rome. San Crisogono was decorated

Apse mosaic in San Crisogono

by Pietro Cavallini – the apse mosaic by his school remains.

Most of the columns were taken from previous buildings, including the great porphyry ones of the triumphal arch. The mosaic floor is the result of recycling precious marble from various Roman ruins.

Caserma dei Vigili della VII Coorte **7**

Via della VII Coorte. **Map** 7 C1. **C** 06-67 10 38 19. 23, 44, 280. 8. **Open** on request – phone first.

NOT ALL ROMAN RUINS are Imperial villas or grand temples; there are also those illustrating the daily life of a busy city. One of these is the barracks of the guards of the VII Coorte, the Roman fire brigade. It was built under Augustus' reign, in the 1st century AD, and the excavated courtyard seen today is where the men would rest while waiting for an alarm.

Santa Cecilia in Trastevere **8**

Piazza di Santa Cecilia. **Map** 8 D1. **C** 06-589 92 89. H, 23, 280. 8. **Open** 10am–noon, 4–5.15pm daily. **Adm charge** for excavations. **Cavallini fresco** can be seen 10am–11.30am Tue & Thu only.

ST. CECILIA, ARISTOCRAT and patron saint of music, was martyred here in AD 230. After an attempt at scalding her to death, she was beheaded. A church was founded – perhaps in the 4th century – on the site of her house (still to be seen beneath the church, with the remains of a Roman tannery). For a long time her body was missing, but it turned up in the Catacombs of San Callisto (see p265). In the 9th century it was reburied here by Pope Paschal I, who rebuilt the church. A fine apse mosaic survives from this period.

The altar canopy by Arnolfo di Cambio and the fresco of *The Last Judgment* by Pietro Cavallini, reached through the adjoining convent, date from the 13th century, one of the few periods when Rome had

Detail of 13th-century fresco by Pietro Cavallini in Santa Cecilia

a distinctive artistic style of its own. In front of the altar is a statue of St. Cecilia by Stefano Maderno, who used her miraculously preserved remains as a model when she was briefly disinterred in 1599.

San Michele a Ripa Grande **9**

Via di San Michele. **Map** 8 D2. **C** 06-584 31. 23, 44, 75, 280. **Open** for special exhibitions only.

THIS HUGE, IMPOSING complex, now housing the Ministry of Culture, stretches 985 ft (300 m) along the river Tiber. It was built on the initiative of Pope Innocent XII and contained a home for the elderly, a boys' reform school, a woollen mill

and various chapels. Today contemporary exhibitions are often held here.

San Francesco a Ripa **10**

Piazza San Francesco d'Assisi 88. **Map** 7 C2. **C** 06-581 90 20. 23, 44, 280. 8. **Open** 7.30am–noon, 4pm–7pm daily.

ST FRANCIS OF ASSISI lived here in a hospice when he visited Rome in 1219 and his stone pillow and crucifix are preserved in his cell. The church was rebuilt by his follower, the nobleman Rodolfo Anguillara, who is portrayed on his tombstone wearing the Franciscan habit.

Entirely rebuilt in the 1680s by Cardinal Pallavicini, the church is rich in sculptures. Particularly flamboyant are the 18th-century Rospigliosi and Pallavicini monuments in the transept chapel.

Not to be missed in the Paluzzi-Albertoni chapel (fourth on the left, along the nave) is Bernini's breathtaking sculpture, the *Ecstasy of Beata Ludovica Albertoni*.

Villa Sciarra **11**

Via Calandrelli 35. **Map** 7 B2. 44, 75. **Park open** 9am–sunset daily. **House closed** for restoration.

IN ROMAN TIMES the site of this small, attractive public park was a nymph's sanctuary. It is especially picturesque in spring when its wisterias are in full bloom. The paths through the park are decorated with Romantic follies, fountains and statues, and there are splendid views of the city over Janiculum's bastions.

Bernini's *Ecstasy of Beata Ludovica Albertoni* (1674) in San Francesco a Ripa

Santa Maria in Trastevere ❻

PROBABLY THE FIRST official Christian place of worship to be built in Rome, this basilica became the focus of devotion to the Virgin Mary. According to legend, the church was founded by Pope Callixtus I in the 3rd century, when Christianity was still a minority cult. Today's church is largely a 12th-century building, remarkable for its mosaics, in particular those by Pietro Cavallini. The 22 granite columns in the nave were taken from the ruins of ancient Roman buildings. Despite some 18th-century Baroque additions, Santa Maria has retained its medieval character. This friendly church has strong links with the local community.

Piazza Santa Maria in Trastevere
The piazza in front of the church is the traditional heart of Trastevere. Today it is surrounded by lively bars and restaurants. Carlo Fontana built the octagonal fountain in the late 17th century.

The floor, relaid in the 1870s, is a re-creation of the Cosmatesque mosaic floor of the 13th century.

The bell tower was built in the 12th century. At the top is a small mosaic of the Virgin.

★ **Facade Mosaics**
The 12th-century mosaic shows Mary feeding the baby Jesus and ten women holding lamps. Eight of the lamps are lit, symbolizing virginity; the veiled women whose lamps have gone out are probably widows.

STAR FEATURES

★ **Cavallini Mosaics**

★ **Facade Mosaics**

MODEST DONORS

Many of Rome's mosaics include a portrait of the pope or cardinal responsible for the building of the church. Often the portrait is dwarfed by the rest of the picture, which glorifies the saint to whom the church is dedicated. On the facade of Santa Maria, two tiny unidentified figures kneel at the Virgin's feet. Were they to stand up, the men would barely reach her knees.

Facade mosaic, detail

The portico was remodeled in 1702 by Carlo Fontana. Statues of four popes decorate the balustrade above.

Front entrance

15th-century wall tabernacle by Mino del Reame

Apse Mosaic
The 12th-century mosaic in the basin of the apse shows the Coronation of the Virgin. She sits on Christ's right hand, surrounded by saints.

★ Cavallini Mosaics
The details in the six mosaics of the Life of the Virgin (1291) display a touching realism.

Madonna della Clemenza
The life-size icon probably dates from the 7th century. A replica is displayed above the altar of the Cappella Altemps.

Tomb of Cardinal Pietro Stefaneschi
The last of his line, Pietro Stefaneschi died in 1417. His tomb is by an otherwise unknown sculptor called Paolo.

TIMELINE

30 BC	AD 200	1150	1400	1650	1900
AD 217–22 Church founded by Pope Callixtus I	*Pope Innocent II*	**1291** Pietro Cavallini adds mosaics of scenes from the life of the Virgin for his patron, Bertoldo Stefaneschi		**1617** Domenichino designs coffered ceiling with octagonal panel of the Assumption of the Virgin	
38 BC Jet of mineral oil spouts from the ground on this site. Later interpreted as a portent of the coming of Christ	**c1138** Pope Innocent II starts rebuilding the church	**1580** Martino Longhi the Elder restores church and builds family chapel for Cardinal Marco Sittico Altemps		**1702** Pope Clement XI has portico rebuilt **1866–77** Church restored by Virginio Vespignani	

JANICULUM

OVERLOOKING THE TIBER on the Trastevere side of the river, the Janiculum Hill has often played its part in the defense of the city. The last occasion was in 1849, when Garibaldi held off attacking French troops. The park at the top of the hill is filled with monuments to Garibaldi and his men. A popular place for walks, the park provides a welcome escape from the densely packed streets of Trastevere.

Puppets in the park at the top of the Janiculum Hill

Visitors will often find puppet shows and other entertainment and activities for children. In medieval times, most of the hill was occupied by monasteries and convents. Bramante built his miniature masterpiece, the Tempietto, in the convent of San Pietro in Montorio. The Renaissance also saw the development of the riverside area along Via della Lungara, where the rich and powerful built large beautiful houses such as the Villa Farnesina.

SIGHTS AT A GLANCE

Churches and Temples
Sant'Onofrio ❻
San Pietro in Montorio ❼
Tempietto ❽

Museums and Galleries
Palazzo Corsini and Galleria Nazionale d'Arte Antica ❷

Historic Buildings
Villa Farnesina pp220–21 ❶

Fountains
Fontana dell'Acqua Paola ❾

Monuments
Garibaldi Monument ❺

Arches and Gates
Porta Settimiana ❸

Parks and Gardens
Botanical Gardens ❹

SEE ALSO

GETTING THERE

The Janiculum (Il Gianicolo) is not the easiest part of Rome to reach by public transport. It can be approached either from the Vatican area *(see p223)* or from Trastevere *(see p207)*. There is only one bus, the 870, that goes up to the top of the hill, but the 44 or 75 will take you from Piazza Venezia to Via Giacinto Carini from where you start your walk up. For sights along Via della Lungara, take the 23 or 280, which go along Lungotevere.

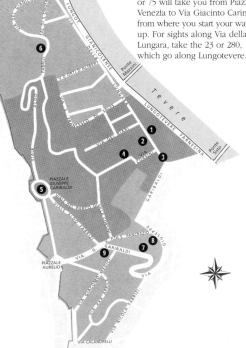

KEY

▨	Tour of the Janiculum map
—	City Wall

0 meters   300
0 yards   300

The staircase fountain in the Botanical Gardens

A Tour of the Janiculum

THE LONG HIKE to the top of the Janiculum is rewarded by wonderful views over the city. The park's monuments include a lighthouse and statues of Garibaldi and his wife, Anita. There is also a cannon that is fired at noon each day. In Via della Lungara, between the Janiculum and the Tiber, stand Palazzo Corsini, with its national art collection, and the Villa Farnesina, decorated by Raphael for his friend and patron, the fabulously wealthy banker Agostino Chigi.

Tasso's Oak is a memorial to the poet Torquato Tasso, who liked to sit here in the days before he died in 1595. The tree was struck by lightning in 1843

The Manfredi Lighthouse, built in 1911, was a gift to the city of Rome from Italians in Argentina.

The Monument to Anita Garibaldi by Mario Rutelli was erected in 1932. The great patriot's Brazilian wife lies buried beneath the statue.

The view from Villa Lante, a beautiful Renaissance summer residence, gives a magnificent panorama of the whole city.

Garibaldi Monument
The inscription on the base of the equestrian statue means "Rome or Death" ⑤

ROMA O MORTE

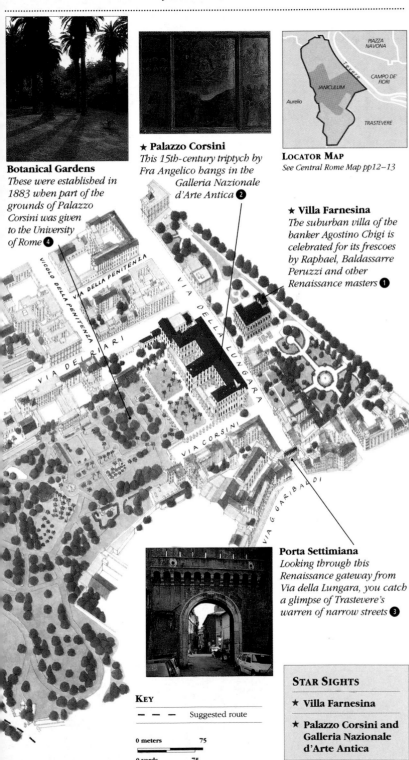

Botanical Gardens
These were established in 1883 when part of the grounds of Palazzo Corsini was given to the University of Rome 4

★ **Palazzo Corsini**
This 15th-century triptych by Fra Angelico hangs in the Galleria Nazionale d'Arte Antica 2

LOCATOR MAP
See Central Rome Map pp12–13

★ **Villa Farnesina**
The suburban villa of the banker Agostino Chigi is celebrated for its frescoes by Raphael, Baldassarre Peruzzi and other Renaissance masters 1

VICOLO DELLA PENITENZA

VIA DELLA PENITENZA

VIA DEI RIARI

VIA DELLA LUNGARA

VIA CORSINI

VIA G. GARIBALDI

Porta Settimiana
Looking through this Renaissance gateway from Via della Lungara, you catch a glimpse of Trastevere's warren of narrow streets 3

KEY

– – – Suggested route

0 meters 75

0 yards 75

STAR SIGHTS

★ Villa Farnesina

★ Palazzo Corsini and Galleria Nazionale d'Arte Antica

Villa Farnesina ❶

See pp220–21.

Palazzo Corsini and Galleria Nazionale d'Arte Antica ❷

Via della Lungara 10. **Map** 4 D5 & 11 A5. **(** *06-68 80 23 23.* **▦** *23, 280.* **Open** *9am–7pm Tue–Fri, 9am–2pm Sat, 9am–1pm Sun & public hols (last adm: 30 mins before closing).* **Closed** *Jan 1, May 1, Aug 15 & Dec 25.* **Adm charge.** ⊘ ♿ ▣

Queen Christina's bedroom in the Palazzo Corsini

The history of Palazzo Corsini is intimately entwined with that of Rome. Built for Cardinal Domenico Riario in 1510–12, it has boasted among its many distinguished guests Bramante, the young Michelangelo, Erasmus and Queen Christina of Sweden, who died here in 1689. The old palazzo was completely rebuilt for Cardinal Neri Corsini by Ferdinando Fuga in 1736. As Via della Lungara is too narrow to allow a good frontal view, Fuga designed the facade so it could be viewed from an angle.

Palazzo Corsini now houses the Galleria Nazionale d'Arte Antica. This outstanding collection includes paintings by Rubens, Van Dyck, Murillo, Caravaggio and Guido Reni, as well as 17th- and 18th-century Italian regional art. The palazzo is also home to the Accademia dei Lincei, a learned society founded in 1603, which once included Galileo among its members.

In 1797 Palazzo Corsini was the backdrop to momentous events: French General Duphot (the fiancé of Napoleon's sister Pauline) was killed here in a skirmish between papal troops and Republicans. The consequent French occupation of the city and the deportation of Pope Pius VI led to the proclamation of a short-lived Roman Republic (1798–9).

Porta Settimiana ❸

Between Via della Scala and Via della Lungara. **Map** 4 D5 & 11 B5. **▦** *23, 280.*

This gate was built in 1498 by Pope Alexander VI Borgia to replace a minor passageway in the Aurelian Wall. The Porta Settimiana marks the start of Via della Lungara, a long straight road built in the early 16th century.

Botanical Gardens ❹

Largo Cristina di Svezia 24, off Via Corsini. **Map** 4 D5. **(** *06-686 41 93.* **▦** *23, 280.* **Open** *9am–6:30pm (Oct-Mar: 5:30pm) Mon–Sat.* **Closed** *Sun, public hols & Aug.* **Adm charge.**

Sequoias, palm trees and splendid collections of orchids and bromeliads are housed in Rome's Botanical Gardens (Orto Botanico). The gardens contain more than 7,000 plant species from all over the world. Indigenous and exotic species are grouped to illustrate their botanical families and their adaptation to different climates and ecosystems. There are also several interesting examples of such plants as the gingko that have survived virtually unchanged from earlier eras. The gardens were originally part of the Palazzo Corsini but since 1983 have belonged to the University of Rome.

Garibaldi Monument ❺

Piazzale Giuseppe Garibaldi. **Map** 3 C5. **▦** *870.*

Base of the Garibaldi Monument

This huge equestrian statue is part of a park that commemorates the heroic events witnessed on the Janiculum when the French army attacked the city in 1849. Garibaldi's Republicans fended off the greatly superior French forces for weeks, until the Italians were overwhelmed. Garibaldi and his men escaped. The monument, erected in 1895, was the work of Emilio Gallori. Around the pedestal are four smaller sculptures in bronze showing battle scenes and allegorical figures.

Steps and tiered fountains at the Botanical Gardens

Courtyard of Sant'Onofrio

Sant'Onofrio ❻

Piazza di Sant'Onofrio 2. **Map** 3 C4.
☎ 06-686 44 98. 🚌 870.
Open 10am–noon Sun & public hols.
Closed Aug, except saint's feast day
on Aug 12. 🔼 **Museum open** by
appt only.

BEATO NICOLA da Forca
Palena, whose tombstone
guards the entrance, founded
this church in 1419 in honor
of the hermit Sant'Onofrio. It
retains the flavor of the 15th
century in the simple shapes
of the portico and the cloister.
In the early 17th century the
portico was decorated with
frescoes by Domenichino.

The monastery next to the
church houses a small museum
dedicated to the 16th-century
poet Torquato Tasso, who
died here in one of the cells.

San Pietro in Montorio ❼

Piazza San Pietro in Montorio 2.
Map 7 B1. ☎ 06-581 39 40. 🚌 44,
75. **Open** 7:30am–noon, 4–6pm
daily. If closed, ring bell at door to
right of church. 🔼

SAN PIETRO IN MONTORIO – the
church of St. Peter on the
Golden Hill – was founded in
the Middle Ages near the spot
where St. Peter was presumed
to have been crucified. It was
rebuilt by order of Ferdinand
and Isabella of Spain at the
end of the 15th century and
decorated by outstanding
artists of the Renaissance.

The facade is typical of a
time when clean, geometric
shapes derived from Classical
architecture were in vogue.
The single nave ends in a
deep apse that once contained

Raphael's *Transfiguration*,
now in the Vatican. Two wide
chapels, one on either side of
the nave, were decorated by
some of Michelangelo's most
famous pupils. The left chapel
was designed by one of the
few artists Michelangelo
admired, Daniele da Volterra,
who was also responsible for
the altar painting, *Baptism of
Christ*. The chapel on the
right was the work of Giorgio
Vasari, who included a self-
portrait (in black, on the left)
in his biblical altar painting,
Conversion of St. Paul.

The first chapel to the right
of the entrance contains the
powerful *Flagellation*, by
Venetian artist Sebastiano del
Piombo (1518); Michelangelo
is said to have provided the
original drawings. Work by
Bernini and his followers can
be seen in the second chapel
on the left and in the flanking
De Raymondi tombs.

Tempietto ❽

Piazza San Pietro in Montorio (in court-
yard of San Pietro in Montorio). **Map** 7
B1. ☎ 06-581 39 40. 🚌 44, 75.
Open 9am–noon, 4pm–6pm daily.
See **The History of Rome** pp30–31.

AROUND 1502 BRAMANTE completed what many consider
to be the first true Renaissance building in Rome – the
Tempietto. The name means
simply "little temple." Its
circular shape echoes early
Christian *martyria*,
chapels built on
the site of a saint's
martyrdom. This
was believed to be
the place where St.
Peter was crucified.

Bramante chose
the Doric order for
the 16 columns
surrounding the
domed chapel.
Above the columns
is a Classical frieze
and a delicate
balustrade. Though
the scale of the
Tempietto is tiny,
Bramante's masterly
use of Classical
proportions creates
a satisfyingly
harmonious whole.

The Tempietto illustrates the
great Renaissance dream that
Rome would relive its ancient
glory.

Fontana dell'Acqua Paola ❾

Via Garibaldi. **Map** 7 B1. 🚌 44, 75.

Fontana dell'Acqua Paola

THIS MONUMENTAL FOUNTAIN
commemorates the
reopening in 1612 of an
aqueduct originally built by
Emperor Trajan in AD 109.
The aqueduct was renamed
the Acqua Paola after Paul V,
the Borghese pope who
ordered its restoration. When
it was first built, the fountain
had five small basins, but in
1690 Carlo Fontana altered the
design, adding the huge basin
you can see today. Despite
many laws intended to deter
them, generations of Romans
used this convenient pool of
fresh water for bathing and
washing their vegetables.

Bramante's round chapel, the Tempietto

Villa Farnesina ❶

THE WEALTHY SIENESE BANKER Agostino Chigi, who had established the headquarters of his far-flung financial empire in Rome, commissioned the villa in 1508 from his compatriot Baldassarre Peruzzi. The simple, harmonious design, with a central block and projecting wings, made this one of the earliest true Renaissance villas. The decoration was carried out between 1510 and 1519, and this has recently been restored. Peruzzi frescoed some of the interiors himself. Later, Sebastiano del Piombo, Raphael and his pupils added more elaborate works. The frescoes illustrate Classical myths, and the vault of the main hall, the Sala di Galatea, is adorned with scenes showing the position of the stars at the time of Chigi's birth. Artists, poets, princes, cardinals and the pope himself were entertained here in style by their wealthy host. In 1577 the villa was bought by Cardinal Alessandro Farnese. Since then, it has been known as the Villa Farnesina.

North Facade
The Loggia of Cupid and Psyche looks out on formal gardens that were used for parties and putting on plays.

Entrance

The Wedding of Alexander and Roxanne by Sodoma
Cherubs are shown helping the bride Roxanne prepare for her marriage.

★ Triumph of Galatea by Raphael
The beautiful sea nymph Galatea was one of the 50 daughters of the god Nereus.

The Gabinetto delle Stampe
sometimes holds exhibitions of rare prints.

Frescoes in the Room of Galatea
Perseus beheads Medusa in a scene from one of Peruzzi's series of mythological frescoes.

THE ARCHITECT

Baldassarre Peruzzi, painter and architect, arrived in Rome from Siena in 1503, at age 20, becoming Bramante's chief assistant. His architectural designs were typical of Classicism, but his painting owes more to Gothic influences – his figurework is highly stylized. On Raphael's death, he became Head of Works at St. Peter's but was captured in the Sack of Rome *(see p31)*, exiled to Siena until 1535 and died in 1536.

Baldassarre Peruzzi

★ Salone delle Prospettive
Peruzzi's frescoes create the illusion of looking out at views of 16th-century Rome through a marble colonnade.

VISITORS' CHECKLIST

Via della Lungara 230. **Map** 4 D5
& 11 A5. 🚌 *23, 280 to
Lungotevere Farnesina.* 📞 *06-
68 80 17 67.* **Open** *9am–1pm
Mon–Sat.* 🚫 🛈 **Adm charge**.
Gabinetto delle Stampe *(rare
print collection)* 📞 *06-66 98 02
30.* **Open** *9am–1pm Tue–Sat for
occasional exhibitions.* 🚫

Fresco from the Salone delle Prospettive
This scene shows the Torre delle Milizie (see p90) as it looked in the 1500s.

★ Loggia of Cupid and Psyche
The model for the figure on the left in Raphael's painting of The Three Graces *was Agostino Chigi's mistress, the courtesan Imperia.*

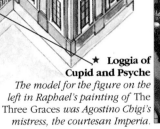

Lunette in the Room of Galatea
Once thought to be by Michelangelo, this giant monochrome head is the work of Peruzzi.

STAR FEATURES

★ **Triumph of Galatea by Raphael**

★ **Loggia of Cupid and Psyche**

★ **Salone delle Prospettive**

VATICAN

As THE SITE where St. Peter was martyred and buried, the Vatican became the residence of the popes who succeeded him. Decisions reached here have shaped the destiny of Europe, and the great basilica of St. Peter's draws pilgrims from all over the Christian world. The papal palaces beside St. Peter's house the Vatican Museums. With the added attractions of Michelangelo's Sistine Chapel and the Raphael Rooms, their wonderful

Nuns in St. Peter's Square

collections of Classical sculpture make them the finest museums in Rome. The Vatican's position as a state within a state was guaranteed by the Lateran Treaty of 1929, marked by the building of a new road, the Via della Conciliazione. This leads from St. Peter's to Castel Sant' Angelo, a monument to a far grimmer past. Built originally as the Emperor Hadrian's mausoleum, this papal fortress and prison has witnessed many fierce battles for control of the city.

SIGHTS AT A GLANCE

Churches and Temples
St. Peter's pp230–3 ❶
Santo Spirito in Sassia ❹
Santa Maria in Traspontina ❾

Museums and Galleries
Vatican Museums pp234–47 ❷

Historic Buildings
Hospital of Santo Spirito ❺
Palazzo del Commendatore ❻
Palazzo dei Convertendi ❼
Palazzo dei Penitenzieri ❽

Palazzo Torlonia ⓬
Castel Sant'Angelo pp248–9 ⓭
Palazzo di Giustizia ⓮

Gates
Porta Santo Spirito ❸

Historic Streets and Piazzas
The Borgo ❿
Vatican Corridor ⓫

GETTING THERE
The quickest way to reach the area is by Metro line A to Ottaviano. This is especially convenient when visiting the Vatican Museums. The 64 bus runs regularly from Piazza dei Cinquecento in front of Termini Station. Other buses that serve the area include the 81 and 492, which stop in Piazza del Risorgimento. There is a regular shuttle bus between St. Peter's and the Vatican Museums.

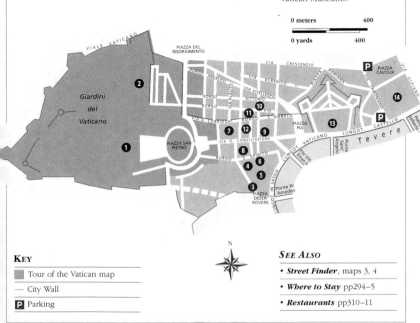

KEY

	Tour of the Vatican map
—	City Wall
P	Parking

SEE ALSO

- *Street Finder*, maps 3, 4
- *Where to Stay* pp294–5
- *Restaurants* pp310–11

Dome of St. Peter's dominating the Vatican skyline

A Tour of the Vatican

THE VATICAN, a center of power for Catholics all over the world and a sovereign state since February 1929, is ruled by the Pope. About 1,000 people live here, staffing the Vatican's facilities. There are shops and a post office; Radio Vatican, broadcasting to the world in over 20 languages; a daily newspaper (*l'Osservatore Romano*), Vatican offices; and a publishing house.

The Madonna of Guadalupe shows the miraculous image of the Madonna that appeared on the cloak of a Mexican Indian in 1531.

Papal heliport

The Grotto of Lourdes is a replica of the grotto in the southwest of France, where in 1858 the Virgin appeared to St. Bernadette.

The Vatican Railway Station, opened in 1930, connects with the line from Rome to Viterbo but is now used only for freight.

Radio Vatican is broadcast from this tower, part of the Leonine Wall built in 847.

The Papal Audience Chamber, by Pier Luigi Nervi, was opened in 1971. It seats up to 12,000.

The information office gives details of tours of the Vatican Gardens.

★ **St. Peter's**
The Chapel of St. Peter is in the grottoes under the basilica. The rich marble decoration was added by Clement VIII at the end of the 16th century ❶

Piazza San Pietro was laid out by Bernini between 1656 and 1667. The narrow space in front of the church opens out into an enormous ellipse flanked by colonnades.

The obelisk was erected here in 1586 with the help of 150 horses and 47 winches.

PIAZZA SANTA MARTA

PIAZZA DEL SANT'UFFIZIO

STAR SIGHTS

★ **St. Peter's**

★ **Vatican Museums**

The Eagle Fountain was built to celebrate the arrival of water from the Acqua Paola aqueduct at the Vatican. The eagle is the Borghese crest.

LOCATOR MAP
See Central Rome Map pp12–13

The Casina of Pius IV is a delightful summerhouse in the Vatican Gardens built by Pirro Ligorio in the mid-16th century.

Entrance to Vatican Museums

★ **Vatican Museums**
Raphael's Madonna of Foligno (1513) is just one of the Vatican's many Renaissance masterpieces ❷

The Galleon Fountain is a perfect scale model of a 17th-century ship in lead, brass and copper. It was made by a Flemish artist for Pope Paul V.

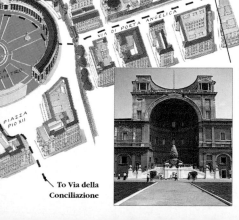

The Cortile della Pigna is mostly the work of Bramante. The niche for the pine cone, once a Roman fountain, was added by Pirro Ligorio in 1562.

KEY

– – – Suggested route

0 meters   75

0 yards   75

To Via della Conciliazione

VIA PIO X

VIA DI PORTA ANGELICA

PIAZZA PIO XII

St. Peter's ❶

See pp230–33.

Vatican Museums ❷

See pp234–47.

Porta Santo Spirito ❸

Via dei Penitenzieri. **Map** 3 C3.
🚌 *34, 46, 46b, 62, 98, 870, 881, 982.*

THIS GATE stands at what was the southern limit of the "Leonine City," the area enclosed within walls by Pope Leo IV as a defense against the Saracens who had sacked Rome in AD 845. The walls measure 2 miles (3 km) in circumference.

Work on the walls started in 846. Pope Leo supervised the huge army of laborers personally, and thanks to his encouragement, the job was completed in four years. He then led a solemn procession to consecrate his massive feat of construction.

Since the time of Pope Leo, the walls have needed much reinforcement and repair. The gateway visible today at Porta Santo Spirito was built by the architect Antonio da Sangallo the Younger in 1543–4. It is framed by two huge bastions that were added in 1564 by Pope Pius IV Medici. Sadly, Sangallo's design for a monumental entrance to the Vatican was never completed; the principal columns come to an end somewhat abruptly in a modern covering of cement.

Santo Spirito in Sassia ❹

Via dei Penitenzieri. **Map** 3 C3.
📞 *06-687 93 10.* 🚌 *23, 34, 62, 64, 982.* **Open** *7am–noon, 3pm–8pm daily.* 🚻 ♿

Nave of Santo Spirito in Sassia

BUILT ON THE SITE of a church erected by King Ine of Wessex, who died in Rome in the 8th century, the church is the work of Antonio da Sangallo the Younger. It was rebuilt (1538–44) after the Sack of Rome had left it in ruins in 1527. The facade was added under Pope Sixtus V (1585–90). The nave and side chapels are decorated with a series of light, lively frescoes. The pretty bell tower is earlier, dating from the reign of Sixtus IV (1471–84). It was probably the work of the pope's architect Baccio Pontelli, who also built the nearby Hospital of Santo Spirito, and the Ponte Sisto *(see p210)* farther down the River Tiber.

Sixtus V's arms over door of Santo Spirito

Hospital of Santo Spirito ❺

Borgo Santo Spirito 2. **Map** 3 C3.
🚌 *34, 46, 46b, 62, 98, 870, 881, 982.* **Octagonal chapel open** *8:30am–2pm daily.*

THE OLDEST HOSPITAL in Rome, this is said to have been founded as a result of a nightmare experienced by Pope Innocent III (1198–1216). In the dream, an angel showed him the bodies of Rome's unwanted babies dredged up from the Tiber River in fishing nets. As a result the pope hastened to build a hospice for sick paupers.

Fresco of an angel in the octagonal chapel of the Hospital of Santo Spirito

In 1475 the hospital was reorganized by Pope Sixtus IV to care for poor pilgrims expected for the Holy Year. Sixtus's hospital was a radical building. Cloisters divided the different types of patient; one area is still reserved for orphans and their nurses.

Unwanted infants were passed through a revolving barrel-like contraption called the *rota*, still visible to the left of the central entrance in Borgo Santo Spirito to guarantee anonymity. Martin Luther, who visited in 1511, was shocked by the number of abandoned children he saw, believing them to be "the sons of the pope himself."

In the center, under the hospital's conspicuous drum, is an octagonal chapel, where mass was said for patients. This room can be visited while the rest of the building still functions as a hospital.

Rusticated doorway of the Palazzo dei Convertendi

The *rota* of Santo Spirito, where mothers left unwanted babies

Palazzo del Commendatore ❻

Borgo Santo Spirito 3. **Map** 3 C3. 🚌 *34, 46, 46b, 62, 64, 98, 870, 881, 982.* ***Courtyard only open*** *to the public.*

As director of the Hospital of Santo Spirito, the Commendatore not only ran the hospital, he was also responsible for its estates and revenues. This important post was originally given to members of the pope's family.

The palazzo, built next door to the hospital, has a spacious 16th-century frescoed loggia appropriate to the dignity and sobriety of its owners. The frescoes represent the story of the founding of the Hospital of Santo Spirito. To the left of the entrance is the Spezieria, or Pharmacy. This still has the wheel used for grinding the bark of the cinchona tree to produce the drug quinine, first introduced here in 1632 by Jesuits from Peru as a cure for malaria.

Above the courtyard is a splendid clock (1827). The dial is divided into six; it was not until 1846 that the familiar division of the day into two periods of 12 hours was introduced in Rome by Pope Pius IX.

Della Rovere arms

Palazzo dei Convertendi ❼

Via della Conciliazione 43. **Map** 3 C3. 🚌 *34, 46, 46b, 62, 64, 98, 870, 881, 982.* ***Not open*** *to the public.*

With the building of Via della Conciliazione in the 1930s, Palazzo dei Convertendi was taken down and later moved to this new site nearby. The house, which is partly attributed to the architect Bramante, is where the artist Raphael died in 1520.

Palazzo dei Penitenzieri ❽

Via della Conciliazione 33. **Map** 3 C3. 📞 *06-686 54 35.* 🚌 *34, 46, 46b, 62, 64, 98, 881. See* **Where to Stay** *p295.*

The palazzo owes its name to the fact that the place was once home to the confessors *(penitenzieri)* of St. Peter's. Their place has now been taken by tourists, as the building has been converted into the Hotel Columbus. Originally built by Cardinal Domenico della Rovere in 1480, the palazzo still bears the family's coat of arms, the oak tree (*rovere* means oak), on its graceful courtyard wellhead. On the cardinal's death, the palazzo was acquired by Pope Julius II della Rovere's favorite, Cardinal Francesco Alidosi. Suspected of treason, the cardinal was murdered in 1511 by the pope's nephew, the duke of Urbino, who also took possession of his palazzo. A few of the rooms still contain beautiful frescoes.

View of the Tiber and the Borgo between Castel Sant'Angelo and St. Peter's by Gaspare Vanvitelli (1653–1736)

Santa Maria in Traspontina ❾

Via della Conciliazione 14.
Map 3 C3. **📞** 06-68 80 64 51.
🚌 23, 34, 62, 64, 870, 982. **Open** 6.30am–noon, 4pm–7.30pm daily. 🚻 ♿

The facade of the Carmelite church of Santa Maria in Traspontina

THE CHURCH occupies the site of an ancient Roman pyramid, believed in the Middle Ages to have been the Tomb of Romulus. The pyramid was destroyed by Pope Alexander VI Borgia, but representations of it survive in the bronze doors at the entrance to St. Peter's and in a Giotto triptych in the Vatican Pinacoteca (see p240).

The present church was begun in 1566 to replace an earlier one which had been in the line of fire of the cannons defending Castel Sant'Angelo during the Sack of Rome in 1527. The papal artillery officers insisted that the dome of the new church should be as low as possible, so it was built without a supporting drum. The first chapel to the right is dedicated to the gunners' patron saint, Santa Barbara, and is decorated with warlike motifs. In the third chapel on the left are two columns, said to be those to which St. Peter and Paul were bound before martyrdom.

The Borgo ❿

Map 3 C3. 🚌 23, 34, 64, 982.

THE WORD BORGO derives from the German *burg*, meaning town. Rome's Borgo is where the first pilgrims to St. Peter's were housed in hostels and hospices, often for quite lengthy periods. The first of these foreign colonies, called "schools", was founded in AD 725 by a Saxon, King Ine of Wessex, who wished to live a life of penance and to be buried near the Tomb of St. Peter. These days hotels and

hostels have made the Borgo a colony of international pilgrims once again. Much of the area's character was destroyed by redevelopment in the 1930s, but it is still enjoyable to explore the old narrow streets on either side of Via della Conciliazione.

Vatican Corridor ⓫

Castel Sant'Angelo to the Vatican.
Map 3 C3. 🚌 23, 34, 64, 982.

Clement VII, who used the Vatican Corridor to evade capture in 1527

LOCALLY KNOWN as the Passetto (small corridor), this long passageway was built into the fortifications during medieval times. Meant to link the Vatican with the fortress of Castel Sant'Angelo, it constituted a fortified escape route which could also be used to control the strategic Borgo area. Arrows and other missiles could be fired from its bastions on to the streets and houses below. The corridor was used in 1494 by Pope Alexander VI Borgia when Rome was invaded by King Charles VIII of France. In 1527 it enabled Pope Clement VII to take refuge in Castel Sant'Angelo, as the troops commanded by the Constable of Bourbon began the Sack of Rome.

Palazzo Torlonia ⑫

Via della Conciliazione 30. **Map** 3 C3.
🚌 *23, 34, 64, 982.* **Not open** to the public.

THE PALAZZO was built in the late 15th century by the wealthy Cardinal Adriano Castellesi, in a style closely resembling Palazzo della Cancelleria *(see p149)*. The cardinal was a much-traveled rogue, who collected vast revenues from the bishopric of Bath and Wells which he was given by his friend King Henry VII of England. In return he gave Henry his palazzo for use as the seat of the English ambassador to the Holy See. Castellesi was finally stripped of his cardinalate by Pope Leo X Medici and disappeared from history.

Pope Leo X

Since then the palazzo has had many owners and tenants. In the 17th century it was rented for a time by Queen Christina of Sweden. The Torlonia family, who acquired the building in 1820, owed its fortune to the financial genius of shopkeeper-turned-banker Giovanni Torlonia. He lent money to the impoverished Roman nobility and bought up their property during the Napoleonic Wars.

Palazzo Torlonia (1496), unaffected by changes to the surrounding area

Castel Sant'Angelo ⑬

See pp248–9.

Palazzo di Giustizia ⑭

Piazza Cavour. **Map** 4 E3. 🚌 *32, 34, 49, 70, 87, 186, 280, 492, 913, 926, 990.* **Not open** to the public.

THE MONUMENTAL Palazzo di Giustizia (Palace of Justice) was built between 1889 and 1910 to house the national law courts. Its riverside facade is crowned with a bronze chariot and fronted by giant statues of the great men of Italian law.

The building was supposed to embody the new order replacing the injustices of papal rule, but it has never endeared itself to the Romans. It was soon dubbed the Palazzaccio (roughly, "the ugly old palazzo") both for its appearance and for the nature of its business. By the 1970s the building was collapsing under its own weight, but it has now been restored.

The ornate travertine facade of the Palazzo di Giustizia

St. Peter's ❶

THE CENTER of the Roman Catholic faith, St. Peter's draws pilgrims from all over the world. Few are disappointed when they enter the sumptuously decorated basilica beneath Michelangelo's vast dome.

A shrine was erected on the site of St. Peter's tomb in the 2nd century, and the first great basilica, ordered by the Emperor Constantine, was completed around AD 349. By the 15th century it was falling down, so in 1506 Pope Julius II laid the first stone of a new church. It took more than a century to build, and all the great architects of the Roman Renaissance and Baroque had a hand in its design.

★ Dome of St. Peter's
Designed by Michelangelo, though not finished in his lifetime, the spectacular cupola, 448 ft (136.5 m) high, gives unity to the majestic interior of the basilica.

The nave's total length is 715 ft (218 m).

Papal Altar
The present altar dates from the reign of Clement VIII (1592–1605). The plain slab of marble found in the Forum of Nerva stands under Bernini's baldacchino, over-looking the well of the confessio, the crypt where St. Peter's body is reputedly buried.

Baldacchino
This magnificent canopy of gilded bronze, supported on spiral columns 66 ft (20 m) high, was designed by Bernini in the 17th century.

TIMELINE

AD 61 Burial of St. Peter		1506 Julius II lays first stone	1547 Michelangelo named as chief architect of St. Peter's		1626 New basilica of St. Peter's consecrated
324 Constantine builds basilica	1452 Nicholas V plans restoration			1593 Dome completed	

AD 60	800	1500	1550	1600

| 200 Altar built marking grave of St. Peter | 1503 Pope Julius II chooses Bramante as architect for new basilica | 1538 Antonio da Sangallo the Younger made director of works | 1606 Carlo Maderno extends basilica | 1614 Maderno finishes the facade |
| 800 Charlemagne crowned Holy Roman Emperor in St. Peter's | | 1514 Raphael director of works | 1564 Death of Michelangelo | |

★ **View from the Dome**
The superb symmetry of Bernini's colonnade can be appreciated from the dome.

The two minor cupolas at the corners of the transept are by Vignola.

Pope Urban VIII's Keys
At the base of the columns of the baldacchino, the coat of arms of Pope Urban VIII features the keys to the Kingdom of Heaven.

Facade by Carlo Maderno (1614)

Stairs to the dome

Filarete Door
Finished in 1445, Antonio Averulino's bronze door came from the original basilica.

Entrances

STAR FEATURES

★ **Dome of St. Peter's**

★ **View from the Dome**

Piazza San Pietro
On Sundays and religious occasions the pope blesses the crowds from his balcony above the square.

A Guided Tour of St. Peter's

THE VAST BASILICA'S 615-ft (187-m) long, marble-encrusted interior contains 11 chapels and 45 altars in addition to a wealth of precious works of art. Some were salvaged from the original basilica and others commissioned from late Renaissance and Baroque artists, but much of the elaborate decoration is owed to Bernini's work in the mid-17th century. The two side aisles are 250 ft (76 m) long and converge under Michelangelo's enormous dome. The central focus of the building is the Papal Altar beneath Bernini's great baldacchino, filling the space between four massive piers which support the dome. From the basilica you can visit the Grottoes, the Treasury and St. Peter's Sacristy, or climb up to the terrace for panoramic views.

⑤ **Baldacchino by Bernini**
Commissioned by Pope Urban VIII in 1624, the extravagant Baroque canopy dominates the nave and crowns the Papal Altar, at which only the pope may celebrate mass.

Bernini's Monument to Urban VIII

④ **Throne of St. Peter in Glory**
In the domed apse, look up to the window above Bernini's Baroque sculpture of 1656–65. It lights the image of the Holy Spirit, shown as a dove amid clouds, rays of sunlight and flights of angels.

Entrance to Treasury and Sacristy

HISTORICAL PLAN OF THE BASILICA OF ST. PETER'S

St. Peter was buried in AD 64 in a necropolis near his crucifixion site at the Circus of Nero. Constantine built a basilica on the burial site in AD 324. In the 15th century the old church was found to be unsafe and had to be demolished. It was rebuilt in the 16th and 17th centuries. By 1614 the facade was ready, and in 1626 the new church was consecrated.

KEY

- ⬛ Circus of Nero
- ⬛ Constantinian
- ⬛ Renaissance
- ⬛ Baroque

Entrance to Necropolis

③ **Monument to Pope Alexander VII**
Bernini's last work was finished in 1678 and is in an alcove on the left of the transept. The pope sits among the figures of Truth, Justice, Charity and Prudence.

② **Monument to Leo XI**
On the left beneath the aisle arch is Alessandro Algardi's white marble 1650 monument to Leo XI, whose reign as pope lasted only 27 days.

KEY

- − − − Tour route

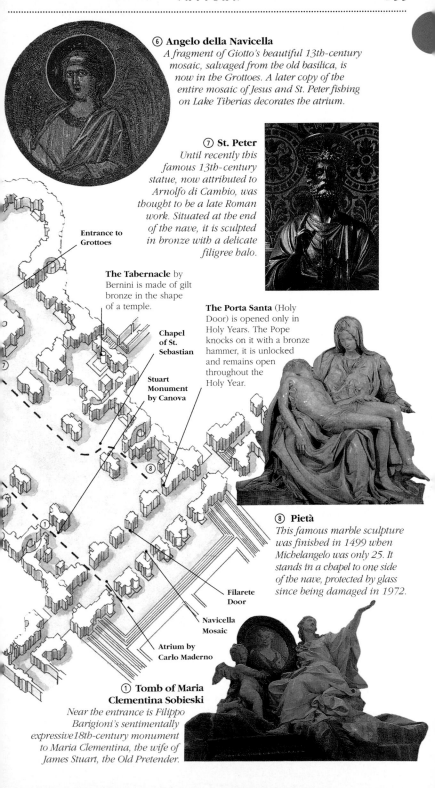

⑥ **Angelo della Navicella**

A fragment of Giotto's beautiful 13th-century mosaic, salvaged from the old basilica, is now in the Grottoes. A later copy of the entire mosaic of Jesus and St. Peter fishing on Lake Tiberias decorates the atrium.

⑦ **St. Peter**

Until recently this famous 13th-century statue, now attributed to Arnolfo di Cambio, was thought to be a late Roman work. Situated at the end of the nave, it is sculpted in bronze with a delicate filigree halo.

Entrance to Grottoes

The Tabernacle by Bernini is made of gilt bronze in the shape of a temple.

Chapel of St. Sebastian

Stuart Monument by Canova

The Porta Santa (Holy Door) is opened only in Holy Years. The Pope knocks on it with a bronze hammer, it is unlocked and remains open throughout the Holy Year.

⑧ **Pietà**

This famous marble sculpture was finished in 1499 when Michelangelo was only 25. It stands in a chapel to one side of the nave, protected by glass since being damaged in 1972.

Filarete Door

Navicella Mosaic

Atrium by Carlo Maderno

① **Tomb of Maria Clementina Sobieski**

Near the entrance is Filippo Barigioni's sentimentally expressive 18th-century monument to Maria Clementina, the wife of James Stuart, the Old Pretender.

Vatican Museums ②

THE BUILDINGS that house one of the world's most important art collections were originally papal palaces built for such Renaissance popes as Sixtus IV, Innocent VIII and Julius II. The long courtyards and galleries, linking Innocent VIII's Belvedere Palace to the other buildings, are by Donato Bramante and were commissioned for Julius II in 1503. Most of the later additions to the buildings were made in the 18th century, when priceless works of art accumulated by earlier popes were first put on display. This complex of museums also houses the Sistine Chapel and the Raphael Rooms, which should not be missed.

★ Atrium of the Four Gates
Built by Camporese from 1792 to 1793, this vast domed edifice was the original entrance to the Vatican Museums.

The Belvedere Palace was commissioned in the late 15th century by Pope Innocent VIII.

★ Cortile della Pigna
This huge bronze pine cone, part of an ancient Roman fountain, once stood in the courtyard of old St. Peter's. Its niche was designed by Pirro Ligorio.

Cortile della Biblioteca

Cortile del Belvedere

Apartment of Pius V

Sistine Chapel

Borgia Tower

Borgia Apartment

Raphael Loggia

Cortile di San Damaso

STAR FEATURES

★ Cortile della Pigna

★ Atrium of the Four Gates

★ Bramante Stairway

Spiral Ramp
The spectacular stairway up to the museums from the street was designed by Giuseppe Momo in 1932.

Entrance

VISITORS' CHECKLIST

Città del Vaticano. Entrance in Viale Vaticano. **Map** 3 B2. 06-69 88 44 66. 49 to entrance, 23, 81, 492, 982 to Piazza del Risorgimento or 64 to St. Peter's. Connecting bus between St. Peter's and museums. Ottaviano. 19 to Piazza del Risorgimento. **Open** Mar–Oct: 8:45am–3:45pm Mon–Fri; 8:45am–12:45pm Sat; Nov–Feb: 8:45am–12:45pm Mon–Sat. **Closed** public & religious hols. Special permit required for Raphael Loggia, Vatican library, Lapidary Gallery & Vatican Archives. **Adm charge**, free last Sun of month. special routes. **Temporary exhibitions, lectures.**

Simonetti Stairway
Built in the 1780s with a vaulted ceiling, these stairs were part of the conversion of the Belvedere Palace into the Pio-Clementine Museum.

Cortile Ottagonale
The inner court of the Belvedere Palace was given its octagonal shape in 1773.

★ **Bramante Stairway**
Pope Julius II built the spiral staircase within a square tower as an entrance to the palace. The staircase could be ridden up on horseback in case of emergency.

Braccio
Nuovo

TIMELINE

1000	1500	1600	1700	1800
1198 Innocent III creates papal palace	**1503** Bramante lays out Belvedere Courtyard **1509** Raphael begins work on Rooms	**1655** Bernini designs Scala Regia	**1756** Foundation of Christian Museum	**1800–23** Chiaramonti Museum founded **1837** Etruscan Museum founded
1473 Pope Sixtus IV builds Sistine Chapel	**1503–13** Pope Julius II starts Classical sculpture collection	*Bramante (1444–1514)*	**1758** Museum of Pagan Antiquities founded **1776–84** Pius VI enlarges museum	**1822** Braccio Nuovo is opened **1970** Pope Paul VI opens Gregorian Museum of Pagan Antiquities

Exploring the Vatican Museums

Four centuries of papal patronage and connoisseurship have resulted in one of the world's great collections of Classical and Renaissance art. The Vatican houses many of the great archaeological finds of central Italy, including the *Laocoön* group, discovered in 1506 on the Esquiline; the *Apollo del Belvedere*; and the Etruscan bronze known as the *Mars of Todi*. During the Renaissance, parts of the museums were decorated with wonderful frescoes commissioned for the Sistine Chapel, the Raphael Rooms and the Borgia Apartment.

Mars of Todi

Gallery of the Candelabra
Once an open loggia (courtyard gallery), this gallery of Greek and Roman sculpture has a view of the Vatican Gardens.

Roo the

Gallery of Tapestries

Etruscan Museum

Siege of Malta
The Gallery of Maps is an important record of 16th-century history and cartography.

Upper floor

Modern Religious Art

Raphael Loggia

Sistine Chapel

Raphael Rooms

GALLERY GUIDE
Visitors have to follow a one-way system. It is best to concentrate on a single collection or to choose one of the suggested itineraries. These are color-coded so that you can follow them throughout the museums. Routes vary in length from 90 minutes to 5 hours. If you are planning a long visit, make sure you allow plenty of time for resting. Conserve your stamina for the Sistine Chapel and the Raphael Rooms; they are 20 to 30 minutes' walk from the entrance, not counting any viewing time along the way.

Sala dei Misteri
This is one of the rooms of the Borgia Apartment, richly decorated with Pinturicchio frescoes.

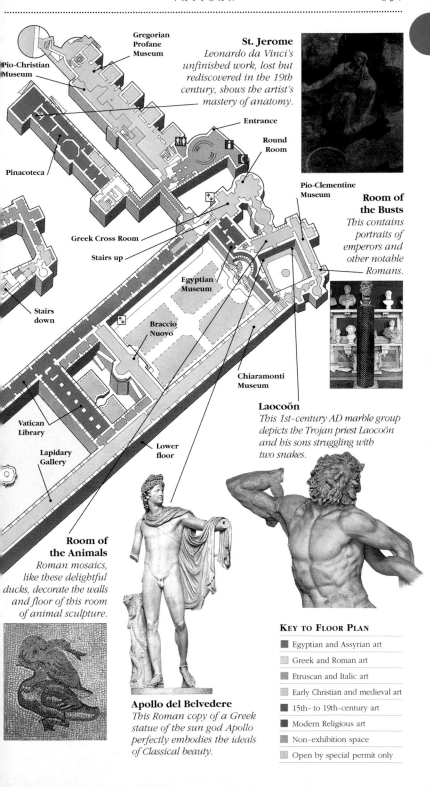

Gregorian Profane Museum

Pio-Christian Museum

St. Jerome
Leonardo da Vinci's unfinished work, lost but rediscovered in the 19th century, shows the artist's mastery of anatomy.

Entrance

Round Room

Pinacoteca

Pio-Clementine Museum

Room of the Busts
This contains portraits of emperors and other notable Romans.

Greek Cross Room

Stairs up

Egyptian Museum

Stairs down

Braccio Nuovo

Chiaramonti Museum

Vatican Library

Laocoön
This 1st-century AD marble group depicts the Trojan priest Laocoön and his sons struggling with two snakes.

Lapidary Gallery

Lower floor

Room of the Animals
Roman mosaics, like these delightful ducks, decorate the walls and floor of this room of animal sculpture.

Apollo del Belvedere
This Roman copy of a Greek statue of the sun god Apollo perfectly embodies the ideals of Classical beauty.

KEY TO FLOOR PLAN

- Egyptian and Assyrian art
- Greek and Roman art
- Etruscan and Italic art
- Early Christian and medieval art
- 15th- to 19th-century art
- Modern Religious art
- Non-exhibition space
- Open by special permit only

Exploring the Vatican's Collections

THE VATICAN'S GREATEST TREASURES are its Greek and
Roman antiquities. These have been on display
since the 18th century. The 19th century saw the
addition of exciting discoveries from Etruscan tombs
and excavations in Egypt. In the Pinacoteca (art gallery)
there is a small, choice collection of painting, including
works by Raphael, Titian and Leonardo. Works by great
painters and sculptors are also displayed throughout the
older parts of the museums in the form of sumptuous
decorations commissioned by the Renaissance popes.

Colored bas-relief from an Egyptian tomb (c. 2400 BC)

EGYPTIAN AND ASSYRIAN ART

THE EGYPTIAN COLLECTION
contains finds from 19th-
and 20th-century excavations
in Egypt and statues that were
brought to Rome in Imperial
times. There are also Roman
imitations of Egyptian art
from Hadrian's Villa (see
p269) and from the Campus
Martius district of ancient
Rome. Egyptian-style statuary
from Hadrian's Villa was used
to decorate the Greek Cross
Room, the entrance to the
new wing built in 1780 by
Michelangelo Simonetti.

The genuine Egyptian works,
exhibited on the lower floor of
the Belvedere Palace, include
statues, mummies, mummy
cases and funerary artifacts.
There is also a large collection
of documents written on
papyrus, the paper the ancient
Egyptians made from reeds.
Among the main treasures is
a colossal granite statue of
Queen Tuia, the mother of
Rameses II, found on the site
of the Horti Sallustiani gardens

(see p251) in 1714. The statue,
which dates from the 13th
century BC, may have been
brought to Rome by the
Emperor Caligula (reigned
AD 37–41), who had an
unhealthy interest in
pharaohs and in his own
mother, Agrippina.

Also noteworthy are
the head of a statue of
Mentuhotep IV (21st
century BC); the
beautiful mummy
case of Queen
Hetep-heret-es;
and the tomb of
Iri, the guardian
of the Pyramid of
Cheops (22nd
century BC).

The Assyrian
Stairway is
decorated with
fragments of
reliefs from
the palaces of
the Kings of
Nineveh (8th century BC).
These depict the military
exploits of King Sennacherib
and his son, Sargon II, and
show scenes from Assyrian
and Chaldean mythology.

ETRUSCAN AND OTHER PRE-ROMAN ART

THIS COLLECTION comprises
artifacts from pre-Roman
civilizations in Etruria and
Latium, from Neolithic times to
the 1st century BC, when
these ancient populations
were assimilated into the
Roman state. Among the finest
objects in the Gregorian
Etruscan Museum are those
from the Regolini-Galassi
tomb, excavated in 1836 at the
necropolis of Cerveteri (see
p271). The tomb was found
intact and yielded numerous
everyday household objects,
plus a throne, a bed and a
funeral cart, all cast in bronze,
dating from the 7th century
BC. Beautiful black vases,
delightful terra-cotta figurines
and such bronze statues as the
famous *Mars of Todi*,
displayed in the Room of the
Bronzes, show the Etruscans
to have been a highly
civilized, sophisticated people.

A number of Greek vases
also found in Etruscan tombs
are on display in the Vase
Collection. The Room of the
Italiot Vases contains only
vases produced locally in the
Greek cities of Southern Italy
and in Etruria itself. These
date from the 3rd to the 1st
century BC.

**Etruscan
gold clasp
(fibula)
from the 7th
century BC**

Head of an athlete in mosaic from the Baths of Caracalla

GREEK AND ROMAN ART

THE GREATER PART of the Vatican Museums is dedicated to Greek and Roman art. Exhibits line connecting corridors and vestibules; walls and floors display fine mosaics; and famous sculptures decorate the main courtyards.

The first serious organization of the collection took place in the reign of Julius II (1503–13) around Bramante's Belvedere Courtyard. The prize pieces form the nucleus of the 18th-century Pio-Clementine Museum. In the pavilions of the Octagonal Courtyard and in the surrounding rooms are sculptures considered among the greatest achievements of Western art. The *Apoxyomenos* (an athlete wiping his body after a race) and the *Apollo del Belvedere* are high-quality Roman copies of Greek originals of about 320 BC. The magnificent *Laocoön*, sculpted by three artists from Rhodes, had long been known to exist from a description by Pliny the Elder. It was rediscovered near the ruins of Nero's Golden House *(see p175)* in 1506. Classical works such as these had a profound influence on Michelangelo and other Renaissance artists.

The much smaller Chiaramonti Museum, named after Pope Pius VII Chiaramonti, was laid out by Canova in the early 19th century. It includes a striking colossal head of the goddess Athene. The Braccio Nuovo, an extension of the Chiaramonti, decorated with Roman floor mosaics, contains a statue of Augustus from the villa of his wife, Livia, at Prima Porta. Its pose is based on the famous *Doryphoros* by the Greek sculptor Polyclitus, a Roman copy of which can be seen on display nearby.

Exhibits in the Vase Rooms range from the Greek geometric style (8th century BC) to black-figure vases from Corinth, such as the famous vase by Exekias, with Achilles and Ajax playing a game similar to checkers (530 BC), and to the later red-figure type, such as the *kylix* (a wide shallow cup) with Oedipus and the Sphinx from the 5th century BC. A stairway links this section to the Gallery of the Candelabra and the Room of the Biga (a two-horse chariot). The horses and harness were added in the 18th century.

The Gregorian Profane Museum, housed in a new wing, charts the evolution of Roman art from dependence upon Greek models to a recognizably Roman style.

The *Doryphoros*, or spear-carrier, a Roman copy in marble of an original Greek bronze

Original Greek works here include large marble fragments from the Parthenon in Athens. There is also a Roman copy of *Athene and Marsyas* by Myron, which was part of the decoration of the Parthenon. Totally Roman in character are two reliefs known as the Rilievi della Cancelleria,

Marble relief of the Emperor Vespasian

because they were discovered beneath the Palazzo della Cancelleria *(see p149)* in the 1930s. They show military parades of the Emperor Vespasian and his son, Domitian. This section also has fine Roman floor mosaics. There are two from the Baths of Caracalla *(see p197)*, depicting athletes and referees. They date from the 3rd century AD. Most striking of all is a mosaic that creates the impression of an unswept floor, covered with debris after a meal. Away from the main Classical collections, in one of the rooms of the Vatican Library, is the *Aldobrandini Wedding*, a beautiful Roman fresco of a bride being prepared for her marriage, dating from the 1st century AD.

Floor mosaic from the Baths of Otricoli in Umbria, in the Round Room

Detail from Giotto's *Stefaneschi Triptych*

EARLY CHRISTIAN AND MEDIEVAL ART

THE MAIN COLLECTION of early Christian antiquities is in the Pio-Christian Museum, founded in the last century by Pope Pius IX and formerly housed in the Lateran Palace. It contains inscriptions and sculpture from catacombs and early Christian basilicas. The sculpture consists chiefly of reliefs decorating sarcophagi, though the most striking work is a free-standing 4th-century statue of the *Good Shepherd*. The sculpture's chief appeal lies in the way it blends biblical episodes with pagan mythology. Christianity adopted Classical images so that its doctrines could be understood in clear visual terms. The idealized pastoral figure of the shepherd, for example, became Christ himself, while bearded philosophers turned into the Apostles. At the same time, Christianity laid claim to be the spiritual and cultural heir of the Roman Empire.

The first two rooms of the Pinacoteca are dedicated to late medieval art, featuring wooden panels tempera-painted that served as altarpieces. The outstanding work is Giotto's altarpiece dating from about 1300, known as the *Stefaneschi Triptych*. It expresses much the same theme as the early Christian works: the continuity between the Classical world of the Roman Empire and the new order of Christian Europe. The crucifixion of St. Peter takes place between two landmarks of ancient Rome, the Pyramid of Caius Cestius *(see p205)*, and the pyramid known in the Middle Ages as the Tomb of Romulus, which stood near the Vatican. The triptych, which decorated the main altar of old St Peter's, includes portraits of Pope St. Celestine V (reigned 1294–6), and of the donor, Cardinal Jacopo Stefaneschi, shown offering the triptych to St. Peter.

The Vatican Library has a number of medieval treasures exhibited rather haphazardly in showcases; these include woven and embroidered cloths, reliquaries, enamels and icons. One of the aims of the 18th-century reorganization of the Vatican collections was to glorify Christian works by contrasting them with earlier pagan creations. In the long Lapidary Gallery, over 3,000 stone tablets with Christian and pagan inscriptions are displayed on opposite walls. The world's greatest collection of its kind, it may be visited only with special permission.

15TH- TO 19TH-CENTURY ART

THE RENAISSANCE POPES, many of whom were cultured connoisseurs of the arts, considered it their duty to sponsor the leading painters, sculptors and goldsmiths of

***Pietà* by the Venetian artist Giovanni Bellini (1430–1516)**

RAPHAEL'S LAST PAINTING

When Raphael died in 1520, the *Transfiguration* was found in his studio, almost complete. The wonderful luminous work was placed at the head of the bier where the great artist's body lay. It depicts the episode in the Gospels in which Christ took three of the Apostles to the top of a mountain, where He appeared to them in divine glory. In the detail shown here, Christ floats above the ground in a halo of ethereal light.

the age. The galleries around the Cortile del Belvedere were all decorated by great artists between the 16th and the 19th century. The Gallery of Tapestries is hung with tapestries woven in Brussels to designs by students of Raphael; the Apartment of Pope Pius V has beautiful 15th-century Flemish tapestries; and the Gallery of Maps is frescoed with 16th-century maps of ancient and contemporary Italy. When you visit the Raphael Rooms *(see pp242–3)*, be sure to also visit the nearby Room of the Chiaroscuri and Pope Nicholas V's tiny private chapel, frescoed by Fra Angelico between 1447 and 1451. Similarly, before reaching the Sistine Chapel *(see pp244–7)*, visit the Borgia Apartment, frescoed in a decorative, flowery style by Pinturicchio and his students in the 1490s. The contrast with Michelangelo's Sistine Chapel ceiling, begun in 1508, could hardly be greater. Another set of fascinating frescoes decorates the Loggia of Raphael, but this requires special permission to visit.

Many important works by Renaissance masters are displayed in the Pinacoteca (art gallery). Highlights among the works by 15th-century painters are a fine *Pietà* by the Venetian Giovanni Bellini and Leonardo da Vinci's unfinished *St. Jerome*. Of the

great 16th-century works, do not miss the fine altarpiece by Titian, the *Crucifixion of St. Peter* by Guido Reni, the *Deposition* by Caravaggio and the *Communion of St. Jerome* by Domenichino. Raphael has a whole room dedicated to his work. It contains the beautiful *Madonna of Foligno* and the *Transfiguration*, as well as eight tapestries made to his designs.

Lunette of the *Adoration of the Magi* by Pinturicchio in the Room of the Liberal Arts in the Borgia Apartment

Town with Gothic Cathedral by Paul Klee (1879–1940)

MODERN RELIGIOUS ART

MODERN ARTISTS exhibited in the Vatican Museums face daunting competition from the great works of the past. Few modern works are displayed conspicuously, the exceptions being Momo's spiral staircase of 1932, which greets visitors as they enter the museums, and Giò Pomodoro's abstract sculpture in the center of the Cortile della Pigna.

In 1973, a contemporary art collection was inaugurated by Pope Paul VI. Housed in the Borgia Apartment, it includes over 800 exhibits by modern artists from all over the world, donated by collectors or the artists themselves. Works in a great variety of media show many contrasting approaches to religious subjects. There are paintings, drawings, engravings and sculptures by 19th- and 20th-century artists, as well as mosaics, stained glass, ceramics and tapestries. Well-known modern painters such as Georges Braque, Paul Klee, Edvard Munch and Graham Sutherland are also represented, and there are drawings by Henry Moore, ceramics by Picasso and stained glass by Fernand Léger. Projects for modern church ornaments include Matisse's decorations for the church of St. Paul de Vence, Luigi Fontana's models for the bronze doors of Milan cathedral and Emilio Greco's panels for the doors of Orvieto cathedral.

Raphael Rooms

P OPE JULIUS II'S PRIVATE APARTMENTS were built above
those of his hated predecessor, Alexander VI, one of
the Borgias, who died in 1503. Julius was impressed with
Raphael's work and chose him to redecorate the four

rooms *(stanze)*. Raphael
and his pupils began the
task in 1508, replacing
existing works by several
better-known artists,
including Raphael's own
teacher, Perugino. The
work took over 16 years,
and Raphael himself died
before its completion.
The frescoes express the
religious and philosophical
ideals of the Renaissance.
They quickly established
Raphael's reputation as an
artist in Rome, putting him
on a par with Michelangelo,
then working on the ceiling
of the Sistine Chapel.

**Detail from *The Expulsion of
Heliodorus from the Temple*,
showing Pope Julius II watching
the scene from his litter**

Cortile del
Belvedere

KEY TO FLOOR PLAN

① Hall of Constantine

② Room of Heliodorus

③ Room of the Segnatura

④ Room of the Fire in the Borgo

HALL OF CONSTANTINE ①

T HE FRESCOES in this room
were started in 1517,
three years before Raphael's
death, but Raphael himself
probably had little hand in
their execution. As a result,
they are not held in the same
high regard as those in the
other rooms. The work was
completed in 1525, during the
reign of Pope Clement VII, by
Giulio Romano and two other
former pupils of Raphael,
Giovanni Francesco Penni
and Raffaellino del Colle.

The theme of the decoration
is the triumph of Christianity
over paganism. The
four major frescoes
show scenes from the
life of Constantine and
include his *Vision of
the Cross* and his
victory over his rival
Maxentius at *The Battle
of the Milvian Bridge*,
for which Raphael had
provided a preparatory
sketch. In both *The
Baptism of Constantine*
and *The Donation of
Constantine*, the figure
of Pope Sylvester *(see
p170)* was given the
features of Clement VII.

ROOM OF HELIODORUS ②

T HIS PRIVATE antechamber
was decorated by Raphael
between 1512 and 1514. The
main frescoes show the
miraculous protection granted
to all the Church's
ministers, doctrines
and property. The
room's name refers
to the fresco on the
right, *The Expulsion
of Heliodorus from
the Temple*. This
shows a story from
Jewish history, in
which a thief called
Heliodorus is felled

**Swiss guards waiting
with papal chair in
*The Mass at Bolsena***

by a horseman as he tries to
make off with the treasure
from the Temple of Jerusalem.
The scene is witnessed by the
pope, borne on a litter by
courtiers. The incident is also
a thinly veiled reference to
Julius II's success in driving
foreign armies out of Italy. In
*The Meeting of Leo I and
Attila*, Raphael pays a similar
compliment to the pope's
political skill. Pope
Leo was originally
given the face of
Julius II, but after
his death, Raphael
substituted the
features of Julius's
successor, Leo X.

*The Mass at
Bolsena* depicts a
miracle that occurred
in 1263. A priest

***The Battle of the Milvian Bridge*, completed by one of Raphael's assistants**

The Liberation of St. Peter, a three-part composition, shows the saint asleep in his cell in the middle section, led out of prison by an angel on the right, while, on the left, the prison guards cower in terror

who doubted that the bread and wine really were the body and blood of Christ suddenly saw the host bleed while he was celebrating mass. Julius II appears in this fresco, accompanied by a colorful group of Swiss guards.

Julius appears again as St. Peter in *The Liberation of St. Peter*. This fresco is remarkable for its dramatic lighting effects, achieved despite the painting's awkward shape and its position above a window.

ROOM OF THE SEGNATURA ③

THE NAME is derived from a special council that met in this room to sign official documents. The frescoes here were completed between 1508 and 1511. The scheme Raphael followed was dictated by Pope Julius II. It reflects the Humanist belief that there could be perfect harmony between Classical culture and Christianity in their mutual search for truth.

The Dispute over the Holy Sacrament, the first fresco completed by Raphael for Pope Julius, represents the triumph of religion and spiritual truth. The consecrated host is shown at the center of the painting. This links the group of learned scholars, who discuss its significance, to the Holy Trinity and the saints floating on clouds up above.

On the opposite wall, *The School of Athens (see p30)* is a bustling scene

centered around the debate on the search for truth between Greek philosophers Plato and Aristotle. It also features portraits of many of Raphael's contemporaries, including Leonardo da Vinci, Bramante and Michelangelo. The other works include a portrait of the bearded Pope Julius II, who in 1511 vowed not to shave until he had rid Italy of all usurpers.

ROOM OF THE *FIRE IN THE BORGO* ④

THIS WAS ORIGINALLY the dining room, but when the decoration was completed under Pope Leo X, it became a music room. All the frescoes exalt the reigning pope by depicting events in the lives of his namesakes, the 9th-century popes Leo III and IV. The main frescoes were finished by two of Raphael's assistants between 1514 and 1517, following their

master's own plans. The most famous, *The Fire in the Borgo*, was painted from Raphael's designs and reflects his maturity as an artist. It celebrates the miracle that took place in 847, when Pope Leo IV extinguished a fire raging in the Borgo *(see p228)* by making the sign of the cross. The incident is likened to the flight of Aeneas from Troy described by Virgil. The figure of Aeneas appears in the foreground carrying his father on his back. This borrowing of an event from Classical legend shows Raphael's new willingness to experiment. Sadly, his pupils did not always follow his designs faithfully, and this, combined with poor restoration, has spoiled the work.

Detail from *The Fire in the Borgo*, showing Aeneas, the Trojan hero, with his father on his back, fleeing from the fire

The Dispute over the Holy Sacrament, the first fresco completed in the Rooms

Sistine Chapel: The Walls

THE MASSIVE WALLS of the Sistine Chapel, the main chapel in the Vatican Palace, were frescoed by some of the finest artists of the 15th and 16th centuries. The 12 paintings on the side walls, by artists including Perugino, Ghirlandaio, Botticelli and Signorelli, show parallel episodes from the life of Moses and of Christ. The decoration of the chapel walls was completed between 1534 and 1541 by Michelangelo, who added the great altar wall fresco, the *Last Judgment*.

KEY TO THE FRESCOES: ARTISTS AND SUBJECTS

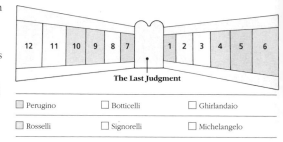

The Last Judgment

☐ Perugino   ☐ Botticelli   ☐ Ghirlandaio

☐ Rosselli   ☐ Signorelli   ☐ Michelangelo

1 Baptism of Christ in the Jordan
2 Temptations of Christ
3 Calling of St. Peter and St. Andrew
4 Sermon on the Mount
5 Handing over the Keys to St. Peter
6 Last Supper
7 Moses's Journey into Egypt
8 Moses Receiving the Call
9 Crossing of the Red Sea
10 Adoration of the Golden Calf
11 Punishment of the Rebels
12 Last Days of Moses

THE LAST JUDGMENT BY MICHELANGELO

REVEALED IN 1993 after a year's restoration, the *Last Judgment* is considered to be the masterpiece of Michelangelo's mature years. It was commissioned by Pope Paul III Farnese, and required the removal of some earlier frescoes and two windows over the altar. A new wall was erected which slanted inwards to stop dust settling on it. Michelangelo worked alone on the fresco for seven years, until its completion in 1541.

The painting depicts the souls of the dead rising up to face the wrath of God, a subject that is rarely used for an altar decoration. The pope chose it as a warning to Catholics to adhere to their faith in the turmoil of the Reformation. In fact the work conveys the artist's own tormented attitude to his faith. It offers neither the certainties of Christian orthodoxy, nor the ordered view of Classicism.

In a dynamic, emotional composition, the figures are caught in a vortex of motion. The dead are torn from their graves and hauled up to face Christ the Judge, whose athletic, muscular figure is the focus of all the painting's movement. Christ shows little sympathy for the agitated saints around him, clutching the instruments of their martyrdom. Neither is any pity shown for the damned, hurled down to the demons in hell. Here Charon, pushing people off his boat into the depths of Hades, and the infernal judge Minos, are taken from Dante's *Inferno*. Minos has ass's ears, and is a portrait of courtier Biagio da Cesena, who had objected to the nude figures in the fresco. Michelangelo's self-portrait is on the skin held by the martyr St. Bartholomew.

Souls meeting the wrath of Christ in Michelangelo's *Last Judgment*

WALL FRESCOES

Detail from Botticelli's fresco
Temptations of Christ

WHEN THE Sistine Chapel was built, the papacy was a strong political power with vast accumulated wealth. In 1475 Pope Sixtus IV was able to summon some of the greatest painters of his day to decorate the chapel. Among the artists employed were Perugino, who was Raphael's master and is often credited with overseeing the project, Sandro Botticelli, Domenico Ghirlandaio, Cosimo Rosselli and Luca Signorelli. Their work on the chapel's frescoes took from 1481 to 1483.

Although frequently overlooked by visitors who concentrate on Michelangelo's work, the frescoes along the side walls of the chapel include some of the finest works of 15th-century Italian art. The two cycles of frescoes represent scenes from the lives of Moses and Christ. Above them in the spaces between the windows are portraits of the earliest popes, painted by various artists, including Botticelli.

The fresco cycles start at the altar end of the chapel, with the story of Christ on the right-hand wall and that of Moses on the left. Originally there were two paintings, *The Birth of Christ* and *The Finding of Moses*, on the wall behind the altar, but these were both destroyed to make way for Michelangelo's *The Last Judgment*.

The final paintings of the two cycles are also lost. They were on the entrance wall, which collapsed during the 16th century. When the wall was restored, they were replaced with poor substitutes.

As was customary at the time, each fresco contains a series of scenes, linked thematically to the central episode. Hidden meanings and symbols connect each painting with its counterpart on the opposite wall, and there are also many allusions to contemporary events.

The elaborate architectural details in the frescoes include familiar Roman monuments. The Arch of Constantine *(see p91)* provides the backdrop for the *Punishment of the Rebels* by Botticelli, the fifth panel in the cycle of Moses, in which the artist himself appears as the last figure but one on the right. Two similar arches appear in the painting opposite, Perugino's *Handing over the Keys to St. Peter*.

Moses was both spiritual and temporal leader of his people. He called down the wrath of God on those who challenged his decisions, thus

The crowd of onlookers in the *Calling of St. Peter and St. Andrew* by Ghirlandaio

setting a precedent for the power exercised by the pope. In *Handing over the Keys to St. Peter*, Christ confers spiritual

and temporal authority on St. Peter by giving him the keys to the Kingdoms of Heaven and Earth. The golden-domed building in the center of the vast piazza represents both the Temple of Jerusalem and the Church, as founded by Peter, the first pope. The fifth figure on the right is thought to be a self-portrait by Perugino.

Botticelli's *Temptations of Christ* includes a view of the

The central episode in Botticelli's *Punishment of the Rebels*

Hospital of Santo Spirito, rebuilt in 1475 by Sixtus IV *(see p226)*. Here the devil is disguised in the habit of a Franciscan monk. Portraits of both Botticelli and Filippino Lippi are visible in the left hand corner. A portrait of the pope's nephew, Girolamo Riario, appears in the painting of the *Crossing of the Red Sea* by Rosselli, in which the sea is literally red. This painting also commemorates the papal victory at Campomorto in 1482.

Perugino's *Handing over the Keys to St. Peter*

Sistine Chapel: The Ceiling

MICHELANGELO FRESCOED the ceiling for Pope Julius II between 1508 and 1512, working on specially designed scaffolding. The main panels, which chart the Creation of the World and Fall of Man, are surrounded by subjects from the Old and New Testaments – except for the Classical Sibyls who are said to have foreseen the birth of Christ. In the 1980s the ceiling was restored revealing colors of an unsuspected vibrancy.

Libyan Sibyl
The pagan prophetess reaches for the Book of Know-ledge. Like most female figures Michelangelo painted, the beautiful Libyan Sibyl was probably modelled on a man.

Illusionistic architecture

KEY TO CEILING PANELS

■ **GENESIS: 1** God Dividing Light from Darkness; **2** Creation of the Sun and Moon; **3** Separating Waters from Land; **4** Creation of Adam; **5** Creation of Eve; **6** Original Sin; **7** Sacrifice of Noah; **8** The Deluge; **9** Drunkenness of Noah.

■ **ANCESTORS OF CHRIST: 10** Solomon with his Mother; **11** Parents of Jesse; **12** Rehoboam with Mother; **13** Asa with Parents; **14** Uzziah with Parents; **15** Hezekiah with Parents; **16** Zerubbabel with Parents; **17** Josiah with Parents.

■ **PROPHETS: 18** Jonah; **19** Jeremiah; **20** Daniel; **21** Ezekiel; **22** Isaiah; **23** Joel; **24** Zechariah.

■ **SIBYLS: 25** Libyan Sibyl; **26** Persian Sibyl; **27** Cumaean Sibyl; **28** Erythrean Sibyl; **29** Delphic Sibyl.

■ **OLD TESTAMENT SCENES OF SALVATION: 30** Punishment of Haman; **31** Moses and the Brazen Serpent; **32** David and Goliath; **33** Judith and Holofernes.

Creation of the Sun and Moon
Michelangelo depicts God as a dynamic but terrifying figure commanding the sun to shed light on the earth.

Original Sin
This shows Adam and Eve tasting the forbidden fruit from the Tree of Knowledge, and their expulsion from Paradise. Michelangelo represents Satan as a snake with the body of a woman.

The Ignudi are athletic male nudes whose significance is uncertain.

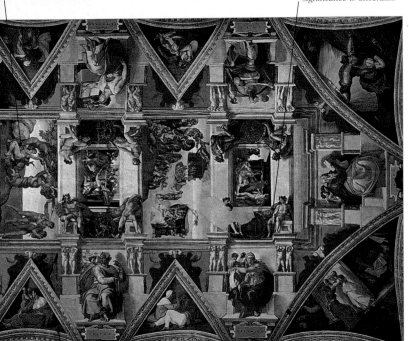

The lunettes are devoted to frescoes of the ancestors of Christ, like Hezekiah.

RESTORATION OF THE SISTINE CEILING

Restorers used computers, photography and spectrum analysis to inspect the fresco before cleaning began. They were therefore able to detect and remove the changes previous restorers had made to Michelangelo's original work. Analysis showed that the ceiling had been cleaned with materials ranging from bread to retsina wine. The restoration then revealed the familiarly dusky, eggshell-cracked figures to have creamy skins, lustrous hair and to be dressed in brightly-colored, luscious robes: "a Benetton Michelangelo" mocked one critic, claiming that a layer of varnish which the artist had added to darken the colors had been removed. However, after examining the work, most experts agreed that the new colors probably matched those painted by Michelangelo.

A restorer cleaning the Libyan Sibyl

Castel Sant'Angelo ⑬

T HE MASSIVE FORTRESS of Castel Sant'Angelo takes its name from the statue of the Archangel Michael on its summit. It began in AD 139 as the Emperor Hadrian's mausoleum. Since then it has had many roles: as part of the Emperor Aurelian's city wall, as a medieval citadel and prison and as the residence of the popes in times of political unrest. From the dank cells in the lower levels to the fine apartments of the Renaissance popes above, a 58-room museum covers all aspects of the castle's history.

Mausoleum of Hadrian
This artist's impression shows the tomb before Aurelian fortified its walls in AD 270 to 275.

Courtyard of Honor
Piles of stone cannonballs decorate the courtyard, once the castle's ammunition store.

The Treasury was probably the original site of Hadrian's burial chamber.

Hall of the Columns

Loggia of Paul III

Hall of the Library

PROTECTING THE POPE

The Vatican Corridor leads from the Vatican Palace to Castel Sant'Angelo. It was built in 1277 to provide an escape route when the pope was in danger. The pentagonal ramparts built around the castle during the 17th century improved its defenses in times of siege.

■ Walls and fortifications
■ Vatican Corridor

The Rooms of Clement VIII are inscribed with the family crest of the Aldobrandini pope (1592–1605).

The Hall of Justice is decorated with a fresco of *The Angel of Justice* by Domenico Zaga (1545).

The spiral ramp was the entrance to the mausoleum.

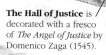

★View from Terrace
The castle's terrace, scene of the last act of Puccini's Tosca, *offers splendid views in every direction.*

The Chamber of the Urns housed the ashes of members of Hadrian's family.

STAR FEATURES

★ Sala Paolina

★ View from Terrace

★ Staircase of Alexander VI

VISITORS' CHECKLIST

Lungotevere Castello (entrance through gardens to the right of building). **Map** 4 D3 & 11 A1.
06-681 91 11. 23, 34, 64, 280 to Lungotevere Castello; 34, 49, 64, 70, 186, 926, 990 to Piazza Cavour. Lepanto.
Open 9am–10pm Tue–Sat, 9am–8pm Sun. **Closed** public hols, 2nd & 4th Tue of month.
Adm charge.
Exhibitions.

Bronze Angel
The gigantic statue of the Archangel Michael is by the 18th-century Flemish sculptor Pieter Verschaffelt.

The Round Hall houses the original model from which Verschaffelt's angel was cast.

★ **Sala Paolina**
The illusionistic frescoes by Perin del Vaga and Pellegrino Tibaldi (1546–8) include one of a courtier entering the room through a painted door.

Hall of Apollo
The room is frescoed with scenes from mythology attributed to the pupils of Perin del Vaga (1548).

Ventilation shaft

★ **Staircase of Alexander VI**
This staircase cuts right through the heart of the building.

Bridge

TIMELINE

AD 139 Mausoleum completed by Antoninus Pius

590 Legendary date of appearance of Archangel Michael above the castle

1493 Pope Alexander VI restores Vatican Corridor

1390 Pope Boniface IX remodels the castle

Facade of Castel Sant'Angelo

AD 100	500	1000	1500

271 Tomb is incorporated into Aurelian Wall and fortified

Cannonballs in the Courtyard of Honor

1527 Castle withstands siege during Sack of Rome

1557 Ramparts built to protect the castle

AD 130 Hadrian begins family mausoleum

1542–9 Sala Paolina and apartments built for Pope Paul III

1870 Castle used as barracks and military prison

VIA VENETO

I N IMPERIAL ROME, this was a suburb where rich families owned luxurious villas and gardens. Ruins from this era can be seen in the excavations in Piazza Sallustio, named after the most extensive gardens in the area, the Horti Sallustiani. After the Sack of Rome in the 5th century, the area reverted to open countryside. Not until the 17th century did it recover its lost splendor, with the building of Palazzo Barberini and the now-vanished Villa Ludovisi.

Film director Federico Fellini

When Rome became capital of Italy in 1870, the Ludovisi sold their land for development. They kept a plot for a new house, but tax on the profits from the sale was so high that they had to sell that, too. By 1900, Via Veneto had become a street with smart modern hotels and cafés. It featured prominently in Fellini's 1960 film *La Dolce Vita*, a scathing satire on the lives of film stars and the idle rich, but since then it has lost its position as the meeting place of the famous.

SIGHTS AT A GLANCE

Churches and Temples
Santa Maria della Concezione ❸
Santa Susanna ❼
Santa Maria della Vittoria ❽

Historic Buildings
Casino dell'Aurora ❷
Palazzo Barberini ❻

Famous Streets
Via Veneto ❶

Fountains
Fontana delle Api ❹
Fontana del Tritone ❺

SEE ALSO
• *Street Finder*, map 5
• *Where to Stay* pp294–5
• *Restaurants* pp310–11

0 meters   200
0 yards   200

N

GETTING THERE
This is one of the easiest parts of Rome to reach by public transportation. Barberini and Repubblica Metro stations on line A are very handy, and Stazione Termini is only 10 to 15 minutes' walk away. The Via Veneto itself starts at Piazza Barberini, well served by buses from all parts of the city. The 95 goes the whole length of Via Veneto to Porta Pinciana. Other useful routes include the 52, 53, 56, 58 and 116 along Via del Tritone.

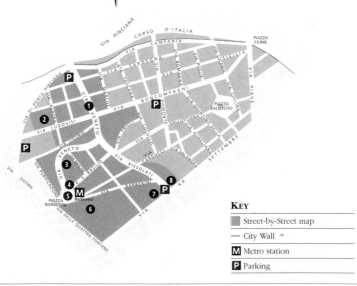

KEY

	Street-by-Street map
—	City Wall ⇒
M	Metro station
P	Parking

The onset of autumn in Via Veneto

Street by Street: Via Veneto

THE STREETS AROUND VIA VENETO, though within the walls of ancient Rome, contain little dating from before the unification of Italy in 1870. With its hotels, restaurants, bars and travel agencies, the area is the center of 20th-century tourism in the way that Piazza di Spagna was the hub of the tourist trade in the Rome of the 18th-century Grand Tour. However, glimpses of the old city can be seen among the modern streets. These include Santa Maria della Concezione, the church of the Capuchin friars, whose convent once stood in its own gardens. In the 17th century, Palazzo Barberini was built here for the powerful papal family. Bernini's Fontana del Tritone and Fontana delle Api have stood in Piazza Barberini since it was the meeting place of cart tracks entering the city from surrounding vineyards.

Casino dell'Aurora
A pavilion is all that remains of the great Ludovisi estate that once occupied most of this quarter of Rome **2**

Santa Maria della Concezione
This church is best known for the macabre collection of bones in its crypt **3**

Fontana delle Api
Bernini's drinking fountain is decorated with bees, emblem of his Barberini patrons **4**

Fontana del Tritone
Bernini's muscular sea god has been spouting water skyward for 350 years **5**

★ **Palazzo Barberini**
Pietro da Cortona worked on his spectacular ceiling fresco The Triumph of Divine Providence *between 1633 and 1639* **6**

The Porta Pinciana
was built in AD 403.
Only the central
arch of white
travertine is
original.

LOCATOR MAP
See Central Rome Map pp12–13

Via Veneto
*Built during the
redevelopment of Rome at
the end of the 19th century,
this street of smart hotels and
spacious pavement cafés
enjoyed its heyday during
the 1950s and 1960s* ❶

Santa Susanna
*This church is
dedicated to a
martyr executed
during Diocletian's
persecution of
Christians in the
3rd century AD* ❼

STAR SIGHTS

★ **Santa Maria
della Vittoria**

★ **Palazzo Barberini**

KEY

– – –   Suggested route

0 meters	75
0 yards	75

★ **Santa Maria
della Vittoria**
*The highlight of this
Baroque church is
the Cornaro Chapel,
designed to resemble a
theater. The center of
the stage is occupied
by Bernini's thrilling
sculpture of the
Ecstasy of St. Teresa* ❽

Sidewalk café on Via Veneto

Via Veneto ❶

Map 5 B1. 🚌 52, 53, 56, 58, 58b, 95, 116, 490, 495 and many other routes to Piazza Barberini. Ⓜ Barberini.

Ⅴᴵᴬ ᴠᴇɴᴇᴛᴏ descends in a lazy curve from the Porta Pinciana to Piazza Barberini, lined in its upper reaches with exuberant turn-of-the-century hotels and canopied sidewalk cafés. It was laid out in 1879 over a large estate sold by the Ludovisi family in the great building boom of Rome's first years as capital of Italy. Palazzo Margherita, intended to be the new Ludovisi family palazzo, was completed in 1890. It now houses the American embassy.

In the 1960s this was the most glamorous street in Rome, its cafés patronized by film stars and plagued by the paparazzi. Most of the people drinking in the cafés today are tourists, as film stars now seem to prefer the livelier Bohemian atmosphere of Trastevere.

Palazzo Margherita, the US embassy

Casino dell'Aurora ❷

Via Lombardia 46. **Map** 5 B2. ☎ 06-48 39 42. 🚌 52, 53, 56, 58, 58b, 95, 116. Ⓜ Barberini. **Open** by appt only.

Tʜᴇ ᴄᴀsɪɴᴏ (a stately country residence) was a summer-house on the grounds of the Ludovisi palace. It was built by Cardinal Ludovisi in the 17th century, and frescoed by Guercino. The ceiling fresco's subject is Aurora, the goddess of dawn. It is a dizzying work creating the impression that the Casino has no roof but lies open to a cloudy sky, across which horses pull Aurora's carriage from the darkness of night toward the light of day.

Santa Maria della Concezione ❸

Via Veneto 27. **Map** 5 B2. ☎ 06-487 27 48. 🚌 52, 53, 56, 58, 58b, 60, 61, 62, 95, 116, 175. Ⓜ Barberini. **Open** 7am–noon, 3:45pm–7:30pm daily. **Crypt open** 9am–noon, 3pm–6pm Fri–Wed. **Donation** expected. ✝

Pᴏᴘᴇ ᴜʀʙᴀɴ ᴠɪɪɪ's brother, Antonio Barberini was a cardinal and a Capuchin friar. In 1626 he founded this plain, unassuming church at what is now the foot of the Via Veneto. When he died, he was buried not in a grand marble sarcophagus like most cardinals, but below a simple flagstone close to the altar, where you can read the bleak epitaph in Latin: "Here lies dust, ashes, nothing."

The grim reality of death is illustrated even more graphically in the crypt beneath the church, where generations of Capuchin friars have decorated the walls of the five vaulted chapels with the bones and skulls of their departed brethren. In all, some 4,000 skeletons were used to create this macabre memento mori. Some of the bones are wired together to form Christian symbols such as crowns of thorns, sacred hearts and crucifixes. There are also a number of complete skeletons, including one of a Barberini princess who died as a child. At the exit, an inscription in Latin reads: "What you are, we used to be. What we are, you will be."
Pope Urban VIII

Fontana delle Api ❹

Piazza Barberini. **Map** 5 B2. 🚌 52, 53, 56, 58, 58b, 60, 61, 62, 95, 116, 175. Ⓜ Barberini.

Tʜᴇ ꜰᴏᴜɴᴛᴀɪɴ of the bees – api are bees, symbol of the Barberini family – is one of Bernini's more modest works. Tucked away in a corner of Piazza Barberini, it is quite easy to miss. Dating from 1644, it pays homage to Pope Urban VIII Barberini, and features rather crablike bees that appear to be sipping the water as it dribbles down into the basin. A Latin inscription informs us that the water is for the use of the public and their animals.

Bernini's Fontana delle Api

Fontana del Tritone ❺

Piazza Barberini. **Map** 5 B3. 🚌 52, 53, 56, 58, 58b, 60, 61, 62, 95, 116, 175. Ⓜ Barberini.

Iɴ ᴛʜᴇ ᴄᴇɴᴛᴇʀ of busy Piazza Barberini is one of Bernini's liveliest fountains, the Triton Fountain. It was created for Pope Urban VIII Barberini in 1642, shortly after the completion of his palace on the ridge above. Acrobatic dolphins stand on their heads, twisting their tails together to support a huge scallop shell on which the sea god Triton kneels, blowing a spindly column of water up into the air through a conch shell. Entwined artistically among the dolphins' tails are the papal tiara, the keys of St. Peter and the Barberini coat of arms.

The Triton and his conch shell in Bernini's Fontana del Tritone

Palazzo Barberini ❻

Via delle Quattro Fontane 13. **Map** 5 B3. 📞 *06-481 45 91.* 🚌 *52, 53, 56, 58, 58b, 60, 61, 62, 95, 116, 175, 492, 590.* Ⓜ *Barberini.* **Open** *9am–7pm Tue–Sat, 9am–1pm Sun & public holidays (last adm: 30 mins before closing).* **Adm charge.**

WHEN MAFFEI BARBERINI became Pope Urban VIII in 1623, he decided to build a grand palace for his family. The site he chose was then on the fringes of the city, over-looking a ruined temple. The architect, Carlo Maderno, designed it as a typical rural villa, with wings extending into the surrounding gardens. Maderno died in 1629, shortly after the foundations had been laid, and Bernini took over, assisted by Borromini. The peculiar pediments on some of the top-floor windows, and the oval staircase inside, are almost certainly by Borromini.

Of the many sumptuously decorated rooms, the most striking is the Gran Salone, with a dazzling illusionistic ceiling fresco by Pietro da Cortona. The palazzo also houses paintings from the 13th to the 16th centuries, part of the Galleria Nazionale d'Arte

Antica, with important works by Filippo Lippi, El Greco and Caravaggio. There is also a Holbein portrait of King Henry VIII of England dressed for his wedding to Anne of Cleves. Of greater local significance are Guido Reni's *Beatrice Cenci,* the young woman executed for planning her father's murder *(see p150),* and *La Fornarina,* traditionally identified as a portrait of Raphael's mistress, but not painted by him.

Santa Susanna ❼

Via XX Settembre 14. **Map** 5 C2. 📞 *06-488 27 48.* 🚌 *60, 61, 62, 175, 492.* Ⓜ *Repubblica.* **Open** *9am–noon, 4pm–7pm daily.*

Facade of Santa Susanna

SANTA SUSANNA'S most striking feature is its vigorous Baroque facade by Carlo Maderno, finished in 1603. Christians have worshiped on the site since at least the 4th century. In the nave, there are four huge frescoes by Baldassarre Croce (1558–1628), painted to resemble tapestries. These depict scenes from the life of Susanna, an obscure Roman saint who was martyred here, and the rather better-known life of the Old Testament Susanna, who was spotted bathing in her husband's garden by two lecherous judges.

Santa Susanna is the Catholic church for Americans in Rome and holds services in English every day.

Santa Maria della Vittoria ❽

Via XX Settembre 17. **Map** 5 C2. 📞 *06-482 61 90.* 🚌 *37, 60, 61, 62, 175, 495, 910.* Ⓜ *Repubblica.* **Open** *6:30am–noon, 4:30–7pm daily.*

SANTA MARIA della Vittoria is an intimate Baroque church with a lavishly decorated candlelit interior. It contains one of Bernini's most ambitious sculptural works, the *Ecstasy of St. Teresa* (1646), centerpiece of the Cornaro Chapel, built to resemble a miniature theater. It even has an audience: sculptures of the chapel's benefactor, Cardinal Federico Cornaro, and his ancestors sit in boxes, as if watching and discussing the scene played out in front of them.

Visitors may be shocked or thrilled by the apparently physical nature of St. Teresa's ecstasy. She lies on a cloud, her mouth half-open and her eyelids closed, with rippling drapery covering her body. Looking over her with a smile, which from different angles can appear either tender or cruel, is a curly-haired angel holding an arrow with which he is about to pierce the saint's body for a second time. The marble figures are framed and illuminated by rays of divine light cast out of bronze.

Bernini's astonishing *Ecstasy of St. Teresa*

FARTHER AFIELD

THE MORE INQUISITIVE visitor to Rome may wish to try a few excursions to the large parks and some of the more isolated churches on the outskirts of the city. With a day to spare, you can explore the villas of Tivoli and the ruins of the ancient Roman port of Ostia. Traditional haunts of the

Dish (3rd century BC) in Villa Giulia

Grand Tour *(see p130)*, such as the catacombs and the ruined aqueducts of Parco Appio Claudio, still offer glimpses of the rapidly vanishing Campagna, the country-side around Rome. More modern sights include the suburb of EUR, built in the Fascist era, and the memorial at the Fosse Ardeatine.

SIGHTS AT A GLANCE

Towns and Areas
EUR 14
Tivoli 18

Historic Roads
Via Appia Antica 8

Churches
Santa Costanza 5
Sant'Agnese fuori le Mura 6
San Lorenzo fuori le Mura 7
San Paolo fuori le Mura 15

Museums and Galleries
Museo e Galleria Borghese pp260–61 2
Villa Giulia pp262–3 3
Galleria Communale d'Arte Moderna 4
Centrale Montemartini 16

Ancient Sites
Hadrian's Villa 21
Ostia Antica 22

Parks and Gardens
Villa Borghese 1
Villa Doria Pamphilj 17
Villa d'Este 19
Villa Gregoriana 20

Tombs and Catacombs
Catacombs of San Callisto 9
Catacombs of San Sebastiano 10
Catacombs of Domitilla 11
Fosse Ardeatine 12
Tomb of Cecilia Metella 13

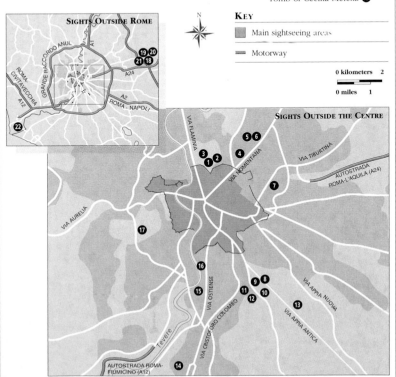

Caryatids beside the canal of the Canopus at Hadrian's Villa

Villa Borghese ●

Map 2 E5. 🚌 *3, 52, 53, 56, 95,116, 490, 495.* 🚋 *19, 30b.*
Park open *dawn to sunset.*
Bioparco *Viale del Giardino Zoologico.*
Map 2 E4. 📞 *06-321 65 64.*
🚌 *3, 52.* 🚋 *19, 19b, 30b.*
Open *daily Mar–Oct: 9.30am–7pm; Nov–Feb: 9.30am–5pm.*
Closed *1 May.* ♿ 🍴 🅿 📷 📷
Galleria Nazionale d'Arte Moderna *Viale delle Belle Arti 131.*
Map 2 D4. 📞 *06-322 981.*
🚋 *19, 19b, 30b.* **Open** *9am–7pm Tue–Sat, 9am–5pm Sun & public hols.* ♿ 📷 📷 📷

British School at Rome, designed by Edwin Lutyens in 1911

T HE VILLA and its park were designed in 1605 for Cardinal Scipione Borghese, nephew of Pope Paul V. The park was the first of its kind in Rome. It contained 400 newly-planted pine trees, garden sculpture by Bernini's father, Pietro, and dramatic waterworks built by Giovanni Fontana. The layout of the formal gardens was imitated by other prominent Roman families at Villa Ludovisi and Villa Doria Pamphilj, but the cardinal's 18th-century successors preferred a more natural-looking park.

In the early 19th century Prince Camillo Borghese assembled the family's magnificent art collection in the Casino Borghese, now the home of the Galleria and Museo Borghese.

In 1901 the park became the property of the Italian state. Within its 4-mile (6-km) circumference there are now museums and galleries, foreign academies and schools of archaeology, a zoo, a riding school, a grassy amphitheatre, an artificial lake, an aviary and an array of summer houses, fountains, Neo-Classical statuary and exotic follies.

There are several ways into the park, including a monumental entrance on Piazzale Flaminio, built for Prince Camillo Borghese in 1825 by Luigi Canina. Other conveniently-sited entrances are at Porta Pinciana at the end of Via Veneto and from the Pincio Gardens *(see p136)*. The main attraction of Italian gardens in hot weather is shade, so the long avenues are lined with hedges and trees. Piazza di Siena, a pleasantly open, grass-covered amphitheatre surrounded by tall umbrella pines, was the inspiration for Ottorino Respighi's famous symphonic poem *The Pines of Rome*, written in 1924. Near Piazza di Siena are the so-called Casina di Raffaello, said to have been owned by Raphael, and the

18th-century Palazzetto dell'Orologio. These were summerhouses from which people enjoyed the beautiful vistas across the park.

Many buildings in the park were originally surrounded by formal gardens: the Casino Borghese and the nearby 17th-century Casino della Meridiana and its aviary (the Uccelliera) have both kept their geometrical flowerbeds. Throughout the park the intersections of paths and avenues are marked by fountains and statues. West of Piazza di Siena is the Fontana dei

Statue of the English poet Byron by Thorvaldsen

Cavalli Marini (the Fountain of the Seahorses) added during the villa's 18th-century remodeling. Walking through the park you will encounter statues of Byron, Goethe and Victor Hugo, and a gloomy equestrian King Umberto I.

Dotted about the park are picturesque temples made to look like ruins, including a circular Temple of Diana between Piazza di Siena and Porta Pinciana, and a Temple of Faustina, wife of Emperor Antoninus Pius, on the hill north of Piazza di Siena. The nearby medieval-looking Fortezzuola by Canina contains the works of the sculptor Pietro Canonica, who lived in the building and died there in 1959. In the garden stands Canonica's *Monument to the Alpino and his Mule,* which honors the humblest

Neo-Classical Temple of Diana

Ionic temple dedicated to Aesculapius, built on the lake island

protagonists in Italy's alpine battles against Austria in World War I.

In the center of the park is the Giardino del Lago, its main entrance marked by an 18th-century copy of the Arch of Septimius Severus.

The garden has an artificial lake complete with an Ionic Temple to Aesculapius, the god of health, by the 18th-century architect Antonio Asprucci. Rowing boats and ducks make the lake a favorite with children, banana trees and bamboo grow around the shore, and clearings are studded with sculptures.

Surrounded by flowerbeds south of the lake is the Art Nouveau Fontana dei Fauni, one of the garden's prettiest sculptures. In a clearing close to the entrance on Viale Pietro Canonica are the original Tritons of the Fontana del Moro in Piazza Navona *(see p120)* – they were moved here and replaced by copies in the 19th century.

From the northwest the park is entered by the Viale delle Belle Arti, where the Galleria Nazionale d'Arte Moderna houses a modest collection of 19th- and 20th-century paintings. The Art Nouveau character of the area dates from the International Exhibition held here in 1911, for which pavilions were built by many nations, the most impressive being the British School at Rome,

by Edwin Lutyens, with a facade adapted from the upper west portico of St Paul's Cathedral in London. Originally a School of Archaeology, the school now teaches literature, fine arts and history. The diverse statues close by include Simon Bolivar and other liberators of Latin America, and the great Persian poet Firdusi.

In the northeastern corner of the park lie the Museo Zoologico and a small re-developed Zoo, known as the Bioparco, where the emphasis is on conservation. Nearby the pretty 16th-century Villa Giulia houses a world-famous collection of Etruscan and

Bioparco symbol

other pre-Roman remains. Another Renaissance building of importance is the Palazzina of Pius IV, close to the Via Flaminia entrance. Designed by the architect Vignola in 1552, it later became an elegant apartment for Pius IV's nephew Carlo Borromeo. It now houses the Italian Embassy to the Holy See.

Museo e Galleria Borghese ❷

See pp260–61.

Villa Giulia ❸

See pp262–3.

A stone lion guarding the ornate entrance to the Zoo

Museo e Galleria Borghese ❷

THE VILLA AND PARK were laid out by Cardinal Scipione Borghese, favorite nephew of Paul V, who had the house designed for pleasure and entertainment. The hedonistic cardinal was also an extravagant patron of the arts and he commissioned sculptures from the young Bernini which now rank among his most famous works. Scipione also opened his pleasure park to the public. Today the villa houses the superb private Borghese collection of sculptures and paintings in the Museo and Galleria Borghese.

Facade of the Villa Borghese
This painting (1613) by the villa's Flemish architect Jan van Santen shows the highly ornate facade of the original design.

MUSEUM GUIDE
The museum is divided into two sections: the sculpture collection (Museo Borghese) occupies the entire ground floor and the picture gallery (Galleria Borghese) is on the upper floor. The Galleria Borghese has reopened to the public after extensive restoration work.

★ **Rape of Proserpine**
One of Bernini's finest works shows Pluto (Hades) abducting his bride. The sculptor's amazing skill with marble can be seen clearly in the twisting figures.

Sleeping Hermaphrodite
Dated around 150 BC, this is a bronze Roman copy of the Greek original by Polycles. The head and mattress were added by Andrea Bergondi in the 17th century.

The Egyptian Room
Frescoes show episodes in Egyptian history and Egyptian motifs.

TIMELINE

1613 15-year-old Bernini sculpts *Aeneas and Anchises*	**Early 1800s** Statues and reliefs are considered too ornate and stripped from the villa's facade	**1809** Much of the collection is sold by Prince Camillo Borghese to France and goes to Louvre	**1902** Villa, grounds and collection bought by the state
1621–5 Bernini sculpts *Pluto and Persephone*			
1625	**1725**	**1825**	
1622–5 Bernini sculpts *Apollo and Daphne*		**1805** Canova sculpts the semi-nude, reclining Pauline Borghese	**Early 1900s** Balustrade round the forecourt is bought by Lord Astor for the Cliveden estate in England
1613–15 The Flemish architect Jan van Santen designs and builds Villa Borghese	*Daphne's fingers turning into leaves*		

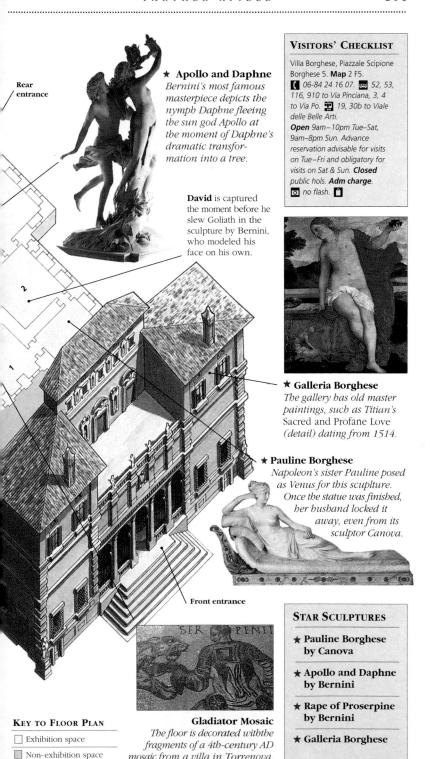

Rear
entrance

★ **Apollo and Daphne**
Bernini's most famous masterpiece depicts the nymph Daphne fleeing the sun god Apollo at the moment of Daphne's dramatic transformation into a tree.

David is captured the moment before he slew Goliath in the sculpture by Bernini, who modeled his face on his own.

VISITORS' CHECKLIST

Villa Borghese, Piazzale Scipione Borghese 5. **Map** 2 F5.
06-84 24 16 07. 52, 53, 116, 910 to Via Pinciana, 3, 4 to Via Po. 19, 30b to Viale delle Belle Arti.
Open 9am–10pm Tue–Sat, 9am–8pm Sun. Advance reservation advisable for visits on Tue–Fri and obligatory for visits on Sat & Sun. **Closed** public hols. **Adm charge.**
no flash.

★ **Galleria Borghese**
The gallery has old master paintings, such as Titian's Sacred and Profane Love *(detail) dating from 1514.*

★ **Pauline Borghese**
Napoleon's sister Pauline posed as Venus for this sculpture. Once the statue was finished, her husband locked it away, even from its sculptor Canova.

Front entrance

STAR SCULPTURES

★ **Pauline Borghese by Canova**

★ **Apollo and Daphne by Bernini**

★ **Rape of Proserpine by Bernini**

★ **Galleria Borghese**

KEY TO FLOOR PLAN

☐ Exhibition space

☐ Non-exhibition space

Gladiator Mosaic
The floor is decorated with the fragments of a 4th-century AD mosaic from a villa in Torrenova.

Villa Giulia ❸

THIS VILLA was built
as a country retreat
for Pope Julius III
and was designed for
entertaining rather than
as a permanent home.
It once housed an
impressive collection of
statues – 160 boatloads
were sent to the Vatican
after the pope died in 1555.
The villa, gardens, pavilions
and fountains were designed
by exceptional architects: Vignola
(designer of the Gesù), Vasari and the
sculptor Ammannati. Michelangelo also
contributed. The villa's main features are
its façade, the courtyard and garden, and
the *nympheum*. Since 1889, Villa Giulia
has housed the Museo Nazionale
Etrusco, with its outstanding collection of
pre-Roman antiquities from central Italy.

**Faliscan Crater
of the Dawn**
*This ornate vase, painted
in the free style of the
4th century BC,
shows Dawn rising
in a chariot.*

Chigi Oinochoe
*Battle and hunting
scenes adorn this
Corinthian vase
from the 6th
century B*

First floor

★ **Husband and
Wife Sarcophagus**
*This 6th-century BC
masterpiece, from
Cerveteri, shows a
dead couple at the
eternal banquet.*

MUSEUM GUIDE
*This is the most
important Etruscan
museum in Italy,
housing artifacts from
most of the major exca-
vations in Tuscany
and Lazio. Rooms
1 to **10** and **23** to **34** are
arranged by site and
include Vulci, Todi,
Veio and Cerveteri,
while private collections
are in rooms **11** to **22**.*

Votive Offering
*The religious
Etruscans made
artifacts, such as
this model of a boy
feeding a bird, in
their gods' honor.*

TIMELINE

1550	1650	1750	1850	1950
1550 Work begins on Villa Giulia under Pope Julius III	**1655** Queen Christina of Sweden stays in villa as Vatican guest	**Late 1700s** First large-scale studies of Etruscan artefacts	**1889** Etruscan museum founded	**1919** Castellani private collection donated to museum
	Late 1500s First, chance finds of Etruscan artefacts raise some scholastic interest		**1908** Barberini private collection bought by the state	**1972** Pesciotti private collection bought by the state
1555 Villa completed				

*Corner decoration
of bronze chariot
used to burn incense*

Facade
The villa's façade dates from 1552 to 1553. The entrance is designed in the form of a triumphal arch.

VISITORS' CHECKLIST

Piazzale di Villa Giulia 9.
Map 1 C4. 06-322 65 71.
52, 926 to Viale Bruno Buozzi, 95, 490, 495 to Viale Washington. 19, 30b to Piazza Thorwaldsen. **Open** 9am–7pm Tue–Sat, 9am–1pm Sun. **Closed** Jan 1, May 1, Dec 25. **Adm charge.** with seven days' notice. **Concerts:** "Notturno Etrusco" evenings held at the Ninfeo (Nympheum) on Saturdays throughout July & August. **Lectures & films.**

★ **Reconstruction of an Etruscan Temple**
Count Adolfo Cozza built the Temple of Alatri here in 1891. He based his design on the accounts of Vitruvius and 19th-century excavations.

Nympheum
Literally, the "area dedicated to the nymphs," this is a sunken courtyard decorated with Classical mosaics, statues and fountains.

STAR EXHIBITS

★ **Husband and Wife Sarcophagus**

★ **Ficoroni Cist**

★ **Reconstruction of an Etruscan Temple**

★ **Ficoroni Cist**
Engraved and beautifully illustrated, this fine bronze marriage coffer dates from the 4th century BC.

Main entrance

Ground floor

KEY TO FLOORPLAN

	Ground floor
	First floor
	Non-exhibition space

Galleria Communale d'Arte Moderna ❹

Via Cagliari 29. (06-474 28 48.
▭ 36, 36b, 38, 38b,58, 58b, 60, 136,
137, 490. **Open** 9am–6.30pm
Tue–Sat, 9pm–1.30pm Sun.
Adm charge.

THE OLD Peroni beer factory
has been restored and
transformed to house the art
collections of the Comune di
Roma. The paintings are not
as "modern" as the name
might imply; most date from
the 19th century and include
works by Rodin, Ximenes,
Balla, De Pissis, Guttuso and
Carrà. There will also be a
cinematheque and videotheque
showing films about art.

Interior of Santa Costanza

Santa Costanza ❺

Via Nomentana 349. (06-861 08 40.
▭ 36, 36b, 37, 60, 62, 136, 137.
Open 9am–noon, 4pm–6pm
Tue–Sat, 4pm–6pm Sun, 9am–noon
Mon. **Adm charge**. & ✦

THE ROUND CHURCH of Santa
Costanza was first built as
a mausoleum for Emperor
Constantine's daughters
Constantia and Helena, in the
early 4th century. The dome
and its drum are supported
by a circular arcade resting on
12 magnificent pairs of granite
columns. The ambulatory that
runs around the outside of

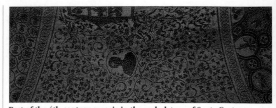

Part of the 4th-century mosaic in the ambulatory of Santa Costanza

the central arcade has a barrel-
vaulted ceiling decorated with
wonderful 4th-century mosaics
of flora and fauna and
charming scenes of a Roman
grape harvest. In a niche on
the far side of the church from
the entrance is a replica of
Constantia's ornately carved
porphyry sarcophagus. The
original was moved to the
Vatican Museums in 1790.

Constantia's sanctity is de-
batable – she was described
by the historian Marcellinus
as a fury incarnate, constantly
goading her equally unpleasant
husband Hannibalianus to
violence. Her canonization
was probably the result of
some confusion with a saintly
nun of the same name.

Sant'Agnese fuori le Mura ❻

Via Nomentana 349. (06-861 08 40.
▭ 36, 36b, 37, 60, 62, 136, 137.
Open 9am–noon, 4pm–6pm Tue–Sat,
4pm–6pm Sun, 9am–noon Mon.
Adm charge to catacombs. & ✦

THE CHURCH OF Sant'Agnese
stands among a group of
early Christian buildings which
includes the ruins of a covered

cemetery, some extensive
catacombs and the crypt where
the 13-year-old martyr St.
Agnes was buried in AD 304.
Agnes was exposed naked by
order of Emperor Diocletian,
furious that she should have
rejected the advances of a
young man at his court, but
her hair miraculously grew to
protect her modesty.

The church is said to have
been built at the request of
the Emperor Constantine's
daughter, Constantia, after
she had prayed at the Tomb
of St. Agnes for delivery
from leprosy.

Though much altered over
the centuries, the form and
much of the structure of the
4th-century basilica remain
intact. In the 7th-century apse
mosaic St Agnes appears as a
bejewelled Byzantine empress
in a stole of gold and a violet
robe. According to tradition
she appeared like this eight
days after her death holding a
white lamb. Every year on
January 21 two lambs are
blessed on the church altar
and a vestment called the
pallium is woven from their
wool. Every newly-appointed
archbishop is sent a *pallium*
by the pope.

Apse mosaic in Sant'Agnese, showing the saint flanked by two popes

Cloister, San Lorenzo fuori le Mura

San Lorenzo fuori le Mura ❼

Piazzale del Verano 3. ☏ 06-49 15 11. 🚌 71, 163, 448, 492. 🚋 19, 30b. **Open** 7am–noon, 4pm–5.30pm (7.30pm in summer) daily. ♿

J UST OUTSIDE the eastern wall of the city stands the church of San Lorenzo. Roasted slowly to death in AD 258, San Lorenzo was one of the most revered of Rome's early Christian martyrs. The first basilica erected over his burial place by Constantine was largely rebuilt in 576 by Pope Pelagius II. Close by stood a 5th-century church dedicated to the Virgin Mary. The intriguing two-leveled church we see today is the result of these two churches being knocked into one. This process, started in the 8th century, was completed in the 13th century by Pope Honorius III, when the nave, the portico and much of the decoration were added. The remains of San Lorenzo are in the choir of the 6th-century church (beneath the 13th-century high altar).

Romanesque bell tower of San Lorenzo

Via Appia Antica ❽

🚌 218, 760. See **Walks** pp284–5.

T HE FIRST PART of the Via Appia was built in 312 BC by the Censor Appius Claudius Caecus. When it was extended to the ports of Benevento, Taranto and Brindisi in 190 BC, the road became Rome's link with its expanding empire in the East. It was the route taken by the funeral processions of the dictator Sulla (78 BC) and Emperor Augustus (AD 14) and it was along this road that St. Paul was led a prisoner to Rome in AD 56.

Gradually abandoned during the Middle Ages, the road was restored in the mid-16th century by Pope Pius IV. It is lined with ruined family tombs and the collective burial places known as columbaria, while beneath the fields on either side lies a vast maze of catacombs. Today the road starts at Porta San Sebastiano (see p196). Major Christian sights include the church of Domine Quo Vadis?, built on the spot where St. Peter is said to have met Christ while fleeing from Rome, and the Catacombs of San Callisto and San Sebastiano. Among the tombs lining the road are those of Cecilia Metella (see p266) and of Romulus, son of the Emperor Maxentius, who died in AD 309.

Catacombs of San Callisto ❾

Via Appia Antica 110. ☏ 06-513 67 25. 🚌 218, 660, 760. **Open** 8.30am– noon, 2.30pm–5.30pm (Oct–Mar: 5pm) Thu–Tue. **Closed** Feb; 1 Jan, Easter Sun & 25 Dec. **Adm charge**. 🚻 🚫 📷 🖥 📷

I N BURYING their dead in underground cemeteries out-side the city walls, the early Christians were simply obeying the laws of the time. They were not forced to use them because of persecution. So many saints were buried that the catacombs became shrines and places of pilgrimage.

The vast Catacombs of San Callisto are on four different

levels and only partly explored. The rooms and connecting passageways are hewn out of volcanic tufa. The dead were placed in niches, known as *loculi*, which held two or three bodies. The most important rooms were decorated with stucco and frescoes. The area that can be visited includes the Crypt of the Popes, where many of the early popes were buried, and the Crypt of Santa Cecilia, where the saint's body was discovered in 820 before being moved to her church in Trastevere (see p211).

Catacombs of San Sebastiano ❿

Via Appia Antica 136. ☏ 06-785 03 50. 🚌 218, 660, 760. **Open** 9am–noon, 2.30pm–5.30pm Fri–Wed. **Closed** Nov. **Adm charge**. 🚻 📷 📷

T HE 17TH-CENTURY church of San Sebastiano, above the catacombs, occupies the site of a basilica from the age of Constantine. Preserved at the entrance to the catacombs is the *triclia*, a building that once stood above ground and was used by mourners for taking funeral refreshments. Its walls are covered with graffiti in-voking St. Peter and St. Paul, whose remains may have been moved here during one of the periods of persecution.

Cypresses lining part of the Roman Via Appia Antica

Catacombs of Domitilla ⑪

Via delle Sette Chiese 282.
☎ 06-511 03 42. 🚌 218, 660, 760.
Open 8.30am–noon, 2.30pm–
5.30pm (Oct–Mar: 5pm) Tue–Sun.
Closed Jan. **Adm charge**. 🚫 📷

THIS NETWORK of catacombs is the largest in Rome. Many of the tombs from the 1st and 2nd centuries AD have no Christian connection. In the burial chambers there are frescoes of both Classical and Christian scenes, including one of the earliest depictions of Christ as the *Good Shepherd*. Above the catacombs stands the basilica of Santi Nereo e Achilleo. After rebuilding and restoration, little remains of the original 4th-century church.

Bronze entrance gates to the Fosse Ardeatine by Mirko Basaldella

Fosse Ardeatine ⑫

Via Ardeatina 174. ☎ 06-513 67 42.
🚌 218. **Open** 8.15am–5.15pm daily
(from 8.45 Sun). Last adm: 30 mins
before closing. **Closed** public hols.

ON THE EVENING of March 24 1944, Nazi forces took 335 prisoners to this abandoned quarry south of Rome and shot them at point blank range. The execution was in response to a bomb attack that had killed 32 German soldiers. The victims included various political prisoners, 73 Jews and ten other civilians, among them a priest and a 14-year-old boy. The Germans blew up the tunnels where the massacre had taken place, but a local peasant had witnessed the scene and later helped

find the corpses. The site is now a memorial to the values of the Resistance against the Germans, which gave birth to the modern Italian Republic. A forbidding bunker-like monument houses the rows of identical tombs containing the victims.

Beside it is a museum of the Resistance. Interesting works of modern sculpture include *The Martyrs*, by Francesco Coccia, and the gates shaped like a wall of thorns by Mirko Basaldella.

Tomb of Cecilia Metella ⑬

Via Appia Antica, km 3.
☎ 06-780 24 65. 🚌 660, 770.
Open 9am–4pm Tue–Sat (6pm in
summer), 9am–12.30pm Mon & Sun.
Closed public hols.

ONE OF THE most famous landmarks on the Via Appia Antica is the huge drum-shaped tomb built for the noblewoman Cecilia Metella. Her father and husband were rich patricians and successful generals of late Republican Rome, but hardly anything is known about the woman herself. Byron muses over her unknown destiny in his poem *Childe Harold*.

In 1302 Pope Boniface VIII donated the tomb to his family, the Caetani. They incorporated it in a fortified castle that blocked the Via Appia, allowing them to control the traffic on the road and exact high tolls.

The marble facing of the tomb was pillaged by another pope, Sixtus V, at the end of the 16th century.

Fragments of marble relief on the Tomb of Cecilia Metella

EUR's Palazzo della Civiltà del Lavoro, the "Square Colosseum"

EUR ⑭

🚌 671, 703, 708, 714, 717, 762 and
other routes. Ⓜ EUR Fermi, EUR
Palasport. **Museo della Civiltà
Romana** Piazza G. Agnelli. ☎ 06-
592 6041. **Open** 9am–7pm Tue–Sat,
9am–1pm Sun and public hols. **Closed**
Jan 1, May 1, Dec 25. **Adm charge**.

THE ESPOSIZIONE Universale di Roma (EUR), a suburb to the south of the city, was built originally for an international exhibition, a kind of "Work Olympics", that was planned for 1942, but never took place because of the war. The architecture was intended to glorify Fascism and to modern eyes the style of the public buildings is very overblown and rhetorical. The eerie shape of the Palazzo della Civiltà del Lavoro (the Palace of the Civilization of Work) is an unmistakable landmark for people arriving from Fiumicino airport.

The scheme was completed in the 1950s. In terms of town planning, EUR has been quite successful and people still flock to live here. The great marble halls house a number of government offices and museums. The Museo della Civiltà Romana displays a vast scale model of Rome at the time of Constantine and casts of the reliefs on the Column of Trajan.

To the south is a lake and park, and the huge domed Palazzo dello Sport built for the 1960 Olympics.

San Paolo fuori le Mura

Via Ostiense 186. 06-541 03 41.
23, 128, 170, 670, 702, 707,
761, 766. San Paolo.
Open 7.30am–6.40pm daily
(last adm: 15 mins before closing).

Today's church is a faithful if somewhat soulless reconstruction of the great 4th-century basilica destroyed by fire on July 15, 1823. Few fragments of the original church survived. The triumphal arch over the nave is decorated on one side with restored 5th-century mosaics. On the other side are mosaics by Pietro Cavallini, originally on the facade. The splendid Venetian apse mosaics (1220) depict Christ with St. Peter, St. Andrew, St. Paul and St. Luke.

The fine marble canopy over the high altar is signed by the sculptor Arnolfo di Cambio (1285) "together with his partner Pietro", who may have been Pietro Cavallini. Below the altar is the *confessio*, the tomb of St. Paul. To the right is an impressive Paschal candlestick by Nicolò di Angelo and Pietro Vassalletto.

The cloister of San Paolo, with its pairs of colorful inlaid

19th-century mosaic on facade of San Paolo fuori le Mura

columns supporting the arcade, was spared completely by the fire. Completed around 1214, it is considered one of the most beautiful in Rome.

Centrale Montemartini

Via Ostiense 106. 06-57991.
23, 702. **Open** 10am–6pm
Tue–Fri, 10am–7pm Sat–Sun.
Closed public hols. **Adm charge.**

An enormous old industrial site has been restored to house the ACEA art centre. Originally, the building was used as the first Roman power

station and its two huge generators still occupy the central machine room and create an intriguing contrast to the exhibitions.

On display are Greek and Roman statues belonging to the Capitoline Museums (*see pp70–73*). These were found in excavations in the late 19th and early 20th centuries but were kept in storage, and this is the first time they have been exhibited to the public.

Casino del Bel Respiro, summer residence in Villa Doria Pamphilj

Villa Doria Pamphilj

Via di San Pancrazio. 44, 75, 710, 870. **Park open** dawn–dusk daily.

One of Rome's largest public parks, the Villa Doria Pamphilj was laid out in the mid-17th century for Prince Camillo Pamphilj. His uncle Pope Innocent X paid for the magnificent summer residence, the Casino del Bel Respiro, fountains and summerhouses, some of which still survive. Today the park is a popular with joggers and dog lovers.

Statue in Centrale Montemarini, former power plant turned art cenre

Day Trips around Rome

Tivoli, a favorite place to escape the heat of the Roman summer

Tivoli ⑱

Town is 20 miles (31 km) northeast of Rome. **FS** *from Roma Termini or Tiburtina.* **☐** *COTRAL from Rebibbia (on Metro line B).*

TIVOLI HAS BEEN a popular summer resort since the days of the Roman Republic. Among the famous men who owned villas here were the poets Catullus and Horace, Caesar's assassins Brutus and Cassius and the Emperors Trajan and Hadrian. Tivoli's main attractions were its clean air and beautiful location on the slopes of the Tiburtini hills, its healthy sulphur springs and the waterfalls of the Aniene – the Emperor Augustus said these had cured him of insomnia. The Romans' luxurious lifestyle was revived in Renaissance times by the owners of the Villa d'Este, the town's most famous sight.

Detail of Fontana dell'Organo at Villa d'Este

In the Middle Ages, Tivoli suffered frequent invasions since its position made it an ideal base for an advance on Rome. In 1461, Pope Pius II built a fortress here, the Rocca Pia, declaring: "It is easier to regain Rome while possessing Tivoli, than to regain Tivoli while possessing Rome."

After suffering heavy bomb damage in 1944, Tivoli's main buildings and churches were speedily restored. The town's cobbled streets are still lined with medieval houses. The Duomo (cathedral) houses a beautiful 13th-century life-size wooden group representing the *Deposition from the Cross.*

Villa d'Este ⑲

Piazza Trento, Tivoli. **☏** *0774-31 20 70.* **☐** *COTRAL from Rebibbia.* **Open** *winter: 9am–4pm Tue–Sun; summer: 9am–6:30pm Tue–Sun.* **Closed** *Jan 1, May 1, Dec 25.* **Adm charge.** **☐**

THE VILLA OCCUPIES the site of an old Benedictine convent. In the 16th century, the estate was developed by Cardinal Ippolito d'Este, son of Lucrezia Borgia. A palace was designed by Pirro Ligorio to make the most of its hilltop situation, but the villa's fame rests more on the terraced gardens and fountains laid out by Ligorio and Giacomo della Porta.

The gardens have suffered from neglect, but the grottoes and fountains still give a vivid impression of the great luxury which the princes of the church enjoyed. From the great loggia of the palace you descend through the shrub-lined paths to the Grotto of Diana and Bernini's Fontana del Bicchierone. Below to the right is the Rometta (little Rome), a model of Tiber Island with allegorical figures and the legendary she-wolf.

The Rometta is at one end of the Viale delle Cento Fontane. Its 100 fountains are in the shape of grotesques, obelisks, ships and the eagles of the d'Este coat of arms, now overgrown with moss. Other fountains have also lost much of their former glory. The Fontana dell'Organo was a water organ, in which the force of the water pumped air through the pipes, but it has long been silent. The garden's lowest level has flower beds, fountains and views out over the plain below.

Terrace of 100 Fountains in the gardens of Villa d'Este

Villa Gregoriana ⑳

Largo Massimo, Tivoli. **FS** *Tivoli, then short walk.* **Open** *9:30am–1 hr before sunset daily.* **Adm charge.**

THE MAIN ATTRACTIONS of this steeply sloping wooded park are the beautiful waterfalls and grottoes created over the centuries by the River Aniene. The park is named after Pope Gregory XVI, who in the 1830s ordered the building of a tunnel as a way of eradicating the danger of flooding. This created a new waterfall, the Grande Cascata, which plunges a full 525 ft (160 m) into the valley behind the town.

The Canopus, extensively restored, with replicas of its original caryatids lining the bank of the canal

Hadrian's Villa ㉑

Villa Adriana, Via Tiburtina. Site is 6 km (4 miles) southwest of Tivoli. ▮ 0774-53 02 03. ▮ Tivoli, then local bus No. 4. ▮ COTRAL from Rebibbia (on line B).
Open Tue–Sun (9am–4pm winter, 9am–6:30pm summer). **Closed** Jan 1, May 1, Dec 25. **Adm charge.** ▯ ▯

BUILT AS a private summer retreat between AD 118 and 134, Hadrian's Villa was a vast open-air museum of the finest architecture of the Roman world. The grounds of the Imperial palace covered an area of 300 acres (120 hectares) and were filled with full-scale reproductions of the emperor's favorite buildings from Greece and Egypt. Although excavations began here in the 16th century, many of the ruins lying scattered in the surrounding fields have yet to be identified with any certainty. The grounds of the villa make

a very picturesque site for a picnic, with scattered fragments of columns lying among olive trees and cypresses.

For an idea of how the whole complex would have looked in its heyday, study the scale model in the building beside the parking area. Important buildings have signs, and several have been partially restored or reconstructed. One of the most impressive is the Maritime Theater. This is a round pool with an island in the middle, surrounded by columns. The island, reached by means of a swing bridge, was probably Hadrian's private studio, where he withdrew from the cares of the Empire to indulge in his favorite pastimes, painting and architecture. There were also theaters; Greek and Latin libraries; two bath houses; extensive housing for guests and the palace staff; and formal gardens with fountains, statues and pools.

Hadrian was a lover of Greek philosophy as well as architecture. One part of the gardens is thought to have been Hadrian's reproduction of the Grove of Academe, where Plato lectured to his students.

Fragment of marble mosaic pavement in the Imperial palace

Hadrian also had a replica of the Stoà Poikile, a beautiful painted colonnade in Athens, from which the Stoic philosophers took their name. Hadrian's Poikile enclosed a piazza with a central pool. The area known as the Hall of the Philosophers near the Poikile was probably a library.

The most ambitious of Hadrian's replicas was the Canopus, a sanctuary of the god Serapis near Alexandria. For this a canal 130 yd (119 m) long was dug and Egyptian statues were imported to decorate the temple and its grounds. This impressive piece of engineering has been restored, and the banks of the canal are lined with caryatids.

Another picturesque spot in the grounds is the Vale of Tempe, the legendary haunt of the goddess Diana, with a stream representing the river Peneios. Below ground, the

Pair of Ionic columns in the vaulted baths of Hadrian's Villa

emperor built a fanciful re-creation of the underworld, Hades, reached through many underground tunnels which linked the various parts of the villa.

Plundered by barbarians who camped here in the 6th and 8th centuries, the villa fell into disrepair. Its marble was burned to make lime for cement, and Renaissance antiquarians contributed further to its destruction. Statues unearthed in the grounds are displayed in museums around Europe. The Vatican's Egyptian Collection (see p238) has many fine works that were found here.

Ostia Antica ㉒

Viale dei Romagnoli 717. Site is 16 miles
(25 km) southwest of Rome. **[** 06-
56 35 80 99. **M** *Magliana on line B,
then train to Ostia Antica.* **Excavations
open** *winter: 9am–4pm daily;
summer: 9am–6pm daily.* **Closed** *Jan
1, May 1, Dec 25.* **Museum open**
9am–1pm daily. **Closed** *public hols.*
Adm charge.

I**N REPUBLICAN TIMES** Ostia was
Rome's main commercial
port and a military base
defending the coastline and
the mouth of the Tiber. The
port continued to flourish
under the Empire, despite the
development of Portus, a new
port slightly to the northwest,
in the 2nd century AD. Ostia's
decline began in the 4th
century, when a reduction in
trade was combined with the
gradual silting up of the
harbor. Worse was to come
when malaria became endemic
in the area, and the city,
whose population is estimated
to have been nearly 100,000 at
its peak, was as a result
totally abandoned.

Buried for centuries by
sand, the city is remarkably
well preserved. The site is
less spectacular than Pompeii
or Herculaneum because
Ostia died a gradual death,
but it gives a more complete
picture of life under the
Roman Empire. People of all
social classes and from all
over the Mediterranean lived
and worked here.

Visitors can understand the
layout of Ostia's streets almost
at a glance. The main road
through the town, the
Decumanus Maximus, would
have been filled with hurrying
slaves and citizens, avoiding
the jostling carriages and

Ruins of shops, offices and houses near Ostia's theater

carts, while tradesmen
pursued their business under
the porticoes lining the street.
The floor plans of the public
buildings along the road are
very clear. Many were bath
houses, such as the Baths of
the Cisiarii (carters) and the
grander Baths of Neptune,
named after their fine black-
and-white floor mosaics.
Beside the restored theater,
three large masks, originally
part of the decoration of the
stage, have been mounted
on large blocks of tufa.
Beneath the great brick
arches that supported the
semicircular tiers of seats
were taverns and shops.
Classical plays are put on
here now in the summer.

The Tiber's course has
changed considerably since
Ostia was the port of Rome. It
once flowed past just to the

**Mask decorating
the theater**

north of Piazzale delle
Corporazioni, the square
behind the theater. The
corporations were the guilds
of the various
trades involved in
fitting out and
supplying ships:
tanners and rope
makers, ship
builders and
timber merchants,
ships' chandlers
and corn weighers.
There were some
60 or 70 offices
around the square.
Mosaics showing
scenes of everyday
life in the port
and the names
and symbols of
the corporations can still be
seen. There were also offices
used by ship-owners and
their agents from places as far
away as Tunisia and the south
of France, Sardinia and Egypt.
In one office, belonging to a
merchant from the town of
Sabratha in North Africa,
there is a delightful mosaic of
an elephant.

The main cargo coming into
Rome was grain from Africa.
Much of this was distributed
free to prevent social unrest.
Although only men received
this *annona*, or corn ration,
at times over 300,000 were
eligible. In the center of the

Mural from Ostia of merchant ship being loaded with grain

square was a temple, probably dedicated to Ceres, goddess of the harvest. Among the buildings excavated are many large warehouses in which grain was stored before it was shipped on to Rome.

The Decumanus leads to the Forum and the city's principal temple, erected by Hadrian in the 2nd century AD and dedicated to Jove, Juno and Minerva. In this rather romantic, lonely spot, it is hard to imagine the Forum as a bustling center where justice

Floor mosaic of Nereid and sea monster in the House of the Dioscuri

Detail of floor mosaic in the Piazzale delle Corporazioni

was dispensed and officials met to discuss the city's affairs. In the 18th century it was used as a sheepfold.

Away from the main street are the buildings where Ostia's inhabitants lived. The great majority lived in rented apartments in blocks three or four stories high, known as *insulae*. These varied widely in their comfort and decor. The House of Diana was one of the more elegant ones, with a balcony around the second floor, a private bathhouse and a central courtyard with a cistern where tenants came to get their water. Around the ground floor of the block were shops, taverns and bars selling snacks and drinks. In the bar at the House of Diana you can see the marble counter used by customers buying their sausages and hot wine sweetened with honey.

For the wealthy there were detached houses *(domus)* such as the House of the Dioscuri, which has fine colored mosaics, and the House of Cupid and Psyche, named after a charming statue found there. This is now in the site's Museo Ostiense, near the Forum, along with other sculptures.

Among the houses and shops there are other buildings, including a laundry and the firemen's barracks.

Various religions are practiced in Ostia. There are no fewer than 18 temples dedicated to the Persian god Mithras, as well as a Jewish synagogue dating from the 1st century AD and a Christian basilica. A plaque records the death of St. Augustine's mother in a hotel here in Ostia in AD 387.

ALSO WORTH SEEING

Anagni FS *from Termini (c 50 min).* Picturesque hill town with papal palace and famous Romanesque cathedral.

Bracciano FS *from Termini or Tiburtina (c 90 min).* 🚌 *from Lepanto, on Metro line A (bus c 90 min).* Volcanic lake with villages and wooded hills. Nice for walks or a visit to Orsini Castle. Swimming in summer.

Cerveteri FS *from Termini, Tiburtina or Ostiense to Cerveteri-Ladispoli, then local bus (c 70 min).* 🚌 *from Via Lepanto, on Metro line A (bus c 80 min).* One of the greatest Etruscan cities. Necropolis with complete streets and houses.

Nemi 🚌 *from Anagnina, on Metro line A (bus c 60 min).* Charming village at volcanic lake in the Castelli Romani. Famous for its wine and strawberries.

Palestrina 🚌 *from Rebibbia, on Metro line B (bus c 70 min).* Impressive Roman sanctuary to goddess Fortuna. Museum and the Mosaic of the Nile.

Pompei FS *to Naples, then change to local train (c 170 min).* 🚌 *Special bus tours from tourist agents.* Excavations of the wealthy and bustling Roman city where the busy daily life was put to a sudden end by the eruption of Vesuvius in AD 79.

Subiaco 🚌 *from Rebibbia, on Metro line B (bus c 120 min).* Birthplace of St. Benedict. Two monasteries to visit.

Tarquinia FS *from Termini or Ostiense (c 180 min).* 🚌 *from Via Lepanto, on Metro line A. Change at Civitavecchia (c 150 min).* Outstanding collection of Etruscan objects and frescoes from Tarquinia's necropolis.

Viterbo FS *from Termini (c 90 min) or COTRAL train from Roma Nord, Piazzale Flaminio, on Metro line A (c 120 min).* 🚌 *from Saxa Rubra reached by the COTRAL train above (bus c 90 min).* Medieval quarter, papal palace and archaeological museum within 13th-century walls.

SIX GUIDED WALKS

ROME IS an excellent city for walking. The distances between major sights in the historic center can easily be covered on foot, and many streets have been pedestrianized. When you get tired, there are plenty of pavement cafés in wonderful settings, such as Piazza Navona and Campo de' Fiori. If you are interested in archaeology, then try a walk across the Forum *(see pp76–87)* and over the Palatine *(see pp96–101)* to take you away from the roaring traffic of modern Rome into a different world of scattered ruins and shady pine trees.

The first of the six suggested walks takes in picturesque quarters on either side of the Tiber, the river that has played such an important part in the city's development. The second

Bernini angel on Ponte Sant'Angelo

walk, along the perfectly straight Via Giulia, gives a vivid impression of the Renaissance city. The next three walks each follow a particular theme. For visitors who wish to savor the glory of ancient Rome, there is a walk taking in the surviving triumphal arches of the emperors. For those who prefer the Middle Ages, there is a tour of early Christian churches with well-preserved mosaics, and for those who enjoy the Roman Baroque, there is a walk concentrating on Bernini's contribution to the city's appearance.

The Romans were famous for their straight roads. The final walk is outside the central sightseeing area, along the best-known Roman road, the Via Appia Antica, parts of which remain after more than 2,000 years of use.

CHOOSING A WALK

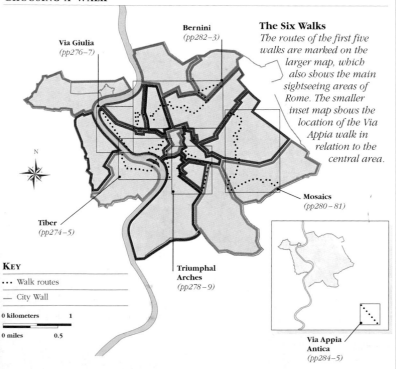

The Six Walks
The routes of the first five walks are marked on the larger map, which also shows the main sightseeing areas of Rome. The smaller inset map shows the location of the Via Appia walk in relation to the central area.

Via Giulia *(pp276–7)*

Bernini *(pp282–3)*

Tiber *(pp274–5)*

Mosaics *(pp280–81)*

Triumphal Arches *(pp278–9)*

Via Appia Antica *(pp284–5)*

KEY

••• Walk routes

— City Wall

0 kilometers   1

0 miles   0.5

Pedestrians strolling across Ponte Sant'Angelo

A Two-Hour Walk by the River Tiber

R OME OWES ITS VERY EXISTENCE to the Tiber; the city grew up around an easy fording point where a market place developed. The river could also be a hazard; shallow and torrent-like, it flooded the city every winter up to 1870, when work began on the massive Lungotevere embankments that run along both sides of the river. These provide many fine views from points along their avenues of plane trees. The walk also explores the neighbourhoods along the riverside, in particular the Jewish Ghetto and Trastevere, which have preserved much of their character from earlier periods in the colourful history of Rome.

From the old port of Rome to Via dei Funari

Starting from the church of Santa Maria in Cosmedin ① *(see p202)*, cross the piazza to the Temples of the Forum Boarium ② *(see p203)*. This was the cattle market that stood near the city's river port. The river here has preserved two less obvious structures from ancient Rome: the mouth of the Cloaca Maxima ③, the city's great sewer, and one arch of a ruined bridge, known as the Ponte Rotto ④. In Via Petroselli stands the rather extraordinary medieval Casa dei Crescenzi ⑤ *(see p203)*, decorated with fragments of Roman temples. Passing the modern Anagrafe (public records office) ⑥, built on the site of the old Roman port, you come to San Nicola in Carcere ⑦ *(see p152)*.

You are now in the Foro Olitorio, Rome's ancient vegetable market. To the east stand the ruins of a Roman portico and the medieval house of the Pierleoni family. Head for the massive Theatre

Santa Maria in Cosmedin ①

of Marcellus ⑧ *(see p151)*, and look for the three Corinthian columns of the Temple of Apollo beside it. Turn into Piazza Campitelli and walk up to Santa Maria in Campitelli ⑨ *(see p151)*. The church honours a miraculous image of the Virgin credited with halting the plague in 1656. The 16th-century piazza was the home of Flaminio Ponzio, its architect, who lived at No. 6. Take Via dei Delfini to Piazza Margana where you should look up at the 14th-century tower of the Margani family ⑩. Retrace your steps, then go up Via dei Funari (Street of the Ropemakers) to the 16th-century facade of Santa Caterina dei Funari ⑪.

The Ghetto

From Piazza Lovatelli take Via Sant'Angelo in Pescheria, which

leads to the ruined Portico of Octavia ⑫ *(see p151)* in the Jewish Ghetto *(see p152)*. The Roman portico, once Rome's fish market, houses the church of Sant'Angelo in Pescheria. Find the marble plaque on the facade: fish longer than this slab were given to the city's *conservatori* (governors). Turn into the Ghetto: two column stumps belonging to the Portico stand in front of a patched-up doorway made of fragments of Roman sculpture. The cramped buildings and streets around Via del Portico

Main altar of Santa Maria in Campitelli ⑨

Arch of the Ponte Rotto ④

d'Ottavia are typical of old Rome: see the Casa di Lorenzo Manilio ⑬ *(see p153)*, and turn down Via delle Cinque Scole, past Palazzo Cenci ⑭ *(see p152),* towards the river. On Lungotevere walk past the Synagogue ⑮ *(see p152)* to the small church of San Gregorio ⑯. Here stood the gates of the Ghetto, which were locked at sundown.

Across the river to Trastevere
Crossing to Tiber Island *(see p152)* by Ponte Fabricio, with its two ancient

Classical relief of Medusa above the doorway of Palazzo Cenci ⑭

much of the spirit of old Trastevere. Walk up to the start of Viale di Trastevere at Piazza Belli. After crossing the road look back

Santa Maria in Trastevere, don't miss the old-fashioned chemist's shop at No. 7. The piazza itself, in front of the magnificent church of Santa Maria in Trastevere ㉒ *(see pp212–13),* has a cheerful atmosphere, and the fountain steps are a favourite meeting place. Go back a little way to Via del Moro. This leads to Piazza Trilussa, dominated by the fountain of the Acqua Paola ㉓, where you emerge on to the bank of the river again. Note the life-like statue, near the fountain, of Roman poet Trilussa, who wrote in the local dialect. From Ponte Sisto ㉔ *(see p210),* look back to Tiber Island and, beyond it, to the medieval bell tower of Santa Maria in Cosmedin, set against the pine trees on the summit of the Palatine.

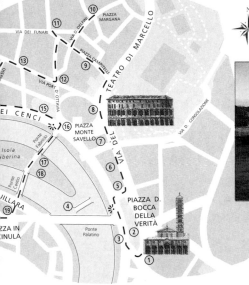

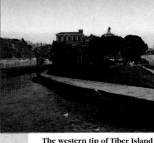

The western tip of Tiber Island

0 metres 250
0 yards 250

stone heads on the parapet, you can enjoy a good view of the river in both directions. On the island itself, you should not miss the Pierleoni Tower ⑰ or the church of San Bartolomeo all'Isola ⑱.

Trastevere
As you cross into Trastevere, you can see the medieval house of the powerful Mattei family ⑲, with its fragments of ancient sculpture. Beyond it, Piazza in Piscinula and the surrounding streets retain

KEY
— Walk route
⚡ Good viewing point

at the medieval tower of the Anguillara ⑳ and the statue honouring the poet Gioacchino Belli ㉑ *(see p209).* As you go down Via della Lungaretta to Piazza

Piazza in Piscinula, old Trastevere

TIPS FOR WALKERS

Starting point: Piazza della Bocca della Verità.
Length: 3.5 km (2 miles).
Getting there: The 23, 44, 75, 81, 160, 280, 628 and 810 buses stop near Santa Maria in Cosmedin.
Best time for walk: This walk can be very romantic in the evenings, but is enjoyable at any time.
Stopping-off points: Piazza Campitelli and Piazza Margana have typical Roman restaurants, and Via del Portico d'Ottavia has restaurants and a bakery. Tiber Island has a bar and the famous Sora Lella restaurant (see p314). In Viale Trastevere there are bars and pizzerias of all kinds. Piazza Santa Maria in Trastevere has lively bars and restaurants with outdoor tables.

A One-Hour Walk along Via Giulia

LAID OUT BY BRAMANTE for Pope Julius II in the early 16th century, Via Giulia was one of the first Renaissance streets to slice through Rome's jumble of medieval alleys. The original plan included new law courts in a central piazza, but this project was abandoned for lack of cash. The street now is dominated by antiques shops and furniture restorers. On summer evenings hundreds of oil lamps light the street while cloisters and courtyards provide romantic settings for a special season of concerts.

Baroque capital on the facade of Sant'Eligio degli Orefici ⑦

From Lungotevere to Largo della Moretta

Starting from Lungotevere dei Tebaldi ① at the eastern end of Via Giulia, you will see ahead of you an archway ② spanning the road. This was the start of Michelangelo's unrealized project linking Palazzo Farnese and its gardens *(see p147)* with the Villa Farnesina *(see pp220–21)* on the other side of the river.

Just before you reach the archway, you will see to your left the curious Fontana del Mascherone ③, in which an ancient grotesque mask and granite basin were combined to create a Baroque fountain.

Beyond the Farnese archway on the left is the lively Baroque facade of the church of Santa Maria dell'Orazione e Morte ④ *(see p147)*. A bit farther along on the same side of the road stands Palazzo Falconieri ⑤, enlarged by Borromini in 1650. Note its two stone falcons glowering at each other across the width of the facade. On the other side of the road, you pass the yellowish facade of Santa Caterina da Siena ⑥, church of the Sienese colony in Rome, which has pretty 18th-century reliefs. The figures of Romulus and Remus symbolize Rome

Relief of Romulus and Remus on Santa Caterina da Siena ⑥

and Siena – there is a legend that the city of Siena was founded by the less fortunate of the twins. After passing the short street that leads down to Sant'Eligio degli Orefici ⑦ *(see p148)* and the facade of Palazzo Ricci ⑧ *(see p149)*, you come to an area of half-demolished buildings around the ruined church of San Filippo Neri ⑨, called Vicolo della Moretta. If you look to the left down to the river, you can see

Fontana del Mascherone ③

Ponte Mazzini and the huge prison of Regina Coeli on the other side of the Tiber. At this point you may like to make a small detour to the right to the beginning of Via del Pellegrino, where there is an inscription ⑩ defining the *pomerium*, or boundary, of the city in the time of the Emperor Claudius.

From Largo della Moretta to the Sofas of Via Giulia

Farther on, facing the narrow Vicolo del Malpasso, are the imposing prisons, the Carceri

Nuove ⑪, built by Pope Innocent X Pamphilj in 1655. When first opened, they were a model of humane treatment of prisoners, but they were replaced by the Regina Coeli prison across the river at the end of the 19th century. The buildings now house offices of the Ministry of Justice and a small Museum of Crime.

At the corner of Via del Gonfalone, a small side street running down to the river,

KEY

— Walk route

☆ Good viewing point

0 meters	250
0 yards	250

Farnese archway across Via Giulia, built to a design by Michelangelo ②

you can see part of the foundations of Julius II's planned law courts. Just down the street stands the small Oratorio di Santa Lucia del Gonfalone ⑫, which is often used for concerts.

The next interesting facade is Carlo Rainaldi's 17th-century Santa Maria del Suffragio ⑬ on the left. On the same side is San Biagio degli Armeni ⑭, the Armenian church in Rome. It is often referred to by local people as San Biagio della Pagnotta (of the loaf of bread). The nickname originates from

the traditional distribution of bread to the poor that took place on the saint's feast day.

On the corner there are more travertine blocks belonging to the foundations of Julius II's projected law courts, known because of their curious shape as the "Sofas of Via Giulia."

The Florentine Quarter

Your next stop should be the imposing Palazzo Sacchetti at No. 66 ⑮. Originally this was the house of Antonio da Sangallo the Younger, the architect of Palazzo Farnese, but it was greatly enlarged by later owners. The porticoed courtyard houses a 15th-century Madonna and a striking Roman relief of the 3rd century AD. Just opposite Palazzo Sacchetti is the beautiful late Renaissance portal of Palazzo Donarelli ⑯. The 16th-century house at No. 93 is richly decorated with stuccoes and coats of arms ⑰. No. 85 is another typical Renaissance palazzo with a heavily rusticated ground floor ⑱. There is a tradition

Plaque honoring Antonio da Sangallo on Palazzo Sacchetti ⑮

that, like many houses of the period, it once belonged to Raphael. Palazzo Clarelli ⑲ was built by Antonio da Sangallo the Younger as his own house. The inscription above the doorway bears the name of Duke Cosimo II de' Medici, whose family later bought the palazzo.

This whole area used to be inhabited by a flourishing Florentine colony, which had its own water mills built on pontoons along the Tiber. Their national church is San Giovanni dei Fiorentini ⑳ *(see p153)*, the final great landmark at the end of Via Giulia. Many Florentine artists and architects had a hand in its design, including Sangallo and Jacopo Sansovino.

Coat of arms of Pope Paul III Farnese on the facade of Via Giulia No. 93 ⑰

Detail on the side of the door of Santa Maria del Suffragio ⑬

TIPS FOR WALKERS

Starting point: Lungotevere dei Tebaldi, by Ponte Sisto.
Length: 1,100 yds (1 km).
Getting there: The 116 goes to and along Via Giulia, or you can take 46, 62 or 64 to Corso Vittorio Emanuele II, then walk down Via dei Pettinari or a 23, 65 or 280 along Lungotevere.
Best time for walk: On summer evenings, oil lamps light the street. At Christmas, there are crèches on display in many shop windows.
Stopping-off points: There are bars in Via Giulia, at Nos. 21 and 84. Campo de' Fiori has better bars, with outdoor tables, and a wide choice of places to eat. These include a fried fish restaurant in Piazza Santa Barbara dei Librai (closed Sun).

A 90-Minute Tour of Rome's Triumphal Arches

ROME'S GREATEST GIFT to architecture was the arch and the Roman people's highest tribute to its victorious generals was the triumphal arch. In Imperial times, arches were erected to honor an emperor's campaign victories almost as a matter of course, promoting his personal cult and ensuring his subsequent deification. Spectacular processions passed through these arches. Conquering generals, cheered by rapturous crowds, rode in their chariots to the Capitol, accompanied by their legions bearing spoils from their campaigns.

Part of the Via Sacra, once spanned by the Arch of Augustus ③

Arches of the Forum

This walk through the Forum and around the base of the Palatine takes in Rome's three great surviving triumphal arches and two arches of more

Relief of barbarian captives on the Arch of Septimius Severus ①

humble design that were used simply as places of business. It starts from the Arch of

TIPS FOR WALKERS

Starting point: The Roman Forum, entrance Largo Romolo e Remo, on Via dei Fori Imperiali.
Length: 2.5 km (1½ miles).
Getting there: The nearest Metro station is Colosseo on line B. Buses 85, 87, 117, 175, 186, 850 stop in Via dei Fori Imperiali, near the Forum entrance.
Best time for walk: Any time of day during Forum opening hours (see p82) is suitable.
Stopping-off points: Several bars and restaurants overlook the Colosseum. There is a small bar in Via dei Cerchi and a smarter one behind San Giorgio in Velabro, in Piazza San Giovanni Decollato (closed Sun). For a meal, try Alvaro al Circo Massimo (closed Mon) in Via di San Teodoro.

Emperor Septimius Severus ① and his sons Geta and Caracalla *(see p83)* in the Forum. Erected in AD 203, it celebrates a successful campaign in the Middle East. Eight years later when Caracalla had his brother killed, all mention of Geta was removed from the inscription.

Look up at the reliefs showing phases of the campaigns. Set in tiers, they are probably the sculptural counterparts of the paintings illustrating the general's feats that were borne aloft in the triumphal procession. On the right, the inhabitants of a fortified city surrender to the Romans' siege machines. Below are smaller friezes showing the triumphal procession itself.

Heading east, make your way through the Forum to the ruins of the Temple of Julius Caesar ②. The temple was built by Augustus in 29 BC, on the site where Caesar's body was cremated after Mark Antony's famous funerary oration. A nearby sign marks the ruins of one of the arches dedicated to Augustus ③, spanning the Via Sacra between the Temple of Castor and Pollux ④ *(see p84)* and the Temple of Caesar. This arch, erected after Augustus had defeated Mark Antony and Cleopatra, was finally demolished in 1545, and its

Capital from Temple of Castor and Pollux ④

materials were used in the new St. Peter's. From here, proceed uphill towards the elegant Arch of Titus ⑤ *(see p87)*. Compared with Septimius Severus's arch, it shows an earlier, simpler style. Look up at the beautiful lettering of the inscription before

KEY

— Walk route
※ Good viewing point
Ⓜ Metro station

0 meters		250
0 yards		250

Arch of Titus in a 19th-century watercolour by the English artist Thomas Hartley Cromek ⑤

you examine the inner bas-reliefs. These show Roman legionaries carrying the spoils looted from the conquest of Jerusalem, heralds holding plaques with the names of vanquished peoples and cities, and Titus riding in triumph in his chariot.

The medieval Frangipane family turned the Colosseum into a vast impregnable stronghold and incorporated the Arch of Titus into their fortifications. Notice the wheelmarks scratched on the inside walls of the arch by generations of carts; they indicate the steady rise in the level of the Forum floor before it was eventually

excavated in the 18th and 19th centuries. Many of the carts that passed through the arch would have been carrying building materials quarried from the Forum's many ruined monuments.

Arch of Constantine

Leave the Forum by heading down the hill towards the Colosseum ⑥ (see pp92–5) and the nearby Arch of Constantine ⑦ (see p91). This arch, hastily built to commemorate the emperor's victory over his rival Maxentius in AD 312, is a patchwork of reliefs from different periods. Stand on the Via di San Gregorio side and compare

Arches of Domitian's extension to the Claudian Aqueduct ⑨

the earlier panels at the top (AD 180–193) with the hectic battle scenes just above the smaller arches, sculpted in AD 315. In the curious dwarf-like soldiers, you can see the transition from Classicism to a cruder medieval style of sculpture.

Now take Via di San Gregorio, which runs the length of the valley between the Palatine and Celian hills. This was the ancient route taken by most triumphal processions. Passing the entrance to the Palatine ⑧ and the well-preserved arches of the Claudian Aqueduct ⑨

on the right, you come to Piazza di Porta Capena ⑩, named after the gate that stood here to mark the beginning of the Via Appia (see p284). After rounding the back of the Palatine, follow Via dei Cerchi, which runs alongside the grassy area that preserves, in an oval outline, all that remains of the Circus Maximus ⑪ (see p205).

Arches of the Forum Boarium

When you reach the church of Sant'Anastasia ⑫, turn right up Via di San Teodoro, then first left down Via del Velabro. Straddling the street is the four-sided Arch of Janus ⑬ (see p202), erected in the 3rd century AD. This is not a triumphal arch but a covered area where merchants could take shelter from the sun or rain when discussing business. Like the Arch of Titus, it became part of a fortress built by the Frangipane family during the Middle Ages.

Tucked away beside the nearby church of San Giorgio in Velabro ⑭ (see p202) is what looks like a large rectangular doorway. This is the Arco degli Argentari, or Moneychangers' Arch ⑮. Look up at the inscription, which says that it was erected by local silversmiths in honor of Septimius Severus and his family in AD 204. As in the emperor's triumphal arch, the name of Geta has been obliterated by his brother and murderer, Caracalla. Geta's figure has also been removed from among the portraits on the panels inside the arch. Triumph in Imperial Rome could be very short-lived.

Four-sided Arch of Janus in the Forum Boarium ⑬

A Three-Hour Tour of Rome's Best Mosaics

IN IMITATION of the audience chambers of Imperial palaces, Rome's early Christian churches were decorated with brilliant mosaics. These were pieced together from cubes of marble, colored stone and fragments of glass. To create a golden background, gold leaf was placed between pieces of glass. These were then heated so that they fused. The glorious colors and subjects portrayed gave the faithful a glimpse of the heavenly court of the King of Kings. This walk concentrates on a few of the churches decorated in this wonderful medium.

Apse mosaic in the Chapel of Santa Rufina ③

San Giovanni

Start from Piazza di Porta San Giovanni, where you can visit the heavily restored mosaic of the Triclinio Leoniano *(see p179)*. Originally in the banqueting hall of Pope Leo III (reigned 795–816) ①, showing Christ among the Apostles. On the left are Pope Sylvester and the Emperor Constantine, on the right, Pope Leo and Charlemagne,

Obelisk and side facade of San Giovanni in Laterano ②

just before he was crowned Holy Roman Emperor in AD 800. Inside the church of San Giovanni in Laterano ② *(see pp182–3)*, the 13th-century apse mosaic shows Christ as he appeared miraculously during the consecration of the church. In the panels by the windows, look for the small figures of two Franciscan friars; these are the artists Jacopo Torriti *(left)* and Jacopo de

Camerino *(right)*. Leave by the exit on the right near the splendid 16th-century organ and head for the octagonal Baptistry of San Giovanni ③, where the Chapel of Santa Rufina has a beautiful apse mosaic dating from the 5th century. In the neighboring Chapel of San Venanzio there are golden 7th-century mosaics, showing the strong influence of the Eastern Church at this time.

Santo Stefano Rotondo to San Clemente

Leave the piazza by the narrow road that leads to the round church of Santo Stefano Rotondo ④ *(see p185)*. One of its chapels contains a 7th-century Byzantine mosaic honoring two martyrs buried here. Farther on, in Piazza della Navicella, is the church of Santa Maria in Domnica ⑤ *(see p193)*. It houses the superb mosaics commissioned by Pope Paschal I, who gave new impetus to Rome's mosaic production in the 9th century. He is represented kneeling beside the Virgin. On leaving the church, notice the facade of San Tommaso in Formis ⑥, which has a charming mosaic of Christ flanked by two freed slaves, one black and one white, dating from the 13th

Ceiling mosaic, Baptistry of San Giovanni ③

Interior of Baptistry of San Giovanni ③

century. From here, head up the steep hill, past the forbidding apse of Santi Quattro Coronati ⑦ *(see p185)*, to the fascinating church of San Clemente ⑧ *(see pp186–7)*. Its 12th-century apse mosaic shows the cross set in a swirling pattern of acanthus leaves. San Clemente also has a fine 12th-century Cosmatesque mosaic floor.

The Colle Oppio
Passing the old entrance to the church, cross Via Labicana and walk up the hill to the small Colle Oppio park ⑨. This has fine views of the Colosseum and contains the ruins of Nero's Golden House ⑩ *(see p175)* and the Baths of Trajan ⑪. Across the park lie San Martino ai Monti ⑫ *(see p170)*, which has a 6th-century mosaic portrait of Pope St. Sylvester near the crypt, and Santa Prassede ⑬ *(see p171)*. Here the Chapel of St. Zeno contains the most important Byzantine mosaics in Rome, reminiscent of the fabulous mosaics of Ravenna. Pope Paschal I erected the chapel as a mausoleum for his

11th-century frieze above the doorway of Santa Pudenziana ⑯

14th-century facade mosaics by Filippo Rusuti. Inside, the 5th-century mosaics in the nave depict Old Testament stories, while the triumphal arch has scenes relating to the birth of Christ, including one of the Magi wearing striped stockings. In the apse is a Coronation of the Virgin by Jacopo Torriti (1295).

On leaving Santa Maria, pass the obelisk ⑮ in the piazza behind the church and go downhill to Via Urbana and Santa Pudenziana ⑯ *(see p171)*. The figures in the apse mosaic, one of the oldest in Rome (AD 390), are remarkable for their naturalism. The two women with crowns are traditionally identified as Santa Prassede and Santa Pudenziana.

Mosaic saint in Santa Prassede ⑬

When you leave the church, you can either retrace your steps to Santa Maria Maggiore or walk down Via Urbana to Via Cavour Metro station.

mother, Theodora. The apse and triumphal arch of the church itself also have fine mosaics. When you move on to Santa Maria Maggiore ⑭ *(see pp172–3)*, go to the column in the center of the piazza in front of the church to see the beautiful

KEY

— Walk route

— City Wall

☆ Good viewing point

Ⓜ Metro station

0 meters 250
0 yards 250

A Two-Hour Walk around Bernini's Rome

GIAN LORENZO BERNINI (1598–1680) is the artist who probably left the strongest personal mark on the appearance of the city of Rome. Favorite architect, sculptor and town-planner to three successive popes, he turned Rome into a uniquely Baroque city. This walk traces his enormous influence on the development and appearance of the center of Rome. It starts from the busy Largo di Santa Susanna just north of Termini station, at the church of Santa Maria della Vittoria.

Facade of Santa Maria in Via ⑬

Quirinale. The long wing of the Palazzo del Quirinale ⑦ *(see p158)*, nicknamed the Manica Lunga (long sleeve), is by Bernini. On the other side of the road is the facade of Sant'Andrea al Quirinale ⑧ *(see p161)*, one of Bernini's greatest churches. When you reach the Piazza del Quirinale ⑨, note the doorway of the palazzo, attributed to Bernini. From the piazza, go down the

composer Donizetti lived at No. 77 and turn into Via Santa Maria in Via, where the church ⑬ has a fine Baroque

Bernini's Fontana del Tritone ②

Through Piazza Barberini

Santa Maria della Vittoria ① *(see p255)* houses the Cornaro Chapel, the setting for one of Bernini's most revolutionary and controversial sculptures, the *Ecstasy of St. Teresa* (1646). From here take Via Barberini to Piazza Barberini. In its centre is Bernini's dramatic Fontana del Tritone ② *(see p254)* and at one side stands the more modest Fontana delle Api ③ *(see p254)*. As you go up Via delle Quattro Fontane, you catch a glimpse of Palazzo Barberini ④ *(see p255)* built by Bernini and several other artists for Pope Urban VIII. The gateway and cornices are decorated with the bees that made up part of the Barberini family crest. Next make your way to the crossroads, decorated by Le Quattro Fontane ⑤ *(see p162)*, to enjoy the splendid views in all four directions.

Passing the diminutive San Carlo alle Quattro Fontane ⑥ *(see p161)*, built by Bernini's rival Borromini, take Via del

stairs to Via della Dataria, and into Vicolo Scanderbeg which leads to a small piazza with the same name ⑩. Scanderbeg was the nickname of the Albanian prince Giorgio Castriota (1403–68), the "Terror of the Turks". His portrait is preserved on the house where he lived.

The Trevi Fountain

Go along the narrow Vicolo dei Modelli ⑪, where male models waited to be chosen by artists, then turn towards the Trevi Fountain ⑫ *(see p159)*. Its energy is clearly inspired by Bernini's work, a tribute to his lasting influence on Roman taste. Leave the piazza along Via delle Muratte where the

Neptune Fountain at the north end of Piazza Navona ⑱

facade by Bernini's follower Carlo Rainaldi. At the top of this street, turn left down to Via del Corso. On the other side of the road, you will see the towering Column of Marcus Aurelius ⑭ *(see p113)* in Piazza Colonna. Beyond this is Palazzo Montecitorio ⑮, begun in 1650 by Bernini and now the home of the Italian parliament *(see p112)*.

Pantheon to Piazza Navona

Via in Aquiro leads you to the Pantheon ⑯ *(see pp110–11)*. Refusing Pope Urban VIII's request for him to redecorate

Collegio Innocenziano by Borromini and Fontana di Moro by Bernini

Angel on Ponte Sant'Angelo

the dome, Bernini said that although St. Peter's had a hundred defects, the Pantheon did not have any. From the Pantheon, make a small detour to Piazza della Minerva where you can see the bizarre Bernini obelisk, supported by a small elephant, by the church of Santa Maria sopra Minerva ⑰ *(see p108)*. Then retrace your steps and take Salita dei Crescenzi to

KEY

— Walk route

❖ Good viewing point

Ⓜ Metro station

0 meters 250

0 yards 250

reach the fabulous Piazza Navona ⑱ *(see p120)* which was remodelled by Bernini for Pope Innocent X Pamphilj. The design for the central fountain, the Fontana dei

Quattro Fiumi *(see p120)*, was by Bernini, though the figures symbolic of the four rivers were sculpted by other artists. The central figure in the Fontana del Moro, however, is by Bernini himself. Bernini's contemporaries were fascinated by the innovative use of shells, rocks and other natural forms in his fountains, and his expert handling of water to create constant movement.

An extended walk

More energetic walkers may like to head towards the river to see the Ponte Sant'Angelo and its Bernini angels; and then on to St. Peter's *(see pp230–33)* where they can admire Bernini's great colonnaded piazza in front of the church, the papal tombs, his altar decorations and the bronze baldacchino.

Tips for Walkers

Starting point: *Largo di Santa Susanna.*
Length: *3.5 km (2 miles).*
Getting there: *Take Metro line A to Repubblica or any bus to Termini, then walk. Buses 60, 61, 62 and 492 stop in Via Barberini.*
Best time for walk: *Go either between 9am and noon for good lighting conditions in the churches, or between 4pm and 7pm.*
Stopping-off points: *The Piazza Barberini and Fontana di Trevi areas have lots of bars and pizzerias for tourists. The many elegant cafés en route include the famous Caffè Giolitti (see p109) and there is a vast choice of outdoor cafés and restaurants around Piazza della Rotonda and Piazza Navona.*

A 90-Minute Walk along the Via Appia Antica

LINED WITH CYPRESSES AND PINES as it was when the ancient Romans came here by torchlight to bury their dead, the Via Appia is wonderfully atmospheric. The fields are strewn with ruined tombs set against the picturesque background of the Alban hills to the south. Although the marble or travertine stone facings of most tombs have been plundered, a few statues and reliefs survive or have been replaced by copies.

Capo di Bove
Start from the Tomb of Cecilia Metella ① *(see p266)*. In the Middle Ages this area acquired the name Capo di Bove (ox head) from the frieze of festoons and ox heads still visible on the tomb. On

Gothic windows in the church of San Nicola ②

the other side of the road you can see the ruined Gothic church of San Nicola ②, which, like the Tomb of Cecilia Metella, was part of the medieval fortress of the Caetani family.

Proceed to the crossroads ③, where there are still many original Roman paving slabs, huge blocks of extremely durable volcanic basalt. Just

The ruined church of San Nicola ②

past the next turning (Via Capo di Bove), you will see on your left the nucleus of a great mausoleum overgrown with ivy, known as the Torre di Capo di Bove ④. Beyond it,

on both sides of the Appia, are other tombs, some still capped with the remains of the medieval towers that were built over them. On the right after passing some private villas, you come to a military zone around the Forte Appio ⑤, one of a series of forts built around the city in the 19th century. On the left, a little further on, stand the ruins of the Tomb of Marcus Servilius ⑥, showing fragments of reliefs excavated in 1808 by the Neo-Classical sculptor Antonio Canova. He was one of the first to work on the principle that excavated tombs and their inscriptions and reliefs should be allowed to remain in situ. On the other side of the road stands a tomb with a relief of a man, naked except for a short cape, known as the

Tomb of Sixtus Pompeus the Righteous ⑨

"Heroic Relief" ⑦. On the left of the road are the ruins of the so-called Tomb of Seneca ⑧. The great moralist Seneca owned a villa near here, where he committed suicide in AD 65 on the orders of Nero.

The next major tomb is that of the family of Sixtus Pompeus the Righteous, a freed slave of the 1st century AD ⑨. The verse inscription records the father's sadness at having to bury his own children, who died young.

Artist's impression of how the mausoleums and tombs lining the Via Appia looked in the 2nd century AD

Section of the Via Appia Antica, showing original Roman paving stones

From Via dei Lugari to Via di Tor Carbone

Just past Via dei Lugari on the right, screened by trees, is the Tomb of Pope St. Urban (reigned 222–230) ⑩. Set back from the road on the left stands a large ruined podium, probably part of a Temple of Jupiter ⑪. The next stretch was excavated by the architect Luigi Canina early in the 19th century. On the right is the Tomb of Caius Licinius ⑫, followed by a smaller Doric tomb ⑬ and the imposing Tomb of Hilarius

Fuscus ⑭, with five portrait busts in relief of members of his family. Next comes the Tomb of Tiberius Claudius Secondinus ⑮, where a group of freedmen of the Imperial household were buried in the 2nd century AD.

Passing a large ruined columbarium, you reach the Tomb of Quintus Apuleius ⑯ and the reconstructed Tomb of the Rabirii freed slaves (1st century BC) ⑰. This has a frieze of three half-length figures above an inscription.

The figure on the right is a priestess of Isis. Behind her you can see the outline of a *sistrum*, the metal rattle used at ceremonies of the cult.

The majority of the tombs are little more than shapeless stacks of eroded brickwork. Two exceptions in the last stretch of this walk are the Tomb of the Festoons ⑱, with its reconstructed frieze of festive putti, and the Tomb of the Frontispiece ⑲, which has a copy of a relief with four portraits. The two central figures are holding hands.

When you reach Via di Tor Carbone, the Via Appia still stretches out ahead of you in a straight line and, if you wish to extend your walk, there are many more tombs and ruined villas to visit along the way.

KEY

— Walk route

⁂ Good viewing point

0 meters 250
0 yards 250

Figure on the Tomb of the Heroic Relief ⑦

TIPS FOR WALKERS

Starting point: Tomb of Cecilia Metella.
Length: 3 km (2 miles).
Getting there: Taking a taxi is the easiest way to reach the tomb. Alternatively, take the 760 from Circo Massimo (Sundays and public holidays only) or the 660 from Colli Albani on Metro Line A.
Best time for walk: Go fairly early, before it gets too hot.
Stopping-off points: There is a bar near the church of Domine Quo Vadis?, before the start of the walk, but it is best to bring your own refreshment. There are also several well-established restaurants on the first stretch of the Appia, including the Cecilia Metella, Via Appia Antica 125/127, tel 06-513 67 43 (closed Mon).

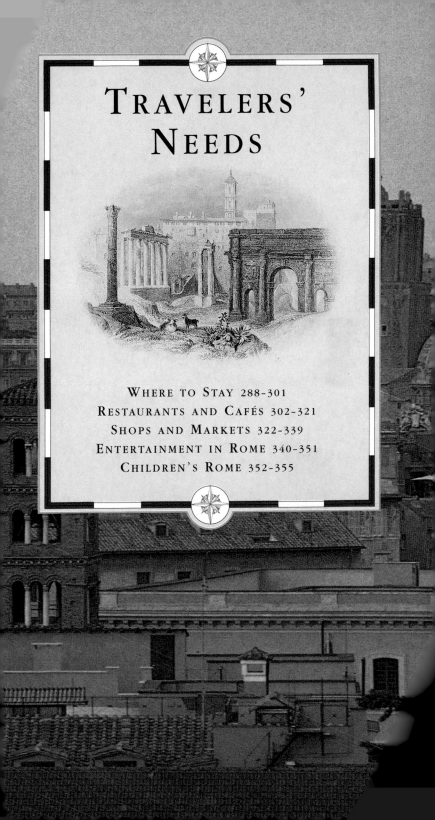

TRAVELERS' NEEDS

WHERE TO STAY

ROME HAS BEEN a major tourist center since the Middle Ages, when pilgrims from all over Europe came to visit the home of Catholicism and its relic-packed churches. The nostalgic can still sleep in a 15th-century hotel or stay around the Campo de' Fiori market, where visiting ecclesiastics were entertained by courtesans in the Renaissance era. Those who prefer their history a little less raffish can stay in an ex-monastery, convent or a still-functioning religious house. Romantics can sleep in the house once occupied by Keats, while the celebrity-conscious can stay

Porter at the Majestic Hotel

in former palaces graced by VIPs of the past and present. Rome offers the full range of accommodations, mainly in historical buildings. *Pensione* (guesthouse) is no longer an official category, but in practice many places retain the name and more personal character that has made them so popular with travelers. Other possibilities include hostels, residential hotels and accommodations with kitchens.

The 72 hotels we have selected are listed in the *Choosing a Hotel* chart *(pp294–5)*, organized *(pp296–301)* according to their price category and area.

WHERE TO LOOK

AROUND the Spanish Steps and Piazza di Spagna lies the traditional heartland of foreign visitors, with some of the most exclusive smaller hotels. Similar places can be found all over the center, to the west of Via del Corso.

While moderately priced accommodations are rare in central Rome, the advantages of staying right on the doorstep of the city's many ancient sights cannot be overestimated; you can walk to the major areas of interest and easily return at midday for a shower, meal and siesta.

If the less expensive hotels we have recommended in the center are full, try the Borgo – close to the Vatican – or the lively quarter of Trastevere.

Those in search of glamour should head for Via Veneto, which has many grand and luxurious hotels.

If you're looking for a peaceful retreat, try the area around the Aventine or one of the high-class hotels next to the Villa Borghese park.

Although many of the streets immediately around Termini Station are somewhat seedy, the area is nonetheless a convenient stopover for travelers. There's also a

concentration of cheap hotels, with some decent (if basic) ones among them. The hotels recommended lie in a fairly safe area on the east side of the station. The approach to the center from Termini has a number of good hotels that are particularly suitable for the business traveler.

HOTEL PRICES

ROME MAY have cheaper accommodations than London or New York, but rates for comparable establishments have caught up. Prices are set by the state, and hotels must display the official rate on the door of each room. VAT is usually included and has been taken into account in the price categories on page 291.

Hotels in Rome generally have low and high season rates, so it is often worth bargaining since you will inevitably be quoted the official rate – even in the winter months before and after Christmas, when competition is less strong. Discounts for long-term visitors and groups are often negotiable.

Rooms without a bathroom can cost about 30% less. Single travelers will find few bargains: though it is possible to find a single room for 60% of the price of a double, on the average you'll pay 70%,

Room in Via Veneto's Majestic Hotel *(see p301)*

The Plaza Minerva *(see p296)*

and occasionally up to 90%. Where breakfast is included in the quoted price, you can ask for the relevant amount to be deducted from your bill if you don't want the meal.

HIDDEN EXTRAS

EVEN IF the price of your room includes service, you are often still expected to give a tip at for room service or for bellboys.

Hotels will often add hefty surcharges to international phone calls and may charge extra for parking and air conditioning. The cost of drinks in minibars can be high – you can buy a cheaper supply from local shops.

FACILITIES

HOTEL STANDARDS have improved of late – you can expect air-conditioning and some bathrooms with hair dryers in middle-range establishments and direct-dial phones in middle-to-lower price rooms, although budget travelers staying in cheaper hotels shouldn't expect much more than a clean room.

Because most hotels occupy historic buildings, room sizes can vary dramatically even within the same establishment (and this is often reflected in the

The Portoghesi Hotel *(see p296)*

pricing), so don't be afraid to ask to see your room before you check in. For the same reason, swimming pools are few and far between, but roof terraces or gardens are common across the range.

First-class hotels will usually have some degree of soundproofing; otherwise, noise levels can be dreadful, in which case ask for a room facing away from the road. The chart on pages 294 to 295 indicates which hotels have a quiet location – this covers both peaceful neighborhoods and certain quiet streets in busy areas.

Parking in central Rome is a problem, though a few hotels have a limited number of parking spaces of their own.

Business visitors to the capital are well provided for, with hotel facilities ranging from fax machines to meeting and conference rooms *(see pp294–5)*.

MAKING RESERVATIONS

THE ITALIAN postal service tends to be unreliable, so it is safer to reserve by phone or fax. You should do this at least two months in advance if you want a particular hotel in May, June, September or October; Easter and Christmas are also busy.

If a deposit is required, you can pay by credit card or international money order. Under Italian law a reservation is valid as soon as the deposit is paid, so you're likely to lose money if you cancel. If you arrive by train, people may approach you at the station with offers of accommodations. They can be of some use if you are looking for a budget hotel, but you should exercise the usual caution. A better bet if you haven't reserved a room anywhere in advance is to head for one of the tourist board offices. Here, staff will reserve you a room within your price range.

Villa San Pio garden *(see p299)*

CHECKING IN AND OUT

ITALIAN HOTELIERS are legally obliged to register you with the police, which is the reason they always ask for your passport. They usually hold on to it for a few hours, but you willl need it if you're going to change money. Everyone in Italy is supposed to carry with them some sort of identification.

In some of Rome's cheaper *pensioni,* don't be surprised if you are asked to pay in advance. To speed up the checking-out process, mention in advance if you intend to pay by credit card.
The Locarno *(see p297)*

TOURIST BOARDS

PROVINCIAL and state tourist boards can provide advice on accommodations. There Is also a free booking service.

Rome Provincial Tourist Board (EPT)
Via Parigi 11, 00185. 📞 06-48 89 91. *Open 8:15am–7:15pm Mon–Fri, 8:15am–1:30pm Sun.*

Leonardo da Vinci Airport, Fiumicino, 00054. 📞 06-65 95 44 71 or 06-65 95 60 74. *Open 8:15am–7:15pm daily.*

Termini Station, Piazza dei Cinquecento, 00185 📞 06-482 40 78 or 06-487 12 70. *Open 8:15am–7:15pm daily.*

Booking Service
📞 06-699 10 00. *Open 7am–10pm daily.*

The reception area of the Regina Hotel Baglioni *(see p301)*

DISABLED TRAVELERS

PROVISION for the disabled is very poor. Small hotels that occupy parts of buildings sometimes offer only rooms that must be reached via several flights of stairs, while certain establishments can accommodate disabled guests only on the ground floor or have only one or two rooms that are appropriate. Ramps, wide doorways and bathroom handrails are rare.

Our entries for wheelchair access in the listings below rely on the establishments' own assessments; any specific requirements should be checked before reserving.

There is a private organization, Associazione Nazionale degli Handicappati at Corso Vittorio 154, which advises disabled travelers. They can be contacted on 06-781 07 72, 9am–6pm Mon–Fri.

TRAVELING WITH CHILDREN

ITALIANS LOVE CHILDREN, and they are usually welcome across the range of hotels. Facilities, however, tend to be unimpressive. Most hotels can provide cribs or small beds, but highchairs, children's meals and babysitting services are rare. However, many establishments – especially smaller, family-run ones – go out of their way to be helpful.

Many hotels do not have any special rates for children, especially in high season, and charge a standard rate if you require an extra bed in a room, whether it's for a baby

or an adult; this can add anything from a few thousand lire to 40% on to the price of a double room. For a family with older children, two-room suites are sometimes to be found. For hotels providing children's facilities, see Choosing a Hotel *(pp294–5)*.

BED & BREAKFAST

A FAIRLY NEW option for visitors to Rome is bed & breakfast accomodation. Roman hosts offer their spare rooms to visitors, generally for a much lower price than an equivalent hotel room. The **Bed & Breakfast Association of Rome** offers an attractive selection of rooms and apartments. **Rome Bed & Breakfast**, based in the US, also has a good range of rooms avaible.

Bed & Breakfast Association of Rome
Piazza del Teatro di Pompeo 2.
📞 FAX *06-687 73 48.*

Rome Bed & Breakfast
📞 *1-619-238 60 76.*
FAX *1-619-531 16 86.*

RESIDENTIAL HOTELS

IF YOU WANT the comfort and privacy of your own apartment coupled with the services of a hotel, you could opt to stay in a *residenza*. Prices range from around L500,000 to over L3 million for a week in a two-bedded room, though some *residenze* are available only for two-week or monthly lets. A full

list is available from tourist board offices *(see p289)*; the following are some of the most central:

Residence Babuino
Via del Babuino 172, 00187.
📞 *06-361 16 63.*

Di Ripetta
Via di Ripetta 231, 00186.
📞 *06-323 11 44.*
FAX *320 39 59.*

In Trastevere
Vicolo Moroni 35–36, 00153.
📞 *06-581 27 68.*

Vittoria
Via Vittoria 60, 00187.
📞 FAX *06-679 75 33.*

RELIGIOUS INSTITUTIONS

IF YOU DON'T MIND an early curfew when the rest of Rome is still swinging, quite a few religious institutions take in paying guests. You do not have to be a practicing Catholic to stay in one of these, but be sure to reserve well in advance since all of the following places cater to groups of students and pilgrims. **Domus Mariae** and **Istituto Madri Pie** are near the Vatican; **Congregazione Suore dello Spirito Santo** is farther out of town, 4 miles (6 km) west of the center. Prices are near those of the cheapest hotels.

Domus Mariae
Via Aurelia 481, 00165.
📞 FAX *06-660 00 576, 06-663 88 23.*

The Gregoriana *(see p297)*

Istituto Madri Pie
Via A. de Gasperi 4, 00165.
06-63 19 67, 06-63 34 41.

Congregazione Suore dello Spirito Santo
Via della Pineta Sacchetti 227, 00168.
FAX 06-305 31 01.

Facade of the Excelsior *(see p301)*

BUDGET ACCOMMODATIONS

EVEN IF YOU'RE TRAVELING on a shoestring, it's possible to find a clean, decent room in Rome. Dormitory accommodations can be found at rock-bottom prices in simple establishments, such as the **Ottaviano.** Youth hostels are a good option – and not just for the young. The **Ostello del Foro Italico** provides bed, breakfast and shower at a very reasonable price.

Women can get single, double or triple rooms at the **Young Women's Christian Association** (YWCA). Its location near Termini Station is convenient but somewhat unsafe, so take care if arriving at night. The **Protezione della Giovane** organization has an information office for women under 25; they will try to find you somewhere safe and cheap to stay.

HOSTEL AND DORMITORY ADDRESSES

Ottaviano
Via Ottaviano 6, 00192.
06-39 73 72 53, or 39 73 81 38.

Associazione Italiana Alberghi per la Gioventù
(Youth Hostel Association)
Via Cavour 44, 00184.
06-487 11 52. FAX 06-488 04 92.

Ostello del Foro Italico
Viale delle Olimpiadi 61, 00194.
06-323 62 79. FAX 06-324 26 13.

Residenza Universitaria de Lollis
Via Cesare de Lollis 20, 00185.
Rooms in August only. Details from Youth Hostel Association, above.

YWCA
Via C. Balbo 4, 00184.
06-488 39 17.
FAX 06-487 10 28.

Protezione della Giovane
Via Urbana 158, 00184.
06-488 14 89.

CAMPING

MOST CAMPSITES are well out of town – suitable for an occasional excursion into Rome – with the exception of **Flaminio**, which is near the Olympic Village, 4 miles (6 km) north of the center.

Flaminio
Via Flaminia Nuova 821, 00191.
06-333 26 04. FAX 06-333 06 53.

USING THE LISTINGS

The hotels on pages 296 to 301 are organized according to area and price. The symbols after the hotel's address show the facilities it offers.

rooms with bath and/or shower available
single-rate rooms available
rooms for more than two people available, or an extra bed can be put in a double room
24-hour room service available
television in all rooms
minibar in all rooms
nonsmoking rooms available
rooms with good view
air-conditioning in all rooms
swimming pool in hotel
business facilities: message-taking service, fax machine for guests, desk and telephone in each room and a meeting room within the hotel
child cribs and baby-sitting service
wheelchair access (phone for details)
elevator
pets allowed in bedrooms (confirm that you are bringing a pet). The majority of hotels accept guide dogs.
hotel parking available
garden/terrace open to guests
bar
restaurant
tourist information
credit cards accepted
AE American Express
DC Diners Club
MC MasterCard/Access
V VISA
JCB Japanese Credit Bureau

Price categories for a double room with bath or shower, including breakfast, tax and service:
L under L100,000
LL L100,000–L199,000
LLL L200,000–L299,000
LLLL L300,000–L400,000
LLLLL over L400,000

The pool in the Aldrovandi Palace garden *(see p301)*

Rome's Best: Hotels

R OMAN HOTELS RANGE from frescoed palaces and *fin-de-siècle* bastions of faded glamor, to family-run guesthouses. Most are within easy reach of restaurants, shops and transport. Whatever the price level, all the hotels shown on this map have something special to offer, whether it's a chic location, or a roof terrace with soaring views across the city. The only drawback is that these places and the others listed on pages 294–301 are exceptions to the many unremarkable hotels in the city, so you should book well in advance. The hotels shown here are the best in their particular style or price range.

Sole al Pantheon
The writers Jean Paul Sartre and Simone de Beauvoir stayed in this superbly located – and recently refurbished – 15th-century palazzo. (See p296.)

0 meters   500

0 yards   500

Raphael
Full of antiques and art, the Raphael offers a central location. (See p297.)

Vatican

Janiculum

Piaz Spa

Piaz Nav

Campo Fiori

R

Traste

Campo de' Fiori
Central Rome's best bargain offers small, well-furnished rooms and terrific views from the sixth-floor roof terrace. (See p298.)

Crowne Plaza Minerva
Smart, post-modern interiors grace this international standard hotel. (See p296.)

Sant'Anselmo
To be sure of getting a room you need to book well in advance at this peacefully located Roman villa. An added bonus is the lovely secluded garden. (See p299.)

Hassler
Luxurious suites and an air of faded grandeur remind visitors of the Hassler's heyday. The roof-top restaurant is Rome's most famous. (See p298.)

Hotel Eden
One of the oldest and most exclusive hotels in Rome, the Eden offers elegant decor and truly innovative cuisine. (See p301.)

Carriage
The serene atmosphere makes this city-center hotel a special haven. (See p297.)

Grand
Good service and extensive facilities are the main features of this old-fashioned, luxury hotel. (See p299.)

Via Veneto

Quirinal

Esquiline

Forum

Palatine

Caracalla

Lateran

Scalinata di Spagna
The prized location at the top of the Spanish Steps, and a large private terrace, make this hotel a popular choice with visitors. (See p298.)

Inghilterra
Sip a cocktail in the Inghilterra's club-like bar, once frequented by Ernest Hemingway. (See p298.)

Choosing a Hotel

THE 71 HOTELS listed in the following pages have all been inspected and assessed. This selection chart includes some of the features that may affect your hotel choice. The hotels are listed alphabetically within their price category. For more detailed information, see pages 296 to 301.

Hotel	Price	Number of Rooms	Large Rooms	Business Facilities	Hotel Parking	Recommended Restaurant	Close to Shops and Restaurants	Quiet Location	24-Hour Room Service
FORUM (see p296)									
Forum	₤₤₤₤	76		■					●
PIAZZA DELLA ROTONDA (see p296)									
Abruzzi	₤₤	25					●		
Mimosa	₤₤	11					●		
Santa Chiara	₤₤₤₤	98					●		
Colonna Palace	₤₤₤₤	110	●				●		
Holiday Inn Crowne Plaza Minerva	₤₤₤₤	134	●	■			●		
Nazionale	₤₤₤₤	87	●	■			●		
Sole al Pantheon	₤₤₤₤	25					●		
PIAZZA NAVONA (see p296)									
Navona	₤₤	21					●	■	
Due Torri	₤₤₤	26					●	■	
Portoghesi	₤₤₤	28					●	■	
Genio	₤₤₤	60					●		
Raphael	₤₤₤₤	72					●	■	
PIAZZA DI SPAGNA (see p297)									
Jonella	₤	5					●		
Firenze	₤₤	25	●				●		●
Homs	₤₤₤	50					●	■	
Locarno	₤₤₤	48		■	●		●		
Lydia	₤₤₤	28					●		
Margutta	₤₤₤	24					●	■	
Mozart	₤₤₤	95					●	■	
Piazza di Spagna	₤₤₤	16	●				●		
Suisse	₤₤₤	12	●				●		
Carriage	₤₤₤₤	27	●				●		
Condotti	₤₤₤₤	16	●				●		
Gregoriana	₤₤₤₤	19					●	■	●
Manfredi	₤₤₤₤	18		■			●		●
Dei Borgognoni	₤₤₤₤₤	50		■	●		●		
Hassler	₤₤₤₤₤	100	●	■	●			■	
D' Inghilterra	₤₤₤₤₤	105		■			●	■	●
Scalinata di Spagna	₤₤₤₤₤	16					●		●
Valadier	₤₤₤₤₤	45		■			●	■	●
CAMPO DE' FIORI (see p298)									
Campo de' Fiori	₤₤	27					●	■	
Della Lunetta	₤₤	35					●		
Piccolo	₤₤	15					●		
Pomezia	₤₤	24					●		
Smeraldo	₤₤	35					●		
Sole	₤₤	58		■	●		●	■	
Rinascimento	₤₤₤	19			●		●	■	
Teatro di Pompeo	₤₤₤	13		■	●		●	■	

Price categories for a double room per night, including breakfast, tax and service:
- Ⓛ under L100,000
- ⓁⓁ L100,000 –L199,000
- ⓁⓁⓁ L200,000 –L299,000
- ⓁⓁⓁⓁ L300,000 –L400,000
- ⓁⓁⓁⓁⓁ over L400,000.

HOTEL PARKING
Car parking facilities attached to the hotel or in the hotel complex.

CLOSE TO SHOPS AND RESTAURANTS
Within a 5-minute walk of a good area for shops, bars, cafés and restaurants.

BUSINESS FACILITIES
Message-taking service, fax machine for guest use, desk and telephone in each room and a meeting room that is available within the hotel.

	Price	Number of Rooms	Large Rooms	Business Facilities	Hotel Parking	Recommended Restaurant	Close to Shops and Restaurants	Quiet Location	24-Hour Room Service
QUIRINAL (see p299)									
Le Grand Hotel	ⓁⓁⓁⓁⓁ	170	●	■		■			●
TERMINI (see p299)									
Katty	Ⓛ	12							
Restivo	Ⓛ	6							
Cervia	ⓁⓁ	28							
Mari	ⓁⓁ	21	●						
Canada	ⓁⓁⓁ	74	●	■					
Hotel Giuliana	ⓁⓁⓁ	21					●		
Venezia	ⓁⓁⓁ	61	●				●		
AVENTINE (see p299)									
Aventino	ⓁⓁ	23	●	■				■	
Domus Aventina	ⓁⓁⓁ	26	●	■				■	●
Sant'Anselmo	ⓁⓁⓁ	46		■					
Villa San Pio	ⓁⓁⓁ	59	●	■	●			■	
TRASTEVERE (see p300)									
Carmel	ⓁⓁ	10							
VATICAN (see p300)									
Alimandi	ⓁⓁ	35			●			■	
Amalia	ⓁⓁⓁ	30					●		
Atlante Star	ⓁⓁⓁⓁ	62	●	■	●		●		●
Columbus	ⓁⓁⓁⓁ	100		■	●				
Hotel dei Mellini	ⓁⓁⓁⓁ	80		■	●			■	●
VIA VENETO (see p300)									
Merano	ⓁⓁ	30					●		
Oxford	ⓁⓁⓁ	58		■					
Residenza	ⓁⓁⓁ	29	●		●		●		
Alexandra	ⓁⓁⓁⓁ	45					●		
Victoria	ⓁⓁⓁⓁ	108		■			●	■	●
Bernini Bristol	ⓁⓁⓁⓁⓁ	126	●	■			●		●
Eden	ⓁⓁⓁⓁⓁ	92	●	■		■	●	■	●
Excelsior	ⓁⓁⓁⓁⓁ	321	●	■	●		●		●
Imperiale	ⓁⓁⓁⓁⓁ	96		■			●		●
Majestic	ⓁⓁⓁⓁⓁ	100			●		●		
Regina Hotel Baglioni	ⓁⓁⓁⓁⓁ	130	●	■	●		●		
Romantik Barocco Hotel	ⓁⓁⓁⓁⓁ	28		■			●		
VILLA BORGHESE (see p301)									
Villa Borghese	ⓁⓁⓁⓁ	31			●				●
Aldrovandi Palace	ⓁⓁⓁⓁⓁ	137		■	●	■			
Lord Byron	ⓁⓁⓁⓁⓁ	37		■		■		■	●

FORUM

Forum

Via Tor de' Conti 25, 00184.
Map 5 B5. **(** 06-679 24 46.
FAX 06-679 67 72. **Rooms:** 76. ▯
▯ ▯ ▯ ▯ ▯ ▯ ▯ ▯
▯ ▯ ▯ ▯ AE, DC, MC, V, JCB.
ⓁⓁⓁⓁ

Occupying a palace built out of
materials from the ruins of the
nearby Imperial Fora, the Forum is
an old-fashioned hotel. It features
mellow wood-paneled public
rooms, and a sunny roof terrace
restaurant giving wonderful views
over the archaeological center.

PIAZZA DELLA ROTONDA

Abruzzi

Piazza della Rotonda 69, 00186.
Map 4 F4 & 12 D3. **(** 06-679 20 21.
Rooms: 25. ▯ ▯ ⓁⓁ

The Abruzzi provides clean, basic
rooms with terra-cotta-tiled floors
in an ochre-colored palazzo overlooking the Pantheon. The rooms
at the back, while not the best, are
quiet. No breakfast is served.

Mimosa

Via di Santa Chiara 61, 00186. **Map**
4 F4 & 12 D3. **(** 06-68 80 17 53.
FAX 06-683 35 57. **Rooms:** 11. ▯ 1.
▯ ▯ ▯ ⓁⓁ

The Mimosa is a clean, if slightly
scruffy, family-run hotel close to
the Pantheon. Rooms are cool, and
the five communal bathrooms and
showers are immaculate. The hotel
is popular with visiting student
groups, so reserve well ahead.

Santa Chiara

Via di Santa Chiara 21, 00186.
Map 4 F4 & 12 D3. **(** 06-687 29 79.
FAX 06-687 31 44. **Rooms:** 98. ▯ ▯
▯ ▯ ▯ ▯ ▯ ▯ AE, DC, MC,
V, JCB. ⓁⓁⓁ

Conveniently located in the historic
center, the Santa Chiara occupies
an apricot-washed palazzo. Public
rooms are cool, particularly the
marble reception area and the
lounge. Bedrooms are carpeted
and have good-quality furnishings.

Colonna Palace

Piazza di Montecitorio 12, 00186.
Map 4 F3 & 12 E2. **(** 06-678 13 41.
FAX 06-678 90 04. **Rooms:** 110. ▯
▯ ▯ ▯ ▯ ▯ ▯ ▯ ▯ ▯
▯ AE, DC, MC, V. ⓁⓁⓁⓁⓁ

The Colonna Palace stands on the
same piazza as Italy's Chamber of
Deputies, and so the area attracts
politicians as well as tourists.
Bedrooms are spacious, though
the bathrooms are small. Breakfast
is served in a basement room
livened up by frescoes. There are
lovely views from the impressive
roof garden, where a Jacuzzi has
recently been installed.

Holiday Inn Crowne Plaza Minerva

Piazza della Minerva 69, 00186.
Map 4 F4 & 12 D3. **(** 06-69 94 18
88. **FAX** 06-679 41 65. **Rooms:** 134.
▯ ▯ ▯ ▯ ▯ ▯ ▯ ▯ ▯
▯ ▯ ▯ ▯ ▯ ▯ AE, DC,
MC, V, JCB. ⓁⓁⓁⓁ

Occupying Palazzo Fonseca
behind the Pantheon, this is
Rome's newest luxury hotel. The
interior was designed by Post-
Modern architect Portoghesi, and
its centerpiece is the lounge,
canopied in semi-translucent
Venetian glass and presided over
by a statue of Minerva. The large
bedrooms are decorated in shades
of beige and coral. Views from the
roof terrace are magnificent,
stretching over the Pantheon,
St. Peter's and the Janiculum Hill.

Nazionale

Piazza di Montecitorio 131, 00186.
Map 4 F3 & 12 E2. **(** 06-69 50 01.
FAX 06-678 66 77. **Rooms:** 87. ▯
▯ ▯ ▯ ▯ ▯ ▯ ▯ ▯ ▯
▯ AE, DC, MC, V.
ⓁⓁⓁⓁ

Home to Robert de Niro while he
was making *Godfather II*, the
Nazionale is usually frequented
by visiting tourists, businesspeople
and politicians – it stands right
on the corner of the Chamber
of Deputies. Public rooms are
comfortable, particularly the
lounge, with its brocade sofas
and flower arrangements. Some of
the rooms are huge, and most are
partially furnished with French and
Italian antiques.

Sole al Pantheon

Piazza della Rotonda 63, 00186.
Map 4 F4 & 12 D3. **(** 06-678
04 41. **FAX** 06-69 94 06 89.
Rooms: 25. ▯ ▯ ▯ ▯ ▯
▯ ▯ ▯ ▯ ▯ AE, DC, MC, V.
ⓁⓁⓁⓁ

A hotel since 1467, the Sole boasts
an illustrious list of former guests –
from Renaissance writer Ariosto to
Jean-Paul Sartre and Simone de
Beauvoir. It is easy to explain its
attraction: its location opposite the
Pantheon is unbeatable, and
though it has been modernized
(60% of the rooms now have

Jacuzzis), there are still bedrooms
with painted, paneled ceilings.

PIAZZA NAVONA

Navona

Via dei Sediari 8, 00186. **Map** 4 F4 &
12 D3. **(** 06-686 42 03. **FAX** 06-68
80 38 02. **Rooms:** 21. ▯ 18. ▯ 1 ▯
▯ ▯ ⓁⓁ

This hotel's superb location –
across from Piazza Navona and
five minutes' stroll from the
Pantheon – means that it's hard to
find a room here unless you
reserve well in advance. The hotel
is run largely by the owners'
Australian son-in-law, who is
extremely helpful. Bedrooms are
basic, and some have bathrooms.
The restaurant opens for groups
of 15 or more.

Due Torri

Vicolo del Leonetto 23, 00186.
Map 4 E3 & 11 C1. **(** 06-687 69 83.
FAX 06-686 54 42. **Rooms:** 26. ▯ 1
▯ ▯ ▯ ▯ ▯ ▯ AE, DC,
MC, V. ⓁⓁⓁⓁ

This amiable hotel is a short walk
from both Piazza Navona and the
Spanish Steps, tucked into an
alleyway in the artisans' district
of the old town. Bedrooms vary:
some are stylish, others plain and
rather small. The lounge is both
elegant and homey, with looped-
back drapes, statuettes, an
immense gilt-framed mirror and
pink velvet sofas.

Portoghesi

Via dei Portoghesi 1, 00186.
Map 4 E3 & 11 C2. **(** 06-686 42
31. **FAX** 06-687 69 76. **Rooms:** 28.
▯ ▯ 1 ▯ ▯ ▯ ▯ ▯ AE, DC,
MC, V. ⓁⓁⓁⓁ

Ideally located on a cobbled street
a brief walk from Piazza Navona,
the Portoghesi is a simple hotel,
with slightly dated bedrooms. The
public rooms, however, are
elegant, and there's a roof terrace
looking out to the dome of the
Portuguese community's church
next door.

Genio

Via Zanardelli 28, 00186. **Map** 4 E3 &
11 C2. **(** 06-683 37 81. **FAX** 06-68 30
72 46. **Rooms:** 60. ▯ ▯ 1 ▯ ▯ ▯
▯ ▯ ▯ ▯ AE, DC, MC, V, JCB.
ⓁⓁⓁⓁ

On a fairly busy road just behind
Piazza Navona, the Genio's
bedrooms are ordinary, though
comfortable. The location,
however, and a roof terrace where
you can picnic with your own
food, make it worth considering.

Raphael

Largo Febo 2, 00186. **Map** 4 E3 & 11 C2. 06-68 28 31. FAX 06-687 89 93. **Rooms:** 72. AE, DC, MC, V, JCB.

The Raphael is curtained with ivy and situated on a cobbled street just off Piazza Navona. The big reception lounge has the air of an exhibition hall, being full of antique statues, modern sculpture and even a painted sled. There is a restaurant in the basement whose outstanding feature is an ornate wine cabinet. Bedrooms are decorated with parquet floors, marbled walls and 18th-century-style furniture as well as paisley curtains. The rooms on the top floor offer terrific views.

PIAZZA DI SPAGNA

Jonella

Via della Croce 41, 00187. **Map** 4 F2. 06-679 79 66. FAX 06-446 23 68. **Rooms:** 5.

The Jonella occupies an orange-colored palazzo on one of the most attractive shopping streets in the Piazza di Spagna area. The decor is somewhat ordinary, but the location and low prices make this place worth considering. The owner occasionally pops out to shop, so if you arrive when no-one's there, be patient and wait for someone to return.

Firenze

Via Due Macelli 106, 00186. **Map** 5 A2 & 12 F1. 06-679 72 40. FAX 06-678 56 36. **Rooms:** 25. AE, MC, V.

The Firenze lies a short distance from Piazza di Spagna on a busy main road. The owner has set her elegant stamp on the hotel: Chinese urns and gilt-framed mirrors greet you in the entrance hall, and the bedrooms are large and beautifully decorated. There is also a leafy terrace where you can take breakfast.

Homs

Via della Vite 71–72, 00187. **Map** 5 A3 & 12 F1. 06-679 29 76. FAX 06-678 04 82. **Rooms:** 50. AE, DC, MC, V.

On one of the quieter, less pretentious shopping streets in the Piazza di Spagna area, the Homs has clean, pleasant rooms with dark-green carpets, white walls and white bathrooms. The breakfast room opens out on to a pleasant terrace.

Locarno

Via della Penna 22, 00186. **Map** 4 F1. 06-361 08 41, 06-361 08 42. FAX 06-321 52 49. **Rooms:** 48. AE, DC, MC, V.

Situated on a small, busy side-street near the Tiber, a brief walk from Piazza del Popolo, the Locarno is an attractive 1920s hotel with an Art Nouveau door and swags of lilac growing across its facade. Old-fashioned touches remain, with a grandfather clock and Tiffany lamp in the reception area, and a marble-topped bar of polished wood. Outside, there's a patio packed with greenery and kept cool by a tiny fountain.

Lydia

Via Sistina 42, 00187. **Map** 5 B2. 06-679 38 15. FAX 06-679 72 63. **Rooms:** 28. 6. AE, DC, MC, V.

The Lydia is a pleasant hotel, popular with students, on a busy road a few minutes' walk from the Spanish Steps. Rooms have pale-blue walls and pastel bedcovers, and two retain their old ceiling frescoes. If you're not lucky enough to get one of these, content yourself with breakfasting in the chandelier-lit dining room, which is also decorated with beautiful frescoes. Some street-facing rooms can be noisy.

Margutta

Via Laurina 34, 00187. **Map** 4 F1. 06-322 36 74. FAX 06-320 03 95. **Rooms:** 24. AE, DC, MC, V.

The Margutta is on a quiet cobbled street just below the Piazza del Popolo. The scruffy facade and slightly grubby seats in the lobby are forgotten as soon as you get into your room, which has white walls and green wrought-iron bedsteads and candleholders. If you wish to stay in one of the three attic rooms that share a pretty roof terrace, be sure to book well in advance.

Mozart

Via dei Greci 236, 00187. **Map** 4 F2. 06-36 00 19 15. FAX 06-36 00 17 35. **Rooms:** 95. AE, DC, MC, V, JCB.

Located on a cobbled street between Piazza del Popolo and Piazza di Spagna, the Mozart is immediately appealing. The attractively worn decor includes a delightful Venetian mirror. There's a small breakfast room, as well as a bar/café, which opens off the stone-lagged reception area. Rooms have ceramic-tiled or parquet floors, and bathrooms tend to be small, most being equipped only with a shower.

Piazza di Spagna

Via Mario de' Fiori 61, 00187. **Map** 5 A2 & 12 F1. 06-679 30 61, 06-679 64 12. FAX 06-679 06 54. **Rooms:** 16. AE, MC, V.

Close to the designer boutiques of Via Condotti, this attractive, small hotel has simple but good-sized rooms with beautiful tiled floors. A couple of bathrooms offer Jacuzzis. The breakfast room and bar are tiny, so most residents decide to take breakfast in the comfort of their own rooms.

Suisse

Via Gregoriana 54–56, 00187. **Map** 5 A2 & 12 F1. 06-678 36 49. FAX 06-678 12 58. **Rooms:** 12. 8.

Occupying the third floor of a dusty palazzo (the entrance is at No. 54), the Suisse is a pleasant small hotel with friendly staff. Chinese prints hang along the corridors and in the rooms. The rooms also have polished floors, molded ceilings and marble-topped dressers and tables. Breakfast is served in the bedrooms.

Carriage

Via delle Carrozze 36, 00187. **Map** 5 A2. 06-699 01 24. FAX 06-678 82 79. **Rooms:** 27. AE, DC, MC, V, JCB.

Situated on a street where the nobility used to park their carriages, this hotel's elegance is immediately evident in the delightful reception area, with its paneling, candelabra and gilt-framed mirrors. The rooms are just as impressive, decorated in a serene shade of blue, with some antique furniture. Two rooms open on to the charming, leafy, terra-cotta-tiled public terrace; two have their own private terraces.

Condotti

Via Mario de' Fiori 37, 00187. **Map** 5 A2 & 12 F1. 06-679 46 61. FAX 06-679 04 57. **Rooms:** 16. AE, DC, MC, V, JCB.

Close to Piazza di Spagna and in the heart of the designer shopping district, the Condotti is a comfortable, inviting hotel with its own ambience and style. Rooms are medium to large and well decorated. One room has its own small terrace, and three others share one.

Gregoriana

Via Gregoriana 18, 00187.
Map 5 A2 & 12 F1. 📞 *06-679 49 88.*
FAX *06-678 42 58.* **Rooms**: *19.*
🛏 ① ㉔ TV 🍷 🔲 ♿ 🔌 📶 🍴
Ⓛ Ⓛ Ⓛ Ⓛ

The Gregoriana is a stylishly congenial hotel, situated close to the Spanish Steps on a tree-lined, quiet street of elegant palazzi. The first- and third-floor corridors are papered with a leopard-spotted print, while that of the second floor is in the style of William Morris. The rooms are all the same: black lacquer doors, terra-cotta-colored carpets, flowery wallpaper and 1920s drawings on the walls. There are no public rooms, so breakfast and drinks are served in the bedrooms.

Manfredi

Via Margutta 61, 00187. **Map** 5 A2.
📞 *06-320 76 76, 06-320 76 95.*
FAX *06-320 77 36.* **Rooms**: *18.* 🛏 ①
⊞ ㉔ TV 🍷 🔲 🛗 ♿ 🔌 🍷 🍴
AE, MC, V, JCB. Ⓛ Ⓛ Ⓛ Ⓛ

This pretty family-run hotel is excellently located, just off Piazza di Spagna, on a peaceful cobbled street of art galleries and antiques shops. The reception area and bar/breakfast room are paved with marble and decorated in soft pastels. The comfortable bedrooms are all soundproofed with pale fabric wallcoverings and co-ordinated furnishings.

Dei Borgognoni

Via del Bufalo 126, 00187. **Map** 5 A3 & 12 F1. 📞 *06-69 94 15 05.* **FAX** *06-69 94 15 01.* **Rooms**: *50.* 🛏 ① ⊞
TV 🍷 🔲 ♿ 🅿 🔌 🍷 🍴
AE, DC, MC, V, JCB. Ⓛ Ⓛ Ⓛ Ⓛ

This elegant hotel is just off Piazza San Silvestro, five minutes from the Spanish Steps. In the public rooms, a modern style is coupled with traditional oil paintings. The bedrooms – some with terraces – are beautifully understated.

Hassler

Piazza Trinità dei Monti 6, 00187.
Map 5 A2. 📞 *06-699 93 40.* **FAX** *06-678 99 91.* **Rooms**: *100.* 🛏 ① 🍴
TV 🍷 🌊 🔲 ♿ 🔌 🍷 🅿 🔌
🍷 🍴 🛗 *AE, DC, MC, V, JCB.*
Ⓛ Ⓛ Ⓛ Ⓛ Ⓛ

Standing at the top of the Spanish Steps, with magnificent views of Rome from its roof terrace, restaurant (*see p313*) and suites, the Hassler was once host to royalty and the glitterati of Europe and America. Its *dolce vita* days are over, but the lounges and bedrooms lit by Venetian glass chandeliers,

the wood-paneled bar and the marble bathrooms retain the air of a more extravagant era.

D' Inghilterra

Via Bocca di Leone 14, 00187. **Map** 5 A2. 📞 *06-69 9 81.* **FAX** *06-69 92 22 43.* **Rooms**: *105.* 🛏 ① ⊞ ㉔ TV 🍷 🔲 🍷 🔲 🛗 ♿ 🔌 🔌 🍴
AE, DC, MC, V. Ⓛ Ⓛ Ⓛ Ⓛ

Liszt and Hemingway are among the writers, artists and musicians who have stayed here. In the heart of Rome's designer shopping area and close to the Spanish Steps, it's still a desirable place to stay. The bedrooms are individually decorated and furnished. The bar could have been lifted straight from a London gentlemen's club, and the restaurant's walls, painted with garden views and sky-frescoed ceiling, create the illusion of dining in the open.

Scalinata di Spagna

Piazza Trinità dei Monti 17, 00187.
Map 5 A2. 📞 *06-69 30 06.*
FAX *06-69 94 05 98.* **Rooms**: *16.* 🛏 ① ⊞ ㉔ TV 🍷 🌊 🔲 🔌 🍴
🔌 *AE, DC, MC, V.* Ⓛ Ⓛ Ⓛ Ⓛ Ⓛ

This hotel occupies a small 18th-century villa at the top of the Spanish Steps. Breakfast is served at a communal table under the gaze of a parrot. Some of the rooms retain their old paneled ceilings. Reserve far in advance if you want to stay in one of the rooms that open out on to the large terrace.

Valadier

Via della Fontanella 15, 00187. **Map** 4 F1. 📞 *06-361 23 44.* **FAX** *06-320 15 58.* **Rooms**: *38.* 🛏 ① ⊞ ㉔ TV 🍷 🔲 ♿ 🔌 🍷 🔌 🍴 *AE, DC, MC, V, JCB.* Ⓛ Ⓛ Ⓛ Ⓛ

Slickly decorated with shiny wood and marble, the Valadier styles itself as an intimate hideaway for those on a romantic visit to Rome. Public rooms are tailor-made for seduction, with low sofas, marble floors and Oriental rugs. If you believe the hotel's publicity, the bizarre art selection is there to provide shy Casanovas with conversation openers.

Campo de' Fiori

Via del Biscione 6, 00186. **Map** 4 E4 & 11 C4. 📞 *06-68 80 68 65.* **FAX** *06-68760 03.* **Rooms**: *27.* 🛏 ① ⊞ 🌊 🔌 🔲 *MC, V.* Ⓛ Ⓛ

This very reasonable mid-range hotel occupies a well-kept house,

just off the Campo de' Fiori market square. You enter the tiny reception area along a passageway in which mirrors intriguingly repeat a series of columns into an illusory optical suggestion of infinity. The small bedrooms have beams and paisley furnishings or sky-painted ceilings, lacy walls and frilly bedcovers. On the sixth floor, a split-level roof garden gives vertiginous but aesthetically rewarding views over the Pantheon, the Victor Emmanuel monument and St. Peter's.

Della Lunetta

Piazza del Paradiso 68, 00186.
Map 4 E4 & 11 C4. 📞 *06-686 10 80.* **FAX** *06-689 20 28.* **Rooms**: *37.* 🛏 13. ① ⊞ 🔌 Ⓛ Ⓛ

On a tiny crumbling piazza, midway between Corso Vittorio Emanuele and Piazza Campo de' Fiori, the Lunetta is a popular well-maintained little hotel with neat, clean rooms and a courtyard. More bathrooms are gradually being installed, and a rooftop garden is being renovated. No breakfast is served.

Piccolo

Via dei Chiavari 32, 00186. **Map** 4 E4 & 11 C4. 📞 *06-68 80 25 60.* **Rooms**: *15.* 🛏 4. ① ⊞ 🔌 🍷 🔲 *AE, MC, V.* Ⓛ

Close to Piazza Campo de' Fiori, the Piccolo is a family-run hotel at the lowest end of the price range. There is, however, nothing cheap about the atmosphere. Cool and serene, featuring clean, simple rooms of various sizes, the Piccolo also has a separate bar/breakfast room with a television.

Pomezia

Via dei Chiavari 12, 00186. **Map** 4 E4 & 12 D4. 📞 *06-686 13 71.* **FAX** *06-686 13 71.* **Rooms**: *24.* 🛏 ① ⊞ 🍷 🔲 *AE, DC, MC, V.* Ⓛ Ⓛ

In the heart of the lively Campo de' Fiori district, the Pomezia was renovated recently and now has spotless, simply decorated rooms and a bar in the reception area to welcome weary arrivals.

Smeraldo

Vicolo dei Chiodaroli 9, 00186.
Map 4 F5 & 12 D4. 📞 *06-687 59 29.*
FAX *06-68 80 54 95.* **Rooms**: *35.* 🛏 23. ① TV 🔌 🔲 🍷 🔲 *AE, MC, V.* Ⓛ Ⓛ

Situated in the heart of the bustling Campo de' Fiori quarter, the Smeraldo offers an oasis of serenity, with clean, simple rooms in an ocher-washed building with shutters over the windows.

Sole

Via del Biscione 76, 00186. **Map** 4 E4 & 11 C4. (06-68 80 52 58. **FAX** 06-689 37 87. **Rooms**: 58. 🛏 31. 1
🔲 24 🛏 🔧 🖿 📷 P 🖲 Ⓛ Ⓛ

Possibly the oldest hotel in Rome, this appealing establishment occupies a palazzo just off the central market square of Campo de' Fiori. Rooms are furnished in a slightly haphazard way, but with some character. There are small sitting areas and a leafy, sunny terrace with a drink-and-snack machine. No breakfast is served.

Rinascimento

Via del Pellegrino 122, 00186. **Map** 4 E4 & 11 B3. (06-687 48 13. **FAX** 06-683 35 18. **Rooms**: 19. 🛏 1
🔲 TV 🔧 🖿 🖳 Y P 🖿 🖡 AE, MC, V. Ⓛ Ⓛ

With an appealing location in the Campo de' Fiori district, close to artisans' workshops and a variety of trattorias, the Rinascimento is housed in an old palazzo with stone arched windows. The bedrooms, however, tend to be slightly worn and have rather cramped bathrooms.

Teatro di Pompeo

Largo del Pallaro 8, 00186. **Map** 4 E4 & 11 C4. (06-687 28 12. **FAX** 06-68 80 55 31. **Rooms**: 12. 🛏 1 🔲 TV
Y 🔧 🖿 🖳 🔧 🖿 P Y
🖡 🖿 AE, DC, MC, V. Ⓛ Ⓛ Ⓛ

This courteously run small hotel sits over the ruins of the first permanent theater in the city, which was completed in 55 BC by Pompey the Great. You can eat breakfast among the original theater arches, and the bar has a terra-cotta floor and marble tables.

Le Grand Hotel

Via V. E. Orlando 3, 00185. **Map** 5 C2. (06-47 091. **FAX** 06-482 38 67. **Rooms**: 170. 🛏 1 🔲 24 TV Y
🖿 🔧 🖳 🔧 🖿 🖡 🖿 AE, DC, MC, V. JCB. Ⓛ Ⓛ Ⓛ Ⓛ

To step into the Grand is to enter another world. Cherubs cavort over the reception area; flowers and fruit are carved on the walls of the lounge, and rich pastel rugs lie on the parquet floor. Facilities include a sauna, beauty salon, hairdresser, and a restaurant renowned as one of the most beautiful in the country. The standard of bedrooms varies, but you might find yourself in an antique bed reading by the light of a genuine Venetian lamp.

Katty

Via Palestro 35, 00185. (06-444 12 16. (06-444 12 16. **Rooms**: 12. 🛏 2. 1 🔲 Ⓛ

The Katty has clean, basic rooms, some of which have an occasional piece of antique furniture. It's extremely popular with British and American students, so either reserve in advance or turn up early, ideally between 8 and 9am. No breakfast is served.

Restivo

Via Palestro 55, 00185. **Map** 6 E2. (06-446 21 72. **Rooms**: 6. 1 🔲 Ⓛ

In the same building as the Mari, the Restivo has six immaculately maintained bedrooms. The elderly owner has a hall full of gifts and postcards from grateful guests who often return again and again.

Cervia

Via Palestro 55, 00185. **Map** 6 E2. (06-49 10 57. **FAX** 06-49 10 56. **Rooms**: 28. 🛏 7. 1 🔲 🖿 AE, DC, MC, V. Ⓛ Ⓛ

The Cervia is a hotel housed in the same palazzo as the Mari and the Restivo. Some of the rooms have been refurbished with sponge-painted walls and private bathrooms, and these are a very good value. The rest, however, tend to be a bit more basic. The public areas are immaculate, and there is also a pleasant modern bar/breakfast room.

Mari

Via Palestro 55, 00185. **Map** 6 E2. (06-446 21 37. **FAX** 06-482 83 13. **Rooms**: 21. 🛏 11. 1 🔲 🖿 MC, V. Ⓛ Ⓛ

This friendly hotel run by three women has clean, pleasant rooms with no frills. If it's full, Mari 2 nearby at Via Calatafimi 38 (tel: 06-474 03 71) has more rooms (half with bathrooms) and is also a good deal. There is a 5% surcharge for paying with credit cards.

Canada

Via Vicenza 58, 00185. **Map** 6 E2. (06-445 77 70. **FAX** 06-445 07 49. **Rooms**: 74. 🛏 1 🔲 TV 🖿 🖳
🔧 🖳 Y 🖿 🖡 🖿 AE, DC, MC, V. Ⓛ Ⓛ Ⓛ

Outside the center, behind Termini Station, the Canada is an above-average mid-range hotel. Rooms are very comfortable, and there's a pleasant lounge with attractive cane seats and comfortable sofas. The service is courteous.

Hotel Giuliana

Via Palermo 36, 00184. **Map** 5 C4. (06-488 07 95. **FAX** 06-482 42 87. **Rooms**: 21. 🛏 1 🔲 TV Y 🖿
🔧 Y 🖿 🖡 🖿 AE, DC, V, JCB. Ⓛ Ⓛ Ⓛ

Within walking distance of many major sights, and 10 minutes from Termini station, this small hotel offers bright, clean accommodation at very reasonable prices. Helpful, English-speaking staff are happy to offer advice on any aspect of your visit, from transport tips to restaurant recommendations.

Venezia

Via Varese 18, 00185. **Map** 6 E2. (06-445 71 01. **FAX** 06-445 76 87. **Rooms**: 61. 🛏 1 🔲 🖿 TV 🖿 🖡 🖿 AE, DC, MC, V, JCB. Ⓛ Ⓛ Ⓛ

One of the nicer mid-sized hotels near Termini station, the Venezia is pleasantly decorated with antique furniture and Murano glass chandeliers in the common areas. The bedrooms are light and airy with smart bathrooms. The hotel offers an especially rich buffet breakfast.

Aventino

Via San Domenico 10, 00153. **Map** 8 D2. (06-574 51 74, 06-578 32 14. **FAX** 06-578 36 04. **Rooms**: 23. 🛏 1 🔲 🖿 🔧 🖳 🖳 Y 🖿 AE, DC, MC, V. Ⓛ Ⓛ

Run by the owners of Villa San Pio and Sant'Anselmo, the Aventino is more modest, with large but fairly simple rooms. However, its lush garden location is gorgeous, and the breakfast room, with a magnificent armoire and stained glass, is a reminder of headier days.

Domus Aventina

Via di Santa Prisca 11B, 00153. **Map** 8 E2. (06-574 61 35. **FAX** 06-57 30 00 44. **Rooms**: 26. 🛏 1 🔲 24 TV
Y 🖿 🔧 🖳 🔧 🖿 🖡 🖿 AE, DC, MC, V, JCB. Ⓛ Ⓛ Ⓛ

This immaculate hotel occupies a 14th-century convent situated at the foot of the Aventine Hill. Rooms are large and simply decorated in pastel tones, and there are wonderful views of the Celian Hill from many of the balconies – 18 rooms have them – and from the huge terrace.

Sant'Anselmo

Piazza di Sant'Anselmo 2, 00153. **Map** 8 D2. (06-574 35 47. **FAX** 06-578 36 04. **Rooms**: 46. 🛏 1 🔲 🖿 🔧 🖿 AE, DC, MC, V. Ⓛ Ⓛ Ⓛ

This pretty villa, among the gardens of the peaceful Aventine, is within walking distance of the Colosseum. The entrance hall ceiling is stenciled with flowers; there are chandeliers and corridors with floors of inlaid marble. The lounge looks out on to the hotel's garden. Reserve well in advance.

Villa San Pio

Via Sant'Anselmo 19, 00153. **Map** 8 E3. 06-578 32 14, 06-574 35 47. **FAX** 06-578 36 04. **Rooms**: 59.
▢▢▢▢▢▢▢▢ AE, DC, MC, V. ⓁⓁⓁ

The Villa San Pio occupies a yellow-and-ocher villa set in a garden graced with statues. The elegant entrance hall is furnished with velvet and brocade chairs and an 18th-century Venetian tapestry. Some of the rooms are simple, others have flower-stenciled furniture; others open on to the garden. There are two bars. Breakfast or drinks can also be taken in the bedrooms or garden.

TRASTEVERE

Carmel

Via Mameli 11, 00153. **Map** 7 C2. **FAX** 06-580 99 21. **Rooms**: 10.
▢ 9. ▢▢▢

The Carmel's most appealing feature is a terrace with its leafy canopy. A couple of rooms open off the terrace. All ten rooms are spotless, and most have bathrooms. The owner is not keen on having children stay, and you must reserve in advance as she closes the hotel if she thinks trade will be slack.

VATICAN

Alimandi

Via Tunisi 8, 00192. **Map** 3 B2. 06-39 72 39 48. **FAX** 06-39 72 39 43. **Rooms**: 35. ▢ 26. ▢▢▢▢▢
▢▢▢ AE, DC, MC, V. ⓁⓁ

On a quietish street just below the entrance to the Vatican Museums, the Alimandi is a simple *pensione* at the cheap end of its price range – hence its popularity with young travelers. Rooms are clean and adequate. Its outstanding feature is the lovely, large roof terrace.

Amalia

Via Germanico 66, 00192. **Map** 3 C2. 06-39 72 33 56, 06-39 72 33 56. **FAX** 06-39 72 33 65. **Rooms**: 30. ▢ 20. ▢▢▢▢▢ AE, MC, V. ⓁⓁⓁ

Situated between the Ottaviano Metro station and the Vatican, the Amalia attracts mainly Italian guests. It has spotless rooms ranged on three floors and a lounge with bar.

Atlante Star

Via Vitelleschi 34, 00193. **Map** 3 C2. 06-687 32 33. **FAX** 06-687 23 00. **Rooms**: 62. ▢▢▢▢▢▢
▢▢▢▢▢▢▢▢ AE, DC, MC, V, JCB. ⓁⓁⓁ

This hotel is a good option for business travelers needing on-site office facilities. The rooftop restaurant has views of St. Peter's, but both service and atmosphere leave much to be desired. Double rooms are modest in size, and singles can be cramped, some of them with only a shower. Avoid street-facing rooms since they can be noisy.

Columbus

Via della Conciliazione 33, 00193. **Map** 3 C3. 06-686 54 35. **FAX** 06-686 48 74. **Rooms**: 100. ▢▢▢▢▢
▢▢▢▢▢▢▢▢ AE, DC, MC, V, JCB. ⓁⓁⓁ

Perfect for anyone wishing to stay near the Vatican, the Columbus occupies an austere former monastery. Heavy wrought-iron light fixtures hang in the reception hall; the magnificent upper lounge has a beamed ceiling and terra-cotta floor; the function room (the old refectory) has kept its frescoes; and there is a walled terrace garden.

Hotel dei Mellini

Via Muzio Clementi 81, 00193. **Map** 4 E2. 06-324 771. **FAX** 06-32 47 78 01. **Rooms**: 80. ▢▢▢▢▢▢
▢▢▢▢▢▢▢ AE, DC, MC, V. ⓁⓁⓁⓁ

Opened in 1996 in a converted late 19th-century building, this hotel has all the modern comfort you could wish for but still feels charming and welcoming. It is located in a quiet residential area near Castel Sant'Angelo and only a short walk across the river from Via Condotti. The reception staff are very helpful and there is a small but nice bar in the lobby and a roof terrace.

VIA VENETO

Merano

Via Veneto 155, 00187. **Map** 5 B2. 06-482 17 96. **FAX** 06-482 18 10. **Rooms**: 30. ▢▢▢▢▢▢
▢ AE, DC, MC, V. ⓁⓁⓁ

The Merano is a friendly small *pensione* in a 19th-century palazzo. The decor is a little dated, and

relatively high prices, for what is essentially a guesthouse, reflect the upscale location. The best feature is its sunny breakfast room.

Oxford

Via Boncompagni 89, 00187. **Map** 5 C1. 06-48 82 89 52. **FAX** 06-42 81 53 49. **Rooms**: 58. ▢▢▢▢▢
▢▢▢▢▢▢▢ AE, DC, MC, V, JCB. ⓁⓁⓁ

On a quiet road off Piazza Fiume, about ten minutes' walk from Via Veneto, the Oxford has stylish public rooms: squashy sofas and modern pictures in the reception area; striped sofas and abstract art in the bar. The bedrooms are more dated, with hessian-covered walls and candlewick bedspreads.

Residenza

Via Emilia 22–24, 00187. **Map** 5 B2. 06-488 07 89. **FAX** 06-48 57 21. **Rooms**: 29. ▢▢▢▢▢
▢▢▢ AE, MC, V. ⓁⓁⓁ

The Residenza is an elegant hotel that occupies a villa on a quiet road off Via Veneto. There is a canopied terrace with pine furniture, and a terra-cotta-tiled roof garden with potted plants. The bedrooms although less stylish than the public rooms, but are comfortable, large and well-equipped.

Alexandra

Via Veneto 18, 00187. **Map** 5 B2. 06-488 19 43. **FAX** 06-487 18.04. **Rooms**: 45. ▢▢▢▢▢
▢▢▢▢▢ AE, DC, MC, V, JCB. ⓁⓁⓁ

One of the less expensive hotels on the upscale Via Veneto, the Alexandra has a pleasant conservatory-style breakfast room and a lounge decorated with chintz and brocade. All the bedrooms are unique; some furnished with antiques, some with splash-painted walls. If you are a light sleeper, ask for an internal room, as the windows do not block out all the traffic noise.

Victoria

Via Campania 41, 00187. **Map** 5 B1. 06-47 39 31. **FAX** 06-487 18 90. **Rooms**: 108. ▢▢▢▢▢▢
▢▢▢▢▢▢▢▢ AE, DC, MC, V. ⓁⓁⓁⓁ

Situated on a quiet road at the top of Via Veneto and overlooking the walls abutting the Porta Pinciana, the Victoria prides itself on being a "hotel for individuals," keeping its personal touch by refusing large group reservations. It is renowned for good service. There are stylish public rooms and an attractive roof terrace, but the bedrooms are rather small and uninspired.

Bernini Bristol

Piazza Barberini 23, 00187. **Map** 5 B3.
06-488 30 51. FAX 06-482 42 66.
Rooms: 125. 🛏 1 ♿ 24 TV 🍸 ❄ 🍴 🔦 ⚓ 🏋 📶 🍽 🚗 *AE, DC, MC, V, JCB.* ⓁⓁⓁⓁ

This unprepossessing brick building overlooks a busy piazza that has Bernini's Triton fountain as its centerpiece. The marble-laden hotel is comfortable, with a roof garden, but the decor is uninspiring and the atmosphere more conducive to work than pleasure. The central location and facilities ensure a steady stream of business visitors.

Eden

Via Ludovisi 49, 00187. **Map** 5 B2.
06-47 81 21. FAX 06-482 15 84.
Rooms: 92. 🛏 1 ♿ TV 24 🍸 🍴 🔦 ⚓ 🏋 🍽 🚗 *AE, DC, MC, V, JCB.* ⓁⓁⓁⓁ

Historically one of Rome's most illustrious hotels, Eden has recently been restored to pristine condition. The roof garden is stunning, giving every justification for the hotel's name; like its biblical namesake, it has its temptations, not least the beautiful La Terrazza restaurant (see p317), which nestles on the roof like a beacon of refinement.

Excelsior

Via Veneto 125, 00187. **Map** 5 B1.
06-470 81. FAX 06-482 62 05.
Rooms: 327. 🛏 1 ♿ 24 TV 🍸 🍴 🔦 ⚓ 🏋 📶 🍽 🚗 *AE, DC, MC, V, JCB.* ⓁⓁⓁⓁ

Exotically sculpted balconies supported by statues set the tone for this extravagant hotel, which houses boutiques, saunas, a restaurant and a famous piano bar. Public rooms are sumptuous, with marble walls and floors, rich carpets and brocade furnishings – and the corridors are paneled with silk or imitation marble. The bedrooms are spacious, with chandeliers, gilded wooden paneling and ornate bathrooms.

Imperiale

Via Veneto 24, 00187. **Map** 5 B2.
06-482 63 51. FAX 06-478 25 43.
Rooms: 95. 🛏 1 ♿ 24 TV 🍸 🍴 🔦 ⚓ 🏋 🍽 🚗 *AE, DC, MC, V.* ⓁⓁⓁⓁ

One of the more reasonably priced Via Veneto hotels, the Imperiale lacks the panache of its more glamorous neighbors, but the friendly staff make for a good relaxed atmosphere. The lounge is more of a place to wait than to spend an evening; but, the bar is quite pleasant, and the bedrooms are well decorated, with pretty coordinating furnishings and small marble bathrooms.

Majestic

Via Veneto 50, 00187. **Map** 5 B2.
06-48 68 41, 06-482 80 14.
FAX 06-488 56 57. *Rooms*: 96. 🛏 1 ♿ TV 🍸 🍴 🔦 ⚓ P 🔦 🍽 🚗 *AE, DC, MC, V, JCB.* ⓁⓁⓁⓁ

Founded in 1889, the Majestic is the oldest of Via Veneto's hotels. Since its five-year refurbishment, it has played host to international stars such as Madonna, Pavarotti, and Stallone. Most of the furniture and much of the décor in the public rooms are original, down to the startling gilded lime-green lounge. Bedrooms and corridors are decorated in a bold, bright style, particularly on the fifth floor, where carpets with a zig-zag pattern provide the background to chintz and brocade.

Regina Hotel Baglioni

Via Veneto 72, 00187. **Map** 5 B2.
06-42 11 11. FAX 06-48 54 83.
Rooms: 130. 🛏 1 ♿ TV 🍸 🍴 🔦 ⚓ 🏋 🍽 🚗 *AE, DC, MC, V.* ⓁⓁⓁⓁ

The exuberance of the Baglioni's exterior – it is painted vanilla and strawberry pink and decorated with grimacing masks – continues in the reception area, where a wrought-iron staircase is guarded by the statue of a sea god. The bedrooms are painted in vivid shades of coral, aqua and blue, and many are very spacious. Double glazing in the rooms overlooking Via Veneto cuts down on some of the noise, but light sleepers might still prefer to ask for a room at the back of the hotel when reserving.

Romantik Barocco Hotel

Via della Purificazione 7, 00187.
Map 5 B3. 06-487 20 01. FAX 06-48 59 94. *Rooms*: 28. 🛏 1 ♿ TV 🍸 🍴 🔦 ⚓ 🏋 🚗 *AE, DC, MC, V, JCB.* ⓁⓁⓁⓁ

Occupying a restored palazzo at the bottom of Via Veneto, the Barocco is ideal for anyone who prefers a small hotel. Bedrooms are pleasant with unobtrusive décor, and some have working areas. There are two small lounges (one with a bar) and a restaurant.

Villa Borghese

Via Pinciana 31, 00198. **Map** 2 F5.
06-841 41 00. FAX 06-841 41 00.
Rooms: 31. 1 ♿ TV 🍸 ❄ P 🔦 🍴 🚗 *AE, DC, MC, V, JCB.* ⓁⓁⓁⓁ

This immediately likable hotel occupies a villa close to Villa Borghese. Although the hotel is on a rather busy main road, the atmosphere is pleasant: more that of a private home than a hotel. Public rooms include an intimate old-fashioned bar, a lounge with comfortable sofas and floral soft furnishings, and there is a courtyard sheltered by a pretty ivy-covered pergola. The rooms are on the small side but they are tastefully decorated.

Aldrovandi Palace

Via Aldrovandi 15, 00197. **Map** 2 E4.
06-322 39 93. FAX 06-322 14 35.
Rooms: 137. 🛏 1 ♿ TV 🍸 ❄ 🍴 🔦 ⚓ P 🔦 🍽 🚗 *AE, DC, MC, V, JCB.* ⓁⓁⓁⓁ

Among the most restful luxury hotels in the city, the Aldrovandi is situated just outside the center of Rome on a fairly busy road overlooking Villa Borghese. The reception lounge is elegant and decorated with rich soft furnishings, carpets, chandeliers and lots of vases of fresh flowers. The real highlight of the hotel, however, is the sunny garden with its attractive swimming pool, which is overlooked by an airy restaurant.

Lord Byron

Via de Notaris 5, 00197. **Map** 2 D4.
06-322 45 41. FAX 06-322 04 05.
Rooms: 37. 🛏 1 ♿ 24 TV 🍸 🍴 🔦 ⚓ 🏋 🍽 🚗 *AE, DC, MC, V.* ⓁⓁⓁⓁ

This refined small hotel is housed in a dazzling white building in the residential district of Parioli. It was originally a monastery, but there is nothing ascetic about its rooms today. The lounge is lavishly furnished with antiques and tapestry-seated chairs, and the tiny sitting room has large sofas and old-fashioned portraits. The restaurant is decorated with plenty of chintz and fresh flowers and serves some of the best food in Rome. All the bedrooms have tapestry and floral soft furnishings with marble coffee tables and are provided with a full decanter of port, which comes with the compliments of the management.

RESTAURANTS AND CAFES

I N ROME, eating out can be both a joy and an entertainment. On warm summer evenings tables flow out onto every conceivable open space, and diners dedicate long hours to the popular social activity of people watching (and of being noticed and admired themselves) in a confusion of passers-by, street performers, rose sellers and traffic. Although Romans have always loved to linger at the table, the lavish feasts of ancient Rome have been scaled down and today's cooking is based on simplicity, freshness and good quality local raw ingredients in

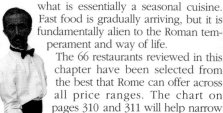

Waiter at Alberto Ciarla (see p316)

what is essentially a seasonal cuisine. Fast food is gradually arriving, but it is fundamentally alien to the Roman temperament and way of life.

The 66 restaurants reviewed in this chapter have been selected from the best that Rome can offer across all price ranges. The chart on pages 310 and 311 will help narrow down your selection, and the map on page 308 shows the highlights of the list. The section *Light Meals and Snacks*, featured on pages 318 to 321, has details of recommended cafés, pizzerias, wine bars and other places for more casual eating.

WHERE TO FIND GOOD RESTAURANTS

E VERY AREA of the city has its own culinary delights. True Roman cooking can be found in the old slaughter-house area of Testaccio and in the Jewish quarter (the Ghetto) near Campo de' Fiori. Around the university, in San Lorenzo, northeast of the city center, you will find lots of cheap pizzerias and *trattorias*.

Near Termini station there's a good selection of African – particularly Ethiopian and Eritrean – restaurants. For dining outdoors, which often means in beautifully secluded piazzas or in impressively ancient parts of the city, try the restaurants in the narrow streets of Trastevere (the old

The interior of Relais le Jardin (see p317)

artists' quarter); around Campo de' Fiori, or along the old Via Appia Antica.

TYPES OF RESTAURANTS

I N GENERAL, a *trattoria* is an unassuming family-run establishment with good home cooking, while a *ristorante* is more elegant and thus more expensive.

Many eating places – where paper tablecloths give a clue to low prices – simply have no name. They

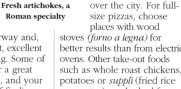

Fresh artichokes, a Roman specialty

offer an open doorway and, more often than not, excellent basic home cooking. Some of them offer a great deal more, and your chances of finding authentic Roman cooking are higher in the best of these establishments than in more expensive restaurants.

There will probably be times when you don't want a full restaurant meal, and Rome offers a huge variety of places for more casual eating (*see pp318–21*). One type of place offering snacks or more substantial dishes is the *enoteca*, which

doubles as a well-stocked wine shop for browsers and connoisseurs.

The sign *Vino e Cucina* (wine and food), sadly fast disappearing, holds the same promise. Other places for a sit-down, informal lunch or dinner are *birrerie*, which are not only for beer drinkers but also offer pizzas or even four-course meals.

There's plenty of interesting take-out food sold throughout the day – *pizza al taglio* (pizza by the slice) – is available all over the city. For full-size pizzas, choose places with wood stoves (*forno a legna*) for better results than from electric ovens. Other take-out foods such as whole roast chickens, potatoes or *supplì* (fried rice croquettes) can be had from *rosticcerie*. A self-service *tavola calda* will serve an impressive array of hot food and is ideal for lunch.

VEGETARIAN FOOD

P URELY VEGETARIAN restaurants are largely unknown in Rome, but everywhere you'll find pasta or rice dishes (*risotto*) using interesting combinations of vegetables, salads, artichokes cooked in different ways or vegetables stuffed and then baked in the oven. Most menus are very adaptable.

The Price of a Meal

WHAT YOU PAY will clearly depend on your choice of establishment. In a *tavola calda*, or Roman pizzeria, for example, you can often eat for as little as L15,000 a head. A local *trattoria* costs perhaps L25,000, whereas in a restaurant expect to pay around L50,000 and up. Bottled wine, as opposed to a jug or carafe of house wine *(vino della casa)*, commands higher prices but should offer a more interesting range of tastes *(see p306)*. House wine is usually acceptable, though.

Reading the Menu

NOT EVERY restaurant automatically provides a menu – the waiter will often tell you the day's specialities *(piatti del giorno)*, usually not mentioned on the standard menu but almost always worth ordering. If you are not sure about these, you can always ask for *la lista* (the menu) and then allow yourself to be guided.

A meal could begin with *antipasti* (appetizers) or *primi piatti* – the latter consisting of *pasta asciutta* (pasta with some kind of sauce), *pasta in brodo* (clear broth with pasta in it), *pasta al forno* (baked pasta), risotto or a substantial soup. You then move on to the *secondi*, the main meat or fish course, for which you'll need to order vegetables *(contorni)* separately if you would like them. Afterward you have a choice of *formaggi* (cheeses), *frutta* (fruit) or *dolci* (desserts). Romans don't usually eat

One of many Trastevere cafés

Outdoor café life in the piazza outside Santa Maria in Trastevere

cheese as well as a sweet dish, but cheese often comes with such fruit as pears, figs and melon. Strong espresso coffee and perhaps a liqueur *(amaro* or *digestivo)* rounds off the meal *(see p306)*. You may want to skip the first course, or you may prefer to choose a salad or vegetable dish. Pasta alone tends not to be seen as a full meal.

Opening Times

RESTAURANTS are generally open from about noon to 3pm and from 8 to 11pm or much later. The busiest times tend to be 9 to 9:30pm for dinner and 1 to 1:30pm for lunch. Dinner is generally the preferred time for more relaxed eating, particularly in summer, when it begins and ends late as the heat of the day subsides. Bars are open all day, often from the early hours, serving all kinds of drinks (alcohol can be sold at any time of day) and snacks. The quietest month is August, when many restaurant owners take their annual vacation (shown by *Chiuso per Ferie* signs).

Reserving a Table

MAKING A RESERVATION *(prenotazione)* is generally advisable, especially for Sunday lunch and often for Saturday evening. Also, check the weekly closing day: many places are closed on Monday, and Sunday evening can also be difficult for reservations.

In summer try to reserve a shady table outside, since air-conditioning is not universal, and indoors the atmosphere may be stuffy.

Wheelchair Access

ROME is slowly adapting to the needs of those in wheelchairs, but a call to the restaurant in advance will help secure the right table.

Taking Children Along

CHILDREN are very welcome, particularly in family-run places. You can usually order half-portions (but expect to pay more than half), or just ask for an extra plate. Highchairs *(seggioline)* may also be available in some establishments.

What to Eat in Rome

Bulb of fresh garlic

THE TRADITIONAL *cucina romanesca* has always relied on local markets full of fresh seasonal vegetables, fruit, cheese and meat from the nearby countryside, plus seafood from the Mediterranean. As in the rest of Italy, pasta is an important part of the menu; one popular dish is the famous *spaghetti alla carbonara*, which was devised in Rome. Many genuinely Roman meat dishes are based on the so-called *quinto quarto* (fifth quarter) – head, innards, tail, pig's feet and so on. Highly flavored with olive oil, herbs, lard, bacon *(pancetta)* or pig's cheek *(guanciale)*, they become a culinary delight. Fish from the Mediterranean is excellent. In season, mushrooms and artichokes may be served in dozens of different ways. *Mesticanza* is also good in season: it's a fresh mix of salad leaves, including the peppery *rughetta* (arugula) and *puntarelle* (curly endive shoots, often served with anchovy dressing). For dessert, be sure to try Italian ice cream or puddings such as the classic *tiramisù*.

Maritozzi alla Panna
These soft buns with raisins and candied peel are filled with whipped cream.

Bruschetta
Toasted bread is rubbed with garlic and olive oil; tomatoes can be added.

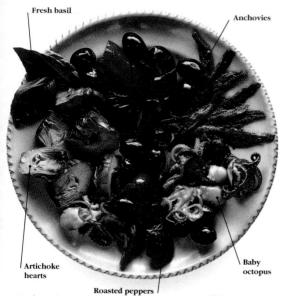

Fresh basil

Anchovies

Artichoke hearts

Roasted peppers

Baby octopus

Antipasti
Italian appetizers may include olives, cured meats, seafood and grilled or preserved vegetables.

Supplì
Fried rice croquettes stuffed with mozzarella make a tasty snack.

Olive Oil and Vinegar
Always on the table, these are for dressing salads and flavoring antipasti.

Filetti di Baccalà
A Jewish specialty, deep-fried cod filets are a typical Roman snack or first course.

Risotto alla Romana
Liver, sweetbreads, Marsala and Romano cheese are used to make this risotto.

TYPICAL ITALIAN PASTA

Penne rigate (quills)

Farfalle (butterflies)

Fusilli (spirals)

Conchigliette (shells)

Cappelletti (small hats)

Bucatini all'Amatriciana
Pasta tubes are served with bacon, tomatoes and onion, with grated Romano on top.

Spaghetti alla Carbonara
Chopped bacon, eggs and cheese are used to prepare this famous local dish.

Gnocchi alla Romana
Small semolina dumplings are served with tomatoes or with butter.

Fiori di Zucca e Carciofi Fritti
Squash blossoms in batter and whole artichokes deep-fried are popular antipasti.

Coda alla Vaccinara
A traditional Roman dish, this is made from braised oxtail with tomatoes.

Saltimbocca alla Romana
Veal with Parma ham and sage, this tasty dish is also served rolled and skewered.

Fave al Guanciale
Fresh springtime broad beans are simmered with bacon and onion.

Parmesan

Italian Cheeses
Parmesan is the best-known Italian cheese, but Rome's classic is pecorino Romano, made from ewe's milk. The mature, hard version is often used grated, but fresh Romano can be eaten as a dessert cheese. Mild buffalo-milk mozzarella is the classic one for pizza.

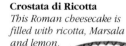

Mozzarella

Tiramisù
Mascarpone cheese, coffee and chocolate are combined for this wonderful dessert.

Crostata di Ricotta
This Roman cheesecake is filled with ricotta, Marsala and lemon.

What to Drink in Rome

ITALY IS ONE OF Europe's most significant wine-producing countries, keeping up a tradition started in the hills around Rome over 2,000 years ago. Today, wine is usually drunk with meals as a matter of course, and knowing the difference between *rosso* (red) and *bianco* (white) may be all the vocabulary you need to get by. Beer is widely available too, as well as good selections of apéritifs and digestifs. Rome's drinking water, another debt to the ancient Romans, is particularly good, fresh and sweet, and in abundant supply.

Roman mosaic showing bird and vines

The vineyards of Frascati, southeast of Rome

WHITE WINE

VINES THRIVE in the warm climate of Lazio, the region around Rome, producing abundant supplies of inexpensive dry white wine for the city's cafés and restaurants. It is usually sold by the carafe. Of local bottled wines, Frascati is the best known, but Castelli Romani, Marino, Colli Albani and Velletri are very similar in style. All are made from one grape variety, the Trebbiano, though better quality versions contain a dash of Malvasia for perfume and flavor. Other central Italian whites worth trying are Orvieto and Verdicchio. Quality white wines from all over Italy, including fine whites from Friuli in the northeast, are widely available in Rome.

Orvieto   **Frascati**

Calcaia comes from Barberani, a reliable producer of Orvieto.

Bigi produces good quality Orvieto, especially the single-vineyard Torricella.

Casal Pilozzo is an easy-drinking white wine from Frascati producers, Colli di Catone. Choose the youngest vintage.

Colle Gaio, with its rich, fruity flavor, stands out among the dry white Frascatis.

WINE TYPE	GOOD VINTAGES	GOOD PRODUCERS
WHITE WINE		
Friuli (Pinot Bianco, Chardonnay, Pinot Grigio, Sauvignon)	The most recent	**Gravner, Jermann, Puiatti, Schiopetto, Volpe Pasini**
Orvieto/ Orvieto Classico	The most recent	**Antinori, Barberani, Bigi, Il Palazzone**
RED WINE		
Chianti/ Chianti Classico/ Chianti Rufina	95, 88, 85	**Antinori, Castello di Ama, Castello di Cacchiano, Castello di Volpaia, Felsina Berardenga, Fontodi, Frescobaldi, Isole e Olena, Il Palazzino, Riecine, Rocca delle Macie, Ruffino, Vecchie Terre di Montefili, Villa Cafaggio**
Brunello di Montalcino/ Vino Nobile di Montepulciano	95, 88, 85	**Altesino, Avignonesi, Biondi Santi, Caparzo, Case Basse, Lisini, Il Poggione, Poliziano, Villa Banfi**
Barolo/ Barbaresco	95, 89, 88, 85, 82, 78	**Aldo Conterno, Altare, Ceretto, Clerico, Gaja, Giacomo Conterno, Giacosa, Mascarello, Ratti, Voerzio**

RED WINE

THOUGH SOME local red wine is made, most of the bottled red wine in Rome comes from other parts of Italy. Tuscany and Piedmont produce very good everyday drinking wines as well as top-grade ones like Barolo. Price should reflect quality – try Dolcetto, Rosso di Montalcino or Montepulciano, all affordable reds.

Tuscan table wine   **Barolo**

Montepulciano d'Abruzzo, a rich and juicy red wine, is always a good choice. It is produced in the Abruzzi region.

Chianti Classico Riserva is older and stronger than a normal Chianti Classico.

Torre Ercolana is produced in small quantities and is generally regarded as one of Lazio's best red wines. It is made from Cesanese and Cabernet grapes and requires at least five years' aging.

READING THE LABEL

ITALY has a two-tier system for labeling quality wine. DOC (*denominazione di origine controllata*) means you can be sure the wine is from the region declared on the label and is made from designated grape varieties. A higher classification – DOCG (*denominazione di origine controllata e garantita*) – is given to top wines such as the reds Barolo, Barbaresco, Chianti Classico and Brunello di Montalcino.

Chianti Classico

APÉRITIFS AND OTHER DRINKS

BITTER, herb-flavored drinks like Martini, Campari or Aperol are the most popular apéritifs. (Ask for an *analcolico* if you prefer a non-alcoholic one.) Italians drink their apéritifs neat or with ice and soda. Strong, herby after-dinner drinks, known as *digestivi* or *amari*, are worth trying if you need to settle your stomach. Italian brandy and grappa can be very fiery. Italian beer, popular with pizza, is made in lager style.

Campari

DRINKING WATER

Unlike many Mediterranean cities, Rome benefits from a constant supply of fresh drinking water, piped down from the hills through a system of pipes and aqueducts that has changed little from ancient Roman times. Only if there is a sign saying *acqua non potabile* is the water not safe to drink.

One of Rome's many fresh water drinking fountains

SOFT DRINKS

ITALIAN FRUIT juices are good and most bars squeeze fresh orange juice (*spremuta*) on the spot. Iced tea and coffee are refreshing in summer, and fruit-flavored tea, such as peach, is very popular.

Refrigerated storage for wine and beer

Coffee is almost more important to Roman life than wine. For strong black coffee, have expresso at any time of day. Try milky cappuccino for breakfast or mid-afternoon or, for extra milk, caffè latte.

Espresso

Cappuccino

Caffè latte

Rome's Best: Restaurants and Cafés

Rome is not particularly known for luxury restaurants, but more for atmospheric places where the focus is on the social side of dining and on regional cooking. An amazing variety can be found. Many places specialize, priding themselves on being the best of their kind – whether they offer superb espresso, or traditional foods like deep-fried salted cod *(baccalà)*. Other restaurants can offer beautiful settings or are the best places to see and be seen. This selection shows some of the many highlights of a city where eating is taken very seriously.

Caffè Giolitti
This historic ice cream shop serves a variety of flavors, to eat in or take away. (See p320.)

Camponeschi
This stylish restaurant offers elegantly prepared dishes and outdoor tables on Piazza Farnese (See p314.)

Filetti di Baccalà
This small, crowded place serves tasty fried fillets of cod – one of Rome's most traditional dishes – and offers a truly Roman experience. (See p320.)

Alberto Ciarla
Fish dominate the exquisite dishes as well as the decor in this elegant restaurant. (See p316.)

Piperno
For over a century, traditional Roman Jewish cooking has been the speciality of Piperno, in the heart of the Jewish Ghetto. (See p314.)

Babington's Tea Rooms
*This old-fashioned, genteel establishment at
the foot of the Spanish Steps serves English
tea and cakes.* (See p320.)

La Terazza
*Gloriously situated in the roof garden
of Hotel Eden, La Terazza offers some
of the finest cuisine in Rome, with views
to match.* (See p317.)

Caffe Greco
*Famous as the
haunt of writers,
artists and
intellectuals in
the 19th century,
this café still
retains the faded
grandeur shown
in this painting.*
(See p320.)

Via Veneto

Quirinal

Capitol

Esquiline

Palatine

Caracalla   Lateran

Aventine

0 meters   500

0 yards   500

Sora Lella
*This Roman trattoria is
famous for its setting on the
Isola Tiberina and for the
fashionable crowd which
it attracts.* (See p314.)

Tazza d'Oro
*This figure graces the
facade of Tazza d'Oro,
where you will find
some of the best espresso
in Rome.* (See p320.)

Choosing a Restaurant

THE RESTAURANTS in this guide have been selected for their good value or exceptional food. This chart highlights some of the factors that may influence your choice. Entries are alphabetical within price category. For more details on the restaurants, see pages 312 to 317. Information on cafés and wine bars is on pages 318 to 321.

	FIXED PRICE MENU	VEGETARIAN DISHES	TABLES OUTSIDE	SEAFOOD SPECIALTIES	LATE OPENING	AIR-CONDITIONING	ATTRACTIVE SETTING
PIAZZA DELLA ROTONDA *(see p312)*							
Il Bacaro ⓁⓁ				●	■	●	
Il Buco ⓁⓁ				●		●	■
Le Due Colonne ⓁⓁ		■		■	●		
Da Gino ⓁⓁ							
Vecchia Locanda ⓁⓁ		■	●	■	●	■	●
Enoteca Capranica ⓁⓁⓁⓁ	●	■		■			●
Sangallo ⓁⓁⓁⓁ						■	
La Rosetta ★ ⓁⓁⓁⓁⓁ				■	●	■	
El Toulà ⓁⓁⓁⓁⓁ	●	■				■	
PIAZZA NAVONA *(see p312)*							
La Taverna ⓁⓁ	●			●	■		■
Osteria dell'Antiquario ⓁⓁⓁ				●		■	●
Papà Giovanni ⓁⓁⓁⓁ		■			●	■	
Il Convivio ⓁⓁⓁⓁ	●			■		■	
PIAZZA DI SPAGNA *(see p313)*							
Al 34 ⓁⓁ		■	●	■			
Birreria Viennese ⓁⓁ	●				●	■	
Mario alle Vite ⓁⓁ			●			■	
Nino ⓁⓁⓁ							
Sogo-Asahi ⓁⓁⓁⓁ	●			■		■	
Porto di Ripetta ⓁⓁⓁⓁ	●			■		■	
Hassler Roof Restaurant ⓁⓁⓁⓁⓁ						■	●
CAMPO DE' FIORI *(see p313)*							
Bella Shanghai Ⓛ	●	■				●	■
Al Pompiere ⓁⓁ							
Il Cardinale ⓁⓁⓁ			■		■	●	■
Il Drappo ⓁⓁⓁ				●		●	
Le Maschere ⓁⓁⓁ		■	●		●		
Sora Lella ⓁⓁⓁ						■	
Vecchia Roma ⓁⓁⓁ		■	●	■	●		●
Piperno ⓁⓁⓁⓁ				●	■		
Camponeschi ⓁⓁⓁⓁⓁ				●	■	●	●
QUIRINAL *(see p314)*							
Colline Emiliane ⓁⓁ						■	
Al Moro ⓁⓁⓁ					■	●	
Il Posto Accanto ⓁⓁⓁ		■		■		●	
Quadrifoglio ⓁⓁⓁ						●	■
TERMINI *(see p314)*							
Gemma alla Lupa Ⓛ	●	■	●			■	
Coriolano ⓁⓁⓁⓁ		■		■		■	
ESQUILINE *(see p314)*							
Trattoria Monti ⓁⓁ							
Cicilardone ⓁⓁⓁ						●	
La Tana del Grillo ⓁⓁⓁ							
Agata e Romeo ⓁⓁⓁⓁⓁ	●					■	

Price categories for a three-course meal for one, half a bottle of house wine and all unavoidable extra charges such as cover, service and tax:
Ⓛ up to L35,000
ⓁⓁ L35–55,000
ⓁⓁⓁ L55–75,000
ⓁⓁⓁⓁ L75–100,000
ⓁⓁⓁⓁⓁ over L100,000.

★ Means highly recommended.

FIXED PRICE MENU
Restaurant offering *menu turistico* (tourist menu): usually three or four courses without wine or coffee, for a set price.

VEGETARIAN DISHES
Restaurant specializing in seafood or fish or serving good seafood selection.

LATE OPENING
Last orders on or after 11:30pm.

ATTRACTIVE SETTING
Restaurant set in a pretty piazza or having a garden terrace or a lovely view.

	Price	FIXED PRICE MENU	VEGETARIAN DISHES	TABLES OUTSIDE	SEAFOOD SPECIALTIES	LATE OPENING	AIR-CONDITIONING	ATTRACTIVE SETTING
LATERAN (see p315)								
Alfredo a Via Gabi	ⓁⓁ						▪	
Charly's Saucière	ⓁⓁ					●	▪	
Cannavota	ⓁⓁⓁ				▪		▪	
AVENTINE (see p316)								
Perilli a Testaccio	ⓁⓁ						▪	
Checchino dal 1887 ★	ⓁⓁⓁⓁ				●			
TRASTEVERE (see p315)								
Da Lucia	Ⓛ			●				
Fricandò	ⓁⓁ		▪	●		●		
La Cornucopia	ⓁⓁⓁ	●		●	▪		▪	●
L'Isola Felice	ⓁⓁⓁ			●			▪	●
Da Paris	ⓁⓁⓁ			●	▪		▪	●
Romolo nel Giardino della Fornarina	ⓁⓁⓁ			●		●		●
Alberto Ciarla ★	ⓁⓁⓁⓁ	●		●	▪	●	▪	
JANICULUM (see p316)								
Antico Arco ★	ⓁⓁ					●	▪	
VATICAN (see p316)								
Macondo	ⓁⓁ		▪	●				
San Luigi	ⓁⓁⓁ		▪				▪	
Les Etoiles	ⓁⓁⓁⓁ			●	▪			
VIA VENETO (see p317)								
Andrea	ⓁⓁⓁ		▪		▪		▪	
Tullio	ⓁⓁⓁ				▪		▪	
Giovanni	ⓁⓁⓁⓁ				▪			
George's ★	ⓁⓁⓁⓁ			●		●	▪	●
Le Sans Souci ★	ⓁⓁⓁⓁ		▪		▪	●	▪	
La Terrazza	ⓁⓁⓁⓁ		▪		▪	●	▪	●
VILLA BORGHESE (see p317)								
Al Ceppo	ⓁⓁⓁ		▪	●	▪		▪	
Relais la Piscine ★	ⓁⓁⓁⓁ	●		●	▪		▪	●
Relais le Jardin ★	ⓁⓁⓁⓁ				▪		▪	

PIAZZA DELLA ROTONDA

Il Bacaro

Via delgli Spagnoli. **Map** 12 D2.
☎ 06-686 41 10. **Open** 8pm–
midnight Mon–Sat. **Closed** 1 week
Jan, 2 weeks Aug. 🎫 💺 🌐 DC,
MC, V, JCB. ⓁⓁ

Located in the historic center of
the city, near the Pantheon, this
tiny restaurant serves meals
cooked in a minute kitchen. The
menu is very much based around
meat and fish dishes and includes
such main courses as fillet steak
with basil sauce. The superb
desserts include an excellent
chocolate mousse.

Il Buco

Via di Sant'Ignazio 8. **Map** 4 F4 &
12 E3. **☎** 06-679 32 98, 06-678 44
67. **Open** 12:30pm–4pm, 7pm–
midnight Tue–Sun. **Closed** Aug,
Christmas. 🎫 💺 🌐 AE, DC,
MC, V. ⓁⓁ

Much has happened since the tiny
buco (hole) opened in 1891 – the
small *osteria* has become a large
restaurant, yet the calm atmosphere, unfailing courtesy and
formidable Tuscan menu remain.
From the traditional *crostini* (liver
pâté canapés), robust *ribollita*
(thick vegetable soup) and huge
Florentine steaks, to the final
tozzetti (almond biscuits) with *vin
santo* (dessert wine), this is a truly
Tuscan experience.

Le Due Colonne

Via del Seminario 122. **Map** 4 F4 &
12 D3. **☎** 06-678 14 49. **Open**
noon–3pm, 7pm–midnight daily.
🅅 👥 💺 🌐 AE, DC, MC, V, JCB.
ⓁⓁ

Evocative of ancient Rome, the
decor of this restaurant includes
two imperial columns, from which
it gets it name, and an ancient
fountain. The cuisine is rich in
Mediterranean flavors, and
includes both Italian and Spanish
dishes. The seafood dishes, such
as *calamari* stuffed with onions
and hard-boiled eggs and giant
shrimp with *Pachino* tomatoes,
are particularly good.

Da Gino

Vicolo Rosini 4 (Piazza del Parlamento).
Map 4 F3 & 12 D1. **☎** 06-687 34 34.
Open 12:45pm–3pm, 8pm–10:30pm
Mon–Sat. **Closed** Aug. 💺 ⓁⓁ

Journalists, politicians and the
initiated scramble for a seat under
the kitsch frescoed pergola of this
ancient, ultra-Roman *trattoria* to

feast on traditional daily dishes:
gnocchi and *osso buco* (Thursdays),
baccalà (Fridays), tripe (Saturdays),
plus classic sturdy soups, dutifully
executed Roman standards and
delectable homemade *tiramisù*.

Vecchia Locanda

Vicolo Sinibaldi 2. **Map** 4 F4 & 12 D3.
☎ 06-68 80 28 31. **Open** 12:30pm–
3pm, 7pm–midnight Mon–Sat. **Closed**
Christmas. 🅅 👥 💺 🌐 AE, DC, V.
ⓁⓁ

Visit this small family-run Ligurian
restaurant in summer, when tables
line the secluded arched street.
Meals are prepared with great
care, and the service is impeccable.
The menu features imaginative
combinations of herbs and vegetables: *risotto* with zucchini blossoms,
porcini crêpes, stuffed truffled
rabbit and lots of fresh fish. There's
a good selection of French and
regional wines.

Enoteca Capranica

Piazza Capranica 99-100. **Map** 12 D2.
☎ 06-69 94 09 92. **Open** noon–3pm,
7pm–11pm Mon–Fri, 7pm–11pm Sat.
Closed Aug. 🅅 👥 💺 🌐 AE,
DC, V, JCB. ⓁⓁⓁ

Housed in part of the impressive
15th-century Palazzo Capranica
(*see p113*), the Enoteca Capranica
offers an extensive menu, mostly
bases around seafood and vegetable dishes. Starters include
delights such as lobster and mango
salad, while exotic main courses
include unusual dishes like *risotto
con zuca e tartufo* (risotto with
pumpkin and truffel) and *spigola
al sale* (sea bass in a salt crust).

Sangallo

Vicolo della Vaccarella 11. **Map** 4 F3
& 12 D2. **☎** 06-686 55 49. **Open**
12:30pm–2:30pm, 7:45pm–10:30pm
Tue–Sat, 12:30pm–2:30pm Mon.
Closed 2 weeks Aug. 🍴 💺
🌐 AE, DC, MC, V. ⓁⓁⓁ

This elegant fish restaurant has an
interesting menu complemented by
an impressive wine list. Antipasti
include *crostini con calamaretti al
radicchio* (baby squid and radicchio
on toast). First courses such as
*fettucelle con gamberi, pomodori e
pecorino* (pasta with shrimp,
tomatoes and pecorino cheese)
are prepared delicately and simply.
Ask about the specialty of the day.

La Rosetta

Via della Rosetta 9. **Map** 4 F4 & 12 D2.
☎ 06-68 30 88 41. **Open** 1pm–3pm,
7:30pm–11:30pm Mon–Fri, 7:30pm–
11:30pm Sat. **Closed** 3 weeks Aug,
Christmas. 💺 🌐 ★ AE, DC,
MC, V, JCB. ⓁⓁⓁⓁ

Despite the exorbitant prices,
people flock nightly (having
reserved in advance) for a seat in
the tightly packed elegant rooms
of this restaurant. Fresh fish and
seafood are bruoght in daily from
Sicily and, cooked in the simplest
ways, achieve close to culinary
perfection. The enthusiastic
service and top quality French
and Italian wines, particularly
the Sicilian whites, available do
justice to the cuisine.

El Toulà

Via della Lupa 29B. **Map** 4 F3 & 12
D1. **☎** 06-687 34 98. **Open**
1pm–3pm, 8pm–11pm Tue–Fri,
8pm–11pm Mon, Sat. **Closed** Aug,
Christmas. 🍴 🅅 👥 💺 🌐 AE,
DC, MC, V, JCB. ⓁⓁⓁⓁⓁ

El Toulà is justly renowned as
one of the most exclusive, traditional and luxurious restaurants
in Rome. The Venetian-inspired
cooking is exactingly prepared to
the highest standards, with forays
into the best classic international
cuisine. In its dignified, formal
surroundings, the service is
exemplary and the selection of
wines superb.

PIAZZA NAVONA

La Taverna

Via del Banco di Santo Spirito 58.
Map 4 D3 & 11 A2. **☎** 06-686 41
16. **Open** noon–3pm, 7pm–11pm
Tue–Sun. 🍴 💺 🎵 🌐 🍽
🌐 AE, DC, MC, V, JCB. ⓁⓁ

Tourists and local residents mingle
in Giovanni's crowded Roman
trattoria to enjoy the family
atmosphere and traditional
regional cooking. Particularly
appreciated are the *rigatoni
all'amatriciana; coda alla
vaccinara*, and, on Thursday,
Friday and Saturday, respectively,
gnocchi, baccalà and tripe.

Osteria dell'Antiquario

Piazzetta San Simeone 27. **Map** 4 E3
& 11 B2. **☎** 06-687 96 94. **Open**
12:30pm–2:30pm, 8pm–11pm Tue–
Sat, 8pm–11pm Mon. **Closed** 2 weeks
Aug, 2 weeks Jan. 🍴 💺 🌐
🌐 AE DC, MC, V, JCB. ⓁⓁ

In the comfort of the elegantly
restructured rooms of an old
antiques shop, Giorgio Nisti
offers an unusual menu dictated
by the whims of the chef and the
daily market, with traditional
dishes creatively adapted to
contemporary health-conscious
tastes. There is an impressive
choice of regional, French and
California wines.

Papà Giovanni

Via dei Sediari 4. **Map** 4 F4 & 12 D3.
📞 06-686 53 08. **Open** 1pm–3pm,
8pm–11:30pm Mon–Sat. 🌿 🅅 ☎
☒ MC, V. ⓁⓁⓁ

Nearly 60 years have passed since
Papà Giovanni first sold his
country wines in Rome; the bottles
lining the walls are testimony to
the past and to the superb cellar of
Giovanni's son, Renato Sentuti.
Here diners sample the best of the
lighter Roman cuisine. Offered are
such classics as *cacio e pepe*, salt
cod and tripe, as well as exotic
salads and truffled dishes. Desserts
include ricotta soufflé with
strawberry sauce, hot chocolate
profiteroles and exquisite sorbets.

Il Convivio

Via dell'Orso 44. **Map** 4 E3 & 11 C2.
📞 06-686 94 32. **Open** 1pm–
2:30pm, 8pm–10:30pm Tue–Sat,
8pm–10:30pm Mon. **Closed** 1 week
Aug. 🍴 ☎ 🅅 ★ ☒ AE, DC, MC, V.
ⓁⓁⓁⓁ

An air of sophisticated tranquillity
pervades this intimate restaurant,
one of the very best specializing
in modern creative cookery. Its
young chef, one of the three
brother/owners from the Marches,
creates both subtle and unusual
combinations of flavors. The highly
personalized menu evolves with
the seasons, and the staff is highly
attentive. The wine list is extensive.

PIAZZA DI SPAGNA

Al 34

Via Mario de' Fiori 34. **Map** 5 A2.
📞 06-679 50 91. **Open** 12:30pm–
3pm, 7:30pm–11pm Tue–Sun. **Closed**
3 weeks Aug. 🅅 ☎ ♿ ☒ AE, DC,
MC, V. ⓁⓁ

This busy, bustling restaurant is an
ideal choice if you're in a hurry, as
the service is speedy and efficient.
Predominantly featuring southern
Italian cooking, the extensive
menu offers an esoteric selection,
particularly where vegetables and
herbs are served with pasta, meat
and fish. Given its location, the
prices are reasonable.

Birreria Viennese

Via della Croce 21. **Map** 5 A2.
📞 06-679 55 69. **Open** noon–
midnight daily. **Closed** 1 week Aug. 🍴
♿ ☒ AE, DC, MC, V, JCB. ⓁⓁ

The stained-glass entrance leads to
a long crowded room where
traditional beers and Austrian
specialties have been sampled for
more than 60 years. Try sausages,
goulash, *Wienerschnitzel*,

sauerkraut or the massive *piatto
di legno della Transilvania* (a
wooden platter heaped with
delights, for two). Wine is also
available. The staff is extremely
helpful and courteous.

Mario alla Vite

Via della Vite 55. **Map** 5 A3 & 12 E1.
📞 06-678 38 18. **Open** 12:30pm–
3pm, 7:30pm–11pm Mon–Sat. **Closed**
Aug. 🍴 ☎ AE, DC, MC, V. ⓁⓁ

Despite an exclusive address,
Mario has kept prices reasonable,
and his food is still simple, honest
Tuscan fare. Elbow-to-elbow
dining, haphazard service and
noisy confusion seem inevitable.
Nevertheless, the food is worth it
– traditional *fagioli al fiasco*
(cannellini beans in oil), *ribollita*
(thick vegetable soup), Florentine
steaks and delicious pastries are
the attractions, along with a wide
selection of wines.

Nino

Via Borgognona 11. **Map** 5 A2 &
12 E1. 📞 06-679 56 76. **Open**
12:30pm–2:30pm, 7:30pm–11pm
Tue–Fri, 7:30pm–11pm Sat. ☎ AE,
DC, MC, V. ⓁⓁ

A reliable restaurant, located
among the fancy shops around
Piazza di Spagna, Nino has been
popular with visitors and locals
alike since it opened in 1934. The
menu features mostly Tuscan
food, so there is always a hearty
soup on offer to go along with
other standards such as a bistecca
alla fiorentina (grilled T-bone
steak). Save room for the deserts,
which are all home-made.

Sogo-Asahi

Via di Propaganda 16. **Map** 5 A2.
📞 06-678 60 93. **Open** noon–
2:30pm, 6:30pm–10pm Mon–Sat.
🍴 ♿ ☎ AE, DC, MC, V, JCB.
ⓁⓁⓁ

This appealing luxury restaurant
is a find for lovers of Japanese
cooking. Traditional specialties
are elegantly served by helpful
and knowledgeable waiters:
sashimi (raw fish) and melt-in-the-
mouth tempura are accompanied
by saké, Japanese beer or a good
Italian wine. The special menus
are particularly inexpensive at
lunch. Sogo-Asahi opens in
August, when most of Rome's
restaurants are closed.

Porto di Ripetta

Via di Ripetta 250. **Map** 4 F2.
📞 06-361 23 76. **Open** 12:45pm–
2:45pm, 8pm–11pm Mon–Sat.
Closed Aug. 🍴 ☎ ☒ AE,
DC, MC, V, JCB. ⓁⓁⓁ

The fame of this restaurant
depends largely on the genius of
chef Maria Romani. With the fish
that arrives daily from her native
Marches, she creates inspired
combinations such as soup with
fish and broad beans or giant
prawns with artichokes. The food
is expensive but worth it; the
business lunch is much cheaper.
There's a selection of excellent
wines to choose from.

Hassler Roof
Restaurant

Piazza Trinità dei Monti 6. **Map** 5 A2.
📞 06-69 93 40. **Open** 7am–
11am, noon–2:30pm, 7:30pm–
10:30pm Mon–Sat, 7am–11am,
12:30pm–3pm, 7:30pm–10pm Sun.
🍴 ☎ ☒ AE, DC, MC, V, JCB.
ⓁⓁⓁⓁ

Perched on the sixth floor of the
Hotel Hassler, overlooking the
Spanish Steps, this roof restaurant
commands a breathtaking view of
Rome. Come for the gargantuan
but pricey Sunday brunch. The
wine list is excellent, the hovering
waiter attentive but discreet. In the
evening, when prices are higher,
there's piano music.

CAMPO DE' FIORI

Bella Shanghai

Corso Vittorio Emanuele II 333.
Map 4 E4 & 11 C3. 📞 06-686 96
51. **Open** 11am–3pm, 6pm–midnight
daily. 🍴 🅅 ☎ AE, DC, MC, V. Ⓛ

This cheerful Vietnamese restaurant
offers a respectable alternative to
Italian food. Eat by candlelight in a
relaxed atmosphere and try the wide
selection of relatively inexpensive
dishes. A waiter patiently explains
the menu for first-timers; recommended are the fried ravioli starters,
chicken in foil (*pollo d'argento*) and
the *tre delizie* (three delights – beef,
chicken and prawns in a special
sauce). There are also affordable
Italian wines, tea, ginseng liqueur
and a selection of grappas.

Al Pompiere

Via S. M. dei Calderari 38. **Map** 4 F5
& 12 D5. 📞 06-686 83 77. **Open**
noon–3pm, 7:30pm–11pm Mon–Sat.
Closed Aug. ☎ ☒ MC, V. Ⓛ

In the heart of the Jewish Ghetto,
Al Pompiere occupies the first
floor of the 16th-century Palazzo
Cenci-Bolognetti. Under its
frescoed open-beamed ceilings,
in a homey atmosphere, all the
classic dishes of the substantial
Roman cuisine are expertly
served: among them fried zucchini
flowers with anchovies, *rigatoni
con la pajata* and baby lamb.

For key to symbols *see p303*.

Il Cardinale

Via delle Carceri 6. **Map** 4 D4 & 11 B3.
[06-686 93 36. **Open** 12:45pm–
3pm, 7:30pm–11:30pm Mon–Sat.
V & 🍴 AE, DC, MC, V. Ⓛ Ⓛ Ⓛ

For genuine regional cooking using
the best local ingredients from the
Castelli Romani, this small, elegant
yet comfortable restaurant near
Via Giulia is highly recommended.
Dishes range from tasty robust
soups to such specialties as
zucchine alla velletrana (baked
squash) and *crema al cocco*
(coconut *crème brûlée*). There are
some very good wines from Lazio.

Il Drappo

Vicolo del Malpasso 9. **Map** 4 D4 &
11 B3. [06-687 73 65. **Open** 8pm–
midnight Mon–Sat. **Closed** Jan 1,
Easter, 2 weeks Aug, Dec 25. & 🍴
🍴 AE, DC, MC, V, JCB. Ⓛ Ⓛ Ⓛ

A small, intimate restaurant with
ceiling drapes (hence the name),
plants and candlelight, Il Drappo
provides an authentic taste of
Sardinia – traditional dishes
imbued with flashes of culinary
creativity. Everything is evocative
of the island, including the wines.
Try the *seada* (sweet cheese-filled
ravioli) for dessert followed by the
mirto liqueur at the end.

Le Maschere

Via Monte della Farina 29. **Map** 4 F5
& 12 D4. [06-687 94 44. **Open**
7pm–12:30am Tue–Sun. **Closed**
Aug. V 🍴 🍴 AE, DC, MC, V,
JCB. Ⓛ Ⓛ Ⓛ

You'll feel an agreeable sensation
of being in the country as you
cross the spacious tiled hall and
descend to the rustic indoor
terrace with its high reed-lined
ceiling, a roofed grill and eerily lit
wall masks. Candles on the tables
and the subdued conversational
hum lull you in preparation for
the fiery Calabrian food to come.
Charming service and good
Calabrian house wine (plus a short
list) ensure an enjoyable evening.

Sora Lella

Via Ponte Quattro Capi 16, Isola
Tiberina. **Map** 8 D1. [06-686 16
01. **Open** 1pm–2:30pm, 8pm–
10:40pm Mon–Sat. **Closed** Aug. &
🍴 AE, DC, MC, V. Ⓛ Ⓛ Ⓛ

Founded by the exuberant Roman
actress Sora Lella, this small, bright
trattoria is a well-known place to
people watch. Sora Lella is now
run by Lella's son, Aldo. Dishes
are based on traditional Roman
cuisine, but prices are very high
for an essentially simple style of
cooking. Go instead for the

beautiful location on the Isola
Tiberina, the often glamorous
clientele and the good service.

Vecchia Roma

Piazza Campitelli 18. **Map** 4 F5 &
12 E5. [06-686 46 04. **Open**
1pm–3pm, 8pm–11:30pm Thu–Tue.
Closed 2 weeks Aug. V & 🍴 🍴
🍴 AE, DC, MC. Ⓛ Ⓛ Ⓛ

Set in a quiet, atmospheric piazza,
this is one of the best places for a
summer evening. Reliable Roman
cooking is offered, with tempting
antipasti, simply cooked fish and
grilled meats, plus a connoisseur's
wine list. Specialties are summer
salads and, in winter, numerous
variations of polenta. Added
pleasures are the 18th-century
interior and the excellent service.

Piperno

Via Monte de' Cenci 9. **Map** 4 F5 &
12 D5. [06-686 11 13. **Open**
12:15pm–2:30pm, 8pm–11pm Tue–
Sat, 12:30pm–3pm Sun. **Closed** Easter,
Aug, Christmas. & 🍴 🍴 AE, DC,
MC, V. Ⓛ Ⓛ Ⓛ

Piperno, in the heart of the old
Jewish Ghetto, has been famed for
over a century for its traditional
Jewish/Roman dishes. Despite the
competition, the restaurant is still
unbeaten for lightly fried zucchini
flowers, vegetable *fritto misto*,
carciofi alla giudia, tripe and
superb fish, served in plain
surroundings. Service is familiarly
attentive and timely. The house
wine is excellent Frascati. Reserve
well in advance.

Camponeschi

Piazza Farnese 50. **Map** 4 E5 & 11 C4.
[06-687 49 27. **Open** 8pm–12:30am
Mon–Sat. **Closed** 10 days Aug. 🍴
🍴 AE, DC, MC, V. Ⓛ Ⓛ Ⓛ Ⓛ Ⓛ

Camponeschi is set in one of the
most attractive piazzas in Rome,
especially beautiful in summer, so
reserving in advance is necessary.
The extensive menu includes
modern and regional Italian
cooking, creative Mediterranean
fish and meat dishes, soufflés and
refined French specialties. There's
a varied regional, French and
Californian wine list.

Colline Emiliane

Via degli Avignonesi 22. **Map** 5 B3.
[06-481 75 38. **Open** 12:45pm–
2:45pm, 7:45pm–10:45pm Sat–Thu.
Closed Aug. & 🍴 MC, V. Ⓛ Ⓛ

Regional dishes are the hallmark
of this small family *trattoria*: one
unpretentious room presenting a

haven from the nearby Via del
Tritone. Enjoy food typical of the
northern province of Emilia
Romagna – salamis and cold meats,
homemade pastas (tagliatelle,
tortellini), boiled meats with *salsa
verde* (spinach, onion and
anchovy sauce) and strictly
Emilian wines.

Al Moro

Vicolo delle Bollette 13. **Map** 5 A3 &
12 F2. [678 34 95. **Open** 1pm–
3:30pm, 8pm–11:30pm Mon–Sat.
Closed Aug. Ⓛ Ⓛ Ⓛ

Franco Romagnoli's *trattoria* is a
reliable choice for traditional
Roman cooking, using fresh local
ingredients. Noisy and crowded,
its closely packed tables do not
encourage intimate dining. Classic
dishes are served: *bucatini
all'amatriciana, spaghetti alla
Moro* (special *carbonara*), fried
vegetables, excellent *baccalà alla
Moro* (salt cod), tripe and
abbacchio. The wine list is vast.

Il Posto Accanto

Via del Boschetto 36A. **Map** 5 B4.
[06-474 30 02. **Open** 12:30pm–
3pm Mon–Fri, 8pm–10pm Mon–Sat.
Closed Aug. V 🍴 & 🍴 AE, DC,
MC, V. Ⓛ Ⓛ Ⓛ

Tiny, intimate and elegant, this
family-run restaurant owes its
success to a carefully chosen short
menu revolving around homemade
pasta (excellent *tagliolini con
asparagi* and *ravioli con zenzero*
– ginger), simply prepared fish
and meat, top-quality vegetables
and familiar desserts *(tiramisù)*,
often prepared within sight of the
lucky diners. There is a range of
wines, as well as good grappas.

Quadrifoglio

Via del Boschetto 19. **Map** 5 B4.
[06-482 60 96. **Open** 7pm–
midnight Mon–Sat. **Closed** Aug. 🍴
🍴 AE, DC, MC, V. Ⓛ Ⓛ Ⓛ

Chef Pino Forlenza has researched
diligently to reproduce authentic
dishes from Naples, Campania and
the tip of Africa. They are tailored to
modern tastes with carefully
selected raw ingredients and
delivered with southern hospitality
and courteous service. Most of the
wines are from Campania.

Gemma alla Lupa

Via Marghera 39. **Map** 6 E3.
[06-49 12 30. **Open** noon–3:30pm,
7pm–11pm Mon–Sat. **Closed** 2
weeks Aug. 🍴 V 🍴 Ⓛ

Gemma's is a modest, family-run, typically Roman *trattoria* which serves up substantial portions of orthodox Roman cooking. Although the main features are its bustling atmosphere and speedy service. it represents a good choice if you want to eat well for a low price.

Coriolano

Via Ancona 14. **Map** 6 D1.
(06-44 24 98 63. **Open** noon–3pm, 7pm–11pm daily. **Closed** 3 weeks Aug. **V** **&** **Y** **AE, DC, MC, V.** **£££££**

This small restaurant aims at perfection with its lacy tablecloths and crystal glasses. The Italian menu changes with the seasons and uses only the freshest of raw ingredients, including fish. Specialties include homemade *ravioli di ricotta e spinaci*, *capretto* (kid) and chocolate *zuppa del contadino*.

Trattoria Monti

Via di San Vito 13A. **Map** 6 D4.
(06-446 65 73. **Open** 12:30pm–3pm, 7:30pm–11pm Wed–Mon. **Closed** Easter, Aug, 3 weeks Dec–Jan. **&** **DC, MC, V.** **££**

This small unpretentious local *trattoria* serves delicate, creative regional dishes from the Marches region. Franca Camerucci cooks, while her husband, Mario, is an attentive waiter and expert sommelier. Specialties include fried stuffed olives, artichokes and *ciauscolo* (salami); *tortello al rosso d'uova* (fresh pasta stuffed with ricotta, spinach and tomato); and *tacchino all'aceto balsamico* (lightly vinegared turkey slices). There is a good Verdicchio house wine and a commendable wine list.

Cicilardone

Via Farini 12. **Map** 6 D4.
(06-48 35 49. **Open** noon–3pm Tue –Sat, 8pm–midnight Mon–Sat. **Closed** mid 2 weeks Aug. **AE, DC, MC, V.** **£££**

Ring at Cicilardone's door and your host – Domenico Lucia – will greet you like an old friend and converse about the gastronomic delights from the region of Basilicata. Try the *menu di assaggini* – a number of dishes to give you an idea of the regional taste, including traditional pastas and hot chocolate profiteroles. There is a selection of some unusual southern wines.

La Tana del Grillo

Via Alfieri 4. **Map** 6 E5. **(** 06-70 45 35 17. **Open** 12:30pm–2:30pm, 7:30pm–11pm Tue–Sat, 7:30pm–11pm Mon. **Closed** Aug. **&** **AE, DC, MC, V.** **£££**

Marisa Balboni runs an elegant and characteristically hospitable Emilian restaurant. Clients are truly pampered, from the comfortable chairs, restful prints and attractive tableware to the wholesome food served with courtesy and care. Particularly recommended are the *polpettone all'emiliana* (meat loaf), *salame al sugo ferrarese* (Ferrarese salami) and *cappellacci con la zucca* (pumpkin-stuffed pasta).

Agata e Romeo

Via Carlo Alberto 45. **Map** 6 D4.
(06-446 58 42. **Open** 1pm–3pm, 7pm–11pm Mon–Sat. **Closed** 2 weeks Jan, 2 weeks Aug. **☉** **V** **&** **Y** **AE, DC, MC, V, JCB.** **££££**

One of the newer *trattoria*-turned-restaurants, its increasing prices sadly reflect recent popular acclaim. Nevertheless, Agata's skill in producing a changing menu of predominantly Roman and southern Italian dishes, and Romeo's impeccable service and range of carefully chosen wines, are hard to beat. Well-spaced, elegantly set tables are ideal for tranquil eating.

Alfredo a Via Gabi

Via Gabi 36. **Map** 10 D3. **(** 06-77 20 67 92. **Open** noon–3pm, 7:30pm–11pm Wed–Mon. **Closed** Aug. **££**

This is a spacious local *trattoria* with a pavement pergola for outdoor eating. Specialties from Rome and the Marches – served in ample portions – include *tonnarelli ai sapori di bosco* (pasta with mushrooms), excellent *porcini* (in season), *straccetti all'ortica* (meat in nettle sauce), and *panna cotta* (rich *crème caramel*) with fruit or chocolate. Service is cheerful and friendly.

Charly's Saucière

Via San Giovanni in Laterano 270.
Map 9 B1. **(** 06-70 49 56 66.
Open 12:45pm–2:30pm, 8pm–11:15pm Tue–Fri, 8pm–midnight Mon, Sat. **Closed** 2 weeks Aug. **&** **AE, MC, V, JCB.** **££**

An old-style, unsurprising and well-established French restaurant, this has scarcely altered over the years and is especially warm and intimate on a winter evening. Diners choose from French and Swiss fare: pâtés,

onion soup, cheese soufflé, fondues, *rösti*, steaks in a variety of sauces, and crêpes, accompanied by a small but careful selection of wines. The service is always highly professional and attentive.

Cannavota

Piazza San Giovanni in Laterano 20.
Map 9 C1. **(** 06-77 20 50 07.
Open 12:30pm–3pm, 7:45pm–11pm Thu–Tue. **Closed** Aug 1–20. **AE, DC, MC, V.** **£££**

Join the enthusiastic regulars who crowd this friendly restaurant if you are feeling especially hungry. Portions are generous, the cooking is traditional Italian and the service is swift. Seafood – shrimp, in particular – is excellent, but meat is also featured on the menu.

Perilli a Testaccio

Via Marmorata 39. **Map** 8 D3.
(06-574 24 15. **Open** 12:30pm–3pm, 7:30pm–11pm Thu–Tue.
Closed Aug. **&** **££**

In the heart of Testaccio, this archetypal Roman *trattoria* is always packed with hungry regulars (and the occasional famous face). On offer are giant-size quantities of robust traditional fare – *rigatoni alla pajata*, *spaghetti alla carbonara* (served in king-size bowls), *coda alla vaccinara*, *carciofi alla romana*. Everything is efficiently served. Ignore the noise and awful murals and enjoy yourself.

Checchino dal 1887

Via di Monte Testaccio 30. **Map** 8 D4.
(06-574 63 18. **Open** Oct–May: 12:30pm–3pm, 8pm–11pm Tue–Sat, 12:30pm–3pm Sun; Jun, Jul, Sep: 12:30pm–3pm, 8pm–11pm Tue–Sat. **Closed** Aug, 1 week at Christmas. **&** **☆** **AE, DC, MC, V.** **££££**

Historic home of Roman cuisine for over 100 years, Checchino specializes in authentic dishes using the *quinto quarto* (offal, tripe, intestines and tail), originally discarded by the old slaughterhouse opposite. At the old convent tables under vaulted ceilings, with an open fire in winter, Ninetta Mariani and her two sommelier sons offer traditional *rigatoni alla pajata*, *coda alla vaccinara*, *crostata di ricotta*, a superb cheese tray and an extraordinary wine selection. Carved into the artificial Monte de' Cocci (made from broken amphoras), its cool, natural wine cellar deserves a special visit.

TRASTEVERE

Da Lucia

Vicolo del Mattonato 2. **Map** 7 B1.
📞 06-580 36 01. **Open** 12:30pm–
3:30pm, 7:30pm–11pm Tue–Sun.
Closed 2 weeks Aug, 1 week
Christmas. 🚶 ♿ 🍴 Ⓛ

Head for this popular well-worn
trattoria off Via Garibaldi if you
want to enjoy genuine Roman
cooking. You won't be disappointed by the *pasta e ceci*,
baccalà, *pollo con i peperoni*
(chicken with peppers), boiled
meats and, incongruously,
Milanese risotto. However the
service is take it or leave it, and
the choice of wine basic. The
outdoor tables make a more
attractive dining area in summer.

Fricandò

Vicolo del Leopardo 39A (off Vicolo del
Cedro). **Map** 7 B1. 📞 06-581 47 38.
Open 7pm–late Mon–Sat. **Closed**
Aug 16–20. 🅥 🚶 ♿ 🍴 AE, V.
Ⓛ Ⓛ

This small, intimate restaurant is
situated in a narrow *vicolo*
(alleyway) reminiscent of a much
older Rome. Sit at one of the
tables outside, below the lines of
washing strung across the street,
and soak up the atmosphere. The
menu features simple Tuscan
dishes such as fettucine with
rabbit, The food is fresh and all
the pastas and cakes are made
on the premises.

La Cornucopia

Piazza in Piscinula 18.
Map 8 D1. 📞 06-580 03 80.
Open 12:30pm–3pm, 8pm–11pm
Mon–Sat. **Closed** 3 weeks Aug–Sep,
Christmas. 🍴 🍷
🌿 AE, MC, V. Ⓛ Ⓛ Ⓛ

One of the better, more expensive
fish restaurants in Trastevere,
La Cornucopia it is particularly
recommended for its candlelight,
elegant place settings and, in
summer, comfortable tables
outside in the piazza. The dishes
are predominantly Mediterranean,
with excellent antipasti, unusual
pasta, such simply cooked fish
as *spigola al vapore* (steamed sea
bass) and selected meats. The
Castelli house will soften the bill.

L'Isola Felice

Vicolo del Leopardo. **Map** 7 B4.
📞 06-581 738. **Open** noon–2:30pm,
9pm–11pm Tue–Sun.
♿ 🍷 🍴 AE, DC, MC, V, JCB.
Ⓛ Ⓛ Ⓛ

This is the way the Romans spell
intimacy. Tucked away in a tiny
backstreet, L'Isola is a secret that
everyone should know about. The
cuisine blends modern Roman and
traditional rural. The starters are
truly excellent – almost a feast in
themselves – and the main courses
add pleasure upon pleasure.

Da Paris

Piazza San Calisto 7A. **Map** 7 C1.
📞 06-581 53 78. **Open** 12:30pm–
3pm, 8pm–11pm Tue–Sat,
12:30pm– 3pm Sun. **Closed** Aug.
🍴 🍷 🌿 AE, DC, MC, V. Ⓛ Ⓛ Ⓛ

This classic Roman/Jewish restaurant is a firm favorite with
choosy diners in Trastevere. Jole
Cappellanti's homemade pasta
and traditional dishes are a must
and include *minestra di arzilla*
(skate) and *trippa* (tripe) *alla
romana*. The *fritto misto vegetale*
is extraordinary, the fish fresh.
There are good desserts and the
owner's personal choice of wines.

Romolo nel Giardino della Fornarina

Via Porta Settimiana 8. **Map** 4 D5 &
11 B5. 📞 06-581 82 84. **Open** noon–
3pm, 7:30pm–midnight Tue–Sun.
Closed Aug 3–26. 🍴 ♿ 🍴
🌿 AE, DC, MC, V. Ⓛ Ⓛ Ⓛ *See p210.*

A Roman institution, this was said
to have been the home of La
Fornarina, Raphael's celebrated
mistress and model. Its atmosphere
is best enjoyed on a summer
evening. Eat out by candlelight in
the walled courtyard, to the
accompaniment of a melancholy
guitar. The food is Roman,
including fried *mozzarella alla
Fornarina* and *cervella e carciofi*
(brains and artichokes).

Alberto Ciarla

Piazza San Cosimato 40. **Map** 7 C1.
📞 06-581 86 68. **Open** 8pm–
midnight Mon–Sat. **Closed** 15 days
Aug, 15 days Jan. 🍴 🍷 🎵 🌿
🍷 ★ 🌿 AE, DC, MC, V, JCB.
Ⓛ Ⓛ Ⓛ Ⓛ Ⓛ

This is the quintessential restaurant for fish lovers – at least, those
who are prepared to splash out.
The elegant, dramatically dark
decor is lit by candlelight. Perfectly executed dishes fluctuate
between the traditional and the
inventive, always with an eye to
what's best in the market, ranging
from the simple to the elaborately
creative. A few innovatory meat
dished can be had. Ciarla, who is
president of the Italian sommeliers,
provides an exceptional wine list,
including many fine French and
Californian wines.

JANICULUM

Antico Arco

Piazzale Aurelio 7. **Map** 7 A1.
📞 06-581 52 74. **Open** 8pm–
midnight Tue–Sat, noon–3pm,
8pm–midnight. 🍷 ★ 🌿 AE,
DC, MC, V. Ⓛ Ⓛ

Since changing managment a few
years ago, the Anitco Arco has
become one of Rome's best places
to eat innovative food and drink
excellent wines without spending
a fortune. Choose from a long list
of interesting wines from all over
Italy and France (with a few
dozen labels available by the
glass). The menu is based on
classic Roman dishes using
seasonal ingredients, but they
have been "revisited" and given a
modern twist. The low-key bistro-
style decor makes it suitable for
an intimate meal as well as
convivial dining.

VATICAN

Macondo

Via Marianna Dionigi 37. **Map** 4 E2.
📞 06-321 26 01. **Open** 8–11pm
Mon–Sat. 🍴 🅥 🌿 Ⓛ Ⓛ

This brightly decorated, friendly
little Caribbean restaurant is just
the place to visit if you fancy a
change from Italian cuisine, but be
warned you will be turned away if
you haven't made a reservation.
The food is fresh, light, and
plentiful and is always beautifully
presented. The star dish is
pabellon criollo (strips of beef,
black beans, rice and fried
plantain). Try such starters as
patacones y guacamole (plantains
and avocado dip), remembering
to leave room for desserts such as
the banana cake soaked in banana
liquor. There is a good selection
of wines at various prices as well
as cocktails and Venezuelan rums.

San Luigi

Via Mocenigo 10. **Map** 3 B2.
📞 06-39 72 07 04. **Open**
noon–3pm, 8pm–11pm Mon–Sat.
Closed Aug. 🍴 🅥 🎵 🌿 AE,
DC, MC, V. Ⓛ Ⓛ Ⓛ

If you have just spent hours in the
Vatican Museums, the pleasure
of a relaxing restaurant with 19th-
century decor and soft music will
soothe your aching limbs. A fixed
menu is offered at lunch and a
choice of traditional Neapolitan
and creative dishes in the evening.
Pastas and desserts are particularly
successful. There's a choice of
good French and Italian wines.

Les Etoiles

Via Vitelleschi 34. **Map** 3 C2. 🔲 06-689 34 34. **Open** 12:30pm–2:30pm, 7:30pm–10:30pm daily. 🍽 🍴 🎵 🚻 ♿ 🅿 *AE, DC, MC, V, JCB.*
Ⓛ Ⓛ Ⓛ Ⓛ

Located at the top of the Atlante Star hotel *(see p300)*, this rooftop restaurant was completely renovated in 1992, and now includes free valet parking and a separate entrance with a lift leading directly to the restaurant levels. The restaurant and its terraces offer panoramic views of the Rome skyline, including St. Peter's. Speciality dishes include snails with truffles on pecorino cheese, quail's eggs on a bed of rocket with mustard dressing, and *tagliolini* (pasta) with clams and *finferli* (mushrooms).

Andrea

Via Sardegna 28. **Map** 5 C1.
🔲 06-482 18 91, 06-474 05 57.
Open 12:30pm–3pm, 7:30pm–11pm Mon–Fri, 7:45pm–11pm Sat.
Closed 2 weeks Aug, Christmas.
🚻 ♿ 🅿 🎵 🍴 *AE, DC, MC, V, JCB.*
Ⓛ Ⓛ Ⓛ

This congenial, refined restaurant offers a superb array of antipasti, ranging from humble *supplì* (rice croquettes) to regal lobster dishes (try it in *insalata catalana*). Leave room for the impressive seasonal first and second courses and for the delicious desserts. There is an extensive choice of French and Italian wines.

Tullio

Via San Nicola da Tolentino 26.
Map 5 B2. 🔲 06-474 55 60. **Open** 12:30pm–3pm, 7:30pm–11pm Mon–Sat. **Closed** Aug. ♿ 🎵 *AE, DC, MC, V, JCB.* Ⓛ Ⓛ Ⓛ

This genuine Tuscan restaurant is frequented by an enthusiastic clientele for its generous helpings and fair prices. Typical dishes include *porcini* mushrooms in every possible form, *pasta e fagioli*, grilled meat and fish and Florentine steaks – served in agreeable surroundings by courteous, speedy waiters.

Giovanni

Via Marche 67. **Map** 5 B1.
🔲 06-482 18 34. **Open** 12:30pm–3pm, 7:30pm–11pm Sun–Thu, 12:30pm–3pm Fri. **Closed** Aug, Christmas. 🎵 *AE, DC, MC, V.*
Ⓛ Ⓛ Ⓛ

A throng of satisfied regulars crowd this classic, well-established restaurant near Via Veneto. The efficient, reliable service is hard to beat. The place is run along traditional lines by the Sbrega family, with a strong regional influence from Lazio and the Marches. They serve such fresh pasta dishes as *tagliolini all'amatriciana*, vegetable soups, boned chicken with rice, unbeatable roast lamb, *osso buco*, fresh fish and *millefeuilles*. The house wines are good.

George's

Via Marche 7. **Map** 5 B2.
🔲 06-42 08 45 75. **Open** 12:30pm–3pm, 7:30pm pm–midnight (piano bar 2am) Mon–Sat. **Closed** Aug. 🍽 🎵 🚻 🅿 ★ 🍴 *AE, DC, MC, V, JCB.*
Ⓛ Ⓛ Ⓛ Ⓛ

Visit this slightly tarnished survivor from the *dolce vita* era for its nostalgic air of luxurious elegance. The softly illuminated rooms, garden terrace, tinkling piano music and impeccable service provide the perfect foil for George's tempting and expertly prepared international dishes. There is also a good selection of French and Italian wines on offer.

Le Sans Souci

Via Sicilia 20-24. **Map** 5 C1.
🔲 06-482 18 14. **Open** 8pm–midnight Tue–Sun. **Closed** Aug.
🚻 🍽 🎵 🅿 ★ 🍴 *AE, DC, MC, V, JCB.* Ⓛ Ⓛ Ⓛ Ⓛ

This restaurant has overcome a glitzy fame to emerge as a sound exponent of elaborate French and Italian cuisine. The decor is black and gold throughout, with 17th-century gilt mirrors and chandeliers. In the sophisticated anteroom you can drink an apéritif at your leisure and consult the menu and magnificent wine list. As you might expect, the service is eagerly efficient.

La Terrazza

Via Ludovisi 49. **Map** 5 B2.
🔲 06-47 81 21. **Open** noon–3:30pm, 7pm–midnight Mon–Sat. **Closed** 2 weeks Aug, Dec 25–Jan 6. 🚻 🍴 *AE, DC, MC, V, JCB.* Ⓛ Ⓛ Ⓛ Ⓛ

Positioned in the roof garden of the Eden Hotel *(see p301)* this spacious establishment has gained a reputation in its own right. The menu is traditional Italian – in this case a guarantee of quality – and the kitchen is just about as spotless as spotless gets. As you might expect from its location, the views of the city are peerless.

Al Ceppo

Via Panama 2. **Map** 2 F3.
🔲 06-841 96 96. **Open** 12:30pm–3pm, 8pm–11pm Tue–Sun. **Closed** 2 weeks Aug. 🚻 🎵 ♿ 🅿 🅿 *AE, DC, MC, V.* Ⓛ Ⓛ Ⓛ

In 20 years, two sisters from the Marches, Cristina and Marisella Milozzi, have won an affectionate following of regulars in this exclusive, notoriously diffident area of Rome. Patrons are attracted by the consistently reliable food and the hospitable yet refined family atmosphere. The strictly seasonal menu concentrates on traditional dishes with a touch of invention, as well as excellent grilled meats, homemade desserts and Italian wines.

Relais la Piscine dell'Aldrovandi Palace Hotel

Via G Mangili 6. **Map** 2 D4.
🔲 06-321 61 26. **Open** 12:30pm–3pm, 7:30pm–11pm daily. 🍽 🍴 ♿ 🚻 🅿 🎵 ★ 🍴 *AE, DC, MC, V.* Ⓛ Ⓛ Ⓛ Ⓛ

The autonomous restaurant of the Aldrovandi Palace Hotel is especially beautiful in summer, when tables are set on the terrace by the pool. Jean Luc Frenat, the young Breton chef, produces an excellent, typically Mediterranean nouvelle cuisine, using prime meat and fish, vegetables and herbs. This is accompanied by meticulous service, wonderful desserts and a fully comprehensive wine list. Business lunches are a specialty.

Relais le Jardin dell'Hotel Lord Byron

Via Giuseppe de Notaris 5.
Map 2 D4. 🔲 06-322 04 04.
Open 12:30pm–2:30pm, 8pm–10:30pm Mon–Sat. **Closed** Aug. 🍽 🍴 ★ 🍴 *AE, DC, MC, V, JCB.* Ⓛ Ⓛ Ⓛ Ⓛ

For many, this is Rome's greatest restaurant, located in the quiet, exclusive and green area of Parioli. Diners here are undaunted by absolutely top prices, high-class, impeccably correct service, and haute cuisine at its finest. The inspired chef draws predominantly on traditional Italian regional cooking, with exceptionally creative combinations of fruit, herbs and vegetables served with top-quality meats and fish. To finish, there are homemade desserts and pastries; the list of French, Italian and Californian wines offers many outstanding choices.

For key to symbols *see p303.*

Light Meals and Snacks

WHERE SHOULD YOU GO for a casual bite to eat? Rome has the ability to satisfy the all-important stomach at most hours of the day and night. A network of *gelaterie, pasticcerie,* pizzerias, wine bars, *rosticcerie* and *tavole calde* mean that many varieties of good food and drink are always just around the corner.

Start with a classic breakfast at your local stand-up bar: cappuccino and a hot *cornetto* (similar to a croissant). A heavy morning's sightseeing may leave you ready for an apéritif in one of Rome's elegant 19th-century bars, followed by lunch at a wine bar or Roman-style fast-food place. In the afternoon, there are plenty of opportunities for coffee and cakes at a *pasticceria*, while the late-night bars, especially those with tables outside, are a source of entertainment. Here you can sip a drink or linger over the final ice cream of the day.

PIZZERIAS

ROMAN PIZZERIAS are the natural choice for in-formal eating: they are noisy, convivial and fun. Most open only in the evening, when the wood ovens are lit and the embers glow reassuringly up until last orders. Look out for the *Forno a Legna* (wood-burning oven) sign – electric ovens simply don't produce the same results. In the best pizzerias you sit in view of the vast marble slabs where the *pizzaioli* flatten the dough and whip the pizzas in and out of the oven on long-handled peels. The turnover is quick, so you may not be en-couraged to linger.

The running order is straightforward: you might have a *bruschetta* (toasted tomato or garlic bread) to start, some *supplì* (fried rice balls) or some fried zucchini flowers Alternatively, try some *filetti di baccalà* (bat-tered cod filets), or a plate of cannellini beans in oil. Follow this with a *calzone* (folded-over pizza) or the classic Roman pizza – round, thin and crunchy – with various toppings: *napoletana* (tomatoes, anchovies, mozza-rella), *margherita* (without anchovies), *capricciosa* (ham, artichokes, eggs, olives) and anything else the *pizzaiolo* fancies. Draft beer is the classic thing to drink, but wine is always available. You should expect to pay around L15,000 a head for a meal.

The most representative Roman pizzerias, from all points of view, are **Da Baffetto**, which can be located by looking for the line outside, and its offspring, **La Montecarlo**. **Remo** in Testaccio and **Ivo** in Trastevere, where tables line the road in summer, are also typically Roman. Another popular place not to be missed is **Panattoni**, where a huge variety of customers patiently line up for a sidewalk seat on Viale Trastevere in summer or clamor for one of the marble-topped tables (from which the restaurant gets its well known nickname "the mortuary") inside.

ENOTECHE (WINE BARS)

ENOTECHE offer a fine selection of wines from Italy and around the world. They are usually run by experts, eager to share their knowledge about the best combinations of wine and food. Some *enoteche* are simply shops for browsing. Others, like **Achilli al Parlamento** and **Bevitoria Navona**, offer the traditional *mescita* – wine and cham-pagne tasting by the glass, accompanied by snacks and canapés. Their prices are reasonable: about L1,500 for a glass on tap, L3,000 upward for a quality wine, to about L8,000 for champagne. **Vineria Reggio** in Campo de' Fiori is a typical spot for *mescita*, especially at night. Here professionals, residents and tourists alike meet for an apéritif or gather round a table to share a bottle.

For more substantial food for as little as L20,000 to L25,000 a head, try the bistro- or restaurant-style *enoteche*, open from lunch until late. Particularly recommended are the innovative **Cul de Sac**, **Trimani Wine Bar**, the tiny **Il Tajut** serving specialties from Friuli and **Cavour 313**.

BIRRERIE (BEER HOUSES)

ROMAN *BIRRERIE* had their heyday in the early years of the 20th century and many have since closed. However, the few that have survived the competition from subsequent pizzerias and *enoteche* are some of the best: German-style beer houses where you can still enjoy beer and substantial snacks in traditional wood-paneled rooms. The permanently crowded **Fratelli Tempera**, serving classic beer-drinkers' fare, is worth a visit for its authentic turn-of-the-century air of decadence. Another place that attracts Italians and foreigners alike is the **Birreria Viennese/Wiener Bierhaus**, with its excellent Transylvanian specialties, which come heaped gener-ously on wooden plates. If you eat here or in the **Birreria Bavarese**, you'll spend around L30,000 to L50,000. Elsewhere will be cheaper if you want to con-centrate more on drinking.

FAST FOOD

ROME HAS PLENTY of homespun fast-food options for when you need something quick and inexpensive to eat. Slices of freshly baked pizza are available for one or two thousand lire from *pizza al taglio* shops. Many of these places also sell spit-roasted chickens, *supplì* and other traditional pizzeria fare. *Rosticcerie* offer deliciously tasty roast chicken and potatoes, as well as ready-made pasta dishes, cooked vegetables, salads and desserts – useful for picnics or for making a complete take-out meal. For a similarly speedy but sit-down snack, bars with a *tavola calda* (hot table) have the same kind of selection, especially at lunch; one of the largest and most popular is **Il Delfino** at Largo Argentina. Vegetarians should seek out the **Centro Macrobiotico** near Piazza di Spagna. The **McDonald's** hamburger outlet in Piazza di Spagna also offers a good range of fresh mixed salads.

Most *alimentari* (grocery shops) will make you up a *panino* (filled roll). Especially delicious are **Paladini's** hot plain pizza pockets stuffed with choices from the shop's counters; here you can also have a glass of wine. Try one of the region's specialties if you see the sign *Porchetta*: whole aromatic roast pig with crackling, sliced into *rosette* (rolls) or thick country-bread sandwiches – there is a good stall selling these at the tram stop in Viale Carlo Felice opposite San Giovanni in Laterano. At the hole-in-the-wall **Er Buchetto** you can even sit down in relative comfort with a glass of wine. For a really typical Roman snack, make a late-afternoon detour to **Filetti di Baccalà**, which serves, as the name suggests, fried cod fillets.

BARS, CAFÉS AND TEA ROOMS

ROMAN BARS are the city's lifeline: they are places to meet, eat, drink, buy supplies of milk and coffee, make phone calls or use the bathroom. Some of them are small, stand-up, basic one-counter bars for grabbing a quick *cornetto* and cappuccino; others are quite luxurious grandiose affairs doubling as cake shops, ice cream parlors, tea rooms or *tavola calda*, or all of these in one. Most open early at around 7:30am, and close late, particularly on weekends, at around midnight or 2am. In summer, tables cover the available outdoor space, and the fight for a place in the shade begins. Traditionally elegant – and pricey – bars for people-watching are the conveniently located **Rosati** and **Doney**, as well as **Caffè Greco**, the 19th-century haunt of artists, writers and composers *(see p133)*, and the carefully restored **La Caffettiera** at the Pantheon. Another popular and well-established bar is the **Antico Caffè della Pace**. **Caffè Flores** (with piano music) and **Selarum** in Trastevere are recommended for late-night drinks, as is **Zodiaco** on Monte Mario for its panoramic views.

Earlier in the day, Rome's favored meeting places are its tea rooms. **Babington's** *(see p134)* is the place to go for an expensive cup of tea and cakes in genteel surroundings; **Dolci e Doni** is more relaxed. Try a *gran caffè speciale* at the counters of **Sant'Eustachio** or one of Rome's best espressos at **Tazza d'Oro**. **Ciampini al Café du Jardin,** with its garden setting and rooftop views, is unbeatable in summer, particularly at the apéritif hour, as is the **Bar Parnaso** in Parioli.

Museum cafés in Rome are seldom open, and even when they are, few are really worth a visit. A welcome exception, however, is the café of the **Palazzo delle Esposizioni** *(see p164)*, which is open throughout the day. and serves an attractive selection of snacks and drinks.

PASTICCERIE (PASTRY SHOPS)

ON SUNDAY mornings you'll often see Romans emerging from the local *pasticceria* with a beautifully wrapped package. This can contain dainty individual pastries, whole cakes or tarts, traditional Easter *colombe* (doves) or Christmas *panettoni* (huge cakes with raisins and candied peel) all for consumption by large gatherings of friends, relatives or family after lunch. The window displays of Rome's cake shops are often fantastic. These, and the aroma of brewing coffee, might tempt you in for a hot *cornetto* or a brioche in the early morning, a midday *pizzetta* or savory tart, or a choux pastry or fruit tart later in the afternoon.

GELATERIE (ICE CREAM PARLORS)

ICE CREAM *(gelato)* is one of summer's particular delights, and nowhere more so than in Rome. Every well-equipped bar has its tubs of homemade ice cream, and in the *gelaterie* the choice is endless – water ices made with a phenomenal variety of fruit; lemon and coffee *granite* (crushed ice); as well as more exotic ice cream specialties such as rice, *zuppa inglese* (English trifle), *zabaglione, tiramisù* and After Eight.

Choose as many varieties as the size of your cone or cup will hold, topped with cream *(panna),* and then go for a stroll or take a break and enjoy an ornate creation with all the trimmings served to you at a table. *Gelaterie* are open all day until late at night, when they become evening entertainment.

Tre Scalini in Piazza Navona is a famous spot for enjoying the expensive yet so heavenly chocolate *tartufo,* while a summer evening in EUR, especially with children, nearly always ends in a trip to **Giolitti**, known historically for ice cream; try also the strategically placed, crowded original parlor near the Pantheon *(see p109),* also serving coffee and pastries. In the same area is the popular **Gelateria della Palma**.

Adults may prefer to pick their nighttime treat at **Chalet del Lago**, again in EUR, while sitting beside the lake. If you happen across a small kiosk bearing the sign *Grattachecche* (most likely in Trastevere and Testaccio), try one of Rome's oldest traditions – ice grated on the spot and enlivened with a variety of classic flavorings.

DIRECTORY

FORUM

Pizzerias
Alle Carrette
Via della Carrette 19,
off Via della Madonna
dei Monti. **Map** 5 B5.

PIAZZA DELLA ROTONDA

Pizzerias
Barroccio
Via dei Pastini 13.
Map 4 F4 & 12 D2.

Er Faciolaro
Via dei Pastini 123.
Map 4 F4 & 12 D2.

Wine Bars
Achilli al Parlamento
Via dei Prefetti 15.
Map 4 F3 & 12 D1.

Corsi
Via del Gesù 88.
Map 4 F4 & 12 E3.

Spiriti
Via di Sant'Eustachio 5.
Map 4 F4 & 12 D3.

Bars, Cafés and Tea Rooms
La Caffettiera
Piazza di Pietra 65.
Map 4 F3 & 12 E2.

Camilloni
Piazza Sant'Eustachio 54.
Map 4 F4 & 12 D3.

Ciampini
Piazza S. Lorenzo in Lucina
29. **Map** 4 F3 & 12 D1.

Sant'Eustachio
Piazza Sant'Eustachio 82.
Map 4 F4 & 12 D3.

Tazza d'Oro
Via degli Orfani 82/84.
Map 4 F4 & 12 D2.

Teichner
Piazza S. Lorenzo in Lucina
17. **Map** 4 F3 & 12 E1.

Ice Cream Parlors
Fiocco di Neve
Via del Pantheon 51.
Map 4 F4 & 12 D2.

Gelateria della Palma
Via della Maddalena 20.
Map 4 F3 & 12 D2.

Giolitti
Via Uffici del Vicario 40.
Map 4 F3 & 12 D2.

PIAZZA NAVONA

Pizzerias
Da Baffetto
Via del Governo Vecchio
114. **Map** 4 E4 & 11 B3.

Corallo
Via del Corallo 10.
Map 4 E4 & 11 B3.

La Montecarlo
Vicolo Savelli 12/13.
Map 4 E4 & 11 C3.

Wine Bars
Bevitoria Navona
Piazza Navona 72.
Map 4 E4 & 11 C2.

Cul de Sac
Piazza Pasquino 73.
Map 4 E4 & 11 C3.

Fast Food
Paladini
Via del Governo Vecchio
28/29. **Map** 4 E4 & 11 B3.

Bars, Cafés and Tea Rooms
Antico Caffè della Pace
Via della Pace 5.
Map 4 E4 & 11 C3.

Pastry Shops
Bella Napoli
Corso Vittorio Emanuele II
246. **Map** 4 E4 & 11 B3.

Ice Cream Parlors
Tre Scalini
Piazza Navona 28.
Map 4 E4 & 11 C3.

PIAZZA DI SPAGNA

Pizzerias
La Capricciosa
Largo dei Lombardi 8.
Map 4 F2.

Il Leoncino
Via del Leoncino 28.
Map 4 F2.

Wine Bars
Antica Enoteca di Via
delle Croce
Via della Croce 76B.
Map 5 A2.

Buccone
Via di Ripetta 19.
Map 4 F1.

Beer Houses
Birreria Bavarese
Via Vittoria 47. **Map** 5 A2.

Birreria Viennese/
Wiener Bierhaus
Via della Croce 21.
Map 5 A2.

Fast Food
Centro Macrobiotico
Via della Vite 14.
Map 5 A3.

Fior Fiore
Via della Croce 17/18.
Map 5 A2.

McDonald's
Piazza di Spagna 46.
Map 5 A2.

Bars, Cafés and Tea Rooms
Babington's Tea Rooms
Piazza di Spagna 23.
Map 5 A2.

Caffè Greco
Via Condotti 86.
Map 5 A2.

Ciampini al Café
du Jardin
Viale Trinità dei Monti.
Map 5 A2.

Dolci e Doni
Via delle Carrozze 85A.
Map 4 F2.

Rosati
Piazza del Popolo 5.
Map 4 F1.

CAMPO DE' FIORI

Wine Bars
Bottega del Vino
da Bleve
Via Santa Maria del Pianto
9A/11.
Map 4 F5 & 12 D5.

Il Goccetto
Via dei Banchi Vecchi 14.
Map 4 D4 & 11 B3.

Vineria Reggio
Piazza Campo de' Fiori 15.
Map 4 E4 & 11 C4.

Fast Food
Il Delfino
Corso Vittorio
Emanuele II 67.
Map 4 F4 & 12 D4.

Filetti di Baccalà
Largo dei Librari 88.
Map 4 E5 & 11 C4.

Da Giovanni
Piazza Campo
de' Fiori 39.
Map 4 E4 & 11 C4.

Bars, Cafés and Tea Rooms
Alberto Pica
Via della Seggiola 12.
Map 4 F5 & 12 D5.

Caffè Flores
Lungotevere
dei Vallati 25/27.
Map 4 E5 & 11 C5.

Pastry Stores
Bernasconi
Largo di Torre
Argentina 1.
Map 4 F4 & 12 D4.

La Dolceroma
Via del Portico
d'Ottavia 20B.
Map 4 F5 & 12 E5.

Il Forno del Ghetto
Via del Portico
d'Ottavia 2.
Map 4 F5 & 12 E5.

QUIRINAL

Pizzerias
Est! Est! Est!
Via Principe Amedeo 4A.
Map 6 D3.

I Rioni
Via dei SS. Quattro
Coronati 24.
Map 9 B1.

Wine Bars
Cavour 313
Via Cavour 313.
Map 5 B5.

Beer Houses
Fratelli Tempera
Via San Marcello 19.
Map 5 A4 & 12 F3.

Fast Food
Bar del Palazzo del Yogobar
Via Mazzarino 8–10.
Map 5 B4.

Er Buchetto
Via del Viminale 2.
Map 5 C3.

McDonald's
Piazza della Repubblica 40.
Map 5 C3.

Nadia e Davide
Via Milano 33.
Map 5 B4.

Bars, Cafés and Tea Rooms
Palazzo delle Esposizioni
Via Milano 9.
Map 5 B4.

Pastry Shops
Dagnino
Via Vittorio Emanuele Orlando 75.
Map 5 C2.

TERMINI

Pizzerias
La Bruschetta
Via Ancona 35.
Map 6 D1.

Formula Uno
Via degli Equi 13.
Map 6 F4.

Le Maschere
Via degli Umbri 16.
Map 6 F4.

Wine Bars
Trimani Wine Bar
Via Cernaia 37B.
Map 6 D2.

Beer Houses
Rive Gauchez
Via dei Sabelli 43.
Map 6 F4.

ESQUILINE

Beer Houses
Marconi
Via di Santa Prassede 9C.
Map 6 D4.

Fast Food
Cottini
Via Merulana 286.
Map 6 D4.

Palazzo del Freddo di Giovanni Fassi
Via Principe Eugenio 65/67.
Map 6 E5.

Bars, Cafés and Tea Rooms
Ristoro della Salute
Piazza del Colosseo 2.
Map 9 A1.

LATERAN

Fast Food
Viale Carlo Felice Porchetta Stall
Viale Carlo Felice.
Map 10 D1.

Ice Cream Parlors
Premiate Gelaterie Fantasia
Via La Spezia 100/102.
Map 10 E1.

AVENTINE

Pizzerias
Remo
Piazza Santa Maria Liberatrice 44.
Map 8 D3.

Wine Bar
Palombi
Piazza Testaccio 48.
Map 8 D3.

TRASTEVERE

Pizzerias
Almacrì
Via F. Benaglia 3.
Map 7 B4.

Dar Poeta
Vicolol del Bologna 45
Map 4 E5 & 11 B5.

Ivo
Via di San Francesco a Ripa 158.
Map 7 C1.

Panattoni
Viale Trastevere 53.
Map 7 C1.

Ar Popi Popi
Via delle Fratte di Trastevere 45.
Map 7 C1.

Piccola Montecarlo
Via Dandolo 26.
Map 7 C2.

Wine Bars
Il Cantiniere di Santa Dorotea
Via di S. Dorotea 9.
Map 4 D5 & 11 B5.

Ferrara
Via del Moro 1/A.
Map 7 C1.

Fast Food
McDonald's
Piazza Sonnino 39/40.
Map 8 D1.

Bars, Cafés and Tea Rooms
Selarum
Via dei Fienaroli 12.
Map 7 C1.

Pastry Shops
Valzani
Via del Moro 37 B.
Map 7 C1.

Ice Cream Parlors
La Fonte della Salute
Via Cardinale Marmaggi 2/4/6. **Map** 7 C1.

Sacchetti
Piazza Santa Maria Cosima 61. **Map** 7 C1.

VATICAN

Pizzerias
Pizzeria San Marco
Via Tacito 29.
Map 4 D2.

Il Tempio della Pizza
Viale Giulio Cesare 91.
Map 3 C1.

Wine Bars
Il Simposio di Piero Costantini
Piazza Cavour 16.
Map 4 E2.

Beer Houses
Penny Lane
Via dei Gracchi 35.
Map 3 C2.

VIA VENETO

Wine Bars
Semidivino
Via Alessandria 230.
Map 6 D1.

Bars, Cafés and Tea Rooms
Doney
Via Veneto 145.
Map 5 B2.

EUR

Fast Food
McDonald's
Piazzale Don Luigi Sturzo 21/22.

Bars, Cafés and Tea Rooms
Chalet del Lago
Lake, EUR.

Ice Cream Parlors
Giolitti
Casina dei Tre Laghi, Viale Oceania 90.

FURTHER AFIELD

Wine Bars
Guerrini
Viale Regina Margherita 205/207.

Il Tajut
Via Albenga 44.
Map 10 E3.

Fast Food
Svizzera Siciliana
Piazza Pio XI 10/11.

Bars, Cafés and Tea Rooms
Bar Parnaso
Piazza delle Muse 22.
Map 2 E2.

Il Cigno
Viale Parioli 16.
Map 2 E3.

Duse
Via Eleonora Duse 1E.
Map 2 F2.

Pannocchi
Via Bergamo 56.
Map 6 D1.

San Filippo
Via di Villa San Filippo 8/10. **Map** 2 F2.

Zodiaco
Viale Parco Mellini 90.

Pastry Shops
Euclide
Via F. Civinini 119.
Map 2 D3.

SHOPS AND MARKETS

ROME HAS BEEN a thriving center for design and cosmopolitan shopping since ancient times. In the heyday of the empire, the finest craftspeople were drawn to Rome, and artifacts and produce of all kinds, including gold, furs, wine and slaves, were imported from far-flung corners of the empire to service the needs of the wealthy Roman population.

Shopping in Rome today in many ways reflects this diverse tradition. Italian designers have

Window shopping in Rome, an absorbing pastime

an international reputation for their luxuriously chic style in fashion, knitwear and leather goods (especially shoes and handbags), as well as in interior design, fabrics, ceramics and glass. The artisan tradition of fine workmanship is strong, and the love of design is apparent in the smallest items. Rome is not a city for bargains (though it often offers better value than Florence or Milan), but even window shopping is a memorable event.

BEST BUYS

LEATHER GOODS of all kinds, including shoes and bags, are a good buy here. Ready-to-wear Italian designer clothes are not cheap, but they are certainly less expensive than designer fashion in other countries. Armani jeans are a good example (see p327). You are also likely to find designer lighting fixtures at lower prices here. Both modern and traditional Italian ceramics and handicrafts can be very beautifully made, and, if you have time to wander around the back streets, unusual unique gifts can often be found.

SALES

SALE TIME (saldi) is from mid-July to mid-September and the period from just before Christmas to the first week in March. Top designers

(see p326) slash prices by half, but their clothes are still very expensive even then. Good bargains can be found in the young designer shops (see p327), and good-quality large shoe sizes are sold very cheaply (most Italians have small feet). Both of the Cesari shops (see pp 328 and 333) are well known for their sales. In general, though, sales in Rome do not offer huge discounts.

Both the original and the sale price should be quoted on each reduced item. Liquidazioni (closing-down sales) are usually genuine and can sometimes be worth investigating. However, other signs in shop windows, such as Vendite Promozionali (special introductory prices) and Sconti (discounts) are often only lures to get you into the shop. The sign on the door saying Entrata Libera means "Browsers Welcome."

Antiques at Acanto (see p336)

WHEN TO SHOP

SHOPS ARE GENERALLY open from 9am to 1pm and from 3:30 to 7:30pm (4 to 8pm in the summer months). Some of the shops in the center stay open all day from 10:30am to 7:30pm. Most shops are closed on Sunday (except immediately before Christmas). Shops are also closed on Monday morning, apart from most food stores, which close on Thursday afternoons in winter and Saturday afternoons in summer.

August brings the city to a virtual standstill as Roman families escape the heat and go to the sea or the mountains. Signs saying Chiuso per Ferie (Closed for Vacation) appear everywhere in the shops. Most shops close for at least two weeks around August 15, the national holiday.

Flower stalls in Piazza Campo de' Fiori (see p338)

SHOPPING ETIQUETTE

APART FROM a few department stores, most Roman shops are small, specializing in just one field. Browsing at leisure may at first seem daunting if you are used to large shopping centers. Customers will almost always receive better attention if they dress smartly – the emphasis on *fare la bella figura* (making a good impression) is taken seriously.

Stylish leather gloves on display

Sizes are not always uniform, so it's wise to try clothes on if possible before buying, since refunds and exchanges are not usually given.

HOW TO PAY

MOST SHOPS now accept all the major credit cards, whose signs are displayed on the shop window. Some will also accept foreign currency, though the exchange rate may not be good. When you make a purchase, you are bound by Italian law to leave the shop with a *ricevuta fiscale* (receipt). You can try asking for a discount if paying cash, and you may be lucky, though many shops have a *prezzi fissi* (fixed prices) sign.

VAT EXEMPTION

VALUE-ADDED TAX – VAT (IVA in Italy) – ranges from 12% on clothing to 35% on luxury items such as jewelry and furs. Marked or advertised prices normally include the IVA. It is possible for non–European Union citizens to obtain an IVA refund for individual purchases that exceed L650,000, but be prepared for a long and bureaucratic process. The simplest method is to shop at a place displaying the "Euro Free Tax" sign.

Present your passport when you make your purchase and fill in a form from the shop; the shop then deducts the IVA, gives you a copy of the form, and sends their copy to the Euro Free Tax Organization in Milan, which will then deal with the paperwork.

If you wish to buy something from a shop that is not part of the "Euro Free Tax" scheme, you must get the Italian Customs to stamp the vendor's receipt at your departure, showing them the purchased article, and then mail the stamped receipt back to the shop, which should then send you a refund.

Mercato delle Stampe *(see p338)*

DEPARTMENT STORES AND SHOPPING CENTERS

DEPARTMENT STORES, known as *grandi magazzini*, are few and far between in Rome. **La Rinascente** and **Coin** are good for ready-to-wear clothes, household linens and haberdashery and have well-stocked perfume counters. La Rinascente gives 10% discount to tourists on perfumes and cosmetics if you show your passport. The **Standa** and **Upim** chain stores offer moderately priced medium-quality clothes and household goods.

Another alternative for the zealous shopper is to head for one of Rome's two shopping centers. **Cinecittà Due Centro Commerciale**, built in 1988, offers around 100 shops plus bars, banks,

Bargains in Via Sannio *(see p339)*

and restaurants within easy reach of the center by Metro (line A to Cinecittà). An even bigger center, called **I Granai**, has now opened in Via Laurentina, reachable by Metro (line B to Laurentina).

Cinecittà Due Centro Commerciale
Via Palmiro Togliatti 2.
📞 06-722 09 10.

Coin
Piazzale Appio 7. **Map** 10 D2.
📞 06-708 00 20.

I Granai
Via del Rigamonti 100.
📞 06-51 95 57 77.

La Rinascente
Via del Corso 189. **Map** 5 A3 & 12 E2.
📞 06-679 76 91.

Piazza Fiume. **Map** 6 D1.
📞 06-884 12 31.

Standa
Via Cola di Rienzo 153. **Map** 4 D2.
📞 06-324 32 83.

Viale Trastevere 62. **Map** 7 C2.
📞 06-581 60 36.

Via Appia Nuova 181. **Map** 10 D2.
📞 06-702 48 96.

Upim
Via del Tritone 172. **Map** 5 A3.
📞 06-678 33 36.

Via Nazionale 211. **Map** 5 C3.
📞 06-48 45 02.

Via Gioberti 64. **Map** 6 D4.
📞 06-446 55 79.

Craftsmen near Piazza Navona

Rome's Best: Shopping Streets and Markets

THE MOST INTERESTING shops in Rome are in the old center, so shopping is easy to combine with sightseeing. The shops are often housed in medieval or Renaissance buildings, and their window displays can be exquisite. Just like shopkeepers in the past, today's traders tend to specialize in one type of merchandise. Street names often refer to the old tradesmen: locksmiths in Via dei Chiavari, leather jerkin makers in Via dei Giubbonari and chair makers in Via dei Sediari. Today, antiques merchants have taken over from the rosary sellers on Via dei Coronari. The top names in fashion and modern design dominate the Via Condotti area, and the artisan-craftsperson tradition is still strong around Campo de' Fiori and Piazza Navona.

Via dei Coronari

Art Nouveau and antiques enthusiasts will love browsing in the shops that line this charming street just northwest of Piazza Navona. But be prepared for high prices as most of the items are imported.

Via Cola di Rienzo

Situated close to the Vatican Museums, this long wide street has the finest food shops and is also good for clothes, books and gifts.

Via del Pellegrino

Bookstores and art shops abound here next to working artisans in the historic center. Don't miss the mirror-lined alley near Campo de' Fiori.

Via dei Cappellari

This narrow medieval street is a great place for watching furniture restorers and other artisans plying their crafts in the open air.

Porta Portese

You can buy anything from antiques to a tin whistle at Trastevere's Sunday-morning flea market. (See p339.)

Via Margutta
Upscale antiques shops mix with genteel restaurants on this peaceful cobbled street.

Via del Babuino
This street is renowned for designer furniture, lighting and glass, as well as interesting antiques and fashion shops.

DESIGNER SHOPPING

All the well-known stars of the Italian fashion scene, plus exclusive jewelers, gift shops, shoe designers and tailors, are concentrated in this cluster of chic and stylish shopping streets by the Spanish Steps *(see pp326–31)*. Romans love to stroll here in the early evening.

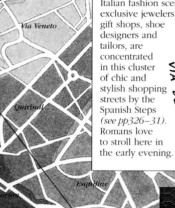

MISSONI
GIORGIO ARMANI
TRUSSARDI
valentino
GUCCI
FENDI
MaxMara
VIA CONDOTTI
VIA BORGOGNONA
VIA FRATTINA
VIA DEL CORSO
PIAZZA DI SPAGNA

Via Veneto
Quirinal
Capitol
Esquiline
Forum
Palatine
Lateran
Caracalla

Via Borgognona
Crowds flock here to buy, or just gaze at, high-fashion clothes, shoes, leather bags and other accessories.

| 0 meters | 500 |
| 0 yards | 500 |

Testaccio Market
A visual feast of fruit and vegetables greets the eye in this lively market. (See p338.)

Men's and Women's Fashion

I**TALY IS ONE** of the leading lights in high-class fashion, or *alta moda*. Many of the most famous designers are based in Milan, but Rome is home to a cluster of sophisticated and internationally distinguished fashion houses. There is also a wonderful selection of *alta moda* shops. Boutiques displaying an eclectic mix of designer goods are next door to prestigious showrooms devoted to single collections. But even those unable to splurge on genuine designer wear will delight in a stroll down the exclusive streets that radiate out from the Piazza di Spagna, where the window displays are not merely creative but truly spectacular.

Custom-made fashions are beyond most budgets, but designers also offer ready-to-wear alternatives in their boutiques. While not cheap, these provide style at a price far less than that of a tailor-made garment.

– its Roman showrooms have exclusive rights to the original couture collections of avant-garde stylists such as Dolce & Gabbana and Moschino, plus Europeans such as Jean Paul Gaultier. **MaxMara** also has a number of branches here. Chic suits and separates are the mainstays of this popular label. The quality of fabric and finish is superb, and, with suits available for around L1,000,000, its prices are much lower than those of other *alta moda* designers' ready-to-wear lines.

WOMEN'S HIGH FASHION

R**OME'S MOST** famous designer internationally is probably **Valentino**. However, one of the first houses to make a name for Roman fashion was **Sorelle Fontana**. This was *the* salon to be dressed by during the 1950s heyday of Rome's *dolce vita*. Sorelle Fontana has been dressing high society since the 1930s and stocks a wide selection of ready-to-wear clothes and accessories.

Fendi occupies a large tract of the fashion street Via Borgognona. Fendi made its name with high-fashion furs, then branched out into leather goods, accessories and ready-to-wear, collaborating with Karl Lagerfeld, who designed the coveted double-F logo that emblazons its very collectible products. Third-generation family members design the younger, less expensive Fendissime line.

For well over a decade, **Laura Biagiotti** has reigned as Rome's queen of discreet, conservative couture. From her headquarters in a castle just outside Rome, she designs a range of timelessly elegant knitwear and silk separates for women who don't want to sacrifice style for comfort. She is famous for her use of cashmere and white as well as her creative use of fabrics and quality of finish. Her flagship showroom in Via Borgognona stocks her complete collection, which now includes hosiery,

perfumes, swimwear and leather goods. Her scarves make wonderful presents and are often reduced in price during sales; other items from previous collections are available in the shop all year round at very good discounts.

Other internationally known Rome-based designers include **Renato Balestra**, who produces tailored suits and glamorous evening-wear and **Roberto Capucci**, who uses wonderful textures and fabrics in classy suits. **Mila Schön**'s specialty is dramatic eveningwear.

Other luminaries of Italian fashion who have shops in Rome include **Giorgio Armani**, **Gianni Versace** and **Trussardi**. A rising star in ready-to-wear is **Genny**. Based in Ancona, the Genny design team produces some classic, elegant and always stylish collections.

If you're looking for clothes from unconventional designers, **Gente** is the place to go

MEN'S TAILORS AND DESIGNER WEAR

I**TALIAN MEN** are every bit as fashion conscious as the women, and there is no shortage of choice in Rome for the well-dressed man. Suits generally begin at around L1,000,000, jackets at L750,000 and trousers at L250,000.

Most of the "star" designers of women's *alta moda* have a shop for men, like **Valentino Uomo**, **Gianfranco Ferrè** and **Versus by Versace**. The designs are generally less dramatic than the women's, with the accent on understated sophistication and casual sportiness. Valentino's distinctive monogrammed accessories are relatively affordable.

Battistoni is probably the most prestigious designer concentrating on menswear. Giorgio Battistoni and family's fine custom-made shirts and suits have been in demand with film stars and high society for 50 years. **Etro** sells

---

VALENTINO

One of the high priests of Italian fashion, **Valentino Garavani** opened the doors of his Roman atelier in 1959 to a distinguished clientele that included Sophia Loren, Audrey Hepburn and Jackie Kennedy, and has never looked back. He has created some of the most dramatic and flattering evening dresses of the last

three decades. In the 1970s, he began designing ready-to-wear lines for both men and women alongside his *alta moda* collections, and you can now find his very distinctive "V" logo on a wide range of accessories. Valentino's headquarters are in a huge palazzo in Piazza Mignanelli, and he also has a separate ready-to-wear boutique nearby (*see p330*).

classically cut clothes and accessories for men and women in exotic Italian-designed printed fabrics.

Ermenegildo Zenga is housed in a Baroque palazzo setting offers elegant ready-to-wear, and the master tailor Peppino Scarapazzi will also make to measure. **Davide Cenci** has been a mecca those in search of the English country gentleman look since 1926. **Brioni** offers traditional tailor-made and their own ready-to-wear men's clothing. **Trussardi** sells beautifully tailored classics, and **Polidori Uomo** offers sober classics custom-made or ready-to-wear, from its own gorgeous tweeds and wools. **Testa** has impeccably tailored suits that appeal to the younger set, and **Enzo Ceci** is popular for ready-to-wear *alta moda* designs. **Degli Effetti** stocks more avant-garde designers, such as Romeo Gigli and Jean Paul Gaultier.

YOUNG DESIGNER WEAR

THERE IS A HUGE choice for the young. Top designers Valentino and Armani offer their leading fashions translated into more affordable lines at **Oliver** and **Emporio Armani** (Armani jeans are a very good buy at about L100,000). Fendi has its Fendissime line, and Max-Mara's Penny Black label can be found in **Max & Co** branches. Targeted at the younger set, these are good places to pick up stylish, sporty numbers. **Timberland** is another very popular casual label. Average prices are in the region of L100,000 for a shirt, L400,000 for raincoats, L800,000 for suits.

Energie is a big hit and has some of the best window displays in Rome. Teenagers flock here for jeans and T-shirts. **Aria**, **Diesel** and **Box 233** are also very popular these days.

Eventi represents the more avant-garde styles – *dark*, as they call it here – fusing Gothic, New Age and punk influences, which can result in some outrageous window creations. **Luna e L'altra** and

Maga Morgana offers trendy unconventional designer clothes in a pleasant, friendly atmosphere.

HIGH STREET FASHION

ROME IS NOT a good place to look for everyday wear, since there is a distinct lack of mid-price shops bridging the huge gap between the dazzlingly priced *alta moda* designer exclusives and the ultracheap goods sold in markets *(see pp338–9)*. Lower-budget shops do exist, but quality is often poor. If you have the stamina, you may find a bargain along Via del Corso, Via del Tritone, Via Nazionale, Via Cavour, Via Cola di Rienzo, Via Ottaviano or Via dei Giubbonari.

The most convenient places to shop are department stores such as La Rinascente, Standa and Upim *(see p323)*. They may not sound exciting, but you can browse at leisure and find attractive things. It's also worth trying shops mentioned under "Young Designer Wear" – particularly the *alta moda* designers' cheaper lines, such as **Emporio Armani** and **Max & Co**. At **Discount dell'Alta Moda** and **Discount System** you can find end-of-season designer labels at 50% less than the boutique prices. **Scala Quattordici** is a good place to buy simple linen dresses made by the owner. And while you don't need to come to Rome to shop at **Benetton**, there are many shops here which sell the authentic garments in their universal colors.

KNITWEAR

KNITWEAR is a particular strength in Italian design, and in Rome there are plenty of specialist shops. **Laura Biagiotti** is celebrated for her luxurious cashmere separates, and **Missoni Sport** and **Missoni Uomo/Donna** for spectacular kaleidoscopic patterns and colors.

Krizia no longer has a shop in Rome, however, its sophisticated knitwear is available from **Liz**.

Choses de Cachemire has cashmere cardigans, pullovers and knitted suits. Other shops, such as the **Luisa Spagnoli** outlets, offer a wider selection, including lower-priced items.

LINGERIE

THIS IS ANOTHER Italian specialty excelling in both style and quality, with lines such as La Perla exported world-wide. Lingerie is traditionally sold in leading household linen shops *(see p333)* – **Cesari**, for example, is La Perla's main outlet in Rome. There are also boutiques specializing in lingerie and swimwear.

Liberti has a range of swimwear that's ideal for Italian beaches, as well as lingerie and women's night attire. **Brighenti** is said to be where film stars go for their lingerie. **Tomassini** has original designs by Luisa Romagnoli. **Schostal** has more traditional underwear, with a very good men's section.

SECONDHAND CLOTHES

THOSE WHO are willing to browse will find a wide variety of secondhand clothes, whether inspired by a collector's interest in vintage clothes or a low budget. Apart from Via Sannio and Porta Portese markets *(see p339)*, which have many secondhand clothes stalls, the mecca is Via del Governo Vecchio. Among the best shops in this ancient street off Campo de' Fiori are **Mai Visto**, with a range of leather jackets in every color, as well as clothes from the 1970s onwards, and **Moon**, which has mostly 1920s dresses and some hats and jewelry.

Le Gallinelle offers a marvelous selection of period hats and sells both second-hand and vintage clothes. At **Via dei Chiavari 40** you can find smart clothes dating from the 1920s onward, and owner Solange also does some dressmaking on the premises and sells at reasonable prices. Via del Pellegrino is also a good street for shops selling second-hand clothes.

Shoes and Accessories

ITALY'S LEATHER INDUSTRY is renowned all over the world, and shoes, bags and belts are a good buy in Rome. Accessories in general are not just an afterthought but an integral part of an outfit for the well-dressed Roman. The choice of stylish jewelry, scarves, ties and other accessories is excellent.

SHOES

ROME IS FULL of shoe stores, ranging from high-quality stores in the Via Condotti area (where prices tend to start at L250,000) to the more economical shops around the Trevi fountain, and every big market has its bargain shoe stalls on its fringes.

Probably the best-known shop is **Ferragamo** – one of the world's top shoe stores. It stocks classic yet fashion-conscious shoes, as well as women's clothing and leather goods – the silk signature scarves are quite a feature.

Fratelli Rossetti is a close contender for the number one position. Founded by brothers Renzo and Renato over 30 years ago, this company produces classic men's shoes and beautiful, dressy low-heeled shoes for women that reflect the most up-to-the-minute trends. Along with **Campanile** in Via Condotti it represents the epitome of elegance. Its prices, of course, are sky-high but why not buy something small, and at least you'll have the bag! **Bruno Magli**, Bologna's well-known star, has dressy patent-leather pumps and other classic styles.

Rome's own **Raphael Salato** has three extremely elegant, high-priced shops: his shoes are genuine masterpieces of craftsmanship, and many are made of intricately embroidered leather.

Carlotto Rio is one of the more long-lived shoe shops in Rome, having been in business for over a decade, but it can't compete with **Domus**, which opened in 1938. Carlotto Rio sells made-to-measure footwear for both men and women, particularly shoes for special occasions, and also makes bags to customers specifications.

Domus sells a selection of high-quality footwear, specializing in classic shoes for women. They also stock a limited range of bags. **De Bach** has colorful shoe styles for women.

Via Frattina also has other, more moderately-priced shoe stores such as **Pollini,** which makes boots and bags for both men and women in trendy and imaginative styles. **Fausto Santini** stocks original, colorful designs for the younger set at more reasonable prices. The same goes for **Cervone**, which specializes in highly colorful women's shoes, **Borino** stocks simple and elegant, low-heeled designs. The **Mr Boots** chain of shops stock a wide range of trendy boots and casual shoes for men and women, while **Dominici** sells witty, smart and affordable footwear for women.

LEATHER BAGS AND ACCESSORIES

THE MOST FAMOUS of Rome's leather shops is trendy to-the-nth **Gucci**, a dandy's paradise selling shoes, suit-cases, handbags, wallets, belts and other accessories. It has a fashion boutique for men and women and is well known for its silk ties and scarves. **Fendi** also has exquisite leather goods as well as some lower-priced lines in synthetic materials and a range of gift items. Although their famous "stripe" line leather-finished synthetic handbags cost as much as L250,000 (and their all-leather ones start at L300,000), at least they are cheaper to buy here than abroad. **Skin** and **Ginocchi**, both situated in the Via Sistina area, are also quite pricey. Located a short walk to the south of Skin and Ginocchi, near the

Trevi Fountain, is **La Sella**. It sell all things leather, including a range of shoes, bags, purses and belts.

Valextra has high-quality, fairly traditional briefcases, handbags, wallets and purses from Milan.

Mandarina Duck's brightly colored fabric bags and line of luggage are very much in fashion and make an attractive (and vegetarian) alternative to the more traditional leather styles.

There are also some great places to buy artisan leather-work. **Sirni** is at the top end of the scale with elegant bags and briefcases made in a workshop at the back of the shop.

For a more unusual men's present, try **La Cravatta** in Trastevere. In addition to their selection of classy hand-made ties, they also manufacture ties to meet customers specifications. You can choose the design, material, length, and the shape of tie to create the perfect gift.

CLASSIC JEWELRY

WHAT CARTIER is to Paris, Tiffany & Co. is to New York and Asprey's is to London, **Bulgari** is to Rome. This internationally revered jeweler's has passers-by glued to the windows gazing at its large fat gemstones. These "windows" are rather curious small boxes inserted into a wall with one or two pieces of jewelry in each of them, which adds to the feeling of looking at precious items in a case at a museum. Bulgari's watches, especially the men's, are popular and very elegant, as are the famous mesh necklaces. It specializes in large, colorful stones in High Renaissance-style settings but also produces a selection of contemporary designs. This was one of Andy Warhol's favorite shops, and it is definitely the most palatial shop on Via Condotti. Inside, the shop's atmosphere is one of almost religious awe and contemplation.

Buccellati is an offshoot of the famous Florentine dynasty, which was begun by Mario Buccellati in the 1920s and patronized by the poet Gabriele D'Annunzio. Its delicately engraved designs are inspired by the Italian Renaissance, and are real classics displaying superb craftsmanship.

Ansuini designs are fashionable yet classic, with strong, imaginative themes being introduced for each new collection. **Massoni**, founded in 1790, is one of Rome's oldest jewelry houses. Its refined one-of-a-kind pieces and brooches are quite outstanding. At **Moroni Gioielli** you will also find imaginative, unique pieces of the highest-quality workmanship. **Petocchi**, which was jeweler to the former Italian monarchy (1861–1946), the House of Savoy, has both traditional and contemporary styles on display.

Peroso is an old-fashioned store that has been going since 1891 and specializes in antique jewelry and silverware. **Boncompagni Sturni** sells traditional designs with the emphasis on quality and craftsmanship. You have to ring the bell to be admitted to both of these stores, and they are extremely expensive.

COSTUME JEWELRY

FOR LESS conventional tastes, there are several shops selling innovative, avant-garde pieces, often using semi-precious metals and stones. **Via dei Coronari 193** is worth trying. **Delettré** produces bold, unique designs influenced by Art Deco styles. You are as likely to find rock crystal here as diamonds. Their logo of a crescent moon and five stars was specially designed by Karl Lagerfeld.

Tempi Moderni has an interesting collection of Art Deco and Liberty period jewelry. You can also find some nice pieces from the 1920s and 1930s in Cose Cosi (*see p336*). **Bozart** is the place for trendy, flashy costume jewelry. **Siragusa** puts beautiful 3rd- and 4th-century BC beads and coins into handmade gold chains, in a museum-like shop just off the Piazza di Spagna.

TRADITIONAL GOLDSMITHS AND SILVERSMITHS

THE MAINSTAY of Rome's jewelry industry is still the traditional artisan goldsmith and silversmith, working to order in tiny studio workshops. These are concentrated in the old Jewish Ghetto area, Campo de' Fiori, Ponte Sisto near Via Giulia, and Montepietà (where the pawnbrokers live). Artisan jewelry can also be found in Via dei Coronari, Via dell'Orso, Via del Pellegrino. The jewelers create individual pieces to their own designs and have often learned their profession from their parents and grandparents. They also do repair work, or take old gold jewelry, melt it down and make it into something to suit you. **Oddi e Seghetti** produces some traditional artisan jewelry and always works to customers' commissions.

GLOVES, HATS AND HOSIERY

IF YOU'RE LOOKING for top quality, you will find an expensive line of gloves and scarves at **Merola**. **Di Cori** and **Sermoneta** stock every imaginable kind of glove. **Catello d'Auria** specializes in gloves and hosiery. **Borsalino** is the place for hats. **Calza e Calze** has the best range of hosiery in Rome – the friendly staff will serve you with almost any color or pattern of tights and stockings that you could wish for.

SIZE CHART

For Australian sizes follow British and American convention.

Children's clothing

Italian	2-3	4-5	6-7	8-9	10-11	12	14	14+ (years)
British	2-3	4-5	6-7	8-9	10-11	12	14	14+ (years)
American	2-3	4-5	6-6x	7-8	10		12	14	16 (size)

Children's shoes

Italian	24	25½	27	28	29	30	32	33	34
British	7	8	9	10	11	12	13	1	2
American	7½	8½	9½	10½	11½	12½	13½	1½	2½

Women's dresses, coats and skirts

Italian	38	40	42	44	46	48	50
British	8	10	12	14	16	18	20
American	6	8	10	12	14	16	18

Women's blouses and sweaters

Italian	81	84	87	90	93	96	99 (cms)
British	31	32	34	36	38	40	42 (inches)
American	6	8	10	12	14	16	18 (size)

Women's shoes

Italian	36	37	38	39	40	41
British	3	4	5	6	7	8
American	5	6	7	8	9	10

Men's suits

Italian	44	46	48	50	52	54	56	58 (size)
British	34	36	38	40	42	44	46	48 (inches)
American	34	36	38	40	42	44	46	48 (inches)

Men's shirts (collar size)

Italian	36	38	39	41	42	43	44	45 (cms)
British	14	15	15½	16	16½	17	17½	18 (inches)
American	14	15	15½	16	16½	17	17½	18 (inches)

Men's shoes

Italian	39	40	41	42	43	44	45	46
British	6	7	7½	8	9	10	11	12
American	7	7½	8	8½	9½	10½	11	11½

DIRECTORY

WOMEN'S HIGH FASHION

Fendi
Via Borgognona 39.
Map 5 A2.
📞 06-679 76 41.

Genny
Piazza di Spagna 27.
Map 5 A2.
📞 06-679 60 74.

Gente
Via del Babuino 81.
Map 4 F1.
📞 06-320 76 71.
Also: Via Frattina 69.
Map 5 A2.
📞 06-678 91 32.
Also: Via dei Due Macelli 62. **Map** 5 A3 & 12 F1.
📞 06-679 27 27.

Gianni Versace
Via Bocca di Leone 26.
Map 5 A2.
📞 06-678 05 21.

Giorgio Armani
Via Condotti 77.
Map 5 A2. 📞 06-699 14 61. Also: Via del Babuino 140. **Map** 4 F1.
📞 06-36 00 21 97.

Laura Biagiotti
Via Borgognona 43–44.
Map 5 A2.
📞 06-679 12 05.

Max & Co
Via Condotti 46.
Map 5 A2.
📞 06-678 79 46.

MaxMara
Via Frattina 28.
Map 5 A2.
📞 06-679 36 38.

Mila Schön
Via Condotti 51-52.
Map 5 A2.
📞 06-678 48 05.

Renato Balestra
Via Sistina 67. **Map** 5 A2.
📞 06-679 55 37.

Roberto Capucci
Via Gregoriana 56.
Map 5 A2.
📞 06-679 51 80.

Sorelle Fontana
Salita S. Sebastianello 5.
Map 5 A2.
📞 06-679 86 52.

Trussardi
Via Condotti 49–50.
Map 5 A2.
📞 06-679 21 51.

Valentino
Via Bocca di Leone 15.
Map 5 A2.
📞 06-679 58 62.

MEN'S TAILORS AND DESIGNER WEAR

Battistoni
Via Condotti 61A.
Map 5 A2.
📞 06-678 62 41.

Brioni
Via Barberini 79.
Map 5 A2.
📞 06-678 36 35.

Davide Cenci
Via Campo Marzio 1–7.
Map 4 F3 & 12 D2.
📞 06-699 06 81.

Degli Effetti
Piazza Capranica 79.
Map 4 F3 & 12 D2.
📞 06-679.02.02.

Enzo Ceci
Via della Vite 52.
Map 5 A3 & 12 E1.
📞 06-679 88 82.

Ermenegildo Zegna
Via Borgognona 7E.
Map 5 A2.
📞 06-678 91 43.

Etro
Via del Babuino 102.
Map 5 A2.
📞 06-678 82 57.

Gianfranco Ferrè
Via Borgognona 6.
Map 5 A2.
📞 06-679 74 45.

Polidori Uomo
Via Borgognona 4C
Map 5 A2.
📞 06-699 41 171.

Testa
Via Borgognona 13.
Map 5 A2.
📞 06-679 61 74.
Also: Via Frattina 104.
Map 5 A2.
📞 06-679 12 96.

Trussardi
See Women's High Fashion.

Valentino Uomo
Via Condotti 13.
Map 5 A2.
📞 06-678 36 56.

Versus by Versace
Via Borgognona 34.
Map 5 A2.

YOUNG DESIGNER WEAR

Aria
Via Nazionale 239.
Map 5 C3.
📞 06-48 44 21.

Box 233
Via Nazionale 233.
Map 5 C3.
📞 06-481 45 18.

Diesel
Via del Corso 185.
Map 4 F3 & 12 E1.
📞 06-678 66 41.

Emporio Armani
Via del Babuino 140.
Map 4 F1.
📞 06-322 15 84.

Energie
Via del Corso 408–409.
Map 4 F2.
📞 06-687 12 58.
687 10 04.
Also: Via del Corso 486–487. **Map** 4 F2.
📞 06-322 70 46.

Eventi
Via dei Serpenti 134.
Map 5 B4.
📞 06-48 49 60.

Luna e L'Altra
Via del Governo
Vecchio 105.
Map 4 E4 & 11 B3.
📞 06-68 80 49 95.

Maga Morgana
Via del Governo Vecchio
27. **Map** 4 E4 & 11 C3.
📞 06-687 99 95.

Max & Co
Via Nazionale 56.
Map 5 C3.
📞 06-48 90 31 10.
Also: Via Appia Nuova
201–203. **Map** 10 D2.
📞 06-701 44 13.

Oliver
Via del Babuino 61.
Map 4 F1.
📞 06-360 01 906.

Timberland
Via del Babuino 75.
Map 4 F1.
📞 06-679 08 36.

HIGH STREET FASHION

Benetton
Via Condotti 59.
Map 5 A2.
📞 06-679 79 82.

Discount dell'Alta Moda
Via di Gesù e Maria 16A.
Map 4 F2.
📞 06-361 37 96.

Discount System
Via del Viminale 35.
Map 5 C3.
📞 06-482 39 17.

Emporio Armani
See Young Designer Wear.

Max & Co
See Young Designer Wear.

Scala Quattordici
Via della Scala 14.
Map 4 D5 & 11 B5.

KNITWEAR

Choses de Cachemire
Via del Babuino 105.
Map 4 F1 📞 06-679 84 88.

Laura Biagiotti
See Women's High Fashion.

Liz
Via Appia Nuova 90.
Map 10 D2.
📞 06-700 36.09.

Luisa Spagnoli
Via del Corso 385.
Map 5 A4 & 12 F3.
📞 06-679 81 89.
Also: Via Vittorio
Veneto 130. **Map** 5 B1.
📞 06-420 11 81.
Also: Via Frattina 84B.
Map 5 A2.
📞 06-699 17 06.

Missoni Sport
Via del Babuino 96A–97.
Map 4 F1.
📞 06-679 79 71.

Missoni Uomo/Donna
Piazza di Spagna 78.
Map 5 A2.
📞 06-679 25 55.

LINGERIE

Brighenti
Via Frattina 7–8.
Map 5 A2.
06-679 14 84.

Cesari
Via del Babuino 195.
Map 5 B3.
06-361 34 51.

Liberti
Via del Tritone 101.
Map 12 F1.
06-488 22 46.

Schostal
Via del Corso 158.
Map 4 F3 & 12 E1.
06-679 12 40.

Tomassini
Via Sistina 119. **Map** 5 A2.
06-488 19 09.

SECOND-HAND CLOTHES

Le Gallinelle
Via del Boschetto 76.
Map 5 B4.
06-488 10 17.

Mai Visto
Via del Governo Vecchio
85. **Map** 11 C3.
06-687 20 26.

Moon
Via del Governo Vecchio
89A. **Map** 4 E4 & 11 B3.

Via dei Chiavari 40
Via dei Chiavari 40.
Map 4 E4 & 11 C4.

SHOES

Borino
Via dei Pettinari 86–87.
Map 4 E5 & 11 C5.
06-687 56 70.

Bruno Magli
Via Vittorio Veneto 70A.
Map 5 B2.
06-488 43 55.

Campanile
Via Condotti 58.
Map 5 A2.
06-678 30 41.

Carlotto Rio
Via dell'Arco della
Ciambella 8. **Map** 12 D3.
06-687 23 08.

Cervone
Via del Corso 99.
Map 4 F2.
06-678 35 22.

De Bach
Via del Babuino 123.
Map 4 F1.
06-678 33 84.

Dominici
Via del Corso 14.
Map 12 E1.
06-361 05 91.

Domus
Via Belsiana 52.
Map 4 F2.
06-678 90 83.

Fausto Santini
Via Frattina 120.
Map 5 A2.
06-678 41 14.

Ferragamo
Via Condotti 73–74.
Map 5 A2.
06-679 15 65.
Also: Via Condotti 66.
Map 5 A2.
06-678 11 30.

Fratelli Rossetti
Via Borgognona 5A.
Map 5 A2.
06-678 26 76.

Mr Boots
Piazza Trilussa 33.
Map 4 E5.
06-580 38 20.
Also: Piazza Re di Roma 10.
Map 10 D3.
06-77 20 86 72.
Also: Via A Brunetti 2.
Map 4F1.
06-321 57 33.

Pollini
Via Frattina 22–24.
Map 5 A2 & 12 E1.
06-678 90 28.

Raphael Salato
Via Veneto 149.
Map 5 B1.
06-482 18 16.

LEATHER GOODS

La Cravatta
Via Santa Cecilia 12.
Map 8 D1.
06-581 66 76.

Fendi
See Women's High Fashion.

Ginocchi
Via Sistina 35. **Map** 5 B2.
06-488 39 25.

Gucci
Via Condotti 8. **Map** 5 A2.
06-678 93 40.

Mandarina Duck
Via di Propaganda 1.
Map 5 A2.
06-69 94 03 20.

La Sella
Via del Lavatore 56.
Map 5 A3 & 12 F1.
06-679 66 54.

Sirni
Via della Stelletta 33.
Map 4 F3 & 12 D2.
06-68 80 52 46.

Skin
Via Capo la Case 41.
Map 5 A3 & 12 F1.
06-678 55 31.

Valextra
Via del Babuino 94.
Map 4 F1.
06-679 23 23.

CLASSIC JEWELRY

Ansuini
Via del Babuino 150D.
Map 4 F1.
06-322 10 72.

Boncompagni
Via del Babuino 115.
Map 4 F1.
06-678 32 39.

Buccellati
Via Condotti 31.
Map 5 A2.
06-679 03 29.

Bulgari
Via Condotti 10.
Map 5 A2.
06-679 38 76.

Massoni
Largo Carlo Goldoni 48.
Map 4 F2 & 12 E1.
06-678 01 82.

Moroni Gioielli
Via Belsiana 32A.
Map 4 F2.
06-678 04 66.

Peroso
Via Sistina 29. **Map** 5 B3.
06-474 79 52.

Petocchi
Piazza di Spagna 23.
Map 5 A2.
06-679 39 47.

COSTUME JEWELRY

Bozart
Via Bocca di Leone 4.
Map 5 A2.
06-678 10 26.

Delettré
Via Fontanella Borghese 39.
Map 4 F2.
06-678 19 12.

Siragusa
Via delle Carrozze 64.
Map 5 A2.
06-679 70 85.

Tempi Moderni
Via del Governo Vecchio
108. **Map** 4 E4 & 11 B3.
06-687 70 07.

**Via dei Coronari
193**
Via dei Coronari 193.
Map 4 E3 & 11 B2.
06-68 80 15 03.

TRADITIONAL GOLDSMITHS AND SILVERSMITHS

Oddi e Seghetti
Via del Cancello 20.
Map 4 E3 & 11 C2.
06-686 13 84.

GLOVES, HATS AND HOSIERY

Borsalino
Via IV Novembre 157B.
Map 5 A4 & 12 F3.
06-679 41 92.

Calza e Calze
Via della Croce 78.
Map 4 F2.
06-678 42 81.

Catello d'Auria
Via dei Due Macelli 55.
Map 5 A2 & 12 F1.
06-679 33 64.

Di Cori
Piazza di Spagna 53.
Map 5 A2.
06-678 44 39.

Merola
Via del Corso 143.
Map 4 F3 & 12 E1.
06-679 19 61.

Sermoneta
Piazza di Spagna 61.
Map 5 A2.
06-679 19 60.

Interior Design

ITALIAN DESIGN belongs to a long-established tradition based on the skills of the master craftsperson, and some firms have a history going back hundreds of years. Rome's stylish interior design shops are worth seeking out, even if it's only to look around and enjoy the ambience. You might well pick up some design ideas for your home, as well as find some interesting or unusual things to buy.

FURNITURE

ALTHOUGH THERE is no distinct area of Rome renowned for its furniture shops, most of the top stores are located to the north of the city center.
Fontana Arte, on Via Giulia, sells highly original furniture and lamps made almost entirely of glass.

Take a look at the nearby **Studio Punto Tre** if you want something different: it's packed with strangely painted chests of drawers, Egyptian-style artifacts and small bits and pieces that would make good presents.

Myricae dazzles with its sensible prices and its covetable Tuscan wrought iron and Venetian painted furniture in sun-drenched or delicate hues.

Spazio Sette, near Largo Argentina, has a spectacular showroom on three levels in the Palazzo Lazzaroni, a former cardinal's palace. It is one of Rome's premier home furnishing stores, and, apart from furniture, it stocks items that would make interesting gifts. The furniture – modern, laminated, stack-up chairs and so forth, plus vases, glass, bowls, and kitchen equipment – is jumbled together in a fascinating display.

Nearby, on Via dei Chaivari, is **Paola Agostara**, another shop that stocks an impressive cornucopia of household objects. Items ranging from hand-painted furniture to glasswear from Eastern Europe are on sale here, along with a collection of designer fabrics and furniture by Paola Agostara herself.

Magazzini Forma & Memoria is an innovative design studio located near the east bank of the Tiber. It displays the latest in furniture and design items from Italy and elsewhere. Also on sale are a range of designer clothes, accessories and toys.

Stildomus, situated approximately half an hour's drive out of the center of the city, has a showroom displaying mainly very fine modern wood furniture.

LIGHTING FIXTURES

LIGHTING FIXTURES are one of the most popular and more easily transportable items to buy, and there are a number of superb showrooms to visit. **Flos Arteluce** is a merger of two design houses whose Roman showroom displays its lights as if they were museum exhibits. The design style is typically minimalist – plenty of black and white, chrome and steel.

Nearby **Artemide** is, like Flos Arteluce, a design house in its own right and is similarly well-known abroad. Its Rome showroom is elegant, with expensive high-tech lighting design similar to that of Flos Arteluce. **Borghini** sells less famous names, and so is more economical.

Paolo Marj is a sculptor working in mixed media such as glass, wood and plastics to create lamps that are original works of art in themselves. Also on sale are a variety of original sculptures by the artist.

Italian lighting and other electrical equipment are designed for 220–240 volts. If you are going to use an item in countries with lower voltages, always ask the shop whether the product needs a transformer, because this can depend on the model. Lighting fixtures generally take screw bulbs, although bayonet bulbs of some designer models may also be ordered.

KITCHENS AND BATHROOMS

ALTHOUGH YOU won't be able to take one home with you, you may like to take a look at a few of the ultramodern high-tech kitchens sold in Rome. For an overview of the latest designs, visit **La Residenza**, which has a selection of about 15 kitchen sets from about 9 or more Italian manufacturers. **Coas Tradizione Casa** in Piazza Cardelli has some interesting combinations in a centrally located showroom.

Italian bathroom shops concentrate almost entirely on modern design. **Odorisio** is the equivalent of La Residenza for bathrooms, and has some luxurious examples. **Ravasini**, nearby, sells very decorative floral fixtures with some matching accessories. **Andreucci** also has a bathroom shop stocking all the latest styles.

TILES

THE ITALIAN ceramic tile tradition is an ancient one. A great variety of tiles is displayed in kitchen and bathroom showrooms, but there are also a number of specialty shops. The most beautiful and the most expensive of these is **Farnese**, looking ancient Roman in style with its mosaic tables. Di Donato uses old-fashioned methods to design and produce the tiles – hence the cost. He is influenced by Roman and Pompeiian art but also produces modern one-of-a-kind designs.

Ceramiche Musa specializes in modern tiles with decorative floral and ancient Roman motifs, which are popular with visitors.

GLASS

DECORATIVE GLASS objects are popular to buy in Rome. **Navona Venetian Glass,** just behind Piazza Navona, sells Murano and other glass items at reasonable prices. This shop is open on Sundays – which can be useful for vistors on short trips to Rome. **Archimede Seguso** also specializes in Murano glass but includes smaller pieces and gift-sized items.

Tupini, the Roman equivalent of the Harrods china department, has quality glass, china and silverware. **Arteque** is a very beautiful shop, with a more traditional flavor. For less expensive gifts, try **Stilvetro**. It is the ideal place for pasta bowls, glass, and ceramics.

Shipment home can usually be arranged at any of these glass establishments so you are able make your purchases without worrying about the heart-stopping hassle of transporting it home without damaging your gifts.

FABRICS

SUMPTUOUS furnishing fabrics are what **Cesari** in Via del Babuino is renowned for. It also has a linen and lingerie shop *(see p.327)*. **Il Sigillo** offers fabrics and wallpapers made to order from a rich assortment of samples. At **Galtrucco** you can choose material for a suit which they will make to measure so that your taste can be combined with their expertise.

If you are looking for worthwhile bargains, take a wander around the old Jewish quarter that runs from Largo Argentina down to the Tiber; it is full of cheaper fabric shops, such as **Paganini**. At sale time, remnants *(scampoli)* can be really good value, and you could find just the right fabric at just the right price.

HOUSEHOLD LINENS AND KITCHENWARE

A SELECTION of lovely sheets can be found at **Frette**. If you enjoy designer kitchenware, don't miss **C.u.c.i.n.a.** in the cellars of No. 118 Via del Babuino. It stocks kitchen utensils from all over the world, as well as pots and pans in both rustic and high-tech styles and countless space-saving accessories. **Single** specializes in stainless steel designs such as Alessi and sells wooden breadboards and assorted containers.

For the budget conscious, there is also **Salvoni**, whose basement is well stocked with cut-price gift ideas. You'll find an arrary of household and kitchenware, including silver, china and crystal items.

Books and Gifts

ROME OFFERS A HUGE SELECTION for gift buying. There are products from all over Italy as well as locally produced artisanwares. Seeking out the smaller shops can be an adventure in itself, as many are in attractive parts of the city that you might not otherwise visit.

Some of the artisan ceramics are very unusual; there are also beautiful books on Italian art and architecture, plus wonderful paper products. Food gifts and drinks are always welcome – especially if they are something really special, such as 20-year-old balsamic vinegar. In addition to the usual souvenirs, there is an abundance of religious artifacts – for obvious reasons – and Michelangelo masterpieces are the most popular icons for T-shirts, statuettes and postcards.

BOOKSHOPS

ROME IS RICH in bookshops, from the encyclopedic to the very specialized. Italian books, both hardcover and softcover, are generally very attractive but also tend to be quite expensive.

Rizzoli, Rome's largest bookshop, has a wide selection on art and cookery, among other subjects, and many books in English and other foreign languages. **Feltrinelli** has three shops in the capital. The most important is situated in Largo Argentina and offers a wide selection of contemporary literature. Milanese **Franco Maria Ricci** offers very beautiful art books, as well as its own glossy magazine, *FMR*. **Libreria Godel** is also good for browsing – it carries books on Rome, great postcards, art calendars and secondhand art books.

Remainder has half-price bargains and sells games for children, too. There are many discount bargains as well as secondhand book stalls in Via delle Terme di Diocleziano and in Largo della Fontanella di Borghese.

MULTIMEDIA AND MUSIC

ROME'S BIGGEST music store is **Ricordi**. In addition to records, cassettes and CDs, it sells musical instruments and musical scores in its four central outlets. By contrast, **Discoteca Frattina** is quite a small, handy music shop that also sells videocassettes. The multimedia shop **Mondadori** sells greeting cards, posters and videos and has good map and music departments as well as books.

STATIONERY AND PAPERCRAFT

A WIDE SELECTION of pretty marbled notebooks, writing paper, files and boxes in various sizes are on offer at **Laboratorio Scatole**.

Pineider, stationery suppliers to the Roman gentry, will print sets of exquisite visiting cards for you. They also sell handsome leather-bound desk diaries. Just as classy, though less traditional, **Vertecchi** is filled with original paper gifts. These include boxes of every size and shape, paper napkins and tablecloths, wrapping paper and a dazzling range of Christmas decorations.

ARTISAN HANDICRAFTS

SPACIOUS and artistically rustic, **La Galleria** is filled with authentic artisanwares, including handwoven textiles and beautiful ceramics that owner Clotilde Sambuco chooses from all parts of Italy. Domenico and Lavinia Sarti's **Bottega Artigiana** nearby is a small shop with ceramics made by the couple in their Anzio studio. You can buy vases and urns in unglazed terra-cotta and attractive terra-cotta light fixtures.

Arti e Mestieri is the workshop of a friendly mother and daughter who make original articles in wood and terra-cotta. **Arte in Città** is a cross between a shop and a gallery. It sells a variety of original craft works by around a hundred artists and artisans, along with a range of handmade cards and postcards. Every month the shop holds an exhibition with a different theme.

For a really original gift, go to **Opificio Romano**, a workshop that reproduces ancient Roman and Pompeian mosaics, where they will re-create any design you choose to order.

SOUVENIRS AND RELIGIOUS ARTIFACTS

MOST OF THE tobacco shops in central Rome sell postcards, stamps and a variety of souvenirs, and many cheap and sometimes appealingly kitsch souvenirs are sold by the mobile stalls around the major tourist attractions.

Bookshops near the main basilicas, such as **Libreria Belardetti**, sell souvenirs and religious mementos. Other shops specialize in religious articles for both the clergy and the layperson. Facing the Vatican gates in Via di Porta Angelica are several shops, such as **Al Pellegrino Cattolico**, selling mementos to visitors and tourists.

FOOD

ONE OF THE unusual things about shopping in Rome is the absence of large-scale supermarkets in the center. It has been local government policy to keep them out in order to protect the little *alimentari*, or delicatessens. There are hundreds of these, not on the main shopping streets, but in small side streets running off them or in the "village" districts, such as Monti, Trastevere, the Ghetto, Borgo and Campo de' Fiori. They are often crammed from floor to ceiling with all the irresistible delicacies that are typical of Italy.

Here you can buy, the day before your departure, your supply of parmesan and pecorino Romano cheese (see p305), Parma ham or prosciutto di montagna, attractive bottles of dark-green extra-virgin unfiltered olive oil, dried porcini mushrooms and sun-dried tomatoes to take home (but check Customs restrictions first). Food is by no means cheap, and most of the above are considered luxury items.

Pietro Franchi is without doubt the most exclusive delicatessen in the city, and its windows are a visual feast of seafood platters, pâtés, cheeses and cold meats. Next door is the famous coffee shop **Castroni**, which has Rome's largest selection of imported products from all over the world. It also stocks Italian olive oils, balsamic vinegars, honeys and preserves and of course coffee.

Via della Croce deserves a special mention for its good selection of well-stocked *alimentari* like **Fratelli Fabbi**. Specialty food shops like **Fior Fiore** sell exquisite little almond and orange peel cakes; ricotta cheese; and piles of artichoke-, spinach- and tomato-flavored pasta; as well as thin, crispy pizza straight from the oven.

Cheese lovers can usually find plenty of Italian varieties in any of the small *alimentari* dotted around the city. However, it's also well worth trying the local cow, sheep and buffalo milk cheeses that are sold at the **Cisternino Cooperativa fra Produttori di Latte di Lazio**, situated near Piazza Campo de' Fiori.

Boxes of chocolates and traditional confectionery and cakes such as *torrone* and *panettone* can generally be bought from good-quality bars. **L'Albero del Pane** sells wonderful wholemeal and rye flour breads and other health foods.

WINE

WINE IS GENERALLY sold in *alimentari* and also in supermarkets. There are, however, many specialty shops (look for the sign *Enoteca*) with a huge stock of wines and spirits. They invariably have a little bar where they serve wine and light snacks or canapés. Here you can find Italian wines, and usually local wines, mostly white, from the nearby Frascati, Colli Albani and Marino vineyards, on tap. One of the most select is **Enoteca Buccone**, which is housed in an old coach-house. Another well-known one is **Antica Enoteca**, which has an old-world feeling to it. The **Enoteca del Corso** is more modern, with a good selection of Italian grappa and jars of marinated fruits. **Enoteca Corsi** in Via del Gesù is also worth a visit,

---

Art and Antiques

ROME'S ART and antiques shops range from exclusive establishments to contemporary art galleries. In response to a fashion for collecting early 20th-century artifacts, new dealers and galleries are springing up throughout Rome – Venini's Murano glass is popular, as are lighting and furniture. Many more sell general bric-a-brac and jewelry. Copies of antique prints can be picked up for a fraction of the originals' price. Rome is not good for bargain antiques, but it's worth looking in shops along Via dei Cappellari and Via del Pellegrino or going to the Porta Portese Sunday market *(see p339)*.

ANTIQUES AND OLD MASTER PAINTINGS

THERE ARE antiques shops dotted all over the center of Rome, though the cream tend to be concentrated in distinct areas. Discreet haggling in the shops is accepted practice, but even if you get a reduction in price, make sure the dealer provides you with the relevant export documents.

The famous Via del Babuino and to a lesser extent Via Margutta, which is more famous for its art galleries, are home to around 30 of Rome's grandest showrooms for antique furniture, Old Master paintings and objets d'art.

Apolloni is owned by top dealer Cesare Lampronti. Aided and complemented by his partner, Carlo Peruzzi, he sells 16th- to 18th-century European paintings, with an emphasis on Roman and Italian works.

Amedeo di Castro, apparently no relation to the other four di Castros on this street, is a fourth-generation dealer in bas-relief sculptures and exquisite pieces from the 18th and early 19th centuries. **Claudio e Laura Moretti's** small, narrow shop is full of antique and later copies of marble busts and statues.

Via Giulia *(see p153)* has over 20 high-quality antiques shops to choose from. Definitely worth a visit is **Antichita Cipriani**, which is a temple to owner Paola Cipriani's love of simply elegant Neo-classical furniture and paintings. She also sells the occasional modern piece.

Another shop not to miss on Via Giulia is **Antiquariato Valligiano**. It's the only place in Rome where you can find 19th-century Italian country furniture – a rustic antidote for those overpowered by the grandiose Baroque.

Via Monserrato, running parallel, is worth scouring for slightly lower quality pieces at more attainable prices.

The area just to the north of the Via Giulia is also a good potential hunting ground. **Mario Prilli**, on Via Banchi Nuovi, is tiny, but don't let that deter you. With every space occupied by a wide variety of antiques, this fascinating shop is worth a look even if you are only browsing. Nearby is **Ad Antiqua Domus**, a treasure trove of antique Italian furniture. Pieces dating from ancient Rome through to the 19th century are on sale

Via dei Coronari is almost exclusively devoted to antiques, with over 40 shops lining both sides of this picturesque street. Quality is very high – as are the prices. It is a good place for Baroque and Empire elaborately inlaid vases, secretaries and consoles.

L'Art Nouveau specializes in high-quality Art Nouveau (usually called *Liberty* here). The **Art Deco Gallery** sells furniture and sculpture from that period.

Piero Tagoni has a superb collection of lighting fixtures from the Baroque through to Art Deco periods.

Slightly farther away lies Via della Stelletta, which is home to a handful of unusual and fascinating shops.

Acanto is an inexpensively priced Aladdin's cave with an eclectic mix of objets d'art. It is the perfect place to search for religious memorabilia, Italian curiosities and prints.

Bilenchi is yet another specialist, but in exquisite, turn-of-the-century lamps.

Another relatively undiscovered area is Via del Boschetto and Via Panisperna. Shops around here tend to specialize in early 20th-century artifacts, with some English Victorian pieces thrown in.

Tad is a great place to come and browse, with a large collection of weird and original design items from all around the world.

Of course there are many perennial favorites apart from these streets. The best way to discover them is through word of mouth or just by chance as you stroll along. **Cose Così**, in the north of the city, is a shop full of decorative pieces from 1800 to 1940 (watches, silver, glass, frames, vases and jewelry), while **Galleria dei Cosmati** is one of the oldest antiques shops in Rome, and definitely one of the largest. It offers an impressive collection of European antiques.

Anticaja e Petrella has an eccentric collection of used junk and printed ephemera stored under Sant'Andrea della Valle *(see p123)*.

MODERN ART

ROME IS RICH in avant-garde galleries exhibiting paintings by recognized modern masters through to the up-and-coming generation of young, mainly Italian, artists.

Rome's art galleries are usually open 10am to 1pm and 5 to 8pm Tuesday to Saturday. Some open only in the afternoon; others also stay open on Monday afternoon. The best times to visit are in the afternoons and early evenings.

As with Rome's antiques shops, the art galleries tend to be concentrated in a couple of distinct areas. The largest of these covers the triangle area between Via del Babuino and Via di Ripetta and adjoining streets, known locally as the Trident. The pioneering **Agenzia d'Arte Moderna**, founded in 1913, promoted Futurism from the start and other modern art movements as well. There are works by Burri and Kounellis always on display.

Sperone, under the owner-directorship of Gian Enzo Sperone, shows works by American artists like Ray Smith, Julio Galan and Jonathan Lasker. Also included are Italian artists like Gallo, Bianchi, Dessi, Paladino and Merzi.

Apollodoro, which sells interesting design artifacts, has an entrance modeled on Borromini's illusionistic perspective in the garden gallery of Palazzo Spada (see p147).

One of this area's highlights is the Via Margutta art fair (see p339), which usually takes place around Christmas and in springtime.

Via Giulia and its surroundings is the next area to investigate: **Galleria Giulia** is a gallery-cum-bookshop with work by artists such as Argeles, Boille, Cano, Cascella, Echaurren, Erba and Lionni, as well as by Bauhaus artists and German Expressionists.

Fabio Sargentini at **L'Attico** follows the latest trends in Italian art from Del Giudice to Corsini and Fabiani.

Trastevere is possibly better for more innovative ventures: The **Galleria Bondho** (previously Alessandra Bonomo) spotlights young Italian and foreign painters, such as Schifano, Boetti, Twombly, Nunzio, Tremlett, LeWitt, Dokoupil. In a stupendous villa situated quite a way out of Rome, **Mauro Vigneti** specializes in both Italian and international artists working in Rome.

ANTIQUE PRINTS AND PHOTOGRAPHS

THE JUSTIFIABLY celebrated **Nardecchia**, named after its cultivated owner, Plinio, is the cream of Rome's print dealers. Look for originals by the 18th-century engraver Piranesi and views of the city and ancient Roman life.

Another Roman institution, **Casali**, has been trading for over 100 years. The family now runs two shops specializing in 16th- to 19th-century drawings and engravings of Roman scenes ranging from museum-standard Piranesi down to relatively inexpensive and delightfully decorative floral scenes by unknowns.

The Florence-based **Alinari** family is renowned for its sepia photographs of Italy from 1890 onward, including shots of Rome at the turn of the century. At its Roman outlet, prices of photographs from the original plates start at around L30,000 and mounted prints at L500,000. Larger sizes can be mounted on wood or board.

Another place definitely worth heading for in search of that perfect print of old Rome and some enjoyable, relaxing, and maybe persuasive, browsing is the **Mercato delle Stampe** (see p338).

DIRECTORY

ANTIQUES AND OLD MASTER PAINTINGS

Acanto
Via della Stelletta 10.
Map 4 F3 & 12 D2.
06-686 54 81.

Ad Antiqua Domus
Via Paola 25–27.
Map 4 D3 & 11 A2.
06-686 15 30.

Amedeo di Castro
Via del Babuino 77–78.
Map 4 F1.
06-320 76 50.

Anticaja e Petrella
Via Monte della Farina 62.
Map 4 F5 & 12D4.

Antichita Cipriani
Via Giulia 122.
Map 4 D4 & 11 A3.
06-68 30 83 44.

Antiquariato Valligiano
Via Giulia 193.
Map 4 E5 & 11 B5.
06-686 95 05.

Apolloni
Via del Babuino 67.
Map 4 F1.
06-36 00 22 16.

Art Deco Gallery
Via dei Coronari 14.
Map 4 E3 & 11 C2.
06-686 53 30.

L'Art Nouveau
Via dei Coronari 221.
Map 4 E3 & 11 C2.
06-68 80 52 30.

Bilenchi
Via della Stelletta 17.
Map 4 F3 & 12 D2.
06-687 52 22.

Claudio e Laura Moretti
Via dei Coronari 233A.
Map 4 E3.

Cose Così
Viale Somalia.
06-68 80 53 63.

Galleria dei Cosmati
Via Vittoria Colonna 11.
Map 4 E2.
06-36 11 41.

Mario Prilli
Via dei Banchi Nuovi 42.
Map 4 D3 & 11 A2.
06-686 88 16.

Piero Tagoni
Via dei Coronari 135.
Map 4 E3 & 11 B2.
06-687 54 50.

Tad
Via San Giacomo 5.
Map 4 F2.

MODERN ART

Agenzia d'Arte Moderna
Piazza del Popolo 3.
Map 4 F1.
06-322 05 38.

Apollodoro
Piazza Mignanelli 17.
Map 5 A2.

L'Attico
Via del Paradiso 41.
Map 4 E4 & 11 C4.
06-686 98 46.

Galleria Bondho
Piazza Sant'Apollonia 3.
Map 7 C1.
06-581 05 79.

Galleria Giulia
Via Giulia 148.
Map 4 D4 & 11 B4.
06-68 80 20 61.

Mauro Vigneti
Via Bel Poggio 4,
Castelnuovo di Porto.
06-90 17 88 55.

Sperone
Via di Pallacorda 15.
Map 4 F3 & 12 D1.
06-689 35 25.

ANTIQUE PRINTS AND PHOTOGRAPHS

Alinari
Via Alibert 16 A.
Map 5 A2.
06-679 29 23.

Casali
Piazza della Rotonda 81 A/82.
Map 4 F4 & 12 D3.
06-678 35 15.

Nardecchia
Piazza Navona 25.
Map 4 E4 & 11 C3.
06-686 93 18.

Outdoor Markets

Rome's outdoor markets are essential to visit if you're interested in experiencing the exuberance and vitality for which Romans are renowned. The markets are wonderfully vivid visually too, as Italian stallholders and vendors have raised the display of even the humblest vegetable to an art form.

The city is dotted with popular, small outdoor food markets, and there are several fascinating well-established ones near the center, along with the most famous flea market over in Trastevere.

It is important to keep your wits about you in all these markets, because pickpockets work with lightning speed in the bustling crowds. However, Roman markets provide such a vibrant source of entertainment, it would be a shame to let such caveats deter you from joining in the fun.

The street fairs that take place throughout the year offer various pleasures and also normally sell a good variety of local produce, handicrafts and clothes. Seasonal fairs also occur, especially around Christmas, when you can stock up on Italian specialties and gifts.

Campo de' Fiori

Piazza Campo de' Fiori. **Map** 4 E4 & 11 C4. H, 46, 62, 64, 70, 81, 116, 492, 628. 8. **Open** 7am–1:30pm Mon–Sat. See p146.

Right in the heart of the old city, Rome's most picturesque market is also its most historical. Its name, Campo de' Fiori, which translates as "field of flowers," sometimes misleads people into expecting a flower market. In fact, the name is said to derive from Campus Florae (Flora's square) – Flora being the lover of the great Roman general Pompey. A market has actually been held for many centuries in this now somewhat shabby, but still beautiful, piazza.

Every morning except Sunday, the piazza is transformed by an array of stalls selling colorful fruit and vegetables, meat, poultry and fish. One or two stalls specialize in legumes, rice, dried fruit and nuts, and there are also flower stalls situated near the fountain. But the huge open baskets of ready-stripped broccoli and spinach, various chopped vegetables for minestrone and freshly prepared green salad mixes are the main attraction for visitors. They provide a real visual display as well as an edible feast.

The excellent delicatessen shops on the square and bread shops nearby complement the market. They make it a great place to stock up for an impromptu picnic if the weather turns out fine and you're tempted to do some *al fresco* dining in one of Rome's many attractive parks.

Mercato delle Stampe

Largo della Fontanella di Borghese. **Map** 4 F3 & 12 D1. 119, also routes to Via Tomacelli. **Open** 7am–1pm Mon–Sat.

This market is a veritable haven for lovers of old prints, books (both genuine antiquarian and less costly secondhand), magazines and other printed ephemera. The quality varies, but it is a good deal more specialized than the *banche*, or stalls, near Termini station which are a more obvious tourist trap. Italian-speaking collectors can enjoy a field day leafing through back issues of specialty magazines. Other visitors might prefer the wonderful selection of illustrated art books and old prints of Rome. It is a good place to pick up that Piranesi print of your favorite Roman vista, ruin or church – but be prepared to bargain hard.

Mercato dei Fiori

Via Trionfale. **Map** 3 B1. Ottaviano. 23, 70. **Open** 10:30am–1pm Tue.

Essentially a trade market, the Flower Market, just north of Via Andrea Doria, is open to the public only on Tuesdays. Housed in a covered hall, it has two floors brimming over with cut flowers upstairs and all kinds of potted plants on the lower floor. Anyone who has an interest in flowers will enjoy this wonderful array of Mediterranean blooms, which are for sale at giveaway prices.

Mercato Andrea Doria

Via Andrea Doria. **Map** 3 B1. Ottaviano. 23, 70. **Open** 7am–1:30pm Mon–Sat.

The market used to stretch the whole length of this wide avenue. It has now been reorganized onto a huge square of open ground between Via Santamaura and Via Tunisi. Apart from the magnificent displays of fruit and vegetables, it has numerous stalls selling meat, poultry, fish and groceries, as well as an interesting clothes and shoe section. Situated northwest of the Vatican Museums, it is a little off the normal beaten track and has remained very much a Roman market that caters to the needs of the large local population.

Mercato di Piazza Vittorio

Piazza Vittorio Emanuele II. **Map** 6 E5. Vittorio Emanuele. 4, 9. **Open** 7am–2pm Mon–Sat. See p174.

Bustling Piazza Vittorio was, until recently, perhaps the most Roman of the city's larger markets.

Organized as a cramped corridor of stalls around a central garden, it is the place where bargain-hunting *popolari*, Rome's bustling shoppers, buy their food. Stallholders offer cheap prices if you buy by the kilo, but watch out for bad fruit.

Lately it has become more international and now features African and Asian food stalls.

Sadly, the market's days are numbered: the city council says that it defaces the 19th-century square. Some stalls have moved to the new site in Via Giolitti; others won't go. The battle is on, but make a visit before a splash of Roman color is lost forever.

Mercato di Testaccio

Piazza Testaccio. **Map** 8 D3. Piramide. 23, 75, 280. **Open** 7:30am–1:30pm Mon–Sat.

The covered market at Testaccio occupies the central area of the Testaccio piazza. The few cheap clothing and shoe stalls skirting the outside are unremarkable, but the inside is well worth a visit. Lined with butchers, grocers and fishsellers, the whole central area is given over to fruit and vegetables – a theater-set array of seductive colors and textures. Very popular with local residents, it offers super-fresh, high-quality produce and reasonable prices. Much of this market's charm for visitors lies in its compact size and relaxed, friendly atmosphere.

Porta Portese

Via Portuense & Via Ippolito Nievo.
Map 7 C3. 🚌 *H, 23, 75.* 🚋 *8.*
Open *6:30am–2pm Sun.*

The *mercato delle pulci*, or flea
market, is relatively new in Roman
terms. Established shortly after the
end of World War II, it is said to
have grown out of the thriving
black market that operated at Tor
di Nona opposite Castel Sant'
Angelo during those lean years.
Stall holders from as far away as
Naples start setting up shop in the
early hours of the morning – if
you happen to be strolling in that
direction after a late night on the
town in Trastevere, it's well worth
pausing just to watch.

Anything and everything seems
to be for sale, piled high on stalls
in carefully arranged disorder –
clothes, shoes, bags, luggage,
camping equipment, linen, towels,
pots, pans, kitchen utensils, plants,
pets, spare parts, cassettes and
CDs, old LPs and 78s.

Furniture stalls tend to be
concentrated around Piazza
Ippolito Nievo along with what
they call "antiques," though you
may have to sort through an awful
lot of junk before finding a real
one. And then you will have to
bargain for it. The technique is to
offer them half the asked price
and then walk away. Many go just
to haggle but usually end up
buying something anyway.

There are also secondhand
clothes – leather or sheepskin
coats and jackets go for L10,000 –
with many of the Via Sannio stall
holders relocating here for the
Sunday trade. The stretch along
Via Ippolito Nievo is monopolized
by "*i Russi di Porta Portese*,"
immigrant Russian stallholders
selling caviar, icons (authenticity
uncertain), lace, other ethnic
handicrafts, old cameras and
binoculars. A must if you have a
Sunday morning to spare.

Mercato di Via Sannio

Via Sannio. **Map** 9 C2. Ⓜ *San
Giovanni.* 🚌 *16, 81, 87.* **Open**
8am–1pm Mon–Fri & 8am–6pm Sat.

In the 1960s and 1970s this used
to be Italy's answer to Carnaby
Street or Soho. Today, at first
glance, it doesn't seem to have
anything very special to offer.
Random stalls sell inexpensive
casual clothes, shoes, bags,
belts, jewelry, toys, kitchen
utensils and music cassettes.
However, toward the end of the
street is a large covered section
that extends back to the Aurelian
Wall *(see p196)*. Here visitors will
find many stalls piled high with
secondhand clothes at very low
prices for those who like to

rummage for bargains. There is
also a section that sells military-
style goods plus camping and
fishing equipment.

Some of these stalls move
their wares to Porta Portese on
Sunday morning.

Local Markets

Generally open *7am–1pm Mon–Sat.*

Piazza delle Coppelle (map 4 F3 &
12 D2), near the Pantheon, is
probably the most picturesque of
all the outdoor food markets
around the city. A tiny market
devoted to food and fruit and

flowers, it offers a charming splash
of color in the heart of the city.

Piazza San Cosimato (map 7 C1)
in Trastevere hosts another lively
local market selling tempting
cheeses and salami.

There is a fairly big market on
Via Alessandria (map 6 D1) in
Nomentana, and other smaller
ones in **Via della Pace** (map 4 E4 &
11 C3) near Piazza Navona, and in
Via Balbo (map 5 C4) and **Via
Milazzo** (map 6 E3) near Termini
Station. You can also visit the trade
market, the **Mercato Generale**
(map 8 D5), in Via Ostiense, which
is open to the public after 8am.

STREET FAIRS

A special and interesting
feature of shopping in
Rome is the street fair.

The **Tevere Expo**
exhibition starts each year
between mid-June and
mid-July on both sides of
the river bank between the
Sant'Angelo and Cavour
bridges. Its stalls display
Italian regional arts and
crafts and also sell pasta,
jam, olive oil, wines and
liqueurs. Most items are
cheaper than in the shops.
The exhibition opens in
the evening (6pm–1am).
The entrance fee is minimal
and also includes a ferry
trip across the Tiber.

There are two antiques
fairs, both known as the
Fiera dell'Antiquariato,
that take place in Via dei
Coronari. The first starts in
the second half of May,
10am to 1pm and 4pm to
11pm daily. It makes a
memorable scene at night,
when lighted torches line
the carpeted street. The
second goes along Via
dell'Orso as well and
normally occurs in mid-
October (or late
September), Monday to
Thursday from 3 to 11pm
and Friday and Saturday
from 10am to 11pm. Stalls
sell leatherwork, jewelry
and gifts.

The **Via Margutta Art
Fair** usually takes place
around Christmas and in
springtime. Set in one of
the most charming and
exclusive streets of the
city, it's an event not to be
missed - although it's more

for browsing because
prices are very high. The
utterly glamorous **Spanish
Steps Alta Moda Fashion
Show** is a fairly new event
and doesn't have a set date.
The seating space is filled
by invitation only. However,
the public can squeeze in
the back to enjoy this
display of Italian designer
fashion. So far it has been
held mid- to late July.

The traditional **Christmas
Fair** held in Piazza Navona
from mid-December until
January 6) is now rather
low-key but still fascinating
for those who have never
seen it. Stalls selling clay
statues for nativities and
sweets that look like pieces
of coal are the main
attraction.

Natale Oggi is a well-
established event taking
place near Christmas in
the Fiera di Roma at EUR,
and it is worth visiting to
have a look at the special
Italian Christmas treats.

Via Giulia hosts art fairs
now and then, plus open
evenings when the antiques
and art galleries stay open
late offering food and wine
to all visitors.

Every year Trastevere
hosts its very own carnival,
known as the **Festa de
Noantri** festival, around
late July, when Viale
Trastevere becomes overrun
with the typical *porchetta*
stalls *(see p341)*, party
lights, gift stalls and people.

The details given here
may change, so check the
local listings or at the
tourist office *(see p359)*.

ENTERTAINMENT IN ROME

THERE'S A PARTICULAR excitement attached to Roman entertainment. Football and opera, for example, are both worth experiencing for sheer atmosphere alone, whether or not you are a fan. The jazz scene is especially good, with international stars appearing alongside local talent. And concerts and films take on an added dimension when performances take place beneath the stars in the many open-air arenas spread across the city. Unexpectedly, given the general shutdown among shops, restaurants and museums, the summer remains Rome's liveliest time for live music and other cultural events. Rome's many graceful Renaissance squares, vast parks, villa gardens, Classical ruins and other open spaces host various major arts festivals. If you prefer sports, or want to try out some Roman nightclubs, there's plenty to choose from.

Gregory Peck and Audrey Hepburn in *Roman Holiday*

WHAT'S HAPPENING

THE HANDIEST source of information about what's happening is *Trovaroma*, the weekly Thursday supplement to *La Repubblica* newspaper. It has a day-by-day rundown of what's on and where, and covers music, exhibitions,

Lester Bowie at Alpheus (*see p344*)

theater, movies, guided tours, restaurants and children's entertainment. Two weekly listings magazines, *Città Aperta* and *Roma c'è,* have an English section covering the "Week in Rome" and there is a *Time Out* in both Italian and English editions. Daily newspapers like *Il Messaggero, Il Manifesto, Paese Sera* and *La Repubblica* usually list that evening's entertainment.

Two biweekly magazines, *Wanted in Rome* and *Metropolitan* (found at Via Veneto newsstands or at English bookshops) provide less detailed listings in English. Also worth getting hold of is *Carnet di Roma,* available at the beginning of each month from the EPT *(see p359)*; it

gives details in English of classical music, festivals, theater and exhibitions in the city and surroundings.

Punctuality is not what Italians are renowned for, so don't be surprised if some events start slightly later than advertised in listings.

RESERVING TICKETS

RESERVING in advance is not part of Italian lifestyle. Two agencies that will reserve theater tickets for you (for a small fee) are **Gesman** and **Box Office**. As a rule, theaters do not accept telephone reservations – you have to visit the box office in person. They will charge you a *prevendita* supplement (about 10% of the normal price) for any tickets sold in advance. The price of a theater ticket can be anywhere between L10,000 and L70,000.

Tickets for classical concerts are usually sold on the spot, and are sometimes for that night only, an arrangement that favors the last-minute

decision to go. Opera is the exception. Tickets are sold months in advance, with just a few held back until two days before the performance.

One of the many stages at Alpheus

It is usually easier (and also cheaper) to get tickets for the Caracalla Festival, which takes place in the summer.

The **Teatro dell'Opera** box office *(see p343)* handles sales for both summer and winter seasons, and they have a high-tech reservation system, with a computer that color-codes unsold seats.

Tickets for most big rock and jazz events can be bought at **Orbis**, **Prontospettacolo**, **Mirabilia** and larger record shops, such as **Rinascita**.

Remember that if you're trying to get hold of a ticket for a particular performance that has already sold out, you're extremely unlikely to be able to obtain one from

Member of contemporary dance group Momix (*see p343*)

unofficial sources – there are few ticket scalpers in Rome, except at major football matches, such as important finals.

DISCOUNT TICKETS

THEATERS and concert venues tend not to offer discounts on tickets since performances are so often oversubscribed. Movie theaters, however, offer people over 60 and disabled people a 30% reduction on weekdays. Many also have cheaper ticket prices for weekday afternoon screenings and for all shows on Wednesday. Some clubs at the beach resorts, such as Fregene, offer reductions: watch for *due per uno* coupons in local bars; they allow two people entrance for the price of one.

FACILITIES FOR THE DISABLED

FEW ROMAN venues provide easy access for people with restricted mobility, and any disabled visitors and their companions are likely to find the lack of provision for them very frustrating.

The situation does improve a little in summer, however, when a great many performances in the city are held in the open air. The Baths of Caracalla have wheelchair access, as do the classical concerts held in the beautiful gardens of Villa Giulia *(see pp262–3)*. For more general information on provisions for the disabled, see page 359.

Summer night outdoor performance among Roman ruins

OPEN-AIR ENTERTAINMENT

Singers performing the Barber of Seville

OPEN-AIR OPERA, movies, classical music and jazz concerts fill the calendar from late June until the end of September. These performances outdoors can be wonderful, with spectacular settings and enthusiastic audiences. Some of them are grand affairs, but small events may be just as evocative – a guitar recital in the cloisters of Santa Maria della Pace *(see p342)*, for example, or jazz in the beautiful gardens of Villa Doria Pamphilj *(see p344)*.

Many movie theaters roll back their ceilings in summer for open-air screenings or else move to outdoor arenas, and there are also annual open-air movie festivals. The Cineporto along the Tiber and the Festival di Massenzio offer films, food and small exhibitions in July and August. Theater, too, moves outside in summer. Greek and Roman plays are staged at Ostia Antica *(see p270)* and other shows take place at the Anfiteatro del Tasso *(see p347)*.

Rome's most important summer festival is month-long RomaEuropa, with main performances in the grounds of the Villa Medici. There are other, smaller festivals, but times and venues change from year to year, so watch for posters around the city for

the most recent information. More traditional is Trastevere's community festival, Festa de Noantri *(see p59)*, with music, fireworks and processions. This religious festival is on the Saturday after July 16, but celebrations continue well into August. The Festa dell'Unità, run by the PDS (the former Communist Party), but not limited to politics, is generally held in September. The celebration includes games, stalls, food and drink.

Finally, if you like your entertainment less structured, and more leisurely, you can always do as the Romans tend to do and take part in the *passeggiata* (early-evening stroll) – the city's favorite spots are Piazza Navona *(see p120)* and along Via del Corso.

TICKET AGENCIES

Gesman
Via Angelo Emo 65. **Map** 3 A2.
Open 9am–1pm & 2pm–6pm Mon–Fri, 9am–1pm Sat. 06-39 74 07 89.

Box Office
Viale Giulio Cesare 88. **Map** 3 C1.
Box office tickets for classical music, rock, pop and jazz concerts and some sporting events. 06-372 02 16.

Mirabilia
Corso Vittorio Emanuele II (in Palazzo Altieri). **Map** 4 F4 & 12 E4.
1478-82211.

Orbis
Piazza dell'Esquilino 37. **Map** 6 D4.
06-47 44 776.

Prontospettacolo
Telephone bookings only.
Open 10am–5pm Mon–Fri.
06-39 38 72 97.

The Teatro dell'Opera *(see p342)*

Classical Music and Dance

CLASSICAL CONCERTS take place in a surprising number of venues: tickets for opera premieres may be hard to get, but those for soloists, groups or orchestras playing in gardens, churches, villas or ancient ruins are more available. World-renowned soloists and orchestras make appearances throughout the year; past visitors have included Luciano Pavarotti and Placido Domingo, Catherine Malfitano and prima ballerina Sylvie Guillem.

Programs are generally international in scope, but some festivals are dedicated to one of Italy's very own, such as Palestrina, the great 16th-century master of polyphonic church music, or Arcangelo Corelli, inventor of the Baroque *concerto grosso*.

MUSIC IN CHURCHES

ONE OF ROME'S main attractions for classical music lovers is the rich repertoire that can be heard in the city's churches. Always sacred in theme (by decree of Pope John Paul II), music is mainly performed as concerts rather than during services.

Programs are posted around the city and outside the churches. You will often find very good musicians playing in the main churches, while the smaller, out-of-the-way churches frequently play host to young musicians and to amateur choirs as well.

St. Peter's (*see p230*) hosts one major RAI (national broadcasting company) concert on December 5 attended by the pope and free for the general public. It has two established choirs. The Coro della Cappella Giulia sing at the 10:30am mass and 5pm vespers on Sunday. The Coro della Cappella Sistina sing whenever the pope celebrates mass here, as on June 29 (St. Peter's and St. Paul's day).

Important choral masses also take place on January 25 in **San Paolo fuori le Mura** (*see p267*), when the Pope attends; on June 24 in **San Giovanni in Laterano** (*p182*); and on December 31 at the **Gesù** (*pp114–5*), where the *Te Deum* is sung. The church of **Sant'Ignazio di Loyola** (*p106*) is another favorite venue for choral concerts.

Gregorian chant can be heard in **Sant'Apollinare** (*p127*) at 11am on Sundays and during religious festivals.

Easter and Christmas are great times for cheap but chilly concerts: there is usually neither an entrance fee nor heating!

ORCHESTRAL, CHAMBER AND CHORAL MUSIC

THE **Auditorium di Santa Cecilia**, the national broadcasting company's **Foro Italico** and **Teatro dell' Opera** are Rome's three main auditoriums, with their own resident orchestras and choirs. The Orchestra e Coro dell' Accademia di Santa Cecilia is the top orchestra, but the Orchestra e Coro di Roma della RAI is also good. All three offer interestingly varied seasons that include visiting groups and soloists from all over the world.

The season at the **Teatro Olimpico** usually offers very good chamber music, some orchestral concerts and ballet, with at least one concert a week. They are advertised on large yellow posters with red borders, easily identifiable in the streets and a hallmark for high-level performances.

Although a variety of classical concerts take place at the **Accademia Filarmonica Romana**, the emphasis is on chamber and choral music, with an internationally renowned series of concerts running from mid-October to mid-May. Performances take place in the Sala Casella, which seats around 180.

Ticket prices for classical concerts vary depending on performers and venue. The **Auditorium del Foro Italico** sells tickets for most concerts

for under L20,000; a ticket for the **Teatro Olimpico** costs between L25,000 and L40,000, but seats for an important concert at **Teatro dell'Opera** may cost as much as L150,000.

The Associazione Musicale Romana sponsors three annual festivals in the **Palazzo della Cancelleria** (*see p149*): the Festival Internazionale di Cembalo (harpsichord festival) in March; Musica al Palazzo in May; and the Festival Internazionale di Organo in September.

It's always worth checking which musicians are playing at the **Teatro Ghione**, the **Oratorio del Gonfalone**, or the **Aula dell' Università la Sapienza**.

OPEN-AIR SUMMER CONCERTS

IN THE SUMMER, music lovers can enjoy concerts in cloisters, palazzo courtyards and ancient ruins. Concerts can be one-time events or part of a festival, regular fixtures or impromptu. Do as the Romans do: don't plan until the last moment and keep an eye on the posters and listings pages (*see p340*) for the latest details.

Open-air opera and dance once had their home in the majestic Baths of Caracalla, but this venue is no longer used. Classical concerts are often part of festivals like RomaEuropa (*see p341*), but there are also a number of open-air festivals and concert series dedicated specifically to classical music. Among the more interesting of these is the Stagione Estiva dell'Orchestra dell'Accademia di Santa Cecilia held at the Ninfeo (*nympheum*) on the grounds of **Villa Giulia** (*see p263*). Also listed as the Concerti a Villa Giulia, the concerts begin in July, with tickets under L20,000.

The Associazione Musicale Romana organizes Serenate in Chiostro – a lively and varied program of concerts held during July in the cloisters of **Santa Maria della Pace** (*see p121*), with tickets on sale for under L20,000. Estate al Tempietto (listed also as Concerti del Tempietto) is the Tempietto orchestra's summer treat, with concerts every evening from July to September in the **Area Archeologica del Teatro di Marcello** *(see p151)*. They're held in the adjacent basilica of San Nicola in Carcere if it rains.

Festival Villa Pamphilj in Musica, in July, is a series of concerts in the gardens of **Villa Doria Pamphilj** *(see p267)*. Programs range from comic opera to jazz and 20th-century classical music.

Brass bands can be heard in the **Pincio Gardens** *(see p136)* on Sunday mornings from the end of April until mid-July – they usually strike up at around 10:30am.

CONTEMPORARY MUSIC

THE **Auditorium del Foro Italico**, the **Auditorium di Santa Cecilia** and the Accademia Filarmonica Romana (usually at the **Teatro Olimpico**) sometimes include modern pieces in their programs but these are generally less popular than the classics; there is no set venue with a regular contemporary program.

International names appear on festival programs and at special concerts. The most interesting festivals are Nuovi Spazi Musicali (now part of RomaEuropa) in the summer, with free concerts transmitted on Italian radio, and the Festival Nuova Consonanza in autumn. Works of modern Italian composers are performed in the Rassegna Nuova Musica Italiana concert series two or three times a year. Also well worth attending are performances by scholars of the French Academy at **Villa Medici** *(see p135)*.

OPERA

I TALY AND OPERA are to many people synonymous. Critics will tell you (justifiably) that Rome's opera is nowhere near the standard of that at Milan's La Scala, or Naples's San Carlo. But that doesn't mean it's not worth visiting – world-class singers do appear here *(see p38)*, mainly in premieres or solo recitals. However you judge the quality of the performances, the surroundings in which they take place are often incomparable. In summer, the visual spectacle of *Aïda*, performed in the open air, is simply magnificent.

The season starts late at **Teatro dell'Opera**, between November and January. In recent years, programs have concentrated on the great popular operas rather than on staging experimental productions or historical adaptations. Tickets range from L25,000 to L250,000. Until recently the Teatro dell'Opera would move outdoors in July and August, to stage opera and ballet in the ancient baths of Caracalla. This celebrated tradition has now stopped as vibrations caused by the basso profundos and by the nimble corps de ballet were deemed to pose a threat to the structure of the Baths.

BALLET AND DANCE

O PPORTUNITIES to watch ballet or contemporary dance are fairly limited in Rome. The opera house's resident company, Corpo di Ballo del Teatro dell'Opera di Roma, performs the great classics as well as Roland Petit–style modern choreographies. Performances are staged at **Teatro dell'Opera**.

Contemporary dance is most likely found during the summer festivals, but foreign companies often perform at **Teatro Olimpico** as well. American modern dance groups of the Moses Pendleton school – Pilobolus, Momix, ISO and Daniel Ezralow – are popular visitors. **Teatro del Vascello** is another venue noted for experimental dance performances. In summer, outdoor performances are organized by **RomaEuropa Festival**.

Rock, Jazz, Folk and World Music

ROME'S NON-CLASSICAL MUSIC SCENE is unpredictable, but if you have the patience, you'll come across a huge variety of music at the many clubs, as well as open-air events with such foreign stars as Madonna, Michael Jackson and Dire Straits. Publicity is often disorganized, but the "Music Box" section of *Trovaroma* or *Roma c'è* (*see p340*) gives an idea of what you can choose from.

It's not possible to reserve tickets in advance at the smaller venues – just turn up with everyone else. You will need to buy a *tessera* (membership card) though, costing anything from L1,000 to L20,000. Well-known musicians may mean a further entrance fee, but local groups are generally included in the membership.

ROCK MUSIC

BIG ROCK CONCERTS are held at EUR in the **Palazzo dello Sport**, or in a stadium: the **Stadio Flaminio**, **Stadio Olimpico**, or out-of-the-way **Ippodromo Capannelle**. Get there at least an hour before the gates open for a good seat. Testaccio's **Villaggio Globale Il Mattatoio** (a converted abattoir) is a large-scale stand-up venue for concerts and other events. The facilities are basic, and again, large crowds mean you should turn up early.

Rome also has several lively clubs and discos which play rock music. Loyal devotees head for the good clubs in large numbers. Some are unpretentious and friendly and some, which are rather sumptuous and stylish, are frequented by the rich and famous. **Frontiera** is one of Rome's largest venues; some nights it features pop groups, including big name bands, and others it becomes a huge disco. However, it is not easy to get to using public transport as it is located well out of the center toward the western end of Via Aurelia. **Horus** is the place to head for if you want to see US and British acts who are just breaking internationally.

Check what's on, too, at the **Antica Carboneria**; at **Black Out**, with concerts held on Thursdays; at the **Mecca Dancing**; and, in the Vatican area, at **Il Castello**, a converted movie theater with rock and jazz festivals and a club. **Forte Prenestino** is an interesting place – a former prison, it was taken over by squatters a few years ago and turned into a social center, hosting rock concerts, debates and art exhibitions. Nearer the center are more traditional establishments. **Big Mama**, the trendy **Palladium** and **Caffè Caruso** are well-known, popular venues for a great variety of live bands.

JAZZ

ROME'S TASTE for jazz has developed over the years as a result of visits from American and other foreign musicians. Miles Davis played one of his last concerts at the Roma Jazz Festival, for instance, and guitarist Pat Metheny, Sonny Rollins, Gil Evans' Band, the Lounge Lizards, Spyrogyra, and Joe Zawinul's Syndicate are frequent visitors. Roma Jazz takes place every year, generally in July, with performances at the **Foro Italico** (*see p351*), sometimes listed as the Stadio del Tennis in *Trovaroma*. Tickets, which cost around L35,000 to 40,000, are obtainable from Orbis (*see p341*) and other agents.

Outside festival times, the best jazz musicians play at **Palladium**, near San Paolo fuori le Mura, or at **Airport Café** and **Alpheus**. **Alpheus** is unique in offering separate concert halls and interesting festivals featuring high-quality jazz ensembles every night. Other, smaller venues, some of which encourage budding talent, include **Vicolo 49**

where you are welcome to join in. Some of Rome's music schools also double as showcases for new performers – these include **Alexanderplatz**.

In summer, many of the music festivals take place outdoors at night. Jazz has featured in the Festival Villa Pamphilj in Musica in recent years, held every July and organized by I Concerti nel Parco. Tickets, costing around L15,000, are available from the Villa Pamphilj itself.

In winter, try the pub-style spot **Stardust**, which opens until late. It offers jazz on Tuesdays and a pianist on other nights. Or try what's offered at **Caffè Latino**, **Caffè Caruso** and **Fonclea**.

Pianist Antonello Salis plays a mix of jazz and Caribbean rhythms. Crystal White and the Supernaturals are a resident Roman jazz-funk formation. Guitar lovers may enjoy Eddie Palermo's fusion, and the major names to be aware of in jazz groups are Roberto Gatto, Maurizio Gianmarco, Massimo Moriconi and Massimo Urbani. Rome's other well-known bands include Orizzonte degli Eventi (fusion), Sestetto Swing di Roma (swing) and Area 2 (not strictly Roman), who play jazz rock.

FOLK MUSIC

AT THE FOREFRONT of folk music in Rome for 30 years, **Folkstudio** in Trastevere is well worth a visit. Founded back in the 1960s, its cramped rooms have an informal, friendly, participatory atmosphere that welcomed up-and-coming stars such as Bob Dylan – a fact that is remembered here with fondness and pride. Irish folk music and American country and western are much in demand, as well as the regional strains of Italian folk music. No drinks are sold, so you must bring your own. You'll need to buy a membership card to enter, costing around L10,000.

A recent arrival on Rome's folk music scene is the **Shamrock** in the Colosseum area, offering country and bluegrass music. If you want to eat, too, head for **Fonclea** near St. Peter's, but check out *Trovaroma* to see who's playing – country music is played only on some nights.

In some of Rome's Irish pubs, you may be lucky and find some spontaneous music-making going on. Places to try are the **Fiddler's Elbow** and **Druid's Den**, both in the Santa Maria Maggiore area. Also find out where the Kay McCarthy Ensemble or Square Dance is performing.

WORLD MUSIC

A STRONG Latin American colony has made its home in Rome since the 1970s. Latin American music is no passing fad here for poseurs and culture hoppers; Romans dance the night away together with the many Brazilian, Argentinian and Peruvian residents and merengue, salsa and soca are all very popular. For the last few years, an open-air summer Caribe festival has taken place in Villa Borghese with live music and other attractions. It's by no means a certain annual event, but its worth keeping an eye out for.

Many venues offer similar opportunities to enjoy Latin American music throughout the year: **El Charango** has South American food as well as music and a small dance area. Also watch for resident Brazilian musicians Brenazil, Carlos de Lima and Alvinho, and local salsa band Xenaya, or check what's on at the **Caffè Latino** and **K.K.** in the Ghetto, at **Caffè Caruso** in Testaccio and the **Bossa Nova** in Trastevere. If you want to get in touch with your inner cha-cha-cha, Latin rhythms pulse seductively against an r'n'b backbeat in Cuba's Roman sub-branch, **St Louis Music City**. Or try **Berimbau**, where you can enjoy a cocktail along with the Brazilian music.

Other regional musical styles have less of a presence, but are nevertheless available for the aficionado. Lovers of African music should seek out performances by Sanganà or Akwaba. African and Italian musicians play together to wonderful effect with Pietro dall'Oglio's group at various places in the city.

DIRECTORY

Airport Café
Via di Porta Castello 44.
Map 4 D3.
06-686 83 28.

Akab
Via di Monte
Testaccio 69.
Map 8 D4.
06-574 41 54.

Alexanderplatz
Via Ostia 9.
Map 3 B1.
06-39 74 21 71.

Alpheus
Via del Commercio 36–8.
Map 8 D5.
06-574 78 26.

Berimbau
Via dei Fienaroli 30.
Map 7 C1.
06-581 32 49.

Big Mama
Vicolo S. Francesco
a Ripa 18.
Map 7 C2.
06-581 25 51.

Black Out
Via Saturnia 18.
Map 9 C3.
06-70 49 67 91.

Bossa Nova
Via degli Orti di
Trastevere 43.
Map 7 C2.
06-581 61 21.

Caffè Caruso
Via di Monte
Testaccio 36.
Map 8 D4.
06-574 50 19.

Caffè Latino
Via di Monte Testaccio 96.
Map 8 D4.
06-57 28 83 84.

El Charango
Via di Sant'Onofrio 28.
Map 3 C4.
06-687 99 08.

Druid's Den
Via S. Martino
ai Monti 28.
Map 6 D4.
06-48 80 02 58.

Fiddler's Elbow
Via dell'Olmata 43.
Map 6 D4.
06-487 21 10.

Folkstudio
Via Frangipane 42.
Map 5 B5.
06-487 10 63.

Fonclea
Via Crescenzio 82 A.
Map 3 C2.
06-689 63 02.

Forte Prenestino
Via F. del Pino.
06-259 70 37.

Frontiera
Via Aurelia 1051.
Map 3 A3.
06-669 28 78.

Horus Club
Corso Sempione 21.
06-86 89 91 81.

**Ippodromo
Capannelle**
Via Appia Nuova km.12.
06-718 31 43.

K.K.
Piazza in Piscinula 20.
Map 8 D1.
06-589 64 21.

Mecca Dancing
Via Tagliamento 9.
06-855 53 98.

Palazzo dello Sport
Viale dell'Umanesimo.
06-592 51 07.

Palladium
Piazza B. Romano 8.
06-511 02 03.

St. Louis Music City
Via Cardello 13.
Map 5 B5.
06-4745 076.

Shamrock
Via Capo d'Africa 26 D.
Map 9 A1.
06-700 25 83.

Stadio Flaminio
Via dello Stadio Flaminio.
Map 1 B2.
06-323 65 39.

Stadio Olimpico
Viale dei Gladiatori.

Stardust
Vicolo de Renzi 4.
Map 7 C1.

Vicolo 49
Vicolo dei Soldati 47.
Map 4 E3 & 11 C2.
06-687 54 40.

**Villaggio Globale Il
Mattatoio**
Lungotevere Testaccio.
Map 8 D4.
06-57 30 03 29.

Movies and Theater

Moviegoing is a popular pastime in Rome, with around 40 films playing on an average weekday; theater-goers, however, have far less choice.

The great majority of Roman movie theaters are *prima visione* (first run) and show the latest international films in dubbed versions. The smaller art theaters are more likely to show subtitled versions of foreign films.

Theater productions are performed in Italian whether the plays are national classics or by foreign playwrights. The main theaters offer a selection by great Italian playwrights. There are also performances of traditional cabaret, avant-garde theater and dance theater. Theater tickets cost between L10,000 and L70,000 and can generally be bought in advance only by visiting the theater box office in person, or through agencies such as **Gesman** and **Box Office** *(see p341)*.

Movies (Prima Visione)

There are over 80 *prima visione* movie theaters in the city. The best in Rome in terms of both decor and comfort are the **Fiamma** (two screens), **Barberini** (three screens) and **Rivoli**.

Foreign films are dubbed into Italian rather than subtitled (Italian dubbers are considered among the best in the world), but the **Alcazar** and **Pasquino** have showings in the original language – mainly English – on Mondays.

Tickets for new films generally cost around L10,000, but a few theaters listed as *prima visione* charge less, namely **Capranichetta** and **Cinema Roma**. Senior citizens and disabled people are normally entitled to a 30% reduction on weekdays. Tickets are reduced for all weekday afternoons and on Wednesdays. Check the newspaper or listings magazines such as *Trovaroma* or *Roma c'è* for details *(see p340)*.

Art Movie Theaters

There are two main types of art movie theaters in Rome: the *cine-clubs* and the *cinema d'essai*. Both are good if you're interested in catching older classics and new foreign films as well as films by some of the contemporary Italian directors.

The *d'essai* theaters now and then show films in the original language (indicated by *v.o.* for *versione originale* in the listings). Try the **Azzurro Scipioni** (one of the few to remain open throughout summer) or the **Nuovo Sacher**. Some of the smaller theaters like the **Labirinto**, are called *cine-clubs* and require membership.

The multimedia arts center **Palazzo delle Esposizioni** usually shows interesting series of international films in the Sala Rossellini (prior reservations are advised).

Cartoons and children's favorites are shown at **Dei Piccoli**. The evening showings for adults, often in the original language, are listed as Dei Piccoli Sera.

The **Tibur**, a small theater with a varied program, is one of the few places where students get a reduction.

English-Language Films

In addition to occasional undubbed showings of British, American and Australasian films in art theaters and the **Alcazar**, Rome has its own English-language movie theater, the **Pasquino**, in Trastevere. Titles change every few days (tickets cost around L12,000).

Summer Movies

Many Roman movie theaters have retractable ceilings used in summer, while other theaters close for the summer. The **Nuovo Sacher** has an outdoor arena that is used for summer screenings.

Rome also has two summer movie festivals: Cineporto and Massenzio. These show several films each night from 9pm until the small hours, with food and drinks on sale and often live music during the intervals. Cineporto (every night, July–September) has a fixed venue in the Parco della Farnesina, but Massenzio moves around (see listings).

It's also worth checking the listings pages *(see p340)* for retrospectives or avant-garde film programs at the **Azzurro Scipioni** and the open-air arts festivals, like Roma-Europa *(see p341)* and Festa dell'Unità *(see p341)*. Sci-fi enthusiasts will surely enjoy the Fantafestival (early June), a science-fiction, fantasy and horror film festival.

Mainstream Theater

The backbone of Rome's theatrical repertoire is Luigi Pirandello's dramas and comedies by 18th-century Venetian Carlo Goldoni and 20th-century Neapolitan Eduardo de Filippo. Major foreign playwrights are also performed from time to time.

The best classic productions are staged at the **Teatro Argentina**, **Teatro Quirino**, **Teatro Valle**, **Teatro Eliseo** and **Teatro Piccolo Eliseo**. **Teatro Argentina**, originally an opera house, is state-owned and home of Rome's permanent theater company. The **Quirino** and **Valle** host productions from other Italian cities. The **Valle** alternates between productions of great Italian classics by famous companies and lesser-known modernist works. Plays at the **Quirino** often feature famous Italian actors. The **Eliseo** and **Piccolo Eliseo** are among the best of the private theaters. Agatha Christie and Alfred Hitchcock are often on at the **Teatro Stabile del Giallo**, which runs crime and detective thrillers, while **Teatro Vittoria** goes in for Noël Coward or Raymond Queneau. The program at

Teatro Sistina usually includes musicals by visiting foreign companies and shows by popular Italian actors.

CONTEMPORARY THEATER

THE HOMES OF contemporary theater are the **Tordinona**, **Politecnico**, **Ateneo** (inside the university), plus a host of small theaters, ingeniously rigged up in cellars, garages, small apartments or tents. The **Colosseo** host some alternative fringe-type productions (known here as *teatro off*), while the **Tordinona**, the **Politecnico** and the **Ateneo** tend to stage works by contemporary authors and occasional avant-garde productions. Some, like the **Teatro dei Cocci**, put on drama school productions.

FOLK, CABARET AND PUPPET THEATER

ROMAN AND Neapolitan folk songs and cabaret can be enjoyed in one of Trastevere's traditional lively cabaret restaurants like **Ciceruacchio**, **Fantasie di Trastevere**, or **Meo Patacca**.

Puppet theater is another Roman tradition. Shows generally take place early in the evening on weekends and sometimes during the week at **Teatro Verde**; **Teatro Mongiovino** and the **English Puppet Theatre**. Puppeteers at the English Puppet Theatre will recite in English if there is enough demand. In the summer, traveling Neapolitan and Sicilian marionette companies give special performances.

OPEN-AIR THEATER

THE OPEN-AIR summer theater season usually features Greek and Roman plays at **Ostia Antica** *(see pp270–71).*

The **Anfiteatro Quercia del Tasso** in the Janiculum park takes its name from the oak tree under which 16th-century poet Tasso used to sit. Comedy shows are staged here in July and September, when the weather permits. In winter the company performs at the **Teatro Anfitrione.**

Nearby is a permanent Neapolitan street puppet theater booth featuring *Pulcinella* (the Italian original of Punch). Shows are usually in the afternoons, with morning shows on Sundays; children love them.

DIRECTORY

MOVIES

Alcazar
Via Card. Merry del Val 14.
Map 7 C1.
[06-588 00 99.

Barberini
Piazza Barberini 52.
Map 5 B3.
[06-482 77 07.

Capranichetta
Piazza di Montecitorio 125.
Map 4 F3 & 12 E2.
[06-679 69 57.

Cinema Roma
Piazza Sonnino 37. **Map**
7 C1. [06-581 28 84.

Fiamma
Via Bissolati 47. **Map** 5 C2.
[06-482 71 00.

Rivoli
Via Lombardia 23. **Map**
5 B2. [06-488 08 83.

ART MOVIES

Azzurro Scipioni
Via degli Scipioni 82. **Map**
3 C2. [06-39 73 71 61.

Dei Piccoli
Viale della Pineta 15. **Map**
5 B1. [06-855 34 85.

Labirinto
Via di Pompeo Magno 27.
Map 4 D1.
[06-321 62 83.

Nuovo Sacher
Largo Ascianghi 1. **Map**
7 C2. [06-581 81 16.

Palazzo delle Esposizioni
Via Milano 9A. **Map** 5 B4.
[06-06-488 54 65.

Tibur
Via degli Etruschi 36.
[06-495 77 62.

ENGLISH-LANGUAGE FILMS

Alcazar
See left.

Pasquino
Vicolo del Piede 19. **Map**
7 C1. [06-580 36 22.

MAINSTREAM THEATER

Teatro Argentina
Largo Argentina 56.
Map 4 F4 & 12 D4.
[06-68 80 46 01.

Teatro Eliseo
Via Nazionale 183.**Map**
5 B4. [06-474 34 31.

Teatro Piccolo Eliseo
Via Nazionale 183. **Map**
5 B4. [06-488 50 95.

Teatro Quirino
Via M. Minghetti 1.
Map 5 A4 & 12 F2.
[06-679 45 85.

Teatro Sistina
Via Sistina 129. **Map** 5 B2.
[06-482 68 41.

Teatro Stabile del Giallo
Via Cassia 871.
[06-30 31 13 35.

Teatro Valle
Via Teatro Valle 23 A.
Map 4 F4 & 12 D3.
[06-68 80 37 94.

Teatro Vittoria
Piazza S. Maria Liberatrice 8.
Map 8 D3.
[06-74 01 70.

CONTEMPORARY THEATER

Teatro Anfitrione
Via di San Saba 24. **Map**
8 E3. [06-575 08 27.

Teatro Ateneo
Viale delle Scienze 3.
Map 6 F3.
[06-49 91 44 35.

Teatro Colosseo
Via Capo d'Africa 5 A.
Map 9 A1.
[06-700 49 32.

Teatro dei Cocci
Via Galvani 69. **Map** 8 D3.
[06-578 35 02.

Teatro Politecnico
Via Tiepolo 13 A. **Map**
1 B3. [06-361 15 01.

Teatro Tordinona
Via degli Acquasparta 16.
Map 4 E3 & 11 C2.
[06-68 80 58 90.

FOLK, CABARET, PUPPET THEATER

Ciceruacchio
Via del Porto 1. **Map** 8 D2.
[06-580 60 46.

English Puppet Theatre
Piazza di Satiri.
[06-589 62 01.

Fantasie di Trastevere
Via di Santa Dorotea 6. **Map**
4 D5. [06-588 16 71.

Meo Patacca
Piazza dei Mercanti 30. **Map**
8 D1. [06-581 61 98.

Teatro Mongiovino
Via Genocchi 15.
[06-513 94 05.

Teatro Verde
Circonvall. Gianicolense 10.
Map 7 B4.
[06-588 20 34.

OPEN-AIR THEATER

Anfiteatro Quercia del Tasso
Passeggiata del Gianicolo.
Map 3 C5.
[06-575 08 27.

Nightclubs

THE CENTER OF ROMAN NIGHTLIFE used to be the Via Veneto area so effectively portrayed by Fellini in his film *La Dolce Vita*. The place still offers plenty of action, but new, less formal and more affordable clubs have emerged, with a more vibrant atmosphere and appealing to a younger and more diverse crowd.

With the new clubs come new areas. The picturesque narrow streets in Trastevere, the Piazza Navona and the Pantheon areas are becoming more popular. Testaccio, too, has become a new mecca for Roman clubbers.

WHAT'S OFFERED

As IN ANY OTHER major city, Rome's nightlife is constantly changing. Roman club-goers are an extremely varied group, and most clubs arrange different nights to appeal to different tastes – so it's essential to keep up-to-date on what's happening by checking in a magazine like *Roma C'E'*, on newsstands every Thursday.

For a more direct source of information, head for the bars around the Piazza Navona and Campo de' Fiori areas. At about 10:30pm the narrow streets and piazzas swarm with people, and any interesting event will soon become common knowledge. *Buoni* (free or reduced-price tickets) may be handed out.

ADMISSION

PREFERRED CLUBBING nights for Romans are Thursday, Friday and, of course, Saturday, when you should expect to pay around L35,000 for entrance. Lines for the most popular places can be long, but provided you arrive before midnight you'll avoid the crush.

Some clubs require a *tessera* (membership card) that you can buy on the spot and that usually replaces the entrance fee. Your ticket, or *tessera*, usually includes a free first drink; your second could well be expensive – as much as L20,000 in some of the plusher clubs.

In these smarter places, how you look is all-important: a jacket and tie are a must, and usually you need an invitation or a personal introduction to get in. It should not be difficult to gain entrance to the traditional discos as long as you dress in designer casual wear, but watch out! A black T-shirt could make you too *alternativo*. All-male groups are never welcome, and in more exclusive clubs neither are unaccompanied men.

CLUBS AND BARS

AN ELEGANT NIGHT out could start in one of the refined piano bars, such as **Le Cornacchie**, **Guilio Passami l'Olio** frequented by the English-speaking community; or the intimate **Tartarughino**, popular with politicians and financiers. Livelier places are the American-style bars, such as **Hemingway**. If you prefer the arts world, head for **Bar del Fico**, **Café les Folies** and **La Vetrina**.

To continue, head for **Gilda**, a favorite with the Roman jet set, featuring two elegant restaurants, a large glitzy dance floor and many VIPs. The famous nightclub of the 1960s, **Jackie O**, has been revamped in lavish style, with a lush interior and an expensive restaurant. In a similar vein and not to be missed are **Open Gate**, and **Club 84**.

The hottest club among the younger and trendier is **Alien**. This club offers house, techno and hip-hop, along with stages, wild lighting effects and "happenings." A smaller dance floor offers a more mellow music selection. Equally funky is **Heaven** which also offers soul and dance music. At **Groove**, acid jazz, rap and soul dominate on Wednesday, Thursday and Friday nights.

An unforgettable place for dancing in a blitzkrieg of beat is **Radio Londra**, designed to look like a World War II bunker, where hard dance music and free entrance attract huge crowds of jive bombers. **Black Out** is one of the few clubs in Rome offering punk and British rock music, with the occasional live concert.

The more traditional disco is at its best at **Mecca Dancing**, the oldest and biggest Roman disco, which totally revamps its interior every season. It's especially popular with the younger crowd, as is **Smile**. **Qube** is a huge disco laid out on several floors with various dance floors playing mainly rave music. There are some disco bars worth noting, too, like **B-Side** and **DDT**.

To find out about events in the more unusual Roman clubs, start the evening at the **Vineria**. The old abattoir (*il Mattatoio*) at Testaccio is the setting for **Villaggio Globale**, a social center hosting concerts, shows, discos and parties. **Circolo degli Artisti** is another social center with a large dance floor, bar, theater and video room, situated in the old milk center. In the southern suburbs, two larger venues offer a variety of concerts and events – the converted movie theater **Palladium** and **Alpheus**.

GAY AND LESBIAN

THE GAY AND LESBIAN SCENE is quite active. Many clubs have fixed gay nights as well as special events, especially during the Maratona Gay Festival in May. The most famous gay club is **Alibi**, where music is a mixture of underground and 1970s hits. **Angelo Azzurro** offers hi-energy and house in Post-Modern surroundings, but is only open at the weekends. Watch for events organized by **Circolo Mario Mieli di Cultura Omosessuale** or go to bars such as **Hangar** to find out what's on. For Lesbians **Angelo Azzurro** has a women-only night on Thursday, and **New Jolie Coeur** often has them on Saturdays.

JAZZ, SALSA AND AFRICAN

THERE ARE plenty of jazz venues *(see p344)* from which to choose while spending time in Rome. The following clubs combine live music with dancing and drinking. **Caffè Latino** (membership club) is best at the weekend. For South American music try **Yes Brazil**, which has live bands and lots of people. **Alpheus** is a four-roomed venue where different kinds of music events take place simultaneously.

African clubs like **Fantasy** (free on Fridays) are lively, friendly and cheap.

CLUBBING IN SUMMER

IN SUMMER, when everything closes down in the city, head for the Roman seaside resorts. At Fregene, for instance, there are 13 clubs; all pretty much the same, where the dress is designer-label casuals. Take along your swimsuit since much of the fun takes place in and around the swimming pools. The clubs include **Gilda on the Beach** and **Miraggio** – the

latter popular with a younger crowd. Most of these seaside clubs have restaurants attached to them as well.

LATE CLUBS

MOST ROMAN clubs stay open until 3 or 4am, However, it is possible to find one or two clubs that remain open until dawn. Before finally heading off to bed, join other diehard clubbers at any of the city's 24-hour bars for a final drink and head for one of the early-morning bakers to buy sweet *cornetti* hot from the oven.

DIRECTORY

Alibi
Via di Monte Testaccio 44.
Map 8 D4.
06-574 34 48.

Alien
Via Velletri 13. **Map** 6 D1.
06-841 22 12.

Alpheus
Via del Commercio 36/8.
Map 8 D5.
06-574 78 26.

Angelo Azzurro
Via Card. Merry del Val 13.
Map 7 C1.
06-580 04 72.

Antico Caffè della Pace
Via della Pace 3–7.
Map 4 E4 & 11 C2.
06-686 12 16.

Bar del Fico
Piazza del Fico 26/8.
Map 11 B2.
06-686 52 05.

Black Out
Via Saturnia 18.
Map 9 C3.
06-70 49 67 91.

B-Side
Via dei Funari 21A.
Map 12 E5.
06-68 83 32 32.

Café les Folies
Via San Francesco a Ripa
165. **Map** 7 C1.
06-588 59 08.

Caffè Latino
Via di Monte Testaccio 96.
Map 8 D4.
06-574 40 20.

Circolo degli Artisti
Via Lamarmora 28.
Map 6 E5.
06-70 30 56 84.

Circolo Mario Mieli di Cultura Omosessuale
Via Ostiense 202.
06-541 39 85.

Club 84
Via Emilia 84.
Map 5 B2.

Le Cornacchie
Piazza Rondanini 53.
Map 4 F4 & 12 D2.
06-68 80 45 50.

DDT
Via dei Sabelli 2.
Map 6 F4.

Fantasy
Via Alba 42.
Map 10 F3.
06-701 67 41.

Gilda
Via Mario de' Fiori 97.
Map 5 A2 & 12 F1.
06-678 48 38.

Giulio Passami l'Olio
Via di Monte Giordano 2.
Map 11 B2.
06-68 80 32 88.

Groove
Vicollo Savelli 10.
Map 11 C3.
06-687 24 27.

Hangar
Via in Selci 69. **Map** 5 C5.
06-448 13 97.

Heaven
Viale di Porta Ardeatina
118A. **Map** 9 B5.
06-574 37 72

Hemingway
Piazza delle Coppelle 10.
Map 4 F3 & 12 D2.
06-686 44 90.

Jackie O
Via Boncompagni 11.
Map 5 B2.
06-42 88 54 57.

Mecca Dancing
Via Tagliamento 9.
06-841 44 59.

New Jolie Coeur
Via Sirte 5.
06-86 21 58 27.

Open Gate
Via San Nicola da
Tolentino 4. **Map** 5 C2.
06-42 00 08 48.

Palladium
Piazza B. Romano 8.
06-511 02 03.

Qube
Via di Portonaccio 212.
06-438 10 05.

Radio Londra
Via Monte Testaccio 65/b.
Map 8 D4.
06-575 00 44.

Safari
Via Aurelia 601.
06-66 41 63 09.

Smile
Via Schiaparelli 29-31.
Map 2 D3.
06-322 12 51.

Tartarughino
Via della Scrofa 1.
Map 4 F3 & 12 D2.
06-686 41 31.

La Vetrina
Via della Vetrina 20.
Map 4 E3 & 11 B2.
06-68 80 84 44.

Villaggio Globale
Lungotevere Testaccio.
Map 8 D4.
06-57 30 03 29.

Vineria Reggio
Campo de' Fiori 5.
Map 4 E4 & 11 C4.
06-68 80 32 68.

Yes Brazil
Via S. Francesco a Ripa
103. **Map** 7 C2.
06-581 62 67.

SUMMER CLUBS

Gilda on the Beach
Lungomare di Ponente 11.
06-66 56 06 49.

Miraggio
Lungomare di Ponente 95.
06-66 56 03 69.

Sports

Don't be surprised if the peace of a Sunday afternoon in Rome is interrupted by people shouting and honking car horns. It simply means that one of the home soccer teams has won at the stadium, and the whole town will vibrate with the excitement.

Soccer is the national sport but other sports also manage to attract a large following. Roman sports fans are never at a loss for varied events and activities.

Times and venues for most spectator sports are listed in *Trovaroma* or *Roma c'è (see p340)*, as well as the local sections of *La Gazzetta dello Sport* or *Corriere dello Sport*.

Soccer

An Italian soccer match is an experience not to miss for the quality of the play, the excitable crowds and the fun atmosphere. Soccer fan troublemakers are rare.

Rome has two teams, Roma and Lazio, and they take turns playing at the **Stadio Olimpico** on Sunday afternoons at 3pm, in the Campionato Italiano (Italian championship league). Seats can be scarce, so get tickets in advance from the stadium (L15,000 to L150,000). The cheapest tickets are in the Le Curve stand; middle-range and most expensive, are in Le Gardinate and La Tribuna, respectively.

On Wednesday evenings, there are international competitions – the Coppa delle Coppe (European Cup Winners Cup), the UEFA cup and the Coppa dei Campioni (European Championship Cup). In between these, teams battle it out for the national Coppa Italia.

Tennis

A major event, the International Championships go on at **Foro Italico** for two weeks in May. The world's top tennis stars thrash it out on clay courts at 1 and 8:30pm from Tuesday to Friday, and at 1pm only on weekends. Buy tickets in advance either directly from the Foro Italico or from a ticket agency.

If you wish to play yourself, there are now over 350 tennis clubs in Rome. It is often essential to reserve at least a week in advance, and there's usually a moderate court fee.

Clubs where membership is not required are the **Tennis Lazio** and the **Circolo della Stampa** in northern Rome and the **Oasis di Pace**, just off the Via Appia Antica. The big hotels offer tennis for a reasonable price. **St. Peter's Holiday Inn** requires a small annual membership fee on top of the court price, which includes the gym and the pool (in the summer).

Horse Racing, Trotting, and Leisure Riding

Important races include the Derby in June and the Premio Roma in November. There are trotting races at the **Ippodromo di Tor di Valle** and flat races and steeple chases at **Concorso Ippico** and the **Ippodromo delle Capannelle**.

The International Horse Show is held at the end of April and the beginning of May in Piazza di Siena, Villa Borghese *(see p258)*. It is one of the most important social and sporting events in the calendar, and the setting makes it a great attraction.

It may be possible to find a riding club that will take you on a hack in the countryside around Rome, but most do not accept short-term members.

Golf

Even the most elite golf clubs will accept a touring golfer with a home membership and handicap. Most clubs are closed on Mondays and on weekends, when they host competitions, and guests cannot play. Prices range from L50,000 to L80,000.

The **Olgiata Golf Club** is open to everybody from Tuesday to Thursday and to guests accompanied by a member on Friday to Sunday. **Country Club Castel Gandolfo** is the newest club, and **Circolo Golf Roma** the oldest and most prestigious. Within the city ring road is the course at the **Sheraton Hotel** (closed Tuesday).

Two of the many important competitions taking place on the golf courses in and around Rome are the National Championships in October and the Rome Masters in April.

Car and Motorcycle Racing

Formula 1 and Formula 3 races take place on Sundays at **Vallelunga**; be prepared for some relatively expensive entrance fees. Frequently on Saturdays official trials are open to spectators, and on some nonracing Sundays Italy's car designers show new models.

Greyhound Racing

The **Cinodromo** track has shed its sleazy image, and the entrance fee and bets are inexpensive. There is usually a lively, animated crowd of all ages in attendance. Races are run every Wednesday and Thursday at 6:30pm and on Sundays at 10:15am.

Rowing

In mid-June, a British Oxbridge crew challenges the historic Aniene crew to a race taking place alternately on the Thames and the Tiber. The best place to view this from is between the Margherita and the Sant' Angelo bridges. The race usually starts at around 6pm. Another event is the battle between the Roma and Lazio crews, from Ponte Milvio to Ponte Flaminio, on the same variable date as the Roma-Lazio soccer Derby.

SWIMMING

SWIMMING POOLS are few and definitely not geared to the short-term visitor. You often have to pay an expensive membership and on top of that a monthly fee. It's also essential, in most pools, to produce a medical certificate assuring your good health.

The state-owned pools can be slightly cheaper, but you still have to pay an initial membership fee.

It's better to try the outdoor pools, often part of the big hotels. The **Shangri-La Hotel** opens its pool to non-residents from July to September. For a higher entrance fee, swim at the **Hilton**, which also opens its pool in summer. The best deal is on Sunday when the sports club and swimming pool **La Margherita** opens to non-members from 10am to 1pm for a reasonable charge. **Piscina delle Rose** in EUR is an Olympic-sized pool (often deserted in the morning) open from June to September 9am to 5:30pm during the week, 9am to 7pm at weekends.

HEALTH CLUBS

JUST AS THE swimming pools, Roman health clubs usually require both a membership and monthly payments. For just a short stay in Rome, it would be much more sensible to try the facilities in your hotel, or, if you are willing to pay, head for one of the private clubs. Use of club facilities may be negotiable – you could possibly be lucky and find that you are waved through for the price of a guest pass.

The **Roman Sports Center** welcomes day members for a reasonable price, and you can use the swimming pools, the gym and sauna. The facilities are open from 9am to 10pm. Be sure to wear Lycra because shorts made from other materials are not allowed.

JOGGING AND CYCLING

ROME'S PERFECT climate and stunning scenery attract thousands of well-dressed joggers and cyclists into the city's many parks. Early week-day mornings or at any time on a Sunday, you'll find the more popular locations looking more like a high-speed fashion show than a track to work up a sweat.

At **Villa Doria Pamphilj** (see p267), is an extensive park situated above the Janiculum, where you can choose among three tracks, plenty of open spaces and a network of paths. **Villa Borghese** (see p258) is another vast popular place with a running track.

Alternatively, jog away your cares under the acacia trees and palms at Villa Torlonia; on the spotlit track at Villa Glori; or combine sport with culture by running the **Via Appia Antica** (see p265) branching off into Parco Caffarella. Other favorite places for inviting exhaustion are Viale delle Terme di Caracalla, Circo Massimo, Parco degli Aquedotti and Parco di Colle Oppio.

All of the above are also ideal for cyclists, and you can rent bikes from many places, including **Collalti**, **Via del Corso** and **I Bike Roma**.

Organized bike trips are advertised in *Trovaroma*.

CHILDREN'S ROME

ITALIANS LOVE HAVING children around, and you can be sure yours will be made welcome wherever they go. But there are few special facilities for children, and the heat, crowds and lack of clean public bathrooms mean that Rome is not an ideal city for a vacation with those under seven. It does, however, have plenty to offer slightly older children, especially those who may have an inter-

Renaissance cherub from the Villa Farnesina

est in history or art. The temptation may be to wear yourself and your children out by packing too many sights into one day. Plan in advance and leave plenty of time to wander around the city, looking at the unusual fountains and monuments, watching knife grinders at work in the markets and spending hours agonizing over the choice of ice cream flavors and special pizza toppings.

PRACTICAL ADVICE

IF YOU ARE bringing your children to Rome, try to come in early spring or late autumn, when the weather is good, but not too hot. Easter is best avoided, since the city is more crowded than usual, and you're constantly jostled on packed buses and streets. Where you stay is crucial. A hotel near the Villa Borghese park will give your children plenty of chance to relax and let off steam, though you may end up spending a lot of time and money to get to and from the town center. A hotel in the old center is ideal, so you can easily go back during the day for a rest and a clean bathroom.

Jogging in Villa Borghese

Since hygienic toilets and changing facilities are rare within the city, it is really not advisable to bring a baby to Rome unless you are visiting friends or family. As with many historic cities, Rome may not instantly appeal to all children, but there is plenty to inspire their imaginations. Use this book to make the buildings and history come alive. Children might also enjoy learning a few Italian words and phrases so they can order food and buy things by themselves.

If lingering over drinks on the café terraces is what you enjoy best, bring your off-spring something to keep them busy once they have finished with their treat: crayons and paper, a computer game or a Walkman. Alternatively, most other adults are very tolerant of children running around and making a noise while they relax and, if yours are reasonably outgoing, they could join in with the local children playing ball games in early evenings on piazzas like Campo de' Fiori.

If you feel the need for a total break, most hotels will be able to provide a babysitter or help you to contact a qualified baby-sitting agency.

In the event of sickness or an accident, see pages 360–61 for information and a list of emergency numbers.

Fairground in the Villa Borghese park

GETTING AROUND

BUMPY COBBLES, narrow streets without sidewalks and overcrowded buses make pushing strollers around tiring work. You will, however, inevitably find some people willing to help you haul a carriage up steps in a Metro station or onto a bus. Mothers with young children are usually allowed ahead in lines and may be offered seats on buses. The Metro is often less crowded. Kids under 3 ft 3 in (1 m) tall travel free on public transportation.

Although the city is not good for cyclists, families with older children could rent bikes to ride along the Via Appia Antica or to take on a regional train into the country. The bike rental hut in the Pincio gardens has free baby seats.

Anyone over the age of 14 can ride a scooter under 50 cc, although Rome is not the best place for novices (see p378).

A rental bike with free baby seat

Pony-pulled trains in the Villa Borghese park

EATING OUT

CHILDREN ARE normally warmly welcomed in neighborhood pizzerias and trattorias, and highchairs are often available for toddlers and babies. If there's no highchair, you can expect the waiters to improvise for you with armloads of cushions or telephone directories. Most places are perfectly happy to serve half portions or to let children share meals.

In trattorias it can sometimes be difficult to be exactly sure what a certain dish contains (especially when there is no menu, and the dishes of the day are reeled off, usually at top speed, by the waiter), so picky eaters are likely to be happier in pizzerias *(see pp318–21)*. Here they can choose their own topping (remember

that *prosciutto*, which is usually translated in menus as ham, is cured). The most entertaining pizzerias for kids are the old-fashioned ones where they can watch the chefs pound, stretch and flip the pizza dough. The best places get busy from around 8:30pm, so it is wise to go early to avoid having to get in line. If all else fails, there are many branches of McDonald's.

PICNICS

PICNICS IN THE parks are ideal, and shopping for the food is often half the fun. There's no problem finding small cartons of fruit juice and branded canned drinks, but these are expensive unless you go to a supermarket – the branch of Standa on Viale Trastevere is the most

convenient. Water from the drinking fountains is hygienic, so it's worth carrying plastic cups around.

In addition to picnic food from bakeries and markets, there are lots of scrumptious takeout foods. Many of them are appealing but messy, so it's wise to bring paper napkins. Try deep-fried fruit and vegetables from Cose Fritte on Via di Ripetta and *supplì al telefono*, rice croquettes with a gooey string of mozzarella inside, from *pizza al taglio* outlets. A *tramezzino* comes quite close to an American sandwich, but if your kids are miserable without peanut butter, you can find it (and other foreign foods) at Ruggieri on Campo de' Fiori.

Feeding pigeons on Piazza Navona

ICE CREAM

ROME, OF COURSE, is famous for ice cream; you and your children are likely to be tempted at every turn. Real ice cream fans may even want to plan their day's sightseeing around one of the best *gelaterie (see pp319–21)*. It's far cheaper to buy either a cone or tub of ice cream to eat in the street, but in some of the more traditional places it's worth paying to sit down. At Fassi, they have an old-fashioned ice cream-making machine on display, and at Giolitti, you can enjoy gargantuan sundaes in the elegant parlor *(see p109)*.

Investigating some of the hundreds of Italian ice cream flavors

Sightseeing with Children

Entrance to the Villa Borghese Zoo

GENERAL TIPS

ROME DOES NOT have many museums with the sort of hands-on exhibits and activities that many other cities provide for children. Instead, it has other things to entertain visitors. Bernini's marble elephant (see p108) and the fat *facchino*, or porter, (p107) delight most children. The Capuchin cemetery at Santa Maria della Concezione (p254), the catacombs (pp264–7) and the Mamertine Prison (p91) are for the young with more ghoulish imaginations.

Look for details like the dirty toenails on figures in Caravaggio's paintings; the Etruscan votives, which were offered to the gods, at the Villa Giulia (pp262–3); and the illusory collapsing ceiling

in the Chiesa Nuova, as well as the fake dome of Sant' Ignazio di Loyola (see p106).

Museums your children will enjoy include the Museo delle Arti e Tradizioni Popolari at EUR, with its antique toys and nativity scene (p267), and the Museo delle Mura, which explores the length of the Aurelian Wall (p196).

Among the churches, St. Peter's, where they can climb to the top of the dome (see p230), and San Clemente, where they can descend to the underground mithreum (see pp186–7), are most fun.

At the Vatican children will like the statues and mosaics in the Animal Gallery and the Sistine Ceiling (p246), especially when they find out that Michelangelo had to paint it hunched up on a scaffolding platform.

ANCIENT RUINS

THE ANCIENT RUINS best appreciated by children are the Colosseum (see pp92–5), and Trajan's Markets (see pp 88–9). You can still make out what both these buildings looked like from their remains. The scant ruins of the Forum and Palatine, on the other hand, may not appeal so strongly. Ostia Antica, where the remains include a theater, shop and 20-seater public toilet, is much more likely to interest them (see pp270–71).

Mosaic from the Vatican

MOSAICS

THERE ARE SCORES of vivid, sometimes quirky, mosaics in buildings all over Rome. Many of these are particularly appealing to children. Details in the mosaics range from brilliantly colored flowers, leaves, animals and buildings (in the churches of San Clemente, Santa Prassede and Santa Maria in Trastevere, see p186, p171 and pp212–13) to the debris of a banquet (in the Vatican's Museo Gregorio Profano, see pp234–5).

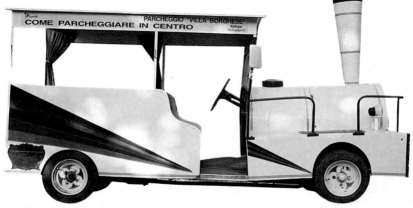
Model trains in Villa Borghese

ENTERTAINMENT

ROME'S CULTURAL offerings for children are a bit sparse. To find out what's on, check the movie pages of the newspapers and the listings in *Trovaroma* and *Roma c'è (see p340)*. Most theaters and cinemas have reduced entry fees for children, but these are only useful if your children can speak Italian.

Language is not a barrier in cartoons and puppet shows. There are cartoons at Villa Borghese's Cinema dei Piccoli and traditional puppet shows every afternoon except Wednesday up on the Janiculum hill. If your hotel has a TV, you'll find plenty of cartoons there to keep your kids entertained.

Stall at the Christmas toy fair on Piazza Navona

Resting on the curb side

One of the most appealing times for children to be in Rome is over Christmas, when Piazza Navona hosts the Chirstmas toy fair, where stalls sell toys and sweets.

PARKS

VILLA BORGHESE *(see p258)* has rowboats to rent and ducks to feed; pony and pony-cart rides; bikes to rent; a mini-cinema; a small fun fair; and a zoo. Villa Celimontana *(see p193)* has bike trails, and open-air theater performances in the summer. The amusement park LUNEUR at EUR *(see p267)* is old-fashioned but can be fun. The Bomarzo Monster Park, 60 miles (95 km) north of Rome, was built in the 16th century for a mad duke. Children can clamber over its giant stone monsters.

TOYS

A VISIT TO a Roman toyshop can be a lot of fun. **Città del Sole** sells a range of delightful educational toys and games, while **Al Sogno** is a wonderland of stuffed animals.

Città del Sole
Via della Scrofa 65.
Map 4 F3 & 12 D2.
06-687 54 04.

Al Sogno
Piazza Navona 53.
Map 4 E4 & 11 C3.
06-686 41 98.

CHILDREN'S CLOTHES

Italians adore dressing their children up, and on Sunday afternoons in particular, you are likely to encounter young children dressed as if they had walked straight out of a costume drama: girls in frills and flounces and boys in velvet breeches or knee-length shorts.

Many shops sell beautifully handcrafted children's shoes and clothes – the downside is that they can often be expensive and impractical: dry-clean-only clothes are common, and shoes are not made for mud.

Lavori Artigianili Femminili sells handmade silk and wool clothes for children up to eight. **Baby House** offers *haute couture* for children, including clothes by top designers, and **Bennetton** sell smart casuals.

Baby House
Via Cola di Rienzo 117. **Map** 3 C2.
06-321 42 91.

Bennetton
Via Condotti 19. **Map** 5 A2.
06-679 79 82.

Lavori Artigianali Femminili
Via Capo le Case 6. **Map** 5 A3 & 12 F1.
06-679 29 92.

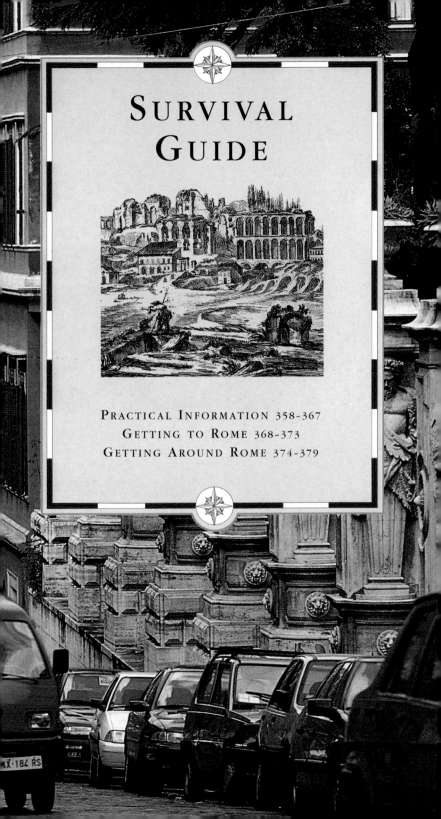

SURVIVAL
GUIDE

PRACTICAL INFORMATION

ROMANS OFTEN SEEM unconcerned by the priceless art treasures and ancient ruins that lie so casually among the buildings and workings of their hectic 20th-century city. Visitors nearly always find these wonders very exciting, but it's not always easy to actually see them. Relaxed local attitudes make for hundreds of variations on opening hours. Most places close for several hours over lunch and reopen in the late afternoon; some museums are open in the mornings only. Bank and shop hours can be just as difficult to pin down. On a more positive note, many of the main sights are within easy walking distance of one another. Start your day early and wear comfortable shoes for the Roman cobblestones. Rome can be a delightfully informal city to visit, but remember to observe dress rules to cover up in churches, as this is one area where the Italians are very strict.

MUSEUMS AND MONUMENTS

MANY MUSEUMS open only in the mornings and close all day on Mondays. If you are particularly eager to see a specific monument or museum, make sure it's open before you set out. Many museums don't allow visitors to enter in the last half an hour or so before they close.

EPT's guide to current exhibitions

There is usually an admission charge for museums and monuments, although some are free on Sundays. Many museums offer a reduced entrance fee for children under 18, students with the appropriate ID and senior citizens from the European Union. If you don't see any reductions advertised it is always worth asking. Entrance to all churches is free, and many contain works of art that are worthy of the world's greatest museums. Some of Rome's sights are accessible only on personal application or by written appointment. Examples include Nero's Aqueduct or the gardens at the Vatican. The *Area by Area* section of this guide gives opening times for each sight and tells you whether there is an admission charge. The **EPT** publishes a useful leaflet called *Musei e Monumenti di Roma*, which gives details of current exhibitions at Rome's

Typical traffic congestion in Via delle Quattro Fontane

TOURIST INFORMATION

THE SERVICE at the main provincial tourist office (**EPT**) is better than at the station. You can pick up details of special tours here. EPT also help with accommodation *(see p289)*. There are also several information kiosks in strategic positions, run by the Commune di Roma, with English-speaking staff providing free maps, leaflets and advice.

Besides the official tourist offices, good travel agents such as **CIT**, **Wagons Lits** or the **American Express** office can also be helpful to visitors. For information on Italian cities and areas outside Rome, contact **ENIT** (the National Tourist Board), who have offices in all the main cities.

A word of warning: prices and opening times change often, without notice, and sights can be closed for what seem to be unbelievably long periods of restoration *(chiuso per restauro)* or because of a strike *(sciopero)*.

ITALIA

ENTE NAZIONALE ITALIANO PER IL TURISMO
ENIT logo

The 116 electric minibus: useful for the historic center

ENTERTAINMENT INFORMATION

THE WEEKLY *Trovaroma*, in *La Repubblica*, and *Roma c'è*, both published on Thursdays are the main guides to

what's on. The bilingual fortnightly *Un Ospite a Roma* (A Guest in Rome) also has entertainment listings and is available free from

Trovaroma   newsagents. English listings are also in *Metropolitan* and *Wanted in Rome*. Full entertainment information is on page 340.

GUIDED TOURS

SEVERAL COMPANIES offer tours with English-speaking guides; these include **CIT**, **American Express**, **Green Line Tours** and **Carrani Tours**. Full-day city tours including lunch cost around L95,000–110,000; half-day tours around L40,000– 50,000. Alternatively, the 110 ATAC bus passes many of the main sights on a three-hour circuit. The total journey costs around L6,000. Tour guides can be hired at many of the major sights, such as the Roman Forum *(see pp78–87)*. Employ only the official guides and make sure you establish the fee in advance; on average they charge around L100,000 for a half-day's tour.

ATAC, the Rome bus company

VISITING CHURCHES

MANY OF ITALY'S churches are very dark, but they usually have light meters to illuminate chapels and works of art. The meters are coin-operated (L100, L200 or L500 coins accepted). Recorded information in several languages is often available at coin-operated machines. Dress codes are firmly upheld in Roman churches; St. Peter's *(see pp230–33)* is especially strict.

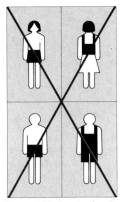

Unacceptable dress in church: both sexes should cover torsos and upper arms.

ETIQUETTE

PEOPLE IN ROME are generally courteous and friendly to foreign visitors. Remember to show consideration for local residents and workers.

Italians are delighted at any effort to speak their language, so it's worth learning a few phrases *(see p431)*. Italians tend to drink only with meals and are unlikely to be seen drunk – drunkenness is frowned upon. Smoking is common in bars and restaurants but banned on public transportation.

Roman style

TIPPING

FOREIGNERS ARE expected to tip, although Italians themselves don't always do so. Leave a few coins in bars or cafés; in restaurants where service is not included, leave around 10%. Keep L1,000 or L2,000 notes and coins handy for taxi drivers, sacristans, chambermaids, doormen, porters and usherettes.

ROME FOR THE DISABLED

ROME IS not particularly well organized to cater for the disabled. Its uneven cobbles and crowded pavements aren't suitable for those in wheelchairs, and even the most agile must be alert when crossing busy roads. Look before crossing at traffic lights and pedestrian crossings – not all vehicles stop when you expect. The seriously disabled will need to arrange help. Ramps, elevators and modified toilets exist in a few places, including Termini station and the Colosseum.

If you have no escort, consider a specially-designed package tour, or contact an organization for disabled travelers before you arrive.

The Vatican Museums, Sistine Chapel and St. Peter's are all accessible by wheelchair. The Vatican Museums *(see pp234–237)* are very accommodating and will offer staff help if needed.

PUBLIC TOILETS

PUBLIC TOILETS are few and far between. There are clean ones by the Colosseum (with facilities for the disabled), at St. Peter's and in the Rinascente store *(see p323)*. Most cafés let you use theirs if you ask. Take your own paper.

USEFUL ADDRESSES

American Express
Piazza di Spagna 38.
Map 5 A2.
06-676 41.

Carrani Tours
Via V. E. Orlando 95.
Map 5 C3.
06-488 05 10.

CIT
Piazza della Repubblica 65.
Map 5 C3.
06-474 65 55.

ENIT
Via Marghera 2.
Map 6 E3.
06-497 11.

EPT
Via Parigi 5.
Map 5 C2.
06-48 89 92 53.
Open 8:15am–7:15pm Mon–Fri, 8:15am–1:30pm Sat.

Green Line Tours
Via Farini 5A.
Map 6 D4.
06-481 57 64.

Personal Security and Health

O N THE WHOLE, Rome is a safe, unthreatening place for visitors, but petty street crime is a problem. Don't carry more money than you'll need for the day and leave other valuables or documents in a hotel safe. Cameras are less likely to be snatched if they're in a carrier bag rather than an obvious case. Take particular care in crowded places, such as stations, or on full buses, and steer clear of bands of innocent-looking children – they may be skillful professional pickpockets.

Pharmacy sign

ADVICE FOR VISITORS

T AKE OUT ADEQUATE property insurance before you travel (it is difficult to arrange once you are in Italy), and guard your belongings all the time once you're in Rome. Some hotels have personal safes in the bedrooms. You can program these with your own number. (Don't use your date of birth; it's on your passport and registration slip.) To be prepared for all eventualities, keep a separate photocopy of all your vital documents, such as your passport, to minimize the problem of replacing them, and take a spare photograph or two. Traveler's checks are the safest way to carry large amounts of cash. Keep the receipts separate from the checks for a refund in case you lose them.

Be wary of bag-snatchers on mopeds who operate on quiet streets. You might want to wear a discreet money belt or a securely fastened, long-strapped shoulder bag, while

Mounted police

equipment like video cameras should be disguised. Pick-pockets (sometimes children) adopt highly sophisticated distraction techniques with cards or newspapers while they deftly separate you from your possessions in seconds. Be especially cautious in market places or on public transportation. Bus route No. 64, which runs between Termini station and the Vatican, is notorious for pickpockets. Thefts from cars are

also common. Nothing portable like a jacket or bag should be left visible inside a car on Rome's streets, and don't carry luggage on a roof rack. The streets to the east and south of Termini station and around the Colosseum are well known for prostitution and drug-peddling and unsavory at night.

Women traveling alone (or even in small groups) may need to take extra care. Italian society is male-dominated, and women who are out without male escorts attract more attention than they do in much of the rest of Europe and North America.

Beware of unauthorized minicab drivers, who are probably not insured and frequently overcharge. They operate in particular near the airport, waiting to profit from

Distinctive *carabinieri* motorcycle

***Carabiniere* – a member of the military police**

***Carabiniere* in traffic police uniform**

Municipal policeman directing traffic

new arrivals. Avoid unofficial vendors and tour guides; instead stick to the official tourist agencies *(see p289 and pp358–9).*

POLICE

T HE VIGILI URBANI, or municipal police, wear blue uniforms in winter and white in summer and can most often be seen regulating traffic. The *carabinieri* are the military police, in red striped trousers. They deal with everything from fine art thefts to speeding offenses. *La polizia* (the state police) wear blue uniforms with white belts and berets, and they specialize in serious crime. Any of these should be able to help you.

MEDICAL MATTERS

N O INOCULATIONS are required for Rome, but take mosquito repellent and sun screen in the summer. The Tiber is polluted, but the water from the taps and from many street fountains is piped straight from the hills, and is fresh and palatable.

Non-EU visitors should take out insurance to cover everything, including emergencies. For insurance claims, make sure you keep all receipts for medical treatment and any medicines prescribed.

For urgent medical attention, contact the First Aid *(Pronto*

Police car

Green cross ambulance

Italian fire engine

Soccorso) department of a main hospital such as **Policlinico Umberto I** or check the Yellow Pages *(Pagine Gialle)* for a doctor *(medico)* or dentist *(dentista).* English speaking doctors can be found at the **Rome American Hospital** or by looking in the English Yellow Pages, available at some hotel receptions and international bookshops. Pharmacists post late-opening rosters on their doors (several stay open all night), and can usually supply the local equivalent of foreign medicines. The **Vatican Pharmacy** stocks some American and British pharmaceutical products.

Many of the words for minor complaints and remedies are similiar in Italian, for example *lassativo* (laxative), *aspirina* (aspirin), and *tranquillante* (tranquilizer).

Policlinico Umberto I
Viale del Policlinico 155.
Map 6 F2.
[06-446 23 41.

Rome American Hospital
Via Emilio Longoni 69.
[06-225 51.

Vatican Pharmacy
Via di Porta Angelica.
Map 3 C2.
[06-686 41 46.

Carabinieri **in dress uniform**

LOST PROPERTY

F OR ITEMS LOST on a bus or metro, contact the numbers below. Otherwise, ask at a police station. If you want to make an insurance claim on your lost property, you will need to report your loss to a police station, and get a signed form. For lost passports, contact your embassy or consulate; for lost traveler's checks, go to the issuing company's office *(see p362).*

Lost Property on Buses
[06-581 60 40. **Open** 7am–6pm.

Lost Property on the Metro
Line A [06-487 43 09. **Open** 9:30am–12:30pm Mon, Wed & Fri.
Line B [06-575 42 95. **Open** 9am–6pm daily.

Commissariato di Polizia – a **police station**

EMERGENCY TELEPHONE NUMBERS

Ambulance
[55 10 or 118.

Automobile Club d'Italia
Car accidents and breakdowns.
[116.

Fire
[115.

General SOS
[113.
Free from any telephone.

Police
[112 (Carabinieri) or 06-46 861 (Polizia).

Samaritans
[06-70 45 44 44.
Line open 1pm–10pm daily.

Traffic Police
[06-888 76 20.

Banking and Local Currency

MONEY SERVICES are not always fast in Rome. Transactions can involve considerable paperwork and a lot of waiting around. On the whole, bank exchange rates are more favorable than those in travel agents and hotels – the deal just takes longer to complete. Small change is indispensable – especially the L100, L200 or L500 coins needed for telephones, tips and for illuminating works of art and chapels in churches *(see p359)*.

Eagle sculpture on the Ministry of Finance

CHANGING MONEY

IT'S BEST to have at least some local currency when you arrive, so you won't have to change money immediately. However, there are increasing numbers of convenient electronic exchange machines at arrival points. There are now several throughout the city too. Multilingual instructions are available. You simply feed in up to 14 notes of the same foreign currency, and should get some lire back. Exchange rates vary from place to place. The Banco di Santo Spirito office at Fiumicino airport offers reasonable rates.

For the best rates, change money at a bank (look for the sign *Cambio*). Hotels tend to give poor rates, even if they charge modest commissions. At the Vatican Museums *(see p235)*, you aren't charged any commission. The American Express office *(see p359)* offers good rates and is open on Saturday mornings. Cardholders may withdraw up to $1,000 (or £500) a week from the cash machine, but you have to pay a fee for this service and need to organize a PIN (personal identification number) linked to your account before you travel.

Automatic exchange machine

CREDIT CARDS

CREDIT CARDS, which used to be regarded with great suspicion in Italy, are now much more widely accepted in larger hotels, shops and restaurants in Rome. Some places, however, prefer Eurocheques, which can be cleared faster. All major credit and charge cards (American Express, Access/Mastercard, Visa, Diners Card) are well known. Banks and cash dispensers are more likely to accept Visa cards for cash advances, but Access (Mastercard) is accepted by more retail outlets in Italy. Take both if you have them. Paying for anything in foreign currency will almost always be expensive.

TRAVELLER'S CHEQUES

IF YOU OPT for traveller's checks, choose a well-known name such as Thomas Cook or American Express, or take those issued through a

major bank. Most issuers charge a 1% commission on traveler's checks. Get some small denominations, so you won't be left with huge amounts of Italian currency at the end of your trip. But don't forget that the minimum commission charged for each transaction (and the amount of time involved) may make changing small amounts of money uneconomical. Always record the traveller's check numbers and refund addresses separately from the checks themselves in case they are stolen. Some places will charge you for each check.

Check the exchange rates before you travel and decide whether lire, dollar or sterling checks are more appropriate. Lire checks are issued only by Italian banks, and may be more difficult to cash in Italy than dollar or sterling ones.

OPENING HOURS

BANKS ARE USUALLY open 8.30am–1.20pm and 3pm–4.30pm Mon–Fri, but opening times vary and banks are closed for public holidays and at weekends.

Bureaux de Change have more generous opening times, similar to shop hours. The exchange office at Termini station *(see p372)* is also open on Sunday mornings.

USING BANKS

LINESS IN BANKS can be long and the form-filling involved in changing money can take up a lot of time. You usually have to line up first at the *cambio*, then at the *cassa* to obtain your cash. Take some form of identity with you, such as a passport. Metal objects may set off emergency detectors as you enter.

Exchange office at one of the Italian national banks

Credito Italiano

One of the major Italian banks

The Bank of Rome, which has branches in other Italian cities

CURRENCY

I TALY'S CURRENCY unit is the lira (plural *lire*) and is usually abbreviated L or £. It became the national currency during the unification process in the mid-19th century.

Lira means pound and the English pound is referred to as *lira sterlina* to distinguish it.

Telephone tokens *(gettoni)* have been phased out so do not accept them if you recieve them in your change.

Shops and bars are usually not very keen on giving change for a high-value note, so ask for smaller denominations of bank notes when you change money. Coins are often in short supply.

The prospect of carrying around millions of units of currency may at first seem alarming. Plans to alter the basic unit have still not been realized, but you'll find in practice that the last three noughts are often ignored in spoken Italian: *sessanta* will usually mean L60,000 and not, as one may think, L60.

Bank Notes

Italian bank notes come in denominations of L100,000, L50,000, L10,000, L5,000, L2,000 and L1,000, which are easily identifiable by their colors and the historic people portrayed. Notes increase in size progressively according to their value. The lira is never divided into smaller units.

1,000 lire

2,000 lire

5,000 lire

10,000 lire

50,000 lire

100,000 lire

Coins

Coins exist in denominations of L500, L200, L100 and L50. Now there is also a L1,000 coin. Several versions of L100 and L50 coins in different sizes are in use (the larger, older ones shown here are still the most common).

50 lire

100 lire

200 lire

500 lire

THE EURO CURRENCY

On 1 Jan 1999, the Euro became the legal currency in 11 European Union countries: Austria, Belgium, Finland, France, Germany, Ireland, Italy, Luxembourg, the Netherlands, Portugal and Spain. Beginning 1 Jan 2002, national currencies will be replaced gradually by the Euro. There will be seven notes in the denominations of 500, 200, 100, 50, 20, 10 and 5 Euros. The eight coins (2 and 1 Euros, 50, 20, 10, 5, 2 and 1 Euro Cents) will have a common European design on one side and the Member States' own national designs on the reverse side.

Using Rome's Telephones

THE ROME TELEPHONE SYSTEM has recently undergone a major upheaval. Many numbers have been changed and new equipment has been installed alongside older machinery. At present, telephone numbers can have any number of digits from four to nine. Any telephone number dialled in Italy, even a local number, now needs to have the relevant local code in front of it.

Telephone company logo

TELEPHONE OFFICES

TELEPHONE OFFICES *(Telefoni)* are run by Telecom Italia (previously called SIP) and ASST, and offer a convenient way of making long-distance or private calls. At the *Telefono* there will be several metered telephones, each in its own sound-proofed booth. An assistant will assign you a booth, and meter your call once you have been connected to the number you want. You do not need large amounts of change as you pay at the desk when you have finished. There is no extra charge for this service, but *Telefoni* opening hours rarely coincide with Italy's cheapest-rate calling times. The one at the **Palazzo delle Poste** on Piazza San Silvestro is an exception – it stays open 24 hours a day. Here you'll also find a 24-hour fax service, to the left of the main entrance. There are other *Telefoni* throughout Rome, including ones at Fiumicino airport, the main hall at Termini railway station, other major post offices and in the underground car park at Villa Borghese. To send an international telegram, either go to a main post office or dial 186 and dictate it over the telephone.

CALL CHARGES

THE CHEAPEST times to phone within Italy are between 6.30pm and 8am Monday to Friday, after 1.30pm Saturday and all day Sunday. Check what time is best if you are making international calls: time variations throughout the world make a difference.

In general, it is cheaper to dial direct for international calls rather than going through the operator or making collect or credit card calls. Telephoning from hotel rooms is usually expensive and is sometimes marked up by several hundred per cent. Normally telephone calls cost more from Italy than they do from North America.

USING A TELECOM ITALIA COIN AND CARD TELEPHONE

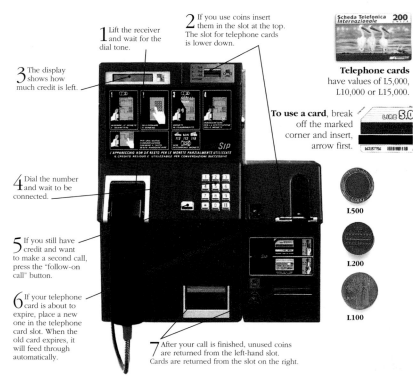

1 Lift the receiver and wait for the dial tone.

2 If you use coins insert them in the slot at the top. The slot for telephone cards is lower down.

3 The display shows how much credit is left.

4 Dial the number and wait to be connected.

5 If you still have credit and want to make a second call, press the "follow-on call" button.

6 If your telephone card is about to expire, place a new one in the telephone card slot. When the old card expires, it will feed through automatically.

7 After your call is finished, unused coins are returned from the left-hand slot. Cards are returned from the slot on the right.

Telephone cards have values of L5,000, L10,000 or L15,000.

To use a card, break off the marked corner and insert, arrow first.

L500

L200

L100

USING PUBLIC TELEPHONES

Newer payphones, called *interurbani*, are orange, and from these you can dial long-distance and most international calls direct. Payphones take L100, L200 and L500 coins. For long-distance direct-dial calls, have at least L2,000 of change ready. If you don't put enough coins in to start with, the telephone simply retains your money and disconnects you. After a successful call, any unused coins are usually returned.

The most up-to-date payphones (pictured opposite) take telephone cards (ask for a *scheda* or *carta telefonica*), costing L5,000, L10,000 or L15,000, as well as coins. Some payphones will now only accept cards. Cards are available from shops, bars

Public telephone sign

REACHING THE RIGHT NUMBER

• The code for Rome is 06 (obligatory also within the city).
• International directory enquiries is on 176.
• International operator assistance is on 170. Reverse charge and credit card calls are also accepted.
• Italian directory enquiries is on 12.
• You can dial direct using the following codes. To reach the operator in your own country to place a collect or credit card call dial 172 then: 0044 for the UK; 1011 for AT&T, US; 1022 for MCI, US; 1877 for US Sprint; 1061 for Telstra, Australia; 1161 for Optus, Australia; and 1001 for Canada.
• *See also* Emergency Numbers *p361*.

Stamps are available at tobacconists

and tobacconists displaying the black and white T sign. Break off the marked corner, insert the card arrow first, and the value of the unexpired units will show on a display window. After your call, the card can be retrieved and reused until its value expires.

For long-distance calls on older telephones it is best to find a metered phone (*telefono a scatti*). Ask if you can phone and the call will be metered. You pay afterwards.

E-MAIL

The internet has made e-mail a viable alternative to the postal service. Two of the most popular places in Rome to access the web are:
Internet Café
Via dei Marrucini, 12. **Map** 6 F3.
06-445 49 53. **Open** 9–2am Mon–Fri, 5pm–2am Sat, Sun.
The Netgate
Piazza Firenze 25. **Map** 12 D1.
06-689 34 45. **Open** 10.30am–10.30pm Mon–Sat (summer).

Sending Letters

The Italian postal service is not especially efficient and it is said that letters travelled faster in the days of the old Roman Empire than they do today, in spite of modern technology. For leisurely postcards, the service is usually fine but expect anything sent abroad to take its

Rome letters   Other destinations

Post Office sign

time; the Italian postal service is particularly slow in August when it can take up to a month for a postcard to reach the US. For anything urgent or important, it's better to use the more expensive express system, which knocks a day or two off the delivery time, or registered post. Otherwise, you can buy ordinary stamps (*francobolli*) at tobacconists with the black and white T sign as well as in post offices. Sub-post office hours are generally from around 8.30am

until 2pm (8.30am–noon on Saturdays and the last day of the month), but main offices stay open 24 hours a day or well into the evening for some services (such as registered post). Among the 24-hour ones are Piazza San Silvestro, at Termini and at the airport. Italian post boxes are red.

POSTE RESTANTE

Letters and parcels which are to be picked up at the post office are sent care of (*c/o*) Palazzo delle Poste, Roma, *Fermo Posta*. Print the surname clearly in block capitals and underline it to make sure the letters are filed correctly. To collect your post, you have to show your passport and pay a small charge. American Express *poste restante* is free to clients.

Vatican post office sign

Vatican postage stamps

VATICAN POST

The Vatican postal service costs the same as the state post, but is faster. Buy cards and stamps at the post office near the Vatican Museums entrance, or in Piazza San Pietro. Letters bearing Vatican stamps can only be posted in blue Vatican post boxes.

Postage stamps

Airmail sticker

Additional Information

Fiumicino airport, point of arrival for most visitors to Rome

CUSTOMS AND IMMIGRATION

E UROPEAN UNION nationals and citizens of the US, Canada, Australia and New Zealand do not need visas for stays of up to three months. All visitors are required to present a full passport on entry and, officially, need to declare their presence to the Italian police within eight days of arrival. If you are staying in a hotel or on a campsite this will be done for you. Otherwise, contact the local **Questura** (police station).

Anyone wishing to stay for more than three months (eight days for citizens of other countries than mentioned above) will have to wade through some complicated Italian bureaucracy to obtain a *permesso di soggiorno* (permit to stay). You can apply for a permit at any main police station, *Questura*, either a permit to work *(lavoro)* or a permit to study *(studio)*.

Duty-free allowances are as follows. Residents of the EU can bring duty-free goods into Italy for their own use: 800 cigarettes, 200 cigars, 400 cigarillos, 1 kg of smoking tobacco, 10 liters of spirits, 90 liters of wine and 100 liters of beer. Duty-free limits for non-EU citizens are much stricter: 400 cigarettes, 100 cigars, 200 cigarillos or 500grams of smoking tobacco, 1 liter of spirits or 2 liters of wine and 50 grams of perfume. To find out what you can take back from Italy to an non-EU country, contact the particular country's customs department.

The refund system for Value Added Tax (IVA in Italy) for non-EU residents is very complex *(see p323)*.

Questura
[06-46 86 1.

CATHOLIC SERVICES

F OR MANY CATHOLICS, a visit to Rome means an audience with the pope. General audiences are usually held every Wednesday at 11am (10am in hot weather) in St. Peter's square, the Audiences room, or at the summer residence at Castel Gandolfo. To attend an audience, apply to the **Prefettura della Casa Pontificia** before your visit. (Rome travel agencies may be able to arrange an audience as part of a coach tour during your stay.) There is no charge. Mass is held daily in the main churches of Rome (High Mass is on Sunday.) Churches where confession is heard include St. Peter's *(see pp230–33)*, San Giovanni in Laterano *(pp182–3)*, San Paolo fuori le Mura *(p267)*, Santa Maria Maggiore *(pp172–3)*, the Gesù *(pp114–15)*, Santa Sabina *(p204)* and Sant'Ignazio *(p106)*. English-speaking Catholic churches include San Silvestro (Piazza San Silvestro) and San Tommaso di Canterbury (Via di Monserrato 45).

Confession box, Gesù

Prefettura della Casa Pontificia
Città del Vaticano, 00120. **Map** 3 B3.
[06-698 82 73.

STUDENT INFORMATION

A N INTERNATIONAL Student Identity Card (ISIC) or a Youth International Educational Exchange Card (YIEE) are worth having for reductions on museum and other charges.

Students on the steps of Santa Maria Maggiore

Contact the **Centro Turistico Studentesco** for general student information. The **Associazione Italiana Alberghi per la Gioventù** (the Italian YHA) has four hostels in the city. **Transalpino** has information on rail discounts for students.

ISIC card

Associazione Italiana Alberghi per la Gioventù
Via Cavour 44, 00184.
Map 3 D3.
[FAX 06-488 04 92.

Centro Turistico Studentesco
Via Genova 16. **Map** 5 C3.
[06-467 91. Also branches at Via Appia Nuova 434 (06-7857 906) and Corso Vittorio Emanuele 297 (06-6872 672).

Transalpino
Piazza Esquilino 10/Z. **Map** 6 D4.
[06-487 08 70. (Branch at Stazione Termini, in main gallery).

The pope on his balcony at St. Peter's

Newspapers available in Rome

NEWSPAPERS, TV, RADIO

ROME'S MAIN newspapers are *La Repubblica* and *Il Messaggero*. British and American newspapers are readily available, and the *International Herald Tribune* is sold on the day of issue. The state TV channels are RAI Uno, Due and Tre; all of them are politically aligned. The advent of satellite and cable TV means there are European channels in many languages, plus sport and CNN news in English. The BBC World Service is broadcast on radio on 15.070MHz (short wave) in the mornings and 648KHz (medium wave) at night. Vatican Radio on 93.3MHz and 105MHz (FM) broadcasts news in English.

EMBASSIES AND CONSULATES

IF YOU LOSE your passport or need other help, contact your national embassy or consulate as listed below.

Australia
Corso Trieste 25/C. **Map** 6 E1.
06-85 27 21.

Canada
Via Zara 30.
06-44 59 81.

New Zealand
Via Zara 28.
06-441 71 71.

United Kingdom
Via XX Settembre 80A. **Map** 6 D2.
06-482 54 41.

United States
Via Veneto 119A/121. **Map** 5 B2.
06-467 41.

ELECTRICAL ADAPTERS

ELECTRIC CURRENT in Italy is 220V AC, with two-pin round-pronged plugs. Adapters can be purchased in most countries. In most hotels of three or more stars, there are hair dryers and shaving outlets in all the bedrooms.

Shaving outlet in hotel bedroom for 110V or 220V

Standard Italian plug

ROME TIME

ROME IS ONE HOUR ahead of Greenwich Mean Time (GMT). Examples of the time difference with Rome for other major cities are as follows: London: -1 hour; New York: -6 hours; Dallas: -7 hours; Los Angeles: -9 hours; Perth: +7 hours; Sydney: +9 hours; Auckland: +11 hours; Tokyo: +8 hours. These figures can vary slightly for brief periods with local changes in summer. For all official purposes, the Italians use the 24-hour clock.

CONVERSION TABLE

Imperial to Metric
1 inch	= 2.54 centimeters
1 foot	= 30 centimeters
1 mile	= 1.6 kilometers
1 ounce	= 28 grams
1 pound	= 454 grams
1 US pint	= 0.5 liters
1 US gallon	= 3.8 liters

Metric to Imperial
1 centimeter	= 0.4 inches
1 meter	= 3 feet 3 inches
1 kilometer	= 0.6 miles
1 gram	= 0.04 ounces
1 kilogram	= 2.2 pounds
1 liter	= 2 US pints

SIGHTSEEING PERMITS

TO VISIT certain sights in Rome, you need to obtain a written permit and book the time of your visit in advance. This applies particularly to archaeological sites, which may sometimes be closed during excavations. Write to the address below, stating your name, the number of people in your party, the reason why you wish to visit the sight (for example study of tourism) and the days on which you are available to make the visit. Try to include a contact phone number in Rome. It is advisable to send the request by fax. Call a few days before to confirm your visit:

Ufficio Monumenti Antichi e Scavi
Via del Portico d'Ottavia 29.
Map 4 F5 & 12 E5.
06-67 10 34 31 or 06-67 10 37 34.
FAX 06-67 10 31 18.

OTHER RELIGIOUS SERVICES

Anglican
All Saints, Via del Babuino 153.
Map 4 F2. 06-36 00 18 81.

American Episcopal
St. Paul's, Via Napoli 58. **Map** 5 C3.
06-488 33 39.

Jewish
Sinagoga, Lungotevere Cenci.
Map 4 F5 & 12 D5. 06-684 00 61.

Methodist
Via Firenze 38. **Map** 5 C3.
06-481 48 11.

Mosque
Viale della Moschea 85 (Parioli district).
Map 2 F1. 06-808 21 67.

Presbyterian
St. Andrew's, Via XX Settembre 7.
Map 5 C3. 06-482 76 27.

The Mosque in Parioli

GETTING TO ROME

MANY NATIONAL AIRLINES, including Italy's Alitalia fly direct to Rome from most European cities and several in North America and Australia. There are no direct flights from New Zealand, but passengers can catch connections from either Frankfurt or London. Rome's Fiumicino airport has expanded considerably in the late 1990s to accommodate the growing number of visitors. Rome also has train and coach links with the rest of Europe. These take a lot longer than flights (about 24 hours from London, compared with about 3 hours by air), but tend to cost about the same, so are only really worthwhile if you want to travel overland. The trains are often crowded in summer.

Alitalia aircraft

Part of the new extension to Fiumicino airport

BY AIR

IF YOU'RE FLYING from the United States, **TWA**, Delta and United Airlines operate regular direct scheduled flights to Rome, with services from about half a dozen cities (including New York, Boston, Washington, Los Angeles and Chicago). Flying time from New York is about eight and a half hours and it's about 13 hours from Los Angeles. **Canadian Airlines** flies from Montreal and Toronto; **Qantas** from Melbourne and Sydney. The Italian state airline, **Alitalia**, also flies between Rome and New York, San Francisco, Philadelphia, Boston, Chicago, Detroit, Washington, Montreal, Toronto and Sydney. It may, however, be considerably cheaper for intercontinental travellers to take a budget flight to London, Paris, Frankfurt or Amsterdam and continue the journey to Rome from there. **British**

Alitalia flight tickets

Airways and Alitalia operate direct scheduled flights from London Heathrow to Rome, and you can fly from Manchester. Among the airlines using Rome as an intercontinental transit point are **Philippine Airlines**, Sudan Airways and Ethiopian Airlines: fares are cheaper, but flights tend to be less frequent and are sometimes subject to long delays.

APEX, PEX, or SuperPEX fares generally offer the best value in scheduled flights, but you must purchase them well in advance (for example, 7 or 14 days ahead in the UK; 21 days in the US). They are subject to penalty clauses if you cancel, so it's advisable to take out insurance as soon as you buy your ticket. If you're based in the UK, it's worth looking in the small ads of newspapers for cut-price charters (though even in low season these are

Check-in area at Fiumicino, Rome's main international airport

becoming increasingly rare). Regular charters run all year round. Most leave from Gatwick and Luton, but there are a couple of flights a week from Manchester and it's usually possible to fly from Glasgow and Birmingham. Fares vary greatly, peaking in summer, and in Holy Week for the Pope's Easter blessing.

If you want to book flights during your stay in Rome, travel agents, such as the **American Express** office, should be able to help.

Easy-to-follow signs at Ostiense

AIRLINE NUMBERS

Alitalia
☏ *1478-656 43 (information), 1478-656 42 (international flights), 1478-656 41 (domestic flights); all these are toll-free numbers that can only be used within Italy.*

American Express
☏ *06-676 41.*

British Airways
☏ *06-52 49 28 00.*

Canadian Airlines
☏ *06-655 71 17 or 1678-622 16 (toll free, within Italy only).*

Qantas
☏ *06-488 81 01 or 06-48 88 09 30.*

TWA
☏ *06-472 11 or 06-65 95 49 21.*

PACKAGE HOLIDAYS

PACKAGE HOLIDAYS to Rome can be much better value than traveling independently. For European visitors there are weekend packages and two- or three-centre holidays; Rome is frequently packaged with Florence and Venice. Those from further afield can visit the city during Europe-wide tours. Most package companies transport you free of charge from the airport to your hotel in Rome. Many, especially the more expensive ones, include a tour guide.

FIUMICINO AIRPORT

ROME HAS TWO international airports. Leonardo da Vinci – commonly known as Fiumicino – handles most scheduled flights, and is situated about 30 km (18 miles) southwest of the city. The airport is currently being expanded to accommodate the increasing number of flights, and will by year 2001 have 3 terminals (two of which were ready in 1999). Terminal A will service domestic flights, Terminal B is for domestic and international flights within the European Community, and Terminal C for international flights.

From Fiumicino there is a train to Fara Sabina station (6.15am– midnight; 30 min journey). It also stops at Trastevere, Ostiense, Tuscolana and Tiburtina stations. A faster, but more expensive, train runs non-stop to Termini every hour (7.50am–10.05pm, return trains departing hourly 7am– 9.15pm). If you are lucky the ticket office (which also sells Metro tickets) will be open; if not, you'll have to tackle the automatic ticket machine *(see p373)*.

Ostiense is linked with Piramide Metro (Line B) where you can catch an underground train to the city center. This Metro line runs from 5.30am until 11.30pm every day. It can be difficult to find a taxi at Ostiense after 9pm, but there's a bus (the No. 95) to Piazza Venezia.

In addition, car hires are also available and have offices at the airport *(see p379)*.

Shuttle bus to car-hire lots at Fiumicino

The train linking Fiumicino airport to Stazione Termini

Efforts are made at Fiumicino to improve both the airport and the surrounding area at the beginning of the new Millennium. These developments include the institution of a People Mover rail transport system for traveling between various points within the airport, the expansion of Terminal A, and a four-star hotel located nearby the terminals.

CIAMPINO AIRPORT

THE OTHER AIRPORT that services Rome is Ciampino, about 15 km (9 miles) southeast and used by the majority of charter flights. Major car hire firms have a rental office at the airport, though you may find it less harrowing to get into the city center on public transport or by taxi.

Although it is more difficult to travel to and from Ciampino via public transportation than Fiumicino, the swiftest way to get to the centre of Rome from Ciampino is by bus to Anagnina Metro station, then by underground train to Termini. Taxis from the airport are expensive; be careful and only use official cabs. In addition, make sure that the fare meter is switched on and showing only the minimum charge before you leave the airport.

Ciampino, a more basic airport used by most charter flights

Arriving in Rome

THIS MAP shows the main bus, rail and Metro links used by travelers arriving in Rome. The connections between Rome's two airports and the city center are shown, as well as links between Rome and the rest of Italy and the international rail routes from neighboring European countries. Travel information, including details of journey times and service frequency, is listed separately in each box.

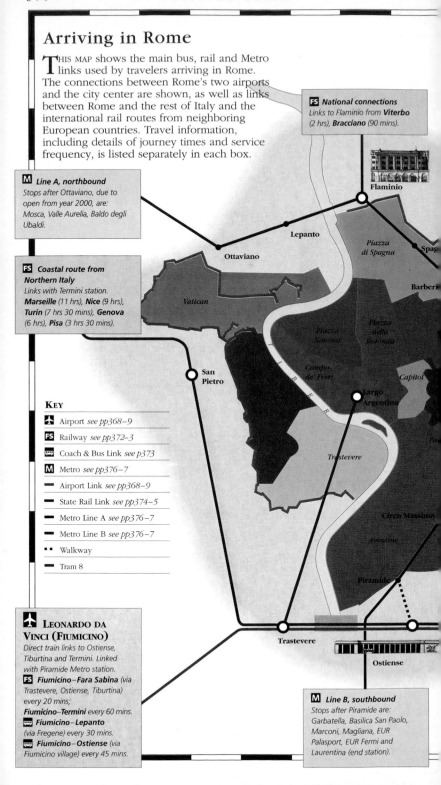

FS National connections
*Links to Flaminio from **Viterbo** (2 hrs), **Bracciano** (90 mins).*

M Line A, northbound
Stops after Ottaviano, due to open from year 2000, are: Mosca, Valle Aurelia, Baldo degli Ubaldi.

FS Coastal route from Northern Italy
*Links with Termini station. **Marseille** (11 hrs), **Nice** (9 hrs), **Turin** (7 hrs 30 mins), **Genova** (6 hrs), **Pisa** (3 hrs 30 mins).*

Flaminio

Lepanto

Ottaviano

Piazza di Spagna

Spag

Vatican

Barberi

Piazza Navona

Piazza della Rotonda

San Pietro

Campo de' Fiori

Capitol

Largo Argentina

Trastevere

Pa

KEY

✈	Airport *see pp368–9*
FS	Railway *see pp372–3*
🚌	Coach & Bus Link *see p373*
M	Metro *see pp376–7*
—	Airport Link *see pp368–9*
—	State Rail Link *see pp374–5*
—	Metro Line A *see pp376–7*
—	Metro Line B *see pp376–7*
••	Walkway
—	Tram 8

Circo Massimo

Aventine

Piramide

✈ **LEONARDO DA VINCI (FIUMICINO)**
Direct train links to Ostiense, Tiburtina and Termini. Linked with Piramide Metro station.
FS *Fiumicino–Fara Sabina (via Trastevere, Ostiense, Tiburtina) every 20 mins;*
Fiumicino–Termini every 60 mins.
🚌 *Fiumicino–Lepanto (via Fregene) every 30 mins.*
🚌 *Fiumicino–Ostiense (via Fiumicino village) every 45 mins.*

Trastevere

Ostiense

M Line B, southbound
Stops after Piramide are: Garbatella, Basilica San Paolo, Marconi, Magliana, EUR Palasport, EUR Fermi and Laurentina (end station).

FS **International and Northern Italy**
Links with Termini. Trains arriving after midnight terminate at Tiburtina.
Paris *(15 hrs)*, **Vienna** *(14 hrs)*, **Geneva** *(14 hrs)*, **Basle** *(13 hrs)*, **Munich** *(11 hrs)*, **Verona** *(7 hrs)*, **Milan** *(5 hrs)*, **Bologna** *(3 hrs 30 mins)*, **Florence** *(2 hrs)*.

Coach connections into Rome
*International and national bus links at **Piazza dei Cinquecento** (in front of Termini). Buses for the Lazio region link at **Lepanto**. Connections to the city center and other parts of Italy link at **Piazzale Ostiense**.*

Coach arriving at Piazzale Ostiense

Piazza Bologna

M **Line B, northbound**
Stops after Tiburtina are: Monti Tiburtini, Pietralata, Santa Maria del Soccorso, Ponte Mammolo and Rebibbia (end station).

Policlinico

Tiburtina

Castro Pretorio

a Veneto

Roma Termini

pubblica

FS **Eastern Italy**
Links with Termini station.
Pescara *(4 hrs)*, **L'Aquila** *(3 hrs 30mins)*.

avour

Vittorio Emanuele

Esquiline

olosseo

Manzoni

Lateran

FS **Southern Italy**
Links with Termini station.
Palermo *(12 hrs)*, **Reggio Calabria** *(9 hrs 30 mins)*, **Bari** *(6 hrs 30 mins)*, **Naples** *(2 hrs)*.

San Giovanni

Caracalla

Re di Roma

Tuscolana

Ponte Lungo

M **Line A, southbound**
Stops after Ponte Lungo are: Furio Camillo, Colli Albani, Arco di Travertino, Porta Furba, Numidio Quadrato, Lucio Sestio, Giulio Agricola, Subaugusta, Cinecittà and Anagnina (end station).

uscita → Linea A

Termini Metro station

✈ **CIAMPINO**
Bus link to Anagnina Metro station (on Line A).
Atac bus *every 30 mins (10–20 mins).* **ACOTRAL bus** *every hour to Anagnina Metro station (10–20 mins). Metro line A links with Termini station.*

Reaching Rome by Train, Coach or Car

Aᴺʸ ᴏᴠᴇʀʟᴀɴᴅ journey to Rome is fastest by train, though there are coach connections to most major European cities. Within Italy, journeys between large cities are usually also best done by train, but when traveling from towns which are not on the main Intercity rail routes, coaches can be quicker. For drivers, the Italian Automobile Club *(see p361)* provides free assistance and excellent maps to members of affiliated automobile clubs from all over the world.

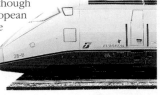

The Eurostar – Italy's fastest train

The foyer of Stazione Termini

STAZIONE TERMINI

Sᴛᴀᴢɪᴏɴᴇ ᴛᴇʀᴍɪɴɪ, Rome's main train station, is also the hub of the urban transport system. Beneath it is the only interchange between the city's two Metro lines, and outside, on Piazza dei Cinquecento, is the central bus terminus. Though it is one of Rome's most stunning 20th-century buildings and was restored in 1999, it also has many unsavory aspects, so it is unwise to linger longer than necessary.

FS logo

If you arrive late, aim to leave the neighborhood as swiftly as you can. There are usually taxis (go to the official queue), even in the small hours, and most of the city's night buses start at Termini.

In summer the station gets very crowded, and you can expect long queues at ticket booths, bureaux de change and at both the transport and tourist information offices. There's a left luggage office, a police station where you should report anything lost or stolen on a train or in the station; and a small Citalia office where you can exchange money as well as

get travel information. In the foyer, there is an international telephone office *(see p364)*, a bookshop, a post office and a tobacconist (where you can stock up on bus and Metro tickets). Other facilities at the station include a burger bar, a café, a ticket office for Transalpino and, downstairs in the gloomy Metro subway, a hairdresser, a pharmacy and an *albergo diurno* (day hotel), where, for a price, you can freshen up with a bath or shower.

Of Rome's other stations, four are most likely to be of interest to tourists. They are

BINARIO 17
Platform sign

← uscita
Exit sign

Ostiense and Trastevere, for trains to Fiumicino airport and Viterbo *(see p271)*; Tiburtina, for some of the trains on the north-south line through Italy; and Roma Nord for trains to Prima Porta.

TRAVELLING BY TRAIN

Iᴛᴀʟɪᴀɴ ꜱᴛᴀᴛᴇ ʀᴀɪʟᴡᴀʏꜱ (Ferrovie dello Stato or FS) have several levels of service, from Locale trains which stop at every station, to the Eurostar, a super-fast and extremely luxurious train, which offers first- and second-class service.

The Eurostar runs between Rome and Milan, Turin, Genoa, Bari, Naples and Venice. You have to reserve and you're charged hefty supplements for the privileges of speed, hostess service and free newspapers. You also pay a supplement on Intercity trains. These trains are for fast long-distance journeys and have both first- and second-class carriages. They run from Rome to Venice, Milan, Florence, Naples and other cities. You should book in high season and at weekends. Booking is obligatory on

Termini, the heart of Italy's rail network and Rome's transport system

An international Eurocity train

some services, which are marked in the timetable by a black R on a white background. Tickets for immediate travel can be bought at the station, but allow plenty of time to queue. To book a ticket in advance or make a seat reservation it is usually much quicker to go to a travel agent displaying the FS symbol.

From Rome you can also take international or Eurocity (EC) trains to destinations all over Europe. It is worth reserving a seat on these services, especially during the summer when trains can become very crowded.

MACHINES FOR FS RAIL TICKETS

These self-service machines are easy to use, and most have instructions in four languages on a printed panel.

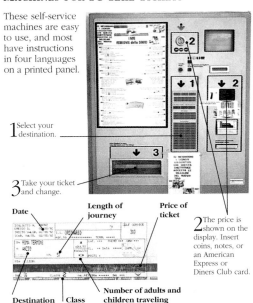

1 Select your destination.

3 Take your ticket and change.

2 The price is shown on the display. Insert coins, notes, or an American Express or Diners Club card.

Date

Length of journey

Price of ticket

Destination | Class

Number of adults and children traveling

COACH TRAVEL

Most regional and long-distance coaches are blue

L ONG-DISTANCE coaches terminate at Tiburtina, which is the city's main coach station. Information and tickets for Euroline coaches to European cities are available from **Lazzi Express**. The **Appian Line** offers regular services within Italy. Its itineraries include Florence, Naples, Capri, Sorrento and Pompei, and, in summer, Venice and Assisi. Local buses, serving villages and towns within the Lazio region, are run by **COTRAL**. All bus stations used by COTRAL are linked

to Metro stations. Tickets for COTRAL services are bought on the spot and cannot be booked in advance. Some day trips from Rome by bus are described on pages 268–71.

Appian Line
Piazza dell'Esquilino 6–7. **Map** 6 D4.
(06-48 78 61.

COTRAL
(167 43 17 84 (toll free).

Lazzi Express
Via Tagliamento 27. **(** 06-884 08 40.

TRAVELLING BY CAR

T O DRIVE YOUR OWN car in Italy you need an international Green Card (for insurance purposes) and the vehicle registration document. A translation of your driving license, available at Italian tourist offices abroad, is also

Blue signs showing A roads and green signs showing motorways

useful. Wearing seatbelts is compulsory in Italy. You must also carry a warning triangle in case of breakdown. Main routes to Rome connect with the Grande Raccordo Anulare (GRA), Rome's ringroad.

Tolls are charged on all Italian motorways. You can buy magnetic motorway toll cards from motoring organizations before entering Italy.

Euroline coach running between Rome and the rest of Europe

GETTING AROUND ROME

ROME'S CENTER is compact, and, although walking absolutely everywhere would be far too overly ambitious, it is a city in which you can spend much of your time on foot. Since the main streets in the center are usually clogged with traffic, driving and cycling are not recommended, but courageous motorcycle or scooter riders can have great

A Roman family's solution to very heavy traffic

fun buzzing around on a rented Vespa. Traveling by bus and tram can be very slow, so use overland public transportation only when you have a long way to go. The Metro, designed to connect the suburbs with the center, has no stops in the historic city center near the Pantheon or Piazza Navona, though it is the swiftest way of crossing the city.

WALKING

WANDERING through Rome's old center is one of the most enjoyable aspects of being in the city. You can take in the architectural details while absorbing the streetlife and stopping as you want at will, or peek into any church, shop or bar that catches your eye. You can easily see several of the main tourist sights in a few hours. The Colosseum, for example, is only about 1.5 miles (2.5 km) from the Spanish Steps. Your route could pass by the Forum, Piazza Venezia and several churches; other sights, such as the Trevi Fountain, the Galleria Doria Pamphilj and the Pantheon, are just a short detour away.

Explore the city area by area, using public transportation when distances are too far.

Avanti: Go! Pedestrians have right of way

Alt: Stop! Traffic has right of way

Only very small patches of central Rome have sidewalks, and a street that is closed to cars will still be used by cyclists and scooter riders. There have been many plans to create more traffic-free zones, and even to ban anything on wheels from some parts of the city – but imposing such measures on a population as insubordinate as Rome's is not easily done.

If you find the summer heat hard to bear, remember that the narrow cobbled streets get little sunlight and remain relatively cool, while walking into an open piazza can be like stepping into a furnace.

During the height of summer, you'll have a more enjoyable time if you follow the example of the Italians. Walk slowly on the shady side of the street; have a long lunch followed by a siesta in the hottest part of the day. You can continue exploring in the late afternoon, when churches and shops reopen and the streets are at their liveliest. Wandering at night is worthwhile, for the streets are cool and many facades floodlit.

Directions for walkers

Pedestrian crossing: only slightly safer than the open road

CROSSING ROADS

FIRST IMPRESSIONS suggest there can be only two sorts of pedestrian in Rome: the quick and the dead. Even if you cross roads by sets of traffic lights and pedestrian crossings strictly in your favor, there is sure to be some van or Vespa hurtling toward you with apparently homicidal intent. Fortunately, Roman drivers have quick reactions. The pious would attribute this to the protection of Santa Francesca Romana (see p87), cynics to the fact that, according to Italian insurance law, drivers are responsible for any road accident. Whatever the inspiration, accidents are quite rare. The best tactic is to be as alert and confident

Pedestrian crossing

Watch out for children

as Romans. The roads are very busy. When crossing try to leave as large a gap as possible between yourself and oncoming traffic. Step purposefully into the road, facing approaching motorists with a determined glare. The trick now is to keep going steadily: don't hesitate or change your course and don't run. As long as a driver can see you, he or she should stop or at least swerve, albeit at the last moment.

Pedestrians and drivers must both take particular care at night, when the traffic lights are switched to a constantly flashing amber, turning the crossings into free-for-alls.

STREET SIGNS

THEORETICALLY, although it may not always seem to be the case, pedestrians have right of way at crossings when the green *avanti* sign is lit up. The red sign *alt* means you must wait. Underground crossings are indicated by a sign reading *sottopassaggio*.

It is easy to get lost in the maze of streets and piazzas that comprise the historic center. Until you know your way around, you can follow the yellow signs marking routes between the sights and piazzas of particular interest to tourists. Routes leading to general landmarks are indicated by signs on a silver-gray background.

No stopping

No parking

One-way street

No through road

DRIVING

DRIVING IN CENTRAL Rome can be an extremely intimidating experience for visitors. The flamboyant aggression of Italian drivers is notorious; pedestrians step out into the roads without warning; and the one-way system operating in much of the center makes retaining a sense of direction impossible. You'll also find motorists passing on the

Directions to parking areas

wrong side, while scooters and Vespas zoom among the lanes of traffic and go the wrong way down one-way streets. A rule to remember is to give way to the right. Unless you are accustomed to driving in Italian cities, leave your car at home – or failing that, in a guarded parking area.

Car thefts are rife in Rome, so never leave anything of value in your car, even out of sight: areas such as Campo de' Fiori are patrolled by gangs watching for anyone leaving cameras, fur coats and other costly items in their trunks. You should also remove your car radio – you won't be the only person carrying one into a bar, restaurant or disco.

Take extra care driving at night. Not only do traffic lights switch to flashing amber, but many Italians are astonishingly cavalier about driving under the influence of alcohol or drugs.

PARKING

THE MOST convenient parking area is below the Villa Borghese. Much of the city center is reserved for residents with permits, but there are around 2,000 metered parking spaces (from 8am–8pm). If you do find a legal place to park, however, you may return and find you've been hemmed in by double-parked cars. Locations of some of the most useful parking areas are on page 379.

GASOLINE

GAS IS VERY expensive. It can be bought from roadside pumps through-out the city, as well as from regular garages,

The state gas company logo

though the former don't always sell lead-free gas (*senza piombo*). In the afternoon and at night, many pumps are self-service, operated by banknotes or credit cards. Late-night gas stations are listed on page 379.

ILLEGAL PARKING

Rome's traffic police are vigilant. If you've parked illegally, your car may be clamped or (if it's causing an obstruction) towed away, so phone 06-676 91 to check before reporting it stolen. No-parking zones should be clearly marked, but look carefully, in case the sign is hidden by a tree.

Signpost for a tow-away area (*zona rimozione*)

A tow truck at work

Traveling by Bus, Tram and Metro

ROME'S PUBLIC TRANSPORT system is comparatively cheap, comprehensive and as efficient as the busy streets allow. Priests, nuns, tourists, pilgrims, businessmen and pickpockets all pile aboard, transforming the buses and trams into mobile saunas during the summer. Short distances are better covered on foot, because heavy traffic often blocks the roads. Getting off at the right stop can be difficult, but other passengers will usually help if you ask for directions. Always keep a tight hold on your valuables.

Weekly travelcard

Monthly travelcard

BUSES AND TRAMS

ROME'S PUBLIC bus and tram company is called **ATAC** (Azienda Tramvie e Autobus del Comune di Roma). Scores of its orange buses and a handful of rattling trams cover most parts of the city. They run from early morning until about midnight. There are also a few night buses.

Apart from a few electric minibuses (115, 116, 117, 119), no buses can run through the narrow streets of the historic center. But there are plenty of bus routes to take you within a short walk of the main sights *(see map inside back cover)*.

Rome's new yellow bus stops comprehensively list the details of routes taken by all the buses using that stop. There are, however, still a number of old-style bus stops left. These list only a few of

ATAC bus No. 64

Rome–Gubbio bus

the streets and piazzas that the buses pass and are mystifying until you know Rome well.

USING BUSES AND TRAMS

THE MAIN TERMINUS is on Piazza dei Cinquecento outside Termini station, but there are other major route hubs throughout the city, most usefully those at Largo Argentina, Piazza Venezia and Piazza del Risorgimento. Information on public transport can be obtained from ATAC kiosks. Tickets can be bought from automatic machines found at main bus stops and also at Metro and train stations or from newsagents and tobacconists.

Most day buses have only a driver; night buses usually also have a conductor who issues tickets. (You can't buy tickets on day buses.)

In the day, if you have a normal ticket, you should board the bus at the back. There will be an orange machine there to time-stamp your ticket. Timed tickets, *biglietto integrale a tempo* (BIT), are valid for 75 minutes or until the end of the journey, if you board before the end of the 75 minutes. BIT tickets can be used on buses and trams and for oneway journeys on the Metro or train.

INFORMATION

ATAC
Piazza dei Cinquecento.
Map 6 D3.
📞 06-46 95 22 52.
Open 7.30am–8pm daily.

Ticket for one day's unlimited travel

Ticket valid for 75 minutes

TICKETS

TICKETS FOR CITY buses, trams and Metros have to be bought before you travel. You can buy them at bars, newsstands and tobacconists, as well as at Metro stations and bus termini. Look out for places displaying ATAC (bus and tram), COTRAL (Metro) and FS (train) stickers. Most of the outlets selling tickets close by mid-evening but there are automatic ticket machines at main bus stops and train and Metro stations which take both coins and notes and distribute change.

BIT tickets are valid for 75 minutes, during which time you can hop on and off as many buses, trams and Metros as many times as you like. If you are going to make four or more journeys in one day, it is worth buying a *biglietto integrato*

New-style bus stop listing details of routes served

A Roman tram in the orange livery of ATAC

giornaliero (BIG) ticket. These give you a day's travel on the buses, trams and the Metros and one-way on urban train lines, except for Fiumicino airport. There are also available weekly tickets and monthly (calendar month) passes which are valid for the whole transport system, with discounts for students and people over 65. Fare-dodging is common, but incurs a hefty on-the-spot fine.

METROPOLITANA

Rome's underground system, the Metropolitana, has two lines (A and B) which cross the city in a rough X-shape, converging at Termini station *(see inside back cover and pp370-71)*. Line A (red) leads from Ottaviano near the Vatican to Anagnina in the southeast of the city,

Metro logo

where buses go to Ciampino airport. Line B (blue) runs from Rebibbia in the northeast, where you can catch a bus to Tivoli, down to EUR in the southwest, where buses leave for the coast. Stations are clearly marked by the Metro logo, a large white M on a red background.

The system was designed to ferry commuters in from the suburbs, so is not very useful within the centre, but the Metro is a relatively speedy way of crossing the city. Useful stations are Colosseo, Spagna, San Giovanni, Ottaviano and Piramide (for trains to Fiumicino). Metro Line C is due to be completed by 2005, linking St. Peter's to the Colosseum. Both metro lines run from 5.30am until 11.30pm every day.

USEFUL BUS AND TRAM ROUTES

This map shows a selection of buses that go through interesting parts of the city with good views of major sights. The 64 is always full of tourists, since it is the one route from Termini to St. Peter's. The other routes are likely to be less crowded. The 30b tram follows a long leisurely route around the southeast of the city, while 23 goes along the Tiber.

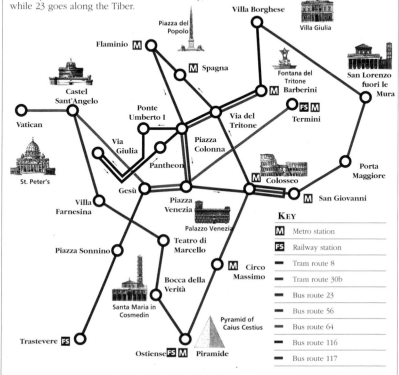

Villa Borghese
Villa Giulia
Piazza del Popolo
Flaminio M
Spagna M
Fontana del Tritone
San Lorenzo fuori le Mura
Castel Sant'Angelo
Barberini M
Vatican
Ponte Umberto I
Via del Tritone
FS M Termini
St. Peter's
Via Giulia
Piazza Colonna
Pantheon
Porta Maggiore
Gesù
Colosseo M
Villa Farnesina
Piazza Venezia
San Giovanni M
Piazza Sonnino
Palazzo Venezia
Teatro di Marcello
Circo Massimo M
Bocca della Verità
Santa Maria in Cosmedin
Pyramid of Caius Cestius
Trastevere FS
Ostiense FS M   Piramide

KEY

M	Metro station
FS	Railway station
—	Tram route 8
—	Tram route 30b
—	Bus route 23
—	Bus route 56
—	Bus route 64
—	Bus route 116
—	Bus route 117

BIKE AND MOPED HIRE

ROME'S NARROW streets and heavy traffic, combined with the seven steep hills on which it was built, make it a challenging place for even the most serious of cyclists. However, there are a few areas, such as the Villa Borghese, the banks of the Tiber and some pockets in the historic center (around the Pantheon and Piazza Navona), where cycling can be a relaxing way to see the city. Make sure that you have a loud bell though – places that are good for cyclists tend to be popular with walkers and strollers too.

Mopeds (motorini) and scooters, called Vespas or

Horse-drawn carriages outside the Pantheon

wasps in Italy because of the buzzing noise they make, are an efficient way of getting through the traffic. You may want to stick to quiet streets to begin with, though.

Although motorcyclists have to wear helmets by law, moped riders over 18 do not. However, you can hire helmets from most hire shops in Rome.

Bikes and mopeds can be hired from **Collalti**, **Roma Rent**, **Scoot-a-Long**, **Happy Rent** and **Scooters for Rent**. **Biciroma** rents from several spots around the city and a **telephone hire service** operates in the summer and autumn.

You may have to leave a credit card as deposit when you pick up the bike.

A Vespa scooter and helmet

HORSE-DRAWN CARRIAGES

THESE ARE NOT as popular in Rome as in Florence, but you can hire horse-drawn caleches (carrozzelle) for a gentle tour of the historic center. Carriages carry up to five people and can be hired from many points: Piazza di Spagna, the Colosseum, Trevi Fountain, St. Peter's, Via Veneto, Villa Borghese, Piazza Venezia and Piazza Navona. Trips last half an hour, an hour, half a day or a day. They tend to be expensive, but prices for longer rides are negotiable; establish the price before you set off and make sure you understand whether the rate is per person, or for the whole carriage.

TAXIS

OFFICIAL TAXIS in Rome are yellow or white and must bear the "taxi" sign on the roof. Only use these taxis, not the ones offered by touts at stations and tourist spots; official taxi drivers do not tout for customers. Official taxis can be hailed either at specially marked stands or on the street (drivers are not meant to stop in the street but many of them do). You can nearly always find them at the main tourist sights, at airports and stations (including

Taxi stand signpost

Termini and Ostiense). Roman taxi drivers are not renowned for their friendliness and may even refuse to take you too far from the lucrative city center.

Taxis aren't a particularly cheap way of getting about, so, unless you have heavy luggage or screaming toddlers, public transport is usually a better option. Taxi drivers always charge supplements for: baggage, night journeys (10pm–7am), journeys on Sundays or public holidays, and fares to or from the airport. As with taxis elsewhere, the meter continues running while

Taxis lining up at Fiumicino

you're at a standstill so traffic jams can become expensive. Drivers may also take suspiciously circuitous routes to your destination. While Native Romans generally tip taxi drivers small amounts or nothing at all, visitors are expected to give at least 10 per cent of the fare.

You can book in advance from **Cosmos Radio Taxi**, **Società Cooperativa Autoradiotaxi Roma** or **Società la Capitale Radio Taxi**. There is a surcharge for taxis booked in advance.

Official taxi with Commune di Roma sign

CAR HIRE

IN ITALY car hire is generally quite expensive, while fuel is among the highest-priced in Europe. Major international companies, including **Avis**, **Europcar**, **Hertz**, **Eurodollar** and **Thrifty** have rental offices at the airports and within the city center. However, you may be able to get a better deal by booking a car before you arrive through a travel agent or tour operator. Local firms (such as **Maggiore**) are generally a lot cheaper, but check that breakdown service and collision damage waiver are included in the hire price.

Prospective renters should be aged 21 or over and have held a driving license for at least one year. Theoretically you should also hold an international license (available from your national automobile association) but most car rental firms do not usually insist on this.

If the expense does not discourage you, the aggressive style of driving might. Accident rates on Italian roads are very high, so make sure you are fully insured against all eventualities. It is also a good idea to join an internationally affiliated automobile association (such as the AA in Britain or the AAA in the US). If you are unfortunate enough to break down, it is best to phone the **ACI** (Italian Automobile Club) for assistance. Although they will tow any car without charging, only members of affiliated associations are entitled to free repairs.

Details of current road and traffic conditions (in Italian) are available from a special **Road Conditions** number. You'll find more information about driving and parking in Rome on page 375.

Car rental offices at Fiumicino airport

DIRECTORY

BIKE AND MOPED HIRE ADDRESSES

Biciroma
Piazza del Popolo.
Map 4 F1.
Also: Piazza di Spagna.
Map 5 A2.
Also: Il Pincio in Villa Borghese.
Map 4 F1.

Collalti
Via del Pellegrino 82.
Map 4 E4 & 11 C4.
📞 06-68 80 10 84 *(bikes)*.

Happy Rent
Via Farini 3.
Map 6 D4.
📞 06-481 81 85 *(bikes, mopeds and scooters)*.

Scoot-a-Long
Via Cavour 302.
Map 5 B5.
📞 06-678 02 06 *(mopeds)*.

Scooters for Rent
Via della Purificazione 84.
📞 06-488 54 85 *(bikes and mopeds)*.

TAXI BOOKING NUMBERS

Cosmos Radio Taxi
📞 06-881 77.

Società la Capitale Radio Taxi
📞 06-49 94.

Società Cooperativa Autoradiotaxi Roma
📞 06-35 70.

CAR HIRE ADDRESSES

Avis
📞 06-41999 *(centralized booking number)*.
Also: Ciampino airport.
📞 06-79 34 01 95.
Also: Fiumicino airport.
📞 06-65 01 15 79.
Also: Via Sardegna 38A.
Map 5 C1.
📞 06-42 82 47 28.

Eurodollar
📞 167 01 86 68 *(toll free)*.

Europcar
Fiumicino airport.
📞 06-65 01 08 79.
Also: Via Lombardia 7.
Map 5 B2.
📞 06-487 12 74.

Hertz
Via Gregorio VII 207.
📞 06-39 37 88 07.
Also: Stazione Termini.
Map 6 D3.
📞 06-474 03 89 or 06-32 68 31.
Also: Fiumicino airport.
📞 06-65 01 14 48.

Maggiore
📞 147 867 07 *(toll free)*.
Stazione Termini.
Map 6 D3.
📞 06-488 00 49.
Also: Via Po 8A.
Map 5 C1.
📞 06-854 86 98 or 06-884 01 37.

Thrifty
Via Ludovisi 60.
Map 5 B2.
📞 06-482 09 66.
Also: Ciampino airport.
📞 06-652 91 34.
Also: Fiumicino airport.
📞 06-79 34 01 37.

CAR BREAKDOWN SERVICES

ACI Breakdown
📞 116.
Autosoccorso CARA
Veientana Vetere 405.
📞 06-332 01 19.
(24-hour rescue service).

Road Conditions
Via Magenta 5. **Map** 6 E3.
📞 06-44 77.

MAIN CAR PARKS

Acqua Acetosa station.
Map 2 E1.
Also: Lepanto Metro station. **Map** 4 D1.
Also: Piazza del Popolo.
Map 4 F1.
Also: EUR Palasport Metro station.

USEFUL 24-HOUR GAS STATIONS

Trastevere
Lungotevere Ripa.
Map 8 D1.

Portuense
Piazza della Radio.
Map 7 B5.

STREET FINDER

MAP REFERENCES given with sights, restaurants, hotels, shops and entertainment venues refer to the maps in this section *(see How the Map References Work opposite)*. A complete index of the street names and places of interest marked on the maps follows on pages 382–91. The key map below shows the area of Rome covered by the *Street Finder*. This includes the sightseeing areas (which are color-coded) as well as the whole of central Rome with all the districts important for restaurants, hotels and entertainment venues. Because the historic centre is so packed with sights, there is a large-scale map of this area on pages 11 and 12.

0 kilometres   2

0 miles   1

How the Map References Work

The first figure tells you which Street Finder map to turn to.

Trevi Fountain ●

Fontana di Trevi. **Map** 5 A3 & 12 F2 🚌 *52, 53, 56, 58, 58b, 60, 61, 62, 71, 95, 115, 116, 117, 492.*

The letter and number are a grid reference. You will find the letters at the top and bottom of the map and the numbers at the sides.

The second reference refers to the large-scale maps of central Rome (11 & 12). It is read in exactly the same way as the first.

The map continues on map 8 of the Street Finder.

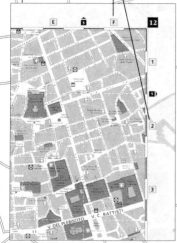

The key to the abbreviations used in the Street Finder is on page 382.

Key to Street Finder

▢	Major sight
▢	Places of interest
▢	Railway station
Ⓜ	Metro station
🚌	Bus terminus
🚋	Tram terminus
🅿	Main car parks
ℹ	Tourist information office
✚	Hospital with emergency unit
🚓	Police station
✝	Church
✡	Synagogue
⊠	Post office
═	Railway line
→	One-way street
▬	Steps
▬	City wall

Scale of Maps 1–10

```
0 meters        250
                            1:13,000
0 yards         250
```

Scale of Maps 11 & 12

```
0 meters        150
                            1:8,000
0 yards         150
```

Street Finder Index

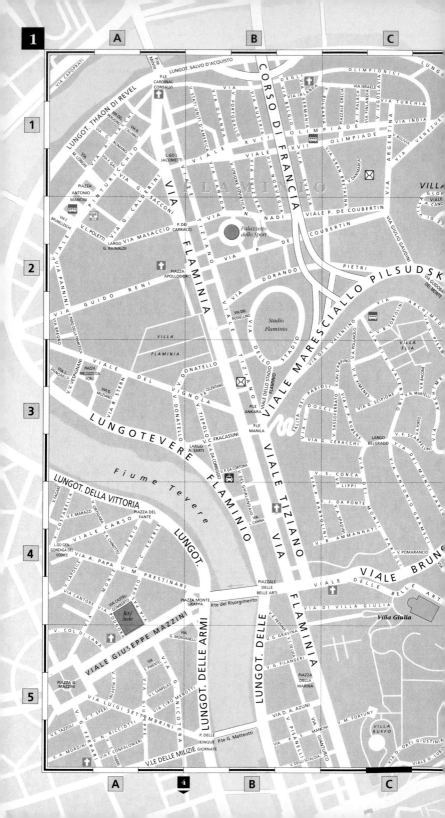

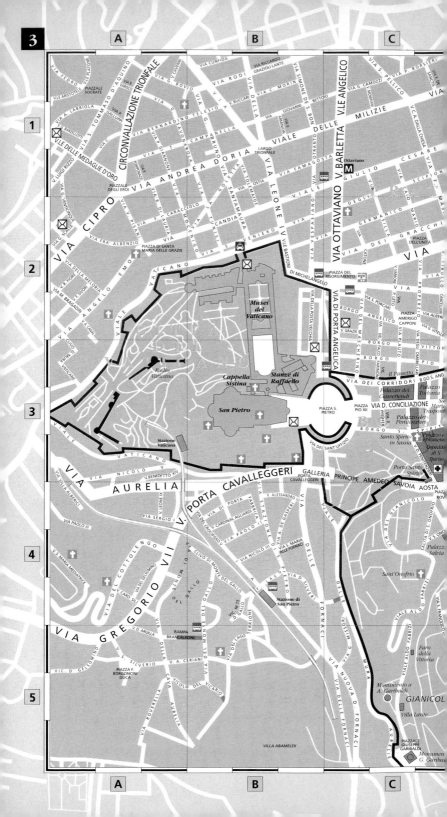

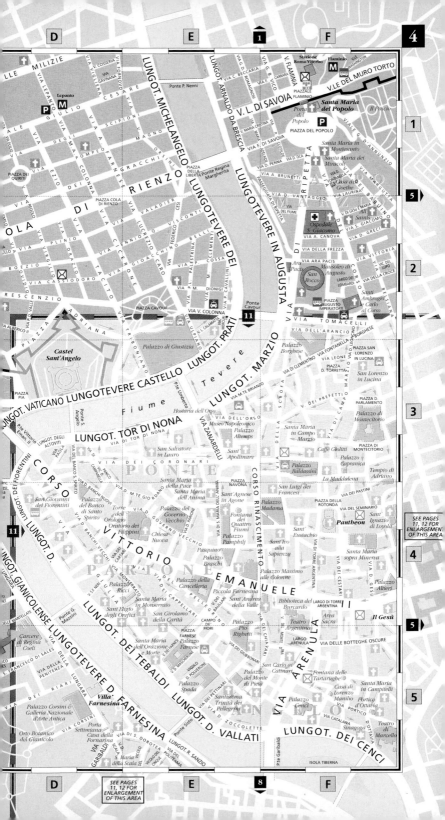

SEE PAGES 11, 12 FOR ENLARGEMENT OF THIS AREA

SEE PAGES 11, 12 FOR ENLARGEMENT OF THIS AREA

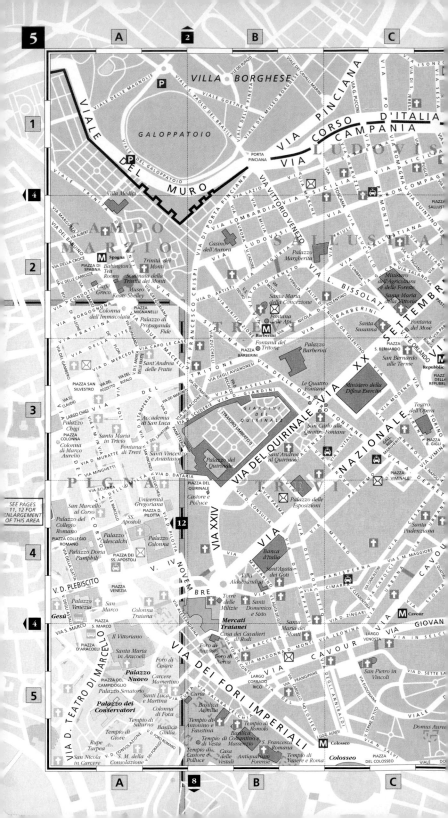

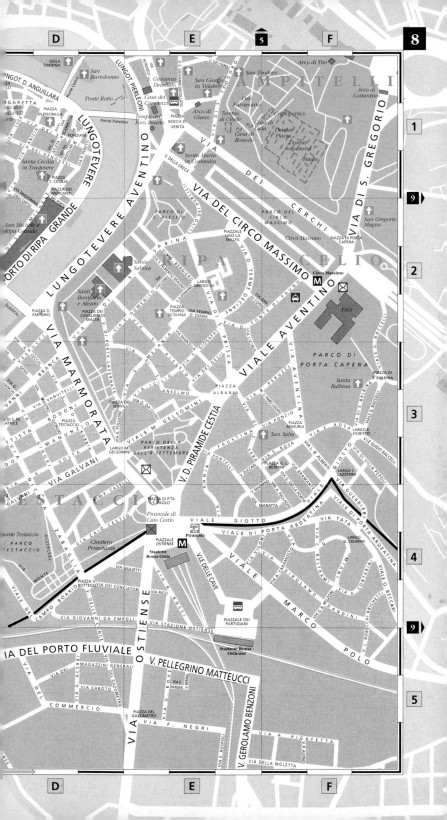

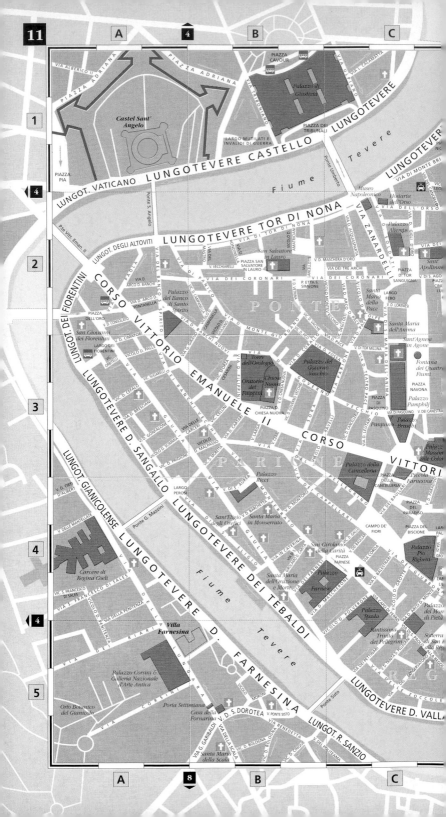

General Index

A

Acknowledgments

DORLING KINDERSLEY would like to thank the following people whose contributions and assistance have made the preparation of this book possible.

MAIN CONTRIBUTORS

Olivia Ercoli is an art historian and tour guide who has lived all her life in Rome. Bilingual in English and Italian, she lectures on art history and writes on a range of subjects for English and Italian publications.

Travel writer Ros Belford conceived the idea of the Virago Woman's Guides, of which she is now series editor, and wrote the *Virago Woman's Guide to Rome*. She has traveled widely in Europe and as well as writing guide books contributes to a variety of publications, including *The Guardian*.

Roberta Mitchell heads the editorial section of the UN's Publishing Division in Rome, where she has lived for many years. An experienced writer and editor with extensive knowledge of the city, she has contributed to a number of guides to Rome, including the *American Express Guide to Rome*.

CONTRIBUTORS

Sam Cole, Mary Jane Cryan Pancani, Daphne Wilson Ercoli, Laura Ercoli, Lindsay Hunt, Adrian James, Christopher McDowall, Davina Palmer, Rodney Palmer, Debra Shipley.

DORLING KINDERSLEY wishes to thank the following editors and researchers at Websters International Publishers: Sandy Carr, Matthew Barrell, Siobhan Bremner, Serena Cross, Valeria Fabbri, Annie Galpin, Gemma Hancock, Celia Woolfrey.

ADDITIONAL PHOTOGRAPHY

Max Alexander, Andy Crawford, Philip Enticknap, Steve Gorton, John Heseltine, Neil Mersh, Poppy, David Sutherland, Martin Woodward.

ADDITIONAL ILLUSTRATIONS

Anne Bowes, Robin Carter, Gillie Newman, Chris D. Orr.

ADDITIONAL PICTURE RESEARCH

Sharon Buckley.

CARTOGRAPHY

Advanced Illustration (Cheshire), Contour Publishing (Derby), Euromap Limited (Berkshire). Street Finder maps: ERA Maptec Ltd. (Dublin) adapted with permission from original survey and mapping from Shobunsha (Japan).

CARTOGRAPHIC RESEARCH

James Anderson, Donna Rispoli, Joan Russell.

RESEARCH ASSISTANCE

Janet Abbott, Flaminia Allvin, Fabrizio Ardito, Licia Bronzin, Lupus Sabene.

DESIGN AND EDITORIAL ASSISTANCE

Hilary Bird, Vanessa Courtier, Kristin Dolina-Adamczyk, Claire Edwards, Jon Eldan, Simon Farbrother, Vanessa Hamilton, Marcus Hardy, Sasha Heseltine, Sally Ann Hibbard, Stephanie Jackson, Steve Knowlden, Mary Lambert, Janette Leung, Jane Middleton, Fiona Morgan, Helen Partington, Naomi Peck, Carolyn Pyrah, Salim Qurashi, Jane Shaw, Clare Sullivan, Andrew Szudek, Daphne Trotter, Diana Vowles, Lynda Warrington.

SPECIAL ASSISTANCE

Dottore Riccardo Baldini, Signor Mario di Bartolomeo of the Soprintendenza dei Beni Artistici e Storici di Roma, Belloni, Dorling Kindersley picture department, David Gleave MW, Debbie Harris, Emma Hutton and Cooling Brown Partnership, Dottoressa Todaro and Signora Camimiti at the Ministero dell'Interno, Trestini.

PHOTOGRAPHY PERMISSIONS

DORLING KINDERSLEY would like to thank the following for their kind permission to photograph at their establishments: Bathsheba Abse at the Keats-Shelley Memorial House, Accademia dei Lincei, Accanto, Aeroporti di Roma, Aldrovandi Palace, Alpheus, Banco di Santo Spirito at Palazzo del Monte di Pietà, Rory Bruck at Babington's, Caffè Giolitti, Caffè Latino, Comune di Roma (Ripartizione X), Comunità Ebraica di Roma, Guido Cornini at Monumenti Musei e Gallerie Ponteficie, Direzione Sanitaria Ospedale di Santo Spirito, Dottoressa Laura Falsini at the

Soprintendenza Archeologica di Etruria Meridionale, Hotel Gregoriana, Hotel Majestic, Hotel Regina Baglioni, Marco Marchetti at Ente EUR, Dottoressa Mercalli at the Museo Nazionale di Castel Sant'Angelo, Ministero dell'Interno, Plaza Minerva, Ristorante Alberto Ciarla, Ristorante Filetti di Baccalà, Ristorante Romolo, Signor Rulli and Signor Angeli at the Soprintendenza Archeologica di Roma, Soprintendenza Archeologica per il Lazio, Soprintendenza per i Beni Ambientali e Architettonici, Soprintendenza per i Beni Artistici e Storici di Roma, Daniela Tabo at the Musei Capitolini, Villa d'Este, Villa San Pio, Mrs. Marjorie Weeke at St. Peter's.

PICTURE CREDITS

t = top; tl = top left; tc = top center;
tr = top right; cla = center left above;
ca = center above; cra = center right above;
cl = center left; c = center; cr = center right;
clb = center left below; cb = center below;
crb = center right below; bl = bottom left;
b = bottom; bc = bottom center;
br = bottom right.

Every effort has been made to trace the copyright holders and we apologize in advance for any unintentional omissions. We would be pleased to insert the appropriate acknowledgments in any subsequent edition of this publication.

Works of art have been reproduced with the permission of the following copyright holders: © DACS: Città con Cattedrale Gotica, 1925 by Paul Klee 241b.

The publishers are grateful to the following individuals, companies and picture libraries for permission to reproduce their photographs:

ACCADEMIA NAZIONALE DI SAN LUCA, Rome: 160b; AFE: 57b, 61cr; Sandro Battaglia 59c, 61clb, 61br, 324br; Louise Goldman 157t; G. La Malfa 251t; AEROPORTI DI ROMA: 368b; AGENZIA SINTESI: Fabio Fiorani 360br, 361t, 361b; Antonella di Girolamo 361c; Marco Marcotulli 360bc; R. Venturi 360bl; ALITALIA: 368t, 369cl; ALLSPORT: David Cannon 39br; ANCIENT ART AND ARCHITECTURE: 16bl, 20tl, 21tl, 25bc, 34crb, 35tc, 44cl; ARTOTHEK, Stadelsches Kunstinstitut Frankfurt, Goethe in the Roman Campagna by J.H.W. Tischbein 136t.

BIBLIOTECA REALE, Torino: 28–29c; BRIDGEMAN ART LIBRARY, LONDON/NEW YORK: 18br, 37tr; Agnew & Sons, London 51tr; Antikenmuseum Staatliches Museum, Berlin 19bl; Biblioteca Publica Episcopal, Barcelona/Index 114bl; Bibliothèque da la Sorbonne 28c, British Museum, London 27ctr; Chateau de Versailles, France/Giraudon 33tr, 54cl; Christie's, London 40, 55tr, 68b, 95t; The Fine Art Society, London 151tr, 279tl; Galleria degli Uffizi, Florence 31bl; Greek Museum, University of Newcastle-upon-Tyne 16br; King Street Galleries, London 33br; Louvre, Paris/Lauros-Giraudon 56br; Louvre, Paris/Giraudon 26br; Roy Miles Gallery, 29 Bruton St, London 228t; Musée des Beaux-Arts, Nantes 53t; Museo e Gallerie Nazionali di Capodimonte, Naples, Detail from the predella of San Ludovico by Simone Martini 26tr; Musée Condé, Chantilly f.71v Très Riches Heures, 26tc; Museum of Fine Arts, Budapest 110bl; Museo Archeologico di Villa Giulia 48cl; Museo Poldi Pezzoli, Milan 54tr; Palazzo Doria Pamphilj, Rome 107b; Piacenza Town Hall, Italy/Index 27br; Private Collection 19br, 22bl, 24br, 27tr, 178b; Pushkin Museum, Moscow 111t; Sotheby's, London 18bl; Vatican Museums & Galleries 41ca, 237tr.

CEPHAS PICTURE LIBRARY: Mick Rock 306tr; VANESSA COURTIER: 355t.

IL DAGHERROTIPO: Stefano Chieppa 152cl, 378b; Giorgio Oddi 53cl; CM DIXON: 17bl, 24c, 268b, 269t, 269b.

ECOLE NATIONALE SUPERIEURE DES BEAUX-ARTS: 21cr, 22–23, 248t, 284–285b; ENTE NAZIONALE ITALIANO PER IL TURISMO: 358cl, cr; ET ARCHIVE: 14, 17tr, 17clb, 18tr, 19tc, 23t, 27cl, 28tl, 31br, 32br, 37br, 48tl, 306tl; MARY EVANS PICTURE LIBRARY: 9, 18cl, 23cl, 24cl, 29br, 30cb, 30b, 31t, 34tl, 34cr, 34bl, 54tl, 56tl, 67bl, 74t, 81b, 91t, 92b, 94bl, 127c, 135t, 213b.

CORALDO FALSINI: 38–39c, 340b, 341t, 341c; WERNER FORMAN ARCHIVE: 17cr, 20bl, 22tl, 23cr, 23bl, 23br, 47tr, 155t, 163tr, 175c; FOLKLORE MUSEUM, Rome: 210br.

GARDEN PICTURE LIBRARY: Bob Challinor 172cb; GIRAUDON: 15b, 28br, 36br, 55tl; RONALD GRANT: 52br, 340t.

SONIA HALLIDAY: 19c, 22br, 25cl; Laura Lushington 24bl; ROBERT HARDING PICTURE LIBRARY: 23cra, 32bl, 79cr, 177t, 268c, 353c;

Mario Carrieri 35tr; Caffè Greco, Rome by Ludwig Passini 309tr; John G Ross 38tl, 59cl, 341b; Sheila Terry 39cl; G White 59br; MICHAEL HOLFORD: 70b; HULTON DEUTSCH: 36tl, 38bc, 57cr, 63, 175b, 287c, 357c.

MAGNUM: Erich Lessing 15t, 17tl, 89br; MANSELL COLLECTION: 19tr, 25bl, 26bc, 31cl, 54bc, 55tc, 56cl, 57cl, 75cl, 75cr, 78tc, 93b, 112c, 122t, 125tr, 126tl, 132br, 133cr, 136bl, 139bl, 139br, 162tr, 172bl, 172 br, 183br, 192bl, 196bl, 210c, 220bl, 227cr, 229cr; Alinari 80br, 141bl, 174t, 254b; Anderson 78cr, 138bl, 163tl, 228b; MORO ROMA: 36cl, 37cl, 38br, 39tr, 39bl.

NATIONAL PORTRAIT GALLERY, London: 55cr, 55b, 56tr, 57tr; © NIPPON TELEVISION NETWORK CORPORATION, Tokyo 1999: 244b and all pictures on 246-7.

LA REPUBBLICA TROVAROMA: 359tl; REX FEATURES: Sipa 366br; Today 39cr.

SCALA: 94t, 278cl, Casa di Augusto 97t, Chiesa del Gesù 115t, Galleria Borghese 32cla, 260tr, Galleria Colonna 157b, Galleria Doria Pamphilj 46br, 105cr, Galleria Spada 46cl, Galleria degli Uffizi 16–17, 27bl, Museo d'Arte Orientale 174t, 174br, Musei Capitolini 47bl, Museo della Civiltà Romana 48tr, 48b, Museo delle Terme 21tr, Museo Napoleonico 49cr, Museo Nazionale, Napoli 21cl, Museo Nazionale, Ravenna 22cl, Museo del Risorgimento, Milano 36clb, 36–37c, Museo del Risorgimento, Roma 37tl, Museo di San

Marco 54bl, Palazzo Barberini 253bl, Palazzo Ducale 8, 19tr, Palazzo della Farnesina 220ct, Palazzo Madama 20cl, Palazzo Venezia 47cr, 66bl, San Carlo alle Quattro Fontane 33cl, 33cr, Santa Cecilia in Trastevere 32tl, San Clemente 35bl, Santa Costanza 24–25c, Santa Maria Antiqua 24tl, Santa Maria dell'Anima 121t, Santa Maria Maggiore 43tr, Santa Maria del Popolo 139tr, 139c, Santa Prassede 26bl, 28bl, Santa Sabina 25tc, 29cl, Vatican Museums 19bc, 25t, 25cr, 25cra, 27cr, 29tl, 29cr, 30tl, 30ct, 31cr, 31bc, 32cr, 32clb, 41tr, 46tl, 48cr, 49bl, 224bl, 225cr, 235t, 238tl, 238br, 240t, 240b, 241t, 241c, 241b, 242tl, 242c, 242b, 243t, 243c, 243b, 245 (all 4); TONY STONE IMAGES: Richard Passmore 1c.

TOPHAM PICTURE SOURCE: 38cl.

ZEFA: 2, 39tl, 230cl, 231br, 356–7, 358t, 372t; Eric Carle 58t; Kohlhas 231t.

JACKET: All special photography except: BRIDGEMAN ART LIBRARY, LONDON/NEW YORK front cover cl; TONY STONE IMAGES: Richard Passmore spine c.

Thanks also to Dottoressa Giulia De Marchi of L'ACCADEMIA NAZIONALE DI SAN LUCA, Rome for 160b, Rettore Padre Libianchi of LA CHIESA DI SANT'IGNAZIO DI LOYOLA for 106t, ENTE NAZIONALE PER IL TURISMO, HASSLER HOTEL, Rome for 293tl, GRAND HOTEL, Rome for 293crb and to LA REPUBBLICA TROVAROMA.

Phrase Book

IN EMERGENCY

Help!	Aiuto!	eye-**yoo**-toh
Stop!	Fermate!	fair-**mah**-teh
Call a	Chiama un	kee-**ah**-mah oon
doctor	medico	**meh**-dee-koh
Call an	Chiama un'	kee-**ah**-mah oon
ambulance	ambulanza	am-boo-**lan**-tsa
Call the	Chiama la	kee-**ah**-mah lah
police	polizia	pol-ee-**tsee**-ah
Call the fire	Chiama i	kee-**ah**-mah ee
brigade	pompieri	pom-pee-**air**-ee
Where is the	Dov'è il telefono?	dov-**eh** eel teh-leh-
telephone?		**foh**-noh?
The nearest	L'ospedale	loss-peh-**dah**-leh pee-
hospital?	più vicino?	oo vee-**chee**-noh?

COMMUNICATION ESSENTIALS

Yes/No	Sì/No	see/noh
Please	Per favore	pair fah-**vor**-eh
Thank you	Grazie	**grah**-tsee-eh
Excuse me	Mi scusi	mee **skoo**-zee
Hello	Buon giorno	buon **jor**-noh
Good bye	Arrivederci	ah-ree-veh-**dair**-chee
Good evening	Buona sera	**bwon**-ah **sair**-ah
morning	la mattina	lah mah-**tee**-nah
afternoon	il pomeriggio	eel poh-meh-**ree**-joh
evening	la sera	lah **sair**-ah
yesterday	ieri	ee-**air**-ee
today	oggi	**oh**-jee
tomorrow	domani	doh-**mah**-nee
here	qui	**kwee**
there	la	lah
What?	Quale?	**kwah**-leh?
When?	Quando?	**kwan**-doh?
Why?	Perchè?	pair-**keh**?
Where?	Dove?	**doh**-veh

USEFUL PHRASES

How are you?	Come sta?	**koh**-meh stah?
Very well,	Molto bene,	**moll**-toh **beh**-neh
thank you.	grazie.	**grah**-tsee-eh
Pleased to	Piacere di	pee-ah-**chair**-eh dee
meet you.	conoscerla.	coh-**noh**-shair-lah
See you soon.	A più tardi.	ah pee-**oo tar**-dee
That's fine.	Va bene.	va **beh**-neh
Where is/are ...?	Dov'è/Dove sono ...?	dov-**eh**/**doveh soh**-noh?
How long does	Quanto tempo ci	**kwan**-toh tem-poh
it take to get to ...?	vuole per	chee voo-**oh**-leh pair
	andare a ...?	an-**dar**-eh ah...?
How do I	Come faccio per	koh-meh **fah**-choh
get to ...?	arrivare a ...?	pair arri-**var**-eh ah..?
Do you speak	Parla inglese?	**par**-lah een-**gleh**-zeh?
English?		
I don't	Non capisco.	non ka-**pee**-skoh
understand.		
Could you speak	Può parlare	pwoh par-**lah**-reh
more slowly,	più lentamente,	pee-oo len-ta-**men**-teh
please?	per favore?	pair fah-**vor**-eh
I'm sorry.	Mi dispiace.	mee dee-spee-**ah**-cheh

USEFUL WORDS

big	grande	**gran**-deh
small	piccolo	**pee**-koh-loh
hot	caldo	**kal**-doh
cold	freddo	**fred**-doh
good	buono	**bwoh**-noh
bad	cattivo	kat-**tee**-voh
enough	basta	**bas**-tah
well	bene	**beh**-neh
open	aperto	ah-**pair**-toh
closed	chiuso	kee-**oo**-zoh
left	a sinistra	ah see-**nee**-strah
right	a destra	ah **dess**-trah
straight on	sempre dritto	**sem**-preh **dree**-toh
near	vicino	vee-**chee**-noh
far	lontano	lon-**tah**-noh
up	su	**soo**
down	giù	**joo**
early	presto	**press**-toh
late	tardi	**tar**-dee
entrance	entrata	en-**trah**-tah
exit	uscita	oo-**shee**-ta
toilet	il gabinetto	eel gab-bee-**net**-toh
free, unoccupied	libero	**lee**-bair-oh
free, no charge	gratuito	grah-**too**-ee-toh

MAKING A TELEPHONE CALL

I'd like to place a	Vorrei fare	vor-**ray far**-eh oona
long-distance call.	una interurbana.	in-tair-oor-**bah**-nah
I'd like to make	Vorrei fare una	vor-**ray far**-eh oona
a reverse-charge	telefonata a carico	teh-leh-fon-**ah**-tah ab
call.	del destinatario.	**kar**-ee-koh dell dess-
		tee-nah-**tar**-ree-oh
I'll try again later.	Ritelefono più	ree-teh-**leh**-foh-noh
	tardi.	pee-oo **tar**-dee
Can I leave a	Posso lasciare	**poss**-oh lash-**ah**-reh
message?	un messaggio?	oon mess-**sah**-joh?
Hold on	Un attimo,	oon **ah**-tee-moh,
	per favore	pair fah-**vor**-eh
Could you speak	Può parlare più	pwoh par-**lah**-reh
up a little please?	forte, per favore?	pee-oo **for**-teh, pair
		fah-**vor**-eh?
local call	la telefonata	lah teh-leh-fon-**ah**-ta
	locale	loh-**kah**-leh

SHOPPING

How much	Quant'è,	kwan-**teh**
does this cost?	per favore?	pair fah-**vor**-eh?
I would like ...	Vorrei ...	vor-**ray**
Do you have ...?	Avete ...?	ah-**veh**-teh.. ?
I'm just looking.	Sto soltanto	stoh sol-**tan**-toh
	guardando.	gwar-**dan**-doh
Do you take	Accettate	ah-chet-**tah**-teh **kar**-teh
credit cards?	carte di credito?	dee **creh**-dee-toh?
What time do	A che ora apre/	ah keh **or**-ah
you open/close?	chiude?	**ah**-preh/kee-**oo**-deh?
this one	questo	**kweh**-stoh
that one	quello	**kwell**-oh
expensive	caro	**kar**-oh
cheap	a buon prezzo	ah bwon **pret**-soh
size, clothes	la taglia	lah **tah**-lee-ah
size, shoes	il numero	eel **noo**-mair-oh
white	bianco	bee-**ang**-koh
black	nero	**neh**-roh
red	rosso	**ross**-oh
yellow	giallo	**jal**-loh
green	verde	**vair**-deh
blue	blu	bloo
brown	marrone	mar-**roh**-neh

TYPES OF SHOP

antique dealer	l'antiquario	lan-tee-**kwah**-ree-oh
bakery	la panetteria	lah pah-net-tair-**ree**-ah
bank	la banca	lah **bang**-kah
bookshop	la libreria	lah lee-breh-**ree**-ah
butcher's	la macelleria	lah mah-chell-eh-**ree**-ah
cake shop	la pasticceria	lah pas-tee-chair-**ee**-ah
chemist's	la farmacia	lah far-mah-**chee**-ah
department store	il grande	eel **gran**-deh
	magazzino	mag-gad-**zee**-noh
delicatessen	la salumeria	lah sah-loo-meh-**ree**-ah
fishmonger's	la pescheria	lah pess-keh-**ree**-ah
florist	il fioraio	eel fee-or-**eye**-oh
greengrocer	il fruttivendolo	eel froo-tee-**ven**-doh-loh
grocery	alimentari	ah-lee-men-**tah**-ree
hairdresser	il parrucchiere	eel par-oo-kee-**air**-eh
ice cream parlour	la gelateria	lah jel-lah-tair-**ee**-ah
market	il mercato	eel mair-**kah**-toh
news-stand	l'edicola	leh-dee-**koh**-lah
post office	l'ufficio postale	loo-**fee**-choh pos-**tah**-leh
shoe shop	il negozio di	eel neh-**goh**-tsioh dee
	scarpe	**skar**-peh
supermarket	il supermercato	su-pair-mair-**kah**-toh
tobacconist	il tabaccaio	lah tah-bak-**eye**-oh
travel agency	l'agenzia di viaggi	lah-jen-**tsee**-ah dee
		vee-**ad**-jee

SIGHTSEEING

art gallery	la pinacoteca	lah peena-koh-**teh**-kah
bus stop	la fermata	lah fair-**mah**-tah
	dell'autobus	dell **ow**-toh-booss
church	la chiesa	lah kee-**eh**-zah
	la basilica	lah bah-**seel**-i-kah
garden	il giardino	eel jar-**dee**-no
library	la biblioteca	lah beeb-lee-oh-**teh**-kah
museum	il museo	eel moo-**zeh**-oh
railway station	la stazione	lah stah-tsee-**oh**-neh
tourist	l'ufficio	loo-**fee**-choh
information	turistico	too-**ree**-stee-koh
closed for the	chiuso per la	kee-**oo**-zoh pair lah
public holiday	festa	**fess**-tah

STAYING IN A HOTEL

Do you have any vacant rooms?	**Avete camere libere?**	*ah-veh-teh kah-mair-eh lee-bair-eh?*
double room	**una camera doppia**	*oona kah-mair-ah dob-pee-ah*
with double bed	**con letto matrimoniale**	*kon let-toh mah-treemoh-nee-ah-leh*
twin room	**una camera con due letti**	*oona kah-mair-ah kon doo-eh let-tee*
single room	**una camera singola**	*oona kah-mair-ah sing-goh-lah*
room with a bath, shower	**una camera con bagno, con doccia**	*oona kah-mair-ah kon ban-yoh, kon dot-chah*
porter	**il facchino**	*eel fah-kee-noh*
key	**la chiave**	*lah kee-ah-veh*
I have a reservation.	**Ho fatto una prenotazione.**	*oh fat-toh oona prehnoh-tah-tsee-oh-neh*

EATING OUT

Have you got a table for ...?	**Avete una tavola per ... ?**	*ah-veh-teh oona tah-voh-lah pair ...?*
I'd like to reserve a table.	**Vorrei riservare una tavola.**	*vor-ray ree-sair-vah-reh oona tah-voh-lah*
breakfast	**colazione**	*koh-lah-tsee-oh-neh*
lunch	**pranzo**	*pran-tsoh*
dinner	**cena**	*cheh-nah*
The bill, please.	**Il conto, per favore.**	*eel kon-toh pair fah-vor-eh*
I am a vegetarian.	**Sono vegetariano/a.**	*soh-noh veh-jeh-tar-ee-ah-noh/nah*
waitress	**cameriera**	*kah-mair-ee-air-ah*
waiter	**cameriere**	*kah-mair-ee-air-eh*
fixed price menu	**il menù a prezzo fisso**	*eel meh-noo ah pret-sob fee-soh*
dish of the day	**piatto del giorno**	*pee-ah-toh dell jor-no*
starter	**antipasto**	*an-tee-pass-toh*
first course	**il primo**	*eel pree-moh*
main course	**il secondo**	*eel seh-kon-doh*
vegetables	**il contorno**	*eel kon-tor-noh*
dessert	**il dolce**	*eel doll-cheh*
cover charge	**il coperto**	*eel koh-pair-toh*
wine list	**la lista dei vini**	*lah lee-stah day vee-nee*
rare	**al sangue**	*al sang-gweh*
medium	**al puntino**	*al poon-tee-noh*
well done	**ben cotto**	*ben kot-toh*
glass	**il bicchiere**	*eel bee-kee-air-eh*
bottle	**la bottiglia**	*lah bot-teel-yah*
knife	**il coltello**	*eel kol-tell-oh*
fork	**la forchetta**	*lah for-ket-tah*
spoon	**il cucchiaio**	*eel koo-kee-eye-oh*

MENU DECODER

apple	**la mela**	*lah meh-lah*
artichoke	**il carciofo**	*eel kar-choff-oh*
baked	**al forno**	*al for-noh*
beans	**i fagioli**	*ee fah-job-lee*
beef	**il manzo**	*eel man-tsoh*
beer	**la birra**	*lah beer-rah*
boiled	**lesso**	*less-oh*
bread	**il pane**	*eel pah-neh*
broth	**il brodo**	*eel brob-doh*
butter	**il burro**	*eel boor-oh*
cake	**la torta**	*lah tor-tah*
cheese	**il formaggio**	*eel for-mad-joh*
chicken	**il pollo**	*eel poll-oh*
baby clams	**le vongole**	*leh von-gob-leh*
coffee	**il caffè**	*eel kah-feh*
dry	**secco**	*sek-koh*
duck	**l'anatra**	*lah-nah-trah*
egg	**l'uovo**	*loo-oh-voh*
eggplant	**la melanzana**	*lah meh-lan-tsah-nah*
fish	**il pesce**	*eel pesh-eh*
french fries	**patatine fritte**	*pah-tah-teen-eh free-teh*
fresh fruit	**frutta fresca**	*froo-tah fress-kah*
garlic	**l'aglio**	*labl-yoh*
grapes	**l'uva**	*loo-vah*
grilled	**alla griglia**	*ab-lah greel-yah*
ham	**il prosciutto**	*eel pro-shoo-toh*
cooked/cured	**cotto/crudo**	*kot-toh/kroo-doh*
ice cream	**il gelato**	*eel jel-lah-toh*
lamb	**l'abbacchio**	*lah-back-kee-oh*
lobster	**l'aragosta**	*lah-rah-goss-tah*
meat	**la carne**	*la kar-neh*
milk	**il latte**	*eel labt-teh*

mineral water fizzy/still	**l'acqua minerale gasata/naturale**	*lah-kwah mee-nair-ah-leh gab-zah-tah/nah-too-rah-leh*
mushrooms	**i funghi**	*ee foon-gee*
oil	**l'olio**	*loll-yoh*
olive	**l'oliva**	*loh-lee-vah*
onion	**la cipolla**	*lah chee-poll-ah*
orange	**l'arancia**	*lah-ran-chah*
orange/lemon juice	**succo d'arancia/ di limone**	*soo-koh dah-ran-chah/dee leh-mob-neh*
peach	**la pesca**	*lah pess-kah*
pepper	**il pepe**	*eel peb-peh*
pork	**carne di maiale**	*kar-neh dee mah-yah-leh*
potatoes	**le patate**	*leh pah-tah-teh*
prawns	**i gamberi**	*ee gam-bair-ee*
rice	**il riso**	*eel ree-zoh*
roast	**arrosto**	*ar-ross-toh*
roll	**il panino**	*eel pah-nee-noh*
salad	**l'insalata**	*leen-sah-lah-tah*
salt	**il sale**	*eel sah-leh*
sausage	**la salsiccia**	*lah sal-see-chah*
seafood	**frutti di mare**	*froo-tee dee mab-reh*
soup	**la zuppa, la minestra**	*lah tsoo-pab, lah mee-ness-trah*
steak	**la bistecca**	*lah bee-stek-kah*
strawberries	**le fragole**	*leh frah-gob-leh*
sugar	**lo zucchero**	*loh zoo-kair-oh*
tea	**il tè**	*eel teh*
herb tea	**la tisana**	*lah tee-zah-nah*
tomato	**il pomodoro**	*eel poh-mob-dor-oh*
tuna	**il tonno**	*ton-noh*
veal	**il vitello**	*vee-tell-oh*
vegetables	**i legumi**	*ee leh-goo-mee*
vinegar	**l'aceto**	*lah-cheh-toh*
water	**l'acqua**	*lah-kwah*
red wine	**vino rosso**	*vee-noh ross-oh*
white wine	**vino bianco**	*vee-noh bee-ang-koh*
zucchini	**gli zucchini**	*lyee dzoo-kee-nee*

NUMBERS

1	**uno**	*oo-noh*
2	**due**	*doo-eh*
3	**tre**	*treh*
4	**quattro**	*kwat-roh*
5	**cinque**	*ching-kweh*
6	**sei**	*say-ee*
7	**sette**	*set-teh*
8	**otto**	*ot-toh*
9	**nove**	*noh-veh*
10	**dieci**	*dee-eh-chee*
11	**undici**	*oon-dee-chee*
12	**dodici**	*dob-dee-chee*
13	**tredici**	*tray-dee-chee*
14	**quattordici**	*kwat-tor-dee-chee*
15	**quindici**	*kwin-dee-chee*
16	**sedici**	*say-dee-chee*
17	**diciassette**	*dee-chah-set-teh*
18	**diciotto**	*dee-chot-toh*
19	**diciannove**	*dee-chah-nob-veh*
20	**venti**	*ven-tee*
30	**trenta**	*tren-tah*
40	**quaranta**	*kwab-ran-tah*
50	**cinquanta**	*ching-kwan-tah*
60	**sessanta**	*sess-an-tah*
70	**settanta**	*set-tan-tah*
80	**ottanta**	*ot-tan-tah*
90	**novanta**	*noh-van-tah*
100	**cento**	*chen-toh*
1,000	**mille**	*mee-leh*
2,000	**duemila**	*doo-eh mee-lah*
5,000	**cinquemila**	*ching-kweh mee-lah*
1,000,000	**un milione**	*oon meel-yoh-neh*

TIME

one minute	**un minuto**	*oon mee-noo-toh*
one hour	**un'ora**	*oon or-ah*
half an hour	**mezz'ora**	*medz-or-ah*
a day	**un giorno**	*oon jor-noh*
a week	**una settimana**	*oona set-tee-mah-nah*
Monday	**lunedì**	*loo-neh-dee*
Tuesday	**martedì**	*mar-teh-dee*
Wednesday	**mercoledì**	*mair-koh-leh-dee*
Thursday	**giovedì**	*joh-veh-dee*
Friday	**venerdì**	*ven-air-dee*
Saturday	**sabato**	*sah-bah-toh*
Sunday	**domenica**	*doh-meh-nee-kah*

DORLING KINDERSLEY *TRAVEL GUIDES*

TITLES AVAILABLE

THE GUIDES THAT SHOW YOU WHAT OTHERS ONLY TELL YOU

COUNTRY GUIDES

AUSTRALIA • CANADA • FRANCE • GREAT BRITAIN
GREECE: ATHENS & THE MAINLAND • THE GREEK ISLANDS
IRELAND • ITALY • MEXICO • PORTUGAL • SCOTLAND
SOUTH AFRICA • SPAIN • THAILAND

REGIONAL GUIDES

BARCELONA & CATALONIA • CALIFORNIA
FLORENCE & TUSCANY • FLORIDA • HAWAII
JERUSALEM & THE HOLY LAND • LOIRE VALLEY
MILAN & THE LAKES • NAPLES WITH POMPEII & THE
AMALFI COAST • PROVENCE & THE COTE D'AZUR • SARDINIA
SEVILLE & ANDALUSIA • SICILY • VENICE & THE VENETO
GREAT PLACES TO STAY IN EUROPE

CITY GUIDES

AMSTERDAM • BERLIN • BUDAPEST • DUBLIN • ISTANBUL
LISBON • LONDON • MADRID • MOSCOW • NEW YORK
PARIS • PRAGUE • ROME • SAN FRANCISCO
ST PETERSBURG • SYDNEY • VIENNA • WARSAW

TRAVEL PLANNERS

AUSTRALIA • FRANCE • FLORIDA
GREAT BRITAIN & IRELAND • ITALY • SPAIN

DK TRAVEL GUIDES CITY MAPS

LONDON • NEW YORK • PARIS • ROME
SAN FRANCISCO • SYDNEY

DK TRAVEL GUIDES PHRASE BOOKS

CONTINUALLY UPDATED